*Applied Econometric
Time Series*

Applied Econometric Time Series

WALTER ENDERS
Iowa State University

JOHN WILEY & SONS, INC.
New York • Chichester • Brisbane • Toronto • Singapore

Acquisitions Editor   Whitney B!ake
Marketing Manager   Karen Allman
Senior Production Editor   Jeanine Furino
Manufacturing Manager   Susan Stetzer
Illustration Coordinator   Gene Aiello
Text Designer   Alan Barnett
Cover Designer   Carol C. Grobe

This book was set in Times Roman by General Graphic Services and
printed and bound by Courier Stoughton. The cover was printed by NEBC.

Recognizing the importance of preserving what has been written, it is a
policy of John Wiley & Sons, Inc. to have books of enduring value published
in the United States printed on acid-free paper, and we exert our best
efforts to that end.

Library of Congress Cataloging-in-Publication Data

Enders, Walter, 1948-
    Applied econometric time series / Walter Enders. — 1st ed.
      p.   cm. — (Wiley series in probability and mathematical statistics)
    Includes bibliographical references.
    ISBN 0-471-03941-1
    I. Econometrics. 2. Time-series analysis. I. Title.
    II. Series.
    HB139.E55   1995
    330'.01'5195—dc20   94-27849
                                                              CIP

Printed in the United States of America

10 9 8 7 6 5 4 3 2 1

To my mother, father, and Linda

PILZ · Bayesian Estimation and Experimental Design in Linear Regression Models
PRESS · Bayesian Statistics: Principles, Models and Applications
PUKELSHEIM · Optimal Experimental Design
PURI and SEN · Nonparametric Methods in General Linear Models
PURI, VILAPLANA, and WERTZ · New Perspectives in Theoretical and Applied
    Statistics
RAO · Asymptotic Theory of Statistical Inference
RAO · Linear Statistical Inference and Its Applications, *Second Edition*
ROBERTSON, WRIGHT, and DYKSTRA · Order Restricted Statistical Inference
ROGERS and WILLIAMS · Diffusions, Markov Processes, and Martingales, Volume II:
    Îto Calculus
ROHATGI · A Introduction to Probability Theory and Mathematical Statistics
ROSS · Stochastic Processes
RUBINSTEIN · Simulation and the Monte Carlo Method
RUZS and SZEKELY · Algebraic Probability Theory
SCHEFFE · The Analysis of Variance
SEBER · Linear Regression Analysis
SEBER · Multivariate Observations
SEBER and WILD · Nonlinear Regression
SERFLING · Approximation Theorems of Mathematical Statistics
SHORACK and WELLNER · Empirical Processes with Applications to Statistics
SMALL and McLEISH · Hilbert Space Methods in Probability and Statistical Inference
STAUDTE and SHEATHER · Robust Estimation and Testing
STOYANOV · Counterexamples in Probability
STYAN · The Collected Papers of T. W. Anderson: 1943–1985
WHITTAKER · Graphical Models in Applied Multivariate Statistics
YANG · The Construction Theory of Denumerable Markov Processes

Applied Probability and Statistics
ABRAHAM and LEDOLTER · Statistical Methods for Forecasting
AGRESTI · Analysis of Ordinal Categorical Data
AGRESTI · Categorical Data Analysis
ANDERSON and LOYNES · The Teaching of Practical Statistics
ANDERSON, AUQUIER, HAUCK, OAKES, VANDAELE, and
    WEISBERG · Statistical Methods for Comparative Studies
*ARTHANARI and DODGE · Mathematical Programming in Statistics
ASMUSSEN · Applied Probability and Queues
*BAILEY · The Elements of Stochastic Processes with Applications to the Natural
    Sciences
BARNETT · Interpreting Multivariate Data
BARNETT and LEWIS · Outliers in Statistical Data, *Second Edition*
BARTHOLOMEW, FORBES, and McLEAN · Statistical Techniques for Manpower
    Planning, *Second Edition*
BATES and WATTS · Nonlinear Regression Analysis and Its Applications
BELSLEY · Conditioning Diagnostics: Collinearity and Weak Data in Regression
BELSLEY, KUH, and WELSCH · Regression Diagnostics: Identifying Influential Data
    and Sources of Collinearity
BHAT · Elements of Applied Stochastic Processes, *Second Edition*
BHATTACHARYA and WAYMIRE · Stochastic Processes with Applications
BIEMER, GROVES, LYBERG, MATHIOWETZ, and SUDMAN · Measurement Errors
    in Surveys
BIRKES and DODGE · Alternative Methods of Regression
BLOOMFIELD · Fourier Analysis of Time Series: An Introduction
BOLLEN · Structural Equations with Latent Variables
BOULEAU · Numerical Methods for Stochastic Processes
BOX · R. A. Fisher, the Life of a Scientist
BOX and DRAPER · Empirical Model-Building and Response Surfaces
BOX and DRAPER · Evolutionary Operation: A Statistical Method for Process
    Improvement

BOX, HUNTER, and HUNTER · Statistics for Experimenters: An Introduction to Design, Data Analysis, and Model Building

BROWN and HOLLANDER · Statistics: A Biomedical Introduction

BUCKLEW · Large Deviation Techniques in Decision, Simulation, and Estimation

BUNKE and BUNKE · Nonlinear Regression, Functional Relations and Robust Methods: Statistical Methods of Model Building

CHATTERJEE and HADI · Sensitivity Analysis in Linear Regression

CHATTERJEE and PRICE · Regression Analysis by Example, *Second Edition*

CLARKE and DISNEY · Probability and Random Processes: A First Course with Applications, *Second Edition*

COCHRAN · Sampling Techniques, *Third Edition*

*COCHRAN and COX · Experimental Designs, *Second Edition*

CONOVER · Practical Nonparametric Statistics, *Second Edition*

CONOVER and IMAN · Introduction to Modern Business Statistics

CORNELL · Experiments with Mixtures, Designs, Models, and the Analysis of Mixture Data, *Second Edition*

COX · A Handbook of Introductory Statistical Methods

*COX · Planning of Experiments

CRESSIE · Statistics for Spatial Data, *Revised Edition*

DANIEL · Applications of Statistics to Industrial Experimentation

DANIEL · Biostatistics: A Foundation for Analysis in the Health Sciences, *Sixth Edition*

DAVID · Order Statistics, *Second Edition*

DEGROOT, FIENBERG, and KADANE · Statistics and the Law

*DEMING · Sample Design in Business Research

DILLON and GOLDSTEIN · Multivariate Analysis: Methods and Applications

DODGE and ROMIG · Sampling Inspection Tables, *Second Edition*

DOWDY and WEARDEN · Statistics for Research, *Second Edition*

DRAPER and SMITH · Applied Regression Analysis, *Second Edition*

DUNN · Basic Statistics: A Primer for the Biomedical Sciences, *Second Edition*

DUNN and CLARK · Applied Statistics: Analysis of Variance and Regression, *Second Edition*

ELANDT-JOHNSON and JOHNSON · Survival Models and Data Analysis

EVANS, PEACOCK, and HASTINGS · Statistical Distributions, *Second Edition*

FISHER and VAN BELLE · Biostatistics: A Methodology for the Health Sciences

FLEISS · The Design and Analysis of Clinical Experiments

FLEISS · Statistical Methods for Rates and Proportions, *Second Edition*

FLEMING and HARRINGTON · Counting Processes and Survival Analysis

FLURY · Common Principal Components and Related Multivariate Models

GALLANT · Nonlinear Statistical Models

GLASSERMAN and YAO · Monotone Structure in Discrete-Event Systems

GROSS and HARRIS · Fundamentals of Queueing Theory, *Second Edition*

GROVES · Survey Errors and Survey Costs

GROVES, BIEMER, LYBERG, MASSEY, NICHOLLS, and WAKSBERG · Telephone Survey Methodology

HAHN and MEEKER · Statistical Intervals: A Guide for Practitioners

HAND · Discrimination and Classification

*HANSEN, HURWITZ, and MADOW · Sample Survey Methods and Theory, Volume I: Methods and Applications

*HANSEN, HURWITZ, and MADOW · Sample Survey Methods and Theory, Volume II: Theory

HEIBERGER · Computation for the Analysis of Designed Experiments

HELLER · MACSYMA for Statisticians

HINKELMAN and KEMPTHORNE: Design and Analysis of Experiments, Volume I: Introduction to Experimental Design

HOAGLIN, MOSTELLER, and TUKEY · Exploratory Approach to Analysis of Variance

HOAGLIN, MOSTELLER, and TUKEY · Exploring Data Tables, Trends and Shapes

HOAGLIN, MOSTELLER, and TUKEY · Understanding Robust and Exploratory Data Analysis

HOCHBERG and TAMHANE · Multiple Comparison Procedures

HOEL · Elementary Statistics, *Fifth Edition*

PREFACE

This book was borne out of frustration. After returning from an enjoyable and productive sabbatical at the University of California at San Diego, I began expanding the empirical content of my graduate-level classes in macroeconomics and international finance. Students' interest surged as they began to understand the concurrent development of macroeconomic theory and time-series econometrics. The difference between Keynesians, monetarists, the rational expectations school, and the real business cycle approach could best be understood by their ability to explain the empirical regularities in the economy. Old-style macroeconomic models were discarded because of their empirical inadequacies, not because of any logical inconsistencies.

Iowa State University has a world-class Statistics Department, and most of our economics students take three of four statistics classes. Nevertheless, students' backgrounds were inadequate for the empirical portion of my courses. I needed to present a reasonable number of lectures on the topics covered in this book. My frustration was that the journal articles were written for those already technically proficient in time-series econometrics. The existing time-series texts were inadequate to the task. Some focused on forecasting, others on theoretical econometric issues, and still others on techniques that are infrequently used in the economics literature. The idea for this text began as my class notes and use of handouts grew inordinately. Finally, I began teaching a new course in applied time-series econometrics.

My original intent was to write a text on time-series macroeconometrics. Fortunately, my colleagues at Iowa State convinced me to broaden the focus; applied microeconomists were also embracing time-series methods. I decided to include examples drawn from agricultural economics, international finance, and some of my work with Todd Sandler on the study of transnational terrorism. You should find the examples in the text to provide a reasonable balance between macroeconomic and microeconomic applications.

The text is intended for those with some background in multiple regression analysis. I presume the reader understands the assumptions underlying the use of ordinary least squares. All of my students are familiar with the concepts of correlation and covariation; they also know how to use t-tests and F-tests within a regression framework. I use terms such as *mean square error, significance level,* and *unbiased estimate* without explaining their meaning. The last two chapters of the text examine multiple time-series techniques. To work through these chapters, it is necessary to know how to solve a system of equations using matrix algebra. Chapter 1, entitled "Difference Equations," is the cornerstone of the text. In my experience, this material and a knowledge of regression are sufficient to bring students to the point where they are able to read the professional journals and to embark on a serious applied study.

I believe in teaching by induction. The method is to take a simple example and build towards more general and more complicated models and econometric procedures. Detailed examples of each procedure are provided. Each concludes with a step-by-step summary of the stages typically employed in using that procedure. The approach is one of learning by doing. A large number of solved problems are included in the body of each chapter. The Questions and Exercises at the end of each chapter are especially important. They have been designed to complement the material in the text. In order to work through the exercises, it is necessary to have access to a software package such as RATS, SAS, SHAZAM, or TSP. Matrix packages such as MATLAB and GAUSS are not as convenient for univariate models. Packages such as MINITAB, SPSSX, and MICROFIT can perform many of the procedures covered in the exercises. You are encouraged to work through as many of the examples and exercises as possible. The answers to all questions are contained in the *Instructor's Manual*. Most of the questions are answered in great detail. In addition, the *Instructor's Manual* contains the data disk and the computer programs that can be used to answer the end of chapter exercises. Programs are provided for the most popular software packages.

In spite of all my efforts, some errors have undoubtedly crept into the text. Portions of the manuscript that are crystal clear to me, will surely be opaque to others. Towards this end, I plan to keep a list of corrections and clarifications. You can receive a copy (of what I hope is a short list) from my Internet address ENDERS@ IASTATE.EDU.

Many people made valuable suggestions for improving the manuscript. I am grateful to my students who kept me challenged and were quick to point out errors. Pin Chung was especially helpful in carefully reading the many drafts of the manuscript and ferreting out numerous mistakes. Selahattan Dibooglu at the University of Illinois at Carbondale and Harvey Cutler at Colorado State University used portions of the text in their own courses; their comments concerning the organization, style, and clarity of presentation are much appreciated. My colleague Barry Falk was more than willing to answer my questions and make helpful suggestions. Hae-Shin Hwang, Texas A and M University; Paul D. McNelis, Georgetown University; Hadi Estahan, University of Illinois; M. Daniel Westbrook, Georgetown University; Beth Ingram, University of Iowa; and Subhash C. Ray, University of Connecticut all provided insightful reviews of various stages of the manuscript. Julio Herrera and Nifacio Velasco, the "food gurus" at the University of Valladolid, helped me survive the final stages of proofreading. Most of all, I would like to thank my loving wife Linda for putting up with me while I was working on the text.

CONTENTS

CHAPTER 4: Testing for Trends and Unit Roots   211

CHAPTER 5: Multiequation Time-Series Models   269

Chapter 1

DIFFERENCE EQUATIONS

The theory of difference equations underlies all the time-series methods employed in later chapters of this text. It is fair to say that time-series econometrics is concerned with the estimation of difference equations containing stochastic components. The traditional use of time-series analysis was to forecast the time path of a variable. Uncovering the dynamic path of a series improves forecasts since the predictable components of the series can be extrapolated into the future. The growing interest in economic dynamics has given a new emphasis to time-series econometrics. Stochastic difference equations arise quite naturally from dynamic economic models. Appropriately estimated equations can be used for the interpretation of economic data and for hypothesis testing.

The aims of this introductory chapter are to:

1. Explain how stochastic difference equations can be used for forecasting and to illustrate how such equations can arise from familiar economic models. The chapter is not meant to be a treatise on the theory of difference equations. Only those techniques that are essential to the appropriate estimation of *linear* time-series models are presented. This chapter focuses on single-equation models; multivariate models are considered in Chapters 5 and 6.

2. Explain what it means to "solve" a difference equation. The solution will determine whether a variable has a stable or an explosive time path. A knowledge of the stability conditions is essential to understanding the recent innovations in time-series econometrics. The contemporary time-series literature pays special attention to the issue of stationary versus nonstationary variables. The stability conditions underlie the conditions for stationarity.

3. Demonstrate how to find the solution to a stochastic difference equation. There are several different techniques that can be used; each has its own relative merits. A number of examples are presented to help you understand the different methods. Try to work through each example carefully. For extra practice, you should complete the exercises at the end of the chapter.

1. TIME-SERIES MODELS

The task facing the modern time-series econometrician is to develop reasonably simple models capable of forecasting, interpreting, and testing hypotheses concerning economic data. The challenge has grown over time; the original use of time-series analysis was primarily as an aid to forecasting. As such, a methodology was developed to decompose a series into a trend, seasonal, cyclical, and an irregular component. Uncovering the dynamic path of a series improves forecast accuracy since each of the predictable components can be extrapolated into the future. Suppose you observe the 50 data points shown in Figure 1.1 and are interested in forecasting the subsequent values. By using the time-series methods discussed in the next several chapters, it is possible to decompose this series into the trend, sea-

Figure 1.1 Hypothetical time series.

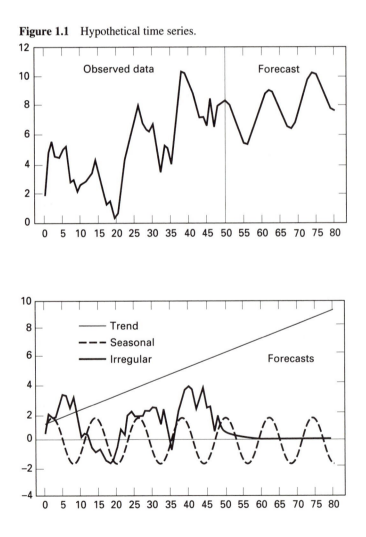

sonal, and irregular components shown in the lower part of the figure. As you can see, the trend changes the mean of the series and the seasonal component imparts a regular cyclical pattern with peaks occurring every 12 units of time. In practice, the trend and seasonal components will not be the simplistic deterministic functions shown in the figure. With economic data, it is typical to find that a series contains stochastic elements in the trend, seasonal, and irregular components. For the time being, it is wise to sidestep these complications so that the projection of the trend and seasonal components into periods 51 and beyond is straightforward.

Notice that the irregular component, while not having a well-defined pattern, is somewhat predictable. If you examine the figure closely, you will see that the positive and negative values occur in runs; the occurrence of a large value in any period tends to be followed by another large value. Short-run forecasts will make use of this positive correlation in the irregular component. Over the entire span, however, the irregular component exhibits a tendency to revert to zero. As shown in the lower part of the figure, the projection of the irregular component past period 50 rapidly decays toward zero. The overall forecast, shown in the top part of the figure, is the sum of each forecasted component.

The general methodology used to make such forecasts entails finding the "equation of motion" driving a stochastic process and using that equation to predict subsequent outcomes. Let y_t denote the value of a data point at period t; if we use this notation, the example in Figure 1.1 assumed we observed y_1 through y_{50}. For $t = 1$ to 50, the equations of motion used to construct components of the y_t series are

$$
\begin{aligned}
\text{Trend:} \quad & T_t = 1 + 0.1t \\
\text{Seasonal:} \quad & S_t = 1.6 \sin(t\pi/2) \\
\text{Irregular:} \quad & I_t = 0.7\,I_{t-1} + \epsilon_t
\end{aligned}
$$

where T_t = value of the trend component in period t
        S_t = value of the seasonal component in t
        I_t = the value of the irregular component in t
        ϵ_t = a pure random disturbance in t

Thus, the irregular disturbance in t is 70% of the previous period's irregular disturbance plus a random disturbance term.

Each of these three equations is a type of **difference equation.** In its most general form, a difference equation expresses the value of a variable as a function of its own lagged values, time, and other variables. The trend and seasonal terms are both functions of time and the irregular term is a function of its own lagged value and the stochastic variable ϵ_t. The reason for introducing this set of equations is to make the point that *time-series econometrics is concerned with the estimation of difference equations containing stochastic components.* The time-series econometrician may estimate the properties of a single series or a vector containing many interdependent series. Both univariate and multivariate forecasting methods are presented in the text. Chapter 2 shows how to estimate the irregular part of a series. The first half of Chapter 3 considers estimating the variance when the data exhibit periods of volatility and tranquility. Estimation of the trend is considered in the last half of Chapter 3 and in Chapter 4. Chapter 4 pays particular attention to the issue of whether the trend is deterministic or stochastic. Chapter 5 discusses the properties of a vector of stochastic difference equations and Chapter 6 is concerned with the estimation of trends in a multivariate model.

Although forecasting was the mainstay of time-series analysis, the growing importance of economic dynamics has generated new uses for time-series analysis. Many economic theories have natural representations as stochastic difference equations. Moreover, many of these models have testable implications concerning the time path of a key economic variable. Consider the following three examples.

1. **The Random Walk Hypothesis:** In its simplest form, the random walk model suggests that day-to-day changes in the price of a stock should have a mean value of zero. After all, if it is known that a capital gain can be made by buying a share on day t and selling it for an expected profit the very next day, efficient speculation will drive up the current price. Similarly, no one will want to hold a stock if it is expected to depreciate. Formally, the model asserts that the price of a stock should evolve according to the stochastic difference equation:

$$y_{t+1} = y_t + \epsilon_{t+1}$$

   or

$$\Delta y_{t+1} = \epsilon_{t+1}$$

   where y_t = the price of a share of stock on day t
   ϵ_{t+1} = a random disturbance term that has an expected value of zero

   Now consider the more general stochastic difference equation:

$$\Delta y_{t+1} = \alpha_0 + \alpha_1 y_t + \epsilon_{t+1}$$

   The random walk hypothesis requires the testable restriction $\alpha_0 = \alpha_1 = 0$. Rejecting this restriction is equivalent to rejecting the theory. Given the information available in period t, the theory also requires that the mean of ϵ_{t+1} be equal to zero; evidence that ϵ_{t+1} is predictable invalidates the random walk hypothesis. Again, the appropriate estimation of a single-equation model is considered in Chapters 2 through 4.

2. **Reduced Forms and Structural Equations:** Often, it is useful to collapse a system of difference equations into separate single-equation models. To illustrate the key issues involved, consider a stochastic version of Samuelson's (1939) classic model:

$$y_t = c_t + i_t \tag{1.1}$$
$$c_t = \alpha y_{t-1} + \epsilon_{ct} \qquad 0 < \alpha < 1 \tag{1.2}$$
$$i_t = \beta(c_t - c_{t-1}) + \epsilon_{it} \qquad \beta > 0 \tag{1.3}$$

where y_t, c_t, and i_t denote real GNP, consumption, and investment in time period t, respectively. In this Keynesian model, y_t, c_t, and i_t are endogenous variables. The previous period's GNP and consumption, y_{t-1} and c_{t-1}, are called predetermined or lagged endogenous variables. The terms ϵ_{ct} and ϵ_{it} are zero mean random disturbances for consumption and investment and the coefficients α and β are parameters to be estimated.

The first equation equates aggregate output (GNP) with the sum of consumption and investment spending. The second equation asserts that consumption spending is proportional to the previous period's income plus a random disturbance term. The third equation illustrates the accelerator principle. Investment spending is proportional to the change in consumption; the idea is that growth in consumption necessitates new investment spending. The error terms ϵ_{ct} and ϵ_{it} represent the portions of consumption and investment not explained by the behavioral equations of the model.

Equation (1.3) is a **structural equation** since it expresses the endogenous variable i_t as being dependent on the current realization of another endogenous variable c_t. A **reduced-form equation** is one expressing the value of a variable in terms of its own lags, lags of other endogenous variables, current and past values of exogenous variables, and disturbance terms. As formulated, the consumption function is already in reduced form; current consumption depends only on lagged income and the current value of the stochastic disturbance term ϵ_{ct}. Investment is not in reduced form since it depends on current period consumption.

To derive a reduced-form equation for investment, substitute (1.2) into the investment equation to obtain

$$i_t = \beta(\alpha y_{t-1} + \epsilon_{ct} - c_{t-1}) + \epsilon_{it}$$
$$= \alpha\beta y_{t-1} - \beta c_{t-1} + \beta\epsilon_{ct} + \epsilon_{it}$$

Notice that the reduced-form equation for investment is not unique. You can lag (1.2) one period to obtain $c_{t-1} = \alpha y_{t-2} + \epsilon_{ct-1}$. Using this expression, we can also write the reduced-form investment equation as

$$i_t = \alpha\beta y_{t-1} - \beta(\alpha y_{t-2} + \epsilon_{ct-1}) + \beta\epsilon_{ct} + \epsilon_{it}$$
$$= \alpha\beta(y_{t-1} - y_{t-2}) + \beta(\epsilon_{ct} - \epsilon_{ct-1}) + \epsilon_{it} \qquad (1.4)$$

Similarly, a reduced-form equation for GNP can be obtained by substituting (1.2) and (1.4) into (1.1):

$$y_t = \alpha y_{t-1} + \epsilon_{ct} + \alpha\beta(y_{t-1} - y_{t-2}) + \beta(\epsilon_{ct} - \epsilon_{ct-1}) + \epsilon_{it}$$
$$= \alpha(1 + \beta)y_{t-1} - \alpha\beta y_{t-2} + (1 + \beta)\epsilon_{ct} + \epsilon_{it} - \beta\epsilon_{ct-1} \qquad (1.5)$$

Equation (1.5) is a **univariate** reduced-form equation; y_t is expressed solely as a function of its own lags and disturbance terms. A univariate model is particularly useful for forecasting since it enables you to predict a series based solely on its own current and past realizations. It is possible to estimate (1.5) using the univariate time-series techniques explained in Chapters 2 through 4. Once you obtain estimates of α and β, it is straightforward to use the observed values of y_1 through y_t to predict all future values in the series (i.e., y_{t+1}, y_{t+2}, ...).

Chapter 5 considers the estimation of multivariate models when all variables are treated as jointly endogenous. The chapter also discusses the restrictions needed to recover (i.e., identify) the structural model from the estimated reduced-form model.

3. **Error Correction: Forward and Spot Prices.** Certain commodities and financial instruments can be bought and sold on the spot market for immediate delivery or for delivery at some specified future date. For example, suppose that the price of a particular foreign currency on the spot market is s_t dollars and the price of the currency for delivery one-period into the future is f_t dollars. Now, consider a speculator who purchased forward currency at the price f_t dollars per unit. At the beginning of period $t + 1$, the speculator receives the currency and pays f_t dollars per unit received. Since spot foreign exchange can be sold at s_{t+1}, the speculator can earn a profit (or loss) of $s_{t+1} - f_t$ per unit transacted.

The unbiased forward rate (UFR) hypothesis asserts that expected profits from such speculative behavior should be zero. Formally, the hypothesis posits the following relationship between forward and spot exchange rates:

$$s_{t+1} = f_t + \epsilon_{t+1} \tag{1.6}$$

where ϵ_{t+1} has a mean value of zero from the perspective of time period t.

In (1.6), the forward rate in t is an unbiased estimate of the spot rate in $t + 1$. Thus, suppose you collected data on the two rates and estimated the regression:

$$s_{t+1} = \alpha_0 + \alpha_1 f_t + \epsilon_{t+1}$$

If you were able to conclude that $\alpha_0 = 0$, $\alpha_1 = 1$ and the regression residuals ϵ_{t+1} have a mean value of zero from the perspective of time period t, the UFR hypothesis could be maintained.

The spot and forward markets are said to be in "long-run equilibrium" when $\epsilon_{t+1} = 0$. Whenever s_{t+1} turns out to differ from f_t, some sort of adjustment must occur to restore the equilibrium in the subsequent period. Consider the adjustment process:

$$s_{t+2} = s_{t+1} - \alpha(s_{t+1} - f_t) + \epsilon_{st+2} \qquad \alpha > 0 \tag{1.7}$$
$$f_{t+1} = f_t + \beta(s_{t+1} - f_t) + \epsilon_{ft+1} \qquad \beta > 0 \tag{1.8}$$

where ϵ_{st+2} and ϵ_{ft+1} both have a mean value of zero from the perspective of time period $t + 1$ and t, respectively.

Equations (1.7) and (1.8) illustrate the type of simultaneous adjustment mechanism considered in Chapter 6. This dynamic model is called an **error-correc-**

tion model since the movement of the variables in any period is related to the previous period's gap from long-run equilibrium. If the spot rate s_{t+1} turns out to equal the forward rate f_t, (1.7) and (1.8) state that the spot and forward rates are expected to remain unchanged. If there is a positive gap between the spot and forward rates so that $s_{t+1} - f_t > 0$, (1.7) and (1.8) lead to the prediction that the spot rate will fall and the forward rate will rise.

2. DIFFERENCE EQUATIONS AND THEIR SOLUTIONS

Although many of the ideas in the previous section were probably familiar to you, it is necessary to formalize some of the concepts used. In this section, we will examine the type of difference equation used in econometric analysis and make explicit what it means to "solve" such equations. To begin our examination of difference equations, consider the function $y = f(t)$. If we evaluate the function when the independent variable t takes on the specific value t^*, we get a specific value for the dependent variable called y_{t^*}. Formally, $y_{t^*} = f(t^*)$. If we use this same notation, y_{t^*+h} represents the value of y when t takes on the specific value $t^* + h$. The first difference of y is defined to be the value of the function when evaluated at $t = t^* + h$ minus the value of the function evaluated at t^*:

$$\begin{aligned} \Delta y_{t^*+h} &\equiv f(t^* + h) - f(t^*) \\ &\equiv y_{t^*+h} - y_{t^*} \end{aligned} \tag{1.9}$$

Differential calculus allows the change in the independent variable (i.e., the term h) to approach zero. Since most economic data are collected over discrete periods, however, it is more useful to allow the length of the time period to be greater than zero. Using difference equations, we normalize units so that h represents a unit change in t (i.e., $h = 1$) and consider the sequence of equally spaced values of the independent variable. Without any loss of generality, we can always drop the asterisk on t^*. We can then form the **first differences:**

$$\begin{aligned} \Delta y_t &= f(t) - f(t - 1) \equiv y_t - y_{t-1} \\ \Delta y_{t+1} &= f(t + 1) - f(t) \equiv y_{t+1} - y_t \\ \Delta y_{t+2} &= f(t + 2) - f(t + 1) \equiv y_{t+2} - y_{t+1} \end{aligned}$$

Often, it will be convenient to express the entire sequence of values $\{\cdots y_{t-2}, y_{t-1}, y_t, y_{t+1}, y_{t+2}, \cdots\}$ as $\{y_t\}$. We can then refer to any one particular value in the sequence as y_t. Unless specified, the index t runs from $-\infty$ to $+\infty$. In time-series econometric models, we will use t to represent "time" and h the length of a time period. Thus, y_t and y_{t+1} might represent the realizations of the $\{y_t\}$ sequence in the first and second quarters of 1995, respectively.

In the same way, we can form the **second difference** as the change in the first difference. Consider

$$\Delta^2 y_t \equiv \Delta(\Delta y_t) = \Delta(y_t - y_{t-1}) = (y_t - y_{t-1}) - (y_{t-1} - y_{t-2}) = y_t - 2y_{t-1} + y_{t-2}$$
$$\Delta^2 y_{t+1} \equiv \Delta(\Delta y_{t+1}) = \Delta(y_{t+1} - y_t) = (y_{t+1} - y_t) - (y_t - y_{t-1}) = y_{t+1} - 2y_t + y_{t-1}$$

The nth difference (Δ^n) is defined analogously. At this point, we risk taking the theory of difference equations too far. As you will see, the need to use second differences rarely arises in time-series analysis. It is safe to say that third- and higher-order differences are never used in applied work.

Since this text considers linear time-series methods, it is possible to examine only the special case of an nth-order linear difference equation with constant coefficients. The form for this special type of difference equation is given by

$$y_t = a_0 + \sum_{i=1}^{n} a_i y_{t-i} + x_t \tag{1.10}$$

The order of the difference equation is given by the value of n. The equation is linear because all values of the dependent variable are raised to the first power. Economic theory may dictate instances in which the various a_i are functions of variables within the economy. However, as long as they do not depend on any of the values of y_t or x_t, we can regard them as parameters. The term x_t is called the **forcing process.** The form of the forcing process can be very general; x_t can be any function of time, current and lagged values of other variables, and/or stochastic disturbances. By appropriate choice of the forcing process, we can obtain a wide variety of important macroeconomic models. Reexamine Equation (1.5), the reduced form equation for GNP. This equation is a second-order difference equation since y_t depends on y_{t-2}. The forcing process is the expression $(1 + \beta)\epsilon_{ct} + \epsilon_{it} - \beta\epsilon_{ct-1}$. You will note that (1.5) has no intercept term corresponding to the expression a_0 in (1.10).

An important special case for the $\{x_t\}$ sequence is

$$x_t = \sum_{i=0}^{\infty} \beta_i \epsilon_{t-i}$$

where the β_i are constants (some of which can equal zero) and the individual elements of the sequence $\{\epsilon_t\}$ are not functions of the y_t. At this point, it is useful to allow the $\{\epsilon_t\}$ sequence to be nothing more than a sequence of unspecified exogenous variables. For example, let $\{\epsilon_t\}$ be a random error term and set $\beta_0 = 1$ and $\beta_1 = \beta_2 = \cdots = 0$, then Equation (1.10) becomes the autoregression equation:

$$y_t = a_0 + a_1 y_{t-1} + a_2 y_{t-2} + \cdots + a_n y_{t-n} + \epsilon_t$$

Let $n = 1$, $a_0 = 0$, and $a_1 = 1$ to obtain the random walk model. Notice that Equation (1.10) can be written in terms of the **difference operator** (Δ). Subtracting y_{t-1} from (1.10), we obtain

$$y_t - y_{t-1} = a_0 + (a_1 - 1)y_{t-1} + \sum_{i=2}^{n} a_i y_{t-i} + x_t$$

or defining $\gamma = (a_1 - 1)$, we get

$$\Delta y_t = a_0 + \gamma y_{t-1} + \sum_{i=2}^{n} a_i y_{t-i} + x_t \qquad (1.11)$$

Clearly, Equation (1.11) is just a modified version of (1.10).

A **solution** to a difference equation expresses the value of y_t as a function of the elements of the $\{x_t\}$ sequence and t (and possibly some given values of the $\{y_t\}$ sequence called **initial conditions**). Examining (1.11) makes it clear that there is a strong analogy to integral calculus when the problem is to find a primitive function from a given derivative. We seek to find the primitive function $f(t)$ given an equation expressed in the form of (1.10) or (1.11). Notice that a solution is a function rather than a number. The key property of a solution is that it satisfies the difference equation for all permissible values of t and $\{x_t\}$. Thus, the substitution of a solution into the difference equation must result in an identity. For example, consider the simple difference equation $\Delta y_t = 2$ (or $y_t = y_{t-1} + 2$). You can easily verify that a solution to this difference equation is $y_t = 2t + c$, where c is any arbitrary constant. By definition, if $2t + c$ is a solution, it must hold for all permissible values of t. Thus for period $t - 1$, $y_{t-1} = 2(t - 1) + c$. Now substitute the solution into the difference equation to form

$$2t + c \equiv 2(t - 1) + c + 2 \qquad (1.12)$$

It is straightforward to carry out the algebra and verify that (1.12) is an identity. This simple example also illustrates that the solution to a difference equation need not be unique; there is a solution for any arbitrary value of c.

Another useful example is provided by the irregular term shown in Figure 1.1; recall that the equation for this expression is $I_t = 0.7I_{t-1} + \epsilon_t$. You can verify that the solution to this first-order equation is

$$I_t = \sum_{i=0}^{\infty} (0.7)^i \epsilon_{t-i} \qquad (1.13)$$

Since (1.13) holds for all time periods, the value of the irregular component in $t - 1$ is given by

$$I_{t-1} = \sum_{i=0}^{\infty} (0.7)^i \epsilon_{t-1-i} \qquad (1.14)$$

Now substitute (1.13) and (1.14) into $I_t = 0.7I_{t-1} + \epsilon_t$ to obtain

$$\epsilon_t + 0.7\epsilon_{t-1} + (0.7)^2\epsilon_{t-2} + (0.7)^3\epsilon_{t-3} + \cdots$$
$$= 0.7[\epsilon_{t-1} + 0.7\epsilon_{t-2} + (0.7)^2\epsilon_{t-3} + (0.7)^3\epsilon_{t-4} + \cdots] + \epsilon_t \quad (1.15)$$

The two sides of (1.15) are identical; this proves that (1.13) is a solution to the first-order stochastic difference equation $I_t = 0.7I_{t-1} + \epsilon_t$. Be aware of the distinction between reduced-form equations and solutions. Since $I_t = 0.7I_{t-1} + \epsilon_t$ holds for all values of t, it follows that $I_{t-1} = 0.7I_{t-2} + \epsilon_{t-1}$. Combining these two equations yields

$$I_t = 0.7(0.7I_{t-2} + \epsilon_{t-1}) + \epsilon_t$$
$$= 0.49I_{t-2} + 0.7\epsilon_{t-1} + \epsilon_t \quad (1.16)$$

Equation (1.16) is a reduced-form equation since it expresses I_t in terms of its own lags and disturbance terms. However, (1.16) does not qualify as a solution since it contains the "unknown" value of I_{t-2}. To qualify as a solution, (1.16) must express I_t in terms of the elements of x_t, t, and any given initial conditions.

3. SOLUTION BY ITERATION

The solution given by (1.13) was simply postulated. The remaining portions of this chapter develop the methods you can use to obtain such solutions. Each method has its own merits; knowing the most appropriate to use in a particular circumstance is a skill that comes only with practice. This section develops the method of **iteration.** Although iteration is the most cumbersome and time-intensive method, most people find it to be very intuitive.

If the value of y in some specific period is known, a direct method of solution is to iterate forward from that period to obtain the subsequent time path of the entire y sequence. Refer to this known value of y as the **initial condition** or value of y in time period 0 (denoted by y_0). It is easiest to illustrate the iterative technique using the first-order difference equation:

$$y_t = a_0 + a_1 y_{t-1} + \epsilon_t \quad (1.17)$$

Given the value of y_0, it follows that y_1 will be given by

$$y_1 = a_0 + a_1 y_0 + \epsilon_1$$

In the same way, y_2 must be

$$y_2 = a_0 + a_1 y_1 + \epsilon_2$$
$$= a_0 + a_1(a_0 + a_1 y_0 + \epsilon_1) + \epsilon_2$$
$$= a_0 + a_0 a_1 + (a_1)^2 y_0 + a_1 \epsilon_1 + \epsilon_2$$

Continuing the process in order to find y_3, we obtain

$$y_3 = a_0 + a_1 y_2 + \epsilon_3$$
$$= a_0[1 + a_1 + (a_1)^2] + (a_1)^3 y_0 + a_1^2 \epsilon_1 + a_1 \epsilon_2 + \epsilon_3$$

You can easily verify that for all $t > 0$, repeated iteration yields

$$y_t = a_0 \sum_{i=0}^{t-1} a_1^i + a_1^t y_0 + \sum_{i=0}^{t-1} a_1^i \epsilon_{t-i} \tag{1.18}$$

Equation (1.18) is a solution to (1.17) since it expresses y_t as a function of t, the forcing process $x_t = \Sigma (a_1)^i \epsilon_{t-i}$, and the known value of y_0. As an exercise, it is useful to show that iteration from y_t back to y_0 yields exactly the formula given by (1.18). Since $y_t = a_0 + a_1 y_{t-1} + \epsilon_t$, it follows that

$$y_t = a_0 + a_1(a_0 + a_1 y_{t-2} + \epsilon_{t-1}) + \epsilon_t$$
$$= a_0(1 + a_1) + a_1 \epsilon_{t-1} + \epsilon_t + a_1^2(a_0 + a_1 y_{t-3} + \epsilon_{t-2})$$

Continuing the iteration back to period 0 yields Equation (1.18).

Iteration Without an Initial Condition

Suppose you were not provided with the initial condition for y_0. The solution given by (1.18) would not be appropriate since the value of y_0 is an unknown. You could not select this initial value of y and iterate forward, nor could you iterate backward from y_t and simply choose to stop at $t = t_0$. Thus, suppose we continued to iterate backward by substituting $a_0 + a_1 y_{-1} + \epsilon_0$ for y_0 in (1.18):

$$y_t = a_0 \sum_{i=0}^{t-1} a_1^i + a_1^t \left(a_0 + a_1 y_{-1} + \epsilon_0 \right) + \sum_{i=0}^{t-1} a_1^i \epsilon_{t-i}$$

$$= a_0 \sum_{i=0}^{t} a_1^i + \sum_{i=0}^{t} a_1^i \epsilon_{t-i} + a_1^{t+1} y_{-1} \tag{1.19}$$

Continuing to iterate backward another m periods, we obtain

$$y_t = a_0 \sum_{i=0}^{t+m} a_1^i + \sum_{i=0}^{t+m} a_1^i \epsilon_{t-i} + a_1^{t+m+1} y_{-m-1} \tag{1.20}$$

Now examine the pattern emerging from (1.19) and (1.20). If $|a_1| < 1$, the term a_1^{t+m+1} approaches zero as m approaches infinity. Also, the infinite sum $[1 + a_1 +$

$(a_1)^2 + \cdots]$ converges to $1/(1 - a_1)$. Thus, if we temporarily assume that $|a_1| < 1$, after continual substitution, (1.20) can be written as

$$y_t = a_0/(1 - a_1) + \sum_{i=0}^{\infty} a_1^i \epsilon_{t-i} \tag{1.21}$$

You should take a few minutes to convince yourself that (1.21) is a solution to the original difference equation (1.17); substitution of (1.21) into (1.17) yields an identity. However, (1.21) is not a unique solution. For any arbitrary value of A, a solution to (1.17) is given by

$$y_t = Aa_1^t + a_0/(1 - a_1) + \sum_{i=0}^{\infty} a_1^i \epsilon_{t-i} \tag{1.22}$$

To verify that *for any arbitrary value of A,* (1.22) is a solution, substitute (1.22) into (1.17) to obtain

$$a_0/(1 - a_1) + Aa_1^t + \sum_{i=0}^{\infty} a_1^i \epsilon_{t-i} = a_0 + a_1 \left[a_0/(1 - a_1) + Aa_1^{t-1} + \sum_{i=0}^{\infty} a_1^i \epsilon_{t-1-i} \right] + \epsilon_t$$

Since the two sides are identical, (1.22) is necessarily a solution to (1.17).

Reconciling the Two Iterative Methods

Given the iterative solution (1.22), suppose that you are now given an initial condition concerning the value of y in the arbitrary period t_0. It is straightforward to show that we can impose the initial condition on (1.22) to yield the same solution as (1.18). Since (1.22) must be valid for all periods (including t_0), then when $t = 0$, it must be true that

$$y_0 = A + a_0/(1 - a_1) + \sum_{i=0}^{\infty} a_1^i \epsilon_{-i} \quad \text{so that}$$

$$A = y_0 - a_0/(1 - a_1) - \sum_{i=0}^{\infty} a_1^i \epsilon_{-i} \tag{1.23}$$

Since y_0 is given, we can view (1.23) as the value of A that renders (1.22) a solution to (1.17) given the initial condition. Hence, the presence of the initial condition eliminates the "arbitrariness" of A. Substituting this value of A into (1.22) yields

$$y_t = \left[y_0 - a_0/(1-a_1) - \sum_{i=0}^{\infty} a_1^i \epsilon_{-i} \right] a_1^t + a_0/(1-a_1) + \sum_{i=0}^{\infty} a_1^i \epsilon_{t-i} \qquad (1.24)$$

Simplification of (1.24) results in

$$y_t = [y_0 - a_0/(1-a_1)]a_1^t + a_0/(1-a_1) + \sum_{i=0}^{t-1} a_1^i \epsilon_{t-i} \qquad (1.25)$$

You should take a moment to verify that (1.25) is identical to (1.18).

Nonconvergent Sequences

Given that $|a_1| < 1$, (1.21) is the limiting value of (1.20) as m grows infinitely large. What happens to the solution in other circumstances? If $|a_1| > 1$, it is not possible to move from (1.20) to (1.21) since the expression $|a_1|^{t+m}$ grows infinitely large as $t + m$ approaches infinity.[1] However, if there is an initial condition, there is no need to obtain the infinite summation. Simply select the initial condition y_0 and iterate forward; the result will be (1.18):

$$y_t = a_0 \sum_{i=0}^{t-1} a_1^i + a_1^t y_0 + \sum_{i=0}^{t-1} a_1^i \epsilon_{t-i}$$

Although the successive values of the $\{y_t\}$ sequence will become progressively larger in absolute value, all values in the series will be finite.

A very interesting case arises if $a_1 = 1$. Rewrite (1.17) as

$$y_t = a_0 + y_{t-1} + \epsilon_t$$

or

$$\Delta y_t = a_0 + \epsilon_t$$

As you should verify by iterating from y_t back to y_0, a solution to this equation is[2]

$$y_t = a_0 t + \sum_{i=1}^{t} \epsilon_i + y_0 \qquad (1.26)$$

After a moment's reflection, the form of the solution is quite intuitive. In every period t, the value of y_t changes by $a_0 + \epsilon_t$ units. After t periods, there are t such changes; hence, the total change is $t a_0$ plus the t values of the $\{\epsilon_t\}$ sequence. Notice

Figure 1.2   Convergent and nonconvergent sequences.

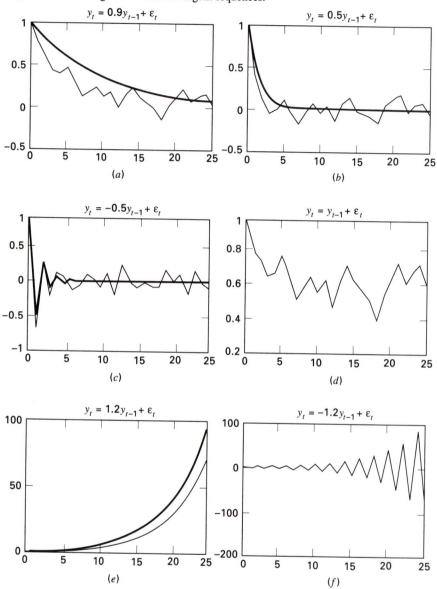

that the solution contains summation of all disturbances from ϵ_1 through ϵ_t. Thus, when $a_1 = 1$, each disturbance has a permanent nondecaying effect on the value of y_t. You should compare this result to the solution found in (1.21). For the case in which $|a_1| < 1$, $|a_1|^t$ is a decreasing function of t so that the effects of past disturbances become successively smaller over time.

The importance of the magnitude of a_1 is illustrated in Figure 1.2. Twenty-five random numbers with a theoretical mean equal to zero were computer-generated and denoted by ϵ_1 through ϵ_{25}. Then the value of y_0 was set equal to unity and the next 25 values of the $\{y_t\}$ sequence were constructed using the formula $y_t = 0.9y_{t-1} + \epsilon_t$. The result is shown by the thin line in part (a) of Figure 1.2. If you substitute $a_0 = 0$ and $a_1 = 0.9$ into (1.18), you will see that the time path of $\{y_t\}$ consists of two parts. The first part, 0.9^t, is shown by the slowly decaying thick line in the (a) panel of the figure. This term dominates the solution for relatively small values of t. The influence of the random part is shown by the difference between the thin and thick lines; you can see that the first several values of $\{\epsilon_t\}$ are negative. As t increases, the influence of the random component becomes more pronounced.

Using the previously drawn random numbers, we again set y_0 equal to unity and a second sequence was constructed using the formula $y_t = 0.5y_{t-1} + \epsilon_t$. This second sequence is shown by the thin line in part (b) of Figure 1.2. The influence of the expression 0.5^t is shown by the rapidly decaying thick line. Again, as t increases, the random portion of the solution becomes more dominant in the time path of $\{y_t\}$. When we compare the first two panels, it is clear that reducing the magnitude of $|a_1|$ increases the rate of convergence. Moreover, the discrepancies between the simulated values of y_t and the thick line are less pronounced in the second part. As you can see in (1.18), each value of ϵ_{t-i} enters the solution for y_t with a coefficient of $(a_1)^i$. The smaller value of a_1 means that the past realizations of ϵ_{t-i} have a smaller influence of the current value of y_t.

Simulating a third sequence with $a_1 = -0.5$ yields the thin line shown in part (c). The oscillations are due to the negative value of a_1. The expression $(-0.5)^t$, shown by the thick line, is positive when t is positive and negative when t is odd. Since $|a_1| < 1$, the oscillations are dampened.

The next three parts of Figure 1.2 all show nonconvergent sequences. Each uses the initial condition $y_0 = 1$ and the same 25 values of $\{\epsilon_t\}$ used in the other simulations. The thin line in part (d) shows the time path of $y_t = y_{t-1} + \epsilon_t$. Since each value of ϵ_t has an expected value of zero, part (d) illustrates a random walk process. Here, $\Delta y_t = \epsilon_t$ so that the change in y_t is random. The nonconvergence is shown by the tendency of $\{y_t\}$ to meander. In part (e), the thick line representing the explosive expression $(1.2)^t$ dominates the random portion of the $\{y_t\}$ sequence. Also notice that the discrepancy between the simulated $\{y_t\}$ sequence and the thick line widens as t increases. The reason is that past values of ϵ_{t-i} enter the solution for y_t with the coefficient $(1.2)^i$. As i increases, the importance of these previous discrepancies becomes increasingly significant. Similarly, setting $a_1 = -1.2$ results in the exploding oscillations shown in the lower-right part of Figure 1.2. The value $(-1.2)^t$ is positive for even values of t and negative for odd values of t.

4. AN ALTERNATIVE SOLUTION METHODOLOGY

Solution by the iterative method breaks down in higher-order equations. The algebraic complexity quickly overwhelms any reasonable attempt to find a solution. Fortunately, there are several alternative solution techniques than can be helpful in solving the *n*th-order equation given by (1.10). Using the principle that you should learn to walk before you learn to run, we see that it is best to step through the first-order equation given by (1.17). Although you will be covering some familiar ground, the first-order case illustrates the general methodology extremely well. To split the procedure into its component parts, consider only the homogeneous portion of (1.17):[3]

$$y_t = a_1 y_{t-1} \tag{1.27}$$

The solution to this homogeneous equation is called the **homogeneous solution;** at times, it will be useful to denote the homogeneous solution by the expression y_t^h. Obviously, the trivial solution $y_t = y_{t-1} = \cdots = 0$ satisfies (1.27). However, this solution is not unique. By setting a_0 and all values of $\{\epsilon_t\}$ equal to zero, (1.18) becomes $y_t = a_1^t y_0$. Hence, $y_t = a_1^t y_0$ must be a solution to (1.27). However, even this solution does not constitute the full set of solutions. It is easy to verify that the expression a_1^t multiplied by any arbitrary constant A satisfies (1.27). Simply substitute $y_t = A(a_1)^t$ and $y_{t-1} = A(a_1)^{t-1}$ into (1.27) to obtain

$$A(a_1)^t = a_1 A(a_1)^{t-1}$$

Since $a_1^t = a_1(a_1)^{t-1}$, it follows that $y_t = A(a_1)^t$ solves (1.27). With the aid of the thick lines in Figure 1.2, we can classify the properties of the homogeneous solution as follows:

1. If $|a_1| < 1$, the expression $(a_1)^t$ converges to zero as t approaches infinity. Convergence is direct if $0 < a_1 < 1$ and oscillatory if $-1 < a_1 < 0$.
2. If $|a_1| > 1$, the homogeneous solution is not stable. If $a_1 > 1$, the homogeneous solution approaches infinity as t increases. If $a_1 < -1$, the homogeneous solution oscillates explosively.
3. If $a_1 = 1$, any arbitrary constant A satisfies the homogeneous equation $y_t = y_{t-1}$. If $a_1 = -1$, the system is *meta-stable*: $(a_1)^t = 1$ for even values of t and -1 for odd values of t.

Now consider (1.17) in its entirety. In the last section, you confirmed that (1.21) is a valid solution to (1.17). Equation (1.21) is called a **particular solution** to the difference equation; all such particular solutions will be denoted by the term y_t^p. The term "particular" stems from the fact that a solution to a difference equation may not be unique; hence, (1.21) is just one particular solution out of the many possibilities.

In moving to (1.22), you verified that the particular solution was not unique. The homogeneous solution Aa_1^t plus the particular solution given by (1.21) constituted the complete solution to (1.17). The **general solution** to a difference equation is defined to be a particular solution plus all homogeneous solutions. Once the general solution is obtained, the arbitrary constant A can be eliminated by imposing an initial condition for y_0.

The Solution Methodology

The results of the first-order case are directly applicable to the nth-order equation given by (1.10). In this general case, it will be more difficult to find the particular solution and there will be n distinct homogeneous solutions. Nevertheless, the solution methodology will always entail the following four steps:

STEP 1: Form the homogeneous equation and find all n homogeneous solutions.

STEP 2: Find a particular solution.

STEP 3: Obtain the general solution as the sum of the particular solution and a linear combination of all homogeneous solutions.

STEP 4: Eliminate the arbitrary constant(s) by imposing the initial condition(s) on the general solution.

Before we address the various techniques that can be used to obtain homogeneous and particular solutions, it is worthwhile to illustrate the methodology using the equation:

$$y_t = 0.9y_{t-1} - 0.2y_{t-2} + 3 \tag{1.28}$$

Clearly, this second-order equation is in the form of (1.10) with $a_0 = 3$, $a_1 = 0.9$, $a_2 = -0.2$, and $x_t = 0$. Beginning with the first of the four steps, form the homogenous equation:

$$y_t - 0.9y_{t-1} + 0.2y_{t-2} = 0 \tag{1.29}$$

In the first-order case of (1.17), the homogeneous solution was $A(a_1)^t$. Section 6 will show you how to find the complete set of homogeneous solutions. For now, it is sufficient to assert that the two homogeneous solutions are $y_{1t}^h = (0.5)^t$ and $y_{2t}^h = (0.4)^t$. To verify the first solution, note that $y_{1t-1}^h = (0.5)^{t-1}$ and $y_{1t-2}^h = (0.5)^{t-2}$. Thus, y_{1t}^h is a solution if it satisfies

$$(0.5)^t - 0.9(0.5)^{t-1} + 0.2(0.5)^{t-2} = 0$$

If we divide by $(0.5)^{t-2}$, the issue is whether

$$(0.5)^2 - 0.9(0.5) + 0.2 = 0$$

Carrying out the algebra $0.25 - 0.45 + 0.2$ does equal zero so that $(0.5)^t$ is a solution to (1.29). In the same way, it is easy to verify that $y^h_{2t} = (0.4)^t$ is a solution since

$$(0.4)^t - 0.9(0.4)^{t-1} + 0.2(0.4)^{t-2} = 0$$

Divide by $(0.4)^{t-2}$ to obtain $(0.4)^2 - 0.9(0.4) + 0.2 = 0.16 - 0.36 + 0.2 = 0$.

The second step is to obtain a particular solution; you can easily confirm that the particular solution $y^p_t = 10$ solves (1.28) as $10 = 0.9(10) - 0.2(10) + 3$.

The third step is to combine the particular solution and a linear combination of both homogeneous solutions to obtain

$$y_t = A_1(0.5)^t + A_2(0.4)^t + 10$$

where A_1 and A_2 are arbitrary constants.

For the fourth step, assume you have two initial conditions for the $\{y_t\}$ sequence. So that we can keep our numbers reasonably round, suppose that $y_0 = 13$ and $y_1 = 11.3$. Thus, for periods zero and one, our solution must satisfy

$$13 = A_1 + A_2 + 10$$
$$11.3 = A_1(0.5) + A_2(0.4) + 10$$

Solving simultaneously for A_1 and A_2, you should find $A_1 = 1$ and $A_2 = 2$. Hence, the solution is

$$y_t = (0.5)^t + 2(0.4)^t + 10$$

Generalizing the Method

To show that the method is applicable to higher-order equations, consider the homogeneous part of (1.10):

$$y_t = \sum_{i=1}^n a_i y_{t-i} \tag{1.30}$$

As shown in Section 6, there are n homongneous solutions that satisfy (1.30). For now, it is sufficient to demonstrate the following proposition: *If y^h_t is a homogeneous solution to (1.30), Ay^h_t is also a solution for any arbitrary constant A.* By assumption, y^h_t solves the homogeneous equation so that

$$y^h_t = \sum_{i=1}^n a_i y^h_{t-i} \tag{1.31}$$

The expression Ay_t^h is also a solution if:

$$Ay_t^h = \sum_{i=1}^{n} a_i A y_{t-i}^h \qquad (1.32)$$

We know (1.32) is satisfied since dividing each term by A yields (1.31). Now suppose that there are two separate solutions to the homogeneous equation denoted by y_{1t}^h and y_{2t}^h. It is straightforward to show that for any two constants A_1 and A_2, the linear combination $A_1 y_{1t}^h + A_2 y_{2t}^h$ is also a solution to the homogeneous equation. If $A_1 y_{1t}^h + A_2 y_{2t}^h$ is a solution to (1.30), it must satisfy

$$A_1 y_{1t}^h + A_2 y_{2t}^h = a_1(A_1 y_{1t-1}^h + A_2 y_{2t-2}^h) + a_2(A_1 y_{1t-2}^h + A_2 y_{2t-2}^h) + \cdots + a_n(A_1 y_{1t-n}^h + A_2 y_{2t-n}^h)$$

Regrouping terms, we want to know if

$$\left(A_1 y_{1t}^h - \sum_{i=1}^{n} A_1 a_i y_{1t-i}^h\right) + \left(A_2 y_{2t}^h - \sum_{i=1}^{n} A_2 a_i y_{2t-i}^h\right) = 0$$

Since $A_1 y_{1t}^h$ and $A_2 y_{2t}^h$ are separate solutions to (1.30), each of the expressions in parentheses is zero. Hence, the linear combination is necessarily a solution to the homogeneous equation. This result easily generalizes to all n homogeneous solutions to an nth-order equation.

Finally, the use of Step 3 is appropriate since *the sum of any particular solution and any linear combination of all homogeneous solutions is also a solution.* To prove the proposition, substitute the sum of the particular and homogeneous solutions into (1.10) to obtain

$$y_t^p + y_t^h = a_0 + \sum_{i=1}^{n} a_i\left(y_{t-i}^p + y_{t-i}^h\right) + x_t \qquad (1.33)$$

Recombining the terms in (1.33), we want to know if

$$\left(y_t^p - a_0 - \sum_{i=1}^{n} a_i y_{t-i}^p - x_t\right) + \left(y_t^h - \sum_{i=1}^{n} a_i y_{t-i}^h\right) = 0 \qquad (1.34)$$

Since y_t^p solves (1.10), the expression in the first set of parentheses of (1.34) is zero. Since y_t^h solves the homogeneous equation, the expression in the second set of parentheses is zero. Thus, (1.34) is an identity; the sum of the homogeneous and particular solutions solves (1.10).

5. THE COBWEB MODEL

An interesting way to illustrate the methodology outlined in the previous section is to consider a stochastic version of the traditional **cobweb model**. Since the model was originally developed to explain the volatility in agricultural prices, let the market for a product—say, wheat—be represented by

$$d_t = a - \gamma p_t \quad . \qquad \gamma > 0 \qquad (1.35)$$
$$s_t = b + \beta p_t^* + \epsilon_t \qquad \beta > 0 \qquad (1.36)$$
$$s_t = d_t \qquad\qquad\qquad (1.37)$$

where d_t = demand for wheat in period t
s_t = supply of wheat in t
p_t = market price of wheat in t
p_t^* = price that farmers expect to prevail at t
ϵ_t = a zero mean stochastic supply shock

and parameters a, b, γ, and β are all positive such that $a > b$.[4]

The nature of the model is such that consumers buy as much wheat as desired at the market clearing price p_t. At planting time, farmers do not know the price prevailing at harvest time; they base their supply decision on the expected price (p_t^*). The actual quantity produced depends on the planned quantity $b + \beta p_t^*$ plus a random supply shock ϵ_t. Once the product is harvested, market equilibrium requires that the quantity supplied equals the quantity demanded. Unlike the actual market for wheat, the model ignores the possibility of storage. The essence of the cobweb model is that farmers form their expectations in a naive fashion; let farmers use last year's price as the expected market price:

$$p_t^* = p_{t-1} \qquad\qquad\qquad (1.38)$$

Point E in Figure 1.3 represents the long-run equilibrium price and quantity combination. Note that the equilibrium concept in this stochastic model differs from that of the traditional cobweb model. If the system is stable, successive prices will *tend* to converge to point E. However, the nature of the stochastic equilibrium is such that the ever-present supply shocks prevent the system from remaining at E. Nevertheless, it is useful to solve for the long-run price. If we set all values of the $\{\epsilon_t\}$ sequence equal to zero, set $p_t = p_{t-1} = \cdots = p$, and equate supply and demand, the long-run equilibrium price is given by $p = (a - b)/(\gamma + \beta)$. Similarly, the equilibrium quantity (s) is given by $s = (a\beta + \gamma b)/(\gamma + \beta)$.

To understand the dynamics of the system, suppose that farmers in t plan to produce the equilibrium quantity s. However, let there be a negative supply shock such that the actual quantity produced turns out to be s_t. As shown by point 1 in Figure 1.3, consumers are willing to pay p_t for the quantity s_t; hence, market equilibrium in t occurs at point 1. Updating one period allows us to see the main result of the cobweb model. For simplicity, assume that all subsequent values of the supply shock are zero (i.e., $\epsilon_{t+1} = \epsilon_{t+2} = \cdots = 0$). At the beginning of period $t + 1$, farmers expect the price at harvest time to be that of the previous period; thus, $p^*_{t+1} = p_t$. Accordingly, they produce and market quantity s_{t+1} (see point 2 in the figure); consumers, however, are willing to buy quantity s_{t+1} only if the price falls to that indicated by p_{t+1} (see point 3 in the figure). The next period begins with farmers expecting to be at point 4. The process continually repeats itself until the equilibrium point E is attained.

As drawn, Figure 1.3 suggests that the market will always converge to the long-run equilibrium point. This result does not hold for all demand and supply curves. To formally derive the stability condition, combine (1.35) through (1.38) to obtain

$$b + \beta p_{t-1} + \epsilon_t = a - \gamma p_t$$

or

$$p_t = (-\beta/\gamma)p_{t-1} + (a - b)/\gamma - \epsilon_t/\gamma \tag{1.39}$$

Clearly, (1.39) is a stochastic first-order linear difference equation with constant coefficients. To obtain the general solution, proceed using the four steps listed at the end of the last section:

1. Form the homogeneous equation: $p_t = (-\beta/\gamma)p_{t-1}$. In the next section, you will learn how to find the solution(s) to a homogeneous equation. For now, it is sufficient to verify that the homogeneous solution is

Figure 1.3   The cobweb model.

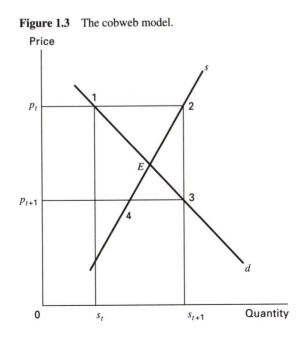

$$p_t^h = A(-\beta/\gamma)^t$$

where A is an arbitrary constant.

2. If the ratio β/γ is less than unity, you can iterate (1.39) backward from p_t to verify that the particular solution for the price is

$$p_t^p = (a-b)/(\gamma+\beta) - (1/\gamma)\sum_{i=0}^{\infty}(-\beta/\gamma)^i \epsilon_{t-i} \qquad (1.40)$$

If $\beta/\gamma \geq 1$, the infinite summation in (1.40) is not convergent. As discussed in the last section, it is necessary to impose an initial condition on (1.40) if $\beta/\gamma \geq 1$.

3. The general solution is the sum of the homogeneous and particular solutions; if we combine these two solutions, the general solution is

$$p_t = (a-b)/(\gamma+\beta) - (1/\gamma)\sum_{i=0}^{\infty}(-\beta/\gamma)^i \epsilon_{t-i} + A(-\beta/\gamma)^t \qquad (1.41)$$

4. In (1.41), A is an arbitrary constant that can be eliminated if we know the price in some initial period. For convenience, let this initial period have a time subscript of zero. Since the solution must hold for every period, *including period zero*, it must be the case that

$$p_0 = (a-b)/(\gamma+\beta) - (1/\gamma)\sum_{i=0}^{\infty}(-\beta/\gamma)^i \epsilon_{-i} + A(-\beta/\gamma)^0$$

Since $(-\beta/\gamma)^0 = 1$, the value of A is given by

$$A = p_0 - (a-b)/(\gamma+\beta) + (1/\gamma)\sum_{i=0}^{\infty}(-\beta/\gamma)^i \epsilon_{-i}$$

Substituting this solution for A back into (1.41) yields

$$p_t = (a-b)/(\gamma+\beta) - (1/\gamma)\sum_{i=0}^{\infty}(-\beta/\gamma)^i \epsilon_{t-i}$$

$$+(-\beta/\gamma)^t \left[p_0 - (a-b)/(\gamma+\beta) + (1/\gamma)\sum_{i=0}^{\infty}(-\beta/\gamma)^i \epsilon_{t-i} \right]$$

and after simplification of the two summations,

$$p_t = (a-b)/(\gamma+\beta) - (1/\gamma)\sum_{i=0}^{t-1}(-\beta/\gamma)^i \epsilon_{t-i} + (-\beta/\gamma)^t[p_0 - (a-b)/(\gamma+\beta)] \quad (1.42)$$

We can interpret (1.42) in terms of Figure 1.3. In order to focus on the stability of the system, temporarily assume that all values of the $\{\epsilon_t\}$ sequence are zero. Subsequently, we will return to a consideration of the effects of supply shocks. If the system begins in long run equilibrium, the initial condition is such that $p_0 = (a-b)/(\gamma+\beta)$. In this case, inspection of Equation (1.42) indicates that $p_t = (a-b)/(\gamma+\beta)$. Thus, if we begin the process at point E, the system remains in long-run equilibrium. Instead, suppose that the process begins at a price below long-run equilibrium: $p_0 < (a-b)/(\gamma+\beta)$. Equation (1.42) tells us that p_1 is

$$p_1 = (a-b)/(\gamma+\beta) + [p_0 - (a-b)/(\gamma+\beta)](-\beta/\gamma)^1 \quad (1.43)$$

Since $p_0 < (a-b)/(\gamma+\beta)$ and $-\beta/\gamma < 0$, it follows that p_1 will be above the long-run equilibrium price $(a-b)/(\gamma+\beta)$. In period 2,

$$p_2 = (a-b)/(\gamma+\beta) + [p_0 - (a-b)/(\gamma+\beta)](-\beta/\gamma)^2$$

Although $p_0 < (a-b)/(\gamma+\beta)$, $(-\beta/\gamma)^2$ is positive; hence, p_2 is below the long-run equilibrium. For the subsequent periods, note that $(-\beta/\gamma)^t$ will be positive for even values of t and negative for odd values of t. Just as we found graphically, the successive values of the $\{p_t\}$ sequence will oscillate above and below the long-run equilibrium price. Since $(\beta/\gamma)^t$ goes to zero if $\beta < \gamma$ and explodes if $\beta > \gamma$, the magnitude of β/γ determines whether the price actually converges to the long-run equilibrium. If $\beta/\gamma < 1$, the oscillations will diminish in magnitude, and if $\beta/\gamma > 1$, the oscillations will be explosive.

The economic interpretation of this stability condition is straightforward. The slope of the supply curve [i.e., $dp_t/d(s_t)$] is $1/\beta$ and the absolute value slope of the demand curve [i.e., $-dp_t/d(d_t)$] is $1/\gamma$. If the supply curve is steeper than the demand curve $1/\beta > 1/\gamma$ or $\beta/\gamma < 1$, so that the system is stable. This is precisely the case illustrated in Figure 1.3. As an exercise, you should draw a diagram with the demand curve steeper than the supply curve and show that the price oscillates and diverges from the long-run equilibrium.

Now consider the effects of the supply shocks. The contemporaneous effect of a supply shock on the price of wheat is the partial derivative of p_t with respect to ϵ_t; from (1.42), we obtain

$$\partial p_t/\partial \epsilon_t = -1/\gamma \quad (1.44)$$

Equation (1.44) is called the **impact multiplier** since it shows the impact effect of a change in ϵ_t on the price in t. In terms of Figure 1.3, a negative value of ϵ_t implies a price above the long-run price p; the price in t rises by $1/\gamma$ units for each unit decline in current period's supply. Of course, this terminology is not specific to the cobweb model; in terms of the nth-order model given by (1.10), the impact multiplier is the partial derivative of y_t with respect to the partial change in the forcing process.[5]

The effects of the supply shock in t persist into future periods. Updating (1.42) by one period yields the **one-period multiplier**:

$$\partial p_{t+1}/\partial \epsilon_t = -(1/\gamma)(-\beta/\gamma)$$
$$= \beta/\gamma^2$$

Point 3 in Figure 1.3 illustrates how the price in $t+1$ is affected by the negative supply shock in t. It is straightforward to derive the result that the effects of the supply shock decay over time. Since $\beta/\gamma < 1$, the absolute value of $\partial p_t/\partial \epsilon_t$ exceeds $\partial p_{t+1}/\partial \epsilon_t$. All the multipliers can be derived analogously; updating (1.42) by two periods yields:

$$\partial p_{t+2}/\partial \epsilon_t = -(1/\gamma)(-\beta/\gamma)^2$$

and after n periods,

$$\partial p_{t+n}/\partial \epsilon_t = -(1/\gamma)(-\beta/\gamma)^n$$

The time path of all such multipliers is called the **impulse response function**. This function has many important applications in time-series analysis since it shows how the entire time path of a variable is affected by a stochastic shock. Here, the impulse response function traces out the effects of a supply shock in the wheat market. In other economic applications, you may be interested in the time path of a money supply shock or a productivity shock on real GNP.

In actuality, the function can be derived without updating (1.42) since it is always the case that:

$$\partial p_{t+j}/\partial \epsilon_t = \partial p_t/\partial \epsilon_{t-j}$$

To find the impulse response function, simply find the partial derivative of (1.42) with respect to the various ϵ_{t-j}. These partial derivatives are nothing more than the coefficients of the $\{\epsilon_{t-j}\}$ sequence in (1.42).

Each of the three components in (1.42) has a direct economic interpretation. The deterministic portion of the particular solution $(a - b)/(\gamma + \beta)$ is the long-run equilibrium price; if the stability condition is met, the $\{p_t\}$ sequence tends to converge to this long-run value. The stochastic component of the particular solution captures the short-run price adjustments due to the supply shocks. The ultimate decay of the coefficients of the impulse response function guarantees that the effects of changes in the various ϵ_t are of a short-run duration. The third component is the expression

$(-\beta/\gamma)^t A = (-\beta/\gamma)^t [p_0 - (a - b)/(\gamma + \beta)]$. The value of A is the initial period's deviation of the price from its long-run equilibrium level. Given that $\beta/\gamma < 1$, the importance of this initial deviation diminishes over time.

6. SOLVING HOMOGENEOUS DIFFERENCE EQUATIONS

Higher-order difference equations arise quite naturally in economic analysis. Equation (1.5)—the reduced-form GNP equation resulting from Samuelson's (1939) model—is an example of a second-order difference equation. Moreover, in time-series econometrics, it is quite typical to estimate second- and higher-order equations. To begin our examination of homogeneous solutions, consider the second-order equation

$$y_t - a_1 y_{t-1} - a_2 y_{t-2} = 0 \tag{1.45}$$

Given the findings in the first-order case, you should suspect that the homogeneous solution has the form $y_t^h = A\alpha^t$. Substitution of this trial solution into (1.45) yields

$$A\alpha^t - a_1 A\alpha^{t-1} - a_2 A\alpha^{t-2} = 0 \tag{1.46}$$

Clearly, any arbitrary value of A is satisfactory. If you divide (1.46) by $A\alpha^{t-2}$, the problem is to find the values of α that satisfy

$$\alpha^2 - a_1\alpha - a_2 = 0 \tag{1.47}$$

Solving this quadratic equation—called the **characteristic equation**—yields two values of α, called the **characteristic roots**. Using the quadratic formula, we find that the two characteristic roots are

$$\begin{aligned}
\alpha_1, \alpha_2 &= \left(a_1 \pm \sqrt{a_1^2 + 4a_2} \right)\big/2 \\
&= \left(a_1 \pm \sqrt{d} \right)\big/2
\end{aligned} \tag{1.48}$$

where d is the discriminant $[(a_1)^2 + 4a_2]$.

Each of these two characteristic roots yields a valid solution for (1.45). Again, these solutions are not unique. In fact, for any two arbitrary constants A_1 and A_2, the linear combination $A_1(\alpha_1)^t + A_2(\alpha_2)^t$ also solves (1.45). As proof, simply substitute $y_t = A_1(\alpha_1)^t + A_2(\alpha_2)^t$ into (1.45) to obtain

$$A_1(\alpha_1)^t + A_2(\alpha_2)^t = a_1[A_1(\alpha_1)^{t-1} + A_2(\alpha_2)^{t-1}] + a_2[A_1(\alpha_1)^{t-2} + A_2(\alpha_2)^{t-2}]$$

Now, regroup terms as follows:

$$A_1[(\alpha_1)^t - a_1(\alpha_1)^{t-1} - a_2(\alpha_1)^{t-2}] + A_2[(\alpha_2)^t - a_1(\alpha_2)^{t-1} - a_2(\alpha_2)^{t-2}] = 0$$

Since α_1 and α^2 each solve (1.45), both terms in brackets must equal zero. As such, the complete homogeneous solution in the second-order case is

$$y_t^h = A_1(\alpha_1)^t + A_2(\alpha_2)^t$$

Without knowing the specific values of a_1 and a_2, we cannot find the two characteristic roots α_1 and α_2. Nevertheless, it is possible to characterize the nature of the solution; there are three possible cases that are dependent on the value of the discriminant d.

CASE 1

If $a_1^2 + 4a_2 > 0$, d is a real number and there will be two distinct real characteristic roots. Hence, there are two separate solutions to the homogeneous equation denoted by $(\alpha_1)^t$ and $(\alpha_2)^t$. We already know that any linear combination of the two is also a solution. Hence,

$$y_t^h = A_1(\alpha_1)^t + A_2(\alpha_2)^t$$

It should be clear that if the absolute value of *either* α_1 or α_2 exceeds unity, the homogeneous solution will explode. Worksheet 1.1 examines two second-order equations showing real and distinct characteristic roots. In the first example, $y_t = 0.2y_{t-1} + 0.35y_{t-2}$, the characteristic roots are shown to be $\alpha_1 = 0.7$ and $\alpha_2 = -0.5$. Hence, the full homogeneous solution is $y_t^h = A_1 (0.7)^t + A_2 (-0.5)^t$. Since both roots are less than unity in absolute value, the homogeneous solution is convergent. As you can see in the graph on the bottom left-hand side of Worksheet 1.1, convergence is not monotonic because of the influence of the expression $(-0.5)^t$.

WORKSHEET 1.1   Homogeneous Solutions: Second-Order Equations

CASE 1: $y_{(t)} = 0.2y_{(t-1)} + 0.35y_{(t-2)}$. Hence, $a_1 = 0.2$, $a_2 = 0.35$.

Form the homogeneous equation: $y_{(t)} - 0.2y_{(t-1)} - 0.35y_{(t-2)} = 0$.

A check of the discriminant reveals $d = (a_1)^2 + 4 \cdot a_2$, so that $d = 1.44$. Given that $d > 0$, the roots will be real and distinct.

Let the trial solution have the form $y_{(t)} = \alpha^t$. Substitute into the homogenous equation $\alpha^t - 0.2 \cdot \alpha^{t-1} - 0.35 \cdot \alpha^{t-2} = 0$.

Divide by α^{t-2} in order to obtain the characteristic equation: $\alpha^t - 0.2 \cdot \alpha^{t-1} - 0.35 \cdot \alpha^{t-2} = 0$

Compute the two characteristic roots:

$$\alpha_1 = 0.5 \cdot (a_1 + \sqrt{d}), \qquad \alpha_2 = 0.5 \cdot (a_1 + \sqrt{d})$$
$$= 0.7 \qquad\qquad\qquad = -0.5$$

The homogeneous solution is $A_1 \cdot 0.7^t + A_2 \cdot (-0.5)^t$. The graph shows the time path of this solution for the case in which the arbitrary constants equal unity and t runs from 1 to 20.

CASE 2: $y_{(t)} = 0.7y_{(t-1)} + 0.35y_{(t-2)}$. Hence, $a_1 = 0.7$, $a_2 = 0.35$.

Form the homogeneous equation: $y_{(t)} - 0.7y_{(t-1)} - 0.35y_{(t-2)} = 0$.

A check of the discriminant reveals $d = (a_1)^2 + 4 \cdot a_2$ so that $d = 1.89$. Given that $d > 0$, the roots will be real and distinct.

Form the characteristic equation: $\alpha^t - 0.7 \cdot \alpha^{t-1} - 0.35 \cdot \alpha^{t-2} = 0$.

Compute the two characteristic roots:

$$\alpha_1 = 0.5 \cdot (a_1 + \sqrt{d}), \qquad \alpha_2 = 0.5 \cdot (a_1 - \sqrt{d})$$
$$= 1.037 \qquad\qquad\qquad = -0.337$$

The homogeneous solution is $A_1 \cdot 1.037^t + A_2 \cdot (-0.337)^t$. The graph shows the time path of this solution for the case in which the arbitrary constants equal unity and t runs from 1 to 20.

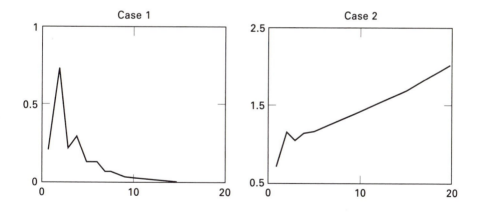

Case 1   Case 2

In the second example, $y_t = 0.7y_{t-1} + 0.35y_{t-2}$. The worksheet indicates how to obtain the solution for the two characteristic roots. Given that one characteristic root is $(1.037)^t$, the $\{y_t\}$ sequence explodes. The influence of the negative root ($\alpha_2 = -0.337$) is responsible for the nonmonotonicity of the time path. Since $(-0.337)^t$ quickly approaches zero, the dominant root is the explosive value 1.037.

CASE 2

If $a_1^2 + 4a_2 = 0$, it follows that $d = 0$ and $\alpha_1 = \alpha_2 = a_1/2$. Hence, a homogeneous solution is $a_1/2$. However, when $d = 0$, there is a second homogeneous solution given by $t(a_1/2)^t$. To demonstrate that $y_t^h = t(a_1/2)^t$ is a homogeneous solution, substitute it into (1.45) to determine whether

$$t(a_1/2)^t - a_1[(t-1)(a_1/2)^{t-1}] - a_2[(t-2)(a_1/2)^{t-2}] = 0$$

Figure 1.4   The homogeneous solution $t \cdot (a_1)^t$.

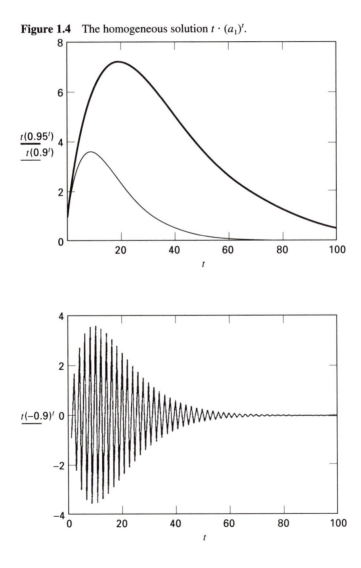

Divide by $(a_1/2)^{t-2}$ and form

$$-[(a_1^2/4) + a_2]t + [(a_1^2/2) + 2a_2] = 0$$

Since we are operating in the circumstance where $a_1^2 + 4a_2 = 0$, each bracketed expression is zero; hence, $t(a_1/2)^t$ solves (1.45). Again, for arbitrary constants A_1 and A_2, the complete homogeneous solution is

$$y_t^h = A_1(a_1/2)^t + A_2t(a_1/2)^t$$

Clearly, the system is explosive if $|a_1| > 2$. If $|a_1| < 2$, the term $A_1(a_1/2)^t$ converges, but you might think that the effect of the term $t(a_1/2)^t$ is ambiguous [since the diminishing $(a_1/2)^t$ is multiplied by t]. The ambiguity is correct in the limited sense that the behavior of the homogeneous solution is not monotonic. As illustrated in Figure 1.4 for $a_1/2 = 0.95$, 0.9, and -0.9, as long as $|a_1| < 2$, $\lim[t(a_1/2)^t]$ is necessarily zero as $t \to \infty$; hence, there is always convergence. For $0 < a_1 < 2$, the homogeneous solution appears to explode before ultimately converging to zero. For $-2 < a_1 < 0$, the behavior is wildly erratic; the homogeneous solution appears to oscillate explosively before the oscillations dampen and finally converge to zero.

CASE 3

If $a_1^2 + 4a_2 < 0$, it follows that d is negative so that the characteristic roots are imaginary. Since $a_1^2 \geq 0$, imaginary roots can occur only if $a_2 < 0$. Although hard to interpret directly, if we switch to polar coordinates, it is possible to transform the roots into more easily understood trigonometric functions. The technical details are presented in Appendix 1 of this chapter. For now, write the two characteristic roots as

$$\alpha_1 = (a_1 + i\sqrt{d})/2, \qquad \alpha_2 = (a_1 - i\sqrt{d})/2$$

where $i = \sqrt{-1}$

As shown in Appendix 1, you can use de Moivre's theorem to write the homogeneous solution as

$$y_t^h = \beta_1 r^t \cos(\theta t + \beta_2) \tag{1.49}$$

where β_1 and β_2 are arbitrary constants, $r = (-a_2)^{1/2}$, and the value of θ is chosen so as to simultaneously satisfy

$$\cos(\theta) = a_1/[2(-a_2)^{1/2}] \tag{1.50}$$

The trigonometric functions impart a wavelike pattern to the time path of the homogeneous solution; note that the frequency of the oscillations is determined by θ.

Since $\cos(\theta t) = \cos(2\pi + \theta t)$, the stability condition is determined solely by the magnitude of $r = (-a_2)^{1/2}$. If $|a_2| = 1$, the oscillations are of unchanging amplitude; the homogeneous solution is periodic. The oscillations will dampen if $|a_2| < 1$ and explode if $|a_2| > 1$.

EXAMPLE: It is worthwhile to work through an exercise using an equation with imaginary roots. The left-hand side of Worksheet 1.2 examines the behavior of the equation $y_t = 1.6y_{t-1} - 0.9y_{t-2}$. A quick check shows that the discriminant d is negative so that the characteristic roots are imaginary. If we transform to polar coordinates, the value of r is given by $(0.9)^{1/2} = 0.949$. From (1.50), $\cos(\theta) = 1.6/(2 \times 0.949) = 0.843$. You can use a trig table or calculator to show that $\theta = 0.567$ [i.e., if $\cos(\theta) = 0.843$, $\theta = 0.567$). Thus, the homogeneous solution is

$$y_t^h = \beta_1(0.949)^t \cos(0.567t + \beta_2) \tag{1.51}$$

The graph on the left-hand side of Worksheet 1.2 sets $\beta_1 = 1$ and $\beta_2 = 0$ and plots the homogeneous solution for $t = 1, ..., 25$. Case 2 uses the same value of a_2 (hence, $r = 0.949$) but sets $a_1 = -0.6$. Again, the value of d is negative; however, for this set of calculations, $\cos(\theta) = -0.316$ so that θ is 1.25. Comparing the two graphs, you can see that increasing the value of θ acts to increase the frequency of the oscillations.

WORKSHEET 1.2   IMAGINARY ROOTS

CASE 1	CASE 2
$y_t - 1.6y_{t-1} + 0.9y_{t-2}$	$y_t + 0.6y_{t-1} + 0.9y_{t-2}$

(a) Check the discriminant $d = a_1^2 + 4a_2$

$d = (-1.6)^2 - 4(0.9)$	$d = (0.6)^2 - 4(0.9)$
$= -1.04$	$= -3.24$

Hence, the roots are imaginary. The homogeneous solution has the form

$$y_t^h = \beta_1 r^t \cos(\theta t + \beta_2)$$

where β_1 and β_2 are arbitrary constants.

(b) Obtain the value of $r = (-a_2)^{1/2}$

$r = (0.9)^{1/2}$	$r = (0.9)^{1/2}$
$= 0.949$	$= 0.949$

(c) Obtain θ from cos(θ) $= a_1/[2(-a_1)^{1/2}]$

$$\cos(\theta) = 1.6/[2(0.9)^{1/2}] \qquad\qquad \cos(\theta) = -0.6/[2(0.9)^{1/2}]$$
$$= 0.843 \qquad\qquad\qquad\qquad = -0.316$$

Given cos(θ), use a trig table to find θ

$$\theta = 0.567 \qquad\qquad\qquad \theta = 1.25$$

(d) Form the homogeneous solution: $y_t^h = \beta_1 r^t \cos(\theta t + \beta_2)$

$$y_t^h = \beta_1(0.949)^t \cos(0.567t + \beta_2) \qquad y_t^h = \beta_1(0.949)^t \cos(1.25t + \beta_2)$$

For $\beta_1 = 1$ and $\beta_2 = 0$, the time paths of the homogeneous solution are

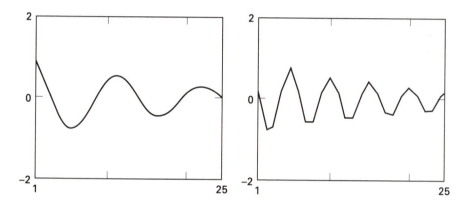

Stability Conditions

The general stability conditions can be summarized using triangle *ABC* in Figure 1.5. Arc *AOB* is the boundary between Cases 1 and 3; it is the locus of points such that $d = a_1^2 + 4a_2 = 0$. The region above *AOB* corresponds to Case 1 (since $d > 0$) and the region below *AOB* corresponds to Case 3 (since $d < 0$).

In Case 1 (in which the roots are real and distinct), stability requires that the largest root be less than unity and the smallest root be greater than −1. The largest characteristic root, $\alpha_1 = (a_1 + \sqrt{d})/2$, will be less than unity if

$$a_1 + (a_1^2 + 4a_2)^{1/2} < 2 \qquad \text{or} \qquad (a_1^2 + 4a_2)^{1/2} < 2 - a_1$$

Hence, $a_1^2 + 4a_2 < 4 - 4a_1 + a_1^2$
or

$$a_1 + a_2 < 1 \qquad\qquad\qquad\qquad (1.52)$$

The smallest root, $\alpha_2 = (a_1 - \sqrt{d})/2$, will be greater than -1 if

$$a_1 - (a_1^2 + 4a_2)^{1/2} > -2 \qquad \text{or} \qquad 2 + a_1 > (a_1^2 + 4a_2)^{1/2}$$

Hence, $4 + 4a_1 + a_1^2 > a_1^2 + 4a_2$

or

$$a_2 < 1 + a_1 \qquad (1.53)$$

Thus, the region of stability in Case 1 consists of all points in the region bounded by $A0BC$. For any point in $A0BC$, conditions (1.52) and (1.53) hold and $d > 0$.

In Case 2 (repeated roots), $a_1^2 + 4a_2 = 0$. The stability condition is $|a_1| < 2$. Hence, the region of stability in Case 2 consists of all points on arc $A0B$. In Case 3 ($d < 0$), the stability condition is $r = (-a_2)^{1/2} < 1$. Hence,

$$-a_2 < 1 \qquad \text{(where } a_2 < 0\text{)} \qquad (1.54)$$

Thus, the region of stability in Case 3 consists of all points in region $A0B$. For any point in $A0B$, (1.54) is satisfied and $d < 0$.

A succint way to characterize the stability conditions is to state that the characteristic roots must lie within the unit circle. Consider the semicircle drawn in Figure 1.6. Real numbers are measured on the horizontal axis and imaginary numbers on

Figure 1.5   Characterizing the stability conditions.

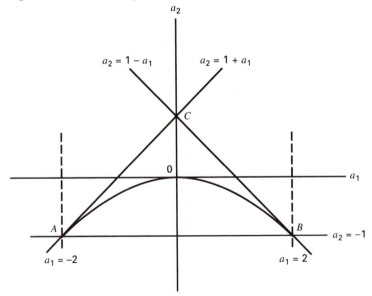

Figure 1.6   Characteristic roots and the unit circle.

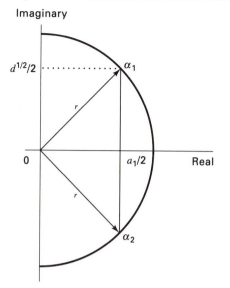

the vertical axis. If the characteristic roots α_1 and α_2 are both real, they can be plotted on the horizontal axis. Stability requires that they lie within a circle of radius 1. Complex roots will lie somewhere in the complex plane. If $\alpha_1 > 0$, the roots $\alpha_1 = (a_1 + i\sqrt{d})/2$ and $\alpha_2 = (a_1 - i\sqrt{d})/2$ can be represented by the two points shown in Figure 1.6. For example, α_1 is drawn by moving $a_1/2$ units along the real axis and $\sqrt{d}/2$ units along the imaginary axis. Using the distance formula, we can give the length of the radius r by

$$r = \sqrt{(a_1/2)^2 + (d^{1/2}i/2)^2}$$

and using the fact that $i^2 = -1$, we obtain

$$r = -a_2/2$$

The stability condition requires that $r < 1$. Hence, when plotted on the complex plane, the two roots α_1 and α_2 must lie within a circle of radius equal to unity. In the time-series literature, it is simply stated that *stability requires that all characteristic roots lie within the unit circle.*

Higher-Order Systems

The same method can be used to find the homogeneous solution to higher-order difference equations. The homogeneous equation for (1.10) is

$$y_t - \sum_{i=1}^{n} a_i y_{t-i} = 0 \qquad (1.55)$$

Given the results in Section 4, you should suspect each homogeneous solution to have the form $y_t^h = A\alpha^t$, where A is an arbitrary constant. Thus, to find the value(s) of α, we seek the solution for

$$A\alpha^t - \sum_{i=1}^{n} a_i A\alpha^{t-i} = 0 \qquad (1.56)$$

or, dividing through by α^{t-n}, we seek the values of α that solve

$$\alpha^n - a_1\alpha^{n-1} - a_2\alpha^{n-2} \cdots -a_n = 0 \qquad (1.57)$$

This nth-order polynomial will yield n solutions for α. Denote these n characteristic roots by α_1, α_2, ..., α_n. Given the results in Section 4, the linear combination $A_1\alpha_1^t + A_2\alpha_2^t + \cdots + A_n\alpha_n^t$ is also a solution. The arbitrary constants A_1 through A_n can be eliminated by imposing n initial conditions on the general solution. The α_i may be real or complex numbers. Stability requires that all real-valued α_i be less than unity in absolute value. Complex roots will necessarily come in pairs. Stability requires that all roots lie within the unit circle shown in Figure 1.6.

In most circumstances, there is little need to directly calculate the characteristic roots of higher-order systems. Many of the technical details are included in Appendix 2 to this chapter. However, there are some useful rules to check the stability conditions in higher-order systems.

1. In an nth-order equation, a necessary condition for all characteristic roots to lie inside the unit circle is

$$\sum_{i=1}^{n} a_i < 1$$

2. Since the values of the a_i can be positive or negative, a sufficient condition for all characteristic roots to lie inside the unit circle is

$$\sum_{i=1}^{n} |a_i| < 1$$

3. At least one characteristic root equals unity if

$$\sum_{i=1}^{n} a_i = 1$$

Any sequence that contains one or more characteristic roots that equal unity is called a **unit root** process.

4. For a third-order equation, the stability conditions can be written as

$$1 - a_1 - a_2 - a_3 > 0$$
$$1 + a_1 - a_2 + a_3 > 0$$
$$1 - a_1 a_3 + a_2 - a_3^2 > 0$$
$$3 + a_1 + a_2 - 3a_3 > 0 \quad \text{or} \quad 3 - a_1 + a_2 + 3a_3 > 0$$

Given that the first three inequalities are satisfied, either of the last two can be checked. One of the last conditions is redundant given that the other three hold.

7. FINDING PARTICULAR SOLUTIONS FOR DETERMINISTIC PROCESSES

Finding the particular solution to a difference equation is often a matter of ingenuity and perseverance. The appropriate technique depends crucially on the form of the $\{x_t\}$ process. We begin by considering those processes that contain only deterministic components. Of course, in econometric analysis, the forcing process will contain both deterministic and stochastic components.

CASE 1

$x_t = 0$. When all elements of the $\{x_t\}$ process are zero, the difference equation becomes

$$y_t = a_0 + a_1 y_{t-1} + a_2 y_{t-2} + \cdots + a_n y_{t-n} \tag{1.58}$$

Intuition suggests that an unchanging value of y (i.e., $y_t = y_{t-1} = \cdots = c$) should solve the equation. Substitute the trial solution $y_t = c$ into (1.58) to obtain

$$c = a_0 + a_1 c + a_2 c + \cdots + a_n c$$

so that

$$c = a_0/(1 - a_1 - a_2 - \cdots - a_n) \tag{1.59}$$

As long as $(1 - a_1 - a_2 - \cdots - a_n)$ does not equal zero, the value of c given by (1.59) is a solution to (1.58). Hence, the particular solution to (1.58) is given by $y_t^p = a_0/(1 - a_1 - a_2 - \cdots - a_n)$.

If $1 - a_1 - a_2 - \cdots - a_n = 0$, the value of c in (1.59) is undefined; it is necessary to try some other form for the solution. The key insight is that $\{y_t\}$ is a unit root process if $\Sigma a_i = 1$. Since $\{y_t\}$ is not convergent, it stands to reason that the constant solution does not work. Instead, recall equations (1.12) and (1.26); these solutions suggest that a linear time trend can appear in the solution of a unit root process. As such, try the solution $y_t^p = ct$. For ct to be a solution, it must be the case that

$$ct = a_0 + a_1 c(t - 1) + a_2 c(t - 2) + \cdots + a_n c(t - n)$$

or combining like terms, we obtain

$$(1 - a_1 - a_2 - \cdots - a_n)ct = a_0 - c(a_1 + 2a_2 + 3a_3 + \cdots + na_n)$$

Since $1 - a_1 - a_2 - \cdots - a_n = 0$, select the value of c such that

$$c = a_0/(a_1 + 2a_2 + 3a_3 + \cdots + na_n)$$

For example, let

$$y_t = 2 + 0.75y_{t-1} + 0.25y_{t-2}$$

Here, $a_1 = 0.75$ and $a_2 = 0.25$; $\{y_t\}$ is a unit root process since $a_1 + a_2 = 1$. The particular solution has the form ct, where $c = 2/[0.75 + 2(0.25)] = 1.6$. In the event that the solution ct fails, sequentially try the solutions $y_t^p = ct^2, ct^3, \cdots, ct^n$. For an nth-order equation, one of these solutions will always be the particular solution.

CASE 2

The Exponential Case. Let x_t have the exponential form $b(d)^{rt}$, where b, d, and r are constants. Since r has the natural interpretation as a growth rate, we would expect to encounter this type of forcing process case in a growth context. We illustrate the solution procedure using the first-order equation:

$$y_t = a_0 + a_1 y_{t-1} + bd^{rt} \tag{1.60}$$

To try to gain an intuitive feel for the form of the solution, notice that if $b = 0$, (1.60) is a special case of (1.58). Hence, you should expect a constant to appear in the particular solution. Moreover, the expression d^{rt} grows at the constant rate r. Thus, you might expect the particular solution to have the form $y_t^p = c_0 + c_1 d^{rt}$, where c_0 and c_1 are constants. If this equation is actually a solution, you should be able to substitute it back into (1.60) and obtain an identity. Making the appropriate substitutions, we get

$$c_0 + c_1 d^{rt} = a_0 + a_1[c_0 + c_1 d^{r(t-1)}] + bd^{rt} \tag{1.61}$$

For this solution to "work," it is necessary to select c_0 and c_1 such that

$$c_0 = a_0/(1 - a_1) \qquad \text{and} \qquad c_1 = bd^r/(d^r - a_1)$$

Thus, a particular solution is

$$y_t^p = [a_0/(1 - a_1)] + [bd^r/(d^r - a_1)]d^{rt}$$

The nature of the solution is that y_t^p equals the constant $a_0/(1 - a_1)$ plus an expression that grows at the rate r. Note that for $|d^r| < 1$, the particular solution converges to $a_0/(1 - a_1)$.

If either $a_1 = 1$ or $a_1 = d^r$, use the "trick" suggested in Case 1. If $a_1 = 1$, try the solution $c_0 = ct$, and if $a_1 = d^r$, try the solution $c_1 = t(bd^r)/(d^r - a_1)$. Use precisely the same methodology in higher-order systems.

CASE 3

Deterministic time trend. In this case, let the $\{x_t\}$ sequence be represented by the relationship $x_t = bt^d$ where b is a constant and d a positive integer. Hence,

$$y_t = a_0 + \sum_{i=1}^{n} a_i y_{t-i} + bt^d \tag{1.62}$$

Since y_t depends on t^d, it follows that y_{t-1} depends on $(t - 1)^d$, y_{t-2} depends on $(t - 2)^d$, etc. As such, the particular solution has the form $y_t^p = c_0 + c_1 t + c_2 t^2 + \cdots + c_d t^d$. To find the values of the c_i, substitute the particular solution into (1.62). Then select the value of each c_i that result in an identity. Although various values of d are possible, in economic applications it is common to see models incorporating a linear time trend ($d = 1$). For illustrative purposes, consider the second-order equation $y_t = a_0 + a_1 y_{t-1} + a_2 y_{t-2} + bt$. Posit the solution $y_t^p = c_0 + c_1 t$, where c_0 and c_1 are undetermined coefficients. Substituting this "challenge solution" into the second-order difference equation yields

$$c_0 + c_1 t = a_0 + a_1[c_0 + c_1(t - 1)] + a_2[c_0 + c_1(t - 2)] + bt \tag{1.63}$$

Now select values of c_0 and c_1 so as to force Equation (1.63) to be an identity for all possible values of t. If we combine all constant terms and all terms involving t, the required values of c_0 and c_1 are

$$c_1 = b/(1 - a_1 - a_2)$$
$$c_0 = [a_0 - (2a_2 + a_1)c_1]/(1 - a_1 - a_2)$$

so that

$$c_0 = [a_0/(1 - a_1 - a_2)] - [b/(1 - a_1 - a_2)^2]$$

Thus, the particular solution will also contain a linear time trend. You should have no difficulty foreseeing the solution technique if $a_1 + a_2 = 1$. In this circumstance—which is applicable to higher-order cases also—try multiplying the original challenge solution by t.

8. THE METHOD OF UNDETERMINED COEFFICIENTS

At this point, it is appropriate to introduce the first of two useful methods of finding particular solutions when there are stochastic components in the $\{y_t\}$ process. The key insight of the **method of undetermined coefficients** is that the particular solution to a linear difference equation is necessarily linear. Moreover, the solution can depend only on time, a constant, and the elements of the forcing process $\{x_t\}$. Thus, it is often possible to know the exact *form* of the solution even though the coefficients of the solution are unknown. The technique involves positing a solution—called a **challenge solution**—that is a linear function of all terms thought to appear in actual solution. The problem becomes one of finding the set of values for these undetermined coefficients that solve the difference equation.

The actual technique for finding the coefficients is straightforward. Substitute the challenge solution into the original difference equation and solve for the values of the undetermined coefficients that yield an identity for all possible values of the included variables. If it is not possible to obtain an identity, the form of the challenge solution is incorrect. Try a new trial solution and repeat the process. In fact, we used the method of undetermined coefficients when positing the challenge solutions $y_t^p = c_0 + c_1 d^{rt}$ and $y_t^p = c_0 + c_1 t$ for Cases 2 and 3 in Section 7.

To begin, reconsider the simple first-order equation $y_t = a_0 + a_1 y_{t-1} + \epsilon_t$. Since you have solved this equation using the iterative method, the equation is useful for illustrating the method of undetermined coefficients. The nature of the $\{y_t\}$ process is such that the particular solution can depend only on a constant term, time, and the individual elements of the $\{\epsilon_t\}$ sequence. Since t does not explicitly appear in the forcing process, t can be in the particular solution only if the characteristic root is unity. Since the goal is to illustrate the method, posit the challenge solution:

$$y_t = b_0 + b_1 t + \sum_{i=0}^{\infty} \alpha_i \epsilon_{t-i} \tag{1.64}$$

where b_0, b_1, and all the α_i are the coefficients to be determined.

Substitute (1.64) into the original difference equation to form

$$b_0 + b_1 t + \alpha_0 \epsilon_t + \alpha_1 \epsilon_{t-1} + \alpha_2 \epsilon_{t-2} + \cdots$$
$$= a_0 + a_1[b_0 + b_1(t - 1) + \alpha_0 \epsilon_{t-1} + \alpha_1 \epsilon_{t-2} + \cdots] + \epsilon_t$$

Collecting like terms, we obtain

$$(b_0 - a_0 - a_1 b_0 + a_1 b_1) + b_1(1 - a_1)t + (\alpha_0 - 1)\epsilon_t + (\alpha_1 - a_1 \alpha_0)\epsilon_{t-1}$$
$$+ (\alpha_2 - a_1 \alpha_1)\epsilon_{t-2} + (\alpha_3 - a_1 \alpha_2)\epsilon_{t-3} + \cdots = 0 \quad (1.65)$$

Equation (1.65) must hold for all values of t and all possible values of the $\{\epsilon_t\}$ sequence. Thus, each of the following conditions must hold:

$$\alpha_0 - 1 = 0$$
$$\alpha_1 - a_1 \alpha_0 = 0$$
$$\alpha_2 - a_1 \alpha_1 = 0$$
$$.$$
$$.$$
$$b_0 - a_0 - a_1 b_0 + a_1 b_1 = 0$$
$$b_1 - a_1 b_1 = 0$$

Notice that the first set of conditions can be solved for the α_i recursively. The solution of the first condition entails setting $\alpha_0 = 1$. Given this solution for α_0, the next equation requires $\alpha_1 = a_1$. Moving down the list, we obtain $\alpha_2 = a_1 \alpha_1$ or $\alpha_2 = a_1^2$. Continuing the recursive process, we find $\alpha_i = a_1^i$. Now consider the last two equations. There are two possible cases depending on the value of a_1. If $a_1 \neq 1$, it immediately follows that $b_1 = 0$ and $b_0 = a_0/(1 - a_1)$. For this case, the particular solution is

$$y_t = [a_0/(1 - a_1)] + \sum_{i=0}^{\infty} a_1^i \epsilon_{t-i}$$

Compare this result to (1.21); you will see that it is precisely the same solution found using the iterative method. The general solution is the sum of this particular solution plus the homogeneous solution Aa_1^t. Hence, the general solution is

$$y_t = [a_0/(1 - a_1)] + \sum_{i=0}^{\infty} a_1^i \epsilon_{t-i} + Aa_1^t$$

Now, if there is an initial condition for y_0, it follows that

$$y_0 = [a_0/(1 - a_1)] + \sum_{i=0}^{\infty} a_1^i \epsilon_{-i} + A$$

Combining these two equations so as to eliminate the arbitrary constant A, we obtain

$$y_t = [a_0/(1-a_1)] + \sum_{i=0}^{\infty} a_1^i \epsilon_{t-i} + a_1^t \left\{ y_0 - [a_0/(1-a_1)] - \sum_{i=0}^{\infty} a_1^i \epsilon_{-i} \right\}$$

so that

$$y_t = [a_0/(1-a_1)] + \sum_{i=0}^{t-1} a_1^i \epsilon_{t-i} + a_1^t \left\{ y_0 - [a_0/(1-a_1)] \right\} \qquad (1.66)$$

It is easily verified that (1.66) is identical to (1.25). Instead, if $a_1 = 1$, b_0 can be any arbitrary constant and $b_1 = a_0$. The improper form of the solution is

$$y_t = b_0 + a_0 t + \sum_{i=0}^{\infty} \epsilon_{t-i}$$

The form of the solution is "improper" since the sum of the $\{\epsilon_t\}$ sequence may not be finite. Hence, it is necessary to impose an initial condition. If the value y_0 is given, it follows that

$$y_0 = b_0 + \sum_{i=0}^{\infty} \epsilon_{-i}$$

Imposing the initial condition on the improper form of the solution yields (1.26)

$$y_t = y_0 + a_0 t + \sum_{i=1}^{t} \epsilon_i$$

To take a second example, consider the equation

$$y_t = a_0 + a_1 y_{t-1} + \epsilon_t + \beta_1 \epsilon_{t-1} \qquad (1.67)$$

Again, the solution can depend only on a constant, the elements of the $\{\epsilon_t\}$ sequence, and t raised to the first power. As in the previous example, t does not need to be included in the challenge solution if the characteristic root differs from unity. To reinforce this point, use the challenge solution given by (1.64). Substitute this tentative solution into (1.67) to obtain

$$b_0 + b_1 t + \sum_{i=0}^{\infty} \alpha_i \epsilon_{t-i} = a_0 + a_1 \left[b_0 + b_1(t-1) + \sum_{i=0}^{\infty} \alpha_i \epsilon_{t-1-i} \right] + \epsilon_t + \beta_1 \epsilon_{t-1}$$

Matching coefficients on all terms containing $\epsilon_t, \epsilon_{t-1}, \epsilon_{t-2}, \cdots$ yields

$$\alpha_0 = 1$$
$$\alpha_1 = a_1 \alpha_0 + \beta_1 \qquad \text{[so that } \alpha_1 = a_1 + \beta_1]$$
$$\alpha_2 = a_1 \alpha_1 \qquad \text{[so that } \alpha_2 = a_1(a_1 + \beta_1)]$$
$$\alpha_3 = a_1 \alpha_2 \qquad \text{[so that } \alpha_3 = (a_1)^2(a_1 + \beta_1)]$$

.
.

$$\alpha_i = a_1 \alpha_{i-1} \qquad \text{[so that } \alpha_i = (a_1)^{i-1}(a_1 + \beta_1)]$$

Matching coefficients of intercept terms and coefficients of terms containing t, we get

$$b_0 = a_0 + a_1 b_0 - a_1 b_1$$
$$b_1 = a_1 b_1$$

Again, there are two cases. If $a_1 \neq 1$, then $b_1 = 0$ and $b_0 = a_0/(1 - a_1)$. The particular solution is

$$y_t = [a_0/(1-a_1)] + \epsilon_t + (a_1 + \beta_1) \sum_{i=1}^{\infty} a_1^{i-1} \epsilon_{t-i}$$

The general solution augments the particular solution with the term Aa_1^t. You are left with the exercise of imposing the initial condition for y_0 on the general solution. Now consider the case in which $\alpha_1 = 1$. The undetermined coefficients are such that $b_1 = a_0$ and b_0 is an arbitrary constant. The improper form of the solution is

$$y_t = b_0 + a_0 t + \epsilon_t + (1 + \beta_1) \sum_{i=1}^{\infty} \epsilon_{t-i}$$

If y_0 is given, it follows that

$$y_0 = b_0 + \epsilon_0 + (1 + \beta_1) \sum_{t=1}^{\infty} \epsilon_{-i}$$

Hence, imposing the initial condition, we obtain

$$y_t = y_0 + a_0 t + \epsilon_t + (1 + \beta_1) \sum_{i=1}^{t-1} \epsilon_{t-i}$$

Higher-Order Systems

The identical procedure is used for higher-order systems. As an example, let us find the particular solution to the second-order equation:

$$y_t = a_0 + a_1 y_{t-1} + a_2 y_{t-2} + \epsilon_t \tag{1.68}$$

Since we have a second-order equation, we use the challenge solution:

$$y_t = b_0 + b_1 t + b_2 t^2 + \alpha_0 \epsilon_t + \alpha_1 \epsilon_{t-1} + \alpha_2 \epsilon_{t-2} + \cdots$$

where b_0, b_1, b_2, and the α_i are the undetermined coefficients.

Substituting the challenge solution into (1.68) yields

$$(b_0 + b_1 t + b_2 t^2) + \alpha_0 \epsilon_t + \alpha_1 \epsilon_{t-1} + \alpha_2 \epsilon_{t-2} + \cdots = a_0 + a_1 [b_0 + b_1(t-1) + b_2(t-1)^2$$
$$+ \alpha_0 \epsilon_{t-1} + \alpha_1 \epsilon_{t-2} + \alpha_2 \epsilon_{t-3} + \cdots] + a_2 [b_0 + b_1(t-2) + b_2(t-2)^2$$
$$+ \alpha_0 \epsilon_{t-2} + \alpha_1 \epsilon_{t-3} + \alpha_2 \epsilon_{t-4} + \cdots] + \epsilon_t$$

The necessary and sufficient conditions for the values of the α_i's to render the equation above an identity for all possible realizations of the $\{\epsilon_t\}$ sequence are

$$\alpha_0 = 1$$
$$\alpha_1 = a_1 \alpha_0 \qquad [\text{so that } \alpha_1 = a_1]$$
$$\alpha_2 = a_1 \alpha_1 + a_2 \alpha_0 \qquad [\text{so that } \alpha_2 = (a_1)^2 + a_2]$$
$$\alpha_3 = a_1 \alpha_2 + a_2 \alpha_1 \qquad [\text{so that } \alpha_3 = (a_1)^3 + 2a_1 a_2]$$
$$\cdot$$
$$\cdot$$

Notice that for any value of $j \geq 2$, the coefficients solve the second-order difference equation $\alpha_j = a_1 \alpha_{j-1} + a_2 \alpha_{j-2}$. Since we know α_0 and α_1, we can solve for all the α_j iteratively. The properties of the coefficients will be precisely those discussed when considering homogeneous solutions, namely the following:

1. Convergence necessitates $|a_2| < 1$, $a_1 + a_2 < 1$, and $a_2 - a_1 < 1$. Notice that convergence implies that past values of the $\{\epsilon_t\}$ sequence ultimately have a successively smaller influence on the current value of y_t.

2. If the coefficients converge, convergence will be direct if $(a_1^2 + 4a_2) > 0$, will follow a sine/cosine pattern if $(a_1^2 + 4a_2) < 0$, and will "explode" and then converge if $(a_1^2 + 4a_2) = 0$. Appropriately setting the α_i, we are left with the remaining expression:

$$b_2(1 - a_1 - a_2)t^2 + [b_1(1 - a_1 - a_2) + 2b_2(a_1 + 2a_2)]t$$
$$+ [b_0(1 - a_1 - a_2) - a_0 + a_1(b_1 - b_2) + 2a_2(b_1 - 2b_2)] = 0 \quad (1.69)$$

Equation (1.69) must equal zero for all values of t. First, consider the case in which $a_1 + a_2 \neq 1$. Since $(1 - a_1 - a_2)$ does not vanish, it is necessary to set the value of b_2 equal to zero. Given that $b_2 = 0$ and the coefficient of t must equal zero, it follows that b_1 must also be set equal to zero. Finally, given that $b_1 = b_2 = 0$, we must set $b_0 = a_0/(1 - a_1 - a_2)$. Instead, if $a_1 + a_2 = 1$, the solutions for the b_i depend on the specific values of a_0, a_1, and a_2. The key point is that *the stability condition for the homogeneous equation is precisely the condition for convergence of the particular solution. If the characteristic roots of the homogeneous equation are equal to unity, a polynomial time trend will appear in the particular solution. The order of the polynomial is the number of unitary characteristic roots.* This result generalizes to higher-order equations.

If you are really clever, you can combine the discussion of the last section with the method of undetermined coefficients. Find the deterministic portion of the particular solution using the techniques discussed in the last section. Then use the method of undetermined coefficients to find the stochastic portion of the particular solution. In (1.67), for example, set $\epsilon_t = \epsilon_{t-1} = 0$ and obtain the solution $a_0/(1 - a_1)$. Now use the method of undetermined coefficients to find the particular solution of $y_t = a_1 y_{t-1} + \epsilon_t + \beta_1 \epsilon_{t-1}$. Add together the deterministic and stochastic components to obtain all components of the particular solution.

A Solved Problem

To illustrate the methodology using a second-order equation, augment (1.33) with the stochastic term ϵ_t so that

$$y_t = 3 + 0.9y_{t-1} - 0.2y_{t-2} + \epsilon_t \quad (1.70)$$

You have already verified that the two homogeneous solutions are $A_1(0.5)^t$ and $A_2(0.4)^t$ and the deterministic portion of the particular solution is $y_t^p = 10$. To find the stochastic portion of the particular solution, form the challenge solution:

$$y_t = \sum_{i=0}^{\infty} \alpha_i \epsilon_{t-i}$$

In contrast to (1.64), the intercept term b_0 is excluded (since we have already found the deterministic portion of the particular solution) and the time trend $b_1 t$ is excluded (since both characteristic roots are less than unity). For this challenge to "work," it must satisfy

$$\alpha_0 \epsilon_t + \alpha_1 \epsilon_{t-1} + \alpha_2 \epsilon_{t-2} + \alpha_3 \epsilon_{t-3} + \cdots = 0.9(\alpha_0 \epsilon_{t-1} + \alpha_1 \epsilon_{t-2} + \alpha_2 \epsilon_{t-3} + \alpha_3 \epsilon_{t-4} + \cdots)$$
$$- 0.2[\alpha_0 \epsilon_{t-2} + \alpha_1 \epsilon_{t-3} + \alpha_2 \epsilon_{t-4} + \alpha_3 \epsilon_{t-5} + \cdots] + \epsilon_t \quad (1.71)$$

Since (1.71) must hold for all possible realizations of $\epsilon_t, \epsilon_{t-1}, \epsilon_{t-2}, \cdots$, each of the following conditions must hold:

$$\alpha_0 = 1$$
$$\alpha_1 = 0.9\alpha_0$$

so that $\alpha_1 = 0.9$, and for all $i \geq 2$,

$$\alpha_i = 0.9\alpha_{i-1} - 0.2\alpha_{i-2} \tag{1.72}$$

Now, it is possible to solve (1.72) iteratively so that $\alpha_2 = 0.9\alpha_1 - 0.2\alpha_0 = 0.61$, $\alpha_3 = 0.9(0.61) - 0.2(0.9) = 0.369$, etc. A more elegant solution method is to view (1.72) as a second-order difference equation in the α_i with initial conditions $\alpha_0 = 1$ and $\alpha_1 = 0.9$. The solution to (1.72) is

$$\alpha_i = 5(0.5)^i - 4(0.4)^i \tag{1.73}$$

To obtain (1.73), note that the solution to (1.72) is $\alpha_i = A_3(0.5)^i + A_4(0.4)^i$, where A_3 and A_4 are arbitrary constants. Imposing the conditions $\alpha_0 = 1$ and $\alpha_1 = 0.9$ yields (1.73). If we use (1.73), it follows that $\alpha_0 = 5(0.5)^0 - 4(0.4)^0 = 1$; $\alpha_1 = 5(0.5)^1 - 4(0.4)^1 = 0.9$; $\alpha_2 = 5(0.5)^2 - 4(0.4)^2 = 0.61$, etc.

The general solution to (1.70) is the sum of the two homogeneous solutions and the deterministic and stochastic portions of the particular solution:

$$y_t = 10 + A_1(0.5)^t + A_2(0.4)^t + \sum_{i=0}^{\infty} \alpha_i \epsilon_{t-i} \tag{1.74}$$

where the α_i are given by (1.73).

Given initial conditions for y_0 and y_1, it follows that A_1 and A_2 must satisfy

$$y_0 = 10 + A_1 + A_2 + \sum_{i=0}^{\infty} \alpha_i \epsilon_{-i} \tag{1.75}$$

$$y_1 = 10 + A_1(0.5) + A_2(0.4) + \sum_{i=0}^{\infty} \alpha_i \epsilon_{1-i} \tag{1.76}$$

Although the algebra becomes messy, (1.75) and (1.76) can be substituted into (1.74) to eliminate the arbitrary constants:

$$y_t = 10 + (0.4)^t[5(y_0 - 10) - 10(y_1 - 10)] + (0.5)^t[10(y_1 - 10) - 4(y_0 - 10)] + \sum_{i=0}^{t-2} \alpha_i \epsilon_{t-i}$$

9. LAG OPERATORS

If it is not important to know the actual values of the coefficients appearing in the particular solution, it is often more convenient to use lag operators than the method of undetermined coefficients. The **lag operator** L is defined to be a *linear* operator such that for any value y_t

$$L^i y_t \equiv y_{t-i} \qquad (1.77)$$

Thus, L^i preceding y_t simply means to lag y_t by i periods. It is useful to remember the following properties of lag operators:

1. The lag of a constant is a constant: $Lc = c$.
2. The distributive law holds for lag operators. We can set $(L^i + L^j)y_t = L^i y_t + L^j y_t = y_{t-i} + y_{t-j}$.
3. The associative law of multiplication holds for lag operators. We can set $L^i L^j y_t = L^i(L^j y_t) = L^i y_{t-j} = y_{t-i-j}$. Similarly, we can set $L^i L^j y_t = L^{i+j} y_t = y_{t-i-j}$. Note that $L^0 y_t = y_t$.
4. L raised to a negative power is actually a *lead* operator: $L^{-i} y_t = y_{t+i}$. To explain, define $j = -i$ and form $L^j y_t = y_{t-j} = y_{t+i}$.
5. For $|a| < 1$, the infinite sum $(1 + aL + a^2 L^2 + a^3 L^3 + \cdots)y_t = y_t/(1 - aL)$. This property of lag operators may not seem intuitive, but it follows directly from properties 2 and 3 above.

   Proof: Multiply each side by $(1 - aL)$ to form $(1 - aL)(1 + aL + a^2 L^2 + a^3 L^3 + \cdots)y_t = y_t$. Multiply the two expressions to obtain $(1 - aL + aL - a^2 L^2 + a^2 L^2 - a^3 L^3 + \cdots)y_t = y_t$. Given that $|a| < 1$, the expression $a^n L^n y_t$ converges to zero as n approaches infinity. Thus, the two sides of the equation are equal.
6. For $|a| > 1$, the infinite sum $[1 + (aL)^{-1} + (aL)^{-2} + (aL)^{-3} + \cdots]y_t = -aLy_t/(1 - aL)$.

   Hence, $y_t/(1 - aL) = -(aL)^{-1} \sum_{i=0}^{\infty} (aL)^{-i} y_t$

   Proof: Multiply by $(1 - aL)$ to form $(1 - aL)[1 + (aL)^{-1} + (aL)^{-2} + (aL)^{-3} + \cdots]y_t = -aLy_t$. Perform the indicated multiplication to obtain: $[1 - aL + (aL)^{-1} - 1 + (aL)^{-2} - (aL)^{-1} + (aL)^{-3} - (aL)^{-2} \cdots]y_t = -aLy_t$. Given that $|a| > 1$, the expression $a^{-n} L^{-n} y_t$ converges to zero as n approaches infinity. Thus, the two sides of the equation are equal.

Lag operators provide a concise notation for writing difference equations. Using lag operators, we can write the pth-order equation $y_t = a_0 + a_1 y_{t-1} + \cdots + a_p y_{t-p} + \epsilon_t$ as

$$(1 - a_1 L - a_2 L^2 - \cdots - a_p L^p)y_t = a_0 + \epsilon_t$$

or more compactly as

$$A(L)y_t = a_0 + \epsilon_t$$

where $A(L)$ is the polynomial $(1 - a_1L - a_2L^2 - \cdots - a_pL^p)$.

Since $A(L)$ can be viewed as a polynomial in the lag operator, the notation $A(1)$ is used to denote the sum of the coefficients:

$$A(1) = 1 - a_1 - a_2 \cdots - a_p.$$

As a second example, lag operators can be used to express the equation $y_t = a_0 + a_1y_{t-1} + \cdots + a_py_{t-p} + \epsilon_t + \beta_1\epsilon_{t-1} + \cdots + \beta_q\epsilon_{t-q}$ as

$$A(L)y_t = a_0 + B(L)\epsilon_t$$

where $A(L)$ and $B(L)$ are polynomials of orders p and q, respectively.

It is straightforward to use lag operators to solve linear difference equations. Again, consider the first-order equation $y_t = a_0 + a_1y_{t-1} + \epsilon_t$, where $|a_1| < 1$. Use the definition of L to form

$$y_t = a_0 + a_1Ly_t + \epsilon_t \tag{1.78}$$

Solving for y_t, we obtain

$$y_t = (a_0 + \epsilon_t)/(1 - a_1L) \tag{1.79}$$

From property 1, we know that $La_0 = a_0$, so that $a_0/(1 - a_1L) = a_0 + a_1a_0 + a_1^2a_0 + \cdots = a_0/(1 - a_1)$. From property 5, we know that $\epsilon_t/(1 - a_1L) = \epsilon_t + a_1\epsilon_{t-1} + a_1^2\epsilon_{t-2} + \cdots$. Combining these two parts of the solution, we obtain the particular solution given by (1.21).

For practice, we can use lag operators to solve (1.67): $y_t = a_0 + a_1y_{t-1} + \epsilon_t + \beta_1\epsilon_{t-1}$, where $|a_1| < 1$. Use property 2 to form $(1 - a_1L)y_t = a_0 + (1 + \beta_1L)\epsilon_t$. Solving for y_t yields

$$y_t = [a_0 + (1 + \beta_1L)\epsilon_t]/(1 - a_1L)$$

so that

$$y_t = [a_0/(1 - a_1)] + [\epsilon_t/(1 - a_1L)] + [\beta_1\epsilon_{t-1}/(1 - a_1L)] \tag{1.80}$$

Expanding the last two terms of (1.80) gives the same solution found using the method of undetermined coefficients.

Now suppose $y_t = a_0 + a_1y_{t-1} + \epsilon_t$ but that $|a_1| > 1$. The application of property 5 to (1.79) is inappropriate since it implies that y_t is infinite. Instead, expand (1.79) using property 6:

$$y_t = [a_0/(1-a_1)] - (a_1 L)^{-1} \sum_{i=0}^{\infty} (a_1 L)^{-i} \epsilon_t \tag{1.81}$$

$$= [a_0/(1-a_1)] - (1/a_1) \sum_{i=0}^{\infty} (a_1 L)^{-i} \epsilon_{t+1}$$

$$= [a_0/(1-a_1)] - (1/a_1) \sum_{i=0}^{\infty} a_1^{-i} \epsilon_{t+1+i} \tag{1.82}$$

Lag Operators in Higher-Order Systems

We can also use lag operators to transform the *n*th-order equation $y_t = a_0 + a_1 y_{t-1} + a_2 y_{t-2} + \cdots + a_n y_{t-n} + \epsilon_t$ into

$$(1 - a_1 L - a_2 L^2 - \cdots - a_n L^n) y_t = a_0 + \epsilon_t$$

or

$$y_t = (a_0 + \epsilon_t)/(1 - a_1 L - a_2 L^2 - \cdots a_n L^n)$$

From our previous analysis (also see Appendix 2 in this chapter), we know that the stability condition is such that the characteristic roots of the equation $\alpha^n - a_1 \alpha^{n-1} - \cdots - a_n = 0$ all lie *within* the unit circle. Notice that the values of α solving the characteristic equation are the reciprocals of the values of L that solve the equation $1 - a_1 L \cdots - a_n L^n = 0$. In fact, the expression $1 - a_1 L \cdots - a_n L^n$ is then called the inverse characteristic equation. Thus, in the literature, it is often stated that the stability condition is for the characteristic roots of $(1 - a_1 L \cdots - a_n L^n)$ to lie *outside* of the unit circle.

In principle, one could use lag operators to actually obtain the coefficients of the particular solution. To illustrate using the second-order case, consider $y_t = (a_0 + \epsilon_t)/(1 - a_1 L - a_2 L^2)$. If we knew the factors of the quadratic equation were such that $(1 - a_1 L - a_2 L^2) = (1 - b_1 L)(1 - b_2 L)$, we could write

$$y_t = (a_0 + \epsilon_t)/[(1 - b_1 L)(1 - b_2 L)]$$

If both b_1 and b_2 are less than unity in absolute value, we can apply property 5 to obtain

$$y_t = \frac{[a_0/(1-b_1)] + \sum_{i=0}^{\infty} b_1^i \epsilon_{t-i}}{1 - b_2 L}$$

Reapply the rule to $a_0/(1 - b_1)$ and to each of the elements in the summation $\Sigma b_1^i \epsilon_{t-i}$ to obtain the particular solution. If you want to know the actual coefficients of the process, it is preferable to use the method of undetermined coefficients. The beauty of lag operators is that they can be used to denote such particular solutions succinctly. The general model

$$A(L)y_t = a_0 + B(L)\epsilon_t$$

has the particular solution:

$$y_t = a_0/A(L) + B(L)\epsilon_t/A(L)$$

10. FORWARD - VERSUS BACKWARD-LOOKING SOLUTIONS

As suggested by (1.82), there is a **forward-looking** solution to any linear difference equation. The text will not make much use of the forward-looking solution since future realizations of stochastic variables are not directly observable. However, knowing how to obtain forward-looking solutions is useful for solving rational expectations models. Let us return to the simple iterative technique to consider the forward-looking solution to the first-order equation $y_t = a_0 + a_1 y_{t-1} + \epsilon_t$. Solving for y_{t-1}, we obtain

$$y_{t-1} = -(a_0 + \epsilon_t)/a_1 + y_t/a_1 \tag{1.83}$$

Updating one period yields

$$y_t = -(a_0 + \epsilon_{t+1})/a_1 + y_{t+1}/a_1 \tag{1.84}$$

Since $y_{t+1} = (y_{t+2} - a_0 - \epsilon_{t+2})/a_1$, begin iterating forward:

$$
\begin{aligned}
y_t &= -(a_0 + \epsilon_{t+1})/a_1 + (y_{t+2} - a_0 - \epsilon_{t+2})/(a_1)^2 \\
&= -(a_0 + \epsilon_{t+1})/a_1 - (a_0 + \epsilon_{t+2})/(a_1)^2 + y_{t+2}/(a_1)^2 \\
&= -(a_0 + \epsilon_{t+1})/a_1 - (a_0 + \epsilon_{t+2})/(a_1)^2 + (y_{t+3} - a_0 - \epsilon_{t+3})/(a_1)^3
\end{aligned}
$$

Therefore, after n iterations,

$$y_t = -a_0 \sum_{i=1}^{n} a_1^{-i} - \sum_{i=1}^{n} a_1^{-i}\epsilon_{t+i} + y_{t+n}/a_1^n \tag{1.85}$$

If we maintain that $|a_1| < 1$, this forward-looking solution will diverge as n becomes infinitely large. However, if $|a_1| > 1$, the expression a_1^{-n} goes to zero while

$-a_0(a_1^{-1} + a_1^{-2} + a_1^{-3} + \cdots)$ converges to $a_0/(1 - a_1)$. Hence, we can write the forward-looking particular solution for y_t as

$$y_t = a_0/(1-a_1) - \sum_{i=1}^{\infty} a_1^{-i} \epsilon_{t+i} \qquad (1.86)$$

Note that (1.86) is similar in form to (1.82); the difference is that the *future* values of the disturbances affect the present. Clearly, if $|a_1| > 1$, the summation is convergent so that (1.86) is a legitimate particular solution to the difference equation. Given an initial condition, a stochastic difference equation will have a forward- and backward-looking solution. For example, using lag operators, we can write the particular solution to $y_t = a_0 + a_1 y_{t-1} + \epsilon_t$ as $(a_0 + \epsilon_t)/(1 - a_1 L)$. Now multiply the numerator and denominator by $-a_1^{-1}L^{-1}$ to form

$$y_t = a_0/(1 - a_1) - a_1^{-1}L^{-1}\epsilon_t/(1 - a_1^{-1}L^{-1})$$

$$= a_0/(1-a_1) - \sum_{i=1}^{\infty} a_1^{-i} \epsilon_{t+i} \qquad (1.87)$$

More generally, we can always obtain a forward-looking solution for any nth-order equation. (For practice in using the alternative methods of solving difference equations, try to obtain this forward-looking solution using the method of undetermined coefficients.)

Properties of the Alternative Solutions

The backward- and forward-looking solutions are two mathematically valid solutions to any n.th order difference equation. In fact, since the equation itself is linear, it is straightforward to show that any linear combination of the forward- and backward-looking solutions is also a solution. For economic analysis, however, the distinction is important since the time paths implied by these alternative solutions are quite different. First consider the backward-looking solution. If $|a_1| < 1$, the expression a_1^i converges toward zero as $i \to \infty$. Also, notice that the effect of ϵ_{t-i} on y_t is a_1^i; if $|a_1| < 1$, the effects of the past ϵ_t also diminish over time. Suppose instead that $|a_1| > 1$; in this instance, the backward-looking solution for y_t explodes.

The situation is reversed using the forward solution. Here, if $|a_1| < 1$, the expression a_1^{-i} gets infinitely large as i approaches ∞. Instead, if $|a_1| > 1$, the forward-looking solution leads to a finite sequence for $\{y_t\}$. The reason is that a_1^{-i} converges to zero as i increases. Note that the effect of ϵ_{t+i} on y_t is a_1^{-i}; if $|a_1| > 1$, the effects of the future values of ϵ_{t+i} have a diminishing influence on the current value of y_t.

From a purely mathematical point of view, there is no "most appropriate" solution. However, economic theory may suggest that a sequence be **bounded** in the sense that the limiting value for any value in the sequence is finite. Real interest rates, real per capita income, and many other economic variables can hardly be expected to approach either plus or minus infinity. Imposing boundary restrictions entails using the backward-looking solution if $|a_1| < 1$ and the forward-looking solution if $|a_1| > 1$. Similar remarks hold for higher-order equations.

Cagan's Money Demand Function

Cagan's model of hyperinflation provides an excellent example of choosing the appropriateness of forward- versus backward-looking solutions. Let the demand for money take the form

$$m_t - p_t = \alpha - \beta(p_{t+1}^e - p_t) \qquad \beta > 0 \qquad (1.88)$$

where m_t = logarithm of the nominal money supply in t
         p_t = the logarithm of price level in t
         p_{t+1}^e = the logarithm of the price level expected in period $t + 1$

The key point of the model is that the demand for real money balances $(m_t - p_t)$ is negatively related to the expected rate of inflation $(p_{t+1}^e - p_t)$. Because Cagan was interested in the relationship between inflation and money demand, all other variables were subsumed into the constant α. Since our task is to work with forward-looking solutions, let the money supply function simply be the process

$$m_t = m + \epsilon_t$$

where m = the average value of the money supply
         ϵ_t = a disturbance term with a mean value of zero

As opposed to the cobweb model, let individuals have forward-looking perfect foresight so the expected price for $t + 1$ equals the price that actually prevails:

$$p_{t+1}^e = p_{t+1}$$

Under perfect foresight, agents in period t are assumed to know the price level in $t + 1$. In the context of the example, agents are able to solve difference equations and can simply "figure out" the time path of prices. Thus, we can write the money market equilibrium condition as

$$m + \epsilon_t - p_t = \alpha - \beta[p_{t+1} - p_t]$$

or

$$p_{t+1} - (1 + 1/\beta)p_t = -(m - \alpha)/\beta - \epsilon_t/\beta \qquad (1.89)$$

For practice, we use the method of undetermined coefficients to obtain the particular solution. (You should check your abilities by repeating the exercise using lag operators.) We use the forward-looking solution since the coefficient on $(1 + 1/\beta)$ is greater than unity in absolute value. Try the challenge solution:

$$p_t^p = b_0 + \sum_{i=0}^{\infty} \alpha_i \epsilon_{t+i}$$

Substituting this challenge solution into the above, we obtain

$$b_0 + \sum_{i=0}^{\infty} \alpha_i \epsilon_{t+1+i} - ((1+\beta)/\beta)\left(b_0 + \sum_{i=0}^{\infty} \alpha_i \epsilon_{t+i}\right) = (\alpha - m - \epsilon_t)/\beta \qquad (1.90)$$

For (1.90) to be an identity for all possible realizations of $\{\epsilon_t\}$, it must be the case that

$$
\begin{array}{ll}
b_0 - b_0(1+\beta)/\beta = (\alpha - m)/\beta & \Rightarrow b_0 = m - \alpha \\
-\alpha_0(1+\beta)/\beta = -1/\beta & \Rightarrow \alpha_0 = 1/(1+\beta) \\
\alpha_0 - \alpha_1(1+\beta)/\beta = 0 & \Rightarrow \alpha_1 = \beta/(1+\beta)^2 \\
\cdot \\
\cdot \\
\cdot \\
\alpha_i - \alpha_{i+1}(1+\beta)/\beta = 0 & \Rightarrow \alpha_i = \beta^i/(1+\beta)^{i+1}
\end{array}
$$

In compact form, the particular solution can be written as

$$p_t^p = m - \alpha + (1/\beta)\sum_{i=0}^{\infty} [\beta/(1+\beta)]^{1+i}\epsilon_{t+i} \qquad (1.91)$$

The next step is to find the homogeneous solution. Form the homogeneous equation, $p_{t+1} - (1 + 1/\beta)p_t = 0$. For any arbitrary constant A, it is easy to verify that the solution is

$$p_t^h = A(1 + 1/\beta)^t$$

Hence, the general solution is

$$p_t = m - \alpha + (1/\beta)\sum_{i=0}^{\infty} [\beta/(1+\beta)]^{1+i}\epsilon_{t+i} + A(1+1/\beta)^t \qquad (1.92)$$

If you examine (1.92) closely, you will note that the impulse response function is convergent; the expression $[\beta/(1 + \beta)]^{1+i}$ converges to zero as i approaches infinity.

However, the homogeneous portion of the solution is divergent. For (1.92) to yield a nonexplosive price sequence, we must be able to set the arbitrary constant equal to zero. To understand the economic implication of setting $A = 0$, suppose that the initial condition is such that the price level in period zero is p_0. If we impose this initial condition, (1.92) becomes

$$p_0 = m - \alpha + (1/\beta) \sum_{i=0}^{\infty} [\beta/(1+\beta)]^{1+i} \epsilon_i + A$$

Solving for A yields

$$A = p_0 + \alpha - m - (1/\beta) \sum_{i=0}^{\infty} [\beta/(1+\beta)]^{1+i} \epsilon_i$$

Thus, the initial condition must be such that

$$A = 0 \quad \text{or} \quad p_0 = m - \alpha + (1/\beta) \sum_{i=0}^{\infty} [\beta/(1+\beta)]^{1+i} \epsilon_i \qquad (1.93)$$

Examine the three separate components of (1.92). The deterministic expression $m - \alpha$ is the same type of long-run "equilibrium" condition encountered on several other occasions; a stable sequence tends to converge toward the deterministic portion of its particular solution. The second component of the particular solution consists of the short-run responses induced by the various ϵ_t shocks. These movements are necessarily of a short-term duration because the coefficients of the impulse response function must decay. The point is that the particular solution captures the overall long-run and short-run equilibrium behavior of the system. Finally, the homogeneous solution can be viewed as a measure of disequilibrium in the initial period. Since (1.91) is the overall equilibrium solution for period t, it should be clear that the value of p_0 in (1.93) is the equilibrium value of the price for period zero. After all, (1.93) is nothing more than (1.91) with the time subscript lagged t periods. Thus, the expression $A(1 + 1/\beta)^t$ must be zero if the deviation from equilibrium in the initial period is zero.

Imposing the requirement that the $\{p_t\}$ sequence be bounded necessitates that the general solution be

$$p_t = m - \alpha + (1/\beta) \sum_{i=0}^{\infty} [\beta/(1+\beta)]^{1+i} \epsilon_{t+i}$$

Notice that the price in each and every period t is proportional to the mean value of the money supply; this point is easy to verify since all variables are expressed in logarithms and $\partial p_t/\partial m = 1$. Temporary changes in the money supply behave in an interesting fashion. The impulse response function indicates that *future* increases in the money supply, represented by the various ϵ_{t+i}, serve to increase the price level in the *current* period. The idea is that future money supply increases imply higher prices in the future. Forward-looking agents reduce their current money holdings, with a consequent increase in the current price level, in response to this anticipated inflation.

SUMMARY AND CONCLUSIONS

Time-series econometrics is concerned with the estimation of difference equations containing stochastic components. Originally, time-series models were used for forecasting. Uncovering the dynamic path of a series improves forecasts since the predictable components of the series can be extrapolated into the future. The growing interest in economic dynamics has given a new emphasis to time-series econometrics. Stochastic difference equations arise quite naturally from dynamic economic models. Appropriately estimated equations can be used for the interpretation of economic data and for hypothesis testing.

This introductory chapter focused on methods of "solving" stochastic difference equations. Although iteration can be useful, it is impractical in many circumstances. The solution to a linear difference equation can be divided into two parts: a *particular* solution and *homogeneous* solution. One complicating factor is that the homogeneous solution is not unique. The *general* solution is a linear combination of the particular solution and all homogeneous solutions. Imposing n initial conditions on the general solution of an nth-order equation yields a unique solution.

The homogeneous portion of a difference equation is a measure of the "disequilibrium" in the initial period(s). The homogeneous equation is especially important in that it yields the characteristic roots; an nth-order equation has n such characteristic roots. If all the characteristic roots lie within the unit circle, the series will be convergent. As you will see in Chapter 2, there is a direct relationship between the stability conditions and the issue of whether an economic variable is stationary or nonstationary.

The method of undetermined coefficients and use of lag operators are powerful tools for obtaining the particular solution. The particular solution will be a linear function of the current and past values of the forcing process. In addition, this solution may contain an intercept term and a polynomial function of time. Unit roots and characteristic roots outside of the unit circle require the imposition of an initial condition for the particular solution to be meaningful. Some economic models allow for forward-looking solutions; in such circumstances, anticipated future events have consequences for the present period.

The tools developed in this chapter are aimed at paving the way for the study of time-series econometrics. It is a good idea to work all the exercises presented below. Characteristic roots, the method of undetermined coefficients, and lag operators will be encountered throughout the remainder of the text.

QUESTIONS AND EXERCISES

1. Consider the difference equation $y_t = a_0 + a_1 y_{t-1}$ with the initial condition y_0. Jill solved the difference equation by iterating backward:

$$y_t = a_0 + a_1 y_{t-1}$$
$$= a_0 + a_1(a_0 + a_1 y_{t-2})$$
$$= a_0 + a_0 a_1 + a_0 a_1^2 + \cdots + a_0 a_1^{t-1} + a_1^t y_0$$

   Bill added the homogeneous and particular solutions to obtain $y_t = a_0/(1 - a_1) + a_1^t[y_0 - a_0/(1 - a_1)]$.

   A. Show that the two solutions are identical for $|a_1| < 1$.

   B. Show that for $a_1 = 1$, Jill's solution is equivalent to $y_t = a_0 t + y_0$. How would you use Bill's method to arrive at this same conclusion in the case $a_1 = 1$?

2. The cobweb model in Section 5 assumed *static* price expectations. Consider an alternative formulation called *adaptive expectations*. Let the expected price in t (denoted by p_t^*) be a weighted average of the price in $t - 1$ and the price expectation of the previous period. Formally,

$$p_t^* = \alpha p_{t-1} + (1 - \alpha)p_{t-1}^*, \qquad 0 < \alpha \le 1$$

   Clearly, when $\alpha = 1$, the static and adaptive expectations schemes are equivalent. An interesting feature of this model is that it can be viewed as a difference equation expressing the expected price as a function of its own lagged value and the forcing variable p_{t-1}.

   A. Find the homogeneous solution for p_t^*.

   B. Use lag operators to find the particular solution. Check your answer by substituting your answer in the original difference equation.

3. Suppose that the money supply process has the form $m_t = m + \rho m_{t-1} + \epsilon_t$, where m is a constant and $0 < \rho < 1$.

   A. Show that it is possible to express m_{t+n} in terms of the known value m_t and the sequence $\{\epsilon_{t+1}, \epsilon_{t+2}, \dots, \epsilon_{t+n}\}$.

   B. Suppose that all values of ϵ_{t+i} for $i > 0$ have a mean value of zero. Explain how you could use your result in part A to forecast the money supply n periods into the future.

4. Find the particular solutions for each of the following:

   i. $y_t = a_1 y_{t-1} + \epsilon_t + \beta_1 \epsilon_{t-1}$

ii. $y_t = a_1 y_{t-1} + \epsilon_{1t} + \beta \epsilon_{2t}$ (*Hint:* The form of the solution is $y_t = \Sigma c_i \epsilon_{1t-i} + \Sigma d_i \epsilon_{2t-i}$.)

5. The *unit root problem* in time-series econometrics is concerned with character-istic roots that are equal to unity. In order to preview the issue:

   A. Find the homogeneous solution to each of the following: (*Hint:* Each has at least one unit root.)

   i. $y_t = a_0 + 1.5 y_{t-1} - 0.5 y_{t-2} + \epsilon_t$ ii. $y_t = a_0 + y_{t-2} + \epsilon_t$

   iii. $y_t = a_0 + 2 y_{t-1} - y_{t-2} + \epsilon_t$ iv. $y_t = a_0 + y_{t-1} + 0.25 y_{t-2} - 0.25 y_{t-3} + \epsilon_t$

   B. Show that each of the backward-looking solutions is not convergent.

   C. Show that Equation i can be written entirely in first differences; that is, $\Delta y_t = a_0 + 0.5 \Delta y_{t-1} + \epsilon_t$. Find the particular solution for Δy_t. (*Hint:* Define $y_t^* = \Delta y_t$ so that $y_t^* = a_0 - 0.5 y_{t-1}^* + \epsilon_t$. Find the particular solution for y_t^* in terms of the $\{\epsilon_t\}$ sequence.)

   D. Similarly transform the other equations into their first-difference form. Find the backward-looking particular solution, if it exists, for the transformed equations.

   E. Given the initial condition y_0, find the solution for $y_t = a_0 - y_{t-1} + \epsilon_t$.

6. A researcher estimated the following relationship for the inflation rate (π_t):

$$\pi_t = -0.05 + 0.7\pi_{t-1} + 0.6\pi_{t-2} + \epsilon_t$$

   A. Suppose that in periods 0 and 1, the inflation rate was 10 and 11%, respec-tively. Find the homogeneous, particular, and general solutions for the in-flation rate.

   B. Discuss the shape of the impulse response function. Given that the United States is not headed for runaway inflation, why do you believe that the re-searcher's equation is poorly estimated?

7. Consider the stochastic process $y_t = a_0 + a_2 y_{t-2} + \epsilon_t$.

   A. Find the homogeneous solution and determine the stability condition.

   B. Find the particular solution using the method of undetermined coefficients.

8. Reconsider the Cagan demand for money function in which $m_t - p_t = a - \beta(p_{t+1} - p_t)$.

   A. Show that the backward-looking particular solution for p_t is divergent.

B. Obtain the forward-looking particular solution for p_t in terms of the $\{m_t\}$ sequence. In forming the general solution, why is it necessary to assume that the money market is in long-run equilibrium?

C. Find the impact multiplier. How does an increase in m_{t+2} affect p_t? Provide an intuitive explanation of the shape of the entire impulse response function.

9. For each of the following, verify that the posited solution satisfies the difference equation. The symbols c, c_0, and a_0 denote constants:

Equation	Solution
A. $y_t - y_{t-1} = 0$	$y_t = c$
B. $y_t - y_{t-1} = a_0$	$y_t = c + a_0 t$
C. $y_t - y_{t-2} = 0$	$y_t = c + c_0(-1)^t$
D. $y_t - y_{t-2} = \epsilon_t$	$y_t = c + c_0(-1)^t + \epsilon_t + \epsilon_{t-2} + \epsilon_{t-4} + \cdots$

10. Part 1: For each of the following, determine whether $\{y_t\}$ represents a stable process. Determine whether the characteristic roots are real or imaginary and the real parts are positive or negative.

A. $y_t - 1.2y_{t-1} + 0.2y_{t-2}$ 　　 B. $y_t - 1.2y_{t-1} + 0.4y_{t-2}$

C. $y_t - 1.2y_{t-1} - 1.2y_{t-2}$ 　　 D. $y_t + 1.2y_{t-1}$

E. $y_t - 0.7y_{t-1} - 0.25y_{t-2} + 0.175y_{t-3} = 0$
　　[Hint: $(x - 0.5)(x + 0.5)(x - 0.7) = x^3 - 0.7x^2 - 0.25x + 0.175$.]

Part 2: Write each of the above equations using lag operators. Determine the characteristic roots of the inverse characteristic equation.

11. Consider the stochastic difference equation:

$$y_t = 0.8y_{t-1} + \epsilon_t - 0.5\epsilon_{t-1}$$

A. Suppose that the initial conditions are such that $y_0 = 0$ and $\epsilon_0 = \epsilon_{-1} = 0$. Now suppose that $\epsilon_1 = 1$. Determine the values y_1 through y_5 by forward iteration.

B. Find the homogeneous and particular solutions.

C. Impose the initial conditions in order to obtain the general solution.

D. Trace out the time path of an ϵ_t shock on the entire time path of the $\{y_t\}$ sequence.

12. Use Equation (1.5) to determine the restrictions on α and β necessary to ensure that the $\{y_t\}$ process is stable.

ENDNOTES

1. Another possibility is to obtain the forward-looking solution; such solutions are discussed in Section 10.
2. Alternatively, you can substitute (1.26) into (1.17). Note that when ϵ_t is a pure random disturbance, $y_t = a_0 + y_{t-1} + \epsilon_t$ is called a **random walk plus drift** model.
3. Any linear equation in the variables x_1 through x_n is homogeneous if has the form $a_1 x_1 + a_2 x_2 + \cdots + a_n x_n = 0$. To obtain the homogeneous portion of (1.10), simply set the intercept term a_0 and forcing process x_t equal to zero. Hence, the homogeneous equation for (1.10) is $y_t = a_1 y_{t-1} + a_2 y_{t-2} + \cdots + a_n y_{t-n}$.
4. If $b > a$, the demand and supply curves do not intersect in the positive quadrant. The assumption $a > b$ guarantees that the equilibrium price is positive.
5. For example, if the forcing process is $x_t = \epsilon_t + \beta_1 \epsilon_{t-1} + \beta_2 \epsilon_{t-2} + \cdots$, the impact multiplier can be taken as the partial derivative of y_t with respect to x_t. However, this text follows the usual practice of considering multipliers with respect to the $\{\epsilon_t\}$ process.

APPENDIX 1   Imaginary Roots and de Moivre's Theorem

Consider a second-order difference equation $y_t = a_1 y_{t-1} + a_2 y_{t-2}$ such that the discriminant d is negative (i.e., $d = a_1^2 + 4a_2 < 0$). From Section 6, we know that the full homogeneous solution can be written in the form

$$y_t^h = A_1 \alpha_1^t + A_2 \alpha_2^t \tag{A1.1}$$

where the two imaginary characteristic roots are

$$\alpha_1 = (a_1 + i\sqrt{d})/2 \quad \text{and} \quad \alpha_2 = (a_1 - i\sqrt{d})/2 \tag{A1.2}$$

The purpose of this appendix is to explain how to rewrite and interpret (A1.1) in terms of standard trigonometric functions. You might first want to refresh your memory concerning two useful trig identities. For any two angles θ_1 and θ_2,

$$\sin(\theta_1 + \theta_2) = \sin(\theta_1)\cos(\theta_2) + \cos(\theta_1)\sin(\theta_2)$$
$$\cos(\theta_1 + \theta_2) = \cos(\theta_1)\cos(\theta_2) - \sin(\theta_1)\sin(\theta_2) \tag{A1.3}$$

If $\theta_1 = \theta_2$, we can drop subscripts and form

$$\sin(2\theta) = 2\sin(\theta)\cos(\theta)$$
$$\cos(2\theta) = \cos(\theta)\cos(\theta) - \sin(\theta)\sin(\theta) \tag{A1.4}$$

The first task is to demonstrate how to express imaginary numbers in the complex plane. Consider Figure A1.1 in which the horizontal axis measures real numbers and the vertical axis imaginary numbers. The complex number $a + bi$ can be represented by the point a units from the origin along the horizontal axis and b

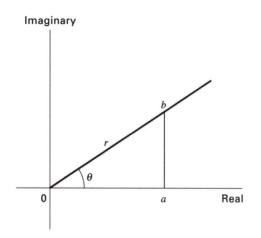

Figure A1.1 A graphical representation of complex numbers.

units from the origin along the vertical axis. It is convenient to represent the distance from the origin by the length of the vector denoted by r. Consider angle θ in triangle $0ab$ and note that $\cos(\theta) = a/r$ and $\sin(\theta) = b/r$. Hence, the lengths a and b can be measured by

$$a = r\cos(\theta) \quad \text{and} \quad b = r\sin(\theta)$$

In terms of (A1.2), we can define $a = a_1/2$ and $b = \sqrt{d}/2$. Thus, the characteristic roots α_1 and α_2 can be written as

$$\alpha_1 = a + bi = r[\cos(\theta) + i\sin(\theta)]$$
$$\alpha_2 = a - bi = r[\cos(\theta) - i\sin(\theta)] \quad \text{(A1.5)}$$

The next step is to consider the expressions α_1^t and α_2^t. Begin with the expression α_1^2 and recall that $i^2 = -1$:

$$\alpha_1^2 = \{r[\cos(\theta) + i\sin(\theta)]\}\{r[\cos(\theta) + i\sin(\theta)]\}$$
$$= r^2[\cos(\theta)\cos(\theta) - \sin(\theta)\sin(\theta) + 2i\sin(\theta)\cos(\theta)]$$

From (A1.4),

$$\alpha_1^2 = r^2[\cos(2\theta) + i\sin(2\theta)]$$

If we continue in this fashion, it is straightforward to demonstrate that

$$\alpha_1^t = r^t[\cos(t\theta) + i\sin(t\theta)] \quad \text{and} \quad \alpha_2^t = r^t[\cos(t\theta) - i\sin(t\theta)] \quad \text{(A1.6)}$$

Since y_t^h is a real number and α_1 and α_2 are complex, it follows that A_1 and A_2 must be complex. Although A_1 and A_2 are arbitrary complex numbers, they must have the form

$$A_1 = B_1[\cos(B_2) + i\sin(B_2)] \qquad \text{and} \qquad A_2 = B_1[\cos(B_2) - i\sin(B_2)]$$

where B_1 and B_2 are arbitrary real numbers measured in radians.

In order to calculate $A_1(\alpha_1^t)$, use (A1.6) and (A1.7) to form

$$\begin{aligned}
A_1\alpha_1^t &= B_1[\cos(B_2) + i\sin(B_2)]r^t[\cos(t\theta) + i\sin(t\theta)] \\
&= B_1r^t[\cos(B_2)\cos(t\theta) - \sin(B_2)\sin(t\theta) + i\cos(t\theta)\sin(B_2) + i\sin(t\theta)\cos(B_2)]
\end{aligned}$$

Using (A1.3) and (A1.4), we obtain

$$A_1\alpha_1^t = B_1r^t[\cos(t\theta + B_2) + i\sin(t\theta + B_2)] \tag{A1.8}$$

You should use the same technique to convince yourself that

$$A_2\alpha_2^t = B_1r^t[\cos(t\theta + B_2) - i\sin(t\theta + B_2)] \tag{A1.9}$$

Since the homogeneous solution y_t^h is the sum of (A1.8) and (A1.9),

$$\begin{aligned}
y_t^h &= B_1r^t[\cos(t\theta + B_2) + i\sin(t\theta + B_2)] + B_1r^t[\cos(t\theta + B_2) - i\sin(t\theta + B_2)] \\
&= 2B_1r^t\cos(t\theta + B_2)
\end{aligned} \tag{A1.10}$$

Since B_1 is arbitrary, the homogeneous solution can be written in terms of the arbitrary constants B_1 and B_3

$$y_t^h = B_3r^t\cos(t\theta + B_2) \tag{A1.11}$$

Now imagine a circle with a radius of unity superimposed on Figure $A1.1$. The stability condition is for the distance $r = 0b$ to be less than unity. Hence, in the literature it is said that the stability condition is for the characteristic roots to lie within this unit circle.

APPENDIX 2 Characteristic Roots in Higher-Order Equations

The characteristic equation to an nth-order difference equation is

$$\alpha^n - a_1\alpha^{n-1} - a_2\alpha^{n-2} \cdots - a_n = 0 \tag{A1.12}$$

As stated in Section 6, the n values of α that solve this **characteristic equation** are called the **characteristic roots.** Denote the n solutions by $\alpha_1, \alpha_2, \cdots, \alpha_n$. Given the results in Section 4, the linear combination $A_1\alpha_1^t + A_2\alpha_2^t + \cdots + A_n\alpha_n^t$ is also a solution to (A1.12).

A priori, the characteristic roots can take on any values. There is no restriction that they be real versus complex nor any restriction concerning their sign or magnitude. Consider the following possibilities:

1. **All the α_i are real and distinct**. There are several important subcases. First suppose that each value of α_i is less than unity in absolute value. In this case, the homogeneous solution (A1.12) converges since the limit of each α_i^t equals zero as t approaches infinity. For a negative value of α_i, the expression α_i^t is positive for even values of t and negative for odd values of t. Thus, if any of the α_i are negative (but less than 1 in absolute value), the solution will tend to exhibit some oscillation. If any of the α_i are greater than unity in absolute value, the solution will diverge.

2. **All the α_i are real but $m \leq n$ of the roots are repeated**. Let the solution be such that $\alpha_1 = \alpha_2 = \cdots = \alpha_m$. Call the single distinct value of this root α^* and let the other $n-m$ roots be denoted by α_{m+1} through α_n. In the case of a second-order equation with a repeated root, you saw that one solution was $A_1\alpha^t$ and the other was $A_2t\alpha^t$. With m repeated roots, it is easily verified that $t\alpha^{*t}$, $t^2\alpha^{*t}$, $\cdots$, $t^{m-1}\alpha^{*t}$ are also solutions to the homogeneous equation. With m repeated roots, the linear combination of all these solutions is

$$A_1\alpha^{*t} + A_2t\alpha^{*t} + A_3t^2\alpha^{*t} + \cdots + A_mt^{m-1}\alpha^{*t} + A_{m+1}\alpha_{m+1}^t + \cdots + A_n\alpha_n^t \quad \text{(A1.13)}$$

3. **Some of the roots are complex**. Complex roots (which necessarily come in conjugate pairs) have the form $\alpha_i \pm i\theta$, where α_i and θ are real numbers and i is defined to be $\sqrt{-1}$. For any such pair, a solution to the homogeneous equation is $A_1(\alpha_1 + i\theta)^t + A_2(\alpha_1 - i\theta)^t$, where A_1 and A_2 are arbitrary constants. Transforming to polar coordinates, we can write the associated two solutions in the form $\beta_1r^t\cos(\theta t + \beta_2)$ with arbitrary constants β_1 and β_2. Here stability hinges on the magnitude of r^t; if $|r| < 1$, the system converges. However, even if there is convergence, convergence is not direct since the sine and cosine functions impart oscillatory behavior to the time path of y_t. For example, if there are three roots, two of which are complex, the homogeneous solution has the form

$$\beta_1r^t\cos(\theta t + \beta_2) + A_3\alpha_3^t$$

Stability of Higher-Order Systems: In practice, it is difficult to find the actual values of the characteristic roots. Unless the characteristic equation is easily factored, it is necessary to use numerical methods to obtain the characteristic roots. However, for most purposes, it is sufficient to know the qualitative properties of the solution; usually, it is sufficient to know whether all the roots lie within the unit circle. The **Schur theorem** gives the necessary and sufficient conditions for stability. Given the characteristic equation of (A1.12), the theorem states that if all the n determinants below are positive, the real parts of all characteristic roots are less than 1 in absolute value:

$$\Delta_1 = \begin{vmatrix} 1 & -a_n \\ -a_n & 1 \end{vmatrix}$$

$$\Delta_2 = \begin{vmatrix} 1 & 0 & -a_n & -a_{n-1} \\ -a_1 & 1 & 0 & -a_n \\ -a_n & 0 & 1 & -a_1 \\ -a_{n-1} & -a_n & 0 & 1 \end{vmatrix}, \quad \Delta_3 = \begin{vmatrix} 1 & 0 & 0 & -a_n & -a_{n-1} & -a_{n-2} \\ -a_1 & 1 & 0 & 0 & -a_n & -a_{n-1} \\ -a_2 & -a_1 & 1 & 0 & 0 & -a_n \\ -a_n & 0 & 0 & 1 & -a_1 & -a_2 \\ -a_{n-1} & -a_n & 0 & 0 & 1 & -a_1 \\ -a_{n-2} & -a_{n-1} & -a_n & 0 & 0 & 1 \end{vmatrix} \cdots$$

$$\Delta_n = \begin{vmatrix} 1 & 0 & 0 & . & . & 0 & -a_n & -a_{n-1} & . & . & . & -a_1 \\ -a_1 & 1 & 0 & . & . & 0 & 0 & -a_n & . & . & . & -a_2 \\ -a_2 & -a_1 & 1 & . & . & 0 & 0 & 0 & -a_n & . & . & -a_3 \\ . & . & . & . & . & . & . & . & . & . & . & . \\ -a_{n-1} & -a_{n-2} & -a_{n-3} & . & . & 1 & 0 & 0 & 0 & . & . & -a_n \\ -a_n & 0 & 0 & . & . & 0 & 1 & -a_1 & -a_2 & . & . & -a_{n-1} \\ -a_{n-1} & -a_n & 0 & . & . & 0 & 0 & 1 & . & . & . & -a_{n-2} \\ . & . & . & . & . & . & . & . & . & . & . & . \\ -a_2 & -a_3 & -a_4 & . & . & 0 & 0 & 0 & . & . & 1 & -a_1 \\ -a_1 & -a_2 & -a_3 & . & . & -a_n & 0 & 0 & . & . & . & 1 \end{vmatrix}$$

To understand the way each determinant is formed, note that each can be partitioned into four subareas. Each subarea of Δ_i is a triangular $i \times i$ matrix. The northwest subarea has the value 1 on the diagonal and all zeros above the diagonal. The subscript increases by 1 as we move down any column beginning from the diagonal. The southeast subarea is the transpose of the northwest subarea. Notice that the northeast subarea has a_n on the diagonal and all zeros below the diagonal. The subscript decreases by 1 as we move up any column beginning from the diagonal. The southwest subarea is the transpose of the northeast subarea. As defined above, the value of a_0 is unity.

Special Cases: As stated above, the Schur theorem gives the necessary and sufficient conditions for all roots to lie in the unit circle. Rather than calculate all these determinants, it is often possible to use the simple rules discussed in Section 6. Those of you familiar with matrix algebra may wish to consult Samuelson (1941) for formal proofs of these conditions.

Chapter 2

STATIONARY TIME-SERIES MODELS

The theory of linear difference equations can be extended to allow the forcing process $\{x_t\}$ to be stochastic. This class of linear stochastic difference equations underlies much of the theory of time-series econometrics. Especially important is the Box–Jenkins (1976) methodology for estimating time-series models of the form:

$$y_t = a_0 + a_1 y_{t-1} + \cdots + a_p y_{t-p} + \epsilon_t + \beta_1 \epsilon_{t-1} + \cdots + \beta_q \epsilon_{t-q}$$

Such models are called autoregressive integrated moving average (ARIMA) time-series models. The aims of this chapter are to:

1. Present the theory of stochastic linear difference equations and consider the time-series properties of stationary ARIMA models; a stationary ARIMA model is called an ARMA model. It is shown that the stability conditions of the previous chapter are necessary conditions for stationarity.

2. Develop the tools used in estimating ARMA models. Especially useful are the autocorrelation and partial autocorrelation functions. It is shown how the Box–Jenkins methodology relies on these tools to estimate an ARMA model from sample data.

3. Consider various test statistics to check for model adequacy. Several examples of estimated ARMA models are analyzed in detail. It is shown how a properly estimated model can be used for forecasting.

1. STOCHASTIC DIFFERENCE EQUATION MODELS

In this chapter, we continue to work with **discrete**, rather than continuous, time-series models. Recall from the discussion in Chapter 1 that we can evaluate the function $y = f(t)$ at t_0 and $t_0 + h$ to form

$$\Delta y = f(t_0 + h) - f(t_0)$$

As a practical matter, most economic time-series data are collected for discrete time periods. Thus, we consider only the equidistant intervals t_0, $t_0 + h$, $t_0 + 2h$, $t_0 + 3h$, ... and conveniently set $h = 1$. Be careful to recognize, however, that a discrete time series implies t, but not necessarily y_t, is discrete. For example, although Scotland's annual rainfall is a continuous variable, the sequence of such annual rainfall totals for years 1 through t is a discrete time series. In many economic applications, t refers to "time" so that h represents the change in time. However, t need not refer to the type of time interval as measured by a clock or calendar. Instead of allowing our measurement units to be minutes, days, quarters, or years, we can use t to refer to an ordered event number. We could let y_t denote the outcome of spin t on a roulette wheel; y_t can then take on any of the 38 values 00, 0, 1, ..., 36.

A discrete variable y is said to be a **random** variable (i.e., stochastic) if for any real number r, there exists a probability $p(y \le r)$ that y takes on a value less than or equal to r. This definition is fairly general; in common usage, it is typically implied that there is at least one value of r for which $0 < p(y = r) < 1$. If there is some r for which $p(y = r) = 1$, y is deterministic rather than random.

It is useful to consider the elements of an observed time series $\{y_0, y_1, y_2, \ldots, y_t\}$ as being realizations (i.e., outcomes) of a stochastic process. As in Chapter 1, we continue to let the notation y_t refer to an element of the entire sequence $\{y_t\}$. In our roulette example, y_t denotes the outcome of spin t on a roulette wheel. If we observe spins 1 through T, we can form the sequence $y_1, y_2, \ldots, y_T$, or more compactly, $\{y_t\}$. In the same way, the term y_t could be used to denote GNP in time period t. Since we cannot forecast GNP perfectly, y_t is a random variable. Once we learn the value of GNP in period t, y_t becomes one of the realized values from a stochastic process. (Of course, measurement error may prevent us from ever knowing the "true" value of GNP.)

For discrete variables, the probability distribution of y_t is given by a formula (or table) that specifies each possible realized value of y_t and the probability associated with that realization. If the realizations are linked across time, there exists the joint probability distribution $p(y_1 = r_1, y_2 = r_2, \ldots, y_T = r_T)$, where r_i is the realized value of y in period i. Having observed the first t realizations, we can form the expected value of $y_{t+1}, y_{t+2}, \ldots$, conditioned on the observed values of y_1 through y_t.[1] This conditional mean, or expected value, of y_{t+i} is denoted by $E_t(y_{t+i} | y_t, y_{t-1}, \ldots, y_1)$ or $E_t y_{t+i}$.

Of course, if y_t refers to the outcome of spinning a fair roulette wheel, the probability distribution is easily characterized. In contrast, we may never be able to completely describe the probability distribution for GNP. Nevertheless, the task of economic theorists is to develop models that capture the essence of the true data-generating process. Stochastic difference equations are one convenient way of modeling dynamic economic process. To take a simple example, suppose that the Federal Reserve's money supply target grows 3% each year. Hence,

$$m_t^* = 1.03 m_{t-1}^* \qquad (2.1)$$

or given the initial condition m_0^*, the particular solution is

$$m_t^* = (1.03)^t m_0^*$$

where m_t^* = the logarithm of the money supply target in year t
m_0^* = the initial condition for the target money supply in period zero

Of course, the actual money supply m_t and target need not be equal. Suppose that at the end of period $t - 1$, there exist m_{t-1} outstanding dollars that are carried forward into period t. Hence, at the beginning of t there are m_{t-1} dollars so that the gap between actual and desired money holdings is $m_t^* - m_{t-1}$. Suppose that the Fed cannot perfectly control the money supply but attempts to change the money supply by ρ percent ($\rho < 100\%$) of any gap between the desired and actual money supply. We can model this behavior as

$$\Delta m_t = \rho(m_t^* - m_{t-1}) + \epsilon_t$$

or using (2.1), we obtain

$$m_t = \rho(1.03)^t m_0^* + (1 - \rho)m_{t-1} + \epsilon_t \qquad (2.2)$$

where ϵ_t = the uncontrollable portion of the money supply

We assume the mean of ϵ_t is zero in all time periods.

Although the economic theory is overly simple, the model does illustrate the key points discussed above. Note the following:

1. Although the money supply is a continuous variable, (2.2) is a discrete difference equation. Since the forcing process $\{\epsilon_t\}$ is stochastic, the money supply is stochastic; we can call (2.2) a linear stochastic difference equation.

2. If we knew the distribution of $\{\epsilon_t\}$, we could calculate the distribution for each element in the $\{m_t\}$ sequence. Since (2.2) shows how the realizations of the $\{m_t\}$ sequence are linked across time, we would be able to calculate the various joint probabilities. Notice that the distribution of the money supply sequence is completely determined by the parameters of the difference equation (2.2) and distribution of the $\{\epsilon_t\}$ sequence.

3. Having observed the first t observations in the $\{m_t\}$ sequence, we can make forecasts of $m_{t+1}, m_{t+2}, \ldots$. For example, if we update (2.2) by one period and take the conditional expectation, the forecast of m_{t+1} is $\rho(1.03)^{t+1} m_0^* + (1 - \rho)m_t$. Hence, $E_t m_{t+1} = \rho(1.03)^{t+1} m_0^* + (1 - \rho)m_t$.

Before we proceed too far along these lines, let us go back to the basic building block of discrete stochastic time-series models: the **white-noise** process. A sequence $\{\epsilon_t\}$ is a white-noise process if each value in the sequence has a mean of zero, a constant variance, and is serially uncorrelated. Formally, if the notation $E(x)$ denotes the theoretical mean value of x, the sequence $\{\epsilon_t\}$ is a white-noise process if for each time period t,

$$E(\epsilon_t) = E(\epsilon_{t-1}) = \cdots = 0$$
$$E(\epsilon_t^2) = E(\epsilon_{t-1}^2) = \cdots = \sigma^2 \qquad [\text{or } \text{var}(\epsilon_t) = \text{var}(\epsilon_{t-1}) = \cdots = \sigma^2]$$

and for all j

$$E(\epsilon_t\,\epsilon_{t-s}) = E(\epsilon_{t-j}\,\epsilon_{t-j-s}) = 0 \text{ for all } s \qquad [\text{or } \text{cov}(\epsilon_t, \epsilon_{t-s}) = \text{cov}(\epsilon_{t-j}, \epsilon_{t-j-s}) = 0]$$

In the remainder of this text, $\{\epsilon_t\}$ will always refer to a white-noise process and σ^2 to the variance of that process. When it is necessary to refer to two or more white-noise processes, symbols such as $\{\epsilon_{1t}\}$ and $\{\epsilon_{2t}\}$ will be used. Now, use a white-noise process to construct the more interesting time series:

$$x_t = \sum_{i=0}^{q} \beta_i \epsilon_{t-i} \tag{2.3}$$

For each period t, x_t is constructed by taking the values $\epsilon_t, \epsilon_{t-1}, \ldots, \epsilon_{t-q}$ and multiplying each by the associated value of β_i. A sequence formed in this manner is called a **moving average** of order q and denoted by MA(q). To illustrate a typical moving average process, suppose you win \$1 if a fair coin shows a head and lose \$1 if it shows a tail. Denote the outcome on toss t by ϵ_t (i.e., for toss t, ϵ_t is either +\$1 or −\$1). If you wish to keep track of your "hot streaks," you might want to calculate your average winnings on the last four tosses. For each coin toss t, your average winnings on the last four tosses are $1/4\epsilon_t + 1/4\epsilon_{t-1} + 1/4\epsilon_{t-2} + 1/4\epsilon_{t-3}$. In terms of (2.3), this sequence is a moving average process such that $\beta_i = 0.25$ for $i \leq 3$ and zero otherwise.

Although the $\{\epsilon_t\}$ sequence is a white-noise process, the constructed $\{x_t\}$ sequence will *not* be a white-noise process if two or more of the β_i differ from zero. To illustrate using an MA(1) process, set $\beta_0 = 1$, $\beta_1 = 0.5$, and all other $\beta_i = 0$. In this circumstance, $E(x_t) = E(\epsilon_t + 0.5\epsilon_{t-1}) = 0$ and $\text{var}(x_t) = \text{var}(\epsilon_t + 0.5\epsilon_{t-1}) = 1.25\sigma^2$. You can easily convince yourself that $E(x_t) = E(x_{t-s})$ and $\text{var}(x_t) = \text{var}(x_{t-s})$ for all s. Hence, the first two conditions for $\{x_t\}$ to be a white-noise process are satisfied. However, $E(x_t x_{t-1}) = E[(\epsilon_t + 0.5\epsilon_{t-1})(\epsilon_{t-1} + 0.5\epsilon_{t-2})] = E[\epsilon_t\epsilon_{t-1} + 0.5(\epsilon_{t-1})^2 + 0.5\epsilon_t\epsilon_{t-2} + 0.25\epsilon_{t-1}\epsilon_{t-2}] = 0.5\sigma^2$. Given there exists a nonzero value of s such that $E(x_t x_{t-s}) \neq 0$, the $\{x_t\}$ sequence is not a white-noise process.

Exercise 1 at the end of this chapter asks you to find the mean, variance, and covariance of your "hot streaks" in coin tossing. For practice, you should complete that exercise before continuing.

2. ARMA MODELS

It is possible to combine a moving average process with a linear difference equation to obtain an autoregressive moving average model. Consider the pth-order difference equation:

$$y_t = a_0 + \sum_{i=1}^{p} a_i y_{t-i} + x_t \tag{2.4}$$

Now let $\{x_t\}$ be the MA(q) process given by (2.3) so that we can write

$$y_t = a_0 + \sum_{i=1}^{p} a_i y_{t-i} + \sum_{i=0}^{q} \beta_i \epsilon_{t-i} \tag{2.5}$$

We follow the convention of normalizing units so that β_0 is always equal to unity. If the characteristic roots of (2.5) are all in the unit circle, $\{y_t\}$ is called an **autoregressive moving average** (ARMA) model for y_t. The autoregressive part of the model is the "difference equation" given by the homogeneous portion of (2.4) and the moving average part is the $\{x_t\}$ sequence. If the homogeneous part of the difference equation contains p lags and the model for x, q lags, the model is called an ARMA(p, q) model. If $q = 0$, the process is called a pure autoregressive process denoted by AR(p), and if $p = 0$, the process is a pure moving average process denoted by MA(q). In an ARMA model, it is perfectly permissible to allow p and/or q to be infinite. In this chapter, we consider only models in which all the characteristic roots of (2.4) are within the unit circle. However, if one or more characteristic roots is greater than or equal to unity, the $\{y_t\}$ sequence is said to be an **integrated** process and (2.5) is called an autoregressive integrated moving average (ARIMA) model.

Treating (2.5) as a difference equation suggests that we can "solve" for y_t in terms of the $\{\epsilon_t\}$ sequence. The solution of an ARMA(p, q) model expressing y_t in terms of the $\{\epsilon_t\}$ sequence is the **moving average representation** of y_t. The procedure is no different from that discussed in Chapter 1. For the AR(1) model $y_t = a_0 + a_1 y_{t-1} + \epsilon_t$, the moving average representation was shown to be

$$y_t = a_0/(1-a_1) + \sum_{i=0}^{\infty} a_1^i \epsilon_{t-i}$$

For the general ARMA(p, q) model, rewrite (2.5) using lag operators so that

$$\left(1 - \sum_{i=1}^{p} a_i L^i\right) y_t = a_0 + \sum_{i=0}^{q} \beta_i \epsilon_{t-i}$$

so that the *particular* solution for y_t is

$$y_t = \frac{a_0 + \sum_{i=0}^{q} \beta_i \epsilon_{t-i}}{1 - \sum_{i=1}^{p} a_i L^i} \tag{2.6}$$

Fortunately, it will not be necessary for us to expand (2.6) to obtain the specific coefficient for each element in $\{\epsilon_t\}$. The important point to recognize is that the expansion will yield an MA(∞) process. The issue is whether such an expansion is convergent so that the stochastic difference equation given by (2.6) is stable. As you will see in the next section, the stability condition is that the characteristic roots of the polynomial $(1 - \Sigma a_i L^i)$ must lie outside of the unit circle. It is also shown that if y_t *is a linear stochastic difference equation, the stability condition is a necessary condition for the time series $\{y_t\}$ to be stationary.*

3. STATIONARITY

Suppose that the quality control division of a manufacturing firm samples four machines each hour. Every hour, quality control finds the mean of the machines' output levels. The plot of each machine's hourly output is shown in Figure 2.1. If y_{it} represents machine y_i's output at hour t, the means ($\bar{y}_t$) are readily calculated as

$$\bar{y}_t = \sum_{i=1}^{4} y_{it}/4$$

For hours 5, 10, and 15, these mean values are 5.57, 5.59, and 5.73, respectively.

The sample variance for each hour can similarly be constructed. Unfortunately, applied econometricians do not usually have the luxury of being able to obtain an **ensemble** (i.e., multiple time-series data of the same process over the same time period). Typically, we observe only one set of realizations for any particular series. Fortunately, if $\{y_t\}$ is a **stationary** series, the mean, variance, and autocorrelations can usually be well approximated by sufficiently long **time averages** based on the single set of realizations. Suppose you observed only the output of machine 1 for 20 periods. If you knew that the output was stationary, you could approximate the mean level of output by

$$\bar{y}_t = \sum_{t=1}^{20} y_{1t}/20$$

In using this approximation, you would be assuming that the mean was the same for each period. In this example, the means of the four series are 5.45, 5.66, 5.45,

Figure 2.1   Hourly output of four machines.

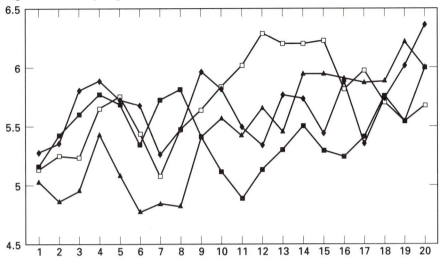

and 5.71. Formally, a stochastic process having a finite mean and variance is **co-variance stationary** if for all t and $t-s$,

$$E(y_t) = E(y_{t-s}) = \mu \tag{2.7}$$

$$E[(y_t - \mu)^2] = E[(y_{t-s} - \mu)^2] = \sigma_y^2 \qquad [\text{var}(y_t) = \text{var}(y_{t-s}) = \sigma_y^2] \tag{2.8}$$

$$E[(y_t - \mu)(y_{t-s} - \mu)] = E[(y_{t-j} - \mu)(y_{t-j-s}\,\mu)] = \gamma_s$$

$$[\text{cov}(y_t, y_{t-s}) = \text{cov}(y_{t-j}, y_{t-j-s})] \tag{2.9}$$

where μ, σ_y^2 *and all* γ_s *are constants*

In (2.9), allowing $s = 0$ means that γ_0 is equivalent to the variance of y_t. Simply put, a time series is covariance stationary if its mean and all autocovariances are unaffected by a change of time origin. In the literature, a covariance stationary process is also referred to as a weakly stationary, second-order stationary, or wide-sense stationary process. A **strongly** stationary process need not have a finite mean and/or variance (i.e., μ and/or γ_0 need not be finite); this terminology implies that weak stationarity can be a more stringent condition than strong stationarity. The text considers only covariance stationary series so that there is no ambiguity in using the terms stationary and covariance stationary interchangeably. One further word about terminology. In multivariate models, the term autocovariance is reserved for the covariance between y_t and its own lags. Cross-covariance refers to the covariance between one series and another. In univariate time-series models, there is no ambiguity and the terms autocovariance and covariance are used interchangeably.

For a covariance stationary series, we can define the **autocorrelation** between y_t and y_{t-s} as

$$\rho_s \equiv \gamma_s / \gamma_0$$

where γ_0 and γ_s are defined by (2.9).

Since γ_s and γ_0 are time-independent, the autocorrelation coefficients ρ_s are also time-independent. Although the autocorrelation between y_t and y_{t-1} can differ from the autocorrelation between y_t and y_{t-2}, the autocorrelation between y_t and y_{t-1} must be identical to that between y_{t-s} and y_{t-s-1}. Obviously, $\rho_0 = 1$.

Stationarity Restrictions for an AR(1) Process

For expositional convenience, first consider the necessary and sufficient conditions for an AR(1) process to be stationary. Let

$$y_t = a_0 + a_1 y_{t-1} + \epsilon_t$$

where ϵ_t = white noise

Suppose that the process started in period zero, so that y_0 is a deterministic initial condition. In Section 3 of the last chapter, it was shown that the solution to this equation is (also see Question 2 at the end of this chapter)

$$y_t = a_0 \sum_{i=0}^{t-1} a_1^i + a_1^t y_0 + \sum_{i=0}^{t-1} a_1^i \epsilon_{t-i} \tag{2.10}$$

Taking the expected value of (2.10), we obtain

$$Ey_t = a_0 \sum_{i=0}^{t-1} a_1^i + a_1^t y_0 \tag{2.11}$$

Updating by s periods yields

$$Ey_{t+s} = a_0 \sum_{i=0}^{t+s-1} a_1^i + a_1^{t+s} y_0 \tag{2.12}$$

If we compare (2.11) and (2.12), it is clear that both means are time-dependent. Since Ey_t is not equal to Ey_{t+s}, the sequence cannot be stationary. However, if t is large, we can consider the limiting value of y_t in (2.10). If $|a_1| < 1$, the expression $(a_1)^t y_0$ converges to zero as t becomes infinitely large and the sum $a_0[1 + a_1 + (a_1)^2 + (a_1)^3 + \cdots]$ converges to $a_0/(1 - a_1)$. Thus, as $t \to \infty$ and if $|a_1| < 1$

$$\lim y_t = a_0/(1-a_1) + \sum_{i=0}^{\infty} a_1^i \epsilon_{t-i} \tag{2.13}$$

Now take expectations of (2.13) so that for sufficiently large values of t, $Ey_t = a_0/(1 - a_1)$. Thus, the mean value of y_t is finite and time-independent so that $Ey_t =$

$Ey_{t-s} = \mu$ for all t. Turning to the limiting value of the variance, we find

$$E(y_t - \mu)^2 = E[(\epsilon_t + a_1\epsilon_{t-1} + (a_1)^2\epsilon_{t-2} + \cdots)^2]$$
$$= \sigma^2[1 + (a_1)^2 + (a_1)^4 + \cdots] = \sigma^2/[1 - (a_1)^2]$$

which is also finite and time-independent. Finally, it is easily demonstrated that the limiting values of all autocovariances are finite and time-independent:

$$E[(y_t - \mu)(y_{t-s} - \mu)] = E\{[\epsilon_t + a_1\epsilon_{t-1} + (a_1)^2\epsilon_{t-2} + \cdots][\epsilon_{t-s} + a_1\epsilon_{t-s-1} + (a_1)^2\epsilon_{t-s-2} + \cdots]\}$$
$$= \sigma^2(a_1)^s[1 + (a_1)^2 + (a_1)^4 + \cdots]$$
$$= \sigma^2(a_1)^s/[1 - (a_1)^2] \tag{2.14}$$

In summary, if we can use the limiting value of (2.10), the $\{y_t\}$ sequence will be stationary. For any given y_0 and $|a_1| < 1$, it follows that t must be sufficiently large. Thus, if a sample is generated by a process that has recently begun, the realizations may not be stationary. It is for this very reason that many econometricians assume that the data-generating process has been occurring for an infinitely long time. In practice, the researcher must be wary of any data generated from a "new" process. For example, $\{y_t\}$ could represent the daily change in the dollar/mark exchange rate beginning immediately after the demise of the Bretton Woods fixed exchange rate system. Such a series may not be stationary due to the fact there were deterministic initial conditions (exchange rate changes were essentially zero in the Bretton Woods era). The careful researcher wishing to use stationary series might consider excluding some of these earlier observations from the period of analysis.

Little would change had we not been given the initial condition. Without the initial value y_0, the sum of the homogeneous and particular solutions for y_t is

$$y_t = a_0/(1 - a_1) + \sum_{i=0}^{\infty} a_1^i\epsilon_{t-i} + A(a_1)^t \tag{2.15}$$

where A = an arbitrary constant

If we take the expectation of (2.15), it is clear that the $\{y_t\}$ sequence cannot be stationary unless the expression $A(a_1)^t$ is equal to zero. Either the sequence must have started infinitely long ago (so that $a_1^t = 0$) or the arbitrary constant A must be zero. Recall that the arbitrary constant has the interpretation of a deviation from long-run equilibrium. A succinct way to state the stability conditions is the following:

1. The homogeneous solution must be zero. Either the sequence must have started infinitely far in the past or the process must always be in equilibrium (so that the arbitrary constant is zero).

2. The characteristic root a_1 must be less than unity in absolute value.

These two conditions readily generalize to all ARMA(p, q) processes. We know that the homogeneous solution to (2.5) has the form

$$\sum_{i=1}^{p} A_i \alpha_i^t$$

or if the roots are repeated,

$$\alpha \sum_{i=1}^{m} A_i t^i + \sum_{i=m+1}^{p} A_i \alpha_i^t$$

where the A_i represent p arbitrary values, α are the repeated roots, and the α_i are the $(p - m)$ distinct roots.

If any portion of the homogeneous equation is present, the mean, variance, and all covariances will be time-dependent. Hence, for any ARMA(p, q) model, stationarity necessitates that the homogeneous solution be zero. The next section addresses the stationarity restrictions for the particular solution.

4. STATIONARITY RESTRICTIONS FOR AN ARMA(p, q) MODEL

As a prelude to the stationarity conditions for the general ARMA(p, q) model, first consider the restrictions necessary to ensure that an ARMA(2, 1) model is stationary. Since the magnitude of the intercept term does not affect the stability (or stationarity) conditions, set $a_0 = 0$ and write

$$y_t = a_1 y_{t-1} + a_2 y_{t-2} + \epsilon_t + \beta_1 \epsilon_{t-1} \tag{2.16}$$

From the previous section, we know that the homogeneous solution must be zero. As such, it is only necessary to find the particular solution. Using the method of undetermined coefficients, we can write the challenge solution as

$$y_t = \sum_{i=0}^{\infty} \alpha_i \epsilon_{t-i} \tag{2.17}$$

For (2.17) to be a solution of (2.16), the various α_i must satisfy

$$\alpha_0 \epsilon_t + \alpha_1 \epsilon_{t-1} + \alpha_2 \epsilon_{t-2} + \alpha_3 \epsilon_{t-3} + \cdots = a_1(\alpha_0 \epsilon_{t-1} + \alpha_1 \epsilon_{t-2} + \alpha_2 \epsilon_{t-3} + \alpha_3 \epsilon_{t-4} + \cdots)$$
$$+ a_2(\alpha_0 \epsilon_{t-2} + \alpha_1 \epsilon_{t-3} + \alpha_2 \epsilon_{t-4} + \alpha_3 \epsilon_{t-5} + \cdots) + \epsilon_t + \beta_1 \epsilon_{t-1}$$

To match coefficients on the terms containing $\epsilon_t, \epsilon_{t-1}, \epsilon_{t-2}, \ldots$, it is necessary to set

1. $\alpha_0 = 1$
2. $\alpha_1 = a_1 \alpha_0 + \beta_1$ $\Rightarrow \alpha_1 = a_1 + \beta_1$
3. $\alpha_i = a_1 \alpha_{i-1} + a_2 \alpha_{i-2}$ for all $i \geq 2$

The key point is that for $i \geq 2$, the coefficients satisfy the difference equation $\alpha_i = a_1\alpha_{i-1} + a_2\alpha_{i-2}$. If the characteristic roots of (2.16) are within the unit circle, the $\{\alpha_i\}$ must constitute a convergent sequence. For example, reconsider the case in which $a_1 = 1.6$, $a_2 = -0.9$, and let $\beta_1 = 0.5$. Worksheet 2.1 shows that the coefficients satisfying (2.17) are 1, 2.1, 2.46, 2.046, 1.06, −0.146, ... (also see Worksheet 1.2 of the previous chapter).

WORKSHEET 2.1   Coefficients of the ARMA(2,1) Process: $y_t = 1.6y_{t-1} - 0.9y_{t-2} + \epsilon_t + 0.5\epsilon_{t-1}$.

If we use the method of undetermined coefficients, the α_i must satisfy

$$\alpha_0 = 1$$
$$\alpha_1 = 1.6 + 0.5 \qquad \text{hence, } \alpha_1 = 2.1$$
$$\alpha_i = 1.6 \cdot \alpha_{i-1} - 0.9 \cdot \alpha_{i-2} \qquad \text{for all } i = 2, 3, 4 \ldots$$

Notice that the coefficients follow a second-order difference equation with imaginary roots. With de Moivre's theorem, the coefficients will satisfy

$$\alpha_i = 0.949^i \beta_1 \cos(0.567i + \beta_2)$$

Imposing the initial conditions for α_0 and α_1 yields

$$1 = \beta_1 \cos(\beta_2) \qquad \text{and} \qquad 2.1 = 0.949\beta_1 \cos(0.567 + \beta_2)$$

Since $\beta_1 = 1/\cos(\beta_2)$, we seek the solution to

$$\cos(\beta_2) - (0.949/2.1) \cdot \cos(0.567 + \beta_2) = 0$$

From a trig table, the solution for β_2 is −1.197. Hence, the α_i satisfy

$$- 1/1.197 \cdot 0.949^i \cdot \cos(0.567 \cdot i - 1.197)$$

Alternatively, we can use the initial values of α_0 and α_1 to find the other α_i by iteration. The sequence of the α_i is shown in the graph below.

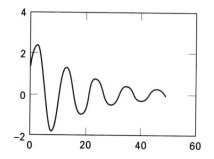

The first 10 values of the sequence are

i	0	1	2	3	4	5	6	7	8	9	10
α_i	1.00	2.10	2.46	2.046	1.06	−0.146	1.187	−1.786	−1.761	−1.226	−0.378

To verify that the $\{y_t\}$ sequence generated by (2.17) is stationary, take the expectation of (2.17) to form $Ey_t = Ey_{t-i} = 0$ for all t and i. Hence, the mean is finite and time-invariant. Since the $\{\epsilon_t\}$ sequence is assumed to be a white-noise process, the variance of y_t is constant and time-independent, that is,

$$\text{Var}(y_t) = E[\alpha_0\epsilon_t + \alpha_1\epsilon_{t-1} + \alpha_2\epsilon_{t-2} + \alpha_3\epsilon_{t-3} + \cdots)^2]$$

$$= \sigma^2 \sum_{i=0}^{\infty} \alpha_i^2$$

Hence, $\text{var}(y_t) = \text{var}(y_{t-s})$ for all t and s. Finally, the covariance between y_t and y_{t-s} is

$$\text{Cov}(y_t,y_{t-1}) = E[(\epsilon_t + \alpha_1\epsilon_{t-1} + \alpha_2\epsilon_{t-2} + \cdots)(\epsilon_{t-1} + \alpha_1\epsilon_{t-2} + \alpha_2\epsilon_{t-3} + \alpha_3\epsilon_{t-4} + \cdots)]$$
$$= \sigma^2(\alpha_1 + \alpha_2\alpha_1 + \alpha_3\alpha_2 + \cdots)$$
$$\text{Cov}(y_t, y_{t-2}) = E[(\epsilon_t + \alpha_1\epsilon_{t-1} + \alpha_2\epsilon_{t-2} + \cdots)(\epsilon_{t-2} + \alpha_1\epsilon_{t-3} + \alpha_2\epsilon_{t-4} + \alpha_3\epsilon_{t-5} + \cdots)]$$
$$= \sigma^2(\alpha_2 + \alpha_3\alpha_1 + \alpha_4\alpha_2 + \cdots)$$

so that

$$\text{Cov}(y_t, y_{t-s}) = \sigma^2(\alpha_s + \alpha_{s+1}\alpha_1 + \alpha_{s+2}\alpha_2 + \cdots) \tag{2.18}$$

Hence, $\text{cov}(y_t, y_{t-s})$ is constant and independent of t. Instead, if the characteristic roots of (2.16) do not lie within the unit circle, the $\{\alpha_i\}$ sequence will *not* be convergent. As such, the $\{y_t\}$ sequence *cannot* be convergent.

It is not too difficult to generalize these results to the entire class of ARMA(p, q) models. Begin by considering the conditions ensuring the stationarity of a pure MA(∞) process. By appropriately restricting the β_i, all the finite-order MA(q) processes can be obtained as special cases. Consider

$$x_t = \sum_{i=0}^{\infty} \beta_i\epsilon_{t-i}$$

where $\{\epsilon_t\}$ = a white-noise process with variance σ^2

We have already determined that $\{x_t\}$ is not a white-noise process; now the issue is whether $\{x_t\}$ is covariance stationary? (If you need to refresh your memory concerning mathematical expectations, you should consult the appendix to this chapter before proceeding.) Considering conditions (2.7), (2.8), and (2.9), we ask the following:

1. Is the mean finite and time-independent? Take the expected value of x_t and remember that the expectation of a sum is the sum of the individual expectations. Hence,

$$E(x_t) = E(\epsilon_t + \beta_1\epsilon_{t-1} + \beta_2\epsilon_{t-2} + \cdots)$$
$$= E\epsilon_t + \beta_1 E\epsilon_{t-1} + \beta_2 E\epsilon_{t-2} + \cdots = 0$$

Repeat the procedure with x_{t-s}:

$$E(x_{t-s}) = E(\epsilon_{t-s} + \beta_1\epsilon_{t-s-1} + \beta_2\epsilon_{t-s-2} + \cdots) = 0$$

Hence, all elements in the $\{x_t\}$ sequence have the same finite mean ($\mu = 0$).

2. Is the variance finite and time-independent? Form var(x_t) as

$$\text{Var}(x_t) = E[(\epsilon_t + \beta_1\epsilon_{t-1} + \beta_2\epsilon_{t-2} + \cdots)^2]$$

Square the term in parentheses and take expectations. Since $\{\epsilon_t\}$ is a white-noise process, all terms $E\epsilon_t\epsilon_{t-s} = 0$ for $s \neq 0$. Hence,

$$\text{Var}(x_t) = E(\epsilon_t)^2 + (\beta_1)^2 E(\epsilon_{t-1})^2 + (\beta_2)^2 E(\epsilon_{t-2})^2 + \cdots$$
$$= \sigma^2[1 + (\beta_1)^2 + (\beta_2)^2 + \cdots]$$

As long as $\Sigma(\beta_i)^2$ is finite, it follows that var(x_t) is finite. Thus, $\Sigma(\beta_i)^2$ being finite is a necessary condition for $\{x_t\}$ to be stationary. To determine whether var(x_t) = var(x_{t-s}), form

$$\text{Var}(x_{t-s}) = E[(\epsilon_{t-s} + \beta_1\epsilon_{t-s-1} + \beta_2\epsilon_{t-s-2} + \cdots)]^2 = \sigma^2[1 + (\beta_1)^2 + (\beta_2)^2 + \cdots]$$

Thus, var(x_t) = var(x_{t-s}) for all t and $t - s$.

3. Are all autocovariances finite and time-independent? First form $E(x_t x_{t-s})$ as

$$E(x_t x_{t-s}) = E[(\epsilon_t + \beta_1\epsilon_{t-1} + \beta_2\epsilon_{t-2} + \cdots)(\epsilon_{t-s} + \beta_1\epsilon_{t-s-1} + \beta_2\epsilon_{t-s-2} + \cdots)]$$

Carrying out the multiplication and noting that $E(\epsilon_t\epsilon_{t-s}) = 0$ for $s \neq 0$, we get

$$E(x_t x_{t-s}) = \sigma^2(\beta_s + \beta_1\beta_{s+1} + \beta_2\beta_{s+2} + \cdots)$$

Restricting the sum $\beta_s + \beta_1\beta_{s+1} + \beta_2\beta_{s+2} + \cdots$ to be finite means that $E(x_t x_{t-s})$ is finite. Given this second restriction, it is clear that the covariance between x_t and x_{t-s} depends on only the number of periods separating the variables (i.e., the value of s), but *not* the time subscript t.

In summary, the necessary and sufficient conditions for any MA process to be stationary are for the sums of (1), $\Sigma(\beta_i)^2$, and of (2), $(\beta_s + \beta_1\beta_{s+1} + \beta_2\beta_{s+2} + \cdots)$, to be finite. Since (2) must hold for all values of s and $\beta_0 = 1$, condition (1) is redundant. The direct implication is that a finite-order MA process will always be stationary. For an infinite-order process, (2) must hold for all $s \geq 0$.

Stationarity Restrictions for the Autoregressive Coefficients

Now consider the pure autoregressive model:

$$y_t = a_0 + \sum_{i=1}^{p} a_i y_{t-i} + \epsilon_t \tag{2.19}$$

If the characteristic roots of the homogeneous equation of (2.19) all lie inside the unit circle, it is possible to write the particular solution as

$$y_t = \frac{a_0}{1 - \sum_{i=1}^{p} a_i} + \sum_{i=0}^{\infty} \alpha_i \epsilon_{t-i} \tag{2.20}$$

where   the α_i = undetermined coefficients

Although it is possible to find the undetermined coefficients $\{\alpha_i\}$, we know that (2.20) is a convergent sequence so long as the characteristic roots of (2.19) are inside the unit circle. To sketch the proof, the method of undetermined coefficients allows us to write the particular solution in the form of (2.20). We also know that the sequence $\{\alpha_i\}$ will eventually solve the difference equation:

$$\alpha_i - a_1\alpha_{i-1} - a_2\alpha_{i-2} - \cdots - a_p\alpha_{i-p} = 0 \tag{2.21}$$

If the characteristic roots of (2.21) are all inside the unit circle, the $\{\alpha_i\}$ sequence will be convergent. Although (2.20) is an infinite-order moving average process, the convergence of the MA coefficients implies that $\Sigma\alpha_i^2$ is finite. Hence, we can use (2.20) to check the three conditions for stationarity. Since $\alpha_0 = 1$,

1. $Ey_t = Ey_{t-s} = a_0/(1 - \Sigma a_i)$

You should recall from Chapter 1 that a necessary condition of all characteristic roots to lie inside the unit circle is $1 - \Sigma a_i \neq 0$. Hence, the mean of the sequence is finite and time-invariant:

2. $\text{Var}(y_t) = E[(\epsilon_t + \alpha_1\epsilon_{t-1} + \alpha_2\epsilon_{t-2} + \alpha_3\epsilon_{t-3} + \cdots)^2] = \sigma^2\Sigma\alpha_i^2$

and

$$\text{Var}(y_{t-s}) = E[(\epsilon_{t-s} + \alpha_1\epsilon_{t-s-1} + \alpha_2\epsilon_{t-s-2} + \alpha_3\epsilon_{t-s-3} + \cdots)^2] = \sigma^2\Sigma\alpha_i^2$$

Given that $\Sigma\alpha_i^2$ is finite, the variance is finite and time-independent.

3. $\text{Cov}(y_t, y_{t-s}) = E[(\epsilon_t + \alpha_1\epsilon_{t-1} + \alpha_2\epsilon_{t-2} + \cdots)(\epsilon_{t-s} + \alpha_1\epsilon_{t-s-1} + \alpha_2\epsilon_{t-s-2} + \cdots)]$

$\qquad\qquad\quad = \sigma^2(\alpha_s + \alpha_1\alpha_{s+1} + \alpha_2\alpha_{s+2} + \cdots)$

Thus, the covariance between y_t and y_{t-s} is constant and time-invariant for all t and $t - s$.

Nothing of substance is changed by combining the AR(p) and MA(q) models into the general ARMA(p, q) model:

$$y_t = a_0 + \sum_{i=1}^{p} a_i y_{t-i} + x_t$$

$$x_t = \sum_{i=0}^{q} \beta_i \epsilon_{t-i} \tag{2.22}$$

If the roots of the inverse characteristic equation lie outside of the unit circle [i.e., if the roots of the homogeneous form of (2.22) lie inside the unit circle] and the $\{x_t\}$ sequence is stationary, the $\{y_t\}$ sequence will be stationary. Consider

$$y_t = \frac{a_0}{1 - \displaystyle\sum_{i=1}^{p} a_i} + \frac{\epsilon_t}{1 - \displaystyle\sum_{i=1}^{p} a_i L^i} + \frac{\beta_1\epsilon_{t-1}}{1 - \displaystyle\sum_{i=1}^{p} a_i L^i} + \frac{\beta_2\epsilon_{t-2}}{1 - \displaystyle\sum_{i=1}^{p} a_i L^i} + \cdots \tag{2.23}$$

With very little effort, you can convince yourself that the $\{y_t\}$ sequence satisfies the three conditions for stationarity. Each of the expressions on the right-hand side of (2.23) is stationary as long as the roots of $1 - \Sigma a_i L^i$ are outside the unit circle. Given that $\{x_t\}$ is stationary, only the roots of the autoregressive portion of (2.22) determine whether the $\{y_t\}$ sequence is stationary.

What about the possibility of using the forward-looking solution? For example, in Cagan's monetary model you saw that the forward-looking solution yields a convergent sequence. Time-series econometrics rules out this type of perfect foresight/forward-looking solution. It is the *expectation* of future events (not the realized value of future events) that affects the present. After all, if you had perfect foresight, econometric forecasting would be unnecessary.

5. THE AUTOCORRELATION FUNCTION

The autocovariances and autcorrelations of the type found in (2.18) serve as useful tools in the Box–Jenkins (1976) approach to identifying and estimating time-series models. We illustrate by considering four important examples: the AR(1), AR(2), MA(1) and ARMA(1, 1) models. For the AR(1) model, $y_t = a_0 + a_1 y_{t-1} + \epsilon_t$, (2.14) shows

$$\gamma_0 = \sigma^2/[1 - (a_1)^2]$$
$$\gamma_s = \sigma^2 (a_1)^s/[1 - (a_1)^2]$$

Forming the autocorrelations by dividing each γ_s by γ_0, we find that $\rho_0 = 1$, $\rho_1 = a_1$; $\rho_2 = (a_1)^2, \ldots, \rho_s = (a_1)^s$. For an AR(1) process, a necessary condition for stationarity is for $|a_1| < 1$. Thus, the plot of ρ_s against s—called the autocorrelation function (ACF) or **correlogram**—should converge to zero geometrically if the series is stationary. If a_1 is positive, convergence will be direct, and if a_1 is negative, the autocorrelations will follow a dampened oscillatory path around zero. The first two graphs on the left-hand side of Figure 2.2 show the theoretical autocorrelation functions for $a_1 = 0.7$ and $a_1 = -0.7$, respectively. Here, ρ_0 is not shown since its value is necessarily unity.

The Autocorrelation Function of an AR(2) Process

Now consider the more complicated AR(2) process $y_t = a_1 y_{t-1} + a_2 y_{t-2} + \epsilon_t$. We omit an intercept term (a_0) since it has no effect on the ACF. For the second-order process to be stationary, we know that it is necessary to restrict the roots of $(1 - a_1 L - a_2 L^2)$ to be outside the unit circle. In Section 4, we derived the autocovariances of an ARMA(2, 1) process by use of the method of undetermined coefficients. Now we want to illustrate an alternative technique using the **Yule–Walker** equations. Multiply the second-order difference equation by y_{t-s} for $s = 0$, $s = 1$, $s = 2, \ldots$ and take expectations to form

$$Ey_t y_t = a_1 Ey_{t-1} y_t + a_2 Ey_{t-2} y_t + E\epsilon_t y_t$$
$$Ey_t y_{t-1} = a_1 Ey_{t-1} y_{t-1} + a_2 Ey_{t-2} y_{t-1} + E\epsilon_t y_{t-1}$$
$$Ey_t y_{t-2} = a_1 Ey_{t-1} y_{t-2} + a_2 Ey_{t-2} y_{t-2} + E\epsilon_t y_{t-2}$$
$$\cdot$$
$$\cdot$$
$$Ey_t y_{t-s} = a_1 Ey_{t-1} y_{t-s} + a_2 Ey_{t-2} y_{t-s} + E\epsilon_t y_{t-s} \qquad (2.24)$$

By definition, the autocovariances of a stationary series are such that $Ey_t y_{t-s} = Ey_{t-s} y_t = Ey_{t-k} y_{t-k-s} = \gamma_s$. We also know that the coefficient on ϵ_t is unity so that $E\epsilon_t y_t = \sigma^2$. Since $E\epsilon_t y_{t-s} = 0$, we can use the equations in (2.24) to form

$$\gamma_0 = a_1 \gamma_1 + a_2 \gamma_2 + \sigma^2 \qquad (2.25)$$

Figure 2.2 Theoretical ACF and PACF patterns.

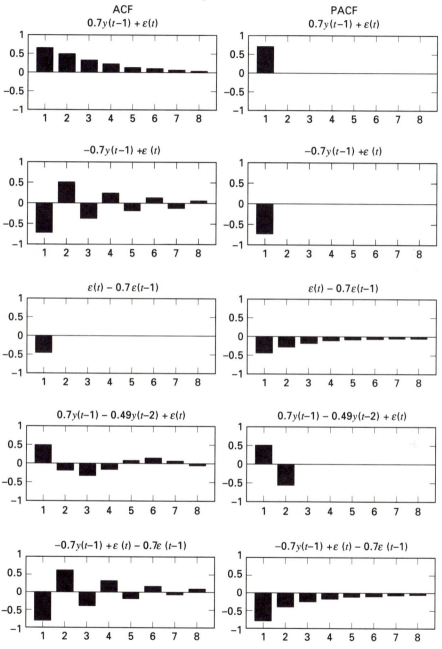

$$\gamma_1 = a_1\gamma_0 + a_2\gamma_1 \tag{2.26}$$
$$\gamma_s = a_1\gamma_{s-1} + a_2\gamma_{s-2} \tag{2.27}$$

Dividing (2.26) and (2.27) by γ_0 yields

$$\rho_1 = a_1\rho_0 + a_2\rho_1 \tag{2.28}$$
$$\rho_s = a_1\rho_{s-1} + a_2\rho_{s-2} \tag{2.29}$$

We know that $\rho_0 = 1$, so that from (2.28), $\rho_1 = a_1/(1 - a_2)$. Hence, we can find all ρ_s for $s \geq 2$ by solving the difference equation (2.29). For example, for $s = 2$ and $s = 3$,

$$\rho_2 = (a_1)^2/(1 - a_2) + a_2$$
$$\rho_3 = a_1[(a_1)^2/(1 - a_2) + a_2] + a_2a_1/(1 - a_2)$$

Although the values of the ρ_s are cumbersome to derive, we can easily characterize their properties. Given the solutions for ρ_0 and ρ_1, the key point to note is that the ρ_s all satisfy the difference equation (2.29). As in the general case of a second-order difference equation, the solution may be oscillatory or direct. Note that the stationarity condition for y_t necessitates that the characteristic roots of (2.29) lie inside of the unit circle. Hence, the $\{\rho_s\}$ sequence must be convergent. The correlogram for an AR(2) process must be such that $\rho_0 = 1$ and ρ_1 is determined by (2.28). These two values can be viewed as "initial values" for the second-order difference equation (2.29).

The fourth graph on the left-hand side of Figure 2.2 shows the ACF for the process $y_t = 0.7y_{t-1} - 0.49y_{t-2} + \epsilon_t$. The properties of the various ρ_s follow directly from the homogeneous equation $y_t = 0.7y_{t-1} + 0.49y_{t-2} = 0$. The roots are obtained from the solution to

$$\alpha = \{0.7 \pm [(-0.7)^2 - 4(0.49)]^{1/2}\}/2$$

Since the discriminant $d = (-0.7)^2 - 4(0.49)$ is negative, the characteristic roots are imaginary so that the solution oscillates. However, since $a_2 = -0.49$, the solution is convergent and the $\{y_t\}$ sequence is stationary.

Finally, we may wish to find the covariances rather than the autocorrelations. Since we know all the autocorrelations, if we can find the variance of y_t (i.e., γ_0), we can find all the other γ_s. To find γ_0, use (2.25) and note that $\rho_i = \gamma_i/\gamma_0$, so

$$\text{Var}(y_t)(\rho_0 - a_1\rho_1 - a_2\rho_2) = \sigma^2$$

Substitution for ρ_0, ρ_1, and ρ_2 yields

$$\gamma_0 = \text{var}(y_t) = [(1 - a_2)/(1 + a_2)]\left[\frac{\sigma^2}{(a_1 + a_2 - 1)(a_2 - a_1 - 1)}\right]$$

The Autocorrelation Function of an MA(1) Process

Next consider the MA(1) process $y_t = \epsilon_t + \beta\epsilon_{t-1}$. Again, obtain the Yule–Walker equations by multiplying y_t by each y_{t-s} and take expectations:

$$\gamma_0 = \text{var}(y_t) = Ey_ty_t = E[(\epsilon_t + \beta\epsilon_{t-1})(\epsilon_t + \beta\epsilon_{t-1})] = (1 + \beta^2)\sigma^2$$
$$\gamma_1 = Ey_ty_{t-1} = E[(\epsilon_t + \beta\epsilon_{t-1})(\epsilon_{t-1} + \beta\epsilon_{t-2})] = \beta\sigma^2$$

and

$$\gamma_s = Ey_ty_{t-s} = E[(\epsilon_t + \beta\epsilon_{t-1})(\epsilon_{t-s} + \beta\epsilon_{t-s-1})] = 0 \qquad \text{for all } s > 1$$

Hence, by dividing each γ_s by γ_0, it is immediately seen that the ACF is simply $\rho_0 = 1$, $\rho_1 = \beta/(1 + \beta^2)$, and $\rho_s = 0$ for all $s > 1$. The third graph on the left-hand side of Figure 2.2 shows the ACF for the MA(1) process $y_t = \epsilon_t - 0.7\epsilon_{t-1}$. As an exercise, you should demonstrate that the ACF for the MA(2) process $y_t = \epsilon_t + \beta_1\epsilon_{t-1} + \beta_2 \epsilon_{t-2}$ has two spikes and then cuts to zero.

The Autocorrelation Function of an ARMA(1, 1) Process

Finally, let $y_t = a_1y_{t-1} + \epsilon_t + \beta_1\epsilon_{t-1}$. Using the now familiar procedure, we find the Yule–Walker equations:

$$Ey_ty_t = a_1Ey_{t-1}y_t + E\epsilon_ty_t + \beta_1E\epsilon_{t-1}y_t \quad \Rightarrow \gamma_0 = a_1\gamma_1 + \sigma^2 + \beta_1(a_1 + \beta_1)\sigma^2 \quad (2.30)$$
$$Ey_ty_{t-1} = a_1Ey_{t-1}y_{t-1} + E\epsilon_ty_{t-1} + \beta_1E\epsilon_{t-1}y_{t-1} \quad \Rightarrow \gamma_1 = a_1\gamma_0 + \beta_1\sigma^2 \quad (2.31)$$
$$Ey_ty_{t-2} = a_1Ey_{t-1}y_{t-2} + E\epsilon_ty_{t-2} + \beta_1E\epsilon_{t-1}y_{t-2} \quad \Rightarrow \gamma_2 = a_1\gamma_1 \quad (2.32)$$
$$\cdot$$
$$\cdot$$
$$Ey_ty_{t-s} = a_1Ey_{t-1}y_{t-s} + E\epsilon_ty_{t-s} + \beta_1E\epsilon_{t-1}y_{t-s} \quad \Rightarrow \gamma_s = a_1\gamma_{s-1} \quad (2.33)$$

Solving (2.30) and (2.31) simultaneously for γ_0 and γ_1 yields

$$\gamma_0 = \frac{1 + \beta_1^2 + 2a_1\beta_1}{(1 - a_1^2)}\sigma^2$$

$$\gamma_1 = \frac{(1 + a_1\beta_1)(a_1 + \beta_1)}{(1 - a_1^2)}\sigma^2$$

Hence,

$$\rho_1 = \frac{(1 + a_1\beta_1)(a_1 + \beta_1)}{(1 + \beta_1^2 + 2a_1\beta_1)} \qquad (2.34)$$

and $\rho_s = a_1\rho_{s-1}$ for all $s \geq 2$.

Thus, the ACF for an ARMA(1, 1) process is such that the magnitude of ρ_1 depends on both a_1 and β_1. Beginning with this value of ρ_1, the ACF of an ARMA(1, 1) process looks like that of the AR(1) process. If $0 < a_1 < 1$, convergence will be direct, and if $-1 < a_1 < 0$, the autocorrelations will oscillate. The ACF for the function $y_t = -0.7y_{t-1} + \epsilon_t - 0.7\epsilon_{t-1}$ is shown in the last graph on the left-hand side of Figure 2.2. The top portion of Worksheet 2.2 derives these autocorrelations.

We leave you with the exercise of deriving the correlogram of the ARMA(2, 1) process used in Worksheet 2.1. You should be able to recognize the point that the correlogram can reveal the pattern of the autoregressive coefficients. For an ARMA(p, q) model beginning at lag q, the values of the ρ_i will satisfy

$$\rho_i = a_1\rho_{i-1} + a_2\rho_{i-2} + \cdots + a_p\rho_{i-p}$$

The first $p - 1$ values can be treated as initial conditions that satisfy the Yule–Walker equations.

6. THE PARTIAL AUTOCORRELATION FUNCTION

In an AR(1) process, y_t and y_{t-2} are correlated even though y_{t-2} does not directly appear in the model. The correlation between y_t and y_{t-2} (i.e., ρ_2) is equal to the correlation between y_t and y_{t-1} (i.e., ρ_1) multiplied by the correlation between y_{t-1} and y_{t-2} (i.e., ρ_1 again) so that $\rho_2 = \rho_1^2$. It is important to note that all such "indirect" correlations are present in the ACF of any autoregressive process. In contrast, the **partial autocorrelation** between y_t and y_{t-s} eliminates the effects of the intervening values y_{t-1} through y_{t-s+1}. As such, in an AR(1) process, the partial autocorrelation between y_t and y_{t-2} is equal to zero. The most direct way to find the partial autocorrelation function is to first form the series $\{y_t^*\}$ by subtracting the mean of y (μ) from each observation: $y_t^* \equiv y_t - \mu$. Next, form the first-order autoregression equation:

$$y_t^* = \phi_{11}y_{t-1}^* + e_t$$

where: e_t = an error term

Here, the symbol $\{e_t\}$ is used since this error process may not be white-noise.

Since there are no intervening values, ϕ_{11} is both the autocorrelation and partial autocorrelation between y_t and y_{t-1}. Now form the second-order autoregression equation:

$$y_t^* = \phi_{21}y_{t-1}^* + \phi_{22}y_{t-2}^* + e_t$$

Here, ϕ_{22} is the partial autocorrelation coefficient between y_t and y_{t-2}. In other words, ϕ_{22} is the correlation between y_t and y_{t-2} controlling for (i.e., "netting out") the effect of y_{t-1}. Repeating this process for all additional lags s yields the partial autocorrelation function (PACF). In practice, with sample size T, only $T/4$ lags are used in obtaining the sample PACF.

Since most statistical computer packages perform these transformations, there is little need to elaborate on the computational procedure. However, it should be pointed out that a simple computional method relying on the so-called Yule–Walker equations is available. One can form the partial autocorrelations from the autocorrelations as

$$\phi_{11} = \rho_1 \tag{2.35}$$
$$\phi_{22} = (\rho_2 - \rho_1^2)/(1 - \rho_1^2) \tag{2.36}$$

and for additional lags,

$$\phi_{ss} = \frac{\rho_s - \sum_{j=1}^{s-1} \phi_{s-1,j}\rho_{s-j}}{1 - \sum_{j=1}^{s-1} \phi_{s-1,j}\rho_j}, \qquad s = 3, 4, 5, \ldots \tag{2.37}$$

where $\phi_{sj} = \phi_{s-1,j} - \phi_{ss}\phi_{s-1,s-j}, j = 1, 2, 3, \ldots, s - 1$.

For an AR(p) process, there is no direct correlation between y_t and y_{t-s} for $s > p$. Hence, all values of ϕ_{ss} for $s > p$ will be zero and the PACF for a pure AR(p) process should cut to zero for all lags greater than p. This is a useful feature of the PACF that can aid in the identification of an AR(p) model. In contrast, consider the PACF for the MA(1) process $y_t = \epsilon_t + \beta\epsilon_{t-1}$. As long as $\beta \neq -1$, we can write $y_t/(1 + \beta L) = \epsilon_t$, which we know has the infinite-order autoregressive representation:

$$y_t - \beta y_{t-1} + \beta^2 y_{t-2} - \beta^3 y_{t-3} + \cdots = \epsilon_t$$

As such, the PACF will *not* jump to zero since y_t will be correlated with all its own lags. Instead, the PACF coefficients exhibit a geometrically decaying pattern. If $\beta < 0$, decay is direct, and if $\beta > 0$, the PACF coefficients oscillate.

Worksheet 2.2 illustrates the procedure used in constructing the PACF for the ARMA(1, 1) model shown in the fifth graph on the right-hand side of Figure 2.2:

$$y_t = -0.7y_{t-1} + \epsilon_t - 0.7\epsilon_{t-1}$$

First calculate the autocorrelations. Clearly, $\rho_0 = 1$; use Equation (2.34) to calculate as $\rho_1 = -0.8445$. Thereafter, the ACF coefficients decay at the rate $\rho_i = (-0.7)\rho_{i-1}$ for $i \geq 2$. Using (2.35) and (2.36), we obtain $\phi_{11} = -0.8445$ and $\phi_{22} = -0.4250$. All subsequent ϕ_{ss} and ϕ_{sj} can be calculated from (2.37) as in Worksheet 2.2.

WORKSHEET 2.2   Calculation of the partial autocorrelations of
$y_t = -0.7y_{t-1} + \epsilon_t - 0.7\epsilon_{t-1}$

STEP 1: Calculate the autocorrelations. Use (2.34) to calculate ρ_1 as

$$\rho_1 = \frac{(1+0.49)(-0.7-0.7)}{1+0.49+2(0.49)} = -0.8445$$

The remaining correlations decay at the rate $\rho_i = -0.7\rho_{i-1}$, so that

$$\rho_2 = 0.591 \qquad \rho_3 = -0.414 \qquad \rho_4 = 0.290 \qquad \rho_5 = -0.203$$
$$\rho_6 = 0.142 \qquad \rho_7 = -0.010 \qquad \rho_8 = 0.070 \qquad \rho_9 = -0.049$$

STEP 2: Calculate the first two partial autocorrelations using (2.35) and (2.36). Hence,

$$\phi_{11} = \rho_1 = -0.844$$
$$\phi_{22} = [0.591 - (-0.8445)^2]/[1 - (-0.8445)^2] = -0.425$$

STEP 3: Construct all remaining ϕ_{ss} iteratively using (2.37). To find ϕ_{33}, note that $\phi_{21} = \phi_{11} - \phi_{22}\phi_{11} = -1.204$ and form

$$\phi_{33} = \left(\rho_3 - \sum_{j=1}^{2} \phi_{2j}\rho_{3-j} \right)\left(1 - \sum_{j=1}^{2} \phi_{2j}\rho_j \right)^{-1}$$

$$= [-0.414 - (-1.204)(0.591) - (-0.425)(-0.8445)]/$$
$$[1 - (-1.204)(-0.8445) - (-0.425)(0.591)]$$
$$= -0.262$$

Similarly, to find ϕ_{44}, use

$$\phi_{44} = \left(\rho_4 - \sum_{j=1}^{3} \phi_{3j}\rho_{4-j} \right)\left(1 - \sum_{j=1}^{3} \phi_{3j}\rho_j \right)^{-1}$$

Since $\phi_{3j} = \phi_{2j} - \phi_{33}\phi_{2,2-j}$, it follows that $\phi_{31} = -1.315$ and $\phi_{32} = -0.74$. Hence,

$$\phi_{44} = -0.173$$

If we continue in this fashion, it is possible to demonstrate that $\phi_{55} = -0.117$, $\phi_{66} = -0.081$, $\phi_{77} = -0.056$, and $\phi_{88} = -0.039$.

Table 2.1: **Properties of the ACF and PACF**

Process	ACF	PACF
White-noise	All $\rho_s = 0$.	All $\phi_{ss} = 0$.
AR(1): $a_1 > 0$	Direct exponential decay: $\rho_s = a_1^s$.	$\phi_{11} = \rho_1$; $\phi_{ss} = 0$ for $s \geq 2$.
AR(1): $a_1 < 0$	Oscillating decay: $\rho_s = a_1^s$.	$\phi_{11} = \rho_1$; $\phi_{ss} = 0$ for $s \geq 2$.
AR(p)	Decays toward zero. Coefficients may oscillate.	Spikes through lag p. All ϕ_{ss} $= 0$ for $s > p$.
MA(1): $\beta > 0$	Negative spike at lag 1. $\rho_s = 0$ for $s \geq 2$.	Oscillating decay: $\phi_{11} < 0$.
MA(1): $\beta < 0$	Positive spike at lag 1. $\rho_s = 0$ for $s \geq 2$.	Oscillating decay: $\phi_{11} > 0$.
ARMA(1, 1): $a_1 > 0$	Exponential decay beginning at lag 1. Sign $\rho_1 = \text{sign}(a_1 + \beta)$.	Oscillating decay beginning at lag 1. $\phi_{11} = \rho_1$.
ARMA(1, 1): $a_1 < 0$	Oscillating decay beginning at lag 1. Sign $\rho_1 = \text{sign}(a_1 + \beta)$.	Exponential decay beginning at lag 1. $\phi_{11} = \rho_1$ and sign(ϕ_{ss}) $= \text{sign}(\phi_{11})$.
ARMA (p, q)	Decay (either direct or oscillatory) beginning at lag q.	Decay (either direct or oscillatory) beginning at lag p.

More generally, the PACF of a stationary ARMA(p, q) process must ultimately decay toward zero beginning at lag p. The decay pattern depends on the coefficients of the polynomial $(1 + \beta_1 L + \beta_2 L^2 + \cdots + \beta_q L^q)$. Table 2.1 summarizes some of the properties at the ACF and PACF for various ARMA processes. Also, the right-hand-side graphs of Figure 2.2 show the partial autocorrelation functions of the five indicated processes.

For stationary processes, the key points to note are the following:

1. The ACF of an ARMA(p, q) process will begin to decay at lag q. Beginning at lag q, the coefficients of the ACF (i.e., the ρ_i) will satisfy the difference equation $(\rho_i = a_1\rho_{i-1} + a_2\rho_{i-2} + \cdots + a_p\rho_{i-p})$. Since the characteristic roots are inside the unit circle, the autocorrelations will decay beginning at lag q. Moreover, the pattern of the autocorrelation coefficients will mimic that suggested by the characteristic roots.

2. The PACF of an ARMA(p, q) process will begin to decay at lag p. Beginning at lag p, the coefficients of the PACF (i.e., the ϕ_{ss}) will mimic the ACF coefficients from the model $y_t/(1 + \beta_1 L + \beta_2 L^2 + \cdots + \beta_q L^q)$.

We can illustrate the usefulness of the ACF and PACF functions using the model $y_t = a_0 + 0.7y_{t-1} + \epsilon_t$. If we compare the top two graphs of Figure 2.2, the ACF shows the monotonic decay of the autocorrelations, while the PACF exhibits the single spike at lag 1. Suppose that a researcher collected sample data and plotted the ACF and PACF functions. If the actual patterns compared favorably to the theoretical patterns, the researcher might try to estimate data using an AR(1) model.

Correspondingly, if the ACF exhibited a single spike and the PACF monotonic decay (see the third graph of the figure for the model $y_t = \epsilon_t - 0.7\epsilon_{t-1}$), the researcher might try an MA(1) model.

7. SAMPLE AUTOCORRELATIONS OF STATIONARY SERIES

In practice, the theoretical mean, variance, and autocorrelations of a series are unknown to the researcher. Given that a series is stationary, we can use the sample mean, variance, and autocorrelations to estimate the parameters of the actual data-generating process. Let there be T observations labeled y_1 through y_T. We can let $\bar{y}$, $\hat{\sigma}^2$, and r_s be estimates of μ, σ^2, and ρ_s, respectively, where:

$$\bar{y} = \frac{\sum_{t=1}^{T} y_t}{T} \tag{2.38}$$

$$\hat{\sigma}^2 = \frac{\sum_{t=1}^{T}(y_t - \bar{y})^2}{T} \tag{2.39}$$

and for each value of $s = 1, 2, \ldots$,

$$r_s = \frac{\sum_{t=s+1}^{T}(y_t - \bar{y})(y_{t-s} - \bar{y})}{\sum_{t=1}^{T}(y_t - \bar{y})^2} \tag{2.40}$$

The sample autocorrelation function [i.e., the ACF derived from (2.40)] and PACF can be compared to various theoretical functions to help identify the actual nature of the data-generating process. Box and Jenkins (1976) discuss the distribution of the sample values of r_s under the null that y_t is stationary with normally distributed errors. Allowing var(r_s) to denote the sampling variance of r_s, they obtain

$$\text{Var}(r_s) = T^{-1} \qquad \text{for } s = 1$$

$$= \left(1 + 2\sum_{j=1}^{s-1} r_j^2\right) T^{-1} \qquad \text{for } s > 1 \tag{2.41}$$

if the true value of $r_s = 0$ [i.e., if the true data-generating process is an MA($s - 1$) process]. Moreover, in large samples (i.e., for large values of T), r_s will be normally distributed with a mean equal to zero. For the PACF coefficients, under the null hypothesis of an AR(p) model (i.e, under the null that all $\phi_{p+i,p+i}$ are zero), the variance of the $\phi_{p+i,p+i}$ is approximately T^{-1}.

In practice, we can use these sample values to form the sample autocorrelation and partial autocorrelation functions and test for significance using (2.41). For example, if we use a 95% confidence interval (i.e., two standard deviations), and the calculated value of r_1 exceeds $2T^{-1/2}$, it is possible to reject the null hypothesis that the first-order autocorrelation is not statistically different from zero. Rejecting this hypothesis means rejecting an MA($s-1$) = MA(0) process and accepting the alternative $q > 0$. Next, try $s = 2$; var(r_2) is $(1 + 2r_1^2)/T$. If r_1 is 0.5 and T 100, the variance of r_2 is 0.015 and the standard deviation about 0.123. Thus, if the calculated value of r^2 exceeds 2(0.123), it is possible to reject the hypothesis $r_2 = 0$. Here, rejecting the null means accepting the alternative that $q > 1$. Repeating for the various values of s is helpful in identifying the order to the process. In practice, the maximum number of sample autocorrelations and partial autocorrelations to use is $T/4$.

When looking over a large number of autocorrelations, we will see that some exceed two standard deviations as a result of pure chance even though the true values in the data-generating process are zero. The Q-statistic can be used to test whether a group of autocorrelations is significantly different from zero. Box and Pierce (1970) used the sample autocorrelations to form the statistic

$$Q = T \sum_{k=1}^{s} r_k^2$$

If the data are generated from a stationary ARMA process, Q is asymptotically χ^2 distributed with s degrees of freedom. The intuition behind the use of the statistic is that high sample autocorrelations lead to large values of Q. Certainly, a white-noise process (in which all autocorrelations should be zero) would have a Q value of zero. If the calculated value of Q exceeds the appropriate value in a χ^2 table, we can reject the null of no significant autocorrelations. Note that rejecting the null means accepting an alternative that at least one autocorrelation is not zero.

A problem with the Box–Pierce Q-statistic is that it works poorly even in moderately large samples. Ljung and Box (1978) report superior small sample performance for the modified Q-statistic calculated as

$$Q = T(T+2) \sum_{k=1}^{s} r_k^2 / (T-k) \tag{2.42}$$

If the sample value of Q calculated from (2.42) exceeds the critical value of χ^2 with s degrees of freedom, then *at least* one value of r_k is statistically different from zero at the specified significance level. The Box–Pierce and Ljung–Box Q-statistics also serve as a check to see if the *residuals* from an estimated ARMA(p, q) model behave as a white-noise process. However, when we form the s correlations from an estimated ARMA(p, q) model, the degrees of freedom are reduced by the number of estimated coefficients. Hence, if using the residuals of an ARMA(p, q) model, Q has a χ^2 with s-p-q degrees of freedom (if a constant is included, the degrees of freedom are s-p-q-1).

Model Selection Criteria

One natural question to ask of any estimated model is: How well does it fit the data? Adding additional lags for p and/or q will necessarily reduce the sum of squares of the estimated residuals. However, adding such lags entails the estimation of additional coefficients and an associated loss of degress of freedom. Moreover, the inclusion of extraneous coefficients will reduce the forecasting performance of the fitted model. There exist various model selection criteria that trade off a reduction in the sum of squares of the residuals for a more **parsimonious** model. The two most commonly used model selection criteria are the Akaike information criterion (AIC) and Schwartz Bayesian criterion (SBC), calculated as

$$AIC = T \ln(\text{residual sum of squares}) + 2n$$
$$SBC = T \ln(\text{residual sum of squares}) + n \ln(T)$$

where $n =$ number of parameters estimated ($p + q +$ possible constant term);
        $T =$ number of usable observations.

Typically in creating lagged variables, some observations are lost. To adequately compare the alternative models, T should be kept fixed. For example, with 100 data points, estimate an AR(1) and AR(2) using only the last 98 observations in each estimation. Compare the two models using $T = 98$.[2]

Ideally, the AIC and SBC will be as small as possible (note that both can be negative). We can use these criteria to aid in selecting the most appropriate model; model A is said to fit better than model B if the AIC (or SBC) for A is smaller than that for model B. In using the criteria to compare alternative models, we must estimate over the same sample period so that they will be comparable. For each, increasing the number of regressors increases n, but should have the effect of reducing the residual sum of squares. Thus, if a regressor has no explanatory power, adding it to the model will cause both the AIC and SBC to increase. Since $\ln(T)$ will be greater than 2, the SBC will always select a more parsimonious model than the AIC; the marginal cost of adding regressors is greater with the SBC than the AIC.

Of the two criteria, the SBC has superior large sample properties. Let the true order of the data-generating process be (p^*, q^*) and suppose that we use the AIC and SBC to estimate all ARMA models of order (p, q) where $p \geq p^*$ and $q \geq q^*$. Both the AIC and SBC will select models of orders greater than or equal to (p^*, q^*) as the sample size approaches infinity. However, the SBC is asymptotically consistent, whereas the AIC is biased toward selecting an overparameterized model.

Estimation of an AR(1) Model

Let us use a specific example to see how the sample autocorrelation function and partial autocorrelation function can be used as an aid in identifying an ARMA model. A computer program was used to draw 100 normally distributed random numbers with a theoretical variance equal to unity. Call these random variates ϵ_t, where t runs from 1 to 100. Beginning with $t = 1$, values of y_t were generated using the formula $y_t = 0.7y_{t-1} + \epsilon_t$ and initial condition $y_0 = 0$. Note that the problem of nonstationarity is avoided since the initial condition is consistent with long-run equilibrium. The upper-left-hand graph of Figure 2.3 shows the sample correlogram and upper-right-hand graph the sample PACF. You should take a minute to compare the ACF and PACF to those of the theoretical processes illustrated in Figure 2.2.

In practice, we never know the true data-generating process. However, suppose we were presented with these 100 sample values and asked to uncover the true process. The first step might be to compare the sample ACF and PACF to those of the various theoretical models. The decaying pattern of the ACF and the single

Figure 2.3   ACF and PACF for two simulated processes.

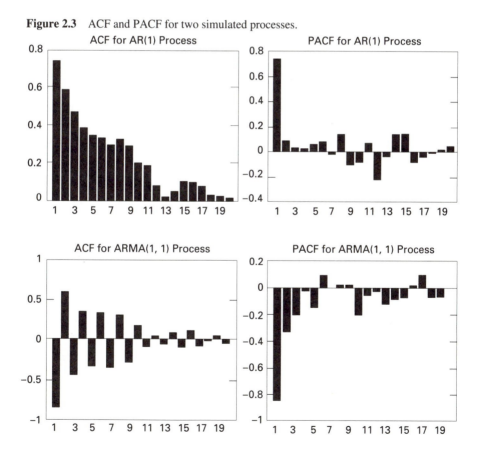

large spike in the sample PACF suggest an AR(1) model. The first three autocorrelations are $r_1 = 0.74$, $r_2 = 0.58$, and $r_3 = 0.47$, which are somewhat greater than the theoretical values of 0.7, 0.49 ($0.7^2 = 0.49$), and 0.343. In the PACF, there is a sizable spike of 0.74 at lag one and all other partial autocorrelations (except for lag 12) are very small.

Under the null hypothesis of an MA(0) process, the standard deviation of r_1 is $T^{-1/2} = 0.1$. Since the sample value of $r_1 = 0.74$ is more than seven standard deviations from zero, we can reject the null that r_1 equals zero. The standard deviation of r_2 is obtained by applying (2.41) to the sampling data, where $s = 2$:

$$\text{Var}(r_2) = [1 + 2(0.74)^2]/100 = 0.021$$

Since $(0.021)^{1/2} = 0.1449$, the sample value of r_2 is approximately four standard deviations from zero; at conventional significance levels, we can reject the null hypothesis that r_2 equals zero. We can similarly test the significance of the other values of the autocorrelations.

As you can see in the second part of the figure, other than $\phi_{1,1}$, all partial autocorrelations (except for lag 12) are less than $2T^{-1/2} = 0.2$. The decay of the ACF and single spike of the PACF give the strong impression of a first-order autoregressive model. If we did not know the true underlying process and happened to be using monthly data, we might be concerned with the significant partial autocorrelation at lag 12. After all, with monthly data we might expect some direct relationship between y_t and y_{t-12}.

Although we know that the data were actually generated from an AR(1) process, it is illuminating to compare the estimates of two different models. Suppose we estimate an AR(1) model and also try to capture the spike at lag 12 with an MA coefficient. Thus, we can consider the two tentative models:

$$\text{Model 1: } y_t = a_1 y_{t-1} + \epsilon_t$$
$$\text{Model 2: } y_t = a_1 y_{t-1} + \epsilon_t + \beta_{12}\epsilon_{t-12}$$

Table 2.2 reports the results of the two estimations.[3] The coefficient of model 1 satisfies the stability condition $|a_1| < 1$ and has a low standard error (the associated t-statistic for a null of zero is more than 12). As a useful diagnostic check, we plot the correlogram of the **residuals** of the fitted model in Figure 2.4. The Q-statistics for these residuals indicate that each one of the autocorrelations is less than two standard deviations from zero. The Ljung–Box Q-statistics of these residuals indicate that *as a group*, lags 1 through 8, 1 through 16, and 1 through 24 are not significantly different from zero. This is strong evidence that the AR(1) model "fits" the data well. After all, if residual autocorrelations were significant, the AR(1) model would not be utilizing all available information concerning movements in the $\{y_t\}$ sequence. For example, suppose we wanted to forecast y_{t+1} conditioned on all available information up to and including period t. With model 1, the value of y_{t+1} is: $y_{t+1} = a_1 y_t + \epsilon_{t+1}$. Hence, the forecast from model 1 is $a_1 y_t$. If the residual au-

Table 2.2: **Estimates of an AR(1) Model**

	Model 1 $y_t = a_1 y_{t-1} + \epsilon_t$	Model 2 $y_t = a_1 y_{t-1} + \epsilon_t + \beta_{12}\epsilon_{t-12}$
Degrees of freedom	99	98
Sum of squared residuals	85.21	85.17
Estimated a_1 (standard error)	0.7910 (0.0622)	0.7953 (0.0683)
Estimated β (standard error)		−0.033 (0.1134)
AIC/SBC	AIC = 442.07/SBC = 444.67	AIC = 444.01/SBC = 449.21
Ljung–Box Q-statistics for the residuals (significance level in parentheses)	$Q(8) = 6.43(0.490)$ $Q(16) = 15.86\ (0.391)$ $Q(24) = 21.74\ (0.536)$	$Q(8) = 6.48\ (0.485)$ $Q(16) = 15.75\ (0.400)$ $Q(24) = 21.56\ (0.547)$

tocorrelations had been significant, this forecast would not be capturing all the available information set.

Examining the results for model 2, note that both models yield similar estimates for the first-order autoregressive coefficient and associated standard error. However, the estimate for β_{12} is of poor quality; the insignificant t value suggests that it should be dropped from the model. Moreover, comparing the AIC and SBC values of the two models suggests that any benefits of a reduced residual sum of squares are overwhelmed by the detrimental effects of estimating an additional parameter. All these indicators point to the choice of model 1.

Figure 2.4 ACF of residuals from model 1.

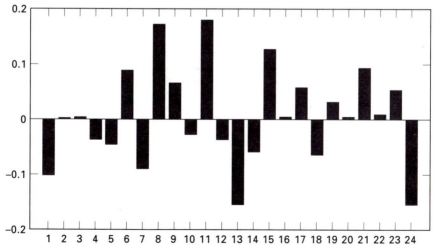

Exercise 7 at the end of this chapter entails various estimations using this data set. In this exercise you are asked to show that the AR(1) model performs better than some alternative specifications. It is important that you complete this exercise.

Estimation of an ARMA(1, 1) Model

A second $\{y_t\}$ sequence was constructed to illustrate the estimation of an ARMA-(1, 1). Given 100 normally distributed values of the $\{\epsilon_t\}$, 100 values of $\{y_t\}$ were generated using

$$y_t = -0.7y_{t-1} + \epsilon_t - 0.7\epsilon_{t-1}$$

where y_0 and ϵ_0 were both set equal to zero.

Both the sample ACF and PACF from the simulated data (see the second set of graphs in Figure 2.3) are roughly equivalent to those of the theoretical model shown in Figure 2.2. However, if the true data-generating process was unknown, the researcher might be concerned about certain discrepancies. An AR(2) model could yield a sample ACF and PACF similar to those in the figure. Table 2.3 reports the results of estimating the data using the following three models:

$$\text{Model 1: } y_t = a_1 y_{t-1} + \epsilon_t$$
$$\text{Model 2: } y_t = a_1 y_{t-1} + \epsilon_t + \beta_1 \epsilon_{t-1}$$
$$\text{Model 3: } y_t = a_1 y_{t-1} + a_2 y_{t-2} + \epsilon_t$$

In examining Table 2.3, notice that all the estimated values of a_1 are highly significant; each of the estimated values is *at least* eight standard deviations from zero. It is clear that the AR(1) model is inappropriate. The Q-statistics for model 1 indicate that there is significant autocorrelation in the residuals. The estimated ARMA(1, 1) model does not suffer from this problem. Moreover, both the AIC and SBC select model 2 over model 1.

Table 2.3:   **Estimates of an ARMA(1, 1) Model**

	Estimates[a]	Q-Statistics[b]	AIC/SBC
Model 1	a_1: −0.835 (0.053)	Q(8) = 26.19 (0.000) Q(24) = 41.10 (0.001)	AIC = 507.3 SBC = 509.9
Model 2	a_1: −0.679 (0.076) β_1: −0.676 (0.081)	Q(8) = 3.86 (0.695) Q(24) = 14.23 (0.892)	AIC = 481.4 SBC = 486.6
Model 3	a_1: −1.16 (0.093) a_2: −0.378 (0.092)	Q(8) = 11.44 (0.057) Q(24) = 22.59 (0.424)	AIC = 492.5 SBC = 497.7

[a]Standard errors in parentheses.
[b]Ljung–Box Q-statistics of the residuals from the fitted model. Significance levels in parentheses.

With the same type of reasoning, model 2 is preferred to model 3. Note that for each model, the estimated coefficients are highly significant and the point estimates imply convergence. Although the Q-statistic at 24 lags indicates that these two models do not suffer from correlated residuals, the Q-statistic at 8 lags indicates serial correlation in the residuals of model 3. Thus, the AR(2) model does not capture short-term dynamics as well as the ARMA(1, 1) model. Also note that the AIC and SBC both select model 2.

Estimation of an AR(2) Model

A third data series was simulated as

$$y_t = 0.7y_{t-1} - 0.49y_{t-2} + \epsilon_t$$

The estimated coefficients of the ACF and PACF of the series are

ACF:

Lag:						
1:	0.4655046	−0.1607289	−0.3216291	−0.1077528	−0.0518159	−0.1649841
7:	−0.0995764	0.1283475	0.1795718	0.0343415	−0.0869808	−0.1133948
13:	−0.1639613	−0.0579051	0.1151097	0.2540039	0.0460659	−0.1745434
19:	−0.1503307	0.0100510	0.0318942	−0.0869327	−0.0456013	0.0516806

PACF:

1:	0.4655046	−0.4818344	0.0225089	0.0452089	−0.2528370	−0.1206075
7:	0.1011489	0.0367555	−0.0758751	0.0229422	−0.0203879	−0.1391730
13:	−0.1671389	0.2066915	0.0074996	0.0851050	−0.2156580	0.0131360
19:	−0.0223151	−0.0324078	0.0148130	−0.0609358	0.0374894	−0.1842465

Note the large autocorrelation at lag 16 and large partial autocorrelations at lags 14 and 17. Given the way the process was simulated, the presence of these autocorrelations is due to nothing more than chance. However, an econometrician unaware of the actual data-generating process might be concerned about these autocorrelations. By using the 100 observations of the series, the coefficients of the AR(2) model are estimated as

Coefficient	Estimate	Standard Error	t-Statistic	Significance
a_1	0.692389807	0.089515769	7.73484	0.00000000
a_2	−0.480874620	0.089576524	−5.36831	0.00000055

AIC = 219.87333,   SBC = 225.04327

Overall, the model appears to be adequate. However, the two AR(2) coefficients are unable to capture the correlations at very long lags. For example, the partial autocorrelations of the *residuals* for lags 14 and 17 are both greater than 0.2 in absolute value. The calculated Ljung–Box statistic for 16 lags is 24.6248 (which is significant at the 0.038 level). At this point, it might be tempting to try to model the correlation at lag 16 by including the moving average term $\beta_{16}\epsilon_{t-16}$. Such an estimation results in

Coefficient	Estimate	Standard Error	t-Statistic	Significance
a_1	0.716681247	0.091069451	7.86961	0.00000000
a_2	−0.464999924	0.090958095	−5.11224	0.00000165
β_{16}	0.305813568	0.109936945	2.78172	0.00652182

$$AIC = 213.40055, \qquad SBC = 221.15545$$

All estimated coefficients are significant and the Ljung–Box Q-statistics are all insignificant at conventional levels. In conjunction with the fact that the AIC and SBC both select this second model, the researcher unaware of the true process might be tempted to conclude that the data-generating process includes a moving average term at lag 16.

A useful check of model adequacy is to split the sample into two parts. If a coefficient is present in the data-generating process, its influence should be seen in both subsamples. If the simulated data are split into two parts, the ACF and PACF using observations 50 through 100 are

ACF:

1:	0.4599901	−0.2066698	−0.2803821	0.0347391	0.0954499	−0.1525615
7:	−0.1329561	0.1017190	0.1807890	0.0274346	−0.0085572	0.0085072
13:	−0.0582938	−0.0876270	0.0426585	0.2051536	0.0643034	−0.1615533
19:	−0.1839472	−0.0504421	−0.0328661	−0.1452760	−0.1071579	−0.0360288

PACF:

1:	0.4599901	−0.5305123	0.1926653	0.0632359	−0.1967718	−0.1295519
7:	0.2337759	−0.0784309	0.0035535	0.0647291	0.1537812	−0.2568410
13:	0.0258134	0.1455056	0.0384080	0.0042725	−0.0542786	−0.0094085
19:	−0.1372884	−0.0763979	−0.0341192	−0.0830831	−0.0287218	−0.2200985

As you can see, the size of partial autocorrelations at lags 14 and 17 is diminished. Now, estimating a pure AR(2) model over this second part of the sample yields

Coefficient	Estimate	Standard Error	t-Statistic	Significance
a_1	0.713855785	0.120541523	5.92207	0.00000031
a_2	−0.537843744	0.120420318	−4.46639	0.00004687

$$Q(8) = 7.8296, \quad \text{significance level } 0.25085764$$
$$Q(16) = 15.9331, \quad \text{significance level } 0.31747712$$
$$Q(24) = 26.0648, \quad \text{significance level } 0.24890909$$

All estimated coefficients are significant and the Ljung–Box Q-statistics do not indicate any significant autocorrelations in the residuals. In fact, this model does estimate the actual data-generating process quite well. In this example, the large spurious autocorrelations of the long lags do not appear in the second sample period. Thus, it is hard to maintain that the correlation at lag 16 is meaningful. Most sophisticated practitioners are cautious about trying to fit any model to the very long lags. As you can infer from (2.41), the variance of r_s can be sizable when s is large. Moreover, in small samples, a few "unusual" observations can create the appearance of significant autocorrelations at long lags. Since econometric estimation involves unknown data-generating processes, the more general point is that we always need to be wary of our estimated model. Fortunately, Box and Jenkins (1976) established a set of procedures that can be used to check a model's adequacy.

8. BOX–JENKINS MODEL SELECTION

The estimates of the AR(1), ARMA(1, 1) and AR(2) models in the previous section illustrate the Box–Jenkins (1976) strategy for appropriate model selection. Box and Jenkins popularized a three-stage method aimed at selecting an appropriate model for the purpose of estimating and forecasting a univariate time series. In the **identification stage**, the researcher visually examines the time plot of the series, autocorrelation function, and partial correlation function. Plotting each observation of the $\{y_t\}$ sequence against t provides useful information concerning outliers, missing values, and structural breaks in the data. Nonstationary variables may have a pronounced trend or appear to meander without a constant long-run mean or variance. Missing values and outliers can be corrected at this point. At one time, the standard practice was to first-difference any series deemed to be nonstationary. Currently, a large literature is evolving that develops formal procedures to check for nonstationarity. We defer this discussion until Chapter 4 and assume that we are working with stationary data. A comparison of the sample ACF and PACF to those of various theoretical ARMA processes may suggest several plausible models. In the **estimation stage**, each of the tentative models is fit and the various a_i and β_i coefficients are examined. In this second stage, the estimated models are compared using the criteria listed below.

Parsimony

A fundamental idea in the Box–Jenkins approach is the principle of **parsimony**. Parsimony (meaning sparseness or stinginess) should come as second nature to economists. Incorporating additional coefficients will necessarily increase fit (e.g., the value of R^2 will increase) at a cost of reducing degrees of freedom. Box and

Jenkins argue that parsimonious models produce better forecasts than overparameterized models. A parsimonious model fits the data well without incorporating any needless coefficients. The aim is to approximate the true data-generating process but not to pin down the exact process. The goal of parsimony suggested eliminating the MA(12) coefficient in the simulated AR(1) model above.

In selecting an appropriate model, the econometrician needs to be aware that several very different models may have very similar properties. As an extreme example, note that the AR(1) model $y_t = 0.5y_{t-1} + \epsilon_t$ has the equivalent infinite-order moving average representation $y_t = \epsilon_t + 0.5\epsilon_{t-1} + 0.25\epsilon_{t-2} + 0.125\epsilon_{t-3} + 0.0625\epsilon_{t-4} +$ .... In most samples, approximating this MA(∞) process with an MA(2) or MA(3) model will give a very good fit. However, the AR(1) model is the more parsimonious model and is preferred.

Also be aware of the **common factor problem**. Suppose we wanted to fit the ARMA(2, 3) model:

$$(1 - a_1 L - a_2 L^2)y_t = (1 + \beta_1 L + \beta_2 L^2 + \beta_3 L^3)\epsilon_t \qquad (2.43)$$

Also suppose that $(1 - a_1 L - a_2 L^2)$ and $(1 + \beta_1 L + \beta_2 L^2 + \beta_3 L^3)$ can each be factored as $(1 + cL)(1 + aL)$ and $(1 + cL)(1 + b_1 L + b_2 L^2)$, respectively. Since $(1 + cL)$ is a common factor to each, (2.43) has the equivalent, but more parsimonious, form:[4]

$$(1 + aL)y_t = (1 + b_1 L + b_2 L^2)\epsilon_t \qquad (2.44)$$

In order to ensure that the model is parsimonious, the various a_i and β_i should all have t-statistics of 2.0 or greater (so that each coefficient is significantly different from zero at the 5% level). Moreover, the coefficients should not be strongly correlated with each other. Highly collinear coefficients are unstable; usually one or more can be eliminated from the model without reducing forecast performance.

Stationarity and Invertibility

The distribution theory underlying the use of the sample ACF and PACF as approximations to those of the true data-generating process assumes that the $\{y_t\}$ sequence is stationary. Moreover, t-statistics and Q-statistics also presume that the data are stationary. The estimated autoregressive coefficients should be consistent with this underlying assumption. Hence, we should be suspicious of an AR(1) model if the estimated value of a_1 is close to unity. For an ARMA(2, q) model, the characteristic roots of the estimated polynomial $(1 - a_1 L - a_2 L^2)$ should lie outside of the unit circle.

The Box–Jenkins approach also necessitates that the model be **invertible**. Formally, $\{y_t\}$ is invertible if it can be represented by a finite-order or convergent autoregressive process. Invertibility is important because the use of the ACF and PACF implicitly assumes that the $\{y_t\}$ sequence can be well approximated by an autoregressive model. As a demonstration, consider the simple MA(1) model:

$$y_t = \epsilon_t - \beta_1 \epsilon_{t-1} \tag{2.45}$$

so that if $|\beta_1| < 1$,

$$y_t/(1 - \beta_1 L) = \epsilon_t$$

or

$$y_t + \beta_1 y_{t-1} + \beta_1^2 y_{t-2} + \beta_1^3 y_{t-3} + \cdots = \epsilon_t \tag{2.46}$$

If $|\beta_1| < 1$, (2.46) can be estimated using the Box–Jenkins method. However, if $|\beta_1| \geq 1$, the $\{y_t\}$ sequence cannot be represented by a finite-order AR process; as such, it is not invertible. More generally, for an ARMA model to have a convergent AR representation, the roots of the polynomial $(1 + \beta_1 L + \beta_2 L^2 + \cdots + \beta_q L^q)$ must lie outside of the unit circle. Note that there is nothing "improper" about an invertible model. The $\{y_t\}$ sequence implied by $y_t = \epsilon_t - \epsilon_{t-1}$ is stationary in that it has a constant time-invariant mean $(Ey_t = Ey_{t-s} = 0$, a constant time-invariant variance $[\text{var}(y_t) = \text{var}(y_{t-s}) = \sigma^2(1 + \beta_1^2)]$, and the autocovariances $\gamma_1 = -\beta_1 \sigma^2$ and all other $\gamma_s = 0$. The problem is that the technique does not allow for the estimation of such models. If $\beta_1 = 1$, (2.46) becomes

$$y_t = -y_{t-1} + y_{t-2} - y_{t-3} + y_{t-4} + \cdots$$

Clearly, the autocorrelations and partial autocorrelations between y_t and y_{t-s} will never decay.

Goodness of Fit

A good model will fit the data well. Obviously, R^2 and the average of the residual sum of squares are common "goodness-of-fit" measures in ordinary least squares. The problem with these measures is that the "fit" necessarily improves as more parameters are included in the model. Parsimony suggests using the AIC and/or SBC as more appropriate measures of the overall fit of the model. Also, be cautious of estimates that fail to converge rapidly. Most software packages estimate the parameters of an ARMA model using non-linear search procedures. If the search fails to converge rapidly, it is possible that the estimated parameters are unstable. In such circumstances, adding an additional observation or two can greatly alter the estimates.

The third stage in the Box–Jenkins methodology involves **diagnostic checking**. The standard practice is to plot the residuals to look for outliers and evidence of periods in which the model does not fit the data well. If all plausible ARMA models show evidence of a poor fit during a reasonably long portion of the sample, it is wise to consider using intervention analysis, transfer function analysis, or any other of the multivariate estimation methods discussed in later chapters. If the variance of the residuals is increasing, a logarithmic transformation may be appropriate. Alternatively, you may wish to actually model any tendency of the variance to change using the ARCH techniques discussed in Chapter 3.

It is particularly important that the residuals from an estimated model be serially uncorrelated. Any evidence of serial correlation implies a systematic movement in the $\{y_t\}$ sequence that is not accounted for by the ARMA coefficients included in the model. Hence, any of the tentative models yielding nonrandom residuals should be eliminated from consideration. To check for correlation in the residuals, construct the ACF and PACF of the *residuals* of the estimated model. You can then use (2.41) and (2.42) to determine whether any or all of the residual autocorrelations or partial autocorrelations are statistically significant.[5] Although there is no significance level that is deemed "most appropriate," be wary of any model yielding (1) several residual correlations that are marginally significant and (2) a Q-statistic that is barely significant at the 10% level. In such circumstances, it is usually possible to formulate a better performing model.

In the previous section, recall that the estimated AR(1) model had Box–Ljung Q-statistics indicating a possible MA term at lag 12. As a result, we also estimated the model $y_t = 0.7953y_{t-1} + \epsilon_t - 0.033\epsilon_{t-12}$. The procedure of adding another coefficient is called **overfitting**. Overfit a model if the initial ACF and PACF yield ambiguous implications concerning the proper form of the ARMA coefficients. In the first example, the AR(1) model (i.e., model 1) outperformed the ARMA(1, 1) model. Obviously, in other circumstances, the "overfitted" model may outperform the first model. As an additional diagnostic check, some researchers will overfit a model by including a coefficient at some randomly selected lag. If such overfitting greatly affects the model, the estimated model is likely to yield poor forecasts.

If there are sufficient observations, fitting the same ARMA model to each of two subsamples can provide useful information concerning the assumption that the data-generating process is unchanging. In the estimated AR(2) model in the last section, the sample was split in half. In general, suppose you estimated an ARMA(p, q) model using a sample size of T observations. Denote the sum of the squared residuals as SSR. Divide the T observations into two subsamples with t_m observations in the first and $t_n = T - t_m$ observations in the second. Use each subsample to estimate the two models:

$$y_t = a_0(1) + a_1(1)y_{t-1} + \cdots + a_p(1)y_{t-p} + \epsilon_t + \beta_1(1)\epsilon_{t-1} + \cdots + \beta_q(1)\epsilon_{t-q}$$
$$\text{using } t_1, \ldots, t_m$$

$$y_t = a_0(2) + a_1(2)y_{t-1} + \cdots + a_p(2)y_{t-p} + \epsilon_t + \beta_1(2)\epsilon_{t-1} + \cdots + \beta_q(2)\epsilon_{t-q}$$
$$\text{using } t_{m+1}, \ldots, t_T$$

Let the sum of the squared residuals from each model be SSR_1 and SSR_2, respectively. To test the restriction that all coefficients are equal [i.e., $a_0(1) = a_0(2)$ and

$a_1(1) = a_1(2)$ and $\ldots$ $a_p(1) = a_p(2)$ and $\beta_1(1) = \beta_1(2)$ and $\ldots$ $\beta_q(1) = \beta_q(2)$], use an F-test and form:[6]

$$F = \frac{(\text{SSR} - \text{SSR}_1 - \text{SSR}_2)/(n)}{(\text{SSR}_1 + \text{SSR}_2)/(T - 2n)} \tag{2.47}$$

where n = number of parameters estimated ($n = p + q + 1$ if an intercept is included and $p + q$ otherwise)
the number of degrees of freedom are (n, T $-$ 2n).

Intuitively, if the restriction that the two sets of coefficients is not binding, the total from the two models (i.e., $\text{SSR}_1 + \text{SSR}_2$) should equal the sum of the squared residuals from the entire sample estimation. Hence, F should equal zero. The larger the calculated value of F, the more restrictive is the assumption that the two sets of coefficients are equal.

Similarly, the model can be estimated over nearly all the sample period. If we use 20 years of quarterly data, for example, the model might be estimated using only the first 19 years of data. Then, the model can be used to make forecasts of the last year of data. For each period t, the forecast error is the difference between the forecast and known value of y_t. The sum of the squared forecast errors is a useful way to compare the adequacy of alternative models. Those models with poor *out-of-sample* forecasts should be eliminated. Some of the details in constructing out-of-sample forecasts are discussed in the next section.

9. THE FORECAST FUNCTION

Perhaps the most important use of an ARMA model is to forecast future values of the $\{y_t\}$ sequence.[7] To simplify the discussion, it is assumed that the actual data-generating process and current and past realizations of the $\{\epsilon_t\}$ and $\{y_t\}$ sequences are known to the researcher. First, consider the forecasts from the AR(1) model $y_t = a_0 + a_1 y_{t-1} + \epsilon_t$. Updating one period, we obtain

$$y_{t+1} = a_0 + a_1 y_t + \epsilon_{t+1}$$

If you know the coefficients a_0 and a_1, you can forecast y_{t+1} conditioned on the information available at period t as

$$E_t y_{t+1} = a_0 + a_1 y_t \tag{2.48}$$

where $E_t y_{t+j}$ = a short-hand way to write the conditional expectation of y_{t+j} given the information available at t

Formally, $E_t y_{t+j} = E(y_{t+j} | y_t, y_{t-1}, y_{t-2}, \ldots, \epsilon_t, \epsilon_{t-1}, \ldots)$.

In the same way, since $y_{t+2} = a_0 + a_1 y_{t+1} + \epsilon_{t+2}$, the forecast of y_{t+2} conditioned on the information available at period t is

$$E_t y_{t+2} = a_0 + a_1 E_t y_{t+1}$$

and using (2.48), we obtain

$$E_t y_{t+2} = a_0 + a_0 a_1 + a_1^2 y_t \tag{2.49}$$

It should not require too much effort to convince yourself that

$$E_t y_{t+3} = a_0 + a_0 a_1 + a_0 a_1^2 + a_1^3 y_t$$

and in general,

$$E_t y_{t+j} = a_0 (1 + a_1 + a_1^2 + \cdots + a_1^{j-1}) + a_1^j y_t \tag{2.50}$$

Equation (2.50)—called the **forecast function**—yields the j-step ahead forecasts for each value y_{t+j}. Since $|a_1| < 1$, (2.50) yields a convergent sequence of forecasts. If we take the limit of $E_t y_{t+j}$ as $j \to \infty$, we find that $E_t y_{t+j} \to a_0/(1 - a_1)$. This result is really quite general. *For any stationary ARMA model, the conditional forecast of y_{t+j} converges to the unconditional mean as $j \to \infty$.* Unfortunately, the forecasts from an ARMA model will not be perfectly accurate. Forecasting from time period t, we can define the j-step ahead forecast error, $f_t(j)$—as the difference between the realized value of y_{t+j} and forecasted value:

$$f_t(j) \equiv y_{t+j} - E_t y_{t+j}$$

Hence, the one-step ahead forecast error is: $f_t(1) = y_{t+1} - E_t y_{t+1} = \epsilon_{t+1}$ (i.e., the "unforecastable" portion of y_{t+1} given the information available in t). To find the two-step ahead forecast error, we need to form $f_t(2) = y_{t+2} - E_t y_{t+2}$. Since $y_{t+2} = a_0 + a_1 a_0 + a_1^2 y_t + \epsilon_{t+2} + a_1 \epsilon_{t+1}$ and $E_t y_{t+2} = a_0 + a_1 a_0 + a_1^2 y_t$, it follows that

$$f_t(2) = \epsilon_{t+2} + a_1 \epsilon_{t+1}$$

You should take a few moments to demonstrate that for the AR(1) model, the j-step ahead forecast error is given by

$$f_t(j) = \epsilon_{t+j} + a_1 \epsilon_{t+j-1} + a_1^2 \epsilon_{t+j-2} + a_1^3 \epsilon_{t+j-3} + \cdots + a_1^{j-1} \epsilon_{t+1} \tag{2.51}$$

Equation (2.51) shows that the forecasts from (2.50) yield unbiased estimates of each value y_{t+j}. The proof is trivial; since $E_t \epsilon_{t+j} = E_t \epsilon_{t+j-1} = \cdots = E_t \epsilon_{t+1} = 0$, the conditional expectation of (2.51) is $E_t f_t(j) = 0$. Since the expected value of the forecast error is zero, the forecasts are unbiased.

Although unbiased, the forecasts from an ARMA model are necessarily inaccurate. To find the variance of the forecast error, continue to assume that the elements of the $\{\epsilon_t\}$ sequence are independent with variance σ^2. Hence, from (2.51) the variance of the forecast error is

$$\text{Var}[f_t(j)] = \sigma^2[1 + a_1^2 + a_1^4 + a_1^6 + \cdots + a_1^{2(j-1)}] \tag{2.52}$$

Since the one-step forecast error variance is σ^2, the two-step ahead forecast error variance is $\sigma^2(1 + a_1^2)$, etc. The essential point to note is that the variance of the forecast error is an increasing function of j. As such, you can have more confidence in short-term rather than long-term forecasts. In the limit as $j \to \infty$, the forecast error variance converges to $\sigma^2/(1 - a_1^2)$; hence, the forecast error variance converges to the unconditional variance of the $\{y_t\}$ sequence.

Moreover, assuming that the $\{\epsilon_t\}$ sequence is normally distributed, you can place confidence intervals around the forecasts. The one-step ahead forecast of y_{t+1} is $a_0 + a_1 y_t$, and the variance is σ^2. As such, the 95% confidence interval for the one-step ahead forecast can be constructed as

$$a_0 + a_1 y_t \pm 1.96\sigma$$

In the same way, the two-step ahead forecast is $a_0(1 + a_1) + a_1^2 y_t$ and (2.52) indicates that var$[f_t(2)]$ is $\sigma^2(1 + a_1^2)$. Thus, the 95% confidence interval for the two-step ahead forecast is

$$a_0(1 + a_1) + a_1^2 y_t \pm 1.96\sigma(1 + a_1^2)^{1/2}$$

Of course, if there is any uncertainty concerning the parameters, the confidence intervals will be wider than those reported here.

Iterative Forecasts

The derivation of (2.50)—the forecast function for an AR(1) model—relied on forward iteration. To generalize the discussion, it is possible to use the iterative technique to derive the forecast function for any ARMA(p, q) model. To keep the algebra simple, consider the ARMA(2, 1) model:

$$y_t = a_0 + a_1 y_{t-1} + a_2 y_{t-2} + \epsilon_t + \beta_1 \epsilon_{t-1} \tag{2.53}$$

Updating one period yields

$$y_{t+1} = a_0 + a_1 y_t + a_2 y_{t-1} + \epsilon_{t+1} + \beta_1 \epsilon_t$$

If we continue to assume that (1) all coefficients are known; (2) all variables subscripted t, $t - 1$, $t - 2$, etc. are known at period t; and (3) $E_t \epsilon_{t+j} = 0$ for $j > 0$, the conditional expectation of y_{t+1} is

$$E_t y_{t+1} = a_0 + a_1 y_t + a_2 y_{t-1} + \beta_1 \epsilon_t \tag{2.54}$$

Equation (2.54) is the one-step ahead forecast of y_{t+1}. To find the two-step ahead forecast, update (2.53) by two periods:

$$y_{t+2} = a_0 + a_1 y_{t+1} + a_2 y_t + \epsilon_{t+2} + \beta_1 \epsilon_{t+1}$$

The conditional expectation of y_{t+2} is

$$E_t y_{t+2} = a_0 + a_1 E_t y_{t+1} + a_2 y_t \tag{2.55}$$

Equation (2.55) expresses the two-step ahead forecast in terms of the one-step ahead forecast and current value of y_t. Combining (2.54) and (2.55) yields

$$
\begin{aligned}
E_t y_{t+2} &= a_0 + a_1(a_0 + a_1 y_t + a_2 y_{t-1} + \beta_1 \epsilon_t) + a_2 y_t \\
&= a_0(1 + a_1) + (a_1^2 + a_2)y_t + a_1 a_2 y_{t-1} + a_1 \beta_1 \epsilon_t
\end{aligned}
$$

You should be able to demonstrate that the three-step ahead forecast is

$$
\begin{aligned}
E_t y_{t+3} &= a_0 + a_1 E_t y_{t+2} + a_2 E_t y_{t+1} \\
&= a_0 + a_1\{a_0(1 + a_1) + [a_1^2 + a_2]y_t + a_1 a_2 y_{t-1} + a_1 \beta_1 \epsilon_t\} + \\
&\qquad\qquad\qquad\qquad\qquad a_2(a_0 + a_1 y_t + a_2 y_{t-1} + \beta_1 \epsilon_t) \\
&= a_0(1 + a_1 + a_1^2 + a_2) + (a_1^3 + 2a_1 a_2)y_t + (a_1^2 a_2 + a_2^2)y_{t-1} + \beta_1(a_1^2 + a_2)\epsilon_t \tag{2.56}
\end{aligned}
$$

Finally, all j-step ahead forecasts can be obtained from

$$E_t y_{t+j} = a_0 + a_1 E_t y_{t+j-1} + a_2 E_t y_{t+j-2}, \qquad j \geq 2 \tag{2.57}$$

Equations (2.56) and (2.57) suggest that the forecasts will satisfy a second-order difference equation. As long as the characteristic roots of (2.57) lie inside the unit circle, the forecasts will coverge to the unconditional mean $a_0/(1 - a_1 - a_2)$.

An Alternative Derivation of the Forecast Function

Instead of using the iterative technique, it is often preferable to derive the forecast function using the solution methodology discussed in Section 4 of Chapter 1. For any ARMA(p, q) model, the solution technique entails (1) finding all homogeneous solutions; (2) finding the particular solution; (3) forming the general solution as the sum of the homogeneous and particular solutions; and (4) imposing the initial conditions. This solution methodology will express y_t in terms of the p initial conditions $y_0, y_1, \ldots, y_{p-1}$ and q initial values $\epsilon_0, \epsilon_1, \ldots \epsilon_{q-1}$. The only twist is that the forecast function expresses y_{t+j} in terms of $y_t, y_{t-1}, \ldots, y_{t-p+1}$ and $\epsilon_t, \epsilon_{t-1}, \ldots, \epsilon_{t-q+1}$. To illustrate the appropriate modification of the time subscripts, consider the AR(2) model:

$$y_t = 3 + 0.9y_{t-1} - 0.2y_{t-2} + \epsilon_t$$

In Section 8 of Chapter 1, it was shown that the solution is

$$y_t = 10 + (0.4)^t[5(y_0 - 10) - 10(y_1 - 10)] + (0.5)^t[10(y_1 - 10) - 4(y_0 - 10)] + \sum_{i=0}^{t-2} \alpha_i \epsilon_{t-i}$$

where the values of α_i satisfy $\alpha_i = 5(0.5)^i - 4(0.4)^i$.

The problem is to modify this equation so as to express y_{t+j} in terms of y_t, y_{t-1}, and the $\{\epsilon_t\}$ sequence. Updating by j periods, we find

$$y_{t+j} = 10 + (0.4)^j[5(y_{t-1} - 10) - 10(y_t - 10)]$$
$$+ (0.5)^j[10(y_t - 10) - 4(y_{t-1} - 10)] + \sum_{i=0}^{j-1} \alpha_i \epsilon_{t+j-i}$$

Taking the conditional expectation of y_{t+j} yields the forecast function:

$$E_t y_{t+j} = 10 + (0.4)^j[5(y_{t-1} - 10) - 10(y_t - 10)] + (0.5)^j[10(y_t - 10) - 4(y_{t-1} - 10)]$$

Obviously, as j increases, the forecast approaches the unconditional mean of 10. For practice, try the ARMA(1, 1) model:

$$y_t = a_0 + a_1 y_{t-1} + \epsilon_t + \beta_1 \epsilon_{t-1}$$

where $\{\epsilon_t\}$ is a white-noise process, $|a_1| < 1$, and there is a given initial condition for y_0.

You should recognize that the homogeneous equation $y_t - a_1 y_{t-1} = 0$ has the solution $A(a_1)^t$, where A is an arbitrary constant. Next, use lag operators to obtain the particular solution as

$$y_t = a_0/(1 - a_1) + \epsilon_t/(1 - a_1 L) + \beta_1 \epsilon_{t-1}/(1 - a_1 L) \qquad (2.58)$$

so that the general solution is

$$y_t = a_0/(1 - a_1) + \sum_{i=0}^{\infty} a_1^i \epsilon_{t-i} + \beta_1 \sum_{i=0}^{\infty} a_1^i \epsilon_{t-1-i} + A a_1^t \qquad (2.59)$$

Now impose the initial condition for y_0. Since (2.59) must hold for all periods, including period zero, it follows that

$$y_0 = a_0/(1 - a_1) + \sum_{i=0}^{\infty} a_1^i \epsilon_{-i} + \beta_1 \sum_{i=0}^{\infty} a_1^i \epsilon_{-1-i} + A \qquad (2.60)$$

Solving (2.60) for A eliminates the arbitrary constant. Combining (2.59) and (2.60), we get

$$y_t = a_0/(1 - a_1) + \sum_{i=0}^{\infty} a_1^i \epsilon_{t-i} + \beta_1 \sum_{i=0}^{\infty} a_1^i \epsilon_{t-1-i}$$
$$+ \left[y_0 - a_0/(1 - a_1) - \sum_{i=0}^{\infty} a_1^i \epsilon_{-i} - \beta_1 \sum_{i=0}^{\infty} a_1^i \epsilon_{-1-i} \right] a_1^t$$

so that

$$y_t = a_0/(1 - a_1) + \sum_{i=0}^{t-1} a_1^i \epsilon_{t-i} + \beta_1 \sum_{i=0}^{t-1} a_1^i \epsilon_{t-1-i} + [y_0 - a_0/(1 - a_1)] a_1^t \qquad (2.61)$$

To this point, (2.61) is simply the general solution to the stochastic difference equation represented by an ARMA(1, 1) process. This solution expresses the current value of y_t in terms of the constants a_0, a_1, and β_1, $\{\epsilon_t\}$ sequence, and initial value of y_0.

The important point is that (2.61) can be used to forecast y_t conditioned on information available at period zero. Given $E_0 \epsilon_i = 0$ for $i > 0$, it follows that

$$E_0 y_t = a_0/(1 - a_1) + \beta_1 a_1^{t-1} \epsilon_0 + [y_0 - a_0/(1 - a_1)] a_1^t \qquad (2.62)$$

Equation (2.62) can be viewed as the *t-step ahead* forecast function given information available in period zero. To form the *j-step ahead* forecasts conditioned on information available at t, first change the time subscript in (2.62) so that the *j*-step ahead forecasts are

$$E_0 y_j = a_0/(1 - a_1) + \beta_1 a_1^{j-1} \epsilon_0 + [y_0 - a_0/(1 - a_1)] a_1^j$$
$$= [a_0/(1 - a_1)](1 - a_1^j) + \beta_1 a_1^{j-1} \epsilon_0 + y_0 a_1^j \qquad (2.63)$$

Next, update (2.63) by t periods so that

$$E_t y_{t+j} = [a_0/(1 - a_1)](1 - a_1^j) + \beta_1 a_1^{j-1} \epsilon_t + y_t a_1^j \qquad (2.64)$$

Equation (2.64) is in the desired form; (2.64) expressed the forecast of y_{t+j} conditioned on information available at period t. The various *j*-step ahead forecasts are

$$E_t y_{t+1} = a_0 + \beta_1 \epsilon_t + a_1 y_t$$
$$E_t y_{t+2} = [a_0/(1 - a_1)](1 - a_1^2) + \beta_1 a_1 \epsilon_t + y_t a_1^2$$
$$E_t y_{t+3} = [a_0/(1 - a_1)](1 - a_1^3) + \beta_1 a_1^2 \epsilon_t + y_t a_1^3$$
$$\cdots$$

Given that $|a_1| < 1$, the limiting value of the forecast as $j \to \infty$ is the unconditional mean: $\lim E_t y_{t+j} = a_0/(1 - a_1)$.

As a check, you can compare (2.64) to (2.50); after all, the AR(1) and ARMA(1, 1) models are equivalent if $\beta_1 = 0$. If $\beta_1 = 0$, (2.64) becomes

$$E_t y_{t+j} = [a_0/(1 - a_1)](1 - a_1^j) + y_t a_1^j \qquad (2.65)$$

Note that (2.65) is identical to (2.50); for $|a_1| < 1$,

$$a_0 \sum_{i=0}^{j-1} a_1^i = [a_0/(1 - a_1)](1 - a_1^j)$$

The example illustrates the basic point that for any ARMA(p, q) model, the forecast function for y_{t+j} will have the form

$$E_t y_{t+j} = \alpha_0(j) + \alpha_1(j)y_t + \alpha_2(j)y_{t-1} + \cdots + \alpha_p(j)y_{t-p+1} + \gamma_1(j)\epsilon_t + \cdots + \gamma_q \epsilon_{t-q+1} \qquad (2.66)$$

where all values of $_i(j)$ and $\gamma_i(j)$ are undetermined coefficients.

The notation $a_i(j)$ and $\gamma_i(j)$ is designed to stress the point that the coefficients are a function of j. Since we are working with stationary and invertible processes, we know the nature of the solution is such that as $j \to \infty$, $\alpha_0(j) \to a_0/(1 - \Sigma a_i)$, $\alpha_i(j) \to 0$, and that $\Sigma[\gamma_i(j)]^2$ is finite.

In practice, you will not know the actual order of the ARMA process or coefficients of that process. Instead, to create out-of-sample forecasts, it is necessary to use the estimated coefficients from what you believe to be the most appropriate form of an ARMA model. The rule of thumb is that forecasts from an ARMA model should never be trusted if the model is estimated with fewer than 50 observations. Suppose you have T observations of the $\{y_t\}$ sequence and choose to fit an ARMA(2, 1) model to the data. Let a hat or caret (i.e.: a ^) over a parameter denote the estimated value of a parameter and let $\{\hat{\epsilon}_t\}$ denote the residuals of the estimated model. Hence, the estimated AR(2, 1) model can be written as

$$y_t = \hat{a}_0 + \hat{a}_1 y_{t-1} + \hat{a}_2 y_{t-2} + \hat{\epsilon}_t + \beta_1 \hat{\epsilon}_{t-1}$$

Given that the sample contains T observations, the out-of-sample forecasts are easily constructed. For example, you can use (2.54) to forecast the value of y_{T+1} as

$$E_T y_{T+1} = \hat{a}_0 + \hat{a}_1 y_T + \hat{a}_2 y_{T-1} + \beta_1 \hat{\epsilon}_T \qquad (2.67)$$

Given the estimated values of $\hat{a}_0$, $\hat{a}_1$, and $\hat{a}_2$, (2.67) can easily be constructed using the actual values y_T, y_{T-1}, and $\hat{\epsilon}_T$ (i.e., the last residual of your estimated model). Similarly, the forecast of y_{T+2} can be constructed as

$$E_T y_{T+2} = \hat{a}_0 + \hat{a}_1 E_T y_{T+1} + \hat{a}_2 y_T$$

where $E_T y_{T+1}$ = the forecast from (2.67)

Given these two forecasts, all subsequent forecasts can be obtained from the difference equation:

$$E_T y_{T+j} = a_0 + a_1 E_T y_{T+j-1} + a_2 E_T y_{T+j-2} \qquad \text{for } j \geq 2$$

10. A MODEL OF THE WPI

The ARMA estimations performed in Section 8 were almost too straightforward. In practice, we rarely find a data series precisely conforming to a theoretical ACF or PACF. This section is intended to illustrate some of the ambiguities frequently encountered in the Box–Jenkins technique. These ambiguities may lead two equally skilled econometricians to estimate and forecast a series using very different ARMA processes. Many view the necessity to rely on the researcher's judgment and experience as a serious weakness of a procedure that is designed to be scientific.

It is useful to illustrate the Box–Jenkins modeling procedure by estimating a quarterly model of the U.S. Wholesale Price Index (WPI). The file labeled WPI.WK1 on the data disk contains the data used in this section. Exercise 10 at the end of this chapter will help you to reproduce the results reported below.

The top graph of Figure 2.5 clearly reveals that there is little point in modeling the series as being stationary; there is a decidedly positive trend or drift throughout the period 1960:I to 1990:IV. The first difference of the series seems to have a constant mean, although inspection of the middle graph suggests that the variance is an increasing function of time. As shown in the bottom graph of the same figure, the first difference of the logarithm (denoted by $\Delta lwpi$) is the most likely candidate to be covariance stationary. The large volatility of the WPI accompanying the oil price shocks in the 1970s should make us somewhat wary of the assumption that the process is covariance stationary. At this point, some researchers would make additional transformations intended to reduce the volatility exhibited in the 1970s. However, it seems reasonable to estimate a model of the $\{\Delta lwpi_t\}$ sequence. As always, you should maintain a healthy skepticism of the accuracy of your model.

Before reading on, you should examine the autocorrelation and partial autocorrelation functions of the $\{\Delta lwpi_t\}$ sequence shown in Figure 2.6. Try to identify the tentative models that you would want to estimate. In making your decision, note the following:

1. The ACF and PACF converge to zero reasonably quickly. We do not want to *overdifference* the data and try to model the $\{\Delta^2 lwpi_t\}$ sequence.

2. The theoretical ACF of a pure MA(q) process cuts off to zero at lag q and the theoretical ACF of an AR(1) model decays geometrically. Examination of the

two graphs of Figure 2.6 suggests that neither of these specifications seems appropriate for the sample data.

3. The PACF is such that $\phi_{1,1} = 0.609$ and cuts off to 0.252 abruptly (i.e., $\phi_{2,2} = 0.252$). Overall, the PACF suggests that we should consider models such as $p = 1$ and $p = 2$. The ACF is suggestive of an AR(2) process or a process with both autoregressive and moving average components.

4. Note the jump in ACF at lag 4 and the small spike in the PACF at lag 4 ($\phi_{4,4} = 0.198$). Since we are using quarterly data, we might want to incorporate a seasonal factor at lag 4.

Figure 2.5   U.S. wholesale price index (1985 = 100).

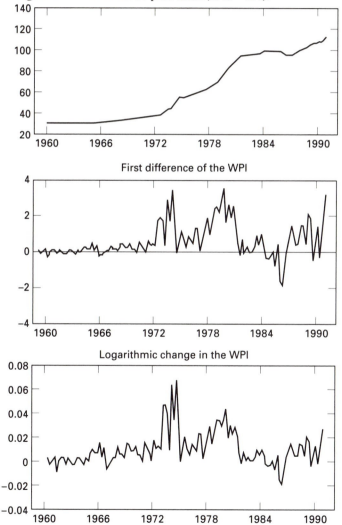

Figure 2.6   ACF and PACF for the logarithmic change in the WPI.

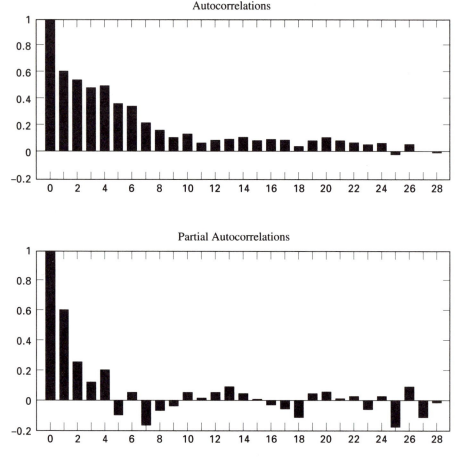

Autocorrelations

Partial Autocorrelations

Points 1 to 4 suggest an ARMA(1, 1) or AR(2) model. In addition, we might want to consider models with a seasonal term at lag 4. Since computing time is inexpensive, we can estimate a variety of models and compare their results. Table 2.4 reports estimates of five tentative models; note the following points:

1. The estimated AR(1) model confirms our analysis in the identification stage. Although the estimated value of a_1 (0.618) is less than unity in absolute value and more than eight standard deviations from zero, the AR(1) specification is inadequate. Forming the Ljung–Box Q-statistic for 12 lags of the residuals yields a value of 23.6; we can reject the null that $Q = 0$ at the 1% significance level. Hence, the lagged residuals of this model exhibit substantial serial autocorrelation. Then we must eliminate this model from consideration.

2. The AR(2) model is an improvement over the AR(1) specification. The estimated coefficients ($a_1 = 0.456$ and $a_2 = 0.258$) are each significantly different from zero at the 1% level and imply characteristic roots in the unit circle. Q-statistics indicate that the autocorrelations of the residuals are not statistically significant. As measured by the AIC, the fit of the AR(2) model is superior to that of the AR(1); the SBC is the same for the two models. Overall, the AR(2) model dominates the AR(1) specification.

3. The ARMA(1, 1) specification dominates the AR(2) model. The estimated coefficients are of high quality (with t values of 14.9 and -4.22). The estimated value of a_1 is positive but less than unity, and the Q-statistics indicate that the autocorrelations of the residuals are not statistically significant. Moreover, all goodness-of-fit measures select the ARMA(1, 1) specification over the AR(2) model. Thus, there is little reason to maintain the AR(2) specification.

Table 2.4: **Estimates of the WPI (Logarithmic First Differences)**

	$p = 1$ $q = 0$	$p = 2$ $q = 0$	$p = 1$ $q = 1$	$p = 1$ $q = 1, 4$	$p = 1$ $q = 2$
a_0	0.011 (4.14)	0.011 (3.31)	0.012 (2.63)	0.011 (2.76)	0.012 (2.62)
a_1	0.618 (8.54)	0.456 (5.11)	0.887 (14.9)	0.791 (9.21)	0.887 (13.2)
a_2		0.258 (2.89)			
β_1			−0.484 (−4.22)	−0.409 (−3.62)	−0.483 (−4.19)
β_2					−0.002 (−0.019)
β_4				0.315 (3.36)	
SSR	0.0156	0.0145	0.0141	0.0134	0.0141
AIC	−503.3	−506.1	−513.1	−518.2	−511.1
SBC	−497.7	−497.7	−504.7	−507.0	−499.9
$Q(12)$	23.6 (0.008)	11.7 (0.302)	11.7 (0.301)	4.8 (0.898)	11.7 (0.301)
$Q(24)$	28.6 (0.157)	15.6 (0.833)	15.4 (0.842)	9.3 (0.991)	15.3 (0.841)
$Q(30)$	40.1 (0.082)	22.8 (0.742)	22.7 (0.749)	14.8 (0.972)	22.6 (0.749)

Notes: Each coefficient is reported with the associated t-statistic for the null hypothesis that the estimated value is equal to zero.

SSR is the sum of squared residuals.

$Q(n)$ reports the Ljung–Box Q-statistic for the autocorrelations of the n residuals of the estimated model. With 122 observations, $T/4$ is approximately equal to 30. Significance levels are in parentheses.

4. In order to account for the possibility of seasonality, we estimated the ARMA(1, 1) model with an additional moving average coefficient at lag 4, that is, we estimated a model of the form $y_t = a_0 + a_1 y_{t-1} + \epsilon_t + \beta_1 \epsilon_{t-1} + \beta_4 \epsilon_{t-4}$. More sophisticated seasonal patterns are considered in the next section. For now, note that the additive expression $\beta_4 \epsilon_{t-4}$ is often preferable to an additive autoregressive term of the form $a_4 y_{t-4}$. For truly seasonal shocks, the expression $\beta_4 \epsilon_{t-4}$ best captures spikes—not decay—at the quarterly lags. The coefficients of the estimated ARMA[1, (1, 4)] model are all highly significant with t-statistics of 9.21, −3.62, and 3.36.[8] The Q-statistics are all very low, implying that the autocorrelations of the residuals are statistically equal to zero. Moreover, the AIC and SBC strongly select this model over the ARMA(1, 1) model.

5. In contrast, the ARMA(1, 2) contains a superfluous coefficient. The t-statistic for β_2 is sufficiently low that we should eliminate this model.

Having identified and estimated a plausible model, we want to perform additional diagnostic checks of model adequacy. Due to the high volatility in the 1970s, the sample was split into the two subperiods: 1960:I to 1971:IV and 1972:I to 1990:IV. Model estimates for each subperiod are

$$\Delta lwpi_t = 0.004 + 0.641 \Delta lwpi_{t-1} + \epsilon_t - 0.351 \epsilon_{t-1} + 0.172 \epsilon_{t-4} \qquad (1960:I–1971:IV)$$

and

$$\Delta lwpi_t = 0.016 + 0.753 \Delta lwpi_{t-1} + \epsilon_t - 0.394 \epsilon_{t-1} + 0.335 \epsilon_{t-4} \qquad (1972:I–1990:IV)$$

The coefficients of the two models appear to be quite similar; we can formally test for the equality of coefficients using (2.47). Respectively, the sums of squared residuals for the two models are $SSR_1 = 0.001359$ and $SSR_2 = 0.011681$, and from Table 2.4 we can see that $SSR = 0.0134$. Since $T = 122$ and $n = 4$ (including the intercept means there are four estimated coefficients), (2.47) becomes

$$F = [(0.0134 - 0.001359 - 0.011681)/4]/[(0.001359 + 0.011681)/(122\text{-}8)]$$
$$= 0.78681$$

With 4 degrees of freedom in the numerator and 114 in the denominator, we cannot reject the null of no structural change in the coefficients (i.e., we accept the hypothesis that there is no change in the structural coefficients).

As a final check, out-of-sample forecasts were constructed for each of the two models. By using additional data through 1992:II, the variance of the out-of-sample forecast errors of the ARMA(1, 1) and ARMA[1, (1,4)] models were calculated to be 0.00011 and 0.00008, respectively. Clearly, all the diagnostics select the ARMA[1, (1,4)] model. Although the ARMA[1, (1,4)] model appears to be adequate, other researchers might have selected a decidedly different model. Consider some of the alternatives listed below:

1. **Trends**: Although the logarithmic change of the WPI wholesale appears to be stationary, the ACF converges to zero rather slowly. Moreover, both the ARMA(1, 1) and ARMA[1, (1,4)] models yield estimated values of a_1 (0.887 and 0.791, respectively) that are close to unity. Some researchers might have chosen to model the second difference of the series. Others might have de-trended the data using a deterministic time trend. Chapter 4 discusses formal tests for the appropriate form of the trend.

2. The seasonality of the data was modeled using a moving average term at lag 4. However, there are many other plausible ways to model the seasonality in the data, as discussed in the next section. For example, many computer programs are capable of estimating multiplicative seasonal coefficients. Consider the multiplicative seasonal model:

$$(1 - a_1L)y_t = (1 + \beta_1 L)(1 + \beta_4 L^4)\epsilon_t$$

Here, the seasonal expression $\beta_4 \epsilon_{t-4}$ enters the model in a multiplicative, rather than a linear, fashion. Experimenting with various multiplicative seasonal coefficients might be a way to improve forecasting performance.

3. Given the volatility of the $\{\Delta lwpi_t\}$ sequence during the 1970s, the assumption of a constant variance might not be appropriate. Transforming the data using a square root, rather than the logarithm, might be more appropriate. A general class of transformations was proposed by Box and Cox (1964). Suppose that all values of $\{y_t\}$ are positive so that it is possible to construct the transformed $\{y_t^*\}$ sequence as

$$y_t^* = (y_t^\lambda - 1)/\lambda, \qquad \lambda \neq 0$$
$$= \ln(y_t), \qquad \lambda = 0$$

The common practice is to transform the data using a preselected value of λ. Selecting a value of λ that is close to zero acts to "smooth" the sequence. As in the WPI example (which simply set $\lambda = 0$), an ARMA model can be fit to the transformed data. Although some software programs have the capacity to simultaneously estimate λ along with the other parameters of the ARMA model, this approach has fallen out of fashion. Instead, it is possible to actually model the variance using the methods discussed in Chapter 3.

11. SEASONALITY

Many economic processes exhibit some form of seasonality. The agricultural, construction, and travel sectors have obvious seasonal patterns resulting from their dependence on the weather. Similarly, the Thanksgiving–Christmas holiday season has a pronounced influence on the retail trade. In fact, the seasonal variation of some series may account for the preponderance of its total variance. Forecasts that ignore important seasonal patterns will have a high variance. In the last section, we saw how the inclusion of a four-quarter seasonal factor could help improve the model of the WPI. This section expands that discussion by illustrating some of the techniques that can be used to identify seasonal patterns.

Too many people fall into the trap of ignoring seasonality if they are working with **deseasonalized** or **seasonally adjusted** data. Suppose you collect a data set that the U.S. Bureau of the Census has "seasonally adjusted" using its X-11 method.[9] In principle, your seasonally adjusted data should have the seasonal pattern removed. However, caution is necessary. Although a standardized procedure may be necessary for a government agency reporting hundreds of series, the procedure might not be best for an individual wanting to model a single series. Even if you use seasonally adjusted data, a seasonal pattern might remain. This is particularly true if you do not use the entire span of data; the portion of the data used in your study can display more (or less) seasonality than the overall span. There is another important reason to be concerned about seasonality when using deseasonalized data. Implicit in any method of seasonal adjustment is a two-step procedure. First, the seasonality is removed, and second, the autoregressive and moving average coefficients are estimated using Box–Jenkins techniques. As surveyed in Bell and Hillmer (1984), often the seasonal and ARMA coefficients are best identified and estimated jointly. In such circumstances, it is wise to avoid using seasonally adjusted data.

Models of Seasonal Data

The Box–Jenkins technique for modeling seasonal data is no different from that of nonseasonal data. The twist introduced by seasonal data of period s is that the seasonal coefficients of the ACF and PACF appear at lags s, $2s$, $3s$, . . . , rather than at lags 1, 2, 3, ... For example, two purely seasonal models for quarterly data might be

$$y_t = a_4 y_{t-4} + \epsilon_t, \qquad |a_4| < 1 \qquad (2.68)$$

and

$$y_t = \epsilon_t + \beta_4 \epsilon_{t-4} \qquad (2.69)$$

You can easily convince yourself that the theoretical correlogram for (2.68) is such that $\rho_i = (a_4)^{i/4}$ if $i/4$ is an integer, and $\rho_i = 0$ otherwise; thus, the ACF exhibits decay at lags 4, 8, 12, ... For model (2.69), the ACF exhibits a single spike at lag 4 and all other correlations are zero.

In practice, identification will be complicated by the fact that the seasonal pattern will interact with the nonseasonal pattern in the data. The ACF and PACF for a combined seasonal/nonseasonal process will reflect both elements. Note that the final model of the wholesale price index estimated in the last section had the form

$$y_t = a_1 y_{t-1} + \epsilon_t + \beta_1 \epsilon_{t-1} + \beta_4 \epsilon_{t-4} \qquad (2.70)$$

Alternatively, an autoregressive coefficient at lag 4 might have been used to capture the seasonality:

$$y_t = a_1 y_{t-1} + a_4 y_{t-4} + \epsilon_t + \beta_1 \epsilon_{t-1} \tag{2.71}$$

Both these methods treat the seasonal coefficients additively; an AR or MA coefficient is added at the seasonal period. **Multiplicative seasonality** allows for the interaction of the ARMA and seasonal effects. Consider the multiplicative specifications:

$$(1 - a_1 L)y_t = (1 + \beta_1 L)(1 + \beta_4 L^4)\epsilon_t \tag{2.72}$$

$$(1 - a_1 L)(1 - a_4 L^4)y_t = (1 + \beta_1 L)\epsilon_t \tag{2.73}$$

Equation (2.72) differs from (2.70) in that it allows the moving average term at lag 1 to interact with the seasonal moving average effect at lag 4. In the same way, (2.73) allows the autoregressive term at lag 1 to interact with the seasonal autoregressive effect at lag 4. Many researchers prefer the multiplicative form since a rich interaction pattern can be captured with a small number of coefficients. Rewrite (2.72) as

$$y_t = a_1 y_{t-1} + \epsilon_t + \beta_1 \epsilon_{t-1} + \beta_4 \epsilon_{t-4} + \beta_1 \beta_4 \epsilon_{t-5} \tag{2.74}$$

Estimating only three coefficients (i.e., a_1, β_1, and β_4) allows us to capture the effects of an autoregressive term at lag 1 and the effects of moving average terms at lags 1, 4, and 5. Of course, you do not really get something for nothing. The estimates of the three moving average coefficients are interrelated. A researcher estimating the unconstrained model $y_t = a_1 y_{t-1} + \epsilon_t + \beta_1 \epsilon_{t-1} + \beta_4 \epsilon_{t-4} + \beta_5 \epsilon_{t-5}$ would necessarily obtain a smaller residual sum of squares, since β_5 is not constrained to equal $\beta_1 \beta_4$. However, (2.72) is clearly the more parsimonious model. If the unconstrained value of β_5 approximates the product $\beta_1 \beta_4$, the multiplicative model will be preferable. For this reason, most software packages have routines capable of estimating multiplicative models. Otherwise, there are no theoretical grounds leading us to prefer one form of seasonality over another. As illustrated in the last section, experimentation and diagnostic checks are probably the best way to obtain the most appropriate model.

Seasonal Differencing

Spain is undoubtedly the most popular destination for European vacationers. During the months of July and August, the beaches along the Mediterranean coast swell with tourists basking in the sun. Figure 2.7 shows the monthly number of tourists visiting Spain between January 1970 and March 1989; the strong seasonal pattern dominates the movement in the series. You will also note that Spain's popularity has been growing; the series appears to be nonstationary in that the mean is increasing over time.

Figure 2.7   Tourism in Spain.

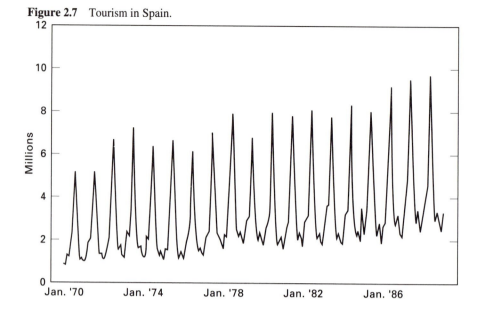

This combination of strong seasonality and nonstationarity is often found in economic data. The ACF for a nonstationary seasonal process is similar to that for a nonstationary nonseasonal process; with seasonal data the spikes at lags s, $2s$, $3s$, ... do not exhibit rapid decay. The other autocorrelations are dwarfed by the seasonal effects. Notice ACF for the Spanish tourism data shown in Figure 2.8. The autocorrelation coefficients at lags 12, 24, 36, and 48 are all close to unity and the seasonal peaks decay slowly. The coefficients at lags 6, 18, 30, and 42 are all negative since tourism is always low 6 months from the summer boom.

Let y_t denote the log of number of tourists visiting Spain each month; the first step in the Box–Jenkins method is to difference the $\{y_t\}$ sequence so as to make it stationary. In contrast to the other series we examined, the appropriate way to difference strongly seasonal data is at the seasonal period. Formal tests for seasonal differencing are examined in Chapter 4. For now, it is sufficient to note that the seasonal difference $(1 - L^{12})y_t = y_t - y_{t-12}$ will have a smaller variance than the first difference $y_t - y_{t-1}$. In the Spanish data, the strong seasonality means that January-to-January and July-to-July changes are not as pronounced as the changes between June and July. Figure 2.9 shows the first and twelfth differences of the data; clearly, the twelfth difference has less variation and should be easier to identify and estimate.

The logarithmic twelfth difference (i.e., $y_t - y_{t-12}$) displays a flat ACF showing little tendency to decay. The first 12 of the autocorrelations are

ρ_1	ρ_2	ρ_3	ρ_4	ρ_5	ρ_6	ρ_7	ρ_8	ρ_9	ρ_{10}	ρ_{11}	ρ_{12}
0.26	0.31	0.26	0.28	0.23	0.24	0.19	0.21	0.19	0.20	0.15	−0.17

There is no reasonable way to fit a low-order model to the seasonally differenced data; the seasonal differencing did not eliminate the time-varying mean. In order to impart stationarity into the series, the next step is to take the first difference of the already seasonally differenced data. The ACF and PACF for the series $(1 - L)$ $(1 - L^{12})y_t$ are shown in Figure 2.10; the properties of this series are much more amenable to the Box–Jenkins methodology. For the first 10 coefficients, the single spike in the ACF and uniform decay of the PACF suggest an MA(1) model. The significant coefficients at lags 11, 12, and 13 might result from additive or multiplicative seasonal factors. The estimates of the following three models are reported in Table 2.5:

$$(1 - L^{12})(1 - L)(1 - a_{12}L^{12})y_t = (1 + \beta_1 L)\epsilon_t \quad \text{Model 1: Autoregressive}$$
$$(1 - L^{12})(1 - L)y_t = (1 + \beta_1 L)(1 + \beta_{12}L^{12})\epsilon_t \quad \text{Model 2: Multiplicative moving average}$$
$$(1 - L^{12})(1 - L)y_t = (1 + \beta_1 L + \beta_{12}L^{12})\epsilon_t \quad \text{Model 3: Additive moving average}$$

The point estimates of the coefficients all imply stationarity and invertibility. Moreover, all are at least six standard deviations from zero. However, the diagnostic statistics all suggest that model 2 is preferred. Model 2 has the best fit in that it has the lowest sum of squared residuals (SSR). Moreover, the Q-statistics for lags

Figure 2.8   Correlogram of tourism in Spain.

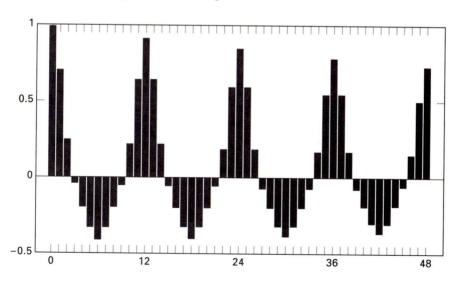

Figure 2.9   First and twelfth differences.

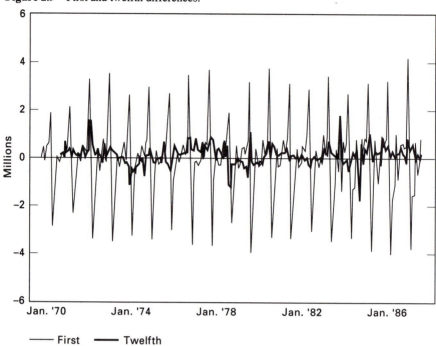

——— First   ▬▬▬ Twelfth

Table 2.5:   **Three Models of Spanish Tourism**

	Model 1[1]	Model 2	Model 3
a_{12}	−0.408 (−6.54)		
β_1	−0.738 (−15.56)	0.740 (−16.14)	−0.640 (−14.75)
β_{12}		−0.671 (−13.02)	−0.306 (−7.00)
SSR	2.823	2.608	3.367
AIC	217.8	212.98	268.70
SBC	224.5	219.75	275.47
$Q(12)$	8.59 (0.571)	4.38 (0.928)	25.54 (0.004)
$Q(24)$	41.11 (0.007)	15.71 (0.830)	66.58 (0.000)
$Q(48)$	67.91 (0.019)	37.61 (0.806)	99.31 (0.000)

Clearly, there is no difference between an additive seasonality and multiplicative seasonality when all other autoregressive coefficients are zero.

12, 24, and 48 indicate that the residual autocorrelations are insignificant. In contrast, the residual correlations for model 1 are significant at long lags [i.e., $Q(24)$ and $Q(48)$ are significant at the 0.007 and 0.019 levels] and the residual correlations for model 3 are significant for lags 12, 24, and 48. Other diagnostic methods including overfitting and splitting the sample suggest that model 2 is appropriate.

The procedures illustrated in this example of fitting a model to highly seasonal data are typical of many other series. With highly seasonal data, it is necessary to supplement the Box–Jenkins method:

1. In the identification stage, it is necessary to seasonally difference the data and check the ACF of the resultant series. Often, the seasonally differenced data will not be stationary. In such instances, the data may also need to be first-differenced.

2. Use the ACF and PACF to identify potential models. Try to estimate models with low-order nonseasonal ARMA coefficients. Consider both additive and multiplicative seasonality. Allow the appropriate form of seasonality to be determined by the various diagnostic statistics.

A compact notation has been developed that allows for the efficient representation of intricate models. As in previous sections, the dth difference of a series is denoted by Δ^d. For example,

$$\Delta^2 y_t = \Delta(y_t - y_{t-1})$$
$$= y_t - 2y_{t-1} + y_{t-2}$$

Figure 2.10   ACF and PACF for Spanish Tourism.

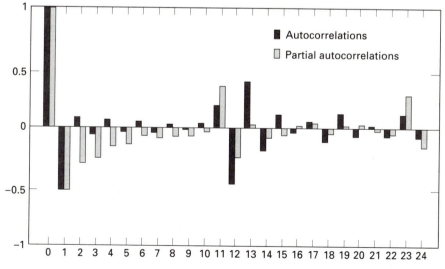

Seasonally adjusted and first-differenced

A seasonal difference is denoted by Δ_s, where s is the period of the data. The Dth such seasonal difference is Δ_s^D. For example, if we wanted the second seasonal difference of the Spanish data, we could form

$$\begin{aligned}
\Delta_{12}^2 y_t &= \Delta_{12}(y_t - y_{t-12}) \\
&= \Delta_{12} y_t - \Delta_{12} y_{t-12} \\
&= y_t - y_{t-12} - (y_{t-12} - y_{t-24}) \\
&= y_t - 2y_{t-12} + y_{t-24}
\end{aligned}$$

Combining the two types of differencing yields $\Delta^d \Delta_s^D$. Multiplicative models are written in the form ARIMA(p, d, q)(P, D, Q)$_s$

where p and q = the nonseasonal ARMA coefficients
       d = number of nonseasonal differences
      P = number of multiplicative autoregressive coefficients;
      D = number of seasonal differences
      Q = number of multiplicative moving average coefficients
      s = seasonal period

Using this notation, we can say that the fitted model of Spanish tourism is an ARIMA(0, 1, 1)(0, 1, 1)$_{12}$ model. In applied work, the ARIMA(0, 1, 1)(0, 1, 1)$_s$ model occurs routinely; it is called the "airline model" ever since Box and Jenkins (1976) used this model to analyze airline travel data.

SUMMARY AND CONCLUSIONS

The chapter focuses on the Box–Jenkins (1976) approach to identification, estimation, diagnostic checking, and forecasting a univariate time series. ARMA models can be viewed as a special class of linear stochastic difference equations. By definition, an ARMA model is covariance stationary in that it has a finite and time-invariant mean and covariances. For an ARMA model to be stationary, the characteristic roots of the difference equation must lie inside the unit circle. Moreover, the process must have started infinitely far in the past or the process must always be in equilibrium.

In the identification stage, the series is plotted and the sample autocorrelations and partial correlations are examined. As illustrated using the U.S. Wholesale Price Index, a slowly decaying autocorrelation function suggests nonstationarity behavior. In such circumstances, Box and Jenkins recommend differencing the data. Formal tests for nonstationarity are presented in Chapter 4. A common practice is to use a logarithmic or Box–Cox transformation if the variance does not appear to be constant. Chapter 3 presents some modern techniques that can be used to model the variance.

The sample autocorrelations and partial correlations of the suitably transformed data are compared to those of various theoretical ARMA processes. All plausible models are estimated and compared using a battery of diagnostic criteria. A well-estimated model (1) is parsimonious; (2) has coefficients that imply stationarity and invertibility; (3) fits the data well; (4) has residuals that approximate a white-noise process; (5) has coefficients that do not change over the sample period; and (6) has good out-of-sample forecasts.

In utilizing the Box–Jenkins methodology, you will find yourself making many seemingly ad hoc choices. The most parsimonious model may not have the best fit or out-of-sample forecasts. You will find yourself addressing the following types of questions: What is the most appropriate data transformation? Is an ARMA(2, 1) model more appropriate than an ARMA(1, 2) specification? How to best model seasonality? Given this latitude, many view the Box–Jenkins methodology as an art rather than a science. Nevertheless, the technique is best learned through experience. The exercises at the end of this chapter are designed to guide you through the types of choices you will encounter in your own research.

QUESTIONS AND EXERCISES

1. In the coin-tossing example of Section 1, your winnings on the last four tosses (w_t) can be denoted by

    $$w_t = 1/4\epsilon_t + 1/4\epsilon_{t-1} + 1/4\epsilon_{t-2} + 1/4\epsilon_{t-3}$$

    A. Find the expected value of w_t. Find the expected value given that $\epsilon_{t-3} = \epsilon_{t-2} = 1$.

    B. Find var(w_t). Find var(w_t) conditional on $\epsilon_{t-3} = \epsilon_{t-2} = 1$.

    C. Find: i. Cov(w_t, w_{t-1})   ii. Cov(w_t, w_{t-2})   iii. Cov(w_t, w_{t-5})

2. Substitute (2.10) into $y_t = a_0 + a_1 y_{t-1} + \epsilon_t$. Show that the resulting equation is an identity.

    A. Find the homogeneous solution to $y_t = a_0 + a_1 y_{t-1} + \epsilon_t$.

    B. Find the particular solution given that $|a_1| < 1$.

    C. Show how to obtain (2.10) by combining the homogeneous and particular solutions.

3. Consider the second-order autoregressive process $y_t = a_0 + a_2 y_{t-2} + \epsilon_t$, where $|a_2| < 1$.

    A. Find: i. $E_{t-2} y_t$ ii. $E_{t-1} y_t$ iii. $E_t y_{t+2}$

    iv. Cov(y_t, y_{t-1})   v. Cov(y_t, y_{t-2})   vi. The partial autocorrelations ϕ_{11} and ϕ_{22}

    B. Find the impulse response function. Given y_{t-2}, trace out the effects on an ϵ_t shock on the $\{y_t\}$ sequence.

C. Determine the forecast function $E_t y_{t+s}$. The forecast error f_s is the difference between y_{t+s} and $E_t y_{t+s}$. Derive the correlogram of the $\{f_s\}$ sequence. [*Hint:* Find $E_t f_s$, var(f_s), and $E(f_s \, f_{s-j})$ for $j = 0$ to s.]

4. Two different balls are drawn from a jar containing three balls numbered 1, 2, and 4. Let x = number on the first ball drawn and y = sum of the two balls drawn.

   A. Find the joint probability distribution for x and y; that is, find prob($x = 1$, $y = 3$), prob($x = 1$, $y = 5$), ..., and prob($x = 4$, $y = 6$).

   B. Find each of the following: $E(x)$, $E(y)$, $E(y \,|\, x = 1)$, $E(x \,|\, y = 5)$, var($x \,|\, y = 5$), and $E(y^2)$.

   C. Consider the two functions $w_1 = 3x^2$ and $w^2 = x^{-1}$. Find $E(w_1 + w_2)$ and $E(w_1 + w_2 \,|\, y = 3)$.

   D. How would your answers change if the balls were drawn with replacement?

5. The general solution to an nth-order difference equation requires n arbitrary constants. Consider the second-order equation $y_t = a_0 + 0.75 y_{t-1} - 0.125 y_{t-2} + \epsilon_t$.

   A. Find the homogeneous and particular solutions. Discuss the shape of the impulse response function.

   B. Find the values of the initial conditions (and A_1 and A_2) that ensure the $\{y_t\}$ sequence is stationary. (*Note:* A_1 and A_2 are the arbitrary constants in the homogeneous solution.)

   C. Given your answer to part B, derive the correlogram for the $\{y_t\}$ sequence.

6. Consider the second-order stochastic difference equation $y_t = 1.5 y_{t-1} - 0.5 y_{y-2} + \epsilon_t$.

   A. Find the characteristic roots of the homogeneous equation.

   B. Demonstrate that the roots of $1 - 1.5L + 0.5L^2$ are the reciprocals of your answer in part A.

   C. Given initial conditions for y_0 and y_1, find the solution for y_t in terms of the current and past values of the $\{\epsilon_t\}$ sequence. Explain why it is not possible to obtain the backward-looking solution for y_t unless such initial conditions are given.

   D. Find the forecast function for y_{t+s}.

   E. Find: $E y_t$, $E y_{t+1}$, var(y_t), var(y_{t+1}), and cov(y_{t+1}, y_t).

7. The file entitled SIM_2.WK1 contains the simulated data sets used in this chapter. The first column contains the 100 values of the simulated AR(1)

process used in Section 7. This first series is entitled Y1. Use this series to perform the following tasks. (*Note:* Due to differences in data handling and rounding, your answers need only approximate those presented here.)

A. Plot the sequence against time. Do the data appear to be stationary? Show that the properties of the sequence are

Sample mean	−0.5707418062	Variance	1.939987
Skewness	−0.31011	Significance Level (Sk=0)	0.21239328

B. Verify that the first 12 coefficients of the ACF and PACF are

ACF:

1: 0.7394472	0.5842742	0.4711050	0.3885974	0.3443779	0.3350913
7: 0.2972263	0.3251532	0.2689484	0.2007989	0.1886648	0.0824283

PACF:

1: 0.7394472	0.0827240	0.0302925	0.0255945	0.0601115	0.0889358
7: −0.0165339	0.1438633	−0.1002335	−0.0653566	0.0699036	−0.2040202

Ljung–Box Q-statistics: $Q(8) = 177.5774,$
$$Q(16) = 197.8423, \quad Q(24) = 201.2825$$

C. Use the data to verify the results given in Table 2.2.

D. Determine whether it is appropriate to include a constant in the AR(1) process. You should obtain the following estimates:

Coefficient	Estimate	Standard Error	t-Statistic	Significance Level
1. CONSTANT	−0.538045291	0.380434146	−1.41429	0.16044514
2. AR{1}	0.756861387	0.067241069	11.25594	0.00000000

E. Estimate the series as an AR(2) process without an intercept. You should obtain:

Coefficient	Estimate	Standard Error	t-Statistic	Significance Level
1. AR{1}	0.7048671016	0.0993987373	7.09131	0.00000000
2. AR{2}	0.1094585628	0.0986680252	1.10936	0.26998889

Ljung–Box Q-statistics: $Q(8) = 5.1317, \quad Q(16) = 15.8647, \quad Q(24) = 21.0213$

F. Estimate the series as an ARMA(1, 1) process without an intercept. You should obtain:

Coefficient	Estimate	Standard Error	t-Statistic	Significance Level
1. AR{1}	0.846376753	0.068533381	12.34985	0.00000000
2. MA{1}	−0.148770547	0.125784398	−1.18274	0.23977273

Verify that the first 12 coefficients of the ACF and PACF of the *residuals* are:

ACF:

1: −0.0069909	−0.0365955	−0.0375520	−0.0749124	−0.0683620	0.0546530
7: −0.0808082	0.1598166	0.0732022	−0.0080406	0.1686742	−0.0484844

PACF:

1: −0.0069909	−0.0366462	−0.0381264	−0.0770739	−0.0733243	0.0460005
7: −0.0923797	0.1542973	0.0630681	0.0027253	0.1917630	−0.0374165

Ljung–Box Q-statistics: $Q(8) = 5.2628$, significance level 0.51057476
$Q(16) = 15.7449$, significance level 0.32919794
$Q(24) = 21.0950$, significance level 0.51487365

G. Compare the AIC and SBC values from the models estimated in parts D, E, and F.

8. The second column in file entitled SIM_2.WK1 contains the 100 values of the simulated ARMA(1, 1) process used in Section 7. This series is entitled Y2. Use this series to perform the following tasks. (*Note:* Due to differences in data handling and rounding, your answers need only approximate those presented here.)

A. Plot the sequence against time. Do the data appear to be stationary? Show that the properties of the sequence are:

Sample mean	0.02254818000	Variance	5.743104
Skewness	−0.06175	Significance level (Sk = 0)	0.80390523

ACF:

1: −0.8343833	0.5965289	−0.4399659	0.3497724	−0.3187446	0.3316348
7: −0.3371782	0.3166057	−0.2761498	0.1789268	−0.0839171	0.0375968

PACF:

1: −0.8343833	−0.3280611	−0.1942907	−0.0145160	−0.1398293	0.0891764
7: 0.0004335	0.0143663	0.0166776	−0.1987829	−0.0462213	−0.0212410

B. Verify the results in Table 2.3.

C. Estimate the process using a pure MA(2) model. You should obtain:

Coefficient	Estimate	Standard Error	t-Statistic	Significance Level
1. MA{1}	−1.152648087	0.087208938	−13.21709	0.00000000
2. MA{2}	0.521919469	0.087336869	5.97594	0.00000004

D. Verify that the first 12 coefficients of the ACF and PACF of the *residuals* are

ACF:

1: −0.1281102	0.2841720	−0.2721070	0.0641308	−0.1690135	0.1591088
7: −0.1711865	0.1009624	−0.2300744	0.0202238	−0.0918914	−0.0507396

PACF:

1: −0.1281102	0.2722277	−0.2314021	−0.0521753	−0.0407344	0.0989550
7: −0.1253922	−0.0203505	−0.1278106	−0.0870339	0.0170745	−0.1709188

Ljung–Box Q-statistics: $Q(8) = 28.4771$, significance level 0.00007638
$Q(16) = 37.4666$, significance level 0.00062675
$Q(24) = 38.8424$, significance level 0.01470990

9. The third column in SIM_2.WK1 contains the 100 values of an AR(2) process; this series is entitled Y3. Use this series to perform the following tasks. (*Note:* Due to differences in data handling and rounding, your answers need only approximate those presented here.)

A. Plot the sequence against time. Verify the ACF and PACF coefficients reported in Section 7. Compare the sample ACF and PACF to those of a theoretical AR(2) process.

B. Estimate the series as an AR(1) process. You should find:

Coefficient	Estimate	Standard Error	t-Statistic	Significance Level
1. AR{1}	0.4676067905	0.0892951880	5.23664	0.00000093

ACF of the Residuals:

1: 0.2226399	−0.3349466	−0.3386407	0.0569540	0.0807033	−0.1656232
7: −0.1358947	0.1490039	0.1810292	−0.0022135	−0.0893884	−0.0245175

PACF of the Residuals:

1: 0.2226399	−0.4045690	−0.1809423	0.0803672	−0.1663664	−0.2353309
7: −0.0327129	0.0578083	−0.0587342	0.0005358	0.0422312	−0.0381843

Ljung–Box Q-statistics: $Q(8) = 36.9968$,   significance level 0.00000470
                        $Q(16) = 55.8708$,   significance level 0.00000127
                        $Q(24) = 69.0486$,   significance level 0.00000170

C. Why is the AR(1) model inadequate?

D. Could an ARMA(1, 1) process generate the type of sample ACF and PACF found in part A? Estimate the series as an ARMA(1, 1) process. You should obtain:

Coefficient	Estimate	Standard Error	t-Statistic	Significance Level
1. AR{1}	0.1861328174	0.1592235925	1.16900	0.24526729
2. MA{1}	0.5057665581	0.1407905283	3.59233	0.00051680

ACF of the Residuals:

1: 0.0284101	−0.1131579	−0.3143993	0.0716440	0.0162748	−0.1298382
7: −0.1197985	0.1392267	0.1194444	0.0174992	−0.1155456	0.0427301

PACF of the Residuals:

1: 0.0284101	−0.1140571	−0.3118831	0.0757999	−0.0596767	−0.2396433
7: −0.0872039	0.1041284	−0.0272326	−0.0175071	−0.0164607	0.0486076

Ljung–Box Q-Statistics: $Q(8) = 17.7685$,   significance level 0.00683766
                        $Q(16) = 37.0556$,   significance level 0.00072359
                        $Q(24) = 44.9569$,   significance level 0.00268747

Why is the ARMA(1, 1) model inadequate?

E. Estimate the series as an AR(2) process to verify the results reported in the text. Also show that

ACF of the Residuals:

1: 0.0050856	0.0167033	−0.1311013	0.0737802	−0.0183142	−0.1857531
7: −0.1223167	0.1169804	0.0827464	−0.0445903	−0.1014803	0.0879798
13: −0.1499004	0.0365971	−0.1062701	0.2608459	−0.0365855	−0.1119749
19: −0.0855518	0.0179101	0.0695385	−0.1661957	−0.0183144	0.0479631

PACF of the Residuals:

1: 0.0050856	0.0166779	−0.1313096	0.0764420	−0.0160463	−0.2098313
7: −0.1023138	0.1265615	0.0378627	−0.0653412	−0.0679885	0.0629571
13: −0.2287224	0.0563135	−0.0068239	0.2076758	−0.0936362	−0.1587757
19: −0.0419646	−0.0410407	0.0716762	−0.1014686	0.0384143	−0.0779761

Ljung–Box Q-Statistics: $Q(8) = 9.2697$,   significance level 0.15896993
$\qquad\qquad\qquad Q(16) = 24.6248$,   significance level 0.03845761
$\qquad\qquad\qquad Q(24) = 31.8487$,   significance level 0.08001287

The Q-statistics indicate that the autocorrelations at longer lags are statistically different from zero at the usual significance levels. Why might you choose *not* to model such long lags when using actual economic data?

F. Now estimate the series as an AR(2) but also include a moving average term at lag 16. Show that the residuals are such that

ACF of the Residuals:

1: 0.0265736	0.0040771	−0.0933018	0.0858766	0.0225622	−0.1521287
7: −0.1643954	0.0947202	0.1447444	0.0017055	−0.0718022	0.0512581
13: −0.1023376	0.0151149	−0.1029252	0.0174225	−0.0629532	−0.1078434
19: −0.0754905	−0.0307818	0.0130560	−0.1275938	0.0223896	0.0338157

PACF of the Residuals:

1: 0.0265736	0.0033733	−0.0935665	0.0917077	0.0182999	−0.1663372
7: −0.1432380	0.1106009	0.1204167	−0.0169905	−0.0350092	0.0517180
13: −0.1887574	0.0078523	0.0014991	0.0232808	−0.0985569	−0.1417484
19: −0.0753388	−0.0797882	0.0086627	−0.1045587	0.0291697	−0.0227024

Ljung–Box Q-statistics: $Q(8) = 8.2222$,   significance level 0.14440657
$\qquad\qquad\qquad Q(16) = 13.9801$,   significance level 0.37524746
$\qquad\qquad\qquad Q(24) = 19.0856$,   significance level 0.57964913

C. Compare the AIC and SBC values from the models estimated in parts B, D, E, and F.

10. The file called WPI.WK1 contains the U.S. Wholesale Price Index from 1960:QI to 1992:Q2. Make the data transformations indicated in the text.

A. Use the sample from 1960:Q1 to 1990:Q4 in order to reproduce the results of Section 10.

B. Use the fitted model to create "out-of-sample" forecasts for the 1991:Q1 to 1992:Q2 period.

C. Consider some of the plausible alternative models suggested in the text.

   i. Try to fit a model to the second-difference of the logarithm of the WPI.

   ii. Estimate the multiplicative seasonal model

D. Compare these models to that of part B.

11. The file entitled US.WK1 contains quarterly value of the U.S. money supply (M1) from 60:Q1 to 91:Q4.

   A. Plot the sequence against time. Verify that the properties of the sequence are

   Sample mean 3.80169890625   Variance   5.260577E+22
   Skewness   0.83949   Significance level (Sk = 0) 0.00012712

   B. Detrend the data by estimating the regression:

   $$\Delta \log(M1) = a_0 + b(\text{time}) + \epsilon_t$$

   The ACF of the residuals is

1:	0.8835022	0.8752123	0.8064355	0.8334758	0.7165115	0.6968231
7:	0.6249026	0.6437679	0.5285896	0.5118881	0.4507793	0.4770092

   Ljung–Box Q-statistics: $Q(8) = 630.0809$,   significance level 0.000
   $\qquad\qquad\qquad\qquad\qquad Q(16) = 836.4612$,   significance level 0.000

   Does detrending seem to render the sequence stationary?

   C. Calculate the ACF and PACF of the first difference of $\log(M1)$. You should obtain:

   ACF:
1:	0.5394848	0.3234781	−0.5573607	0.8528067	−0.5168406	0.2986240
7:	−0.5523817	0.7950047	−0.5096188	0.2695013	−0.5425407	0.7549618

   PACF:
1:	−0.5394848	0.0457493	−0.5175494	0.7167389	−0.0356317	−0.1396979
7:	−0.0457462	0.1998479	−0.0995162	−0.1475262	−0.0125845	0.0905883

   Explain the observed pattern at lags 4, 8, and 12.

   D. Seasonally difference the money supply as $\Delta_4 \log(M1) = \Delta \log(M1)_t - \Delta \log(M1)_{t-4}$. You should find that the ACF and PACF are

   ACF:
1:	0.8585325	0.7148654	0.5452426	0.3963377	0.3401345	0.2636718
7:	0.1814409	0.0991204	0.0554050	0.0287039	0.0423198	0.0651970

   PACF:
1:	0.8585325	−0.0844838	−0.1831526	−0.0283342	0.2688532	−0.1594976
7:	−0.1789985	−0.0055668	0.2312324	−0.0787959	−0.0015501	0.0736405

E. For convenience, let ml_t denote $\Delta_4 \log(M1)$. Estimate the seasonally differenced log of the money supply as the AR(1) process:

$$ml_t = a_0 + a_1 ml_{t-1} + \epsilon_t$$

Coefficient	Estimate	Standard Error	t-Statistic	Significance Level
CONSTANT	0.06217	0.0090502490	6.86967	0.000000
AR{1}	0.86241	0.0446622831	19.30970	0.000000

Examine the diagnostic statistics to show that this model is inappropriate.

F. Estimate $\log(M1)$ using each of the following:

$$ARIMA(1, 0, 0)(0, 1, 1)$$
$$ARIMA[1, 0, (4)](0, 1, 0)$$

Why is each inadequate?

G. Define $\Delta ml_t = ml_t - ml_{t-1}$ so that Δml_t is the first difference of the seasonal difference of the money supply. Estimate Δml_t as

$$\Delta ml_t = (1 + \beta_4 L^4)\epsilon_t$$

You should obtain:

Coefficient	Estimate	Standard Error	t-Statistic	Significance Level
MA{4}	−0.672328387	0.071121156	−9.45328	0.00000000

ACF of Residuals:

1: 0.0616653	0.1387445	−0.0388472	0.0720538	0.0875724	0.0110692
7: −0.0622441	−0.0953258	−0.0131446	−0.1265891	−0.0802878	−0.0407282

PACF of Residuals:

1: 0.0616653	0.1354570	−0.0558297	0.0601665	0.0952727	−0.0207820
7: −0.0826424	−0.0831404	0.0052625	−0.1232642	−0.0717116	0.0263945

Ljung–Box Q-statistics: $Q(8) = 6.5331$, significance level 0.479
$Q(16) = 10.3813$, significance level 0.795
$Q(24) = 14.0666$, significance level 0.925
$Q(32) = 17.4491$, significance level 0.976

Explain why this model is superior to any of those in part F.

ENDNOTES

1. The appendix to this chapter provides a review of constructing joint probabilities, expected values, and variances.
2. Some authors let T equal the maximum number of observations that can be used in the estimation; hence, T changes with the number of parameters estimated. Since there is no underlying distributional theory associated with the AIC and SBC, this procedure cannot be said to be incorrect. Also be aware that there are several equivalent formulations of the AIC and SBC. Your software package may not yield the precise numbers reported in the text.
3. Nearly all econometric software packages contain a Box–Jenkins estimation procedure. Mechanics of the estimation usually entail nothing more than specifying the number of autoregressive and moving average coefficients to include in the estimated model.
4. Most software programs will not be able to estimate (2.43) since there is not a unique set of parameter values that minimizes the likelihood function.
5. Some software programs report the Durbin–Watson test statistic as a check for first-order serial correlation. This well-known test statistic is biased toward finding no serial correlation in the presence of lagged dependent variables. Hence, it is ususally not used in ARMA models.
6. Estimation of an AR(p) model usually entails a loss of the number of usable observations. Hence, to estimate a sample using T observations, it will be necessary to have ($T + p$) observations. Also note that the procedure outlined necessitates that the second subsample period incorporate the lagged values $t_m, t_{m-1}, \ldots, t_{m-p+1}$.
7. Many of the details concerning optimal forecasts are contained in the appendix to Chapter 3.
8. In essence, the estimated equation is an ARMA(1, 4) model with the coefficients β_2 and β_3 constrained to be equal to zero. In order to distinguish between the two specifications, the notation ARMA[1, (1,4)] is used to indicate that only the moving average terms at lags 1 and 4 are included in the model.
9. The details of the X-11 procedure are not important for our purposes. The SAS statistical package can preform the X-11 procedure. The technical details of the procedure are explained in the Bureau of the Census report (1969).

APPENDIX   Expected Values and Variance

1. **Expected value of a discrete random variable**

   A random variable x is defined to be discrete if the range of x is countable. If x is discrete, there is a finite set of numbers $x_1, x_2, \ldots, x_n$ such that x takes on values only in that set. Let $f(x_j) = $ the probability that $x = x_j$. The mean or **expected value** of x is defined to be

$$E(x) = \sum_{j=1}^{n} x_j f(x_j)$$

Note the following:

1. We can let n go to infinity; the notion of a discrete variable is that the set be "denumerable" or a countable infinity. For example, the set of all positive integers is discrete.
2. If $\Sigma\, x_j f(x_j)$ does not converge, the mean is said not to exist.
3. $E(x)$ is an "average" of the possible values of x; in the sum, each possible x_j is weighted by the probability that $x = x_j$, that is,

$$E(x) = w_1 x_1 + w_2 x_2 + \cdots + w_n x_n$$

where $\Sigma w_j = 1$

2. Expected value of a continuous random variable

Now let x be a continuous random variable. Denote the probability that x is in the interval (x_0, x_1) be denoted by $f(x_0 \leq x \leq x_1)$. If the function $f(x)$ is depicted by Figure A2.1, it follows that

$$f(x_0 \leq x \leq x_1) = \int_{x_0}^{x_1} f(x)\, dx$$

The mean, or expected value, of x is

$$E(x) = \int_{-\infty}^{\infty} xf(x)\, dx$$

3. Expected value of a function

Let x be a random variable and $g(x)$ a function. The mean or expected value of $g(x)$ is

$$E[g(x)] = \sum_{j=1}^{n} g(x_j) f(x_j)$$

Figure A2.1 Frequency of x.

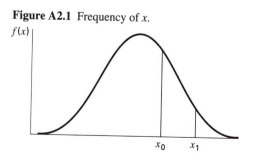

for discrete x or

$$E[g(x)] = \int_{-\infty}^{\infty} g(x)f(x)\, dx$$

for continuous x. *Note:* If $g(x_j) \equiv x_j$, we obtain the simple mean.

4. **Properties of the expectations operator**

   1. The expected value of a constant c is the value of the constant. That is, $E(c) = c$.

      Proof:

      $$g(x) = c \int_{-\infty}^{\infty} cf(x)\, dx = c \int_{-\infty}^{\infty} f(x)\, dx = c$$

   2. The expected value of a constant times a function is the constant times the expected value of the function.

      Proof:

      $$E[cg(x)] = \int_{-\infty}^{\infty} cg(x)f(x)\, dx = c \int_{-\infty}^{\infty} g(x)f(x)\, dx = cE[g(x)]$$

   3. The expected value of a sum is the sum of the expectations:

      $$E[c_1 g_1(x) \pm c_2 g_2(x)] = c_1 E g_1(x) \pm c_2 E g_2(x)$$

      Proof:

      $$\int_{-\infty}^{\infty} [c_1 g_1(x) \pm c_2 g_2(x)]f(x)\, dx = \int_{-\infty}^{\infty} c_1 g_1(x)f(x)\, dx \pm \int_{-\infty}^{\infty} c_2 g_2(x)f(x)\, dx$$

      $$= c_1 E[g_1(x)] \pm c_2 E[g_2(x)]$$

5. **Variance of a Random Variable**

   The variance of x is defined such that $\operatorname{var}(x) = E\{[x - E(x)]^2\}$:

   $$\operatorname{Var}(x) = E[x^2 - 2x\, E(x) + E(x)\, E(x)]$$

Since $E(x)$ is a constant, $E[E(x)] = E(x)$ and $E[xE(x)] = [E(x)]^2$. Using these results and the property that the expectation of a sum is the sum of the expectations, we obtain

$$Var(x) = E(x^2) - 2E[x\,E(x)] + E(x)^2$$
$$= E(x^2) - [E(x)]^2$$

6. Jointly Distributed Discrete Random Variables

Let x and y be random variables such that x takes on values $x_1, x_2, \ldots, x_n$ and y values $y_1, y_2, \ldots, y_m$. Also let f_{ij} denote the probability that $x = x_i$ *and* $y = y_j$. If $g(x, y)$ denotes a function of x and y, the expected value of the function is

$$E[g(x,\,y)] = \sum_{i=1}^{n}\sum_{j=1}^{m} f_{ij}g(x_i,\,y_j)$$

Expected value of a sum

Let the function $g(x, y)$ be $x + y$. The expected value of $x + y$ is:

$$E(x+y) = \sum_{i}\sum_{j} f_{ij}(x_i + y_j)$$

$$= \sum_{i}\sum_{j} f_{ij}x_i + \sum_{i}\sum_{j} f_{ij}y_j$$

$$= \sum_{j} (f_{1j}x_1 + f_{2j}x_2 + \cdots + f_{nj}x_n) + \sum_{i} (f_{i1}y_1 + f_{i2}y_2 + \cdots + f_{im}y_m)$$

Note that $(f_{11} + f_{12} + f_{13} + \cdots + f_{1m})$ is the probability that x takes on the value x_1 denoted by f_1. More generally, $(f_{i1} + f_{i2} + f_{i3} + \cdots + f_{im})$ is the probability that x takes on the value x_i denoted by f_i or $f(x_i)$. Since $(f_{1i} + f_{2i} + f_{3i} + \cdots + f_{ni})$ is the probability that $y = y_i$ denoted by $f(y_i)$, the two summations above can be written as

$$E(x + y) = \Sigma x_i f(x_i) + \Sigma y_i f(y_i)$$
$$= E(x) + E(y)$$

Hence, we have generalized the result of 4.3 above to show that the expected value of a sum is the sum of the expectations.

7. Covariance and Correlation

The covariance between x and y, $cov(x, y)$, is defined to be

$$Cov(x, y) = E\{[x - E(x)][y - E(y)]\} \equiv \sigma_{xy}$$

Multiply $[x - E(x)]$ by $[y - E(y)]$ and use the property that the expected value of a sum is the sum of the expectations:

$$\text{Cov}(x, y) = E(xy) - E[xE(y)] - E[yE(x)] + E[E(x)E(y)]$$
$$= E(xy) - E(x)E(y)$$

The **correlation coefficient** between x and y is defined to be

$$\rho_{xy} = \frac{\text{cov}(x, y)}{\sqrt{\text{var}(x)}\sqrt{\text{var}(y)}}$$

Since $\text{cov}(x, y) = E(xy) - E(x)E(y)$, we can express the expectation of the product of x and y, $E(xy)$, as

$$E(xy) = E(x)E(y) + \text{cov}(x, y)$$
$$= E(x)E(y) + \rho_{xy}\, \sigma_x \sigma_y$$

where the standard deviation of variable z (denoted by σ_z) = the positive square root of z.

8. **Conditional Expectation**

   Let x and y be jointly distributed random variables, where f_{ij} denotes the probability that $x = x_i$ and $y = y_j$. Each of the f_{ij} values is a **conditional probability**; each is the probability that x takes on the value x_i given that y takes on the specific value y_j.

   The expected value of x conditional on y taking on the value y_j is:

   $$E(x \mid y_j) = f_{1j}x_1 + f_{2j}x_2 + \cdots + f_{nj}x_n$$

9. **Statistical Independence**

   If x and y are **statistically independent**, the probability of $x = x_i$ and $y = y_j$ is the probability that $x = x_i$ multiplied by the probability that $y = y_j$. If we use the notation in number 6 above, *two events are statistically independent if and only if* $f_{ij} = f(x_i)f(y_j)$. For example, if we simultaneously toss a fair coin and roll a fair die, the probability of obtaining a head *and* a three is 1/12; the probability of a head is 1/2 and the probability of obtaining a three is 1/6.

   An extremely important implication follows directly from this definition. If x and y are independent events, the expected value of the product of the outcomes is the product of the expected outcomes:

   $$E(xy) = E(x)E(y)$$

   The proof is straightforward. Form $E(xy)$ as

$$E(xy) = f_{11}x_1y_1 + f_{12}x_1y_2 + f_{13}x_1y_3 + \cdots + f_{1m}x_1y_m + f_{21}x_2y_1 + f_{22}x_2y_2$$
$$+ f_{23}x_2y_3 + \cdots + f_{2m}x_2y_m + \cdots + f_{n1}x_ny_1 + f_{n2}x_ny_2 + f_{n3}x_ny_3 + \cdots f_{nm}x_ny_m$$

Since x and y are independent, $f_{ij} = f(x_i)f(y_i)$. Hence

$$E(xy) = \sum_{i=1}^{n} f_{i1}x_iy_1 + \cdots + \sum_{i=1}^{n} f_{im}x_iy_m$$

$$= \sum_{i=1}^{n} f(x_i)f(y_1)x_iy_1 + \sum_{i=1}^{n} f(x_i)f(y_2)x_iy_2 + \cdots + \sum_{i=1}^{n} f(x_i)f(y_m)x_iy_m$$

$$= f(y_1)y_1 \sum_{i=1}^{n} f(x_i)x_i + \cdots + f(y_m)y_m \sum_{i=1}^{n} f(x_i)x_i$$

Recall that $\Sigma f(x_i)x_i = E(x)$. Thus

$$E(xy) = E(x)[f(y_1)y_1 + f(y_2)y_2 + \cdots + f(y_m)y_m]$$

so that $E(xy) = E(x)E(y)$. Since $cov(x, y) = E(xy) - E(x)E(y)$, it immediately follows that the covariance and correlation coefficient of two independent events is zero.

10. **An Example of Conditional Expectation**
Since the concept of conditional expectation plays such an important role in modern macroeconomics, it is worthwhile to consider the specific example of tossing dice. Let x denote the number of spots showing on die 1, y the number of spots on die 2, and S the sum of the spots ($S = x + y$). Each die is fair so that the probability of any face turning up is 1/6. Since the outcomes on die 1 and die 2 are independent events, the probability of any specific values for x and y is the product of the probabilities. The possible outcomes and the probability associated with each outcome S are

S	2	3	4	5	6	7	8	9	10	11	12
$f(S)$	1/36	2/36	3/36	4/36	5/36	6/36	5/36	4/36	3/36	2/36	1/36

To find the expected value of the sum S, multiply each possible outcome by the probability associated with that outcome. As you well know if you have been to Las Vegas, the expected value is 7. Suppose that you roll the dice sequentially and that the roll turns up 3 spots. What is the expected value of the sum given that $x = 3$? We know that y can take on values 1 through 6 each with a probability of 1/6. Given $x = 3$, the possible outcomes for S are 4 through 9, each with a probability of 1/6. Hence, the conditional probability of S given three spots on die 1 is $E(S \mid x = 3) = (1/6)4 + (1/6)5 + (1/6)6 + (1/6)7 + (1/6)8 + (1/6)9 = 6.5$.

Chapter 3

MODELING ECONOMIC TIME SERIES: TRENDS AND VOLATILITY

Many economic time series do not have a constant mean and most exhibit phases of relative tranquility followed by periods of high volatility. Much of the current econometric research is concerned with extending the Box–Jenkins methodology to analyze this type of time-series behavior. The aims of this chapter are to:

1. Examine the so-called *stylized facts* concerning the properties of economic time-series data. Casual inspection of GNP, financial aggregates, interest and exchange rates suggests they do not have a constant mean and variance. A stochastic variable with a constant variance is called **homoskedastic** as opposed to **heteroskedastic.**[1] For series exhibiting volatility, the unconditional variance may be constant even though the variance during some periods is unusually large. You will learn how to use the tools developed in Chapter 2 to model such conditional heteroskedasticity.

2. Formalize simple models of variables with a time-dependent mean. Certainly, the mean value of GNP, various price indices, and the money supply have been increasing over time. The trends displayed by these variables may contain deterministic and/or stochastic components. Learning about the properties of the two types of trends is important. It makes a great deal of difference if a series is estimated and forecasted under the hypothesis of a deterministic versus stochastic trend.

3. Illustrate the difference between stochastic and deterministic trends by considering the modern view of the business cycle. A methodology that can be used to decompose a series into its temporary and permanent components is presented.

1. ECONOMIC TIME SERIES: THE STYLIZED FACTS

Figures 3.1 through 3.8 illustrate the behavior of some of the more important variables encountered in macroeconomic analysis. Casual inspection does have its perils and formal testing is necessary to substantiate any first impressions. However,

Figure 3.1   U.S. GNP (1985 prices).

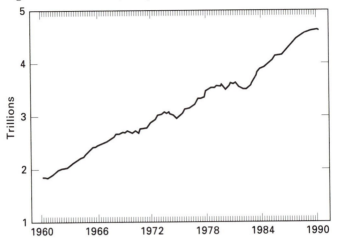

the strong visual pattern is that these series are *not* stationary; the sample means do not appear to be constant and/or there is the strong appearance of heteroskedasticity. We can characterize the key features of the various series with these "stylized facts":

1. **Most of the series contain a clear trend.** Real GNP and its subcomponents and the supplies of short-term financial instruments exhibit a decidedly upward trend. For some series (interest, and inflation rates), the positive trend is interrupted by a marked decline, followed by a resumption of the positive growth. Nevertheless, it is hard to maintain that these series do have a time-invariant mean. As such, they are not stationary.

Figure 3.2   Investment and government consumption (1985 prices).

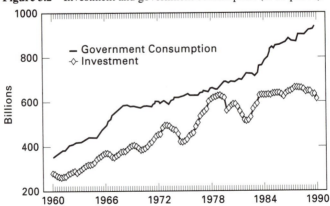

Figure 3.3   Checkable deposits and money market instruments.

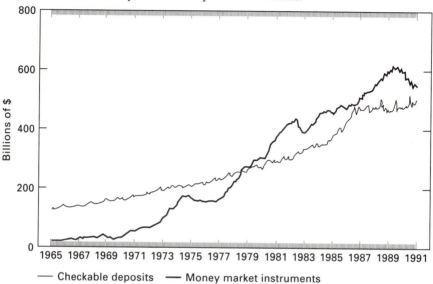

— Checkable deposits   — Money market instruments

2. **Some series seem to meander.** The pound/dollar exchange rate shows no particular tendency to increase or decrease. The pound seems to go through sustained periods of appreciation and then depreciation with no tendency to revert to a long-run mean. This type of "random walk" behavior is typical of nonstationary series.

3. **Any shock to a series displays a high degree of persistence.** Notice that the Federal Funds Rate experienced a violently upward surge in 1973 and remained at the higher level for nearly 2 years. In the same way, U.K. industrial production plummeted in the late 1970s, not returning to its previous level until the mid–1980s.

4. **The volatility of many series is not constant over time.** During the 1970s, U.S. producer prices fluctuated wildly as compared with the 1960s and 1980s. Real investment grew smoothly throughout most of the 1960s, but became highly variable in the 1970s also. Such series are called **conditionally heteroskedastic** if the unconditional (or long-run) variance is constant but there are periods in which the variance is relatively high.

5. **Some series share comovements with other series.** Large shocks to U.S. industrial production appear to be timed similarly to those in the U.K. and Canada. Short- and long-term interest rates track each other quite closely. The presence of such comovements should not be too surprising. We might expect that the underlying economic forces affecting U.S. industry also affect industry internationally.

Figure 3.4   U.S. money supply: M2.

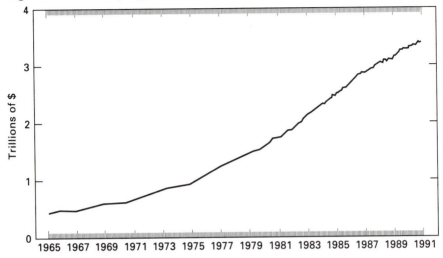

Please be aware that "eyeballing" the data is not a substitute for formally testing for the presence of conditional heteroskedasticity or nonstationary behavior.[2] Although most of the variables shown in the figures are probably nonstationary, the issue will not always be so obvious. Fortunately, it is possible to modify the tools developed in the last chapter to help in the identification and estimation of such series. The remainder of this chapter considers the issue of conditional heteroskedasticity and presents simple models of trending variables. Formal tests for the pres-

Figure 3.5   Short- and long-term U.S. interest rates.

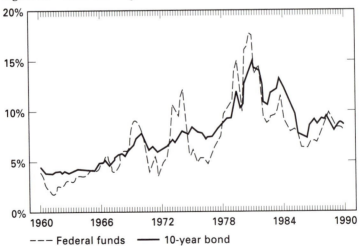

Figure 3.6   U.S. price indices (percent change).

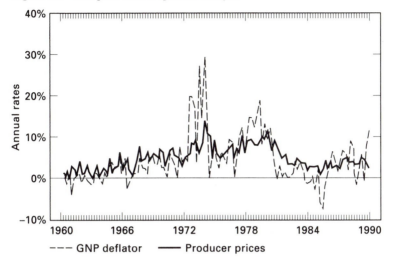

--- GNP deflator   —— Producer prices

ence of trends (either deterministic and/or stochastic) are contained in the next chapter. The issue of comovements must wait until Chapter 6.

2. ARCH PROCESSES

In conventional econometric models, the variance of the disturbance term is as-sumed to be constant. However, Figures 3.1 through 3.8 demonstrate that many economic time series exhibit periods of unusually large volatility followed by peri-ods of relative tranquility. In such circumstances, the assumption of a constant vari-ance (**homoskedasticity**) is inappropriate. It is easy to imagine instances in which you might want to forecast the conditional variance of a series. As an asset holder, you would be interested in forecasts of the rate of return *and* its variance over the holding period. The unconditional variance (i.e., the long-run forecast of the vari-ance) would be unimportant if you plan to buy the asset at t and sell at $t + 1$.

One approach to forecasting the variance is to explicitly introduce an indepen-dent variable that helps to predict the volatility. Consider the simplest case in which

$$y_{t+1} = \epsilon_{t+1} x_t$$

where y_{t+1} = the variable of interest
  ϵ_{t+1} = a white-noise disturbance term with variance σ^2
  x_t = an independent variable that can be observed at period t

If $x_t = x_{t-1} = x_{t-2} = \cdots =$ constant, the $\{y_t\}$ sequence is the familiar white-noise process with a constant variance. However, when the realizations of the $\{x_t\}$ se-

Figure 3.7   Exchange rate indices (currency/dollar).

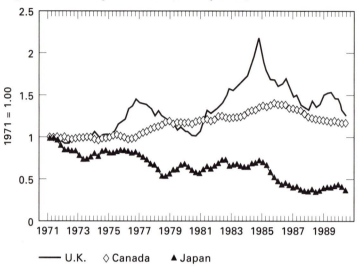

quence are not all equal, the variance of y_{t+1} conditional on the observable value of x_t is

$$\mathrm{Var}(y_{t+1} \mid x_t) = x_t^2 \sigma^2$$

Here, the conditional variance of y_{t+1} is dependent on the realized value of x_t. Since you can observe x_t at time period t, you can form the variance of y_{t+1} conditionally on the realized value of x_t. If the magnitude $(x_t)^2$ is large (small), the variance of y_{t+1} will be large (small) as well. Furthermore, if the successive values of $\{x_t\}$ exhibit positive serial correlation (so that a large value of x_t tends to be followed by a large value of x_{t+1}), the conditional variance of the $\{y_t\}$ sequence will exhibit positive serial correlation as well. In this way, the introduction of the $\{x_t\}$ sequence can explain periods of volatility in the $\{y_t\}$ sequence. In practice, you might want to modify the basic model by introducing the coefficients a_0 and a_1 and estimating the regression equation in logarithmic form as

$$\ln(y_t) = a_0 + a_1 \ln(x_{t-1}) + e_t$$

where e_t = the error term [formally, $e_t = \ln(\epsilon_t)$]

The procedure is simple to implement since the logarithmic transformation results in a linear regression equation; OLS can be used to estimate a_0 and a_1 directly. A major difficulty with this strategy is that it assumes a specific cause for the changing variance. Often, you may not have a firm theoretical reason for selecting one candidate for the $\{x_t\}$ sequence over other reasonable choices. Was it the oil price shocks, a change in the conduct of monetary policy, and/or the breakdown of the Bretton–Woods system that was responsible for the volatile WPI during the 1970s? Moreover, the technique necessitates a transformation of the data such that the resulting series has a constant variance. In the example at hand, the $\{e_t\}$ sequence is assumed to have a constant variance. If this assumption is violated, some other transformation of the data is necessary.

ARCH Processes

Instead of using ad hoc variable choices for x_t and/or data transformations, Engle (1982) shows that it is possible to simultaneously model the mean *and* variance of a series. As a preliminary step to understanding Engle's methodology, note that conditional forecasts are vastly superior to unconditional forecasts. To elaborate, suppose you estimate the stationary ARMA model $y_t = a_0 + a_1 y_{t-1} + \epsilon_t$ and want to forecast y_{t+1}. The conditional forecast of y_{t+1} is:

$$E_t y_{t+1} = a_0 + a_1 y_t$$

If we use this conditional mean to forecast y_{t+1}, the forecast error variance is $E_t[(y_{t+1} - a_0 - a_1 y_t)^2] = E_t \epsilon_{t+1}^2 = \sigma^2$. Instead, if unconditional forecasts are used, the unconditional forecast is always the long-run mean of the $\{y_t\}$ sequence that is equal to $a_0/(1 - a_1)$. The unconditional forecast error variance is

$$E\{[y_{t+1} - a_0/(1 - a_1)]^2\} = E[(\epsilon_{t+1} + a_1 \epsilon_t + a_1^2 \epsilon_{t-1} + a_1^3 \epsilon_{t-2} + \cdots)^2]$$
$$= \sigma^2/(1 - a_1^2)$$

Figure 3.8   Industrial production.

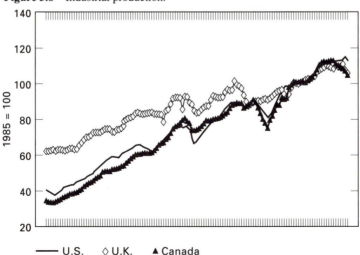

— U.S.   ◇ U.K.   ▲ Canada

Since $1/(1 - a_1^2) > 1$, the unconditional forecast has a greater variance than the conditional forecast. Thus, conditional forecasts (since they take into account the known current and past realizations of series) are preferable.

Similarly, if the variance of $\{\epsilon_t\}$ is not constant, you can estimate any tendency for sustained movements in the variance using an ARMA model. For example, let $\{\hat{\epsilon}_t\}$ denote the estimated residuals from the model $y_t = a_0 + a_1 y_{t-1} + \epsilon_t$, so that the conditional variance of y_{t+1} is

$$\mathrm{Var}(y_{t+1} \mid y_t) = E_t[(y_{t+1} - a_0 - a_1 y_t)^2]$$
$$= E_t \epsilon_{t+1}^2$$

Thus far, we have set $E_t \epsilon_{t+1}^2$ equal to σ^2. Now suppose that the conditional variance is not constant. One simple strategy is to model the conditional variance as an AR(q) process using the *square* of the estimated residuals:

$$\hat{\epsilon}_t^2 = \alpha_0 + \alpha_1 \hat{\epsilon}_{t-1}^2 + \alpha_2 \hat{\epsilon}_{t-2}^2 + \cdots + \alpha_q \hat{\epsilon}_{t-q}^2 + v_t \tag{3.1}$$

where v_t = a white-noise process

If the values of $\alpha_1, \alpha_2, \ldots, \alpha_n$ all equal zero, the estimated variance is simply the constant α_0. Otherwise, the conditional variance of y_t evolves according to the autoregressive process given by (3.1). As such, you can use (3.1) to forecast the conditional variance at $t + 1$ as

$$E_t \hat{\epsilon}_{t+1}^2 = \alpha_0 + \alpha_1 \hat{\epsilon}_t^2 + \alpha_2 \hat{\epsilon}_{t-1}^2 + \cdots + \alpha_q \hat{\epsilon}_{t+1-q}^2$$

For this reason, an equation like (3.1) is called an **autoregressive conditional heteroskedastic** (ARCH) model. There are many possible applications for ARCH models since the residuals in (3.1) can come from an autoregression, an ARMA model, or a standard regression model.

In actuality, the linear specification of (3.1) is not the most convenient. The reason is that the model for $\{y_t\}$ and the conditional variance are best estimated simultaneously using maximum likelihood techniques. Instead of the specification given by (3.1), it is more tractable to specify v_t as a multiplicative disturbance.

The simplest example from the class of multiplicative conditionally heteroskedastic models proposed by Engle (1982) is

$$\epsilon_t = v_t \sqrt{\alpha_0 + \alpha_1 \epsilon_{t-1}^2} \tag{3.2}$$

where v_t = white-noise process such that $\sigma_v^2 = 1$, v_t and ϵ_{t-1} are independent of each other, and α_0 and α_1 are constants such that $\alpha_0 > 0$ and $0 < \alpha_1 < 1$.

Consider the properties of the $\{\epsilon_t\}$ sequence. Since v_t is white-noise and independent of ϵ_{t-1}, it is easy to show that the elements of the $\{\epsilon_t\}$ sequence have a mean of zero and are uncorrelated. The proof is straightforward. Take the unconditional expectation of ϵ_t. Since $Ev_t = 0$, it follows that

$$E\epsilon_t = E[v_t(\alpha_0 + \alpha_1\epsilon_{t-1}^2)^{1/2}]$$
$$= Ev_t E(\alpha_0 + \alpha_1\epsilon_{t-1}^2)^{1/2} = 0 \qquad (3.3)$$

Since $Ev_t v_{t-i} = 0$, it also follows that

$$E\epsilon_t\epsilon_{t-i} = 0, \qquad i \neq 0 \qquad (3.4)$$

The derivation of the unconditional variance of ϵ_t is also straightforward. Square ϵ_t and take the unconditional expectation to form

$$E\epsilon_t^2 = E[v_t^2(\alpha_0 + \alpha_1\epsilon_{t-1}^2)]$$
$$= Ev_t^2 E(\alpha_0 + \alpha_1\epsilon_{t-1}^2)$$

Since $\sigma_v^2 = 1$ and the unconditional variance of ϵ_t is identical to that of ϵ_{t-1} (i.e., $E\epsilon_t^2 = E\epsilon_{t-1}^2$), the unconditional variance is

$$E\epsilon_t^2 = \alpha_0/(1 - \alpha_1) \qquad (3.5)$$

Thus, the unconditional mean and variance are unaffected by the presence of the error process given by (3.2). Similarly, it is easy to show that the conditional mean of ϵ_t is equal to zero. Given that v_t and ϵ_{t-1} are independent and $Ev_t = 0$, the conditional mean of ϵ_t is

$$E(\epsilon_t \mid \epsilon_{t-1}, \epsilon_{t-2}, \ldots) = Ev_t E(\alpha_0 + \alpha_1\epsilon_{t-1}^2)^{1/2} = 0$$

At this point, you might be thinking that the properties of the $\{\epsilon_t\}$ sequence are not affected by (3.2) since the mean is zero, the variance is constant, and all autocovariances are zero. However, the influence of (3.2) falls entirely on the conditional variance. Since $\sigma_v^2 = 1$, the variance of ϵ_t conditioned on the past history of ϵ_{t-1}, ϵ_{t-2}, ... is

$$E(\epsilon_t^2 \mid \epsilon_{t-1}, \epsilon_{t-2}, \ldots) = \alpha_0 + \alpha_1\epsilon_{t-1}^2 \qquad (3.6)$$

In (3.6), the conditional variance of ϵ_t is dependent on the realized value of ϵ_{t-1}^2. If the realized value of ϵ_{t-1}^2 is large, the conditional variance in t will be large as well. In (3.6) the conditional variance follows a first-order autoregressive process denoted by ARCH(1). As opposed to a usual autoregression, the coefficients α_0 and α_1 have to be restricted. In order to ensure that the conditional variance is never negative, it is necessary to assume that both α_0 and α_1 are positive. After all, if α_0 is negative, a sufficiently small realization of ϵ_{t-1} will mean that (3.6) is negative. Similarly, if α_1 is negative, a sufficiently large realization of ϵ_{t-1} can render a negative value for the conditional variance. Moreover, to ensure the stability of the autoregressive process, it is necessary to restrict α_1 such that $0 < \alpha_1 < 1$.

Equations (3.3), (3.4), (3.5), and (3.6) illustrate the essential features of any ARCH process. In an ARCH model, the error structure is such that the conditional and unconditional means are equal to zero. Moreover, the $\{\epsilon_t\}$ sequence is serially uncorrelated since for all $s \neq 0$, $E\epsilon_t\epsilon_{t-s} = 0$. The key point is that the errors are *not* independent since they are related through their second moment (recall that correlation is a linear relationship). The conditional variance itself is an autoregressive process resulting in conditionally heteroskedastic errors. When the realized value of ϵ_{t-1} is far from zero—so that $\alpha_1(\epsilon_{t-1})^2$ is relatively large—the variance of ϵ_t will tend to be large. As you will see momentarily, the conditional heteroskedasticity in $\{\epsilon_t\}$ will result in $\{y_t\}$ being an ARCH process. Thus, the ARCH model is able to capture periods of tranquility and volatility in the $\{y_t\}$ series.

The four graphs of Figure 3.9 depict two different ARCH models. The upper-left-hand graph (a), representing the $\{v_t\}$ sequence, shows 100 serially uncorrelated and normally distributed random deviates. From casual inspection, the $\{v_t\}$ se-

Figure 3.9   Simulated ARCH processes.

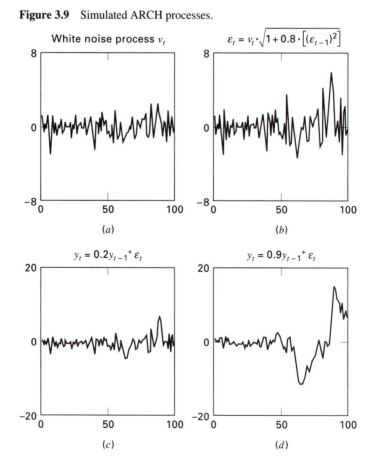

quence appears to fluctuate around a mean of zero and have a constant variance. Note the moderate increase in volatility between periods 50 and 60. Given the initial condition $\epsilon_0 = 0$, these realizations of the $\{v_t\}$ sequence were used to construct the next 100 values of the $\{\epsilon_t\}$ sequence using equation (3.2) and setting $\alpha_0 = 1$ and $\alpha_1 = 0.8$. As illustrated in the upper-right-hand graph (b), the $\{\epsilon_t\}$ sequence also has a mean of zero, but the variance appears to experience an increase in volatility around $t = 50$.

How does the error structure affect the $\{y_t\}$ sequence? Clearly, if the autoregressive parameter a_1 is zero, y_t is nothing more than ϵ_t. Thus, the upper-right-hand graph can be used to depict the time path of the $\{y_t\}$ sequence for the case of $a_1 = 0$. The lower two graphs (c) and (d) show the behavior of the $\{y_t\}$ sequence for the cases of $a_1 = 0.2$ and 0.9, respectively. The essential point to note is that the ARCH error structure and autocorrelation parameters of the $\{y_t\}$ process interact with each other. Comparing the lower two graphs illustrates that the volatility of $\{y_t\}$ is increasing in α_1 and α_1. The explanation is intuitive. Any unusually large (in absolute value) shock in v_t will be associated with a persistently large variance in the $\{\epsilon_t\}$ sequence; the larger α_1, the longer the persistence. Moreover, the greater the autoregressive parameter a_1, the more persistent any given change in y_t. The stronger the tendency for $\{y_t\}$ to remain away from its mean, the greater the variance.

To formally examine the properties of the $\{y_t\}$ sequence, the conditional mean and variance are given by

$$E_{t-1}y_t = a_0 + a_1 y_{t-1}$$

and

$$\begin{aligned} \mathrm{Var}(y_t \mid y_{t-1}, y_{t-2}, \ldots) &= E_{t-1}(y_t - a_0 - a_1 y_{t-1})^2 \\ &= E_{t-1}(\epsilon_t)^2 \\ &= \alpha_0 + \alpha_1 (\epsilon_{t-1})^2 \end{aligned}$$

Since α_1 and ϵ_{t-1}^2 cannot be negative, the minimum value for the conditional variance is α_0. For any nonzero realization of ϵ_{t-1}, the conditional variance of y_t is positively related to α_1. The unconditional mean and variance of y_t can be obtained by solving the difference equation for y_t and then taking expectations. If the process began sufficiently far in the past (so that the arbitrary constant A can safely be ignored), the solution for y_t is

$$y_t = a_0/(1 - a_1) + \sum_{i=0}^{\infty} a_1^i \epsilon_{t-i} \tag{3.7}$$

Since $E\epsilon_t = 0$ for all t, the unconditional expectation of (3.7) is $Ey_t = a_0/(1 - a_1)$. The unconditional variance can be obtained in a similar fashion using (3.7). Given that $E\epsilon_t \epsilon_{t-i}$ is zero for all $i \neq 0$, the unconditional variance of y_t follows directly from (3.7) as

$$\text{Var}(y_t) = \sum_{i=0}^{\infty} a_1^{2i} \, \text{var}(\epsilon_{t-i})$$

From the result that the unconditional variance of ϵ_t is constant [i.e., $\text{var}(\epsilon_t) = \text{var}(\epsilon_{t-1}) = \text{var}(\epsilon_{t-2}) = \cdots = \alpha_0/(1 - \alpha_1)$], it follows that

$$\text{Var}(y_t) = [\alpha_0/(1 - \alpha_1)] \, [1/(1 - a_1^2)]$$

Clearly, the variance of the $\{y_t\}$ sequence is increasing in both α_1 and the absolute value of a_1. Although the algebra can be a bit tedious, the essential point is that the ARCH error process can be used to model periods of volatility within the univariate framework.

The ARCH process given by (3.2) has been extended in several interesting ways. Engle's (1982) original contribution considered the entire class of higher-order ARCH(q) processes:

$$\epsilon_t = v_t \sqrt{\alpha_0 + \sum_{i=1}^{q} \alpha_i \epsilon_{t-i}^2} \tag{3.8}$$

In (3.8), all shocks from ϵ_{t-1} to ϵ_{t-q} have a direct effect on ϵ_t, so that the conditional variance acts like an autoregressive process of order q. Question 2 at the end of this chapter asks you to demonstrate that the forecasts for $E_t\epsilon_{t+1}^2$ arising from (3.1) and (3.8) have precisely the same form.

The GARCH Model

Bollerslev (1986) extended Engle's original work by developing a technique that allows the conditional variance to be an ARMA process. Now let the error process be such that

$$\epsilon_t = v_t \sqrt{h_t}$$

where $\sigma_v^2 = 1$

and

$$h_t = \alpha_0 + \sum_{i=1}^{q} \alpha_i \epsilon_{t-i}^2 + \sum_{i=1}^{p} \beta_i h_{t-i} \tag{3.9}$$

Since $\{v_t\}$ is a white-noise process that is independent of past realizations of ϵ_{t-i}, the conditional and unconditional means of ϵ_t are equal to zero. By taking the expected value of ϵ_t, it is easy to verify that

$$E\epsilon_t = Ev_t\sqrt{h_t} = 0$$

The important point is that the conditional variance of ϵ_t is given by $E_{t-1}\epsilon_t^2 = h_t$. Thus, *the conditional variance of ϵ_t is given by h_t in (3.9).*

This **generalized** ARCH(p, q) model—called GARCH(p, q)—allows for both autoregressive and moving average components in the heteroskedastic variance. If we set $p = 0$ and $q = 1$, it is clear that the first-order ARCH model given by (3.2) is simply a GARCH(0, 1) model. If all the β_i equal zero, the GARCH(p, q) model is equivalent to an ARCH(q) model. The benefits of the GARCH model should be clear; a high-order ARCH model may have a more parsimonious GARCH representation that is much easier to identify and estimate. This is particularly true since all coefficients in (3.9) must be positive. Moreover, to ensure that the conditional variance is finite, all characteristic roots of (3.9) must lie inside the unit circle. Clearly, the more parsimonious model will entail fewer coefficient restrictions.[3]

The key feature of GARCH models is that the conditional variance of the *disturbances* of the $\{y_t\}$ sequence constitutes an ARMA process. Hence, it is to be expected that the residuals from a fitted ARMA model should display this characteristic pattern. To explain, suppose you estimate $\{y_t\}$ as an ARMA process. If your model of $\{y_t\}$ is adequate, the ACF and PACF of the residuals should be indicative of a white-noise process. However, the ACF of the *squared* residuals can help identify the order of the GARCH process. Since $E_{t-1}\epsilon_t = h_t$, it is possible to rewrite (3.9) as

$$E_{t-1}\epsilon_t^2 = \alpha_0 + \sum_{i=1}^{q}\alpha_i\epsilon_{t-i}^2 + \sum_{i=1}^{p}\beta_i h_{t-i} \tag{3.10}$$

Equation (3.10) looks very much like an ARMA(q, p) process in the $\{\epsilon_t^2\}$ sequence. If there is conditional heteroskedasticity, the correlogram should be suggestive of such a process. The technique to construct the correlogram of the squared residuals is as follows:

STEP 1: Estimate the $\{y_t\}$ sequence using the "best-fitting" ARMA model (or regression model) and obtain the squares of the fitted errors $\hat{\epsilon}_t^2$. Also calculate the sample variance of the residuals ($\hat{\sigma}^2$) defined as

$$\hat{\sigma}^2 = \sum_{t=1}^{T}\hat{\epsilon}_t^2/T$$

where T = number of residuals

STEP 2: Calculate and plot the sample autocorrelations of the squared residuals as

$$\rho(i) = \frac{\sum_{t=i+1}^{T} (\hat{\epsilon}_t^2 - \hat{\sigma}^2)(\hat{\epsilon}_{t-i}^2 - \hat{\sigma}^2)}{\sum_{t=1}^{T} (\hat{\epsilon}_t^2 - \hat{\sigma}^2)}$$

STEP 3: In large samples, the standard deviation of $\rho(i)$ can be approximated by $T^{-1/2}$. Individual values of $\rho(i)$ with a value that is significantly different from zero are indicative of GARCH errors. Ljung–Box Q-statistics can be used to test for groups of significant coefficients. As in Chapter 2, the statistic

$$Q = T(T+2) \sum_{i=1}^{n} \rho(i)/(T-i)$$

has an asymptotic χ^2 distribution with n degrees of freedom if the $\hat{\epsilon}_t^2$ are uncorrelated. Rejecting the null hypothesis that the $\hat{\epsilon}_t^2$ are uncorrelated is equivalent to rejecting the null hypothesis of no ARCH or GARCH errors. In practice, you should consider values of n up to $T/4$.

The more formal Lagrange multiplier test for ARCH disturbances has been proposed by Engle (1982). The methodology involves the following two steps:[4]

STEP 1: Use OLS to estimate the most appropriate AR(n) (or regression) model:

$$y_t = a_0 + a_1 y_{t-1} + a_2 y_{t-2} + \cdots + a_n y_{t-n} + \epsilon_t$$

STEP 2: Obtain the squares of the fitted errors $\hat{\epsilon}_t^2$. Regress these squared residuals on a constant and on the q lagged values $\hat{\epsilon}_{t-1}^2, \hat{\epsilon}_{t-2}^2, \hat{\epsilon}_{t-3}^2, \ldots, \hat{\epsilon}_{t-q}^2$, that is, estimate

$$\hat{\epsilon}_t^2 = \alpha_0 + \alpha_1 \hat{\epsilon}_{t-1}^2 + \alpha_2 \hat{\epsilon}_{t-2}^2 + \cdots + \alpha_q \hat{\epsilon}_{t-q}^2 \qquad (3.11)$$

If there are no ARCH or GARCH effects, the estimated values of α_1 through α_q should be zero. Hence, this regression will have little explanatory power so that the coefficient of determination (i.e., the usual R^2-statistic) will be quite low. With a sample of T residuals, under the null hypothesis of no ARCH errors, the test statistic TR^2 converges to a χ_q^2 distribution. If TR^2 is sufficiently large, rejection of the null hypothesis that α_1 through α_q are jointly equal to zero is equivalent to rejecting the null hypothesis of no ARCH errors. On the other hand, if TR^2 is sufficiently low, it is possible to conclude that there are no ARCH effects.

3. ARCH AND GARCH ESTIMATES OF INFLATION

ARCH and GARCH models have become very popular in that they enable the econometrician to estimate the variance of a series at a particular point in time. To illustrate the distinction between the conditional variance and the unconditional variance, consider the nature of the wage bargaining process. Clearly, firms and unions need to forecast the inflation rate over the duration of the labor contract. Economic theory suggests that the terms of the wage contract will depend on the inflation forecasts and uncertainty concerning the accuracy of these forecasts. Let $E_t\pi_{t+1}$ denote the conditional expected rate of inflation for $t + 1$ and $\sigma^2_{\pi t}$ the conditional variance. If parties to the contract have rational expectations, the terms of the contract will depend on $E_t\pi_{t+1}$ and $\sigma^2_{\pi t}$, as opposed to the unconditional mean or unconditional variance. Similarly, as mentioned above, asset pricing models indicate that the risk premium will depend on the expected return and variance of that return. The relevant risk measure is the risk over the holding period, not the unconditional risk.

The example illustrates a very important point. The rational expectations hypothesis asserts that agents do not waste useful information. In forecasting any time series, rational agents use the conditional distribution, rather than the unconditional distribution, of that series. Hence, any test of the wage bargaining model above that uses the historical variance of the inflation rate would be inconsistent with the notion that rational agents make use of all available information (i.e., conditional means and variances). A student of the "economics of uncertainty" can immediately see the importance of ARCH and GARCH models. Theoretical models using *variance as a measure of risk (such as mean variance analysis) can be tested using the conditional variance.* As such, the growth in the use of ARCH/GARCH methods has been nothing short of impressive.

Engle's Model of U.K. Inflation

Although Section 2 focused on the residuals of a pure ARMA model, it is possible to estimate the residuals of a standard multiple-regression model as ARCH or GARCH processes. In fact, Engle's (1982) seminal paper considered the residuals of the simple model of the wage/price spiral for the U.K over the 1958:II to 1977:II period. Let p_t denote the log of the U.K. consumer price index and w_t the log of the index of nominal wage rates. Thus, the rate of inflation is $\pi_t = p_t - p_{t-1}$ and the real wage $r_t = w_t - p_t$. Engle reports that after some experimentation, he chose the following model of the U.K. inflation rate (standard errors appear in parentheses):

$$\pi_t = 0.0257 + 0.334\pi_{t-1} + 0.408\pi_{t-4} - 0.404\pi_{t-5} + 0.0559r_{t-1} + \epsilon_t$$
$$ (0.0057) \quad (0.103) \quad\quad (0.110) \quad\quad (0.114) \quad\quad (0.0136)$$
$$h_t = 0.000089 \tag{3.12}$$

where $h_t =$ the variance of $\{\epsilon_t\}$

The nature of the model is such that increases in the previous period's real wage increase the current inflation rate. Lagged inflation rates at $t - 4$ and $t - 5$ are intended to capture seasonal factors. All coefficients have a t-statistic greater than 3.0, and a battery of diagnostic tests did not indicate the presence of serial correlation. The estimated variance was the constant value 8.9E–5. In testing for ARCH errors, the Lagrange multiplier test for ARCH(1) errors was not significant, but the test for an ARCH(4) error process yielded a value of TR^2 equal to 15.2. At the 0.01 significance level, the critical value of χ^2 with four degrees of freedom is 13.28; hence, Engle concludes that there are ARCH errors.

Engle specified a ARCH(4) process forcing the following declining set of weights on the errors:

$$h_t = \alpha_0 + \alpha_1(0.4\epsilon_{t-1}^2 + 0.3\epsilon_{t-2}^2 + 0.2\epsilon_{t-3}^2 + 0.1\epsilon_{t-4}^2) \tag{3.13}$$

The rationale for choosing a two-parameter variance function was to ensure the nonnegativity and stationarity constraints that might not be satisfied using an unrestricted estimating equation. Given this particular set of weights, the necessary and sufficient conditions for the two constraints to be satisfied are $\alpha_0 > 0$ and $0 < \alpha_1 < 1$.

Engle shows that the estimation of the parameters of (3.12) and (3.13) can be considered separately without loss of asymptotic efficiency. One procedure is to estimate (3.12) using OLS and save the residuals. From these residuals, an estimate of the parameters of (3.13) can be constructed, and based on these estimates, new estimates of (3.12) can be obtained. To estimate both with full efficiency, continued iterations can be checked to determine whether the separate estimates are converging. Now that many statistical software packages contain nonlinear maximum likelihood estimation routines, the current procedure is to simultaneously estimate both equations using the methodology discussed in Section 7 below.

Engle's maximum likelihood estimates of the model are

$$\pi_t = 0.0328 + 0.162\pi_{t-1} + 0.264\pi_{t-4} - 0.325\pi_{t-5} + 0.0707r_{t-1} + \epsilon_t$$
$$ (0.0049) \quad (0.108) \quad\quad (0.089) \quad\quad (0.099) \quad\quad (0.0115)$$
$$h_t = 1.4E\text{-}5 + 0.955(0.4\epsilon_{t-1}^2 + 0.3\epsilon_{t-2}^2 + 0.2\epsilon_{t-3}^2 + 0.1\epsilon_{t-4}^2)$$
$$ (8.5) \quad\;\; (0.298) \tag{3.14}$$

The estimated values of h_t are one-step ahead forecast error variances. All coefficients (except the own lag of the inflation rate) are significant at conventional levels. For a given real wage, the point estimates of (3.14) imply that the inflation rate is a convergent process. Using the calculated values of the $\{h_t\}$ sequence, Engle finds that the standard deviation of inflation forecasts more than doubled as the economy moved from the "predictable sixties into the chaotic seventies." The point estimate of 0.955 indicates an extreme amount of persistence.

Bollerslev's Estimates of U.S. Inflation

Bollerslev's (1986) estimate of U.S. inflation provides an interesting comparison of a standard autoregressive time-series model (which assumes a constant variance), model with ARCH errors, and model with GARCH errors. He notes that the ARCH procedure has been useful in modeling different economic phenomena but points out (see pp. 307–308) that

> Common to most . . . applications, however, is the introduction of a rather arbitrary linear declining lag structure in the conditional variance equation to take account of the long memory typically found in empirical work, since estimating a totally free lag distribution often will lead to violation of the non-negativity constraints.

There is no doubt that the lag structure Engle used to model h_t in (3.14) is subject to this criticism. Using quarterly data over the 1948.II to 1983.IV period, Bollerslev (1986) calculates the inflation rate (π_t) as the logarithmic change in the U.S. GNP deflator. He then estimates the autoregression:

$$\pi_t = 0.240 + 0.552\pi_{t-1} + 0.177\pi_{t-2} + 0.232\pi_{t-3} - 0.209\pi_{t-4} + \epsilon_t$$
$$\quad (0.080) \quad (0.083) \quad\quad (0.089) \quad\quad (0.090) \quad\quad (0.080)$$
$$h_t = 0.282 \tag{3.15}$$

Equation (3.15) seems to have all the properties of a well-estimated time-series model. All coefficients are significant at conventional levels (the standard errors appear in parentheses) and the estimated values of the autoregressive coefficients imply stationarity. Bollerslev reports that the ACF and PACF do not exhibit any significant coefficients at the 5% significance level. However, as is typical of ARCH errors, the ACF and PACF of the *squared* residuals (i.e., ϵ_t^2) show significant correlations. The Lagrange multiplier tests for ARCH(1), ARCH(4), and ARCH(8) errors are all highly significant.

Bollerslev next estimates the restricted ARCH(8) model originally proposed by Engle and Kraft (1983). By way of comparison to (3.15), he finds

$$\pi_t = 0.138 + 0.423\pi_{t-1} + 0.222\pi_{t-2} + 0.377\pi_{t-3} - 0.175\pi_{t-4} + \epsilon_t$$
$$\quad (0.059) \quad (0.081) \quad\quad (0.108) \quad\quad (0.078) \quad\quad (0.104)$$

$$h_t = 0.058 + 0.802 \sum_{i=1}^{8} (9-i)/36\epsilon_{t-i}^2$$

$$\quad (0.033)\,(0.265) \tag{3.16}$$

Note that the autoregressive coefficients of (3.15) and (3.16) are similar. The models of the variance, however, are quite different. Equation (3.15) assumes a constant variance, whereas (3.16) assumes the variance (h_t) is a geometrically declining weighted average of the variance in the previous eight quarters.[5]

Hence, the inflation rate predictions of the two models should be similar, but the confidence intervals surrounding the forecasts will differ. Equation (3.15) yields a constant interval of unchanging width. Equation (3.16) yields a confidence interval that expands during periods of inflation volatility and contracts in relatively tranquil periods.

In order to test for the presence of a first-order GARCH term in the conditional variance, it is possible to estimate the equation:

$$h_t = \alpha_0 + \alpha_1 \sum_{i=1}^{8} (9-i)/36\epsilon_{t-i}^2 + \beta_1 h_{t-1} \qquad (3.17)$$

The finding that $\beta_1 = 0$ would imply an absence of a first-order moving average term in the conditional variance. Given the difficulties of estimating (3.17), Bollerslev (1986) uses the simpler Lagrange multiplier test. Formally, the test involves constructing the residuals of the conditional variance of (3.16). The next step is to regress these residuals on a constant and h_{t-1}; the expression TR^2 has a χ^2 distribution with one degree of freedom. Bollerslev finds that $TR^2 = 4.57$; at the 5% significance level, he cannot reject the presence of a first-order GARCH process. He then estimates the following GARCH(1, 1) model:

$$\pi_t = 0.141 + 0.433\pi_{t-1} + 0.229\pi_{t-2} + 0.349\pi_{t-3} - 0.162\pi_{t-4} + \epsilon_t$$
$$\quad\; (0.060) \quad (0.081) \qquad (0.110) \qquad (0.077) \qquad (0.104)$$
$$h_t = 0.007 + 0.135\epsilon_{t-1}^2 + 0.829h_{t-1}$$
$$\quad\; (0.006) \quad (0.070) \qquad (0.068) \qquad\qquad\qquad\qquad (3.18)$$

Diagnostic checks indicate that the ACF and PACF of the squared residuals do not reveal any coefficients exceeding $2T^{-1/2}$. LM tests for the presence of additional lags of ϵ_t^2 and for the presence of h_{t-2} are not significant at the 5% level.

4. ESTIMATING A GARCH MODEL OF THE WPI: AN EXAMPLE

To obtain a better idea of the actual process of fitting a GARCH model, reconsider the U.S. Wholesale Price Index data used in the last chapter. Recall that the Box–Jenkins approach led us to estimate a model of the U.S. rate of inflation (π_t) having the form:

$$\pi_t = a_0 + a_1\pi_{t-1} + \epsilon_t + \beta_1\epsilon_{t-1} + \beta_4\epsilon_{t-4}$$

When we used the standard criteria of the Box–Jenkins procedure, the estimated model performed quite well. All estimated parameters were significant at conventional levels and both the AIC and SBC selected the ARMA[(1, (1, 4)] specification. Diagnostic checks of the residuals did not indicate the presence of serial correlation and there was no evidence of structural change in the estimated coefficients. During the 1970s, however, there was a period of unusual volatility that is characteristic of a GARCH process. The aim of this section is to illustrate a step-by-step analysis of a GARCH estimation of the rate of inflation as measured by the WPI. The data series is contained in the file labeled WPI.WK1 on the data disk. Question 7 at the end of this chapter guides you though the estimation procedure reported below.

In the last chapter, some of the observations were not used in the estimation stage, so that out-of-sample forecasts could be performed. Estimating the same model over the entire 1960:I to 1992:2 sample period yields

$$\pi_t = 0.0101 + 0.7875\pi_{t-1} + \epsilon_t - 0.4374\epsilon_{t-1} + 0.2957\epsilon_{t-4}$$
$$\quad\;\; (0.0039) \quad (0.0865) \qquad\qquad (0.1126) \qquad (0.0904)$$
$$h_t = 1.9193\text{E-4} \tag{3.19}$$

The ACF and PACF of the residuals do not indicate any sign of serial correlation. The only suspect autocorrelation coefficient is for lag 6; the value $\rho(6) = 0.1619$ is about 1.8 standard deviations from zero. All other autocorrelations and partial autocorrelations are less than 0.11. The Ljung–Box Q-statistics for lags of 12, 24, and 36 quarters are 8.47, 15.09, and 28.54; none of these values are significant at conventional levels.

Although the model appears adequate, the volatility during the 1970s suggests an examination of the ACF and PACF of the squared residuals. The autocorrelations of the *squared* residuals are such that $\rho(1) = 0.126$, $\rho(2) = 0.307$, $\rho(3) = 0.115$, and $\rho(4) = 0.292$. Other values for $\rho(i)$ are generally 0.10 or less. The Ljung–Box Q-statistics for the squared are all highly significant; for example, $Q(4) = 27.78$ and $Q(12) = 37.55$, which are both significant at the 0.00001 level. At this point, one might be tempted to plot the ACF and PACF of the squared residuals and estimate the squared residuals using Box–Jenkins methods. The problem with this strategy is that the errors were not generated by the maximum likelihood technique and are not fully efficient. Hence, it is necessary to formally test for ARCH errors.

Alternative Estimates of the Model

Next, let $\hat{\epsilon}_t$ denote the residuals of (3.19) and consider the ARCH(q) model for lag lengths of 1, 4, and 8 quarters:

$$\hat{\epsilon}_t^2 = \alpha_0 + \sum_{i=1}^{q} \alpha_i \hat{\epsilon}_{t-i}^2 \tag{3.20}$$

If we estimate (3.20) using OLS, the calculated values of TR^2 for $q = 1$, 4, and 8 are 22.91, 35.70, and 37.60, respectively. Hence, there appear to be ARCH errors at the 1% significance level; the critical values of χ^2 with one, four, and eight degrees of freedom are 5.41, 11.67, and 18.17, respectively. Since the values of TR^2 for $q = 4$ and $q = 8$ are similar, it seems worthwhile to pin down the lag length to an ARCH(4) process. A straightforward method is to estimate (3.20) for $q = 8$. In this instance, the F-test for the null hypothesis $\alpha_5 = \alpha_6 = \alpha_7 = \alpha_8 = 0$ cannot be rejected at conventional levels.

Another way to determine whether four versus eight lags are most appropriate is to use a Lagrange multiplier test. To use this test, estimate (3.20) with $q = 4$; let $\{\epsilon_{4t}\}$ denote the residuals from this regression. To determine whether lags 5 through 8 contain significant explanatory power, use the $\{\epsilon_{4t}\}$ sequence to estimate the regression:

$$\epsilon_{4t}^2 = \alpha_0 + \sum_{i=1}^{8} \alpha_i \epsilon_{4t-i}^2$$

If lags 5 through 8 contain little explanatory power, TR^2 should be small. Regressing ϵ_{4t} on a constant and eight lags of ϵ_{4t} yielded a value of $TR^2 = 3.85$. With four degrees of freedom, 3.85 is far below the critical value of χ^2; it seems plausible to conclude that the errors are characterized by an ARCH(4) process. The same procedure can be used to test whether the model is an ARCH(1) or ARCH(4) process. Now let $\{\epsilon_{1t}\}$ denote the residuals of (3.20) estimated with $q = 1$. Regressing ϵ_{1t} on a constant and four lags of ϵ_{1t} yielded a value of $TR^2 = 16.32$. At the 0.001 significance level, the critical value of χ^2 with three degrees of freedom is 16.27. Hence, it hardly seems plausible to conclude that an ARCH(1) characterizes the error process; lags 2 through 4 cannot be excluded from (3.20).

Overall, these tests suggest estimating the inflation rate using an ARMA[1, (1, 4)] model by assuming an ARCH(4) error process. The results from a maximum likelihood estimation are

$$\pi_t = 0.0021 + 0.5723\pi_{t-1} + \epsilon_t - 0.1189\epsilon_{t-1} + 0.3108\epsilon_{t-4}$$
$$ (0.0012) \quad (0.1298) \qquad\qquad (0.1135) \qquad (0.0645)$$
$$h_t = 2.1247\text{E-}5 + 0.1433\epsilon_{t-1}^2 + 0.2270\epsilon_{t-2}^2 + 0.0037\epsilon_{t-3}^2 + 0.6755\epsilon_{t-4}^2$$
$$ (0.0000) \qquad (0.1384) \qquad (0.1725) \qquad (0.0709) \qquad (0.2031) \qquad \text{(3.21)}$$

Although each estimated coefficient has the correct sign, we should be somewhat concerned about the number of insignificant coefficients. Note that the estimated coefficient on ϵ_{t-1} in the equation for π_t is about one standard error from zero; we know, however, that eliminating this coefficient from the ARMA[1, (1, 4)] model of inflation leads to residuals that are serially correlated. Moreover, three values of the ARCH(4) error process are not insignificantly different from zero at conventional significance levels. The likely solution to the problem concerns the modeling of the ARCH process; perhaps a more parsimonious model is in order.

One approach to reducing the number of estimated parameters is to constrain the conditional variance to have the same declining weights given by (3.13). The maximum likelihood estimates of this constrained ARCH(4) process are

$$\pi_t = 0.0011 + 0.9201\pi_{t-1} + \epsilon_t - 0.4304\epsilon_{t-1} + 0.1198\epsilon_{t-4}$$
$$(0.0011) \quad (0.0795) \qquad\qquad (0.1476) \quad (0.0929)$$
$$h_t = 6.3767\text{E-}5 + 0.5850(0.4\epsilon_{t-1}^2 + 0.3\epsilon_{t-2}^2 + 0.2\epsilon_{t-3}^2 + 0.1\epsilon_{t-4}^2)$$
$$(1.08\text{E-}3) \quad (0.0795) \tag{3.22}$$

Here, the estimated parameters of the ARCH process are both positive and significantly different from zero. The estimated value of α_1 (=0.5850) implies that h_t is convergent. The problem with this model is that the estimated value of a_1 (=0.9201) is dangerously close to unity (implying a divergent process) and β_4 is significant at only the 0.19 level. Before contemplating the use of second differences or setting $\beta_4 = 0$ and eliminating ϵ_{t-4} from the model, we should be concerned about the validity of the restricted error process. One way to proceed is to try alternative weighting patterns and select the "best" pattern. Of course, this approach is subject to Bollerslev's criticism of being completely ad hoc.

A better alternative is to use a GARCH(1, 1) model. As a first step, the error process was estimated as

$$\pi_t = 0.0013 + 0.7968\pi_{t-1} + \epsilon_t - 0.4014\epsilon_{t-1} + 0.2356\epsilon_{t-4}$$
$$(0.0012) \quad (0.1141) \qquad\qquad (0.1585) \quad (0.1202)$$
$$h_t = 1.5672\text{E-}5 + 0.2226\epsilon_{t-1}^2 + 0.6633h_{t-1}$$
$$(9.34\text{E-}6) \quad (0.1067) \quad (0.1515) \tag{3.23}$$

Notice that the point estimates of the parameters imply stationarity and all coefficients but the intercept term in the π_t equation are significant at the 10% level. The value of the maximized likelihood function is greater for the GARCH(1, 1) model than pure ARCH processes even though all models were estimated over the same time period.[6] The maximized values of the likelihood function for (3.21), (3.22) and (3.23) are 483.25, 491.83, and 496.98, respectively. Moreover, the GARCH(1, 1) model necessitates the estimation of only two parameters. Thus, the GARCH(1, 1) process yields the best fit.

Diagnostic tests did not indicate the need to include other lags in the GARCH(1, 1) model. The Lagrange multiplier tests for the presence of additional values of α_i or β_i were insignificant at conventional levels. Since h_t is an estimate of the conditional variance of π_t, $(h_{t+1})^{1/2}$ is the standard error of the one-step ahead forecast error of π_{t+1}. Figure 3.10 shows a band of $\pm 2 (h_{t+1})^{1/2}$ surrounding the one-step ahead forecast of the WPI.[7] In contrast to the assumption of a constant conditional variance, note that the band width increases in the mid–1970s and latter part of the 1980s.

Figure 3.10   Two-standard-deviation forecast interval for the WPI.

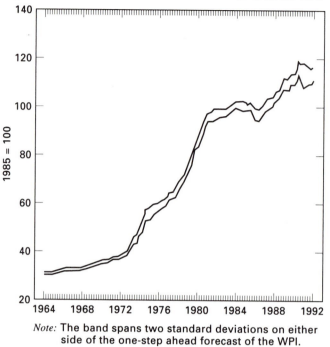

Note: The band spans two standard deviations on either side of the one-step ahead forecast of the WPI.

5. A GARCH MODEL OF RISK

An interesting application of GARCH modeling is provided by Holt and Aradhyula (1990). Their theoretical framework stands in contrast to the cobweb model in that rational expectations are assumed to prevail in the agricultural sector. The aim of the study is to examine the extent to which producers in the U.S. broiler (i.e., chicken) industry exhibit risk-averse behavior. To this end, the supply function for the U.S. broiler industry takes the form:[8]

$$q_t = a_0 + a_1 p_t^e - a_2 h_t - a_3 pfeed_{t-1} + a_4 hatch_{t-1} + a_5 q_{t-4} + \epsilon_{1t} \qquad (3.24)$$

where q_t = quantity of broiler production (in millions of pounds) in t

p_t^e = expected real price of broilers at t conditioned on the information at $t-1$ (so that $p_t^e = E_{t-1} p_t$)

h_t = expected variance of the price of broilers in t conditioned on the information at $t-1$

$pfeed_{t-1}$ = real price of broiler feed (in cents per pound) at $t-1$

$hatch_{t-1}$ = hatch of broiler-type chicks in commercial hatcheries (measured in thousands) in $t-1$

ϵ_{1t} = supply shock in t

and the length of the time period is one quarter.

The supply function is based on the biological fact that the production cycle of broilers is about 2 months. Since bimonthly data are unavailable, the model assumes that the supply decision is positively related to the price expectation formed by producers in the previous quarter. Given that feed accounts for the bulk of production costs, real feed prices lagged one quarter are negatively related to broiler production in t. Obviously, the *hatch* available in $t - 1$ increases the number of broilers that can be marketed in t. The fourth lag of broiler production is included to account for the possibility that production in any period may not fully adjust to the desired level of production.

For our purposes, the most interesting part of the study is the negative effect of the conditional variance of price on broiler supply. The timing of the production process is such that feed and other production costs must be incurred before output is sold in the market. In the planning stage, producers must forecast the price that will prevail 2 months hence. The greater p_t^e, the greater the number of chicks that will be fed and brought to market. If price variability is very low, these forecasts can be held with confidence. Increased price variability decreases the accuracy of the forecasts and decreases broiler supply. Risk-averse producers will opt to raise and market fewer broilers when the conditional volatility of price is high.

In the initial stage of the study, broiler prices are estimated as the AR(4) process:

$$(1 - \beta_1 L - \beta_2 L^2 - \beta_3 L^3 - \beta_4 L^4)p_t = \beta_0 + \epsilon_{2t} \qquad (3.25)$$

Ljung–Box Q-statistics for various lag lengths indicate that the residual series appear to be white-noise at the 5% level. However, the Q-statistic for the squared residuals, that is, the $\{\epsilon_{2t}^2\}$, of 32.4 is significant at the 5% level. Thus, Holt and Aradhyula conclude that the variance of the price is heteroskedastic.

In the second stage of the study, several low-order GARCH estimates of (3.25) are compared. Goodness-of-fit statistics and significance tests suggest a GARCH(1, 1) process. In the third stage, the supply equation (3.24) and a GARCH(1,1) process are simultaneously estimated. The estimated price equation (with standard errors in parentheses) is

$$(1 - 0.511L - 0.129L^2 - 0.130L^3 - 0.138L^4)p_t = 1.632 + \epsilon_{2t} \qquad (3.26)$$
$$ (0.092) \quad (0.098) \quad (0.094) \quad\quad (0.073) \quad\quad (1.347)$$
$$h_t = 1.353 + 0.162\epsilon_{2t-1}^2 + 0.591h_{t-1} \qquad (3.27)$$
$$ (0.747) \quad (0.080) \quad\quad (0.175)$$

Equations (3.26) and (3.27) are well behaved in that (1) all estimated coefficients are significant at conventional significance levels; (2) all coefficients of the conditional variance equation are positive; and (3) the coefficients all imply convergent processes.

Holt and Aradhyula assume that producers use (3.26) and (3.27) to form their price expectations. Combining these estimates with (3.24) yields the supply equation

$$q_t = 2.767p_t^e - 0.521h_t - 4.325pfeed_{t-1} + 1.887hatch_{t-1} + 0.603q_{t-4} + \epsilon_{1t} \quad (3.28)$$
$$(0.585) \quad (0.344) \quad (1.463) \quad\quad (0.205) \quad\quad (0.065)$$

All estimated coefficients are significant at conventional levels and have the appropriate sign. An increase in the expected price increases broiler output. Increased uncertainty, as measured by conditional variance, acts to decrease output. This forward-looking rational expectations formulation is at odds with the more traditional cobweb model discussed in Chapter 1. In order to compare the two formulations, Holt and Aradhyula (1990) also consider an adaptive expectations formulation (see Exercise 2 in Chapter 1). Under adaptive expectations, price expectations are formed according to a weighted average of the previous period's price and the previous period's price expectation:

$$p_t^e = \alpha p_{t-1} + (1 - \alpha)p_{t-1}^e$$

or solving for p_t^e in terms of the $\{p_t\}$ sequence, we obtain

$$p_t^e = \alpha \sum_{i=0}^{\infty} (1-\alpha)^i p_{t-1-i}$$

Similarly, the adaptive expectations formulation for conditional risk is given by

$$h_t = \beta \sum_{i=0}^{\infty} (1-\beta)^i (p_{t-1-i} - p_{t-1-i}^e)^2 \quad (3.29)$$

where $0 < \beta < 1$ and $(p_{t-1-i} - p_{t-1-i}^e)^2 = $ the forecast error variance for period $t - i$.

Note that in (3.29), the expected measure of risk as viewed by producers is not necessarily the actual conditional variance. The estimates of the two models differ concerning the implied long-run elasticities of supply with respect to expected price and conditional variance.[9] Respectively, the estimated long-run elasticities of supply with respect to expected price are 0.587 and 0.399 in the rational expectations and adaptive expectations formulations. Similarly, rational and adaptive expectations formulations yield long-run supply elasticities of conditional variance of −0.030 and −0.013, respectively. Not surprisingly, the adaptive expectations model suggests a more sluggish supply response than the forward-looking rational expectations model.

6. THE ARCH-M MODEL

Engle, Lilien, and Robins (1987) extend the basic ARCH framework to allow the mean of a sequence to depend on its own conditional variance. This class of model, called ARCH-M, is particularly suited to the study of asset markets. The basic insight is that risk-averse agents will require compensation for holding a risky asset. Given that an asset's *riskiness* can be measured by the variance of returns, the risk premium will be an increasing function of the conditional variance of returns.[10] Engle, Lilien, and Robins express this idea by writing the excess return from holding a risky asset as

$$y_t = \mu_t + \epsilon_t \qquad (3.30)$$

where y_t = excess return from holding a long-term asset relative to a one-period treasury bill

μ_t = risk premium necessary to induce the risk-averse agent to hold the long-term asset rather than the one-period bond

ϵ_t = unforecastable shock to the excess return on the long-term asset

To explain (3.30), note that the expected excess return from holding the long-term asset must be just equal to the risk premium:[11]

$$E_{t-1}y_t = \mu_t$$

Engle, Lilien, and Robins assume that the risk premium is an increasing function of the conditional variance of ϵ_t; in other words, the greater the conditional variance of returns, the greater the compensation necessary to induce the agent to hold the long-term asset. Mathematically, if h_t is the conditional variance of ϵ_t, the risk premium can be expressed as

$$\mu_t = \beta + \delta h_t, \qquad \delta > 0 \qquad (3.31)$$

where h_t is the ARCH(q) process:

$$h_t = \alpha_0 + \sum_{i=1}^{q} \alpha_i \epsilon_{t-i}^2 \qquad (3.32)$$

As a set, Equations (3.30), (3.31), and (3.32) constitute the basic ARCH-M model. From (3.30) and (3.31), the conditional mean of y_t depends on the conditional variance h_t. From (3.32), the conditional variance is an ARCH(q) process. It should be pointed out that if the conditional variance is constant (i.e., if $\alpha_1 = \alpha_2 = \cdots = \alpha_q = 0$), the ARCH-M model degenerates into the more traditional case of a constant risk premium.

Figure 3.11 illustrates two different ARCH-M processes. The upper-left-hand graph (a) of the figure shows 60 realizations of a simulated white-noise process denoted by $\{\epsilon_t\}$. Note the temporary increase in volatility during periods 20 to 30. By initializing $\epsilon_0 = 0$, the conditional variance was constructed as the first-order ARCH process:

$$h_t = 1 + 0.65\epsilon_{t-1}^2$$

As you can see in the upper-right-hand graph (b), the volatility in $\{\epsilon_t\}$ translates itself into increases in the conditional variance. Note that large positive *and* negative realizations of ϵ_{t-1} result in a large value of h_t; it is the square of each $\{\epsilon_t\}$ realization that enters the conditional variance. In the lower left graph (c), the values of β and δ are set equal to -4 and $+4$, respectively. As such, the y_t sequence is constructed as $y_t = -4 + 4h_t + \epsilon_t$. You can clearly see that y_t is above its long-run value during the period of volatility. In the simulation, conditional volatility translates itself into increases in the values of $\{y_t\}$. In the latter portion of the sample, the volatility of $\{\epsilon_t\}$ diminishes and the values y_{30} through y_{60} fluctuate around their long-run mean.

The lower-right-hand graph (d) reduces the influence of ARCH-M effects by reducing the magnitude of δ and β (see Exercise 5 at the end of this chapter). Obviously, if $\delta = 0$, there are no ARCH-M effects at all. As you can see by comparing the two lower graphs, y_t more closely mimics the ϵ_t sequence when the magnitude of δ is diminished from $\delta = 4$ to $\delta = 1$.[12]

As in ARCH or GARCH models, the form of an ARCH-M model can be determined using Lagrange multiplier tests exactly as in (3.11). The LM tests are rela-

Figure 3.11   Simulated ARCH-M processes.

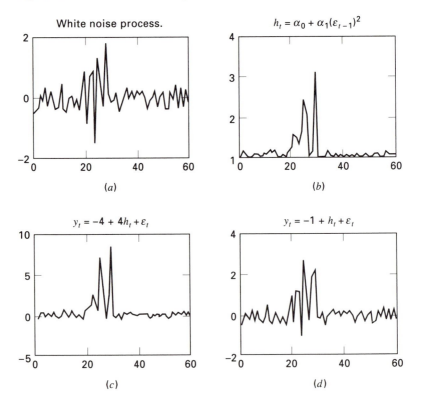

tively simple to conduct since they do not require estimation of the full model. The statistic TR^2 is asymptotically distributed as χ^2 with degrees of freedom equal to the number of restrictions.

Implementation

Using quarterly data from 1960:I to 1984:II, Engle, Lilien, and Robins (1987) constructed the excess yield on 6-month treasury bills as follows. Let r_t denote the quarterly yield on a 3-month treasury bill held from t to $(t + 1)$. Rolling over all proceeds, at the end of two quarters an individual investing \$1 at the beginning of period t will have $(1 + r_t)(1 + r_{t+1})$ dollars. In the same fashion, if R_t denotes the quarterly yield on a 6-month treasury bill, buying and holding the 6-month bill for the full two quarters will result in $(1 + R_t)$ dollars. The excess yield due to holding the 6-month bill is approximately

$$y_t = 2R_t - r_{t+1} - r_t \tag{3.33}$$

The results from regressing the excess yield on a constant are (the t-statistic is in parentheses)

$$y_t = 0.142 + \epsilon_t \tag{3.34}$$
$$(4.04)$$

The excess yield of 0.142% per quarter that is over four standard deviations from zero. The problem with this estimation method is that the post–1979 period showed markedly higher volatility than the earlier sample period. To test for the presence of ARCH errors, the squared residuals were regressed on a weighted average of past squared residuals as in (3.13). The LM test for the restriction $\alpha_1 = 0$ yields a value of $TR^2 = 10.1$, which has a χ^2 distribution with one degree of freedom. At the 1% significance level, the critical value of χ^2 with one degree of freedom is 6.635; hence, there is strong evidence of heteroskedasticity. Thus, there appear to be ARCH errors so that (3.34) is misspecified if individuals demand a risk premium.

The maximum likelihood estimates of the ARCH-M model and associated t-statistics are

$$y_t = -0.0241 + 0.687h_t + \epsilon_t$$
$$(-1.29) \quad (5.15)$$
$$h_t = 0.0023 + 1.64(0.4\epsilon_{t-1}^2 + 0.3\epsilon_{t-2}^2 + 0.2\epsilon_{t-3}^2 + 0.1\epsilon_{t-4}^2)$$
$$(1.08) \quad (6.30)$$

The estimated coefficients imply a time-varying risk premium. The estimated parameter of the ARCH equation of 1.64 implies that the unconditional variance is infinite. Although this is somewhat troublesome, the conditional variance is finite. Shocks to ϵ_{t-i} act to increase the conditional variance so that there are periods of tranquility and volatility. During volatile periods, the risk premium rises as risk-averse agents seek assets that are conditionally less risky.

The next section considers some of the mechanics involved in estimating an ARCH-M model. Exercise 8 at the end of this chapter asks you to estimate such a ARCH-M model using simulated data. The questions are designed to guide you through a typical estimation procedure.

7. MAXIMUM LIKELIHOOD ESTIMATION OF GARCH AND ARCH-M MODELS

Many software packages contain built-in routines that estimate GARCH and ARCH-M models such that the researcher simply specifies the order of the process and the computer does the rest. Even if you have access to an automated routine, it is important to understand the numerical procedures used by your software package. Other packages require user input in the form of a small optimization algorithm. This section explains the maximum likelihood methods required to understand and write a program for ARCH-type models.

Suppose that values of $\{y_t\}$ are drawn from a normal distribution having a mean μ and *constant* variance σ^2. From standard distribution theory, the log likelihood function using T independent observations is

$$\log \mathcal{L} = -(T/2)\,\ln(2\pi) - (T/2)\,\ln\sigma^2 - (1/2\sigma^2)\sum_{t=1}^{T}(y_t - \mu)^2$$

where $\log \mathcal{L} = $ log of the likelihood function

The procedure in maximum likelihood estimation is to select the distributional parameters so as to maximize the likelihood of drawing the observed sample. In the example at hand, the problem is to maximize $\log \mathcal{L}$ with respect to μ and σ^2. The first-order conditions are

$$[(\partial \log \mathcal{L})/\partial\mu] = (1/\sigma^2)\sum_{t=1}^{T}(y_t - \mu)$$

and

$$[(\partial \log \mathcal{L})/\partial\sigma^2] = -(T/2\sigma^2) + (1/2\sigma^4)\sum_{t=1}^{T}(y_t - \mu)^2$$

Setting these partial derivatives equal to zero and solving for the values of μ and σ^2 that yield the maximum value of $\log \mathcal{L}$ (denoted by $\hat{\mu}$ and $\hat{\sigma}^2$), we get

$$\hat{\mu} = \Sigma y_t / T$$

and

$$\hat{\sigma}^2 = \sum (y_t - \hat{\mu})^2 / T$$

Thus, with sample data, the maximum likelihood estimate of the mean is $\hat{\mu}$ and the maximum likelihood estimate of the variance is $\hat{\sigma}^2$. The same principle applies in a regression analysis. Suppose that $\{\epsilon_t\}$ is generated by the following model:

$$\epsilon_t = y_t - \beta x_t$$

In the classical regression model, the mean of ϵ_t is assumed to be zero, the variance is the constant σ^2, and the various realizations of $\{\epsilon_t\}$ are independent. If we use a sample with T observations, the log likelihood equation is a simple modification of the above:

$$\log \mathcal{L} = -(T/2) \ln(2\pi) - (T/2) \ln \sigma^2 - (1/2\sigma^2) \sum_{t=1}^{T} (y_t - \beta x_t)^2$$

Maximizing the likelihood equation with respect to σ^2 and β yields

$$[(\partial \log \mathcal{L}) / \partial \sigma^2] = -(T/2\sigma^2) + (1/2\sigma^4) \sum_{t=1}^{T} (y_t - \beta x_t)^2$$

and

$$[(\partial \log \mathcal{L}) / \partial \beta] = (1/\sigma^2) \sum_{t=1}^{T} (y_t x_t - \beta x_t^2)$$

Setting these partial derivatives equal to zero and solving for the values of β and σ^2 that yield the maximum value of $\log \mathcal{L}$ result in the familiar OLS estimates of the variance and β (denoted by $\hat{\sigma}^2$ and $\hat{\beta}$). Hence,

$$\hat{\sigma}^2 = \Sigma(\epsilon_t)^2 / T$$

and from (3.31),

$$\hat{\beta} = \Sigma x_t y_t / \Sigma(x_t)^2$$

All this should be familiar ground since most econometric texts concerned with regression analysis discuss maximum likelihood estimation. The point to emphasize here is that the first-order conditions are easily solved since they are all linear. Calculating the appropriate sums may be tedious, but the methodology is straightforward. Unfortunately, this is not the case in estimating an ARCH-type model since the first-order equations are nonlinear. Instead, the solution requires some sort of search algorithm. The simplest way to illustrate the issue is to introduce an ARCH(1) error process into the regression model. Continue to assume that ϵ_t is generated by the linear equation $\epsilon_t = y_t - \beta x_t$. Now let ϵ_t be given by (3.2):

$$\epsilon_t = v_t(\alpha_0 + \alpha_1\epsilon_{t-1}^2)^{0.5}$$

so that the conditional variance of ϵ_t is

$$h_t = \alpha_0 + \alpha_1\epsilon_{t-1}^2$$

Although the conditional variance of ϵ_t is not constant, the necessary modifications are clear. Since each realization of ϵ_t has the conditional variance h_t, the appropriate log likelihood function is

$$\log \mathcal{L} = -(T/2)\ln(2\pi) - (T/2)\ln h_t - (1/2h_t)\sum_{t=1}^{T}(y_t - \beta x_t)^2$$

$$\textit{where}\quad h_t = \alpha_0 + \alpha_1\epsilon_{t-1}^2$$
$$= \alpha_0 + \alpha_1(y_{t-1} - \beta x_{t-1})^2$$

Finally, it is possible to combine the above and then to maximize log $\mathcal{L}$ with respect to α_0, α_1, and β. Fortunately, computers are able to select the parameter values that maximize this log likelihood function. In most time-series software packages, the procedure necessary to write such programs is quite simple. For example, RATS uses a typical set of statements to estimate this ARCH(1) model. Consider:[13]

```
NONLIN β α₀ α₁
FRML ε = y − βx
FRML h = α₀ + α₁*ε²₋₁
FRML LIKELIHOOD = −0.5*[log(hₜ) + (ε²ₜ/hₜ)]
COMPUTE β = initial guess, α₀ = initial guess, α₁ = initial guess
MAXIMIZE(RECURSIVE) LIKELIHOOD 2 end
```

The first statement prepares the program to estimate a nonlinear model. The second statement sets up the formula (FRML) for ϵ_t; ϵ_t is defined to be $y_t - \beta x_t$. The third statement sets up the formula for h_t as an ARCH(1) process. The fourth statement is the key to understanding the program. The formula LIKELIHOOD defines the log likelihood for observation t; the program "understands" that it will maximize this sum over all $T - 1$ observations. Note that the constant term $-(T/2)/\log(2\pi)$ is excluded from the definition of LIKELIHOOD; a constant has no effect on the solution to an optimization problem. The program requires initial guesses for β, α_0, and α_1. In practice, a reasonable initial guess for β could come from an OLS regression of $\{y_t\}$ on $\{x_t\}$. The initial guess for α_0 could be the variance of the residuals estimated from this OLS regression. After all, if there is no ARCH effect, OLS and the maximum likelihood methods are identical. The initial guess for α_1 could be a small positive number. The final statement tells the program to maximize LIKELIHOOD from observation 2 (since the initial observation is lost) to the end of the sample.[14]

It is possible to estimate more sophisticated models using a comparable procedure. The key to writing a successful program is to correctly specify the error process and variance. To estimate the ARMA[1, (1, 4)]-ARCH(4) model of the inflation rate given by (3.22), lines 3 and 4 of the program would be replaced with:[15]

$$\text{FRML } \epsilon = \pi_t - a_0 - a_1^* \pi_{t-1} - b_1 \epsilon_{t-1} - b_4 \epsilon_{t-4}$$
$$\text{FRML } h = \alpha_0 + \alpha_1 (0.4 \epsilon_{t-1}^2 + 0.3 \epsilon_{t-2}^2 + 0.2 \epsilon_{t-3}^2 + 0.1 \epsilon_{t-4}^2)$$

Here, the first formula statement defines ϵ_t as the residual from an ARMA[(1, (1, 4)] process. The second statement constrains the lagged coefficients to exhibit a smooth decay. Similarly, the GARCH(1, 1) version of this same model—see (3.23)—uses the program steps:

$$\text{FRML } \epsilon = \pi_t - a_0 - a_1^* \pi_{t-1} - b_1 \epsilon_{t-1} - b_4 \epsilon_{t-4}$$
$$\text{FRML } h = \alpha_0 + \alpha_1 \epsilon_{t-1}^2 + \beta_2 h_{t-1}$$

The program steps for the ARCH-M model of Engle, Lilien, and Robbins (1987) have the form

$$\text{FRML } \epsilon = y - a_0 - a_1 h$$
$$\text{FRML } h = \alpha_0 + \alpha_1 (0.4 \epsilon_{t-1}^2 + 0.3 \epsilon_{t-2}^2 + 0.2 \epsilon_{t-3}^2 + 0.1 \epsilon_{t-4}^2)$$

The first statement defines ϵ_t as the value of y_t less the conditional variance. The second statement defines the conditional variance.

Finally, it is possible to include explanatory variables in the formula for the conditional variance. In the GARCH(1, 1) inflation model, it is possible to write

$$\text{FRML } h = \alpha_0 + \alpha_1 \epsilon_{t-1}^2 + \beta_1 h_{t-1} + \beta_2 z_t$$

where z_t is an explanatory variable for h.

8. DETERMINISTIC AND STOCHASTIC TRENDS

It is helpful to represent the general solution to a linear stochastic difference equation as consisting of the three distinct parts:[16]

$$y_t = \text{trend} + \text{seasonal} + \text{irregular}$$

We have examined how ARMA(p, q) techniques can be used to model the irregular and seasonal components. GARCH and ARCH-M models try to capture the tendency of economic time series to exhibit periods of sustained volatility. The other distinguishing feature of Figures 3.1 through 3.8 is that the series appear to be nonstationary. The mean values for GNP and its subcomponents, the supplies of the financial instruments, and industrial production levels generally appear to be increasing over time. The exchange rate series shown in Figure 3.7 have no obvious tendency for mean reversion.

For some series, such as GNP, the sustained upward trend might be captured by a simple linear time trend. Such an assumption is controversial, however, since it implies a deterministic long-run growth rate of the real economy. Adherents to the "real business cycle" school argue that technological advancements have permanent effects on the trend of the macroeconomy. Given that technological innovations are stochastic, the trend should reflect this underlying randomness. As such, it will be useful to consider models with stochastic and deterministic trends.

A critical task for econometricians is to develop simple stochastic difference equation models that can mimic the behavior of trending variables. The key feature of a trend is that it has a permanent effect on a series. Since the irregular component is stationary, the effects of any irregular components will "die out" while the trending elements will remain in long-term forecasts. Examples of models with deterministic trends include

$$y_t = a_0 + a_1 t + \epsilon_t \qquad \text{(linear time trend)}$$
$$y_t = a_0 + a_1 t + a_2 t^2 + \cdots + a_n t^n + \epsilon_t \qquad \text{(polynomial time trend)}$$

Either of these equations can be augmented with lagged values of the $\{y_t\}$ sequence and/or the $\{\epsilon_t\}$ sequence. However, models with stochastic trends are probabily less familiar to you. The remainder of this section develops time-series models exhibiting a stochastic trend.

The Random Walk Model

Let the current value of y_t be equal to last period's value plus a white-noise term:

$$y_t = y_{t-1} + \epsilon_t \qquad (\text{or } \Delta y_t = \epsilon_t).$$

The random walk model is clearly a special case of the AR(1) process $y_t = a_0 + a_1 y_{t-1} + \epsilon_t$ when $a_0 = 0$ and $a_1 = 1$. Suppose you were betting on the outcome of a coin toss, and a head added $1 to your wealth while a tail cost you $1. We could let $\epsilon_t = +\$1$ if a head appears and $-\$1$ in the event of a tail. Thus, your current wealth (y_t) equals last period's wealth (y_{t-1}) plus the realized value of ϵ_t. If you play again, your wealth in $t + 1$ is $y_{t+1} = y_t + \epsilon_{t+1}$.

If y_0 is a given initial condition, it is readily verified that the general solution to the first-order difference equation represented by the random walk model is

$$y_t = y_0 + \sum_{i=1}^{t} \epsilon_i$$

Taking expected values, we obtain $E(y_t) = E(y_{t-s}) = y_0$; thus, the mean of a random walk is a constant. However, all stochastic shocks have nondecaying effects on the $\{y_t\}$ sequence. Given the first t realizations of the $\{\epsilon_t\}$ process, the conditional mean of y_{t+1} is

$$E_t y_{t+1} = E_t(y_t + \epsilon_{t+1}) = y_t$$

Similarly, the conditional mean of y_{t+s} (for any $s > 0$) can be obtained from

$$y_{t+s} = y_t + \sum_{i=1}^{s} \epsilon_{t+i}$$

so that

$$E_t y_{t+s} = y_t + E_t \sum_{i=1}^{s} \epsilon_{t+i} = y_t$$

The conditional means for all values of y_{t+s} for all positive values of s are equal to y_t. However, an ϵ_t shock has a nondecaying effect on the $\{y_t\}$ sequence so that the $\{y_t\}$ sequence is permanently influenced by an ϵ_t shock. Notice that the variance is time-dependent. Recall that

$$\text{Var}(y_t) = \text{var}(\epsilon_t + \epsilon_{t-1} + \cdots + \epsilon_1) = t\sigma^2$$

so

$$\text{Var}(y_{t-s}) = \text{var}(\epsilon_{t-s} + \epsilon_{t-s-1} + \cdots + \epsilon_1) = (t - s)\sigma^2$$

Since the variance is not constant [i.e., $\text{var}(y_t) \neq \text{var}(y_{t-s})$], the random walk process is nonstationary. Moreover, as $t \to \infty$, the variance of y_t also approaches infinity. Thus, the random walk meanders without exhibiting any tendency to increase or decrease. It is also instructive to calculate the covariance of y_t and y_{t-s}. Since the mean is constant, we can form the covariance γ_{t-s} as

$$E[(y_t - y_0)(y_{t-s} - y_0)] = E[(\epsilon_t + \epsilon_{t-1} + \cdots + \epsilon_1)(\epsilon_{t-s} + \epsilon_{t-s-1} + \cdots + \epsilon_1)]$$
$$= E[(\epsilon_{t-s})^2 + (\epsilon_{t-s-1})^2 + \cdots + (\epsilon_1)^2]$$
$$= (t-s)\sigma^2$$

To form the correlation coefficient ρ_s, we can divide γ_{t-s} by the product of the standard deviation of y_t multiplied by the standard deviation of y_{t-s}. Thus, the correlation coefficient ρ_s is

$$\rho_s = (t-s)/\sqrt{(t-s)t}$$
$$= [(t-s)/t]^{0.5} \tag{3.35}$$

This result plays an important role in the detection of nonstationary series. For the first few autocorrelations, the sample size t will be large relative to the number of autocorrelations formed; for small values of s, the ratio $(t-s)/t$ is approximately equal to unity. However, as s increases, the values of ρ_s will decline. Hence, in using sample data, *the autocorrelation function for a random walk process will show a slight tendency to decay.* Thus, it will not be possible to use the ACF to distinguish between a unit root processes ($a_1 = 1$) and processes such that a_1 is close to unity. In the Box–Jenkins identification stage, a slowly decaying ACF or PACF can be an indication of nonstationarity.

Graph (a) in Figure 3.12 shows the time path of a simulated random walk process. First, 100 normally distributed random deviates were drawn from a theoretical distribution with a mean of zero and variance equal to unity. By setting $y_0 = 0$, each value of y_t ($t = 1, \ldots, 100$) was constructed by adding the random deviate to the value of y_{t-1}. As expected, the simulated series meanders without any tendency to revert to a long-run value. However, there does appear to be a slight positive trend in the simulated data. The reason for the upward trend is that the realized values of the deviates used in this small sample of 100 do not precisely conform to the theoretical distribution. This particular simulation happened to contain more positive values than negative values. The impression of a trend in the true data-generating process is false and serves as a reminder against relying solely on causal inspection.

The Forecast Function

Suppose you collected a sample of values y_0 through y_t and wanted to forecast future values of the data series. From the perspective of time period t, the optimal forecast of y_{t+s} is the mean value of y_{t+s} conditioned on the information available at t:

$$E_t y_{t+s} = y_t$$

Figure 3.12 Four nonstationary models. (a) Random walk model. (b) Random walk plus drift. (c) Random walk plus noise. (d) Local linear trend model.

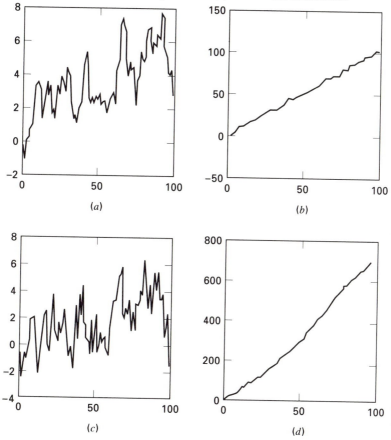

(a) (b) (c) (d)

Hence, the constant value of y_t is the unbiased estimator of all future values of y_{t+s} for all $s > 0$. To interpret, note that an ϵ_t shock has a permanent effect on y_t. The impact multiplier of ϵ_t on y_t (i.e., y_t/ϵ_t) is the same as the multiplier of ϵ_t on all y_{t+s}. This permanence is directly reflected in the forecasting function for y_{t+s}. In the time-series literature, such a sequence is said to have a **stochastic trend** since the expression $\Sigma\epsilon_i$ imparts a permanent, albeit random, change in the conditional mean of the series. Note that the random walk model seems to approximate the behavior of the exchange rates shown in Figure 3.7. The various exchange rate series have no particular tendency to increase or decrease over time; neither do they exhibit any tendency to revert to a given mean value.

The Random Walk plus Drift Model

Now let the change in y_t be partially deterministic and partly stochastic. The random walk plus drift model augments the random walk model by adding a constant term a_0:

$$y_t = y_{t-1} + a_0 + \epsilon_t \tag{3.36}$$

Given the initial condition y_0, the general solution for y_t is:

$$y_t = y_0 + a_0 t + \sum_{i=1}^{t} \epsilon_i \tag{3.37}$$

Here, the behavior of y_t is governed by two nonstationary components: a linear deterministic trend and the stochastic trend $\Sigma \epsilon_i$. If we take expectations, the mean of y_t is $y_0 + a_0 t$ and the mean of y_{t+s} is $E y_{t+s} = y_0 + a_0(t + s)$. To explain, the deterministic change in each realization of $\{y_t\}$ is a_0; after t periods, the cumulated change is $a_0 t$. In addition, there is the stochastic trend $\Sigma \epsilon_i$; each ϵ_i shock has a permanent effect on the mean of y_t. Notice that the first difference of the series is stationary; taking the first difference yields the stationary sequence $\Delta y_t = a_0 + \epsilon_t$.

Graph (b) of Figure 3.12 illustrates a simulated random walk plus drift model. The value of a_0 was set equal to unity and (3.37) simulated using the same 100 deviates used for the random walk model above. Clearly, the deterministic time trend dominates the time path of the series. In a very large sample, asymptotic theory suggests this will always be the case. However, you should not conclude that it is always easy to discern the difference between a random walk model and a model with drift. In a small sample, increasing the variance of $\{\epsilon_t\}$ or decreasing the absolute value of a_0 could cloud the long-run properties of the sequence. Notice that the pattern evident in the random walk plus drift model looks strikingly similar to many of the series—including the money supply and real GNP—shown in Figures 3.1 through 3.8.

The Forecast Function

Updating (3.37) by s periods yields

$$y_{t+s} = y_0 + a_0(t + s) + \sum_{i=1}^{t+s} \epsilon_i$$

$$= y_t + a_0 s + \sum_{i=1}^{s} \epsilon_{t+i}$$

Taking the conditional expectation of y_{t+s}, we get

$$E_t y_{t+s} = y_t + a_0 s$$

In contrast to the pure random walk model, the forecast function is not flat. The fact that the mean change in y_t is always the constant a_0 is reflected in the forecast. In addition to the given value of y_t, we project this deterministic change s times into the future. Thus, the model does not contain an irregular component; the random walk plus drift contains only a deterministic trend and stochastic trend.

The Random Walk plus Noise Model

In the random walk plus noise model, y_t is the sum of a stochastic trend and white-noise component. Formally, this third model is represented by

$$y_t = \mu_t + \eta_t \tag{3.38}$$

and

$$\mu_t = \mu_{t-1} + \epsilon_t \tag{3.39}$$

where $\{\eta_t\}$ is a white-noise process with variance $= \sigma_\eta^2$; and ϵ_t and η_{t-s} are independently distributed for all t and s [i.e., $E(\epsilon_t \eta_{t-s}) = 0$].

It is easy to verify that the $\{\mu_t\}$ sequence represents the stochastic trend. Given the initial condition for μ_0, the solution for μ_t is

$$\mu_t = \mu_0 + \sum_{i=1}^{t} \epsilon_i$$

Combining this expression with the noise term yields

$$y_t = \mu_0 + \sum_{i=1}^{t} \epsilon_i + \eta_t$$

Now recognize that in period zero, the value of y_0 is given by $y_0 = \mu_0 + \eta_0$, so that the solution for the random walk plus noise model can be written as

$$y_t = y_0 - \eta_0 + \sum_{i=1}^{t} \epsilon_i + \eta_t \tag{3.40}$$

The key properties of the random walk plus noise model are as follows:

1. The unconditional mean of the $\{y_t\}$ sequence is constant: $E y_t = y_0 - \eta_0$ and updating by s periods yields $E y_{t+s} = y_0 - \eta_0$. Notice that the successive ϵ_t shocks

have permanent effects on the $\{y_t\}$ sequence in that there is no decay factor on past values of ϵ_{t-i}. Hence, y_t has the stochastic trend μ_t.

2. The $\{y_t\}$ sequence has a pure noise component in that the $\{\eta_t\}$ sequence has only a temporary effect on the $\{y_t\}$ sequence. The current realization of η_t affects only y_t but not the subsequent values y_{t+s}.

3. The variance of $\{y_t\}$ is not constant: $\text{var}(y_t) = t\sigma^2 + \sigma_\eta^2$ and $\text{var}(y_{t-s}) = (t-s)\sigma^2 + \sigma_\eta^2$. As in the other models with a stochastic trend, the variance of y_t approaches infinity as t increases. The presence of the noise component means that the correlation coefficient between y_t and y_{t-s} is smaller than for the pure random walk model. Hence, the sample correlogram will exhibit even faster decay than in the pure random walk model. To derive this result, note that the covariance between y_t and y_{y-s} is

$$\text{Cov}(y_t, y_{t-s}) = E[(y_t - y_0 - \eta_0)(y_{t-s} - y_0 - \eta_0)]$$
$$= E[(\epsilon_1 + \epsilon_2 + \epsilon_3 + \cdots + \epsilon_t + \eta_t)(\epsilon_1 + \epsilon_2 + \epsilon_3 + \cdots + \epsilon_{t-s} + \eta_{t-s})]$$

Since $\{\epsilon_t\}$ and $\{\eta_t\}$ are independent white-noise sequences,

$$\text{Cov}(y_t, y_{t-s}) = (t-s)\sigma^2$$

Thus, the correlation coefficient ρ_s is

$$\rho_s = \frac{(t-s)\sigma^2}{\sqrt{(t\sigma^2 + \sigma_\eta^2)[(t-s)\sigma^2 + \sigma_\eta^2]}}$$

Comparison with (3.35)—that is ρ_s for the random walk model—verifies that the autocorrelations for the random walk plus noise model are always smaller for $\sigma_\eta^2 > 0$.

Consider graph (c) of Figure 3.12 that shows a random walk plus noise model. The series was simulated by setting $\eta_0 = 0$ and drawing a second 100 normally distributed random deviates to represent the η_t series. For each value of t, $\eta_t - \eta_{t-1}$ was added to the value of y_t calculated for the random walk model. If we compare parts (a) and (c) of the figure, it is seen that the two series track each other quite well. The random walk plus noise model could mimic the same set of macroeconomic variables as the random walk model. The effect of the "noise" component, $\{\eta_t\}$, is to increase the variance of $\{y_t\}$ without affecting its long-run behavior. After all, the random walk plus noise series is nothing more than the random walk model with a purely temporary component added.

The Forecast Function

To find the forecast function, update (3.40) by s periods to obtain

$$y_{t+s} = y_0 - \eta_0 + \sum_{i=1}^{t+s} \epsilon_i + \eta_{t+s}$$

$$= y_t - \eta_t + \sum_{i=1}^{s} \epsilon_{t+i} + \eta_{t+s}$$

Taking the conditional expectation, we get

$$E_t y_{t+s} = y_t - \eta_t$$

Thus, the random walk plus noise model contains both a trend and an irregular component. Certainly, η_t has only a temporary effect on y_t; the forecast of y_{t+s} is the current value y_t less the temporary component η_t. The permanent component of $\{y_t\}$ is the stochastic trend $\Sigma\epsilon_t$.

As an exercise, it is useful to show that the random walk plus noise model can also be written in the form

$$y_t = y_{t-1} + \epsilon_t + \eta_t - \eta_{t-1}$$

The proof is straightforward since (3.38) can be written in first differences as $\Delta y_t = \Delta\mu_t + \Delta\eta_t$. Given (3.39), $\Delta\mu_t = \epsilon_t$, so that $\Delta y_t = \epsilon_t + \Delta\eta_t$. Hence, the two forms are equivalent.

The General Trend plus Irregular Model

The random walk plus noise and random walk plus drift model are the building blocks of more complex time-series models. For example, the noise and drift components can easily be incorporated into a single model by modifying (3.39) such that the trend in y_t contains a deterministic and stochastic component. Specifically, replace (3.39) with

$$\mu_t = \mu_{t-1} + a_0 + \epsilon_t \tag{3.41}$$

where a_0 = a constant
$\{\epsilon_t\}$ = a white-noise process

Here, the trend μ_t contains the stochastic change ϵ_t and deterministic change a_0. To establish this point, use (3.37) to obtain the μ_t as

$$\mu_t = \mu_0 + a_0 t + \sum_{i=1}^{t} \epsilon_i$$

Now combine the deterministic and stochastic trends with the noise term to obtain

$$y_t = \mu_0 + a_0 t + \sum_{i=1}^{t} \epsilon_i + \eta_t \tag{3.42}$$

If we impose the initial condition $y_0 = \mu_0 + \eta_0$, the solution for y_t is

$$y_t = y_0 - \eta_0 + a_0 t + \sum_{i=1}^{t} \epsilon_i + \eta_t \tag{3.43}$$

Equations (3.38) and (3.41) are called the **trend plus noise model**; y_t is the sum of a deterministic trend, stochastic trend, and pure white-noise term. Of course, the noise sequence does not need to be a white-noise process. Let $A(L)$ be a polynomial in the lag operator L; it is possible to augment a random walk plus drift process with the stationary noise process $A(L)\eta_t$, so that the **general trend plus irregular model** is

$$y_t = \mu_0 + a_0 t + \sum_{i=1}^{t} \epsilon_i + A(L)\eta_t \tag{3.44}$$

The Local Linear Trend Model

The local linear trend model is built by combining several random walk plus noise processes. Let $\{\epsilon_t\}$, $\{\eta_t\}$, and $\{\delta_t\}$ be three mutually uncorrelated white-noise processes. The local linear trend model can be represented by

$$\begin{aligned} y_t &= \mu_t + \eta_t \\ \mu_t &= \mu_{t-1} + a_t + \epsilon_t \\ a_t &= a_{t-1} + \delta_t \end{aligned} \tag{3.45}$$

The local linear trend model consists of the noise term η_t plus the stochastic trend term μ_t. What is interesting about the model is that the *change in the trend* is a random walk plus noise: that is, $\Delta \mu_t$ is equal to the random walk term a_t plus the noise term ϵ_t. Since this is the most detailed model thus far, it is useful to show that the other processes are special cases of the local linear trend model. For example,

1. **The random walk plus noise:** If all values of the $\{a_t\}$ sequence are equal to zero, (3.45) is a random walk ($\mu_t = \mu_{t-1} + \epsilon_t$) plus noise ($\eta_t$). Let var($\delta$) = 0, so that $a_t = a_{t-1} = \cdots = a_0$. If $a_0 = 0$, $\mu_t = \mu_{t-1} + \epsilon_t$, so that y_t is the random walk μ_t plus the noise term η_t.

2. **The random walk plus drift:** Again, let var(δ) = 0, so that $a_t = a_{t-1} = \cdots = a_0$. Now if a_0 differs from zero, the trend is the random walk plus drift: $\mu_t = \mu_{t-1} + a_0 + \epsilon_t$. Thus, (3.45) becomes trend plus noise model. If we further restrict the model such that var(η) = 0, the model becomes the pure random walk plus drift model.

The solution for y_t can easily be found as follows. First, solve for a_t as

$$a_t = a_0 + \sum_{i=1}^{t} \delta_i$$

Next, use this solution to write μ_t as

$$\mu_t = \mu_{t-1} + a_0 + \sum_{i=1}^{t} \delta_i + \epsilon_t$$

so that

$$\mu_t = \mu_0 + \sum_{i=1}^{t} \epsilon_i + t(a_0 + \delta_1) + \delta_2(t-1) + \delta_3(t-2) + \cdots + \delta_t$$

Since $y_0 = \mu_0 + \eta_0$, the solution for y_t is

$$y_t = y_0 + (\eta_t - \eta_0) + \sum_{i=1}^{t} \epsilon_i + t(a_0 + \delta_1) + (t-1)\delta_2 + (t-2)\delta_3 + \cdots + \delta_t$$

Here, we can see the combined properties of all the other models. Each element in the $\{y_t\}$ sequence contains a deterministic trend, a stochastic trend, and an irregular term. The stochastic trend is $\Sigma\epsilon_i$ and the irregular term η_t. Of course, in a more general version of the model, the irregular term could be given by $A(L)\eta_t$. What is most interesting about the model is the form of the deterministic time trend. Rather than being deterministic, the *coefficient* on time depends on the current and past realizations of the $\{\delta_t\}$ sequence. If in period t, the realized value of the sum $a_0 + \delta_1 + \cdots + \delta_t$ happens to be positive, the coefficient of t will be positive. Of course, this sum can be positive for some values of t and negative for others. The simulated local linear trend model shown in graph (d) happens to have a sustained positive slope since there were more positive draws in the 100 values of $\{\delta_t\}$ than negative values.

The Forecast Function

If we update the solution for y_t by s periods, it is simple to demonstrate that

$$y_{t+s} = y_0 + (\eta_{t+s} - \eta_0) + \sum_{i=1}^{t+s} \epsilon_i + (t+s)(a_0 + \delta_1) + (t+s-1)\delta_2 + (t+s-2)\delta_3$$

$$+ \cdots + \delta_{t+s}$$

so

$$y_{t+s} = y_t + (\eta_{t+s} - \eta_t) + \sum_{i=1}^{s} \epsilon_{t+i} + s(a_0 + \delta_1 + \delta_2 + \cdots + \delta_t) + \sum_{i=1}^{s} (s+1-i)\delta_{t+i}$$

Taking conditional expectations yields

$$E_t y_{t+s} = (y_t - \eta_t) + s(a_0 + \delta_1 + \delta_2 + \cdots + \delta_t)$$

The forecast of y_{t+s} is the current value of y_t less the transitory component η_t plus s multiplied by the slope of the trend term in t.

9. REMOVING THE TREND

You have seen that a trend can have deterministic and stochastic components. The form of the trend has important implications for the appropriate transformation to attain a stationary series. The usual methods for eliminating the trend are **differencing** and **detrending**. Detrending entails regressing a variable on "time" and saving the residuals.[17] We have already examined an ARIMA (p, d, q) model in which the dth difference of a series is stationary. The aim of this section is to compare these two methods of eliminating the trend.

Differencing

First consider the solution for the random walk plus drift model:

$$y_t = y_0 + a_0 t + \sum_{i=1}^{t} \epsilon_i$$

Taking the first difference, we obtain $\Delta y_t = a_0 + \epsilon_t$. Clearly, the $\{\Delta y_t\}$ sequence—equal to a constant plus a white-noise disturbance—is stationary. Viewing Δy_t as the variable of interest, we have

$$E(\Delta y_t) = E(a_0 + \epsilon_t) = a_0$$
$$\text{Var}(\Delta y_t) \equiv E(\Delta y_t - a_0)^2 = E(\epsilon_t)^2 = \sigma^2$$

and

$$\text{Cov}(\Delta y_t, \Delta y_{t-s}) \equiv E[(\Delta y_t - a_0)(\Delta y_{t-s} - a_0)] = E(\epsilon_t \epsilon_{t-s}) = 0$$

Since the mean and variance are constants and the covariance between Δy_t and Δy_{t-s} depends solely on s, the $\{\Delta y_t\}$ sequence is stationary.

The random walk plus noise model is an interesting case study. In first differences, the model can be written as $\Delta y_t = \epsilon_t + \Delta\eta_t$. In this form, it is easy to show that Δy_t is stationary. Notice the following:

$$E(\Delta y_t) = E(\epsilon_t + \Delta\eta_t) = 0$$
$$\text{Var}(\Delta y_t) \equiv E(\Delta y_t)^2 = E[(\epsilon_t + \Delta\eta_t)^2]$$
$$= E[(\epsilon_t)^2 + 2\epsilon_t\Delta\eta_t + (\Delta\eta_t)^2]$$
$$= \sigma^2 + 2E(\epsilon_t\Delta\eta_t) + E[(\eta_t)^2 - 2\eta_t\eta_{t-1} + (\eta_{t-1})^2] = \sigma^2 + 2\sigma_\eta^2$$
$$\text{Cov}(\Delta y_t, \Delta y_{t-1}) = E[(\epsilon_t + \eta_t - \eta_{t-1})(\epsilon_{t-1} + \eta_{t-1} - \eta_{t-2})] = -\sigma_\eta^2$$

and

$$\text{Cov}(\Delta y_t, \Delta y_{t-s}) = E[(\epsilon_t + \eta_t - \eta_{t-1})(\epsilon_{t-s} + \eta_{t-s} - \eta_{t-s-1})] = 0 \qquad \text{for } s \geq 1$$

If we set $s = 1$, the correlation coefficient between Δy_t and Δy_{t-1} is

$$\rho(1) = \frac{\text{cov}(\Delta y_t, \Delta y_{t-1})}{\text{var}(\Delta y_t)} = -\sigma_\eta^2/(\sigma^2 + 2\sigma_\eta^2)$$

Examination reveals $-0.5 \leq \rho(1) \leq 0$ and that all other correlation coefficients are zero. Since the first difference of y_t acts exactly as an MA(1) process, the random walk plus noise model is ARIMA(0, 1, 1). Since adding a constant to a series has no effect on the correlogram, it additionally follows that the trend plus noise model of (3.43) also acts as an ARIMA(0, 1, 1) process.

The local linear trend model acts as an ARIMA(0, 2, 2) model. Taking the first and second difference of y_t in this model, we obtain

$$\Delta y_t = \Delta\mu_t + \Delta\eta_t$$
$$= a_t + \epsilon_t + \Delta\eta_t$$

so that

$$\Delta^2 y_t = \Delta a_t + \Delta\epsilon_t + \Delta^2\eta_t$$
$$= \delta_t + \Delta\epsilon_t + \Delta^2\eta_t$$

Since a_t itself is nonstationary, it is straightforward to show that the first difference of y_t is *not* stationary. Examining $\Delta^2 y_t$, we note

$$E(\Delta^2 y_t) = E(\delta_t + \Delta\epsilon_t + \Delta^2\eta_t) = 0$$

$$\mathrm{Var}(\Delta^2 y_t) = E(\delta_t + \Delta\epsilon_t + \Delta^2\eta_t)^2 = E[(\delta_t)^2 + (\Delta\epsilon_t)^2 + (\Delta^2\eta_t)^2 + \\ 2\delta_t\Delta\epsilon_t + 2\delta_t\Delta^2\eta_t + 2\Delta\epsilon_t\Delta^2\eta_t]$$

$$= \sigma_\delta^2 + 2\sigma^2 + 6\sigma_\eta^2$$

$$\mathrm{Cov}(\Delta^2 y_t, \Delta^2 y_{t-1}) = E[(\delta_t + \Delta\epsilon_t + \Delta^2\eta_t)(\delta_{t-1} + \Delta\epsilon_{t-1} + \Delta^2\eta_{t-1})]$$

$$= E[(\delta_t + \epsilon_t - \epsilon_{t-1} + \eta_t - 2\eta_{t-1} + \eta_{t-2}) \\ (\delta_{t-1} + \epsilon_{t-1} - \epsilon_{t-2} + \eta_{t-1} - 2\eta_{t-2} + \eta_{t-3})]$$

$$= -\sigma^2 - 4\sigma_\eta^2$$

$$\mathrm{Cov}(\Delta^2 y_t, \Delta^2 y_{t-2}) = E[(\delta_t + \Delta\epsilon_t + \Delta^2\eta_t)(\delta_{t-2} + \Delta\epsilon_{t-2} + \Delta^2\eta_{t-2})]$$

$$= E[(\delta_t + \epsilon_t - \epsilon_{t-1} + \eta_t - 2\eta_{t-1} + \eta_{t-2}) \\ (\delta_{t-2} + \epsilon_{t-2} - \epsilon_{t-3} + \eta_{t-2} - 2\eta_{t-3} + \eta_{t-4})]$$

$$= \sigma_\eta^2$$

Note that all other covariance terms are zero. Thus, the local linear trend model acts as an ARIMA(0, 2, 2). You should be able to show that the correlogram is such that $-2/3 \le \rho(1) \le 0$, $0 \le \rho(2) \le 1/6$ and all other values of $\rho(s)$ are zero.

Now consider a general class of ARIMA(p, d, q) models:

$$A(L)y_t = B(L)\epsilon_t \tag{3.46}$$

where $A(L)$ and $B(L)$ are polynomials of orders p and q in the lag operator L.[18]

First suppose that $A(L)$ has a single unit root and $B(L)$ has all roots outside the unit circle.[19] We can factor $A(L)$ into $(1 - L)A^*(L)$ where $A^*(L)$ is a polynomial of order $p - 1$. Since $A(L)$ has only one unit root, it follows that all roots of $A^*(L)$ are outside of the unit circle. Thus, we can write (3.46) as

$$(1 - L)A^*(L)\, y_t = B(L)\epsilon_t$$

Now define $y_t^* = \Delta y_t$, so that

$$A^*(L)y_t^* = B(L)\epsilon_t \tag{3.47}$$

The $\{y_t^*\}$ sequence is stationary since all roots of $A^*(L)$ lie outside the unit circle. The point is that the first difference of a unit root process is stationary. If $A(L)$ has two unit roots, the same argument can be used to show that the second difference of $\{y_t\}$ is stationary. The general point is that the dth difference of a process with d unit roots is stationary. An ARIMA($p, d,$ q) model has d unit roots; the dth difference of such a model is a stationary ARMA(p, q) process. If a series has d unit roots, it is said to be integrated of order d or simply I(d).

Detrending

We have shown that differencing can sometimes be used to transform a nonstationary model into a stationary model with an ARMA representation. This does *not* mean that all nonstationary models can be transformed into a well-behaved ARMA model by appropriate differencing. Consider, for example, a model that is the sum of a deterministic trend component and pure noise component:

$$y_t = y_0 + \alpha_1 t + \epsilon_t$$

The first difference of y_t is not well behaved since

$$\Delta y_t = \alpha_1 + \epsilon_t - \epsilon_{t-1}$$

Here, Δy_t is not *invertible* in the sense that Δy_t cannot be expressed in the form of an autoregressive process. Recall that the invertability of a stationary process requires that the MA component not have a unit root.

Instead, an appropriate way to transform this model is to estimate the regression equation $y_t = \alpha_0 + \alpha_1 t + \epsilon_t$. Subtracting the estimated values of y_t from the observed series yields estimated values of the $\{\epsilon_t\}$ series. More generally, a time series may have the polynomial trend

$$y_t = a_0 + \alpha_1 t + \alpha_2 t^2 + \alpha_3 t^3 + \cdots + \alpha_n t^n + e_t$$

where $\{e_t\}$ = a stationary process

Detrending is accomplished by regressing $\{y_t\}$ on a polynomial time trend. The appropriate degree of the polynomial can be determined by standard t-tests, F-tests, and/or using statistics such as the AIC or SBC. The common practice is to estimate the regression equation using the largest value of n deemed reasonable.

If the t-statistic for α_n is zero, consider a polynomial trend of order $n - 1$. Continue to pare down the order of the polynomial trend until a nonzero coefficient is found. F-tests can be used to determine whether group coefficients—say, α_{n-i} through α_n—are statistically different from zero. The AIC and SBC statistics can be used to reconfirm the appropriate degree of the polynomial.

The difference between the estimated/values of the $\{y_t\}$ sequence from the actual values yields an estimate of the stationary sequence $\{e_t\}$. The detrended process can then be modeled using traditional methods (such as ARMA estimation).

Difference Versus Trend Stationary Models

We have encountered two different types of nonstationary time-series models: those with a stochastic trend and those with a deterministic trend. The economic jargon is such that a **difference stationary** model (DS) can be transformed into a stationary model by differencing and a **trend stationary** model (TS) can be transformed into a stationary model by removing the deterministic trend. A serious problem is encountered when the inappropriate method is used to eliminate trend. We saw an example of the problem in attempting to difference the equation: $y_t = y_0 + \alpha_1 t + \epsilon_t$. Consider, a trend stationary process of the form

$$A(L)y_t = \alpha_0 + \alpha_1 t + e_t$$

where the characteristic roots of the polynomial $A(L)$ are all outside the unit circle and the expression e_t is allowed to have the MA form $e_t = B(L)\epsilon_t$. Subtracting an estimate of the deterministic time trend gives a stationary and invertible ARMA model. However, if we use the notation of (3.47), the first difference of such a model yields

$$A(L)y_t^* = \alpha_1 + (1 - L)B(L)\epsilon_t$$

First-differencing the TS process has introduced a noninvertible unit root process into the MA component of the model. Of course, the same problem is introduced into a model with a polynomial time trend.

In the same way, subtracting a deterministic time trend from a difference stationary process is also inappropriate. In the random walk plus drift model above, subtracting $y_0 + a_0 t$ from each observation does not result in a stationary series since the stochastic trend is not eliminated. More generally, incorporating a deterministic trend component in a regression when none exists results in a misspecification error if the process actually contains a unit root. You might be tempted to think it possible to estimate the deterministic trend from the data using a such regression. Unfortunately, all such coefficients are statistical artifacts in the presence of a nonstationary error term.

The Yen/Dollar Exchange Rate: An Example

The random walk shown in Figure 3.12 might fool a researcher into thinking the series is actually trend stationary. Instead of focusing on simulated data, consider the time path of the yen/dollar exchange rate illustrated in Figure 3.7. Overall, the yen rose by more than 60% during the 21-year period 1971 through 1991. Economic theory suggests no reason to expect the nominal yen/dollar rate to have a deterministic component; in fact, some versions of the efficient market hypothesis suggest that the yen/dollar rate must have a stochastic trend. However, it is interesting to consider the consequences of detrending the yen/dollar rate. If y_t denotes the yen/dollar exchange rate, regressing y_t on a constant and time yields

$$y_t = 0.8479 - 0.0064 \text{ time} + e_t$$
$$ (44.91) \quad (-14.16)$$

The t-statistics (shown in parentheses) indicate that the coefficients are highly significant. The residuals from this regression—the $\{e_t\}$ sequence—are the *de-*

trended values of the yen/dollar exchange rate. The top portion (a) of Figure 3.13 shows the ACF and PACF of the detrended exchange rate; as you can clearly see, the ACF does not die out after 16 quarters! Here, detrending the data does not result in a stationary series. The lower portion (b) of the figure shows the ACF and PACF of the logarithmic change in the yen/dollar rate. The single spike at lag 1 is suggestive of an AR(1) or a MA(1) model. The negative correlation coefficients at lags 5 and 15 do not suggest any particular seasonal patterns and may be spurious. With 70 usable observations, $2T^{-1/2} = 0.239$ is almost exactly equal to the PACF coefficient at lag 5. The results of two alternative estimations of the logarithmic change in the yen/dollar rate are shown in Table 3.1. For both models, the estimated intercept (a_0) is not statistically different from zero at conventional significance levels. The Q-statistics for autocorrelations up to 17 ($T/4 \approx 17$) show that as a group, all can be treated as being equal to zero. However, by a small margin, the SBC selects the MA(1) model. The critical point is that either of these models using differenced data will be vastly superior to a model of the detrended yen/dollar rate.

10. ARE THERE BUSINESS CYCLES?

Traditional business cycle research decomposed real macroeconomic variables into a deterministic secular trend, a cyclical, and an irregular component. The typical decomposition is illustrated by the hypothetical data in Figure 3.14. The secular trend, portrayed by the straight line, was deemed to be in the domain of growth theory. The slope of the trend line was thought to be determined by long-run factors such as technological growth, fertility, and educational attainment levels. One source of the deviations from trend occurs because of the wavelike motion of real economic activity called the **business cycle**. Although the actual period of the cycle was never thought to be as regular as that depicted in the figure, the periods of prosperity and recovery were regarded to be as inevitable as the tides. The goal of monetary and fiscal policy was to reduce the amplitude of the cycle (measured by distance ab). In terms of our previous discussion, the trend is the nonstationary component of growth and the cyclical and irregular components are stationary.

Table 3.1 **Alternative Estimates of the Yen/Dollar Exchange Rate**

	Estimates[a]	Q(17) Statistic[b]	SBC[c]
AR(1)	a_0: −0.0104 (0.0095) a_1: 0.3684 (0.1148)	$Q(17) = 19.06$ (0.3249)	−114.359
MA(1)	a_0: −0.0116 (0.0082) β_1: 0.3686 (0.1123)	$Q(17) = 19.22$ (0.2573)	−114.932

[a]Standard errors are in parentheses.
[b]$T/4$ is approximately 17.
[c]Since both models have the same number of parameters, both the AIC and SBC select the same model.

Figure 3.13

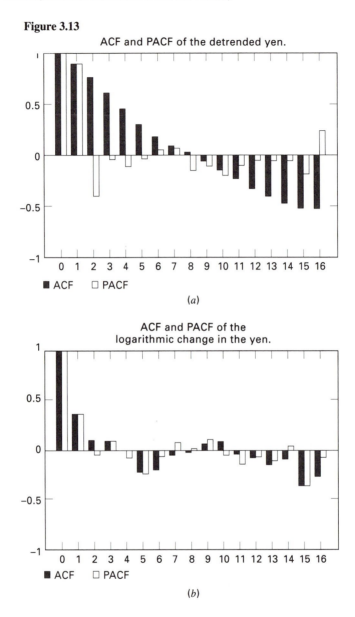

ACF and PACF of the detrended yen.

(a)

ACF and PACF of the logarithmic change in the yen.

(b)

Although there have been recessions and periods of high prosperity, the post–World War II experience taught us that business cycles do not have a regular period. Even so, there is a widespread belief that over the long run, macroeconomic variables grow at a constant trend rate and that any deviations from trend are eventually eliminated by the "invisible hand." The belief that trend is unchanging over time leads to the common practice of "detrending" macroeconomic data using a linear (or polynomial) deterministic regression equation.

This detrending procedure might entail estimating real GNP using the regression $y_t = \alpha_0 + \alpha_1 t + \epsilon_t$. The calculated residuals are the detrended data. Subtracting the trend from each observation might yield something similar to the lower graph of Figure 3.14; the deviations from the cycle are the irregular components of the series. If the residuals are actually stationary, the cyclical and irregular components can be fitted using traditional means.

The problem with this type of analysis is that the trend may not be deterministic. As we have seen, it is improper to subtract a deterministic trend from a difference stationary series. The economic significance of real macroeconomic variables being difference stationary, rather than trend stationary, is profound. If a variable is trend stationary, current economic shocks of any variety will not have any long-run effects on the series. Consider the forecast function from the trend stationary model

Figure 3.14   The business cycle?

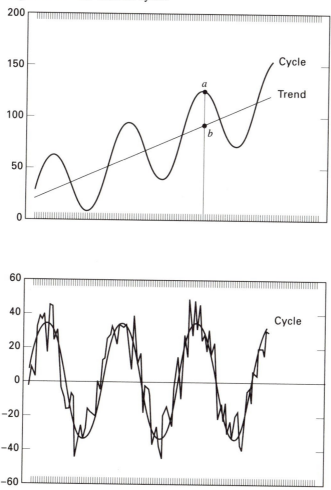

$y_t = \alpha_0 + \alpha_1 t + \epsilon_t$ above. If ϵ_t is a white-noise process, the forecast of y_{t+s} is $\alpha_0 + \alpha_1(t + s)$ for all s; neither current nor past events affect the very long-run forecast of the future y values. More important, given the values α_0 and α_1, the forecast error variance is constant. The forecast error for any s is always ϵ_{t+s}; hence, the forecast error variance for any s is $\mathrm{var}(\epsilon_{t+s})$. Even if $\{\epsilon_t\}$ is serially correlated, long-term forecasts will eventually depend only on α_0 and α_1, and the forecast horizon (s).

This is in stark contrast to the case in which the $\{y_t\}$ series has a stochastic trend. Consider the simple random walk plus noise model $y_t = \mu_t + \eta_t$, where $\mu_t = \mu_{t-1} + \epsilon_t$. Given the initial condition for y_t, we can solve for y_{t+s} as

$$y_{t+s} = y_t + \sum_{i=1}^{s} \epsilon_{t+i} + \eta_{t+s} - \eta_t$$

Notice that the forecast error variance becomes unbounded for long-term forecasts. The s-step ahead forecast of y_{t+s} is

$$E_t y_{t+s} = y_t - \eta_t$$

so that the s-step ahead forecast error variance is

$$\mathrm{Var}(y_{t+s} - E_t y_{t+s}) = \mathrm{var}\left(\sum_{i=1}^{s} \epsilon_{t+i} + \eta_{t+s} \right)$$

$$= s\sigma^2 + \sigma_\eta^2$$

As we forecast further into the future, the confidence interval surrounding our forecasts grows progressively larger. As $s \to \infty$, the variance of the forecast error becomes infinitely large.

Nelson and Plosser (1982) challenged the traditional view by demonstrating that important macroeconomic variables are DS rather than TS processes. They obtained time-series data for 13 important macroeconomic time series: real GNP, nominal GNP, industrial production, employment, unemployment rate, GNP deflator, consumer prices, wages, real wages, money stock, velocity, bond yields, and an index of common stock prices. The sample began as early as 1860 for consumer prices to as late as 1909 for GNP data and ended in 1970 for the entire series. Some of their findings are reported in Table 3.2. The first two columns report the first- and second-order autocorrelations of real and nominal GNP, industrial production, and the unemployment rate. Notice that the autocorrelations of the first three series are strongly indicative of a unit root process. Although $\rho(1)$ for the unemployment rate is 0.75, the second-order autocorrelation is less than 0.5.

First differences of the series yield the first- and second-order sample autocorrelations $r(1)$ and $r(2)$, respectively. Sample autocorrelations of the first differences are indicative of stationary processes. The evidence supports the claim that the data

Table 3.2   **Selected Autocorrelations from Nelson and Plosser**

	ρ(1)	ρ(2)	r(1)	r(2)	d(1)	d(2)
Real GNP	0.95	0.90	0.34	0.04	0.87	0.66
Nominal GNP	0.95	0.89	0.44	0.08	0.93	0.79
Industrial production	0.97	0.94	0.03	−0.11	0.84	0.67
Unemployment rate	0.75	0.47	0.09	−0.29	0.75	0.46

Notes: 1. Full details of the correlogram can be obtained from Nelson and Plosser (1982) who report the first six sample autocorrelations.
   2. Respectively, $\rho(i)$, $r(i)$, and $d(i)$ refer to the ith-order autocorrelation coefficient of each series, first difference of the series, and detrended values of the series.

are generated from DS processes. Nelson and Plosser point out that the positive autocorrelation of differenced real and nominal GNP at lag 1 only is suggestive of an MA(1) process. To further strengthen the argument for DS-generating processes, recall that differencing a TS process yields a noninvertible moving process. None of the differenced series reported by Nelson and Plosser appear to have a unit root in the MA terms.

The results from fitting a linear trend to the data and forming sample autocorrelations of the residuals are shown in the last two columns of the table. An interesting feature of the data is that the sample autocorrelations of the detrended data are reasonably high. This is consistent with the fact that detrending a DS series will not eliminate the nonstationarity. Notice that detrending the unemployment rate has *no effect* on the autocorrelations.

Rather than rely solely on an analysis of correlograms, it is possible to formally test whether a series is difference stationary. We examine such formal tests in the next chapter. The testing procedure is not as straightforward as it might seem. We cannot use the usual statistical techniques since classical procedures all presume that the data are stationary. For now, it suffices to say that Nelson and Plosser are not able to reject the null hypothesis that their data are DS. If this view is correct, macroeconomic variables do not grow at a smooth long-run rate. Some macroeconomic shocks are of a permanent nature; the effects of such shocks are never eliminated.

11. STOCHASTIC TRENDS AND UNIVARIATE DECOMPOSITIONS

Nelson and Plosser's (1982) findings suggest that many economic time series have a stochastic trend and an irregular component. Having observed a series, but not the individual components, is there any way to decompose the series into the constituent parts? Numerous economic theories suggest it is important to distinguish between temporary and permanent movements in a series. A sale (i.e., a temporary price decline) is designed to induce us to purchase now, rather than in the future. Labor economists argue that "hours supplied" is more responsive to a temporary wage increase than a permanent increase. The idea is that workers will temporarily substitute income for leisure time. Certainly, the modern theories of the consumption function that classify an individual's income into permanent and transitory components highlight the importance of such a decomposition.

Any such decomposition is straightforward if it is known that the trend in $\{y_t\}$ is purely deterministic. For example, a linear time trend induces a fixed change each and every period. This deterministic change can be subtracted from the actual change in y_t to obtain the change resulting from the irregular component. If, as in Section 9, there is a polynomial trend, simple detrending using OLS will yield the irregular component of the series.

A difficult conceptual issue arises if the trend is stochastic. For example, suppose you are asked to measure the current phase of the business cycle. If the trend in GNP is stochastic, how is it possible to tell if the GNP is above or below trend? The traditional measurement of a recession by consecutive quarterly declines in real GNP is not helpful. After all, if GNP has a trend component, a negative realization for the irregular component may be outweighed by the positive trend component.

If it is possible to decompose a sequence into its separate permanent and stationary components, the issue can be solved. To better understand the nature of stochastic trends, note that—in contrast to a deterministic trend—a stochastic trend increases *on average* by a fixed amount each period. For example, consider the random-walk plus drift model of (3.36):

$$y_t = y_{t-1} + a_0 + \epsilon_t$$

Since $E\epsilon_t = 0$, the *average* change in y_t is the deterministic constant a_0. Of course, in any period t, the actual change will differ from a_0 by the stochastic quantity ϵ_t. However, each sequential change in $\{y_t\}$ adds to its level, regardless of whether the change results from the deterministic or stochastic component. As we saw in (3.37), the random walk plus drift model has no irregular component; hence, it is a model of pure trend.

The idea that a random walk plus drift is a pure trend has proven especially useful in time-series analysis. Beveridge and Nelson (1981) show how to decompose any ARIMA(p, 1, q) model into the sum of a random walk plus drift and stationary component (i.e., the general trend plus irregular model). Before considering the general case, begin with the simple example of an ARIMA(0, 1, 2) model:

$$y_t = y_{t-1} + a_0 + \epsilon_t + \beta_1\epsilon_{t-1} + \beta_2\epsilon_{t-2} \tag{3.48}$$

If $\beta_1 = \beta_2 = 0$, (3.48) is nothing more than the pure random walk plus drift model. The introduction of the two moving average terms adds an irregular component to the $\{y_t\}$ sequence. The first step in understanding the Beveridge and Nelson (1981) procedure is to obtain the forecast function. For now, keep the issue simple by defining $e_t = \epsilon_t + \beta_1 \epsilon_{t-1} + \beta_2 \epsilon_{t-2}$, so that we can write $y_t = y_{t-1} + a_0 + e_t$. Given an initial condition for y_0, the general solution for y_t is[20]

$$y_t = a_0 t + y_0 + \sum_{i=1}^{t} e_i \tag{3.49}$$

Updating by s periods, we get

$$y_{t+s} = a_0 (t+s) + y_0 + \sum_{i=1}^{t+s} e_i \tag{3.50}$$

Substituting (3.49) into (3.50) so as to eliminate y_0 yields

$$y_{t+s} = a_0 s + y_t + \sum_{i=1}^{s} e_{t+i} \tag{3.51}$$

To express the solution for y_{t+s} in terms of $\{\epsilon_t\}$ rather than $\{e_t\}$, note that

$$\sum_{i=1}^{s} e_{t+i} = \sum_{i=1}^{s} \epsilon_{t+i} + \beta_1 \sum_{i=1}^{s} \epsilon_{t-1+i} + \beta_2 \sum_{i=1}^{s} \epsilon_{t-2+i} \tag{3.52}$$

so the solution for y_{t+s} can be written as

$$y_{t+s} = a_0 s + y_t + \sum_{i=1}^{s} \epsilon_{t+i} + \beta_1 \sum_{i=1}^{s} \epsilon_{t-1+i} + \beta_2 \sum_{i=1}^{s} \epsilon_{t-2+i} \tag{3.53}$$

Now consider the forecast of y_{t+s} for various values of s. Since all values of $E_t \epsilon_{t+i} = 0$ for $i > 0$, it follows that

$$E_t y_{t+1} = a_0 + y_t + \beta_1 \epsilon_t + \beta_2 \epsilon_{t-1}$$
$$E_t y_{t+2} = 2a_0 + y_t + (\beta_1 + \beta_2)\epsilon_t + \beta_2 \epsilon_{t-1}$$
$$\ldots$$
$$E_t y_{t+s} = sa_0 + y_t + (\beta_1 + \beta_2)\epsilon_t + \beta_2 \epsilon_{t-1} \tag{3.54}$$

Here, the forecasts for all $s > 1$ are equal to the expression $sa_0 + y_t + (\beta_1 + \beta_2)\epsilon_t + \beta_2 \epsilon_{t-1}$. Thus, the forecast function converges to a linear function of the forecast horizon s; the slope of the function equals a_0 and the level equals $y_t + (\beta_1 + \beta_2)\epsilon_t + \beta_2 \epsilon_{t-1}$. This stochastic level can be called the trend at t; in terms of our earlier notation, this trend is denoted by μ_t. This trend plus the deterministic value $a_0 s$ constitutes the forecast $E_t y_{t+s}$. There are several interesting points to note:

1. The trend is defined to be the conditional expectation of the limiting value of the forecast function. In lay terms, the trend is the "long-term" forecast. This forecast will differ at each period t as additional realizations of $\{\epsilon_t\}$ become available. At any period t, the irregular component of the series is the difference between y_t and the trend μ_t. Hence, the irregular component of the series is

$$y_t - \mu_t = -(\beta_1 + \beta_2)\epsilon_t - \beta_2\epsilon_{t-1} \tag{3.55}$$

At any point in time, the trend and irregular components are perfectly correlated (the correlation coefficient being -1).

2. By definition, ϵ_t is the innovation in y_t and the variance of the innovation is σ^2. Since the change in the trend resulting from a change in ϵ_t is $1 + \beta_1 + \beta_2$, the variance of the innovation in the trend can exceed the variance of y_t itself. If $(1 + \beta_1 + \beta_2)^2 > 1$, the trend is more volatile than y_t since the negative correlation between the trend and irregular components acts to smooth the $\{y_t\}$ sequence.

3. The trend is a random walk plus drift. Denote the trend at t by μ_t, so that $\mu_t = y_t + (\beta_1 + \beta_2)\epsilon_t + \beta_2\epsilon_{t-1}$. Hence,

$$\begin{aligned}
\Delta\mu_t &= \Delta y_t + (\beta_1 + \beta_2)\Delta\epsilon_t + \beta_2\Delta\epsilon_{t-1} \\
&= (y_t - y_{t-1}) + (\beta_1 + \beta_2)\epsilon_t - \beta_1\epsilon_{t-1} - \beta_2\epsilon_{t-2}
\end{aligned}$$

Since $y_t - y_{t-1} = a_0 + \epsilon_t + \beta_1\epsilon_{t-1} + \beta_2\epsilon_{t-2}$,

$$\Delta\mu_t = a_0 + (1 + \beta_1 + \beta_2)\epsilon_t$$

Thus, $\mu_t = \mu_{t-1} + a_0 + (1 + \beta_1 + \beta_2)\epsilon_t$, so that the trend at t is composed of the drift term a_0 plus the white-noise innovation $(1 + \beta_1 + \beta_2)\epsilon_t$.

Beveridge and Nelson show how to recover the trend and irregular components from the data. In the example at hand, estimate the $\{y_t\}$ series using Box–Jenkins techniques. After the data are differenced, an appropriately identified and estimated ARMA model will yield high-quality estimates of a_0, β_1, and β_2. Next, obtain ϵ_t and ϵ_{t-1} as the one-step ahead forecast errors of y_t and y_{t-1}, respectively. To obtain these values, use the estimated ARMA model to make in-sample forecasts of each observation of y_{t-1} and y_t. The resulting forecast errors become ϵ_t and ϵ_{t-1}. Combining the estimated values of β_1, β_2, ϵ_t, and ϵ_{t-1} as in (3.55) yields the irregular component. Repeating for each value of t yields the entire irregular sequence. From (3.55), this irregular component is y_t less the trend; hence, the permanent component can be obtained directly.

The General ARIMA(p, 1, q) Model

The first-difference of any ARIMA(p, 1, q) series has the stationary infinite-order moving average representation:

$$y_t - y_{t-1} = a_0 + \epsilon_t + \beta_1 \epsilon_{t-1} + \beta_2 \epsilon_{t-2} + \cdots$$

As in the earlier example, it is useful to define $e_t = \epsilon_t + \beta_1 \epsilon_{t-1} + \beta_2 \epsilon_{t-2} + \beta_3 \epsilon_{t-3} + \cdots$, so that it is possible to write the solution for y_{t+s} in the same form as (3.51):

$$y_{t+s} = y_t + a_0 s + \sum_{i=1}^{s} e_{t+i}$$

The next step is to express the $\{e_t\}$ sequence in terms of the various values of the $\{\epsilon_t\}$ sequence. In this general case, (3.52) becomes

$$\sum_{i=1}^{s} e_{t+i} = \sum_{i=1}^{s} \epsilon_{t+i} + \beta_1 \sum_{i=1}^{s} \epsilon_{t-1+i} + \beta_2 \sum_{i=1}^{s} \epsilon_{t-2+i} + \beta_3 \sum_{i=1}^{s} \epsilon_{t-3+i} + \cdots \quad (3.56)$$

Since $E_t \epsilon_{t+i} = 0$, it follows that the forecast function can be written as

$$E_t y_{t+s} = y_t + a_0 s + \left(\sum_{i=1}^{s} \beta_i \right) \epsilon_t + \left(\sum_{i=2}^{s+1} \beta_i \right) \epsilon_{t-1} + \left(\sum_{i=3}^{s+2} \beta_i \right) \epsilon_{t-2} + \cdots \quad (3.57)$$

Now, to find the *stochastic* trend, take the limiting value of the forecast $E_t(y_{t+s} - a_0 s)$ as s becomes infinitely large. As such, the stochastic trend is[21]

$$y_t + \left(\sum_{i=1}^{\infty} \beta_i \right) \epsilon_t + \left(\sum_{i=2}^{\infty} \beta_i \right) \epsilon_{t-1} + \left(\sum_{i=3}^{\infty} \beta_i \right) \epsilon_{t-2} + \cdots$$

The key to operationalizing the decomposition is to recognize that y_{t+s} can be written as

$$y_{t+s} = \Delta y_{t+s} + \Delta y_{t+s-1} + \Delta y_{t+s-2} + \cdots + \Delta y_{t+1} + y_t$$

As such, the trend can be always be written as the current value of y_t plus the sum of all the forecasted changes in the sequence. If we abstract from $a_0 s$, the stochastic portion of the trend is

$$\text{Lim } E_t y_{t+s} = \lim_{s \to \infty} E_t [(y_{t+s} - y_{t+s-1}) + (y_{t+s-1} - y_{t+s-2}) + \cdots$$

$$+ (y_{t+2} - y_{t+1}) + (y_{t+1} - y_t)] + y_t$$

$$= \lim_{s \to \infty} E_t (\Delta y_{t+s} + \Delta y_{t+s-1} + \cdots + \Delta y_{t+2} + \Delta y_{t+1}) + y_t \qquad (3.58)$$

The useful feature of (3.58) is that the Box–Jenkins method allows you to calculate each value of $E_t \Delta y_{t+s}$. For each observation in your data set, find all s-step ahead forecasts and construct the sum given by (3.58). Since the irregular component is y_t minus the sum of the deterministic and stochastic trends, the irregular component can be constructed as

$$y_t - \lim_{s \to \infty} (E_t y_{t+s} - a_0 s) = -\lim_{s \to \infty} E_t (\Delta y_{t+s} + \Delta y_{t+s-1} \cdots + \Delta y_{t+2} + \Delta y_{t+1}) - s a_0$$

Thus, to use the Beveridge and Nelson (1981) technique:

STEP 1: Estimate the first difference of the series using the Box–Jenkins technique. Select the best-fitting ARMA(p, q) model of the $\{\Delta y_t\}$ sequence.

STEP 2: Using the best-fitting ARMA model, for each time period $t = 1, \ldots, T$, find the one-step ahead, two-step ahead, $\ldots$, s-step ahead forecasts: that is, find $E_t \Delta y_{t+s}$ for each value of t and s. For each value of t, use these forecasted values to construct the sums: $E_t (\Delta y_{t+s} + \Delta y_{t+s-1} + \cdots + \Delta y_{t+1}) + y_t$. In practice, it is necessary to find a reasonable approximation to (3.58); in their own work, Beveridge and Nelson let $s = 100$. For example, for the first usable observation (i.e., $t = 1$), find the sum:

$$\mu_1 = E_1 (\Delta y_{101} + \Delta y_{100} + \cdots + \Delta y_2) + y_1$$

The value of y_1 plus the sum of these forecasted changes equals $E_1 y_{101}$; the stochastic portion of trend in period 1 is $E_1 y_{101} - a_0 s$ and the deterministic portion $a_0 s$. Similarly, for $t = 2$, construct

$$\mu_2 = E_2 (\Delta y_{102} + \Delta y_{101} + \cdots + \Delta y_3) + y_2$$

If there are T observations in your data set, the trend component for the last period is

$$\mu_T = E_T (\Delta y_{T+100} + \Delta y_{T+99} + \cdots + \Delta y_{T+1}) + y_T$$

The entire sequence of constructed trends (i.e., $\mu_1, \mu_2, \ldots, \mu_T$) constitutes the $\{\mu_t\}$ sequence.

STEP 3: Form the irregular component at t by subtracting the stochastic portion of the trend at t from the value of y_t. Thus, for each observation t, the irregular component is $-E_t(\Delta y_{t+100} + \Delta y_{t+99} + \cdots + \Delta y_{t+1})$.

Note that for many series, the value of s can be quite small. For example, in the ARIMA(0, 1, 2) model of (3.58), the value of s can be set equal to 2 since all forecasts for $s > 2$ are equal to zero. If the ARMA model that is estimated in Step 1 has slowly decaying autoregressive components, the value of s should be large enough so that the s-step ahead forecasts converge to the deterministic change a_0.

An Example

In Section 9, the natural log of the yen was estimated as the ARIMA(0, 1, 1) process:

$$\Delta y_t = -0.0116 + (1 + 0.3686L)\epsilon_t$$

where Δy_t = the logarithmic change in the yen/dollar exchange rate

Step 2 requires that for each observation, we form the one-step through s-step ahead forecasts. For this model, the mechanics are trivial since for each period t, the one-step forecast is

$$E_t \Delta y_{t+1} = -0.0116 + 0.3686\epsilon_t$$

and all other s-step ahead forecasts are -0.0116.

Thus, for each observation t, the summation $E_t(\Delta y_{t+100} + \Delta y_{t+99} + \cdots + \Delta y_{t+1})$ is equal to $-100(0.0116) + 0.3686\epsilon_t$. For example, for 1973:Q2 (the first usable observation in the sample), the *stochastic* portion of the trend is $y_{1973:Q2} + 0.3686\epsilon_{1973:Q2}$ and the temporary portion of $y_{1973:Q2}$ is $-0.3686\epsilon_{1973:Q2}$. Repeating for each point in the data set yields the irregular and permanent components of the sequence. Figure 3.15 shows the temporary and the permanent portions of the series. As you can clearly see, the trend dominates the movements in the irregular component. Hence, nearly all changes in the yen are permanent changes.

The estimated ARIMA(0, 1, 1) model is the special case of (3.48), in which β_2 is set equal to zero. As such, you should be able to write the equivalent of (3.49) to (3.55) for the yen/dollar exchange rate.

An Alternative Decomposition

The Beveridge and Nelson (1981) decomposition has proven especially useful in that it provides a straightforward method to decompose any ARIMA(p, 1, q) process into a temporary and permanent component. However, it is important to note that *the Beveridge and Nelson decomposition is not unique.* Equations (3.54) and (3.55) provide an example in which the Beveridge and Nelson decomposition forces the innovation in the trend and stationary components to be perfectly correlated.

Figure 3.15 Decomposition of the yen/dollar exchange rate.

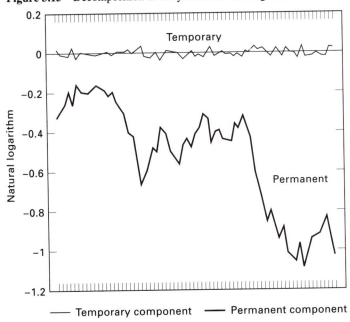

— Temporary component   — Permanent component

In fact, this result applies to the more general ARIMA(p, 1, q) model. Obtaining the irregular as the difference between y_t and its trend forces the correlation coefficient between the innovations to equal -1. However, there is no reason to constrain the two innovations in the two components to be perfectly correlated. To illustrate the point using a specific example, consider the trend plus noise model of (3.41):

$$y_t = \mu_t + \eta_t \qquad (3.59)$$
$$\mu_t = a_0 + \mu_{t-1} + \epsilon_t \qquad (3.60)$$

where $E\epsilon_t\eta_t = 0$

To derive the forecast function, update (3.43) by s periods to obtain

$$y_{t+s} = y_0 - \eta_0 + a_0(t+s) + \sum_{i=1}^{t+s} \epsilon_i + \eta_{t+s}$$

or

$$y_{t+s} = y_t + a_0 s + \sum_{i=1}^{s} \epsilon_{t+i} + \eta_{t+s} - \eta_t$$

The forecast function for all $s > 0$ is such that $E_t y_{t+s} = y_t + a_0 s - \eta_t$; hence, the stochastic level is $y_t - \eta_t$. Thus, the stochastic trend at t is $y_t - \eta_t = \mu_t$, so that the irregular component is η_t. The trend and irregular components are uncorrelated since $E(y_t - \eta_t)\eta_t = E\mu_t\eta_t = 0$. Thus, the Beveridge and Nelson methodology would incorrectly identify the trend and irregular since it would force the two innovations to be perfectly correlated.

Now consider the correct way to identify the two components in (3.59) and (3.60). In Section 9, this trend plus noise model was shown to have an equivalent ARIMA(0, 1, 1) representation such that

$$E\Delta y_t = 0; \quad \mathrm{var}(\Delta y_t) = \sigma^2 + 2\sigma_\eta^2, \quad \text{and } \mathrm{cov}(\Delta y_t, \Delta y_{t-1}) = -\sigma_\eta^2 \quad (3.61)$$

Hence, it is possible to represent (3.59) and (3.60) as the MA(1) process:

$$\Delta y_t = a_0 + e_t + \beta_1 e_{t-1} \quad (3.62)$$

where $e_t = $ an independent white-noise disturbance.

The notation e_t is designed to indicate that shocks to Δy_t come from two sources: ϵ_t and η_t. The problem is to decompose the estimated values of $\{e_t\}$ into these two source components.

In this instance, it is possible to recover, or *identify*, the individual $\{\epsilon_t\}$ and $\{\eta_t\}$ shocks from the estimation of (3.62). The appropriate use of the Box–Jenkins methodology will yield estimates of a_0, β_1 and the elements of the $\{e_t\}$ sequence. If we use these estimates, it is possible to form

$$\mathrm{Var}(\Delta y_t) = \mathrm{var}(e_t + \beta_1 e_{t-1}) = (1 + \beta_1)^2 \, \mathrm{var}(e_t)$$

and

$$\mathrm{Cov}(\Delta y_t, \Delta y_{t-1}) = \beta_1 \, \mathrm{var}(e_t)$$

However, these estimates of the variance and covariance are not arbitrary; for (3.62) to satisfy the restrictions of (3.61), it must be the case that

$$(1 + \beta_1)^2 \, \mathrm{var}(e_t) = \sigma^2 + 2\sigma_\eta^2$$

and

$$\beta_1 \, \mathrm{var}(e_t) = -\sigma_\eta^2$$

Now that we have estimated β_1 and $\mathrm{var}(e_t)$, it is possible to recover σ^2 and σ_η^2 from the data. The individual values of the $\{\epsilon_t\}$ and $\{\eta_t\}$ sequences can be recovered as well. From the forecast function, $E_t y_{t+1} = y_t + a_0 - \eta_t$. Hence, it is possible to use one-step ahead forecasts from (3.62) to find $E_t\Delta y_{t+1} = a_0 + \beta_1 e_t$, so that $E_t y_{t+1} = y_t + a_0 + \beta_1 e_t$. Since the two forecasts must be equivalent, it follows that

$$\beta_1 e_t = -\eta_t$$

Thus, the estimated values of $\beta_1 e_t$ can be used to identify the entire $\{\eta_t\}$ sequence. Given $\{e_t\}$ and $\{\eta_t\}$, the values of $\{\epsilon_t\}$ can be obtained from $\Delta y_t = a_0 + \epsilon_t + \Delta\eta_t$. For each value of t, form $\epsilon_t = \Delta y_t - a_0 - \Delta\eta_t$ using the known values of Δy_t and the estimated values of a_0 and $\Delta\eta_t$.

The point is that it is possible to decompose a series such that the correlation between the trend and irregular components is zero. The example illustrates an especially important point. To decompose a series into a random walk plus drift and stationary irregular component, it is necessary to specify the correlation coefficient between innovations in the trend and irregular components. We have seen two ways to decompose an ARIMA(0, 1, 1) model. In terms of (3.59) and (3.60), the Beveridge and Nelson technique adds the restriction that

$$E\epsilon_t\eta_t/\sigma\sigma_\eta = 1$$

so that the innovations are perfectly correlated, while the second decomposition adds the restriction:

$$E\epsilon_t\eta_t = 0$$

In fact, the correlation coefficient between the two components can be any number in the interval -1 to $+1$. Without the extra restriction concerning the correlation between the innovations, the trend and stationary components cannot be identified; in a sense, we are an equation short. This result carries over to more complicated models since it is always necessary to "cleave" or "partition" the contemporaneous movement of a series into its two constituent parts. The problem is important because economic theory does not always provide the relationship between the two innovations. However, *without a priori knowledge of the relationship between innovations in the trend and stationary components, the decomposition of a series into a random walk plus drift and a stationary component is not unique.*

What if ϵ_t and η_t are uncorrelated, but you incorrectly use a Beveridge and Nelson (1981) decomposition to obtain the temporary and permanent components? Clearly, the in-sample forecasts are invariant to the form of the decomposition. Equation (3.58) has an ARIMA(0, 1, 1) representation that you should properly capture using Step 1 of the Beveridge and Nelson method. As such, there is no way for you to determine that the assumption of perfectly correlated innovations is incorrect. The issue has nothing to do with the correct form of the ARIMA model; rather, the problem is the way in which the innovations in the trend and irregular components are partitioned.

What will the researcher incorrectly partitioning the variances find? Using a Beveridge and Nelson decomposition for an ARIMA(0, 1, 1) model—see (3.48) and (3.54) with $\beta_2 = 0$—the researcher will set the irregular component equal to $-\beta_1$ multiplied by the entire innovation in y_t (i.e., $\epsilon_t + \eta_t$). If, in fact, the innovations are uncorrelated, the actual value of the irregular at t is η_t. The dilemma is that there is no way to identify the "true" model using sample data.

Watson (1986) decomposes the logarithm of GNP under the two alternative assumptions concerning the innovations in the trend and irregular. Using a Beveridge and Nelson decomposition, he estimates the ARIMA(1, 1, 0) model (with standard errors in parentheses):

$$\Delta y_t = 0.005 + 0.406\Delta y_{t-1} + \epsilon_t, \qquad \sigma = 0.0103$$
$$\quad (0.001) \quad (0.077)$$

Assuming that innovations in the trend and irregular components are uncorrelated, Watson estimates $y_t = \mu_t + A(L)\eta_t$:[22]

$$\Delta\mu_t = 0.008 + \epsilon_t, \qquad \sigma = 0.0057$$
$$\quad (0.001)$$
$$A(L)\eta_t = (1 - 1.501L + 0.577L^2)\eta_t, \qquad \sigma_\eta = 0.0076$$
$$\quad (0.121) \qquad (0.125)$$

The short-term forecasts of the two models are quite similar. The standard-error of the one-step ahead forecast of this second model is slightly smaller than that of the first: $(\sigma^2 + \sigma_\eta^2)^{1/2} \cong 0.0095$ is slightly smaller than 0.0103. However, the long-run properties of the two models are quite different. For example, writing $\Delta y_t = (0.005 + \epsilon_t)/(1 - 0.406L)$ yields the impulse response function using the Beveridge and Nelson decomposition. The sum of the coefficients for this impulse response function is 1.68. Hence, a one-unit innovation will eventually increase log GNP by a full 1.68 units. Since all coefficients are positive, following the initial shock, y_t steadily increases to its new level. In contrast, the second model acts as an ARIMA(0, 1, 2) such that the sum of the impulse response coefficients is only 0.57. All coefficients beginning with lag 4 are negative. As such, a one-unit innovation in y_t has a larger effect in the short run than the long run.

SUMMARY AND CONCLUSIONS

Many economic time series exhibit periods of volatility. Conditionally heteroskedastic models (ARCH or GARCH) allow the conditional variance of a series to depend on the past realizations of the error process. A large realization of the current period's disturbance increases the conditional variance in subsequent periods. For a stable process, the conditional variance will eventually decay to the long-run (unconditional) variance. As such, ARCH and GARCH models can capture periods of turbulence and tranquility. The basic GARCH model has been extended by Engle and Bollerslev (1986) to allow for a unit root in the conditional variance.

Such an integrated GARCH (IGARCH) procss allows for shocks to have a permanent effect on the conditional variance.

Conditional variance is a measure of risk. ARCH and GARCH effects have been included in a regression framework to test hypotheses involving risk-averse agents. For example, if producers are risk-averse, conditional price variability will affect product supply. Producers may reduce their exposure by withdrawing from the market in periods of substantial risk. Similarly, asset prices should be negatively related to their conditional volatility. Such ARCH effects in the mean of a series (ARCH-M) are a natural implication of asset-pricing models. The basic GARCH model has been extended to allow the conditional variance to have a unit root. This integrated GARCH, or IGARCH, process is discussed in Engle and Bollerslev (1986).

Nonstationarity due to a time-dependent mean and/or variance is another common feature of economic time series. The trend in a series can contain both stochastic and deterministic components. Differencing can remove a stochastic trend and "detrending" can eliminate a deterministic trend. However, it is inappropriate to difference a trend stationary series and detrend a series containing a stochastic trend. The resultant irregular component of the series can be estimated using Box–Jenkins techniques.

In contrast to traditional theory, the concensus view is that most macroeconomic time series contain a stochastic trend. Decomposing real GNP into its permanent and temporary components, as in Beveridge and Nelson (1981), indicates that innovations in the stochastic trend account for a sizable proportion of the period-to-period movements. However, the Beveridge and Nelson decomposition is not unique in that it forces the correlation coefficient between innovations in the trend and irregular components to be unity. Some of the issues are considered in the appendix to this chapter. In a very technical paper, Quah (1992) takes the issue one step further: He proves that the random walk plus drift model is not a unique form for the trend. In Chapter 5, you will be shown a multivariate technique that allows for a unique decomposition of a series into its temporary and permanent components.

QUESTIONS AND EXERCISES

1. Consider the ARCH-M model represented by Equations (3.30) to (3.32). Recall that $\{\epsilon_t\}$ is a white-noise disturbance; for simplicity, let $E\epsilon_t^2 = E\epsilon_{t-1}^2 = \cdots = 1$.

   A. Find the unconditional mean Ey_t. How does a change in δ affect the mean? Using the example of Section 6, show that changing β and δ from $(-4, 4)$ to $(-1, 1)$ preserves the mean of the $\{y_t\}$ sequence.

   B. Show that the unconditional variance of y_t when $h_t = \alpha_0 + \alpha_1 \epsilon_{t-1}^2$ does not depend on β, δ, or α_0.

2. Suppose that the $\{\epsilon_t\}$ sequence is generated by the ARCH(q) process represented by (3.8)

$$\epsilon_t = v_t(\alpha_0 + \alpha_1\epsilon_{t-1}^2 + \cdots + \alpha_q\epsilon_{t-q}^2)^{1/2}$$

Show that the conditional expectation $E_{t-1}\epsilon_t^2$ has the same form as the conditional expectation of (3.1).

3. Bollerslev (1986) proves that the ACF of the squared residuals resulting from the GARCH(p, q) process represented by (3.9) acts as an ARMA(m, p) process, where $m = \max(p, q)$. You are to illustrate this result using the examples below.

A. Consider the GARCH(1, 2) process $h_t = \alpha_0 + \alpha_1\epsilon_{t-1}^2 + \alpha_2\epsilon_{t-2}^2 + \beta_1 h_{t-1}$. Add the expression $(\epsilon_t^2 - h_t)$ to each side, so that

$$\epsilon_t^2 = \alpha_0 + \alpha_1\epsilon_{t-1}^2 + \alpha_2\epsilon_{t-2}^2 + \beta_1 h_{t-1} + (\epsilon_t^2 - h_t)$$
$$= \alpha_0 + (\alpha_1 + \beta_1)\epsilon_{t-1}^2 + \alpha_2\epsilon_{t-2}^2 - \beta_1(\epsilon_{t-1}^2 - h_{t-1}) + (\epsilon_t^2 - h_t)$$

Define $\eta_t = (\epsilon_t^2 - h_t)$, so that

$$\epsilon_t^2 = \alpha_0 + (\alpha_1 + \beta_1)\epsilon_{t-1}^2 + \alpha_2\epsilon_{t-2}^2 - \beta_1\eta_{t-1} + \eta_t$$

Show that:

  i. η_t is serially uncorrelated.

  ii. The $\{\epsilon_t^2\}$ sequence acts as an ARMA(2, 1) process.

B. Consider the GARCH(2, 1) process $h_t = \alpha_0 + \alpha_1\epsilon_{t-1}^2 + \beta_1 h_{t-1} + \beta_2 h_{t-2}$. Show that it is possible to add η_t to each side so as to obtain

$$\epsilon_t^2 = \alpha_0 + \alpha_1\epsilon_{t-1}^2 + \beta_1 h_{t-1} + \eta_t + \beta_2 h_{t-2}$$

Show that adding and subtracting the terms $\beta_1\eta_{t-1}$ and $\beta_2\eta_{t-2}$ to the right-hand side of this equation yield an ARCH(2, 2) process.

C. Provide an intuitive explanation of the statement: "The Lagrange multiplier test for ARCH errors cannot be used to test the null of white-noise squared residuals against an alternative of a specific GARCH(p, q) process."

D. Sketch the proof of the general statement that the ACF of the squared residuals resulting from the GARCH(p, q) process represented by (3.9) acts as an ARMA(m, p) process, where $m = \max(p, q)$.

4. Given an initial condition for y_0, find and interpret the forecast function for each of the following models:

A. $y_t = y_{t-1} + \epsilon_t + 0.5\epsilon_{t-1}$ B. $y_t = 1.1y_{t-1} + \epsilon_t$

C. $y_t = y_{t-1} + 1 + \epsilon_t$ D. $y_t = y_{t-1} + t + \epsilon_t$

E. $y_t = \mu_t + \eta_t + 0.5\eta_{t-1}$, where $\mu_t = \mu_{t-1} + \epsilon_t$

F. $y_t = \mu_t + \eta_t + 0.5\eta_{t-1}$, where $\mu_t = 0.5 + \mu_{t-1} + \epsilon_t$

G. How can you make the models of parts B and D stationary?

H. Does model E have an ARIMA(p, 1, q) representation?

5. Let $y_0 = 0$ and the first five realizations of the $\{\epsilon_t\}$ sequence be (1, −1, −2, 1, 1). Plot each of the following sequences:

$$\text{Model 1:} \quad y_t = 0.5y_{t-1} + \epsilon_t$$
$$\text{Model 2:} \quad y_t = \epsilon_t - \epsilon_{t-1}^2$$
$$\text{Model 3:} \quad y_t = 0.5y_{t-1} + \epsilon_t - \epsilon_{t-1}^2$$

A. How does the ARCH-M specification affect the behavior of the $\{y_t\}$ sequence? What is the influence of the autoregressive term in model 3?

B. For each of the three models, calculate the sample mean and variance of $\{y_t\}$.

6. The file labeled ARCH.WK1 contains the 100 realizations of the simulated $\{y_t\}$ sequence used to create the lower right-hand graph of Figure 3.9. Recall that this series was simulated as $y_t = 0.9y_{t-1} + \epsilon_t$, where ϵ_t is the ARCH(1) error process $\epsilon_t = v_t(1 + 0.8\epsilon_{t-1})^{1/2}$. You should find that the series has a mean of 0.263369480, a standard deviation of 4.89409139 with minimum and maximum values of −10.8 and 15.15, respectively.

A. Estimate the series using OLS and save the residuals. You should obtain

$$y_t = 0.9444053245y_{t-1} + \epsilon_t$$

The t-statistic for a_1 is 26.50647.
Note that the estimated value of a_1 differs from the theoretical value of 0.9. This is due to nothing more than sampling error; the simulated values of $\{v_t\}$ do not precisely conform to the theoretical distribution. However, can you provide an intuitive explanation of why positive serial correlation in the $\{v_t\}$ sequence might shift the estimate of a_1 upward in small samples?

B. Plot the ACF and PACF of the residuals. Use Ljung–Box Q-statistics to determine whether the residuals approximate white noise. You should find

ACF of the residuals:

1:	0.1489160	0.0044162	−0.0178424	−0.0124788	0.0682729	0.0028705
7:	−0.0994202	−0.1508656	0.0643873	0.1012332	0.0898023	−0.0379116

PACF of the residuals:

1:	0.1489160	−0.0181625	−0.0161712	−0.0074713	0.0727149	−0.0192058
7:	−0.0996379	−0.1234779	0.1115448	0.0731477	0.0606913	−0.0565566

Ljung–Box Q-statistics: $Q(4) = 2.3142$,   significance level 0.50980859
$Q(8) = 6.3861$,   significance level 0.49546069
$Q(24) = 18.4914$,   significance level 0.73031863

C. Plot the ACF and PACF of the squared residuals. You should find

ACF of the squared residuals:

1:	0.4730473	0.1268669	−0.0573466	−0.0777808	0.0570613	0.2424039
7:	0.2727332	0.2140628	0.1368675	−0.0053388	−0.0660162	−0.0942429

PACF of the squared residuals:

1:	0.4730473	−0.1248437	−0.0861060	0.0037908	0.1351502	0.1981716
7:	0.0702680	0.0620095	0.0682656	−0.0656655	−0.0381717	−0.1030398

Ljung–Box Q-statistics: $Q(4) = 25.4702$,   significance level 0.00001231
$Q(8) = 45.2535$,   significance level 0.00000012
$Q(24) = 50.6029$,   significance level 0.00076745

Based on the ACF and PACF of the residuals and squared residuals, what can you conclude about the presence of ARCH errors?

D. Estimate the squared residuals as: $\epsilon_t^2 = \alpha_0 + \alpha_1 \epsilon_{t-1}^2$. You should verify

Coefficient	Estimate	Standard Error	t-Statistic	Significance
α_0	1.5501077352	0.5484906416	2.82613	0.00573246
α_1	0.4745095418	0.0899397119	5.27586	0.00000082

Show that the Lagrange multiplier ARCH(1) errors is $TR^2 = 22.027771$ with a significance level of 0.00000269.

E. For comparison purposes, estimate the squared residuals as an ARCH(4) process. You should find

Coefficient	Estimate	Standard Error	t-Statistic	Significance
α_0	1.934317326	0.653781567	2.95866	0.00394756
α_1	0.520622481	0.105584787	4.93085	0.00000372
α_2	−0.079036621	0.118547940	−0.66671	0.50666555
α_3	−0.089127597	0.118593767	−0.75154	0.45429036
α_4	0.004812599	0.105446847	0.04564	0.96369827

i. Why is this ARCH(4) model inappropriate?

F. Simultaneously estimate the $\{y_t\}$ sequence and ARCH(1) error process using maximum likelihood estimation. You should find

Coefficient	Estimate	Standard Error	*t*-Statistic	Significance
a_1	0.8864631666	0.0270362312	32.78797	0.00000000
α_0	1.1735726519	0.2703953538	4.34021	0.00001423
α_1	0.6663896955	0.2221985284	2.99907	0.00270802

7. The file WPI.WK1 contains the quarterly values of the U.S. Wholesale Price Index (WPI) from 1960:Q1 to 1992:Q2. Use the data to construct the logarithmic change as

$$\Delta lwpi_t = \log(wpi_t) - \log(wpi_{t-1})$$

You should find:

Series	Observations	Mean	Standard Error	Minimum	Maximum
wpi	130	65.09	31.366	30.50	116.2
$\Delta lwpi$	129	0.0101428	0.01452535	−0.02087032	0.06952606

A. Use the entire sample period to estimate Equation (3.19). Perform diagnostic checks to determine whether the residuals appear to be white-noise.

B. Plot the ACF and PACF of the squared residuals.

C. Estimate the various GARCH models given by (3.21), (3.22), and (3.23).

8. Series *Y* on the file labeled ARCHM.PRN contains 100 observations of a simulated ARCH-M process. The properties of the sequence are

Sample mean	1.06988500000	Variance	0.267006
Skewness	0.47442	Significance level (Sk = 0)	0.05642422

A. Plot the ACF and PACF of the $\{y_t\}$ sequence. You should find that the first 12 values are

ACF:

1:	0.0115085	0.0316424	0.2320040	−0.0643045	−0.1395873	−0.3094448
7:	−0.0009952	−0.1573020	−0.2247642	0.1861901	−0.0510400	0.0451368

PACF

1:	0.0115085	0.0315141	0.2315492	-0.0727560	-0.1616008	-0.3873124
7:	0.0369360	-0.0659871	-0.0779783	0.1446746	-0.0821942	-0.0051101

Ljung–Box Q-statistics: $Q(4) = 6.2172$,   significance level 0.18350104
$Q(12) = 31.5695$,   significance level 0.00161190
$Q(24) = 49.8118$,   significance level 0.00149611

B. Estimate the $\{y_t\}$ sequence using the Box–Jenkins methodology. Try to improve on the model:

$$y_t = a_0 + \epsilon_t + \beta_3 \epsilon_{t-3} + \beta_6 \epsilon_{t-6}$$

where

Coefficient	Estimate	Standard Error	t-Statistic	Significance
a_0	1.071771081	0.048009924	22.32395	0.00000000
β_3	0.254214138	0.098929960	2.56964	0.01170287
β_6	-0.262006589	0.099273537	-2.63924	0.00968214

C. Examine the ACF and PACF of the residuals from the MA[(3, 6)] model above. Why might someone conclude that the residuals appear to be white-noise? Now examine the ACF and PACF of the squared residuals. You should find

ACF of the squared residuals:

1:	0.4981203	0.2509847	0.2895971	0.1625192	0.0430988	0.1141240
7:	0.0907499	0.0532747	0.1365066	0.0261814	0.1592152	0.2503240

PACF of the squared residuals:

1:	0.4981203	0.0038049	0.2170029	-0.0878890	-0.0413535	0.1013672
7:	-0.0172378	0.0348213	0.0984692	-0.1475101	0.2890676	0.0322684

Ljung–Box Q-statistics: $Q(4) = 43.7460$,   significance level 0.0000
$Q(8) = 46.5766$,   significance level 0.0000
$Q(12) = 58.9113$,   significance level 0.0000
$Q(24) = 64.5293$,   significance level 0.0000

D. Estimate the $\{y_t\}$ sequence as the ARCH-M process:

$$y_t = a_0 + a_1 h_t + \epsilon_t$$
$$h_t = \alpha_0 + \alpha_1 \epsilon_{t-1}^2$$

You should find

Coefficient	Estimate	Standard Error	t-Statistic	Significance
a_0	0.9081809340	0.0646439764	14.04896	0.00000000
a_1	0.6252387171	0.3491817146	1.79058	0.07336030
α_0	0.1079170551	0.0193136878	5.58759	0.00000002
α_1	0.5973791022	0.2387112973	2.50252	0.01233137

E. Check the ACF and PACF of the estimated $\{\epsilon_t\}$ sequence. Do they appear to be satisfactory? Experiment with several other simple formulations of the ARCH-M process.

9. Consider the ARCH(2) process $E\epsilon_t^2 = \alpha_0 + \alpha_1\epsilon_{t-1}^2 + \alpha_2\epsilon_{t-2}^2$.

A. Suppose that $y_t = a_0 + a_1 y_{t-1} + \epsilon_t$. Find the conditional and unconditional variance of $\{y_t\}$ in terms of of the parameters a_1, α_0, α_1, and α_2.

B. Suppose that $\{y_t\}$ is an ARCH-M process such that the level of y_t is positively related to its own conditional variance. For simplicity, let $y_t = \alpha_0 + \alpha_1\epsilon_{t-1}^2 + \alpha_2\epsilon_{t-2}^2 + \epsilon_t$. Trace out the impulse response function of $\{y_t\}$ to an $\{\epsilon_t\}$ shock. You may assume that the system has been in long-run equilibrium ($\epsilon_{t-2} = \epsilon_{t-1} = 0$) but now $\epsilon_1 = 1$. Thus, the issue is to find the values of y_1, y_2, y_3, and y_4 given that $\epsilon_2 = \epsilon_3 = \cdots = 0$.

C. Use your answer to part B to explain the following result. A student estimated $\{y_t\}$ as an MA(2) process and found the residuals to be white-noise. A second student estimated the same series as the ARCH-M process $y_t = \alpha_0 + \alpha_1\epsilon_{t-1}^2 + \alpha_2\epsilon_{t-2}^2 + \epsilon_t$. Why might both estimates appear reasonable? How would you decide which is the better model?

D. In general, explain why an ARCH-M model might appear to be a moving average process.

10. Given the initial condition y_0, find the general solution and forecast function for the following variants of the trend plus irregular model:

A. $y_t = \mu_t + v_t$, where $u_t = u_{t-1} + \epsilon_t$, $v_t = (1 + \beta_1 L)\eta_t$, and $E\epsilon_t \eta_t = 0$.

B. $y_t = \mu_t + v_t$, where $u_t = u_{t-1} + \epsilon_t$ and $v_t = (1 + \beta_1 L)\eta_t$ and the correlation between ϵ_t and η_t equals unity.

C. Find the ARIMA representation of each model.

11. The columns in the file labeled EXRATES.WK1 contain exchange rate indices for the British pound, French franc, German mark, Italian lira, Canadian dollar, and Japanese yen over the 1973:Q1 to 1990:Q4 period. The units are currency

per U.S. dollar and the values have been converted into indices such that 1971:Q1 = 1.00.

For the yen and Canadian dollar (columns 5 and 6, respectively) you should find the following:

A. Use the data for the yen/dollar exchange rate (i.e., the last colums) to reproduce the results reported in the text.

Series	Observa-tions	Mean	Standard Error	Minimum	Maximum
Yen	72	0.61561729167	0.15471136174	0.34800000000	0.84316700000
Canadian dollar	72	1.16505638889	0.12397561475	0.95716300000	1.39188100000

Form the logarithmic change of each of the two series.

B. Decompose the yen/dollar exchange rate into its temporary and transitory components using the Beveridge and Nelson (1981) decomposition. You should be able to reproduce the results in the text.

C. Detrend the logarithm of the Canadian dollar (denoted by y_t) by estimating the regression $y_t = a_0 + a_1 t + \epsilon_t$. Save the residuals and form the correlogram. You should find that the residuals do not appear to be stationary. For example, the ACF of the residuals is

ACF of the residuals:

1:	0.9381108	0.8516773	0.7656438	0.6707062	0.5656608	0.4646090
7:	0.3665752	0.2619469	0.1602961	0.0668779	-0.0233500	-0.0959095

D. Estimate the logarithmic change in the Canadian dollar as an MA(1) model. You should find

$$\Delta y_t = \epsilon_t + 0.6308671509\epsilon_{t-1}$$

The standard error of β_1 is 0.0927381095, yielding a t-statistic of 6.80267.

E. Perform the appropriate diagnostic checks of the model. Is it necessary to include a constant? What about the autocorrelation coefficient of 0.2249136 at lag 3? You should verify that the Ljung–Box Q-statistics are:

$$Q(4) = 5.6965, \quad \text{significance level of } 0.12734706$$
$$Q(8) = 7.9077, \quad \text{significance level of } 0.34080750$$
$$Q(16) = 16.3652, \quad \text{significance level of } 0.35820258$$

F. To keep the issue as simple as possible, proceed with the Beveridge and Nelson decomposition using the MA(1) model. For each period t, form the various s-step ahead forecasts. Why is it sufficient to set $s = 1$?

G. Form the trend and irregular components of the logarithm of the Canadian dollar. You should be able to verify

Period	Log Canadian $	Trend Component	Temporary Component
1973:02	−0.008634167376	−0.006909245096	−0.001724922281
1973:03	−0.004671896332	−0.003260426492	−0.001411469840
1973:04	−0.008734030846	−0.012187148030	0.003453117184
. . .			
1990:03	0.134045635379	0.132362802801	0.001682832578
1990:04	0.140821380972	0.146157620084	−0.005336239112

H. How would you select s if you found the autoregressive coefficient at lag 3 to be important?

I. Detrend *at least* one of the other exchange rate series in the file (you may convert to logs). Does the detrended series appear to be stationary? Compare with the first diffence of the series.

ENDNOTES

1. Some authors prefer the spelling homoscedastic and heteroscedastic; both forms are correct.

2. If the unconditional variance of a series is not constant, the series is nonstationary. However, *conditional* heteroskedasticy is *not* a source of nonstationarity.

3. Letting $\alpha(L)$ and $\beta(L)$ be polynomials in the lag operator L, we can rewrite h_t in the form:

$$h_t = \alpha_0 + \alpha(L)\epsilon_t^2 + \beta(L)h_{t-1}$$

The notation $\alpha(1)$ denotes the polynomial $\alpha(L)$ evaluated at $L = 1$; that is, $\alpha(1) = \alpha_1 + \alpha_2 + \cdots + \alpha_q$. Bollerslev (1986) shows that the GARCH process is stationary with $E\epsilon_t = 0$, $\text{var}(\epsilon_t) = \alpha_0/[1 - \alpha(1) - \beta(1)]$, and $\text{cov}(\epsilon_t, \epsilon_{t-s}) = 0$ for $s \neq 0$ if $\alpha(1) + \beta(1) < 1$.

4. Unfortunately, there is no available method to test the null of white-noise errors versus the specific alternative of GARCH(p, q) errors. Bollerslev (1986) proves that the ACF of the squared residuals resulting from (3.9) is an ARMA(m, p) model, where $m = \max(p, q)$. Question 3 asks you to illustrate this result.

5. Constraining the coefficients of h_t to follow a decaying pattern conserves degrees of freedom and considerably eases the estimation process. Moreover, the lagged coefficients given by (9-i)/36 (i.e., 8/36, 7/36, . . . , 1/36) are each positive and sum to unity.

6. Estimating a model with n lags usually entails a loss of the first n observations. To correct for this problem, the ARCH and GARCH models should be compared over the

identical sample period. In this way, the number of usable observations will be identical for the two models. In this section, all models were estimated over the 1962:2 to 1992:2 sample period. One observation was lost due to differencing and eight were lost due to the estimation of the ARCH(8) model.

7. The estimated value of h_t is the conditional variance of the logarithmic change in the WPI; in constructing the figure, the interval for the percentage change was converted to the *level* of the WPI.

8. In addition to the intercept term, three seasonal dummy variables were also included in the supply equation.

9. If the underlying data-generating process is autoregressive, adaptive expectations and rational expectations can be perfectly consistent with each other.

10. If the utility function is quadratic and/or the excess returns from holding the asset are normally distributed, an increase in the variance of returns is equivalent to an increase in "risk."

11. Of course, to the individual contemplating the purchase of a risky asset, the value of μ_t is not stochastic. Note that μ_t is the expected return that the individual would demand in order to hold the long-term asset.

12. The unconditional mean of y_t is altered by changing only δ. Changing β and δ commensurately maintains the mean value of the $\{y_t\}$ sequence.

13. The Greek character set and subscripts decending below the line are not permitted in RATS. To actually write such a program, the parameters β, α_0, α_1, and h_t might be denoted by B, $A0$, $A1$, and $H(T)$, respectively.

14. The method is recursive since the program first calculates ϵ_t, then h_t, and then LIKELI-HOOD.

15. In actuality, the program steps in RATS would differ slightly since ϵ could not be defined in terms of its own lagged values. Similar remarks hold for all the program statements below.

16. Many treatments use the representation y_t = trend + cyclical + seasonal + irregular. In the text, any cyclical components are included with the irregular term; the notion is that cyclical economic components are not deterministic.

17. A linguist might want to know why "detrending" entails removing the deterministic trend and not the stochastic trend. The reason is purely historical; originally, trends were viewed as deterministic. Today, subtracting the deterministic time trend is still called "detrending."

18. If $B(L)$ is of infinite order, it is assumed that $\Sigma\beta_i^2$ is finite.

19. If only $B(L)$ has a unit root, the process is invertible. The $\{y_t\}$ sequence is stationary (may be stationary), but the usual estimation techniques are inappropriate. If both $A(L)$ and $B(L)$ have unit roots, the *common factor problem* discussed in Chapter 2 exists. The unit root can be factored from $A(L)$ and $B(L)$.

20. Also assume that all values of ϵ_i are zero for $i < 1$.

21. As an exercise, prove that the first difference of the trend acts as a random walk plus drift. Show that $\mu_t - \mu_{t-1}$ has the intercept a_0 plus a serially uncorrelated error.

22. The assumption that ϵ_t and η_t are uncorrelated places restrictions on the autoregressive and moving average coefficients of Δy_t. For example, in the pure random walk plus noise model, β_1 must be negative. To avoid estimating a constrained ARIMA model, Watson estimates the trend and irregular terms as unobserved components. Many software packages are capable of estimating such equations as time-varying parameter models. Details of the procedure can be obtained in Harvey (1989).

APPENDIX: Signal Extraction and Minimum Mean Square Errors

Linear Least-Squares Projection

The problem for the econometric forecaster is to select an optimal forecast of a random variable y conditional on the observation of a second variable x. Since the theory is quite general, for the time being we ignore time subscripts. Call this conditional forecast y^*, so that the forecast error is $(y - y^*)$ and the mean square forecast error (MSE) $E(y - y^*)^2$. One criterion used to compare forecast functions is the MSE; the optimal forecast function is that with the smallest MSE.

Suppose x and y are jointly distributed random variables with known distributions. Let the mean and variance of x be μ_x and σ_x^2, respectively. Also suppose the value of x is observed before having to predict y. A *linear* forecast will be such that the forecast y^* is a linear function of x. The optimal forecast will necessarily be linear if x and y are linearly related, and/or if they are bivariate normally distributed variables. In this text, only linear relationships are considered; hence, the optimal forecast of y^* has the form

$$y^* = a + b(x - \mu_x)$$

The problem is to select the values of a and b so as to minimize the MSE:

$$\begin{aligned} \text{Min } E(y - y^*)^2 &= E[y - a - b(x - \mu_x)]^2 \\ \{a, b\} \\ &= E[y^2 + a^2 + b^2(x - \mu_x)^2 - 2ay + 2ab(x - \mu_x) - 2by(x - \mu_x)] \end{aligned}$$

Since $E(x - \mu_x) = 0$, $Ey = \mu_y$, $E(x - \mu_x)^2 = \sigma_x^2$, and $E(xy) - \mu_x\mu_y = \text{cov}(x, y) = \sigma_{xy}$, it follows that

$$E(y - y^*)^2 = Ey^2 + a^2 + b^2\sigma_x^2 - 2a\mu_y - 2b\sigma_{xy}$$

Minimizing with respect to a and b yields

$$a = \mu_y, \qquad b = \sigma_{xy}/\sigma_x^2$$

Thus, the optimal prediction formula is

$$y^* = \mu_y - (\sigma_{xy}/\sigma_x^2)\mu_x + (\sigma_{xy}/\sigma_x^2)x$$

The forecast is unbiased in the sense that the mean value of the forecast is equal to the mean value of y. Take the expected value of y^* to obtain

$$Ey^* = E[\mu_y - (\sigma_{xy}/\sigma_x^2)\mu_x + (\sigma_{xy}/\sigma_x^2)x]$$

Since, μ_y, σ_{xy}, and σ_x^2 are constants and $\mu_x = Ex$, it follows that

$$Ey^* = \mu_y$$

You should recognize this formula from standard regression analysis; a regression equation is the minimum mean square error, linear, unbiased forecast of y^*. The argument easily generalizes forecasting y conditional on the observation of the n variables x_1 through x_n and forecasting y_{t+s} conditional on the observation of y_t, $y_{t-1}, \ldots$. For example, if $y_t = a_0 + a_1 y_{t-1} + \epsilon_t$, the conditional forecast of y_{t+1} is $E_t y_{t+1} = a_0 + a_1 y_t$. The forecasts of y_{t+s} can be obtained using the forecast function (or iterative forecasts) discussed in Section 11 of Chapter 2.

Signal Extraction

Signal extraction issues arise when we try to decompose a series into its individual components. Suppose we observe the realizations of a stationary sequence $\{y_t\}$ and want to find the optimal predictor of its components. If we phrase the problem this way, it is clear that the decomposition can be performed using the minimum MSE criterion discussed above. As an example of the technique, consider a sequence composed of two independent white-noise components:

$$y_t = \epsilon_t + \eta_t$$

where $\quad E\epsilon_t \;\; = 0$
$\qquad\quad\; E\eta_t \;\; = 0$
$\qquad\quad\; E\epsilon_t \eta_t = 0$
$\qquad\quad\; E\epsilon_t^2 \;\; = \sigma^2$
$\qquad\quad\; E\eta_t^2 \;\; = \sigma_\eta^2$

Here, the correlation between the innovations is assumed to be equal to zero; it is straightforward to allow nonzero values of $E\epsilon_t \eta_t$. The problem is to find the optimal prediction, or forecast, of ϵ_t (called ϵ_t^*) conditioned of the observation of y_t. The linear forecast has the form

$$\epsilon_t^* = a + by_t$$

In this problem, the intercept term a will be zero, so that the MSE can be written as

$$\begin{aligned}
\text{MSE} &= E(\epsilon_t - \epsilon_t^*)^2 \\
&= E(\epsilon_t - by_t)^2 \\
&= E[\epsilon_t - b(\epsilon_t + \eta_t)]^2
\end{aligned}$$

Hence the optimization problem is to select b so as to minimize:

$$\begin{aligned}
\text{MSE} &= E[(1 - b)\epsilon_t - b\eta_t]^2 \\
&= (1 - b)^2 E\epsilon_t^2 + b^2 E\eta_t^2 \qquad \text{since } E\epsilon_t\eta_t = 0
\end{aligned}$$

The first-order condition is

$$-2(1 - b)\sigma^2 + 2b\sigma_\eta^2 = 0$$

so that

$$b = \sigma^2/(\sigma^2 + \sigma_\eta^2)$$

Here, b partitions y_t in accordance with the relative variance of ϵ_t; that is, $\sigma^2/(\sigma^2 + \sigma_\eta^2)$. As σ^2 becomes very large relative to σ_η^2, $b \to 1$; as σ^2 becomes very small relative to σ_η^2, $b \to 0$. Having extracted ϵ_t, we see that the predicted value of η_t is $\eta_t^* = y_t - \epsilon_t^*$. However, this optimal value of b depends on the assumption that the two innovations are uncorrelated.

Forecasts of a Nonstationary Series Based on Observables
Muth (1960) considers the situation in which a researcher wants to find the optimal forecast of y_t conditional on the observed values of $y_{t-1}, y_{t-2}, \ldots$. Let $\{y_t\}$ be a random walk plus noise. If all realizations of $\{\epsilon_t\}$ are zero for $t \le 0$, the solution for y_t is

$$y_t = \sum_{i=1}^{t} \epsilon_i + \eta_t \tag{A3.1}$$

where y_0 is given and $\mu_0 = 0$.

Let the forecast of y_t be a linear function of the past values of the series, so that

$$y_t^* = \sum_{i=1}^{\infty} v_i y_{t-i} \tag{A3.2}$$

where   the various values of v_i are selected so as to minimize the mean square forecast error.

Use (A3.1) to find each value of y_{t-i} and substitute into (A3.2) so that

$$y_t^* = v_1 \left(\sum_{i=1}^{t-1} \epsilon_i + \eta_{t-1} \right) + v_2 \left(\sum_{i=1}^{t-2} \epsilon_i + \eta_{t-2} \right) + v_3 \left(\sum_{i=1}^{t-3} \epsilon_i + \eta_{t-3} \right) + \cdots$$

Thus, the optimization problem is to select the v_j so as to minimize the MSE:

$$E(y_t - y_t^*)^2 = E\left[\sum_{i=1}^{t} \epsilon_i + \eta_t - v_1 \left(\sum_{i=1}^{t-1} \epsilon_i + \eta_{t-1} \right) - v_2 \left(\sum_{i=1}^{t-2} \epsilon_i + \eta_{t-2} \right) - \cdots \right]^2$$

Since all cross-products are zero, the problem is to select the v_j so as to minimize

$$MSE = \sigma_\epsilon^2 + \sigma_\eta^2 + \sigma_\epsilon^2 \sum_{i=1}^{\infty} \left(1 - \sum_{j=1}^{i} v_j \right) + \sigma_\eta^2 \sum_{j=1}^{\infty} v_j^2$$

For each value of v_k, the first-order condition is

$$2\sigma_\eta^2 v_k - 2\sigma_\epsilon^2 \sum_{j=k}^{\infty} \left(1 - \sum_{i=1}^{j} v_i \right) = 0, \qquad k = 1, 2, \ldots \tag{A3.3}$$

All $\{v_k\}$ will satisfy the difference equation given by (A3.3). To characterize the nature of the solution, set $k = 1$, so that the first equation of (A3.3) is

$$2\sigma_\eta^2 v_1 - 2\sigma_\epsilon^2 \sum_{j=1}^{\infty} \left(1 - \sum_{i=1}^{j} v_i \right) = 0$$

and for $k = 2$,

$$2\sigma_\eta^2 v_2 - 2\sigma_\epsilon^2 \sum_{j=2}^{\infty} \left(1 - \sum_{i=1}^{j} v_i \right) = 0$$

so that by subtraction,

$$\sigma_\epsilon^2 (1 - v_1) + \sigma_\eta^2 (v_2 - v_1) = 0 \tag{A3.4}$$

Now take the second difference of (A3.3) to obtain

$$- v_{k-1} + [2 + (\sigma_\epsilon^2/\sigma_\eta^2)]v_k - v_{k+1} = 0 \qquad \text{for } k = 2, 3, \ldots$$

The solution to this homogeneous second-order difference equation has the form $v_k = A_1\lambda_1^k + A_2\lambda_2^k$, where A_1 and A_2 are arbitrary constants and λ_1 and λ_2 the characteristic roots. If you use the quadratic formula, you will find that the larger root (say, λ_2) is greater than unity; hence, if the $\{v_k\}$ sequence is to be convergent, A_2 must equal zero. The smaller root satisfies

$$\lambda_1^2 - [2 + (\sigma_\epsilon^2/\sigma_\eta^2)] \lambda_1 + 1 = 0 \tag{A3.5}$$

To find the value of A_1, substitute $v_1 = A_1\lambda_1$ and $v_2 = A_1\lambda_1^2$ into (A3.4):

$$\sigma_\epsilon^2(1 - A_1\lambda_1) - \sigma_\eta^2 A_1(\lambda_1^2 - \lambda_1) = 0$$

If you solve (A3.5) for λ_1, it is possible to verify

$$A_1 = (1 - \lambda_1)/\lambda_1$$

Hence, the v_k are determined by

$$v_k = (1 - \lambda_1)\lambda_1^{k-1}$$

The one-step ahead forecast of y_t is

$$y_t^* = (1-\lambda_1)\sum_{j=1}^{\infty} \lambda_1^{j-1} y_{t-j}$$

Since $|\lambda_1| < 1$, the summation is such that $(1 - \lambda_1)\Sigma\lambda_1^{j-1} = 1$. Hence, the optimal forecast of y_t can be formed as a geometrically weighted average of the past realizations of the series.

The Hodrick–Prescott Decomposition
Another method of decomposing a series into a trend and stationary component has been developed by Hodrick and Prescott (1984). Suppose you observe the values y_1 through y_T and want to decompose the series into a trend $\{\mu_t\}$ and stationary component $y_t - \mu_t$. Consider the sum of squares

$$(1/T)\sum_{t=1}^{T}(y_t - \mu_t)^2 + (\lambda/T)\sum_{t=2}^{T-1}[(\mu_{t+1} - \mu_t) - (\mu_t - \mu_{t-1})]^2$$

The problem is to select the $\{\mu_t\}$ sequence so as to minimize this sum of squares. In the minimization problem, λ is an arbitrary constant reflecting the "cost" or penalty of incorporating fluctuations into the trend. In many applications, including Hodrick and Prescott (1984) and Farmer (1993), λ is set equal to 1600. Increasing the value of λ acts to "smooth out" the trend. If $\lambda = 0$, the sum of squares is minimized when $y_t = \mu_t$; the trend is equal to y_t itself. As $\lambda \to \infty$, the trend approaches a linear time trend. Intuitively, for large values of λ, Hodrick-Prescott decomposition forces the change in the trend (i.e., $\Delta\mu_{t+1} - \Delta\mu_t$) to be as small as possible. This occurs when the trend is linear.

The benefit of the Hodrick–Prescott decomposition is that it can extract the same trend from a set of variables. For example, many real business cycle models indicate that all variables will have the same stochastic trend. A Beveridge and Nelson decomposition separately applied to each variable will not yield the same trend for each.

Chapter 4

TESTING FOR TRENDS AND UNIT ROOTS

Inspection of the autocorrelation function serves as a rough indicator of whether a trend is present in a series. A slowly decaying ACF is indicative of a large characteristic root, true unit root process, or trend stationary process. Formal tests can help determine whether or not a system contains a trend and whether that trend is deterministic or stochastic. However, the existing tests have little power to distinguish between near unit root and unit root processes. The aims of this chapter are to:

1. Develop and illustrate the Dickey–Fuller and augmented Dickey–Fuller tests for the presence of a unit root. These tests can also be used to help detect the presence of a deterministic trend. Phillips–Perron tests, which entail less stringent restrictions on the error process, are illustrated.

2. Consider tests for unit roots in the presence of structural change. Structural change can complicate the tests for trends; a policy regime change can result in a structural break that makes an otherwise stationary series appear to be nonstationary.

3. Illustrate a general procedure to determine whether or not a series contains a unit root. Unit root tests are sensitive to the presence of deterministic regressors, such as an intercept term or a deterministic time trend. As such, there is a sophisticated set of procedures that can aid in the identification process. These procedures can be used if it is not known what deterministic elements are part of the true data-generating process. It is important to be wary of the results from such tests since (1) they all have low power to discriminate between a unit root and near unit root process and (2) they may have used an inappropriate set of deterministic regressors.

1. UNIT ROOT PROCESSES

As shown in the last chapter, there are important differences between stationary and nonstationary time series. Shocks to a stationary time series are necessarily temporary; over time, the effects of the shocks will dissipate and the series will revert to its long-run mean level. As such, long-term forecasts of a stationary series will converge to the unconditional mean of the series. To aid in identification, we know that a covariance stationary series:

1. Exhibits **mean reversion** in that it fluctuates around a constant long-run mean.
2. Has a finite variance that is time-invariant.
3. Has a theoretical correlogram that diminishes as lag length increases.

On the other hand, a nonstationary series necessarily has permanent components. The mean and/or variance of a nonstationary series are time-dependent. To aid in the identification of a nonstationary series, we know that:

1. There is no long-run mean to which the series returns.
2. The variance is time-dependent and goes to infinity as time approaches infinity.
3. Theoretical autocorrelations do not decay but, in finite samples, the sample correlogram dies out slowly.

Although the properties of a sample correlogram are useful tools for detecting the possible presence of unit roots, the method is necessarily imprecise. What may appear as a unit root to one observer may appear as a stationary process to another. The problem is difficult because a near unit root process will have the same shaped ACF as a unit root process. For example, the correlogram of a stationary AR(1) process such that $\rho(1) = 0.99$ will exhibit the type of gradual decay indicative of a nonstationary process. To illustrate some of the issues involved, suppose that we know a series is generated from the following first-order process:[1]

$$y_t = a_1 y_{t-1} + \epsilon_t \qquad (4.1)$$

where $\{\epsilon_t\}$ is generated from a white-noise process.

First, suppose that we wish to test the null hypothesis that $a_1 = 0$. Under the maintained null hypothesis of $a_1 = 0$, we can estimate (4.1) using OLS. The fact that ϵ_t is a white-noise process and $|a_1| < 1$ guarantees that the $\{y_t\}$ sequence is stationary and the estimate of a_1 is efficient. Calculating the standard error of the estimate of a_1, the researcher can use a t-test to determine whether a_1 is significantly different from zero.

The situation is quite different if we want to test the hypothesis $a_1 = 1$. Now, under the null hypothesis, the $\{y_t\}$ sequence is generated by the nonstationary process:

$$y_t = \sum_{i=1}^{t} \epsilon_i \qquad (4.2)$$

Thus, if $a_1 = 1$, the variance becomes infinitely large as t increases. Under the null hypothesis, it is inappropriate to use classical statistical methods to estimate and perform significance tests on the coefficient a_1. If the $\{y_t\}$ sequence is generated as in (4.2), it is simple to show that the OLS estimate of (4.1) will yield a biased estimate of a_1. In Section 8 of the previous chapter, it was shown that the first-order autocorrelation coefficient in a random walk model is

$$\rho_1 = [(t-1)/t]^{0.5} < 1$$

Since the estimate of a_1 is directly related to the value of ρ_1, the estimated value of a_1 is biased to be below its true value of unity. The estimated model will mimic that of a stationary AR(1) process with a near unit root. Hence, the usual t-test cannot be used to test the hypothesis $a_1 = 1$.

Figure 4.1 shows the sample correlogram for a simulated random walk process. One hundred normally distributed random deviates were obtained so as to mimic the $\{\epsilon_t\}$ sequence. Assuming $y_0 = 0$, we can calculate the next 100 values in the $\{y_t\}$ sequence as $y_t = y_{t-1} + \epsilon_t$. This particular correlogram is characteristic of most sample correlograms constructed from nonstationary data. The estimated value of ρ_1 is close to unity and the sample autocorrelations die out slowly. If we did not know the way in which the data were generated, inspection of Figure 4.1 might lead us to falsely conclude that the data were generated from a stationary process. With this particular data, estimates of an AR(1) model with and without an intercept yield (standard errors are in parentheses):

$$y_t = 0.9546y_{t-1} + \epsilon_t, \qquad R^2 = 0.86 \qquad (4.3)$$
$$(0.030)$$
$$y_t = 0.164 + 0.9247y_{t-1} + \epsilon_t, \qquad R^2 = 0.864 \qquad (4.4)$$
$$(0.037)$$

Examining (4.3), a careful researcher would not be willing to dismiss the possibility of a unit root since the estimated value of a_1 is only 1.5133 standard deviations from unity. We might correctly recognize that under the null hypothesis of a unit root, the estimate of a_1 will be biased below unity. If we knew the true distribution of a_1 under the null of a unit root, we could perform such a significance test. Of course, if we did not know the true data-generating process, we might estimate the model with an intercept. In (4.4), the estimate of a_1 is more than two standard deviations from unity: $(1 - 0.9247)/0.037 = 2.035$. However, it would be wrong to use this information to reject the null of a unit root. After all, the point of this section has been to indicate that such t-tests are inappropriate under the null of a unit root.

Fortunately, Dickey and Fuller (1979, 1981) devised a procedure to formally test for the presence of a unit root. Their methodology is similar to that used in constructing the data reported in Figure 4.1. Suppose that we generated thousands of such random walk sequences and for each we calculated the estimated value of a_1. Although most all of the estimates would be close to unity, some would be further

Figure 4.1

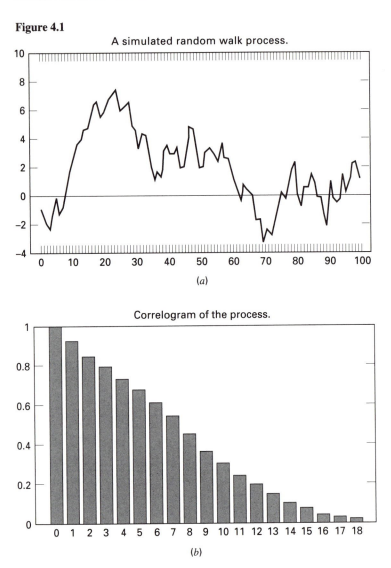

A simulated random walk process.

(a)

Correlogram of the process.

(b)

from unity than others. In performing this experiment, Dickey and Fuller found that in the presence of an intercept:

Ninety percent of the estimated values of a_1 are less than 2.58 standard errors from unity.

Ninety-five percent of the estimated values of a_1 are less than 2.89 standard errors from unity.

Ninety-nine percent of the estimated values of a_1 are less than 3.51 standard errors from unity.[2]

The application of these Dickey–Fuller *critical values* to tests for unit roots is straightforward. Suppose we did not know the true-data generating process and were trying to ascertain whether the data used in Figure 4.1 contained a unit root. Using these Dickey–Fuller statistics, we would not reject the null of a unit root in (4.4). The estimated value of a_1 is only 2.035 standard deviations from unity. In fact, if the true value of a_1 does equal unity, we should find the estimated value to be within 2.58 standard deviations from unity 90% of the time.

Be aware that stationarity necessitates $-1 < a_1 < 1$. Thus, if the estimated value of a_1 is close to -1, you should also be concerned about nonstationarity. If we define $\gamma = a_1 - 1$, the equivalent restriction is $-2 < \gamma < 0$. In conducting a Dickey–Fuller test, *it is possible to check that the estimated value of γ is greater than -2.*[3]

Monte Carlo Simulation

The procedure Dickey and Fuller (1979, 1981) used to obtain their critical values is typical of that found in the modern time series literature. Hypothesis tests concerning the coefficients of non-stationary variables cannot be conducted using traditional *t*-tests or *F*-tests. The distributions of the appropriate test statistics are nonstandard and cannot be analytically evaluated. However, given the trivial cost of computer time, the non-standard distributions can easily be derived using a Monte Carlo simulation.

The first step in the procedure is to computer generate a set of random numbers (sometimes called pseudo-random numbers) from a given distribution. Of course, the numbers cannot be entirely random since all computer algorithms rely on a deterministic number generating mechanism. However, the numbers are drawn so as to mimic a random process having some specified distribution. Usually, the numbers are designed to be normally distributed and serially uncorrelated. The idea is to use these numbers to represent one replication of the entire $\{\epsilon_t\}$ sequence.

All major statistical packages have a built-in random number generator. An interesting experiment is to use your software package to draw a set of 100 random numbers and check for serial correlation. In almost all circumstances, they will be highly correlated. In your own work, if you need to use serially uncorrelated numbers, you can model the computer generated numbers using the Box Jenkins methodology. The residuals should approximate white noise.

The second step is to specify the parameters and initial conditions of the $\{y_t\}$ sequence. Using these parameters, initial conditions, and random numbers, the $\{y_t\}$ can be constructed. Note that the simulated ARCH processes in Figure 3.9 and random-walk process in Figure 4.1 were constructed in precisely this fashion. Similarly, Dickey and Fuller (1979, 1981) obtained 100 values for $\{\epsilon_t\}$, set $a_1 = 1$, $y_0 = 0$, and calculated 100 values for $\{y_t\}$ according to (4.1). At this point, the parameters of interest (such as the estimate of a_1 or the in-sample variance of y_t) can be obtained.

The beauty of the method is that all important attributes of the constructed $\{y_t\}$ sequence are known to the researcher. For this reason, a Monte Carlo simulation is often referred to as an "experiment." The only problem is that the set of random numbers drawn is just one possible outcome. Obviously, the estimates in (4.3) and (4.4) are dependent on the values of simulated $\{\epsilon_t\}$ sequence. Different outcomes for $\{\epsilon_t\}$ will yield different values of the simulated $\{y_t\}$ sequence.

This is why the Monte Carlo studies perform many replications of the process outlined above. The third step is to replicate steps 1 and 2 thousands of times. The goal is to ensure that the statistical properties of the constructed $\{y_t\}$ sequence are in accord with the true distribution. Thus, for each replication, the parameters of interest are tabulated and critical values (or confidence intervals) obtained. As such, the properties your data set can be compared to the properties of the simulated data so that hypothesis tests can be performed. This is the justification for using the Dickey–Fuller critical values to test the hypothesis $a_1 = 1$.

One limitation of a Monte Carlo experiment is that it is specific to the assumptions used to generate the simulated data. If you change the sample size, include (or delete) an additional parameter in the data generating process, or use alternative initial conditions an entirely new simulation needs to be performed. Nevertheless, you should be able to envision many applications of Monte Carlo simulations. As discussed in Hendry, Neale, and Ericsson (1990), they are particularly useful for studying the small sample properties of time-series data. As you will see shortly, Monte Carlo simulations are the workhorse of unit root tests.

Unit Roots in a Regression Model

The unit root issue arises quite naturally in the context of the standard regression model. Consider the regression equation:[4]

$$y_t = a_0 + a_1 z_t + e_t \tag{4.5}$$

The assumptions of the classical regression model necessitate that both the $\{y_t\}$ and $\{z_t\}$ sequences be stationary and the errors have a zero mean and finite variance. In the presence of nonstationary variables, there might be what Granger and Newbold (1974) call a **spurious regression**. A spurious regression has a high R^2, t-statistics that appear to be significant, but the results are without any economic meaning. The regression output "looks good" because the least-squares estimates are not consistent and the customary tests of statistical inference do not hold. Granger and Newbold (1974) provide a detailed examination of the consequences of violating the stationarity assumption by generating two sequences, $\{y_t\}$ and $\{z_t\}$, as *independent* random walks using the formulas:

$$y_t = y_{t-1} + \epsilon_{yt} \tag{4.6}$$

and

$$z_t = z_{t-1} + \epsilon_{zt} \tag{4.7}$$

where ϵ_{yt} and ϵ_{zt} = white-noise processes independent of each other

In their Monte Carlo analysis, Granger and Newbold generated many such samples and for each sample estimated a regression in the form of (4.5). Since the $\{y_t\}$ and $\{z_t\}$ sequences are independent of each other, Equation (4.5) is necessarily meaningless; any relationship between the two variables is spurious. Surprisingly, at the 5% significance level, they were able to reject the null hypothesis $a_1 = 0$ in approximately 75% of the time. Moreover, the regressions usually had very high R^2 values and the estimated residuals exhibited a high degree of autocorrelation.

To explain the Granger and Newbold findings, note that the regression equation (4.5) is necessarily meaningless if the residual series $\{e_t\}$ is nonstationary. Obviously, if the $\{e_t\}$ sequence has a stochastic trend, any error in period t never decays, so that the deviation from the model is permanent. It is hard to imagine attaching any importance to an economic model having permanent errors. The simplest way to examine the properties of the $\{e_t\}$ sequence is to abstract from the intercept term a_0 and rewrite (4.5) as

$$e_t = y_t - a_1 z_t$$

If z_t and y_t are generated by (4.6) and (4.7), we can impose the initial conditions $y_0 = x_0 = 0$, so that

$$e_t = \sum_{i=1}^{t} \epsilon_{yi} - a_1 \sum_{i=1}^{t} \epsilon_{zi} \tag{4.8}$$

Clearly, the variance of the error becomes infinitely large as t increases. Moreover, the error has a permanent component in that $E_t e_{t+1} = e_t$ for all $i \geq 0$. Hence, the assumptions embedded in the usual hypothesis tests are violated, so that any t-test, F-test, or R^2 values are unreliable. It is easy to see why the estimated residuals from a spurious regression will exhibit a high degree of autocorrelation. Updating (4.8), you should be able to demonstrate that the theoretical value of the correlation coefficient between e_t and e_{t+1} goes to unity as t increases.

The essence of the problem is that if $a_1 = 0$, the data generating process in (4.5) is $y_t = a_0 + \epsilon_t$. Given that $\{y_t\}$ is integrated of order one [i.e., I(1)], it follows that $\{e_t\}$ is I(1) under the null hypothesis. However, the assumption that the error term is a unit root process is inconsistent with the distributional theory underlying the use of OLS. This problem will not disappear in large samples. In fact, Phillips (1986) proves that the larger the sample, the more likely you are to falsely conclude that $a_1 \neq 0$.

Worksheet 4.1 illustrates the problem of spurious regressions. The top two graphs show 100 realizations of the $\{y_t\}$ and $\{z_t\}$ sequences generated according to (4.6) and (4.7). Although $\{\epsilon_{yt}\}$ and $\{\epsilon_{zt}\}$ are drawn from white-noise distributions, the realizations of the two sequences are such that y_{100} is positive and z_{100} negative. You can see that the regression of y_t on z_t captures the *within-sample* tendency of the sequences to move in opposite directions. The straight line shown in the scatter plot is the OLS regression line $y_t = -0.31 - 0.46z_t$. The correlation coefficient between $\{y_t\}$ and $\{z_t\}$ is -0.372. The residuals from this regression have a unit root; as such, the coefficients -0.31 and -0.46 are spurious. Worksheet 4.2 illustrates the same problem using two simulated random walk plus drift sequences: $y_t = 0.2 + y_{t-1} + \epsilon_{yt}$ and $z_t = -0.1 + z_{t-1} + \epsilon_{zt}$. The drift terms dominate, so that for small values of t, it appears that $y_t = -2z_t$. As sample size increases, however, the cumulated sum of

WORKSHEET 4.1   Spurious Regressions: Example 1

Consider the two random walk processes:

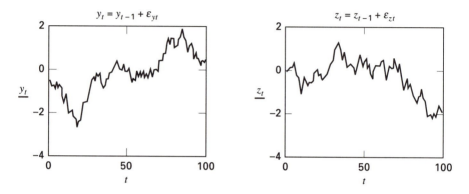

Since the $\{\epsilon_{yt}\}$ and $\{\epsilon_{zt}\}$ sequences are independent, the regression of y_t on z_t is spurious. Given the realizations of the random disturbances, it appears as if the two sequences are related. In the scatter plot of y_t against z_t, you can see that y_t tends to rise as z_t decreases. The regression equation of y_t on z_t will capture this tendency. The correlation coefficient between y_t and z_t is -0.372 and a linear regression yields $y_t = -0.46z_t - 0.31$. However, the residuals from the regression equation are nonstationary.

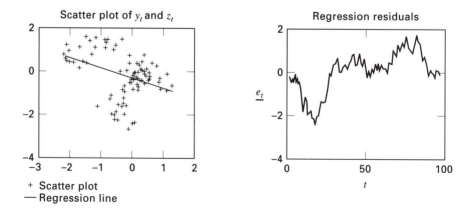

+ Scatter plot
— Regression line

the errors (i.e., Σe_t) will pull the relationship further and further from -2.0. The scatter plot of the two sequences suggests that the R^2 statistic will be close to unity; in fact, R^2 is almost 0.97. However, as you can see in the last graph of Worksheet 4.2, the residuals from the regression equation are nonstationary. All departures from this relationship are necessarily permanent.

The point is that the econometrician has to be very careful in working with nonstationary variables. In terms of (4.5), there are four cases to consider:

CASE 1

Both $\{y_t\}$ and $\{z_t\}$ are stationary. When both variables are stationary, the classical regression model is appropriate.

CASE 2

The $\{y_t\}$ and $\{z_t\}$ sequences are integrated of different orders. Regression equations using such variables are meaningless. For example, replace (4.7) by the stationary process $z_t = \rho z_{t-1} + \epsilon_{zt}$, where $|\rho| < 1$. Now (4.8) is replaced by $e_t = \Sigma\epsilon_{yi} - \Sigma\rho^i\epsilon_{zt-i}$. Although the expression $\Sigma\rho^i\epsilon_{zt-i}$ is convergent, the $\{\epsilon_t\}$ sequence still contains a trend component.[5]

CASE 3

The nonstationary $\{y_t\}$ and $\{z_t\}$ sequences are integrated of the same order and the residual sequence contains a stochastic trend. This is the case in which the regression is spurious. The results from such spurious regressions are meaningless in that all errors are permanent. In this case, it is often recommended that the regression equation be estimated in first differences. Consider the first difference of (4.5):

$$\Delta y_t = a_1\Delta z_t + \Delta e_t$$

Since y_t, z_t, and e_t each contain unit roots, the first difference of each is stationary. Hence, the usual asymptotic results apply. Of course, if one of the trends is deterministic and the other is stochastic, first-differencing each is not appropriate.

CASE 4

The nonstationary $\{y_t\}$ and $\{z_t\}$ sequences are integrated of the same order and the residual sequence is stationary. In this circumstance, $\{y_t\}$ and $\{z_t\}$ are **cointegrated**. A trivial example of a cointegrated system occurs if ϵ_{zt} and ϵ_{yt} are perfectly correlated. If $\epsilon_{zt} = \epsilon_{yt}$, then (4.8) can be set equal to zero (which is stationary) by setting $a_1 = 1$. To consider a more interesting example, suppose that both z_t and y_t are the random walk plus noise processes:

$$y_t = \mu_t + \epsilon_{yt}$$
$$z_t = \mu_t + \epsilon_{zt}$$

where ϵ_{yt} and ϵ_{zt} are white-noise processes and μ_t is the random walk process $\mu_t = \mu_{t-1} + \epsilon_t$. Note that both $\{z_t\}$ and $\{y_t\}$ are unit root processes, but $y_t - z_t = \epsilon_{yt} - \epsilon_{zt}$ is stationary.

All of Chapter 6 is devoted to the issue of cointegrated variables. For now, it is sufficient to note that pretesting the variables in a regression for nonstationarity is extremely important. Estimating a regression in the form of (4.5) is meaningless if

WORKSHEET 4.2   Spurious Regressions: Example 2

Consider the two random walk plus drift processes:

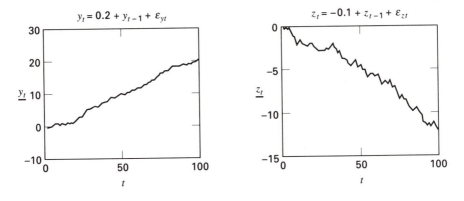

Again, the $\{\epsilon_{yt}\}$ and $\{\epsilon_{zt}\}$ sequences are independent, so that the regression of y_t on z_t is spurious. The scatter plot of y_t against z_t strongly suggests that the two series are related. It is the deterministic time trend that causes the sustained increase in y_t and sustained decrease in z_t. The residuals from the regression equation $y_t = -2z_t + e_t$ are nonstationary.

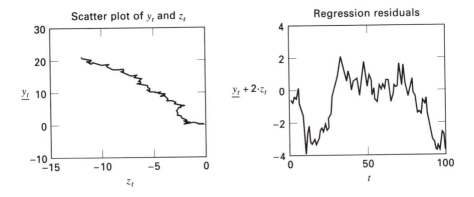

Cases 2 or 3 apply. If the variables are cointegrated, the results of Chapter 6 apply. The remainder of this chapter considers the formal test procedures for the presence of unit roots and/or deterministic time trends.

2. DICKEY–FULLER TESTS

The last section outlined a simple procedure to determine whether $a_1 = 1$ in the model $y_t = a_1 y_{t-1} + \epsilon_t$. Begin by subtracting y_{t-1} from each side of the equation in order to write the equivalent form: $\Delta y_t = \gamma y_{t-1} + \epsilon_t$, where $\gamma = a_1 - 1$. Of course, testing the hypothesis $a_1 = 1$ is equivalent to testing the hypothesis $\gamma = 0$. Dickey and Fuller (1979) actually consider three different regression equations that can be used to test for the presence of a unit root:

$$\Delta y_t = \gamma y_{t-1} + \epsilon_t \tag{4.9}$$
$$\Delta y_t = a_0 + \gamma y_{t-1} + \epsilon_t \tag{4.10}$$
$$\Delta y_t = a_0 + \gamma y_{t-1} + a_2 t + \epsilon_t \tag{4.11}$$

The difference between the three regressions concerns the presence of the deterministic elements a_0 and $a_2 t$. The first is a pure random walk model, the second adds an intercept or *drift* term, and the third includes both a drift and linear time trend.

The parameter of interest in all the regression equations is γ; if $\gamma = 0$, the $\{y_t\}$ sequence contains a unit root. The test involves estimating one (or more) of the equations above using OLS in order to obtain the estimated value of γ and associated standard error. Comparing the resulting t-statistic with the appropriate value reported in the Dickey–Fuller tables allows the researcher to determine whether to accept or reject the null hypothesis $\gamma = 0$.

Recall that in (4.3), the estimate of $y_t = a_1 y_{t-1} + \epsilon_t$ was such that $a_1 = 0.9546$ with a standard error of 0.030. Clearly, the OLS regression in the form $\Delta y_t = \gamma y_{t-1} + \epsilon_t$ will yield an estimate of γ equal to -0.0454 with the same standard error of 0.030. Hence, the associated t-statistic for the hypothesis $\gamma = 0$ is -1.5133 ($-0.0454/0.03 = -1.5133$).

The methodology is precisely the same, regardless of which of the three forms of the equations is estimated. However, be aware that the critical values of the t-statistics do depend on whether an intercept and/or time trend is included in the regression equation. In their Monte Carlo study, Dickey and Fuller (1979) found that the critical values for $\gamma = 0$ depend on the form of the regression and sample size. The statistics labeled τ, τ_μ, and τ_τ are the appropriate statistics to use for Equations (4.9), (4.10), and (4.11), respectively.

Now, look at Table A at the end of this book. With 100 observations, there are three different critical values for the t-statistic $\gamma = 0$. For a regression without the intercept and trend terms ($a_0 = a_2 = 0$), use the section labeled τ. With 100 observations, the critical values for the t-statistic are -1.61, -1.95 and -2.60 at the 10, 5, and 1% significance levels, respectively. Thus, in the hypothetical example with $\gamma = -0.0454$ and a standard error of 0.03 (so that $t = -1.5133$), it is not possible to reject the null of a unit root at conventional significance levels. Note that the appropriate critical values depend on sample size. As in most hypothesis tests, for any given level of significance, the critical values of the t-statistic decrease as sample size increases.

Including an intercept term but not a trend term (only $a_2 = 0$) necessitates the use of the critical values in the section labeled τ_μ. Estimating (4.4) in the form $\Delta y_t = a_0 + \gamma y_{t-1} + \epsilon_t$ necessarily yields a value of γ equal to $(0.9247 - 1) = -0.0753$ with a standard error of 0.037. The appropriate calculation for the τ_μ statistic yields $-0.0753/0.037 = -2.035$. If we read from the appropriate row of Table A, with the same 100 observations, the critical values are -2.58, -2.89, and -3.51 at the 10, 5, and 1% significance levels, respectively. Again, the null of a unit root cannot be rejected at conventional significance levels. Finally, with both intercept and trend, use the critical values in the section labeled τ_τ; now the critical values are -3.45 and -4.04 at the 5 and 1% significance levels, respectively. The equation was not estimated using a time trend; inspection of Figure 4.1 indicates there is little reason to include a deterministic trend in the estimating equation.

As discussed in the next section, these critical values are unchanged if (4.9), (4.10), and (4.11) are replaced by the autoregressive processes:[6]

$$\Delta y_t = \gamma y_{t-1} + \sum_{i=2}^{p} \beta_i \Delta y_{t-i+1} + \epsilon_t \tag{4.12}$$

$$\Delta y_t = a_0 + \gamma y_{t-1} + \sum_{i=2}^{p} \beta_i \Delta y_{t-i+1} + \epsilon_t \tag{4.13}$$

$$\Delta y_t = a_0 + \gamma y_{t-1} + a_2 t + \sum_{i=2}^{p} \beta_i \Delta y_{t-i+1} + \epsilon_t \tag{4.14}$$

The same τ, τ_μ, and τ_τ statistics are all used to test the hypotheses $\gamma = 0$. Dickey and Fuller (1981) provide three additional F-statistics (called ϕ_1, ϕ_2 and ϕ_3) to test **joint** hypotheses on the coefficients. With (4.10) or (4.13), the null hypothesis $\gamma = a_0 = 0$ is tested using the ϕ_1 statistic. Including a time trend in the regression—so that (4.11) or (4.14) is estimated—the joint hypothesis $a_0 = \gamma = a_2 = 0$ is tested using the ϕ_2 statistic and the joint hypothesis $\gamma = a_2 = 0$ is tested using the ϕ_3 statistic.

The ϕ_1, ϕ_2, and ϕ_3 statistics are constructed in exactly the same way as ordinary F-tests are:

$$\phi_i = \frac{[\text{RSS(restricted)} - \text{RSS(unrestricted)}]\ r}{\text{RSS(unrestricted)}\ (T - k)}$$

where   RSS(restricted) and RSS(unrestricted) = the sums of the squared residuals from the restricted and unrestricted models

$$r = \text{number of restrictions}$$
$$T = \text{number of usable observations}$$
$$k = \text{number of parameters estimated in the unrestricted model}$$

Hence, $T - k$ = degrees of freedom in the unrestricted model.

Comparing the calculated value of ϕ_i to the appropriate value reported in Dickey and Fuller (1981) allows you to determine the significance level at which the restriction is binding. The null hypothesis is that the data are generated by the restricted model and the alternative hypothesis is that the data are generated by the unrestricted model. If the restriction is not binding, RSS(restricted) should be close to RSS(unrestricted) and ϕ_i should be small; hence, large values of ϕ_i suggest a binding restriction and rejection of the null hypothesis. Thus, if the calculated value of ϕ_i is smaller than that reported by Dickey and Fuller, you can accept the restricted model (i.e., you do not reject the null hypothesis that the restriction is not binding). If the calculated value of ϕ_i is larger than reported by Dickey and Fuller, you can reject the null hypothesis and conclude that the restriction is binding. The critical values of the three ϕ_i statistics are reported in Table B at the end of this text.

Finally, it is possible to test hypotheses concerning the significance of the drift term a_0 and time trend a_2. Under the null hypothesis $\gamma = 0$, the test for the presence of the time trend in (4.14) is given by the $\tau_{\beta\tau}$ statistic. Thus, this statistic is the test $a_2 = 0$ given that $\gamma = 0$. To test the hypothesis $a_0 = 0$, use the $\tau_{\alpha\tau}$ statistic if you estimate (4.14) and the $\tau_{\alpha\mu}$ statistic if you estimate (4.13). The complete set of test statistics and their critical values for a sample size of 100 are summarized in Table 4.1.

Table 4.1　Summary of the Dickey–Fuller Tests

Model	Hypothesis	Test Statistic	Critical values for 95% and 99% Confidence Intervals
$\Delta y_t = a_0 + \gamma y_{t-1} + a_2 t + \epsilon_t$	$\gamma = 0$	τ_τ	-3.45 and -4.04
	$a_0 = 0$ given $\gamma = 0$	$\tau_{\alpha\tau}$	3.11 and 3.78
	$a_2 = 0$ given $\gamma = 0$	$\tau_{\beta\tau}$	2.79 and 3.53
	$\gamma = a_2 = 0$	ϕ_3	6.49 and 8.73
	$a_0 = \gamma = a_2 = 0$	ϕ_2	4.88 and 6.50
$\Delta y_t = a_0 + \gamma y_{t-1} + \epsilon_t$	$\gamma = 0$	τ_μ	-2.89 and -3.51
	$a_0 = 0$ given $\gamma = 0$	$\tau_{\alpha\mu}$	2.54 and 3.22
	$a_0 = \gamma = 0$	ϕ_1	4.71 and 6.70
$\Delta y_t = \gamma y_{t-1} + \epsilon_t$	$\gamma = 0$	τ	-1.95 and -2.60

Notes:　Critical values are for a sample size of 100.

An Example

To illustrate the use of the various test statistics, Dickey and Fuller (1981) use quarterly values of the logarithm of the Federal Reserve Board's Production Index over the 1950:I to 1977:IV period to estimate the following three equations:

$$\Delta y_t = 0.52 + 0.00120t - 0.119y_{t-1} + 0.498\Delta y_{t-1} + \epsilon_t, \qquad RSS = 0.056448$$
$$\quad (0.15) \quad (0.00034) \quad (0.033) \quad (0.081) \tag{4.15}$$
$$\Delta y_t = 0.0054 + 0.447\Delta y_{t-1} + \epsilon_t, \qquad RSS = 0.063211$$
$$\quad (0.0025) \quad (0.083) \tag{4.16}$$
$$\Delta y_t = 0.511\Delta y_{t-1} + \epsilon_t, \qquad RSS = 0.065966$$
$$\quad (0.079) \tag{4.17}$$

where RSS = residual sum of squares, and standard errors are in parentheses.

To test the null hypothesis that the data are generated by (4.17) against the alternative that (4.15) is the "true" model, use the ϕ_2 statistic. Dickey and Fuller test the null hypothesis $a_0 = a_2 = \gamma = 0$ as follows. Note that the residual sums of squares of the restricted and unrestricted models are 0.065966 and 0.056448 and the null hypothesis entails three restrictions. With 110 usable observations and four estimated parameters, the unrestricted model contains 106 degrees of freedom. Since $0.056448/106 = 0.000533$, the ϕ_2 statistic is given by

$$\phi_2 = (0.065966 - 0.056448)/ 3(0.000533) = 5.95$$

With 110 observations, the critical value of ϕ_2 calculated by Dickey and Fuller is 5.59 at the 2.5% significance level. Hence, it is possible to reject the null hypothesis of a random walk against the alternative that the data contain an intercept and/or a unit root and/or a deterministic time trend (i.e., rejecting $a_0 = a_2 = \gamma = 0$ means that one or more of these parameters does not equal zero).

Dickey and Fuller also test the null hypothesis $a_2 = \gamma = 0$ given the alternative of (4.15). Now if we view (4.16) as the restricted model and (4.15) as the unrestricted model, the ϕ_3 statistic is calculated as

$$\phi_3 = (0.063211 - 0.056448)/ 2(0.000533) = 6.34$$

With 110 observations, the critical value of ϕ_3 is 6.49 at the 5% significance level and 5.47 at the 10% significance level.[7] At the 10% level, they reject the null hypothesis. However, at the 5% level, the calculated value of ϕ_3 is smaller than the critical value; they do not reject the null hypothesis that the data contain a unit root and/or deterministic time trend.

To compare with the τ_τ test (i.e., the hypothesis that only $\gamma = 0$) note that

$$\tau_\tau = -0.119/0.033 = -3.61.$$

which rejects the null of a unit root at the 5% level.

3. EXTENSIONS OF THE DICKEY–FULLER TEST

Not all time-series processes can be well represented by the first-order autoregressive process $\Delta y_t = a_0 + \gamma y_{t-1} + a_2 t + \epsilon_t$. It is possible to use the Dickey–Fuller tests in higher-order equations such as (4.12), (4.13), and (4.14). Consider the pth-order autoregressive process:

$$y_t = a_0 + a_1 y_{t-1} + a_2 y_{t-2} + a_3 y_{t-3} + \cdots + a_{p-2} y_{t-p+2} + a_{p-1} y_{t-p+1} + a_p y_{t-p} + \epsilon_t \quad (4.18)$$

To best understand the methodology of the **augmented Dickey–Fuller** test, add and subtract $a_p y_{t-p+1}$ to obtain:

$$y_t = a_0 + a_1 y_{t-1} + a_2 y_{t-2} + a_3 y_{t-3} + \cdots + a_{p-2} y_{t-p+2} + (a_{p-1} + a_p) y_{t-p+1} - a_p \Delta y_{t-p+1} + \epsilon_t$$

Next, add and subtract $(a_{p-1} + a_p) y_{t-p+2}$ to obtain

$$y_t = a_0 + a_1 y_{t-1} + a_2 y_{t-2} + a_3 y_{t-3} + \cdots - (a_{p-1} + a_p) \Delta y_{t-p+2} - a_p \Delta y_{t-p+1} + \epsilon_t$$

Continuing in this fashion, we get

$$\Delta y_t = a_0 + \gamma y_{t-1} + \sum_{i=2}^{p} \beta_i \Delta y_{t-i+1} + \epsilon_t$$

where $\gamma = -\left(1 - \sum_{i=1}^{p} a_i\right)$

$$\beta_i = \sum_{j=i}^{p} a_j \qquad\qquad (4.19)$$

In (4.19), the coefficient of interest is γ; if $\gamma = 0$, the equation is entirely in first differences and so has a unit root. We can test for the presence of a unit root using the same Dickey–Fuller statistics discussed above. Again, the appropriate statistic to use depends on the deterministic components included in the regression equation. Without an intercept or trend, use the τ statistic; with only the intercept, use the τ_μ statistic; and with both an intercept and trend, use the τ_τ statistic. It is worthwhile pointing out that the results here are perfectly consistent with our study of difference equations in Chapter 1. If the coefficients of a difference equation sum to 1, *at least* one characteristic root is unity. Here, if $\Sigma a_i = 1$, $\gamma = 0$ and the system has a unit root.

Note that the Dickey–Fuller tests assume that the errors are independent and have a constant variance. This raises four important problems related to the fact that we do not know the true data-generating process. First, the true data-generating process may contain both autoregressive and moving average components. We need to know how to conduct the test if the order of the moving average terms (if any) is unknown. Second, we cannot properly estimate γ and its standard error unless all the autoregressive terms are included in the estimating equation. Clearly, the simple regression $\Delta y_t = a_0 + \gamma y_{t-1} + \epsilon_t$ is inadequate to this task if (4.18) is the true data-generating process. However, the true order of the autoregressive process is usually unknown to the researcher, so that the problem is to select the appropriate lag length. The third problem stems from the fact that the Dickey–Fuller test considers only a single unit root. However, a pth-order autoregression has p characteristic roots; if there are $m \leq p$ unit roots, the series needs to be differenced m times to achieve stationarity. The fourth problem is that it may not be known whether an intercept and/or time trend belongs in (4.18). We consider the first three problems below. Section 7 is concerned with the issue of the appropriate deterministic regressors.

Since an invertible MA model can be transformed into an autoregressive model, the procedure can be generalized to allow for moving average components. Let the $\{y_t\}$ sequence be generated from the mixed autoregressive/moving average process:

$$A(L)y_t = C(L)\epsilon_t$$

where $A(L)$ and $C(L)$ = polynomials of orders p and q, respectively

If the roots of $C(L)$ are outside the unit circle, we can write the $\{y_t\}$ sequence as the autoregressive process:

$$A(L)y_t / C(L) = \epsilon_t$$

or, defining $D(L) = A(L)/C(L)$, we get

$$D(L)y_t = \epsilon_t$$

Even though $D(L)$ will generally be an infinite-order polynomial, in principle we can use the same technique as used to obtain (4.19) to form the infinite-order autoregressive model:

$$\Delta y_t = \gamma y_{t-1} + \sum_{i=2}^{\infty} \beta_i \Delta y_{t-i+1} + \epsilon_t \qquad (4.20)$$

As it stands, (4.20) is an infinite-order autoregression that cannot be estimated using a finite data set. Fortunately, Said and Dickey (1984) have shown that an unknown ARIMA(p, 1, q) process can be well approximated by an ARIMA(n, 1, 0) autoregression of order no more than $T^{1/3}$. Thus, we can solve the first problem by using a finite-order autoregression to approximate (4.20). The test for $\gamma = 0$ can be conducted using the aforementioned Dickey–Fuller τ, τ_μ, or τ_τ test statistics.

Now, the second problem concerning the appropriate lag length arises. Including too many lags reduces the power of the test to reject the null of a unit root since the increased number of lags necessitates the estimation of additional parameters and a loss of degrees of freedom. The degrees of freedom decrease since the number of parameters estimated has increased *and* because the number of usable observations has decreased. (We lose one observation for each additional lag included in the autoregression.) On the other hand, too few lags will not appropriately capture the actual error process, so that γ and its standard error will not be well estimated.

How does the researcher select the appropriate lag length in such circumstances? One approach is to start with a relatively long lag length and pare down the model by the usual *t*-test and/or *F*-tests. For example, one could estimate Equation (4.20) using a lag length of n^*. If the *t*-statistic on lag n^* is insignificant at some specified critical value, reestimate the regression using a lag length of $n^* - 1$. Repeat the process until the lag is significantly different from zero. In the pure autoregressive case, such a procedure will yield the true lag length with an asymptotic probability of unity, provided that the initial choice of lag length includes the true length. With seasonal data, the process is a bit different. For example, using quarterly data, one could start with 3 years of lags ($n = 12$). If the *t*-statistic on lag 12 is insignificant at some specified critical value and an *F*-test indicates that lags 9 to 12 are also insignificant, move to lags 1 to 8. Repeat the process for lag 8 and lags 5 to 8 until a reasonable lag length has been determined.

Once a tentative lag length has been determined, diagnostic checking should be conducted. As always, plotting the residuals is a most important diagnostic tool. There should not appear to be any strong evidence of structural change or serial correlation. Moreover, the correlogram of the residuals should appear to be white noise. The Ljung–Box *Q*-statistic should not reveal any significant autocorrelations among the residuals. It is inadvisable to use the alternative procedure of beginning with the most parsimonious model and keep adding lags until a significant lag is found. In Monte Carlo studies, this procedure is biased toward selecting a value of *n* that is less than the true value.

Multiple Roots

Dickey and Pantula (1987) suggest a simple extension of the basic procedure if more than one unit root is suspected. In essence, the methodology entails nothing more than performing Dickey–Fuller tests on successive differences of $\{y_t\}$. When exactly one root is suspected, the Dickey–Fuller procedure is to estimate an equation such as $\Delta y_t = a_0 + \gamma y_{t-1} + \epsilon_t$. Instead, if two roots are suspected, estimate the equation:

$$\Delta^2 y_t = a_0 + \beta_1 \Delta y_{t-1} + \epsilon_t \qquad (4.21)$$

Use the appropriate statistic (i.e., τ, τ_μ, or τ_τ depending on the deterministic elements actually included in the regression) to determine whether β_1 is significantly different from zero. If you cannot reject the null hypothesis that $\beta_1 = 0$, conclude that the $\{y_t\}$ sequence is $I(2)$. If β_1 does differ from zero, go on to determine whether there is a single unit root by estimating

$$\Delta^2 y_t = a_0 + \beta_1 \Delta y_{t-1} + \beta_2 y_{t-2} + \epsilon_t \tag{4.22}$$

Since there are not two unit roots, you should find that β_1 and/or β_2 differ from zero. Under the null hypothesis of a single unit root, $\beta_1 < 0$ and $\beta_2 = 0$; under the alternative hypothesis, $\{y_t\}$ is stationary, so that β_1 and β_2 are both negative. Thus, estimate (4.22) and use the Dickey–Fuller critical values to test the null hypothesis $\beta_1 = 0$. If you reject this null hypothesis, conclude that $\{y_t\}$ is stationary.

As a rule of thumb, economic series do not need to be differenced more than two times. However, in the odd case in which *at most r* unit roots are suspected, the procedure is to first estimate

$$\Delta^r y_t = a_0 + \beta_1 \Delta^{r-1} y_{t-1} + \epsilon_t$$

If $\Delta^r y_t$ is stationary, you should find that $-2 < \beta_1 < 0$. If the Dickey–Fuller critical values for β_1 are such that it is not possible to reject the null of a unit root, you accept the hypothesis that $\{y_t\}$ contains r unit roots. If you reject this null of exactly r unit roots, the next step is to test for $r - 1$ roots by estimating

$$\Delta^r y_t = a_0 + \beta_1 \Delta^{r-1} y_{t-1} + \beta_2 \Delta^{r-2} y_{t-1} + \epsilon_t$$

If both β_1 and β_2 differ from zero, reject the null hypothesis of $r - 1$ unit roots. You can use the Dickey–Fuller statistics to test the null of exactly $r - 1$ unit roots if the τ statistics for β_1 *and* β_2 are both statistically different from zero. If you can reject this null, the next step is to form

$$\Delta^r y_t = a_0 + \beta_1 \Delta^{r-1} y_{t-1} + \beta_2 \Delta^{r-2} y_{t-1} + \beta_3 \Delta^{r-3} y_{t-1} + \epsilon_t$$

As long as it is possible to reject the null hypothesis that the various values of the β_i are nonzero, continue toward the equation:

$$\Delta^r y_t = a_0 + \beta_1 \Delta^{r-1} y_{t-1} + \beta_2 \Delta^{r-2} y_{t-1} + \beta_3 \Delta^{r-3} y_{t-1} + \cdots + \beta_r y_{t-1} + \epsilon_t$$

Continue in this fashion until it is not possible to reject the null of a unit root or the y_t series is shown to be stationary. Notice that this procedure is quite different from the sequential testing for successively greater numbers of unit roots. It might seem tempting to test for a single unit root and, if the null cannot be rejected, go on to test for the presence of a second unit root. In repeated samples, this method tends to select too few roots.

Seasonal Unit Roots

You will recall that the best-fitting model for the monthly Spanish tourism data used in Chapter 2 had the form:

$$(1 - L^{12})(1 - L)y_t = (1 + \beta_1 L)(1 + \beta_{12} L^{12})\epsilon_t$$

Tourist visits to Spain have a unit root and seasonal unit root. Since seasonality is a key feature of many economic series, a sizable literature has developed to test for seasonal unit roots. Before proceeding, note that the first difference of a seasonal unit root process will not be stationary. To keep matters simple, suppose that the quarterly observations of $\{y_t\}$ are generated by

$$y_t = y_{t-4} + \epsilon_t$$

Here, the fourth difference of $\{y_t\}$ is stationary; using the notation of Chapter 2, we can write $\Delta_4 y_t = \epsilon_t$. Given the initial condition $y_0 = y_{-1} = \cdots = 0$, the solution for y_t is:

$$y_t = \epsilon_t + \epsilon_{t-4} + \epsilon_{t-8} + \cdots$$

so that

$$y_t - y_{t-1} = \sum_{i=0}^{t/4} \epsilon_{4i} - \sum_{i=0}^{t/4} \epsilon_{4i-1}$$

Hence, Δy_t equals the difference between two stochastic trends. Since the variance of Δy_t increases without limit as t increases, the $\{\Delta y_t\}$ sequence is not stationary. However, the seasonal difference of a unit root process may be stationary. For example, if $\{y_t\}$ is generated by $y_t = y_{t-1} + \epsilon_t$, the fourth difference (i.e., $\Delta_4 y_t = \epsilon_t + \epsilon_{t-1} + \epsilon_{t-2} + \epsilon_{t-3}$) is stationary. However, the variance of the fourth difference is larger than the variance of the first difference. The point is that the Dickey–Fuller procedure must be modified in order to test for seasonal unit roots and distinguish between seasonal versus nonseasonal roots.

There are several alternative ways to treat seasonality in a nonstationary sequence. The most direct method occurs when the seasonal pattern is purely deterministic. For example, let D_1, D_2, and D_3 represent quarterly seasonal dummy variables such that the value of D_i is unity in season i and zero otherwise. Estimate the regression equation:

$$y_t = \alpha_0 + \alpha_1 D_1 + \alpha_2 D_2 + \alpha_3 D_3 + \hat{y}_t \tag{4.23}$$

where $\hat{y}_t$ is the regression residual, so that $\hat{y}_t$ can be viewed as the deseasonalized value of y_t.

Next, use these regression residuals to estimate the regression:

$$\Delta \hat{y}_t = \gamma \hat{y}_{t-1} + \sum_{i=2}^{p} \beta_i \Delta \hat{y}_{t-i+1} + \epsilon_t$$

The null hypothesis of a unit root (i.e., $\gamma = 0$) can be tested using the Dickey–Fuller τ_μ statistic. Rejecting the null hypothesis is equivalent to accepting the alternative that the $\{y_t\}$ sequence is stationary. The test is possible as Dickey, Bell, and Miller (1986) show that the limiting distribution for γ is not affected by the removal of the deterministic seasonal components. If you want to include a time trend in (4.23), use the τ_τ statistic.

If you suspect a seasonal unit root, it is necessary to use an alternative procedure. To keep the notation simple, suppose you have quarterly observations on the $\{y_t\}$ sequence and want to test for the presence of a seasonal unit root. To explain the methodology, note that the polynomial $(1 - \gamma L^4)$ can be factored, so that there are four distinct characteristic roots:

$$(1 - \gamma L^4) = (1 - \gamma^{1/4}L)(1 + \gamma^{1/4}L)(1 - i\gamma^{1/4}L)(1 + i\gamma^{1/4}L) \qquad (4.24)$$

If y_t has a seasonal unit root, $\gamma = 1$. Equation (4.24) is a bit restrictive in that it only allows for a unit root at an annual frequency. Hylleberg et al. (1990) develop a clever technique that allows you to test for unit roots at various frequencies; you can test for a unit root (i.e., a root at a zero frequency), unit root at a semiannual frequency, or seasonal unit root. To understand the procedure, suppose y_t is generated by

$$A(L)y_t = \epsilon_t$$

where $A(L)$ is a fourth-order polynomial such that

$$(1 - a_1L)(1 + a_2L)(1 - a_3iL)(1 + a_4iL)y_t = \epsilon_t \qquad (4.25)$$

Now, if $a_1 = a_2 = a_3 = a_4 = 1$, (4.25) is equivalent to setting $\gamma = 1$ in (4.24). Hence, if $a_1 = a_2 = a_3 = a_4 = 1$, there is a seasonal unit root. Consider some of the other possible cases:

CASE 1

If $a_1 = 1$, one homogeneous solution to (4.25) is $y_t = y_{t-1}$. As such, the $\{y_t\}$ sequence tends to repeat itself each and every period. This is the case of a nonseasonal unit root.

CASE 2

If $a_2 = 1$, one homogeneous solution to (4.25) is $y_t + y_{t-1} = 0$. In this instance, the sequence tends to replicate itself at 6-month intervals, so that there is a semiannual unit root. For example, if $y_t = 1$, it follows that $y_{t+1} = -1$, $y_{t+2} = +1$, $y_{t+3} = -1$, $y_{t+4} = 1$, etc.

CASE 3

If either a_3 or a_4 is equal to unity, the $\{y_t\}$ sequence has an annual cycle. For example, if $a_3 = 1$, a homogeneous solution to (4.25) is $y_t = iy_{t-1}$. Thus, if $y_t = 1$, $y_{t+1} = i$, $y_{t+2} = i^2 = -1$, $y_{t+3} = -i$, and $y_{t+4} = -i^2 = 1$, so that the sequence replicates itself every fourth period.

To develop the test, view (4.25) as a function of a_1, a_2, a_3, and a_4 and take a Taylor series approximation of $A(L)$ around the point $a_1 = a_2 = a_3 = a_4 = 1$. Although the details of the expansion are messy, first take the partial derivative:

$$\partial A(L)/\partial a_1 = \partial(1 - a_1 L)(1 + a_2 L)(1 - a_3 iL)(1 + a_4 iL)/\partial a_1$$
$$= -(1 + a_2 L)(1 - a_3 iL)(1 + a_4 iL)L$$

Evaluating this derivative at the point $a_1 = a_2 = a_3 = a_4 = 1$ yields

$$-L(1 + L)(1 - iL)(1 + iL) = -L(1 + L)(1 + L^2) = -L(1 + L + L^2 + L^3)$$

Next, form

$$\partial A(L)/\partial a_2 = \partial(1 - a_1 L)(1 + a_2 L)(1 - a_3 iL)(1 + a_4 iL)/\partial a_2$$
$$= (1 - a_1 L)(1 - a_3 iL)(1 + a_4 iL)L$$

Evaluating at the point $a_1 = a_2 = a_3 = a_4 = 1$ yields $(1 - L + L^2 - L^3)L$. It should not take too long to convince yourself that evaluating $\partial A(L)/\partial a_3$ and $\partial A(L)/\partial a_4$ at the point $a_1 = a_2 = a_3 = a_4 = 1$ yields

$$\partial A(L)/\partial a_3 = -(1 - L^2)(1 + iL)iL$$

and

$$\partial A(L)/\partial a_4 = (1 - L^2)(1 - iL)iL$$

Since $A(L)$ evaluated at $a_1 = a_2 = a_3 = a_4 = 1$ is $(1 - L^4)$, it is possible to approximate (4.25) by

$$[(1 - L^4) - L(1 + L + L^2 + L^3)(a_1 - 1) + (1 - L + L^2 - L^3)L(a_2 - 1)$$
$$- (1 - L^2)(1 + iL)iL(a_3 - 1) + (1 - L^2)(1 - iL)iL(a_4 - 1)]y_t = \epsilon_t$$

Define γ_i such that $\gamma_i = (a_i - 1)$ and note that $(1 + iL)i = i - L$ and $(1 - iL)i = i + iL$; hence,

$$(1 - L^4)y_t = \gamma_1(1 + L + L^2 + L^3)y_{t-1} - \gamma_2(1 - L + L^2 - L^3)y_{t-1}$$
$$+ (1 - L^2)[\gamma_3(i - L) - \gamma_4(i + L)]y_{t-1} + \epsilon_t$$

so that

$$(1 - L^4)y_t = \gamma_1(1 + L + L^2 + L^3)y_{t-1} - \gamma_2(1 - L + L^2 - L^3)y_{t-1}$$
$$+ (1 - L^2)[(\gamma_3 - \gamma_4)i - (\gamma_3 + \gamma_4)L]y_{t-1} + \epsilon_t \quad (4.26)$$

To purge the imaginary numbers from (4.26), define γ_5 and γ_6 such that $2\gamma_3 = -\gamma_6 - i\gamma_5$ and $2\gamma_4 = -\gamma_6 + i\gamma_5$. Hence, $(\gamma_3 - \gamma_4)i = \gamma_5$ and $\gamma_3 + \gamma_4 = \gamma_6$. Substituting into (4.26) yields

$$(1 - L^4)y_t = \gamma_1(1 + L + L^2 + L^3)y_{t-1} - \gamma_2(1 - L + L^2 - L^3)y_{t-1}$$
$$+ (1 - L^2)(\gamma_5 - \gamma_6 L)y_{t-1} + \epsilon_t$$

Thus, to implement the procedure, use the following steps:

STEP 1: Form the following variables:

$$y_{1t-1} = (1 + L + L^2 + L^3)y_{t-1} = y_{t-1} + y_{t-2} + y_{t-3} + y_{t-4}$$
$$y_{2t-2} = (1 - L + L^2 - L^3)y_{t-1} = y_{t-1} - y_{t-2} + y_{t-3} - y_{t-4}$$
$$y_{3t-1} = (1 - L^2)y_{t-1} = y_{t-1} - y_{t-3} \qquad \text{so that } y_{3t-2} = y_{t-2} - y_{t-4}$$

STEP 2: Estimate the regression:

$$(1 - L^4)y_t = \gamma_1 y_{1t-1} - \gamma_2 y_{2t-1} + \gamma_5 y_{3t-1} - \gamma_6 y_{3t-2} + \epsilon_t$$

You might want to modify the form of the equation by including an intercept, deterministic seasonal dummies, and a linear time trend. As in the augmented form of the Dickey–Fuller test, lagged values of $(1 - L^4)y_{t-i}$ may also be included. Perform the appropriate diagnostic checks to ensure that the residuals from the regression equation approximate a white-noise process.

STEP 3: Form the *t*-statistic for the null hypothesis $\gamma_1 = 0$; the appropriate critical values are reported in Hylleberg et al. (1990). If you do not reject the hypothesis $\gamma_1 = 0$, conclude that $a_1 = 1$, so there is a nonseasonal unit root. Next, form the *t*-test for the hypothesis $\gamma_2 = 0$. If you do not reject the null hypothesis, conclude that $a_2 = 1$ and there is a unit root with a semiannual frequency. Finally, perform the *F*-test for the hypothesis $\gamma_5 = \gamma_6 = 0$. If the calculated value is less than the critical value reported in Hylleberg et al. (1990), conclude that γ_5 and/or γ_6 is zero, so that there is a unit root with an annual frequency. Be aware that the three null hypotheses are not alternatives; a series may have nonseasonal, semiannual, and annual unit roots.

At the 5% significance level, Hylleberg et al. (1990) report that the critical values using 100 observations are:

	$\gamma_1 = 0$	$\gamma_2 = 0$	$\gamma_5 = \gamma_6 = 0$
Intercept	−2.88	−1.95	3.08
Intercept plus seasonal dummies	−2.95	−2.94	6.57
Intercept plus seasonal dummies plus time trend	−3.53	−2.94	6.60

4. EXAMPLES OF THE AUGMENTED DICKEY–FULLER TEST

The last chapter reviewed the evidence reported by Nelson and Plosser (1982) suggesting that macroeconomic variables are difference stationary rather than trend stationary. We are now in a position to consider their formal tests of the hypothesis. For each series under study, Nelson and Plosser estimated the regression:

$$\Delta y_t = a_0 + a_2 t + \gamma y_{t-1} + \sum_{i=2}^{p} \beta_i \Delta y_{t-1+i} + \epsilon_t$$

The chosen lag lengths are reported in the column labeled p in Table 4.2. The estimated values a_0, a_2, and γ are reported in columns 3, 4, and 5, respectively.

Table 4.2 **Nelson and Plosser's Tests for Unit Roots**

	p	a_0	a_2	γ	$\gamma + 1$
Real GNP	2	0.819 (3.03)	0.006 (3.03)	−0.175 (−2.99)	0.825
Nominal GNP	2	1.06 (2.37)	0.006 (2.34)	−0.101 (−2.32)	0.899
Industrial production	6	0.103 (4.32)	0.007 (2.44)	−0.165 (−2.53)	0.835
Unemployment rate	4	0.513 (2.81)	−0.000 (−0.23)	−0.294* (−3.55)	0.706

Notes: 1. p is the chosen lag length. Coefficients divided by their standard errors are in parentheses. Thus, entries in parentheses represent the *t*-test for the null hypothesis that a coefficient is equal to zero. Under the null of nonstationary, it is necessary to use the Dickey–Fuller critical values. At the 0.05 significance level, the critical value for the *t*-statistic is −3.45.

2. An asterisk (*) denotes significance at the 0.05 level. For real and nominal GNP and industrial production, it is not possible to reject the null $\gamma = 0$ at the 0.05 level. Hence, the unemployment rate appears to be stationary.

3. The expression $\gamma + 1$ is the estimate of the partial autocorrelation between y_t and y_{t-1}.

Recall that the traditional view of business cycles maintains that the GNP and production levels are trend stationary rather than difference stationary. An adherent of this view must assert that γ is different from zero; if $\gamma = 0$, the series has a unit root and is difference stationary. Given the sample sizes used by Nelson and Plosser (1982), at the 0.05 level, the critical value of the t-statistic for the null hypothesis $\gamma = 0$ is -3.45. Thus, only if the estimated value of γ is more than 3.45 standard deviations from zero, is it possible to reject the hypothesis that $\gamma = 0$. As can be seen from inspection of Table 4.2, the estimated values of γ for real GNP, nominal GNP, and industrial production are not statistically different from zero. Only the unemployment rate has an estimated value of γ that is significantly different from zero at the 0.05 level.

Unit Roots and Purchasing-Power Parity

Purchasing-power parity (PPP) is a simple relationship linking national price levels and exchange rates. In its simplest form, PPP asserts that the rate of currency depreciation is approximately equal to the difference between the domestic and foreign inflation rates. If p and p^* denote the logarithms of the U.S. and foreign price levels and e the logarithm of the dollar price of foreign exchange, PPP implies

$$e_t = p_t - p_t^* + d_t$$

where d_t represents the deviation from PPP in period t.

Figure 4.2   Real exchange rates.

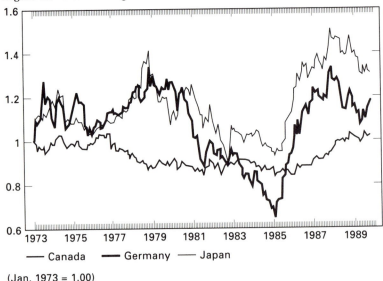

— Canada   — Germany   — Japan

(Jan. 1973 = 1.00)

In applied work, p_t and p_t^* usually refer to national price indices in t relative to a base year, so that e_t refers to an index of the domestic currency price of foreign exchange relative to a base year. For example, if the U.S. inflation rate is 10% while the foreign inflation rate is 15%, the dollar price of foreign exchange should fall by approximately 5%. The presence of the term d_t allows for short-run deviations from PPP.

Because of its simplicity and intuitive appeal, PPP has been used extensively in theoretical models of exchange rate determination. However, as in the well-known Dornbusch (1976) "overshooting" model, real economic shocks, such as productivity or demand shocks, can cause permanent deviations from PPP. For our purposes, the theory of PPP serves as an excellent vehicle to illustrate many time-series testing procedures. One test of long-run PPP is to determine whether d_t is stationary. After all, if the deviations from PPP are nonstationary (i.e., if the deviations are permanent in nature), we can reject the theory. Note that PPP does allow for persistent deviations; the autocorrelations of the $\{d_t\}$ sequence need not be zero. One popular testing procedure is to define the "real" exchange rate in period t as

$$r_t \equiv e_t + p_t^* - p_t$$

Long-run PPP is said to hold if the $\{r_t\}$ sequence is stationary. For example, in Enders (1988), I constructed real exchange rates for three major U.S. trading partners: Germany, Canada, and Japan. The data were divided into two periods: January 1960 to April 1971 (representing the fixed exchange rate period) and January 1973 to November 1986 (representing the flexible exchange rate period). Each nation's Wholesale Price Index (WPI) was multiplied by an index of the U.S. dollar price of the foreign currency and then divided by the U.S. WPI. The log of the constructed series is the $\{r_t\}$ sequence. Updated values of the real exchange rate data used in the study are in the file REAL.PRN contained on the data disk. As an exercise, you should use this data to verify the results reported below.

A critical first step in any econometric analysis is to visually inspect the data. The plots of the three real exchange rate series during the flexible exchange rate period are shown in Figure 4.2. Each series seems to meander in a fashion characteristic of a random walk process. Notice that there is little visual evidence of explosive behavior or a deterministic time trend. Consider Figure 4.3 that shows the autocorrelation function of the Canadian real rate in levels, part (a), and first differences, part (b). This autocorrelation pattern is typical of all the series in the analysis. The autocorrelation function shows little tendency to decay, whereas the autocorrelations of the first differences display the classic pattern of a stationary series. In graph (b), all autocorrelations (with the possible exception of ρ_{11} that equals 0.18) are not statistically different from zero at the usual significance levels.

To formally test for the presence of a unit root in the real exchange rates, augmented Dickey–Fuller tests of the form given by (4.19) were conducted. The regression $\Delta r_t = a_0 + \gamma r_{t-1} + \beta_2 \Delta r_{t-1} + \beta_3 \Delta r_{t-2} + \cdots$ was estimated based on the following considerations:

Figure 4.3   ACF of Canada's real exchange rate.

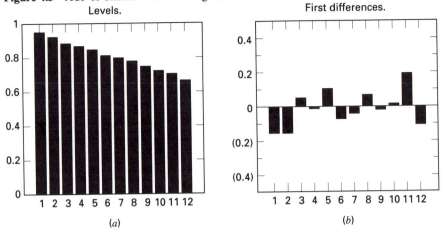

(a)

(b)

1. The theory of PPP does not allow for a deterministic time trend or multiple unit roots. Any such findings would refute the theory as posited. Although all the series decline throughout the early 1980s and all rise during the mid to late 1980s, there is no a priori reason to expect a structural change. Pretesting the data using the Dickey-Pantula (1987) strategy showed no evidence of multiple unit roots. Moreover, there was no reason to entertain the notion of trend stationarity; the expression $a_2 t$ was *not* included in the estimating equation.

2. In both time periods, F-tests and the SBC indicated that β_3 through β_{24} could be set equal to zero. For Germany and Japan during the flexible rate period, β_2 was statistically different from zero; in the other four instances, β_2 could be set equal to zero. In spite of these findings, with monthly data it is always important to entertain the possibility of a lag length no shorter than 12 months. As such, tests were conducted using the short lags selected by the F-tests and SBC *and* using a lag length of 12 months.

For the Canadian case during the 1973 to 1986 period, the t-statistic for the null hypothesis that $\gamma = 0$ is -1.42 using no lags and -1.51 using all 12 lags. Given the critical value of the τ_μ statistic, it is not possible to reject the null of a unit root in the Canadian/U.S. real exchange rate series. Hence, PPP fails for these two nations. In the 1960 to 1971 period, the calculated value of the t-statistic is -1.59; again, it is possible to conclude that PPP fails.

Table 4.3 reports the results of all six estimations using the short lag lengths suggested by the F-tests and SBC. Notice the following properties of the estimated models:

1. For all six models, it is not possible to reject the null hypothesis that PPP fails. As can be seen from the last column of Table 4.3, the absolute value of the t-sta-

tistic for the null $\gamma = 0$ is never more than 1.59. The economic interpretation is that real productivity and/or demand shocks have had a permanent influence on real exchange rates.

2. As measured by the sample standard deviation (SD), real exchange rates were far more volatile in the 1973 to 1986 period than the 1960 to 1971 period. Moreover, as measured by the standard error of the estimate (SEE), real exchange rate volatility is associated with unpredictability. The SEE during the flexible exchange rate period is several hundred times that of the fixed rate period. It seems reasonable to conclude that the change in the exchange rate regime (i.e., the end of Bretton–Woods) affected the volatility of the real exchange rate.

3. Care must be taken to keep the appropriate null hypothesis in mind. Under the null of a unit root, classical test procedures are inappropriate and we resort to the statistics tabulated by Dickey and Fuller. However, classical test procedures (which assume stationary variables) are appropriate under the null that the real rates are stationary. Thus, the following possibility arises. Suppose that the t-statistic in the Canadian case happened to be -2.16 instead of -1.42. Using the Dickey–Fuller critical values, you would not reject the null of a unit root; hence, you could conclude that PPP fails. However, under the null of stationarity (where we can use classical procedures), γ is more than two standard deviations from zero and you would conclude PPP holds since the usual t-test becomes applicable.

   This apparent dilemma commonly occurs when analyzing series with roots close to unity in absolute value. Unit root tests do not have much power in discriminating between characteristic roots close to unity and actual unit roots. The dilemma is only apparent since the two null hypotheses are quite different. It is perfectly consistent to maintain a null that PPP holds and not be able to reject a null that PPP fails! Notice that this dilemma does not actually arise for any of the series reported in Table 4.3; for each, it is not possible to reject a null of $\gamma = 0$ at conventional significance levels.

4. Looking at some of the diagnostic statistics, we see that all the F-statistics indicate that it is appropriate to exclude lags 2 (or 3) through 12 from the regression equation. To reinforce the use of short lags, notice that the first-order correlation coefficient of the residuals (ρ) is low and the Durbin–Watson statistic close to 2. It is interesting that all the point estimates of the characteristic roots indicate that real exchange rates are convergent. To obtain the characteristic roots, rewrite the estimated equations in the autoregressive form $r_t = a_0 + a_1 r_{t-1}$ or $r_t = a_0 + a_1 r_{t-1} + a_2 r_{t-2}$. For the four AR(1) models, the point estimates of the slope coefficients are all less than unity. In the post–Bretton–Woods period (1973–1986), the point estimates of the characteristic roots of Japan's second-order process are 0.931 and 0.319; for Germany, the roots are 0.964 and 0.256. However, this is precisely what we would expect if PPP fails; under the null of a unit root, we know that γ is biased downward.

Table 4.3   **Real Exchange Rate Estimation**

	γ	a_1	a_2	Mean	ρ/DW	F	SD/SEE	H_0: $\gamma = 0$
1973–1986								
Canada	-0.022 (0.0155)	0.978		1.05	0.059 1.88	0.194	5.47 1.16	$t = -1.42$
Japan	-0.047 (0.074)	1.25	-0.297	1.01	-0.007 2.01	0.226	10.44 2.81	$t = -0.635$
Germany	-0.027 (0.076)	1.22	-0.247	1.11	-0.014 2.004	0.858	20.68 3.71	$t = -0.280$
1960–1971								
Canada	-0.031 (0.019)	0.969		1.02	-0.107 2.21	0.434	0.014 0.004	$t = -1.59$
Japan	-0.030 (0.028)	0.970		0.980	0.046 1.98	0.330	0.017 0.005	$t = -1.04$
Germany	-0.016 (0.012)	0.984		1.01	0.038 1.93	0.097	0.026 0.004	$t = -1.23$

Notes: 1.   Standard errors are in parentheses
   2.   Mean is the estimated value of $a_0/(1 - a_1 - a_2)$, SD the standard deviation of the real exchange rate, SEE the estimated standard deviation of the residuals (i.e., the standard error of the estimate). F the significance level of the test that lags 2 (or 3) through 12 can be excluded, DW the Durbin–Watson statistic for first-order serial correlation, and ρ the estimated autocorrelation coefficient.
   3.   Entries are the t-statistic for the hypothesis $\gamma = 0$.

5. PHILLIPS–PERRON TESTS

The distribution theory supporting the Dickey–Fuller tests assumes that the errors are statistically independent and have a constant variance. In using this methodology, care must be taken to ensure that the error terms are uncorrelated and have constant variance. Phillips and Perron (1988) developed a generalization of the Dickey–Fuller procedure that allows for fairly mild assumptions concerning the distribution of the errors.

To briefly explain the procedure, consider the following regression equations:

$$y_t = a_0^* + a_1^* y_{t-1} + \mu_t \tag{4.27}$$

and

$$y_t = \tilde{a}_0 + \tilde{a}_1 y_{t-1} + \tilde{a}_2 (t - T/2) + \mu_t \tag{4.28}$$

where T = number of observations and the disturbance term μ_t is such that $E\mu_t = 0$, but there is no requirement that the disturbance term is serially uncorrelated or homogeneous. Instead of the Dickey–Fuller assumptions of independence and homogeneity, the Phillips–Perron test allows the disturbances to be weakly dependent and heterogeneously distributed.

Phillips and Perron characterize the distributions and derive test statistics that can be used to test hypotheses about the coefficients a_i^* and $\tilde{a}_i$ under the null hypothesis that the data are generated by

$$y_t = y_{t-1} + \mu_t$$

The Phillips–Perron test statistics are modifications of the Dickey–Fuller t-statistics that take into account the less restrictive nature of the error process. The expressions are extremely complex; to actually derive them would take us far beyond the scope of this book. However, many statistical time-series software packages now calculate these statistics, so that they are directly available. For the ambitious reader, the formulas used to calculate these statistics are reported in the appendix to this chapter. The most useful of the test statistics are as follows:

$Z(ta_1^*)$: Used to test the hypothesis $a_1^* = 1$
$Z(t\tilde{a}_1)$: Used to test the hypothesis $\tilde{a}_1 = 1$
$Z(t\tilde{a}_2)$: Used to test the hypothesis $\tilde{a}_2 = 0$
$Z(\phi_3)$: Used to test the hypotheses $\tilde{a}_1 = 1$ and $\tilde{a}_2 = 0$

The critical values for the Phillips–Perron statistics are precisely those given for the Dickey–Fuller tests. For example, the critical values for $Z(ta_1^*)$ and $Z(t\tilde{a}_1)$ are those given in the Dickey–Fuller tables under the headings τ_μ and τ_τ, respectively. The critical values of $Z(\phi_3)$ are given by the Dickey–Fuller ϕ_3 statistic.

Do not be deceived by the apparent simplicity of Equations (4.27) and (4.28). In reality, it is far more general than the type of data-generating process allowable by the Dickey–Fuller procedure. For example, suppose that the $\{\mu_t\}$ sequence is generated by the autoregressive process $\mu_t = [C(L)/B(L)]\epsilon_t$, where $B(L)$ and $C(L)$ are polynomials in the lag operator. Given this form of the error process, we can write Equation (4.27) in the form used in the Dickey–Fuller tests; that is,

$$B(L)y_t = a_0^* B(L) + a_1^* B(L)y_{t-1} + C(L)\epsilon_t$$

or

$$(1 - a_1^* L)B(L)y_t = \alpha + C(L)\epsilon_t$$

where $a_0^* B(L) = \alpha$

Thus, the Phillips–Perron procedure can be applied to mixed processes in the same way as the Dickey–Fuller tests.

Foreign Exchange Market Efficiency

Corbae and Ouliaris (1986) used Phillips–Perron tests to determine whether (1) exchange rates follow a random walk and (2) the return to forward exchange market speculation contains a unit root. Denote the spot dollar price of foreign exchange on day t as s_t. An individual at t can also buy or sell foreign exchange forward. A 90-day forward contract requires that on day $t + 90$, the individual take delivery (or make payment) of a specified amount of foreign exchange in return for a specified amount of dollars. Let f_t denote the 90-day forward market price of foreign exchange purchased on day t. On day t, suppose that an individual speculator buys forward pounds at the price $f_t = \$2.00/\text{pound}$. Thus, in 90 days the individual is obligated to provide $200,000 in return for £100,000. Of course, the agent may choose to immediately sell these pounds on the spot market. If on day $t + 90$, the spot price happens to be $s_{t+90} = \$2.01/\text{pound}$, the individual can sell the £100,000 for $201,000; without transactions costs taken into account, the individual earns a profit of $1000. In general, the profit on such a transaction will be $s_{t+90} - f_t$ multiplied by the number of pounds transacted. (Note that profits will be negative if $s_{t+90} < f_t$.) Of course, it is possible to speculate by selling forward pounds also. An individual selling 90-day forward pounds on day t will be able to buy them on the spot market at s_{t+90}. Here, profits will be $f_t - s_{t+90}$ multiplied by the number of pounds transacted. The efficient market hypothesis maintains that the expected profit or loss from such speculative behavior must be zero. Let $E_t s_{t+90}$ denote the expectation of the spot rate for day $t + 90$ conditioned on the information available on day t. Since we actually know f_t on day t, the efficient market hypothesis for forward exchange market speculation can be written as

$$E_t s_{t+90} = f_t$$

or

$$s_{t+90} - f_t = p_t$$

where p_t = per unit profit from speculation
$E_t p_t = 0$

Thus, the efficient market hypothesis requires that for any time period t, the 90-day forward rate (i.e., f_t) be an unbiased estimator of the spot rate 90 days from t. Suppose that a researcher collected weekly data of spot and forward exchange rates. The data set would consist of the forward rates f_t, f_{t+7}, f_{t+14}, ... and spot rates s_t, s_{t+7}, s_{t+14}, ... By using these exchange rates, it is possible to construct the sequence $s_{t+90} - f_t = p_t$, $s_{t+7+90} - f_{t+7} = p_{t+7}$, $s_{t+14+90} - f_{t+14} = p_{t+14}$, ... Normalize the time period to 1 week, so that $y_1 = p_t$, $y_2 = p_{t+7}$, $y_3 = p_{t+14}$, ... and consider the regression equation (where ~ is dropped for simplicity):

$$y_t = a_0 + a_1 y_{t-1} + a_2 t + \mu_t$$

The efficient market hypothesis asserts that *ex ante* expected profit must equal zero; hence, with quarterly data, it should be the case that $a_0 = a_1 = a_2 = 0$. However, the way that the data set was constructed means that the residuals will be correlated. As Corbae and Ouliaris (1986) point out, suppose that there is relevant exchange market "news" at date T. Agents will incorporate this news into all forward contracts signed in periods subsequent to T. However, the realized returns for all preexisting contracts will be affected by the news. Since there are approximately 13 weeks in a 90-day period, we can expect the μ_t sequence to be an MA(12) process. Although *ex ante* expected returns may be zero, the *ex post* returns from speculation at t will be correlated with the returns from those engaging forward contracts at weeks $t + 1$ through $t + 12$.

Meese and Singleton (1982) assumed white-noise disturbances in using a Dickey–Fuller test to study the returns from forward market speculation. One surprising result was that the return from forward speculation in the Swiss franc contained a unit root. This finding contradicts the efficient market hypothesis since it implies the existence of a permanent component in the sequence of returns. However, the assumption of white-noise disturbances is inappropriate if the $\{\mu_t\}$ sequence is an MA(12) process. Instead, Corbae and Ouliaris use the more appropriate Phillips–Perron procedure to analyze foreign exchange market efficiency; some of their results are contained in Table 4.4.

First, consider the test for the unit root hypothesis (i.e., $a_1 = 1$). All estimated values of a_1 exceed 0.9; the first-order autocorrelation of the returns from speculation appears to be quite high. However, given the small standard errors, all estimated values are over four standard deviations from unity. At the 5% significance level, the critical value for a test of $a_1 = 1$, is -3.43. Note that this critical value is the Dickey–Fuller τ_τ statistic with 250 observations. Hence, as opposed to Meese

Table 4.4   **Returns to Forward Speculation**

	a_0	a_1	a_2
Switzerland	−0.117E-2 (0.106E-2) $Z(ta_0) = -1.28$	0.941 (0.159E-1) $Z(ta_1) = -4.06$	−0.111E-4 (0.834E-5) $Z(ta_2) = -1.07$
Canada	−0.651E-3 (0.409E-3) $Z(ta_0) = -1.73$	0.907 (0.191E-1) $Z(ta_1) = -5.45$	0.116E-5 (0.298E-5) $Z(ta_2) = -1.42$
U.K.	−0.779E-3 (0.903E-3) $Z(ta_0) = -0.995$	0.937 (0.163E-1) $Z(ta_1) = -4.69$	−0.132E-4 (0.720E-5) $Z(ta_2) = -1.50$

Notes: 1. Standard errors are in parentheses.
  2. $Z(ta_0)$ and $Z(ta_2)$ are the Phillips–Perron adjusted *t*-statistics for the hypotheses that $a_0 = 0$ and $a_2 = 0$, respectively. $Z(ta_1)$ is the Phillips–Perron adjusted *t*-statistic for the hypothesis that $a_1 = 1$.

and Singleton (1982), Corbae and Ouliaris are able to reject the null of a unit root in all series examined. Thus, shocks to the return from forward exchange market speculation do not have permanent effects.

A second necessary condition for the efficient market hypothesis to hold is that the intercept term a_0 equal zero. A nonzero intercept term suggests a predictable gap between the forward rate and spot rate in the future. If $a_0 \neq 0$, on average, there are unexploited profit opportunities. It may be that agents are risk-averse or profit-maximizing speculators are not fully utilizing all available information in determining their forward exchange positions. In absolute value, all the $Z(t\tilde{a}_0)$ statistics are *less than* the critical value, so that Corbae and Ouliaris cannot reject the null $a_0 = 0$. In the same way, they are not able to reject the null hypothesis of no deterministic time trend (i.e., that $a_2 = 0$). The calculated $Z(t\tilde{a}_2)$ statistics indicate that the estimated coefficients of the time trend are never more than 1.50 standard errors from zero.

At this point, you might wonder whether it would be possible to perform the same sort of analysis using an augmented Dickey–Fuller (ADF) test. After all, Said and Dickey (1984) showed that the ADF test can be used when the error process is a moving average. The desirable feature of the Phillips–Perron test is that it allows for a weaker set of assumptions concerning the error process. Also, Monte Carlo studies find that the Phillips–Perron test has greater power to reject a false null hypothesis of a unit root. However, there is a cost entailed with the use of weaker assumptions. Monte Carlo studies have also shown that in the presence of *negative* moving average terms, the Phillips–Perron test tends to reject the null of a unit root whether or not the actual data-generating process contains a negative unit root. It is preferable to use the ADF test when the true model contains negative moving average terms and the Phillips–Perron test when the true model contains positive moving average terms.

In practice, the choice of the most appropriate test can be difficult since you never know the true data-generating process. A safe choice is to use both types of unit roots tests. If they reinforce each other, you can have confidence in the results. Sometimes, economic theory will be helpful in that it suggests the most appropriate test. In the Corbae and Ouliaris example, excess returns should be positively correlated; hence, the Phillips–Perron test is a reasonable choice.

6. STRUCTURAL CHANGE

In performing unit root tests, special care must be taken if it is suspected that structural change has occurred. When there are structural breaks, the various Dickey–Fuller and Phillips–Perron test statistics are biased toward the nonrejection of a unit root. To explain, consider the situation in which there is a one-time change in the mean of an otherwise stationary sequence. In the top graph (a) of Figure 4.4, the $\{y_t\}$ sequence was constructed so as to be stationary around a mean of zero for $t = 0, \ldots, 50$ and then to fluctuate around a mean of 6 for $t = 51, \ldots, 100$. The sequence was formed by drawing 100 normally and independently distributed values for the $\{\epsilon_t\}$ sequence. By setting $y_0 = 0$, the next 100 values in the sequence were generated using the formula:

$$y_t = 0.5y_{t-1} + \epsilon_t + D_L \tag{4.29}$$

where D_L is a dummy variable such that $D_L = 0$ for $t = 1, \ldots, 50$ and $D_L = 3$ for $t = 51, \ldots, 100$. The subscript L is designed to indicate that the *level* of the dummy changes. At times, it will be convenient to refer to the value of the dummy variable in period t as $D_L(t)$; in the example at hand, $D_L(50) = 0$ and $D_L(51) = 3$.

In practice, the structural change may not be as apparent as the break shown in the figure. However, the large simulated break is useful for illustrating the problem of using a Dickey–Fuller test in such circumstances. The straight line shown in the figure highlights the fact that the series appears to have a deterministic trend. In fact, the straight line is the best-fitting OLS equation:

$$y_t = a_0 + a_2 t + e_t$$

In the figure, you can see that the fitted value of a_0 is negative and the fitted value of a_2 is positive. The proper way to estimate (4.29) is to fit a simple AR(1) model and allow the intercept to change by including the dummy variable D_L. However, suppose that we unsuspectingly fit the regression equation:

$$y_t = a_0 + a_1 y_{t-1} + e_t \tag{4.30}$$

As you can infer from Figure 4.4, the estimated value of a_1 is necessarily biased toward unity. The reason for this upward bias is that the estimated value of a_1 cap-

Figure 4.4   Two models of structural change.

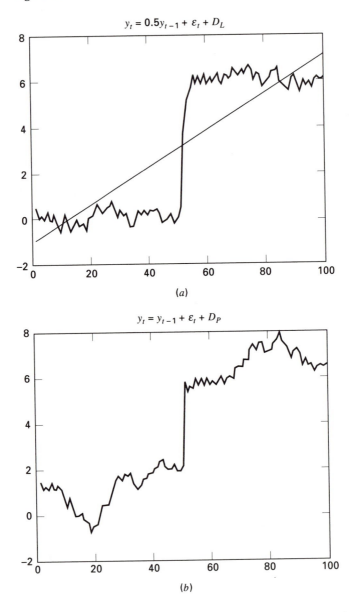

tures the property that "low" values of y_t (i.e., those fluctuating around zero) are followed by other low values and "high" values (i.e., those fluctuating around a mean of 6) are followed by other high values. For a formal demonstration, note that as a_1 approaches unity, (4.30) approaches a random walk plus drift. We know that the solution to the random walk plus drift model includes a deterministic trend, that is,

$$y_t = y_0 + a_0 t + \sum_{i=1}^{t} \epsilon_i$$

Thus, the misspecified equation (4.30) will tend to mimic the trend line shown in Figure 4.4 by biasing a_1 toward unity. This bias in a_1 means that the Dickey–Fuller test is biased toward accepting the null hypothesis of a unit root, *even though the series is stationary within each of the subperiods.*

Of course, a unit root process can exhibit a structural break also. The lower graph (b) of Figure 4.4 simulates a random walk process with a structural change occurring at $t = 51$. This second simulation used the same 100 realizations for the $\{\epsilon_t\}$ sequence and set $y_0 = 2$. The 100 realizations of the $\{y_t\}$ sequence were constructed as

$$y_t = y_{t-1} + \epsilon_t + D_P$$

where $D_P(51) = 4$ and all other values of $D_P = 0$.

Here, the subscript P refers to the fact that there is a single *pulse* in the dummy variable. In a unit root process, a single pulse in the dummy will have a permanent effect on the level of the $\{y_t\}$ sequence. In $t = 51$, the pulse in the dummy is equivalent to an ϵ_{t+51} shock of four extra units. Hence, the *one-time* shock to $D_P(51)$ has a *permanent* effect on the mean value of the sequence for $t \geq 51$. In the figure, you can see that the level of the process takes a discrete jump in $t = 51$, never exhibiting any tendency to return to the prebreak level.

The bias in the Dickey–Fuller tests was confirmed in a Monte Carlo experiment. Perron (1989) generated 10,000 replications of a stationary process like that of (4.29). Each replication was formed by drawing 100 normally and independently distributed values for the $\{\epsilon_t\}$ sequence. For each of the 10,000 replicated series, Perron used OLS to estimate a regression in the form of (4.30).[8] As could be anticipated from our earlier discussion, he found that the estimated values of a_1 were biased toward unity. Moreover, the bias became more pronounced as the magnitude of the break increased.

Testing for Structural Change

Returning to the two graphs of Figure 4.4, we see that there may be instances in which the unaided eye cannot easily detect the difference between the alternative types of sequences. One econometric procedure to tests for unit roots in the presence of a structural break involves splitting the sample into two parts and using Dickey–Fuller tests on each part. The problem with this procedure is that the degrees of freedom for each of the resulting regressions are diminished. It is preferable to have a single test based on the full sample.

Perron (1989) goes on to develop a formal procedure to test for unit roots in the presence of a structural change at time period $t = \tau + 1$. Consider the null hypothesis of a one-time jump in the level of a unit root process against the alternative of a one-time change in the intercept of a trend stationary process. Formally, let the null and alternative hypotheses be

$$H_1: y_t = a_0 + y_{t-1} + \mu_1 D_P + \epsilon_t \tag{4.31}$$

$$A_1: y_t = a_0 + a_2 t + \mu_2 D_L + \epsilon_t \tag{4.32}$$

where D_P represents a *pulse* dummy variable such that $D_P = 1$ if $t = \tau + 1$ and zero otherwise, and D_L represents a *level* dummy variable such that $D_L = 1$ if $t > \tau$ and zero otherwise.

Under the null hypothesis, $\{y_t\}$ is a unit root process with a one-time jump in the level of the sequence in period $t = \tau + 1$. Under the alternative hypothesis, $\{y_t\}$ is trend stationary with a one-time jump in the intercept. Figure 4.5 can help you to visualize the two hypotheses. Simulating (4.31) by setting $a_0 = 1$ and using 100 realizations for the $\{\epsilon_t\}$ sequence, the erratic line in Figure 4.5 illustrates the time path under the null hypothesis. You can see the one-time jump in the level of the process occurring in period 51. Thereafter, the $\{y_t\}$ sequence continues the original random walk plus drift process. The alternative hypothesis posits that the $\{y_t\}$ sequence is stationary around the broken trend line. Up to $t = \tau$, $\{y_t\}$ is stationary around $a_0 + a_2 t$ and beginning $\tau + 1$, y_t is stationary around $a_0 + a_2 t + \mu_2$. As illustrated by the broken line, there is a one-time increase in the intercept of the trend if $\mu_2 > 0$.

The econometric problem is to determine whether an observed series is best modeled by (4.31) or (4.32). The implementation of Perron's (1989) technique is straightforward:

Figure 4.5
Alternative representations of structural change.

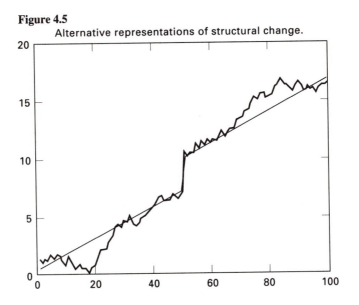

STEP 1: Detrend the data by estimating the alternative hypothesis and calling the residuals $\hat{y}_t$.

Hence, each value of $\hat{y}_t$ is the residual from the regression $y_t = a_0 + a_2 t + \mu_2 D_L + \hat{y}_t$.

STEP 2: Estimate the regression:

$$\hat{y}_t = a_1 \hat{y}_{t-1} + \epsilon_t$$

Under the null hypothesis of a unit root, the theoretical value of a_1 is unity. Perron (1989) shows that when the residuals are identically and independently distributed, the distribution of a_1 depends on the proportion of observations occurring prior to the break. Denote this proportion by: $\lambda = \tau/T$

where $T =$ total number of observations.

STEP 3: Perform diagnostic checks to determine if the residuals from Step 2 are serially uncorrelated. If there is serial correlation, use the augmented form of the regression:

$$\hat{y}_t = a_1 \hat{y}_{t-1} + \sum_{i=1}^{k} \beta_i \Delta \hat{y}_{t-i} + \epsilon_t$$

where $\hat{y}_t =$ is the detrended series.

STEP 4: Calculate the *t*-statistic for the null hypothesis $a_1 = 1$. This statistic can be compared to the critical values calculated by Perron. Perron generated 5000 series according to H_1 using values of λ ranging from 0 to 1 by increments of 0.1. For each value of λ, he estimated the regressions $\hat{y}_t = a_1 \hat{y}_{t-1} + \epsilon_t$ and calculated the sample distribution of a_1. Naturally, the critical values are identical to the Dickey–Fuller statistics when $\lambda = 0$ and $\lambda = 1$; in effect, there is no structural change unless $0 < \lambda < 1$. The maximum difference between the two statistics occurs when $\lambda = 0.5$. For $\lambda = 0.5$, the critical value of the *t*-statistic at the 5% level of significance is -3.76 (which is larger in absolute than the corresponding Dickey–Fuller statistic of -3.41). If you find a *t*-statistic greater than the critical value calculated by Perron, it is possible to reject the null hypothesis of a unit root.

Of course, it is possible to incorporate Step 1 directly into Steps 2 or 3. To combine Steps 1 and 3, simply estimate the equation:

$$y_t = a_0 + a_1 y_{t-1} + a_2 t + \mu_2 D_L + \sum_{i=1}^{k} \beta_i \Delta y_{t-i} + \epsilon_t$$

The t-statistic for the null $a_1 = 1$ can then be compared to the appropriate critical value calculated by Perron. In addition, the methodology is quite general in that it can also allow for a one-time change in the drift or one-time change in both the mean and drift. For example, it is possible to test the null hypothesis of a permanent change magnitude of the drift term versus the alternative of a change in the slope of the trend. Here, the null hypothesis is

$$H_2: y_t = a_0 + y_{t-1} + \mu_2 D_L + \epsilon_t$$

where $D_L = 1$ if $t > \tau$ and zero otherwise. With this specification, the $\{y_t\}$ sequence is generated by $\Delta y_t = a_0 + \epsilon_t$ up to period τ and $\Delta y_t = (a_0 + \mu_2) + \epsilon_t$ thereafter. If $\mu_2 > 0$, the slope coefficient of the deterministic trend increases for $t > \tau$. Similarly, a slowdown in trend growth occurs if $\mu_2 < 0$.

The alternative hypothesis posits a trend stationary series with a change in the slope of the trend for $t > \tau$:

$$A_2: y_t = a_0 + a_2 t + \mu_3 D_T + \epsilon_t$$

where $D_T = t - \tau$ for $t > \tau$ and zero otherwise. For example, suppose that the break occurs in period 51 so that $\tau = 50$. Thus, $D_T(1)$ through $D_T(50)$ are all zero, so that for the first 50 periods, $\{y_t\}$ evolves as $y_t = a_0 + a_2 t + \epsilon_t$. Beginning with period 51, $D(51)_T = 1$, $D(52)_T = 2, \ldots$, so that for $t > \tau$, $\{y_t\}$ evolves as $y_t = a_0 + (a_2 + \mu_3)t + \epsilon_t$. Hence, D_T changes the slope of the deterministic trend line. The slope of the trend is a_2 for $t \leq \tau$ and $a_2 + \mu_3$ for $t > \tau$.

To be even more general, it is possible to combine the two null hypotheses H_1 and H_2. A change in both the level and drift of a unit root process can be represented by

$$H_3: y_t = a_0 + y_{t-1} + \mu_1 D_P + \mu_2 D_L + \epsilon_t$$

where D_P and D_L = the pulse and level dummies defined above

The appropriate alternative for this case is

$$A_3: y_t = a_0 + a_2 t + \mu_2 D_L + \mu_3 D_T + \epsilon_t$$

Again, the procedure entails estimating the regression A_2 or A_3. Next, using the residuals $\hat{y}_t$, estimate the regression:

$$\hat{y}_t = a_1 \hat{y}_{t-1} + e_t$$

If the errors from this second regression equation do not appear to be white-noise, estimate the equation in the form of an augmented Dickey–Fuller test. The t-statistic for the null hypothesis $a_1 = 1$ can be compared to the critical values calculated by Perron (1989). For $\lambda = 0.5$, Perron reports the critical value of the t-statistic at the 5% significance level to be -3.96 for H_2 and -4.24 for H_3.

Perron's Test for Structural Change

Perron (1989) used his analysis of structural change to challenge the findings of Nelson and Plosser (1982). With the very same variables used, his results indicate that most macroeconomic variables are *not* characterized by unit root processes. Instead, the variables appear to be TS processes coupled with structural breaks. According to Perron (1989), the stock market crash of 1929 and dramatic oil price increase of 1973 were exogenous shocks having permanent effects on the mean of most macroeconomic variables. The crash induced a one-time fall in the mean. Otherwise, macroeconomic variables appear to be trend stationary.

All variables in Perron's study (except real wages, stock prices, and the stationary unemployment rate) appeared to have a trend with a constant slope and exhibited a major change in the level around 1929. In order to entertain various hypotheses concerning the effects of the stock market crash, consider the regression equation:

$$y_t = a_0 + \mu_1 D_P + \mu_2 D_L + a_2 t + a_1 y_{t-1} + \sum_{i=1}^{k} \beta_i \Delta y_{t-i} + \epsilon_t$$

where $D_P(1930)$ = 1 and zero otherwise
D_L = 1 for all t beginning in 1930 and zero otherwise

Under the presumption of a one-time change in the mean of a unit root process, $a_1 = 1$, $a_2 = 0$, and $\mu_2 = 0$. Under the alternative hypothesis of a permanent one-time break in the trend stationary model, $a_1 < 1$ and $\mu_1 = 0$. Perron's (1989) results using real GNP, nominal GNP, and industrial production are reported in Table 4.5. Given the length of each series, the 1929 crash means that λ is 1/3 for both real and nominal GNP and equal to 2/3 for industrial production. Lag lengths (i.e., the values of k) were determined using t-tests on the coefficients β_i. The value k was selected if the t-statistic on β_k was greater than 1.60 in absolute value and the t-statistic on β_i for $i > k$ was less than 1.60.

First, consider the results for real GNP. When we examine the last column of the table, it is clear that there is little support for the unit root hypothesis; the estimated value of $a_1 = 0.282$ is significantly different from unity at the 1% level. Instead, real GNP appears to have a deterministic trend (a_2 is estimated to be over five standard deviations from zero). Also note that the point estimate $\mu_1 = -0.189$ is significantly different from zero at conventional levels. Thus, the stock market crash is estimated to have induced a permanent one-time decline in the intercept of real GNP.

These findings receive additional support since the estimated coefficients and their t-statistics are quite similar across the three equations. All values of a_1 are about five standard deviations from unity, whereas the coefficients of the deterministic trends (a_2) are all over five standard deviations from zero. Since all estimated values of μ_1 are significant at the 1% level and negative, the data seem to support the contention that real macroeconomic variables are TS, except for a structural break resulting from the stock market crash.

Table 4.5   **Retesting Nelson and Plosser's Data for Structural Change**

	T	λ	k	a_0	μ_1	μ_2	a_2	a_1
Real GNP	62	0.33	8	3.44	−0.189	−0.018	0.027	0.282
				(5.07)	(−4.28)	(−0.30)	(5.05)	(−5.03)
Nominal GNP	62	0.33	8	5.69	−3.60	0.100	0.036	0.471
				(5.44)	(−4.77)	(1.09)	(5.44)	(−5.42)
Industrial production	111	0.66	8	0.120	−0.298	−0.095	0.032	0.322
				(4.37)	(−4.56)	(−.095)	(5.42)	(−5.47)

Notes: 1. T = number of observations
λ = proposition of observations occurring before the structural change
k = lag length
2. The appropriate *t*-statistics are in parentheses. For a_0, μ_1, μ_2, and a_2, the null is that the coefficient is equal to zero. For a_1, the null hypothesis is $a_1 = 1$. Note that all estimated values of a_1 are significantly different from unity at the 1% level.

Tests with Simulated Data

To further illustrate the procedure, 100 random numbers were drawn to represent the $\{\epsilon_t\}$ sequence. By setting $y_0 = 0$, the next 100 values in the $\{y_t\}$ sequence were drawn as

$$y_t = 0.5y_{t-1} + \epsilon_t + D_L$$

where $D_L = 0$ for $t = 1, \ldots, 50$
$D_L = 1$ for $t = 51, \ldots, 100$

Thus, the simulation is identical to (4.29), except that the magnitude of the structural break is diminished. This simulated series is on the data file labeled BREAK.PRN; you should try to reproduce the following results. If you were to plot the data, you would see the same pattern as in Figure 4.4. However, if you did not plot the data or were otherwise unaware of the break, you might easily conclude that the $\{y_t\}$ sequence has a unit root. The ACF of the $\{y_t\}$ sequence suggests a unit root process; for example, the first six autocorrelations are

Lag:	*1*	*2*	*3*	*4*	*5*	*6*
	0.94	0.88	0.84	0.81	0.77	0.72

and the ACF of the first differences is:

Lag:	*1*	*2*	*3*	*4*	*5*	*6*
	−0.002	−0.201	−0.112	0.079	−0.010	−0.061

Dickey–Fuller tests yield

$\Delta y_t = -0.0233y_{t-1} + \epsilon_t,$ *t*-statistic for $\gamma = 0$: -0.98495

$\Delta y_t = 0.0661 - 0.0566y_{t-1} + \epsilon_t,$ *t*-statistic for $\gamma = 0$: -1.70630

$\Delta y_t = -0.0488 - 0.1522y_{t-1} + 0.004t + \epsilon_t,$ *t*-statistic for $\gamma = 0$: -2.73397

Diagnostic tests indicate that longer lags are not needed. Regardless of the presence of the constant or the trend, the $\{y_t\}$ sequence appears to be difference stationary. Of course, the problem is that the structural break biases the data toward suggesting a unit root.

Now, with the Perron procedure, the first step is to estimate the model $y_t = a_0 + a_2t + \mu_2 D_L + \hat{y}_t$. The residuals from this equation are the detrended $\{\hat{y}_t\}$ sequence. The second step is to test for a unit root in the residuals by estimating $\hat{y}_t = a_1 \hat{y}_{t-1} + \epsilon_t$. The resulting regression is:

$$\hat{y}_t = 0.4843\, \hat{y}_{t-1} + \epsilon_t$$

In the third step, all the diagnostic statistics indicate that $\{\epsilon_t\}$ approximates a white-noise process. Finally, the *t*-statistic for $a_1 = 1$ is 5.396. Hence, we can reject the null of a unit root and conclude that the simulated data are stationary around a breakpoint at $t = 51$.

Some care must be used in using Perron's procedure since it assumes that the date of the structural break is known. In your own work, if the date of the break is uncertain, you should consult Perron and Vogelsang (1992). In fact, entire issue of the July 1992 *Journal of Business and Economic Statistics* is devoted to breakpoints and unit roots.

7. PROBLEMS IN TESTING FOR UNIT ROOTS

There is a substantial literature concerning the appropriate use of the various Dickey–Fuller test statistics. The focus of this ongoing research concerns the power of the test and presence of the deterministic regressors in the estimating equations. Although many details are beyond the level of this text, it is important to be aware of some of the difficulties entailed in testing for the presence of a trend (either deterministic or stochastic) in the data-generating process.

Power

Formally, the **power** of a test is equal to the probability of rejecting a false null hypothesis (i.e., 1 minus the probability of a type II error). Monte Carlo simulations have shown that the power of the various Dickey–Fuller and Phillips–Perron tests is very low; unit root tests do not have the power to distinguish between a unit root and near unit root process. Thus, these tests will too often indicate that a series contains a unit root. Moreover, they have little power to distinguish between trend stationary and drifting processes. In finite samples, any trend stationary process can be arbitrarily well approximated by a unit root process, and a unit root process can be arbitrarily well approximated by a trend stationary process. These results should not be too surprising after examining Figure 4.6. The top graph (a) of the figure shows a stationary process and unit root process. So as not to bias the results in any particular direction, the simulation uses the same 100 values of $\{\epsilon_t\}$ that were used in Figure 4.4. Using these 100 realizations of $\{\epsilon_t\}$, we constructed two sequences as:

$$y_t = 1.1y_{t-1} - 0.1y_{t-2} + \epsilon_t$$
$$z_t = 1.1z_{t-1} - 0.15z_{t-2} + \epsilon_t$$

The $\{y_t\}$ sequence has a unit root; the roots of the $\{z_t\}$ sequence are 0.9405 and 0.1595. Although $\{z_t\}$ is stationary, it can be called a near unit root process. If you did not know the actual data-generating processes, it would be difficult to tell that only $\{z_t\}$ is stationary.

Similarly, as illustrated in the lower graph (b) of Figure 4.6, it can be quite difficult to distinguish between a trend stationary and unit root plus drift process. Still using the same 100 values of $\{\epsilon_t\}$, we can construct two other sequences as:

$$w_t = 1 + 0.02t + \epsilon_t$$
$$x_t = 0.02 + x_{t-1} + \epsilon_t/3$$

where $x_0 = 1$

Here, the trend and drift terms dominate the time paths of the two sequences. Again, it is very difficult to distinguish between the sequences. This is especially true since dividing each realization of ϵ_t by 3 acts to smooth out the $\{x_t\}$ sequence. Just as it is difficult for the naked eye to perceive the differences in the sequences, it is also difficult for the Dickey–Fuller and Phillips–Perron tests to select the correct specification.

It is easy to show that a trend stationary process can be made to mimic a unit root process arbitrarily well. As discussed in Chapter 3, it is possible to write the random walk plus noise model in the form:

$$y_t = \mu_t + \eta_t$$
$$\mu_t = \mu_{t-1} + \epsilon_t$$

where η_t and ϵ_t are both independent white-noise processes with variances of σ_η^2 and σ^2, respectively. Suppose that we can observe the $\{y_t\}$ sequence, but cannot directly observe the separate shocks affecting y_t. If the variance of ϵ_t is not zero, $\{y_t\}$ is the unit root process:

$$y_t = \mu_0 + \sum_{i=1}^{t} \epsilon_i + \eta_t \tag{4.33}$$

Figure 4.6

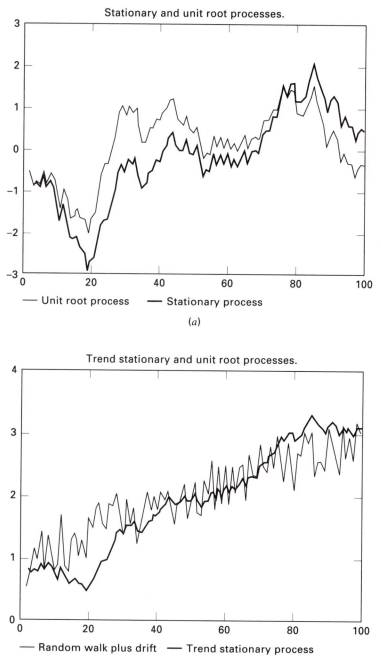

Stationary and unit root processes.

— Unit root process   — Stationary process

(a)

Trend stationary and unit root processes.

— Random walk plus drift   — Trend stationary process

(b)

On the other hand, if $\sigma^2 = 0$, then all values of $\{\epsilon_t\}$ are constant, so that: $\epsilon_t = \epsilon_{t-1} = \cdots = \epsilon_0$. To maintain the same notation as in previous chapters, define this initial value of ϵ_0 as a_0. It follows that $\mu_t = \mu_0 + a_0 t$, so $\{y_t\}$ is the trend stationary process:

$$y_t = \mu_0 + a_0 t + \eta_t \tag{4.34}$$

Thus, the difference between the difference stationary process of (4.33) and trend process of (4.34) concerns the variance of ϵ_t. Having observed the composite effects of the two shocks—but not the individual components η_t and ϵ_t—we see that there is no simple way to determine whether σ^2 is *exactly* equal to zero. This is particularly true if the data-generating process is such that σ_η^2 is large relative to σ^2. In a finite sample, arbitrarily increasing σ_η^2 will make it virtually impossible to distinguish between a TS and DS series.

It also follows that a trend stationary process can arbitrarily well approximate a unit root process. If the stochastic portion of the trend stationary process has sufficient variance, it will not be possible to distinguish between the unit root and trend stationary hypotheses. For example, the random walk plus drift model (a difference stationary process) can be arbitrarily well represented by the model $y_t = a_0 + a_1 y_{t-1} + \epsilon_t$ by increasing σ^2 and allowing a_1 to get sufficiently close to unity. Both these models can be approximated by (4.34).

Does it matter that is often impossible to distinguish between borderline stationary, trend stationary, and unit root processes? The realistic answer is that it depends on the question at hand. In borderline cases, the short-run forecasts from the alternative models may have nearly identical forecasting performance. In fact, Monte Carlo studies indicate that when the true data-generating process is stationary but has a root close to unity, the one-step ahead forecasts from a differenced model are usually superior to the forecasts from a stationary model. However, the long-run forecasts of a model with a deterministic trend will be quite different from those of the other models.[9]

Determination of the Deterministic Regressors

Unless the researcher knows the actual data-generating process, there is a question concerning whether it is most appropriate to estimate (4.12), (4.13) or (4.14). It might seem reasonable to test the hypothesis $\gamma = 0$ using the most general of the models, that is,

$$\Delta y_t = a_0 + \gamma y_{t-1} + a_2 t + \sum_{i=2}^{p} \beta_i \Delta y_{t-i+1} + \epsilon_t \tag{4.35}$$

After all, if the true process is a random walk process, this regression should find that $a_0 = \gamma = a_2 = 0$. One problem with this line of reasoning is that the presence of the additional estimated parameters reduces degrees of freedom and the power of the test. Reduced power means that the researcher will conclude that the process contains a unit root when, in fact, none is present. The second problem is that the appropriate statistic (i.e., the τ, τ_μ, and τ_τ) for testing $\gamma = 0$ depends on which regressors are included in the model. As you can see by examining the three Dickey–Fuller tables, for a given significance level, the confidence intervals around $\gamma = 0$ dramatically expand if a drift and time trend are included in the model. This is quite different from the case in which $\{y_t\}$ is stationary. The distribution of the *t*-statistic does not depend on the presence of the other regressors when stationary variables are used.

The point is that it is important to use a regression equation that mimics the actual data-generating process. If we inappropriately omit the intercept or time trend, the power of the test can go to zero.[10] For example, if as in (4.35), the data-generating process includes a trend, omitting the term $a_2 t$ imparts an upward bias in the estimated value of γ. On the other hand, extra regressors increase the absolute value of the critical values so that you may fail to reject the null of a unit root.

To illustrate the problem, suppose that the time series $\{y_t\}$ is assumed to be generated by the random walk plus drift process:

$$y_t = a_0 + a_1 y_{t-1} + \epsilon_t, \qquad a_0 \neq 0 \text{ and } a_1 = 1 \qquad (4.36)$$

where the initial condition y_0 is given and $t = 1, 2, \ldots, T$.

If there is no drift, it is inappropriate to include the intercept term since the power of the Dickey–Fuller test is reduced. When the drift is actually in the data-generating process, omitting a_0 from the estimating equation also reduces the power of the test in finite samples. How do you know whether to include a drift or time trend in performing the tests? The key problem is that *the tests for unit roots are conditional on the presence of the deterministic regressors and tests for the presence of the deterministic regressors are conditional on the presence of a unit root.*

Campbell and Perron (1991) report the following results concerning unit root tests:

1. When the estimated regression includes *at least* all the deterministic elements in the actual data-generating process, the distribution of γ is nonnormal under the null of a unit root. The distribution itself varies with the set of parameters included in the estimating equation.

2. If the estimated regression includes deterministic regressors that are not in the actual data-generating process, the power of the unit root test against a stationary alternative decreases as additional deterministic regressors are added.

3. If the estimated regression omits an important deterministic trending variable present in the true data-generating process, such as the expression $a_2 t$ in (4.35), the power of the *t*-statistic test goes to zero as the sample size increases. If the estimated regression omits a nontrending variable (i.e., the mean or a change in the mean), the *t*-statistic is consistent, but the finite sample power is adversely affected and decreases as the magnitude of the coefficient on the omitted component increases.

4. Estimating (4.13) or (4.14), we observe that the τ_μ, τ_τ, ϕ_1, ϕ_2, and ϕ_3 statistics have the *asymptotic* distributions tabulated by Dickey and Fuller (1979, 1981). The critical values of the various statistics depend on sample size. However, the *sample* variance of $\{y_t\}$ will be dominated by the presence of a trend or drift. We saw an example of this phenomenon in Figure 3.12 of Chapter 3. The time path of the random walk plus drift model in graph (b) is swamped by the presence of the drift term. The fact that the stochastic trend is precisely the same as in graph (a) has little effect on the overall appearance of the series. Although the proof is beyond the scope of this text, the τ_μ and τ_τ statistics converge to the standardized normal. Specifically,

$$\sum_{t=1}^{T} y_t^2 \Rightarrow a_2^2 T^5 \quad 20 \qquad if\ a_2 \neq 0$$

$$\Rightarrow a_0^2 T^3 \quad 3 \qquad if\ a_0 \neq 0\ and\ a_2 = 0$$

Only when both a_0 and a_2 equal zero in the regression equation and data-generating process do the nonstandard Dickey–Fuller distributions dominate. If the data-generating process is known to contain a trend or drift, *the null hypothesis $\gamma = 0$ can be tested using the standardized normal distribution.*

The direct implication of these four findings is that the researcher may fail to reject the null hypothesis of a unit root because of a misspecification concerning the deterministic part of the regression. Too few or too many regressors may cause a failure of the test to reject the null of a unit root. Although we can never be sure that we are including the appropriate deterministic regressors in our econometric model, there are some useful guidelines. Doldado, Jenkinson, and Sosvilla-Rivero (1990) suggest the following procedure to test for a unit root when the form of the data-generating process is unknown. The following is a straightforward modification of their method:

STEP 1: As shown in Figure 4.7, start with the least restrictive of the plausible models (which will generally include a trend and drift) and use the τ_τ statistic to test the null hypothesis $\gamma = 0$. Unit root tests have low power to reject the null hypothesis; hence, if the null hypothesis of a unit root is *rejected,* there is no need to proceed. Conclude that the $\{y_t\}$ sequence does not contain a unit root.

STEP 2: If the null hypothesis is *not rejected,* it is necessary to determine whether too many deterministic regressors were included in Step 1 above.[11] Test for the significance of the trend term under the null of a unit root (e.g., use the $\tau_{\beta\tau}$ statistic to test the significance of a_2). You should try to gain additional confirmation for this result by testing the hypothesis $a_2 = \gamma = 0$ using the ϕ_3 statistic. If the trend is not significant, proceed to Step 3. Otherwise, if the trend is significant, retest for the presence of a unit root (i.e., $\gamma = 0$) using the standardized normal distribution. After all, if a trend is inappropriately included in the estimating equation, the limiting distribution of a_2 is the standardized normal. If the null of a unit root is rejected, proceed no further; conclude that the $\{y_t\}$ sequence does not contain a unit root. Otherwise, conclude that the $\{y_t\}$ sequence contains a unit root.

STEP 3: Estimate (4.35) without the trend [i.e., estimate a model in the form of (4.13)]. Test for the presence of a unit root using the τ_μ statistic. If the null is rejected, conclude that the model does not contain a unit root. If the null hypothesis of a unit root is not rejected, test for the significance of the constant (e.g., use the $\tau_{\alpha\mu}$ statistic to test the significance of a_0 given $\gamma = 0$). Additional confirmation of this result can be obtained by testing the hypothesis $a_0 = \gamma = 0$ using the ϕ_1 statistic. If the drift is not significant, estimate an equation in the form of (4.12) and proceed to Step 4. If the drift is significant, test for the presence of a unit root using the standardized

Figure 4.7   A procedure to test for unit roots.

Estimate $\Delta y_t = a_o + \gamma y_{t-1} + a_2 t + \Sigma \beta_i \Delta y_{t-i} + \varepsilon_t$

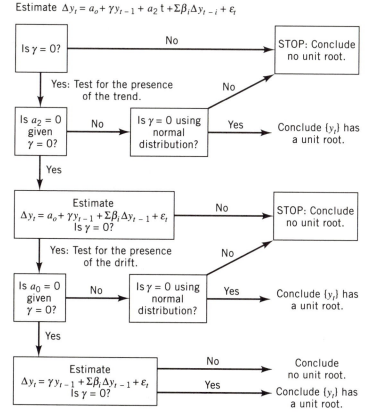

normal. If the null hypothesis of a unit root is rejected, conclude that the $\{y_t\}$ sequence does not contain a unit root. Otherwise, conclude that the $\{y_t\}$ sequence contains a unit root.

STEP 4: Estimate (4.35) without the trend or drift, that is, estimate a model in the form of (4.12). Use τ to test for the presence of a unit root. If the null hypothesis of a unit root is rejected, conclude that the $\{y_t\}$ sequence does not contain a unit root. Otherwise, conclude that the $\{y_t\}$ sequence contains a unit root.

Remember, this procedure is not designed to be applied in a completely mechanical fashion. Plotting the data is usually an important indicator of the presence of deterministic regressors. The data shown in Figure 4.1 could hardly be said to contain a deterministic trend. Moreover, theoretical considerations might suggest the appropriate regressors. The efficient market hypothesis is inconsistent with the presence of a deterministic trend in an asset market price. However, the procedure is a sensible way to test for unit roots when the form of the data-generating process is completely unknown.

GDP and Unit Roots

Although the methodology outlined in Figure 4.7 can be very useful, it does have its problems. Each step in the procedure involves a test that is conditioned on all the previous tests being correct; the significance level of each of the cascading tests is impossible to ascertain.

The procedure and its inherent dangers are nicely illustrated by trying to determine if real gross domestic product (GDP) has a unit root. The data are contained in the file entitled US.WK1 on the data disk; it is a good idea to replicate the results reported below. If we use quarterly data over the 1960:1 to 1991:4 period, the correlogram of the logarithm of real GDP exhibits slow decay. However, the first 12 autocorrelations and partial autocorrelations of the logarithmic first difference are

ACF of the logarithmic first difference of real GDP:

Lag 1:   0.3093189   0.2316683   0.0572363   0.0556556 −0.0604932   0.0336679
   7: −0.0476200 −0.1453376 −0.0461222   0.0600729   0.0101171 −0.1695323

PACF of the logarithmic first difference of real GDP:

Lag 1:   0.3093189   0.1503780 −0.0567524   0.0220048 −0.0876589   0.0696282
   7: −0.0507211 −0.1605942   0.0669240   0.1200468 −0.0353431 −0.2423071

Despite the somewhat large partial correlation at lag 12, the Box–Jenkins procedure yields the ARIMA(0, 1, 2) model:

$$\Delta LGDP_t = 0.007018 + (1 + 0.262169L + 0.197547L^2)\epsilon_t$$
$$(0.001144) \qquad (0.088250) \quad (0.082663)$$

where $LGDP_t = \log(GDP_t)$, so that $\Delta LGDP_t$ is the growth rate of real GDP, and standard errors are in parentheses.

The model is well estimated in that the residuals appear to be white-noise and all coefficients are of high quality. For our purposes, the interesting point is that the $\Delta\log(GDP_t)$ series appears to be a stationary process. Integrating suggests that $\log(GDP_t)$ has a stochastic and deterministic trend. The deterministic quarterly growth rate of 0.007018—close to a 3% annual rate—appears to be quite reasonable. Now consider the three augmented Dickey–Fuller equations with t-statistics in parentheses:

$$\Delta LGDP_t = 0.79018 - 0.05409 LGDP_{t-1} + 0.000348t$$
$$\quad (2.56548) \quad (-2.54309) \quad (2.27941)$$
$$+ 0.24961\Delta LGDP_{t-1} + 0.17273\Delta LGDP_{t-2} \quad (4.37)$$
$$(2.83349) \quad\quad\quad (1.94841)$$
$$RSS = 0.0089460783$$

$$\Delta LGDP_t = 0.09600 - 0.00611 LGDP_{t-1} + 0.23613\Delta LGDP_{t-1}$$
$$\quad (2.05219) \quad (-1.96196) \quad\quad (2.64113)$$
$$+ 0.13535\Delta LGDP_{t-2} \quad (4.38)$$
$$(1.52736)$$
$$RSS = 0.0093334206$$

$$\Delta LGDP_t = 0.000279 LGDP_{t-1} + 0.26331\Delta LGDP_{t-1} + 0.15443\Delta LGDP_{t-2} \quad (4.39)$$
$$\quad (3.82135) \quad\quad (2.93959) \quad\quad (1.72964)$$
$$RSS = 0.0096582756$$

From (4.37), the t-statistic for the null hypothesis $\gamma = 0$ is -2.54309. Critical values with 125 usable observations are not reported in the Dickey–Fuller table.[12] However, with 100 observations, the critical value of τ_τ at the 5% significance level is -3.45; hence, it is not possible to reject the null hypothesis of a unit root given the presence of the drift term and time trend.

The power of the test may have been reduced due to the presence of an unnecessary time trend and/or drift term. In Step 2, you test for the presence of the time trend given the presence of a unit root. In (4.37), the t-statistic for the null hypothesis that $a_2 = 0$ is 2.27941. Do not let this large value fool you into thinking that a_2 is significantly different from zero. Remember, in the presence of a unit root, you cannot use the critical values of a t-table; instead, the appropriate critical values are given by the Dickey–Fuller $\tau_{\beta\tau}$ statistic. As you can see in Table 4.1, the critical value of $\tau_{\beta\tau}$ at the 5% significance level is 2.79; hence, it is reasonable to conclude that $a_2 = 0$. The ϕ_3 statistic to test the joint hypothesis $a_2 = \gamma = 0$ reconfirms this result. If we view (4.37) as the unrestricted model and (4.39) as the restricted model, there are two restrictions and 120 degrees of freedom in the unrestricted model; the ϕ_3 statistic is

$$\phi_3 = [(0.0096582756 - 0.0089460783)/2] \,/\,(0.0089460783/120)$$
$$= 4.7766$$

Since the critical value of ϕ_3 is 6.49, it is possible to conclude that the restriction $a_2 = \gamma = 0$ is not binding. Thus, proceed to Step 3 where you estimate the model without the trend. In (4.38), the t-statistic for the null hypothesis $\gamma = 0$ is -1.96196. Since the critical value of the τ_μ statistic is -2.89 at the 5% significance level, the null hypothesis of a unit root is not rejected at conventional significance levels. Again, the power of this test will have been reduced if the drift term does not belong in the model. To test for the presence of the drift, use the $\tau_{\alpha\tau}$ statistic. The calculated t-statistic is 2.05219, whereas the critical value at the 5% significance level is 2.54. The ϕ_1 statistic also suggests that the drift term is zero. Comparing (4.38) and (4.39), we obtain

$$\phi_1 = (0.0096582756 - 0.0093334206)/(0.0093334206/121)$$
$$= 4.21147365$$

Proceeding to Step 4 yields (4.39). The point is that the procedure has worked itself into an uncomfortable corner. The problem is that the positive coefficient for γ (i.e., the estimated value of $\gamma = 0.000279$ is almost four standard deviations from zero) suggests an *explosive* process. In Step 3, it was probably unwise to conclude that the drift term is equal to zero. As you should verify in Exercise 4 at the end of this chapter, the simple Box–Jenkins ARIMA(0, 1, 2) model with an intercept of 0.007018 performs better than any of the alternatives.

SUMMARY AND CONCLUSIONS

In finite samples, the correlogram of a unit root process will decay slowly. As such, a slowly decaying ACF can be indicative of a unit root or near unit root process. The issue is especially important since many economic time series appear to have a nonstationary component. When you encounter such a time series, do you detrend, do you first-difference, or do you do nothing since the series might be stationary?

Adherents of the Box–Jenkins methodology recommend differencing a nonstationary variable or variable with a near unit root. For very short-term forecasts, the form of the trend is nonessential. Differencing also reveals the pattern of the other autoregressive and moving average coefficients. However, as the forecast horizon expands, the precise form of the trend becomes increasingly important. Stationarity implies the absence of a trend and long-run mean reversion. A deterministic trend implies steady increases (or decreases) into the infinite future. Forecasts of a series with a stochastic trend converge to a steady level. As illustrated by the distinction between real business cycles and the more traditional formulations, the nature of the trend may have important theoretical implications.

The usual t-statistics and F-statistics are not applicable to determine whether or not a sequence has a unit root. Dickey and Fuller (1979, 1981) provide the appropriate test statistics to determine whether a series contains a unit root, unit root plus drift, and/or unit root plus drift plus a time trend. The tests can also be modified to account for seasonal unit roots. If the residuals of a unit root process are heterogeneous or weakly dependent, the alternative Phillips–Perron test can be used.

Structural breaks will bias the Dickey–Fuller and Phillips–Perron tests toward the nonrejection of a unit root. Perron (1989) shows how it is possible to incorporate a known structural change into the tests for unit roots. Caution needs to be exercised since it is always possible to argue that structural change has occurred; each year has something different about it than the previous year. In an interesting extension, Perron and Vogelsang (1992) show how to test for a unit root when the precise date of the structural break is unknown.

All the aforementioned tests have very low power to distinguish between a unit root and near unit root process. A trend stationary process, can be arbitrarily well approximated by a unit root process, and a unit root process can be arbitrarily well approximated by a trend stationary process. Moreover, the testing procedure is confounded by the presence of the deterministic regressors (i.e., the intercept and deterministic trend). Too many or too few regressors reduce the power of the tests.

An alternative is to take a Bayesian approach and avoid specific hypothesis testing altogether. West and Harrison (1989) provide an accessible introduction to Bayesian analysis in the context of regression analysis. Zellner (1988) discusses some of the philosophical underpinnings of the approach and Leamer (1986) provides a straightforward application to estimating the determinants of inflation. Sims (1988) is the standard reference for the Bayesian approach to unit roots.

QUESTIONS AND EXERCISES

1. The columns in the file labeled REAL.PRN contain the logarithm of the real exchange rates for Canada, Japan, Germany, and the U.K. The four series are called RCAN, RGER, RJAP, and RUK, respectively. As in Section 4, each series is constructed as $r_t = e_t + p_t^* - p_t$

   where r = log of the real exchange rate
              e = log of the dollar price of foreign exchange
             p^* = log of the foreign wholesale price index
              p = log of the U.S. wholesale price index

   All series run from February 1973 through December 1989, and each is expressed as an index number such that February 1973 = 1.00.

You should find that the data have the following properties:

Series	Observa-tions	Mean	Standard Error	Minimum	Maximum
RCAN	203	0.93041911330	0.05685010789	0.83472000000	1.03930000000
RGER	203	1.07711822660	0.15732887872	0.64541000000	1.34009000000
RJAP	203	1.16689172414	0.13981473422	0.91620000000	1.50787000000
RUK	203	1.09026873892	0.14524762980	0.70991900000	1.38482000000

A. For each sequence, find the ACF and PACF of (i) the level of the real exchange rate; (ii) the first difference of the real exchange rate; and (iii) the detrended real exchange rate. For example, for Canada you should find

ACF:

1:	0.95109959	0.91691527	0.89743824	0.86897993	0.84708012	0.81911904
7:	0.79706303	0.77888188	0.75410092	0.72946966	0.70020306	0.65782904

ACF of the first difference:

1:	−0.1562001	−0.1531103	0.0443029	−0.0152957	0.1053500	−0.0740475
7:	−0.0475489	0.0597755	−0.0255490	0.0142241	0.1810469	−0.1151413

B. Explain why it is not possible to determine whether the seqence is stationary or nonstationary by the simple examination of the ACF and PACF.

C. Including a constant, use Dickey–Fuller and augmented Dickey–Fuller tests (with 12 monthly lags) to test whether the series are unit root processes. You should find that the t-statistics for $\gamma = 0$ are

Series	No lags	12 lags	Trend + 12 lags
RCAN	−1.81305	−1.50810	−0.85650
RJAP	−1.81978	−2.30579	−2.61854
RGER	−1.64297	−2.10719	−2.09955
RUK	−1.55877	−2.51668	−2.57493

i. The last entry in the table means that γ is more than 2.57 standard deviations from zero. A student's t-table indicates that at the 95% significance level, the critical value is about 1.96 standard deviations. Why is it incorrect to conclude that the null hypothesis of a unit root can be *rejected* since the calculated t-statistic is more than 1.96 standard deviations from zero?

ii. For each entry reported in the table, what are the appropriate statistics to use (τ, τ_μ, or τ_τ) in order to test the null hypothesis of a unit root?

D. If your software package can perform Phillips–Perron tests, reestimate part C using the Phillips–Perron rather than Dickey–Fuller procedure. You should find that the t-statistics for $\gamma = 0$ are

Series	No lags	12 lags	Trend + 12 lags
RCAN	−1.82209	−1.60022	−1.10882
RJAP	−1.82886	−2.03795	−2.19736
RGER	−1.65117	−1.85319	−1.88371
RUK	−1.56654	−1.81530	−2.01424

E. Why do you suppose the results from parts C and D are so similar?

F. Determine whether an intercept term belongs in the regression equations. Determine whether the time trend should be included in the equations. Determine whether the intercept *and* time trend belong in the equations.

G. Use the Japanese data to show that you can reject the null hypothesis of two unit roots.

2. The second column in the file labeled BREAK.PRN contains the simulated data used in Section 6. You should find:

Series	Observa-tions	Mean	Standard Error	Minimum	Maximum
Y1	100	0.98802	0.99373	−0.78719	2.654697

A. Plot the data to see if you can recognize the effects of the structural break.

B. Verify the results reported in Section 6.

3. The third column in the file labeled BREAK.PRN contains another simulated data set with a structural break at $t = 51$. You should find

Series	Observa-tions	Mean	Standard Error	Minimum	Maximum
Y2	100	2.21080	1.7816	−1.3413	5.1217

A. Plot the data. Compare your graph to those of Figures 4.4 and 4.5.

B. Obtain the ACF and PACF of the $\{Y2_t\}$ sequence and first difference of the sequence. Do the data appear to be difference stationary?

C. If as in (4.11), a Dickey–Fuller test is performed including a constant and trend, you should obtain

Coefficient	Estimate	Standard Error	t-Statistic	Significance
Constant	0.072445666	0.071447971	1.01396	0.31314869
TREND	−0.000101438	0.002120465	−0.04784	0.96194514
$Y2_{t-1}$	−0.022398360	0.034013944	−0.65851	0.51178974

    i. In what ways is this regression equation inadequate?

    ii. What diagnostic checks would you want to perform?

D. Estimate the equation $Y2_t = a_0 + a_2 t + \mu_2 D_L$ and save the residuals. You should obtain

Coefficient	Estimate	Standard Error	t-Statistic	Significance
Constant	0.4185991020	0.1752103414	2.38912	0.01882282
DUMMY	2.8092054550	0.3097034669	9.07063	0.00000000
TREND	0.0076752509	0.0053644896	1.43075	0.15571516

E. Perform a Dickey–Fuller test on the saved residuals. You should find $\hat{y}_t = 0.9652471\hat{y}_{t-1} + \epsilon_t$, where the standard error of $a_1 = 0.0372$. Also perform the appropriate diagnostic tests on this regression to ensure that the residuals approximate white noise. You should conclude that the series is a unit root process with a one-time pulse at $t = 51$.

F. Return to part D but now eliminate the insignificant time trend. How is your answer to part E affected?

4. The sixth column in the file labeled US.WK1 contains the real GDP data used in Section 7. The quarterly series runs from 1960:1 to 1991:4 and each entry is expressed in 1985 dollars. You should find that the properties of the series are such that

Series Name	Observations	Mean
GDP85	128	$3.220373E+12$

A. Plot the logarithm of real GDP. Do the data suggest any particular form of the trend?

B. Use the Box–Jenkins methodology to verify that an ARIMA(0, 1, 2) model performs better than an ARIMA(2, 1, 0) model.

C. Calculate the various Dickey–Fuller statistics reported in Section 7. Are there any indications that might be inappropriate to accept the hypothesis $a_0 = 0$?

D. Repeat the procedure using the Phillips–Perron tests.

ENDNOTES

1. Issues concerning the possibility of higher-order equations, longer lag lengths, serial correlation in the residuals, structural change, and the presence of deterministic components will be considered in due course.
2. The critical values are reported in Table A at the end of this text.
3. Suppose that the estimated value of γ is -1.9 (so that the estimate of a_1 is -0.9) with a standard error of 0.04. Since the estimated value of γ is 2.5 standard errors from -2 [$(2 - 1.9)/0.04 = 2.5$], the Dickey–Fuller statistics indicate that we cannot reject the null hypothesis $\gamma = -2$ at the 95% significance level. Unless stated otherwise, the discussion in the text assumes that a_1 is positive. Also note that if there is no prior information concerning the sign of a_1, a two-tailed test can be conducted.
4. Here we use the notation e_t, rather than ϵ_t, to highlight that the residuals from such a regression will generally not be white-noise.
5. For the same reason, it is also inappropriate to use one variable that is trend stationary and another that is difference stationary. In such instances, "time" can be included as a so-called *explanatory* variable or the variable in question can be detrended.
6. Tests using lagged changes in the $\{\Delta y_t\}$ sequence are called augmented Dickey–Fuller tests.
7. In their simulations, Dickey and Fuller (1981) found that 90% of the calculated ϕ_3 statistics were 5.47 or less and 95% were 6.49 or less when the actual data were generated according to the null hypothesis.
8. Perron's Monte Carlo study allows for a drift and deterministic trend. Nonetheless, the value of a_1 is biased toward unity in the presence of the deterministic trend.
9. Moreover, Evans and Savin (1981) find that for an AR(1) model, the limiting distribution of the autoregressive parameter has a normal asymptotic distribution (for $\rho < 1$). However, when the parameter is near 1, the unit root distribution is a better finite sample approximation than the asymptotic correct distribution.
10. Campbell and Perron (1991) report that omitting a variable that is growing at least as fast as any other of the appropriately included regressors causes the power of the tests to approach zero.
11. Using the most general model in Step 1 is meant to address the problem of omitting important deterministic regressors.
12. The sample period 1960:1 to 1991:4 contains 128 total observations. Three observations are lost by creating the two lagged changes.

APPENDIX: Phillips–Perron Test Statistics

Suppose that we observe observations $1, 2, \ldots, T$ of the $\{y_t\}$ sequence and estimate the regression equation:

$$y_t = \tilde{a}_0 + \tilde{a}_1 y_{t-1} + \tilde{a}_2(t - T/2) + u_t$$

In this appendix, we modify our notation slightly for those wishing to read the work of Phillips and Perron. Fortunately, the changes are minor; simply replace $\tilde{a}_0$ with μ, $\tilde{a}_1$ with α, and $\tilde{a}_2$ with β. Thus, suppose we have estimated the regression:

$$y_t = \mu + \beta(t - T/2) + \alpha y_{t-1} + u_t$$

where μ, β, and α are the conventional least-squares regression coefficients.

Phillips–Perron derive test statistics for the regression coefficients under the null hypothesis that the data are generated by

$$y_t = y_{t-1} + u_t$$

where the disturbance term u_t is such that $Eu_t = 0$.

There is no requirement that the disturbance term be serially uncorrelated or homogeneous. Instead, the Phillips–Perron test allows the disturbances to be weakly dependent and heterogeneously distributed.

The Phillips–Perron statistics modify the Dickey–Fuller t-statistics by allowing for an adjustment to account for heterogeneity in the error process. Let t_μ, t_α, and t_β be the usual t-test statistics for the null hypotheses $\mu = 0$, $\alpha = 1$, and $\beta = 0$, respectively. (*Note:* In terms of our usual notation, these are equivalent to $\tilde{a}_0 = 0$, $\tilde{a}_1 = 1$, and $\tilde{a}_2 = 0$.) The Phillips–Perron statistics are

$$Z(t_\alpha) = (\tilde{S}/\tilde{\sigma}_{T\omega})t_\alpha - (T^3/4\sqrt{3}D_x^{1/2}\,\tilde{\sigma}_{T\omega})(\tilde{\sigma}_{T\omega}^2 - \tilde{S}^2)$$

$$Z(t_\mu) = (\tilde{S}/\tilde{\sigma}_{T\omega})t_\mu + (T^3/24D_x^{1/2}E_x\,\tilde{\sigma}_{T\omega})(\tilde{\sigma}_{T\omega}^2 - \tilde{S}^2)(T^{-3/2}\Sigma y_{t-1})$$

$$Z(t_\beta) = (\tilde{S}/\tilde{\sigma}_{T\omega})t_\beta + (T^3/2D_x^{1/2}\tilde{\sigma}_{T\omega})[T^{-2}\Sigma(y_{t-1} - \bar{y}_{-1})^2]^{-1/2}$$
$$(\tilde{\sigma}_{T\omega}^2 - \tilde{S}^2)[(1/2)T^{-3/2}\Sigma y_{t-1} - T^{-5/2}\Sigma t y_{t-1}]$$

where $D_X = \det(X'X)$, the determinant of the regressor matrix X,

$$E_x = [T^{-6}D_x + (1/12)(T^{-3/2}\Sigma y_{t-1})^2]^{1/2}$$

$\tilde{S}$ is the standard error of the regression,

$$\tilde{\sigma}_{T\omega}^2 = T^{-1}\Sigma_1^T u_t^2 + 2T^{-1}\Sigma_{s=1}^1\Sigma_{t=s+1}^T u_t u_{t-s}$$

and ω is the number of estimated autocorrelations.

Note that $\tilde{S}^2$ and $\tilde{\sigma}_{T\omega}^2$ are consistent estimates of $\sigma_u^2 = \lim_{T\to\infty} E(u_T^2)$ and $\sigma^2 = \lim_{T\to\infty} E(T^{-1}S_T^2)$,

where $S_T = \Sigma u_t$ and all summations run over t.

For the joint hypothesis $\beta = 0$ and $\alpha = 1$, use the $Z(\phi_3)$ statistic:

$$Z(\phi_3) = (S^2/\sigma_{T\omega}^2)\phi_3 - (1/2\sigma_{T\omega}^2)(\sigma_{T\omega}^2 - S^2)[T(\alpha - 1) - (T^6/48D_x)(\sigma_{T\omega}^2 - S^2)]$$

If a deterministic trend is not included in the regression equation, the hypothesis $\alpha = 1$ is tested using

$$Z(ta_1^*) = Z(t\alpha*) = (S/\sigma_{T\omega})t_{\alpha*} - (1/2\sigma_{T\omega})(\sigma_{T\omega}^2 - S^2)[T^{-2}\Sigma(y_{t-1} - Y_{-1})^2]^{-1/2}$$

where

$$Y_{-1} = T^{-1}\sum_{t=1}^{T} y_{t-1}$$

Chapter 5

MULTIEQUATION
TIME-SERIES MODELS

$\mathbf{A}$s we have seen in previous chapters, you can capture many interesting dynamic relationships using single-equation time-series methods. In the recent past, many time-series texts would end with nothing more than a brief discussion of multi-equation models. However, one of the most fertile areas of contemporary time-series research concerns multiequation models. The specific aims of this chapter are to:

1. Introduce **intervention analysis** and **transfer function analysis.** These two techniques generalize the univariate methodology by allowing the time path of the "dependent" variable to be influenced by the time path of an "independent" or "exogenous" variable. If it is known that there is no feedback, intervention and transfer function analysis can be very effective tools for forecasting and hypothesis testing.

2. Introduce the concept of a vector autoregression (VAR). The major limitation of intervention and transfer function models is that many economic systems do exhibit feedback. In practice, it is not always known if the time path of a series designated to be the "independent" variable has been unaffected by the time path of the so-called "dependent" variable. The most basic form of a VAR treats all variables symmetrically without making reference to the issue of dependence versus independence.

3. The tools employed by VAR analysis—Granger causality, impulse response analysis, and variance decompositions—can be helpful in understanding the interrelationships among economic variables and in the formulation of a more structured economic model. These tools are illustrated using examples concerning the fight against transnational terrorism.

4. Develop two new techniques, **structural VARs** and **multivariate decompositions,** that blend economic theory and multiple time-series analysis. Economic

theories contain behavioral, structural, and/or reduced-form relationships that can be incorporated into a VAR analysis. In a structural VAR, the restrictions of a particular economic model are imposed on the contemporaneous relationship among the variables. The dynamic response of each variable to various economic shocks can be obtained and the restrictions of the model tested. Similarly, long run neutrality restrictions can aid in decomposing a series into its temporary and permanent components. As opposed to the class of univariate decompositions considered in Chapter 3, decompositions in a VAR framework can be exactly identified.

1. INTERVENTION ANALYSIS

Beginning in the late 1960s, the international community experienced a serious threat from transnational terrorism. Terrorists engage in a wide variety of operations including assassinations, armed attacks, bombings, kidnappings, and skyjackings. Such incidents are particularly heinous since they are often directed at innocent victims who are not part of the decision-making apparatus that the terrorists seek to influence. Although the downing of Pan Am flight 103 over Lockerbie, Scotland on December 21, 1988 captured the attention of the international community, skyjacking incidents are actually quite numerous.

A critical response to the rise in skyjackings occurred when the United States began to install metal detectors in all U.S. airports in January 1973. Other international authorities followed shortly. The summation of all transnational plus U.S. domestic skyjackings is shown in Figure 5.1. Although the number of skyjacking incidents appears to take a sizable and permanent decline at this date, we might be interested in actually measuring the effects of installing the metal detectors. If $\{y_t\}$ represents the quarterly total of skyjackings, one might try to take the mean value of $\{y_t\}$ for all $t < 1973{:}1$ and compare it to the mean value of $\{y_t\}$ for all $t \geq 1973{:}1$. However, such a test is probably inappropriate in time-series analysis. Since successive values of y_t are serially correlated, some of the effects of the premetal detector regime could "carry over" to the postintervention date. For example, some planned skyjacking incidents already in the pipeline might not be deterred as readily as others.

Intervention analysis allows for a formal test of a change in the mean of a time series. Consider the model used in Enders, Sandler, and Cauley (1990) to study the impact of the metal detector technology on the number of skyjacking incidents:

$$y_t = a_0 + a_1 y_{t-1} + c_0 z_t + \epsilon_t, \qquad |a_1| < 1 \qquad (5.1)$$

where z_t = the intervention (or dummy) variable that takes on the value of zero prior to 1973:1 and unity beginning in 1973:1

ϵ_t = is a white-noise disturbance

To explain the nature of the model, notice that for $t < 1973{:}1$, the value z_t is zero.[1] As such, the intercept term is a_0 and the long-run mean of the series $a_0/$

Figure 5.1   Skyjackings.

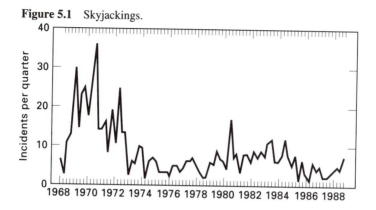

$(1 - a_1)$. Beginning in 1973, the intercept term jumps to $a_0 + c_0$ (since $z_{1973:1}$ jumps to unity). Thus, the initial or **impact effect** of the metal detectors is given by the magnitude of c_0. The statistical significance of c_0 can be tested using a standard *t*-test. We would conclude that metal detectors reduced the number of skyjacking incidents if c_0 is negative and statistically different from zero.

The long-run effect of the intervention, given by $c_0/(1 - a_1)$, is equal to the new long-run mean $(a_0 + c_0)/(1 - a_1)$ minus the value of the original mean $a_0/(1 - a_1)$. The various transitional effects can be obtained from the impulse response function. Using lag operators, rewrite (5.1) as

$$(1 - a_1 L)y_t = a_0 + c_0 z_t + \epsilon_t$$

so that

$$y_t = a_0/(1 - a_1) + c_0 \sum_{i=0}^{\infty} a_1^i z_{t-i} + \sum_{i=0}^{\infty} a_1^i \epsilon_{t-i} \tag{5.2}$$

Equation (5.2) is an impulse response function; the interesting twist added by the intervention variable is that we can obtain the responses of the $\{y_t\}$ sequence to the interventions. To trace out the effects of metal detectors on skyjackings, suppose that $t = 1973:1$ (so that $t + 1 = 1973:2$, $t + 2 = 1973:3$, etc.). For time period t, the impact of z_t on y_t is given by the magnitude of the coefficient c_0. The simplest way to derive the remaining impulse responses is to recognize that (1) $dy_t/dz_{t-i} = dy_{t+i}/dz_t$ and (2) $z_{t+i} = z_t = 1$ for all $i > 0$.

Hence, differentiate (5.2) with respect to z_{t-1} and update by one period, so that

$$dy_{t+1}/dz_t = c_0 + c_0 a_1$$

The presence of the term c_0 reflects the direct impact of z_{t+1} on y_{t+1}, and the second term $c_0 a_1$ reflects the effect of z_t on y_t ($= c_0$) multiplied by the effect of y_t on

y_{t+1} (= a_1). Continuing in this fashion, we can trace out the entire impulse (or impact) response function as

$$dy_{t+j}/dz_t = c_0[1 + a_1 + \cdots + (a_1)^j]$$

since $z_{t+1} = z_{t+2} = \cdots = 1$.

Taking limits as $j \to \infty$, we can reaffirm that the long-run impact is given by $c_0/(1 - a_1)$. If it is assumed that $0 < a_1 < 1$, the absolute value of the magnitude of the impacts is an increasing function of j. As we move further away from the date in which the policy was introduced, the greater the absolute value of the magnitude of the policy response. If $-1 < a_1 < 0$, the policy has a damped oscillating effect on the $\{y_t\}$ sequence. After the initial jump of c_0, the successive values of $\{y_t\}$ oscillate above and below the long-run level of $c_0/(1 - a_1)$.

There are several important extensions to the intervention example provided here. Of course, the model need not be a first-order autoregressive process. A more general ARMA(p, q) intervention model has the form:

$$y_t = a_0 + A(L)y_{t-1} + c_0 z_t + B(L)\epsilon_t$$

where $A(L)$ and $B(L)$ = polynomials in the lag operator L

Also, the intervention need not be the pure jump illustrated in the upper-left-hand graph (a) of Figure 5.2. In our study, the value of the intervention sequence jumps from zero to unity in 1973:1. However, there are several other possible ways to model the intervention function:

1. *Impulse function.* As shown in the upper-right-hand graph (b) of the figure, the function z_t is zero for all periods except in one particular period in which z_t is unity. This pulse function best characterizes a purely temporary intervention. Of course, the effects of the single impulse may last many periods due to the autoregressive nature of the $\{y_t\}$ series.

2. *Gradually changing function.* An intervention may not reach its full force immediately. Although the United States began installing metal detectors in airports in January 1973, it took almost a full year for installations to be completed at some major international airports. Our intervention study of the impact of metal detectors on quarterly skyjackings also modeled the z_t series as 1/4 in 1973:1, 1/2 in 1973:2, 3/4 in 1973:3, and 1.0 in 1973:4 and all subsequent periods. This type of intervention function is shown in the lower-left-hand graph (c) of the figure.

3. *Prolonged impulse function.* Rather than a single pulse, the intervention may remain in place for one or more periods and then begin to decay. For a short time, sky marshals were put on many U.S. flights to deter skyjackings. Since the sky marshal program was allowed to terminate, the $\{z_t\}$ sequence for sky marshals might be represented by the decaying function shown in the lower-right-hand graph (d) of Figure 5.2.

Figure 5.2 Typical intervention functions.

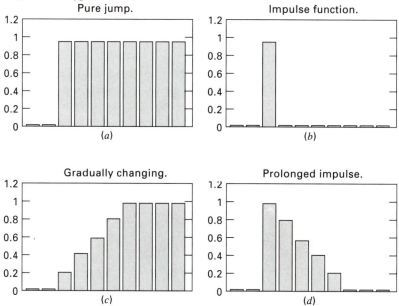

Be aware that the effects of these interventions change if $\{y_t\}$ has a unit root. From the discussion of Perron (1989) in Chapter 4, you should recall that a pulse intervention will have a permanent effect on the level of a unit root process. Similarly, if $\{y_t\}$ has a unit root, a pure jump intervention will act as a drift term. As indicated in Question 1 at the end of this chapter, an intervention will have a temporary effect on a unit root process if all values of $\{z_t\}$ sum to zero (e.g, $z_t = 1$, $z_{t+1} = -0.5$, $z_{t+2} = -0.5$, and all other values of the intervention variable equal zero).

Often, the shape of the intervention function is clear from a priori reasoning. When there is an ambiguity, estimate the plausible alternatives and then use the standard Box–Jenkins model selection criteria to choose the most appropriate model. The following two examples illustrate the general estimation procedure.

Estimating the Effect of Metal Detectors on Skyjackings

The linear form of the intervention model $y_t = a_0 + A(L)y_{t-1} + c_0 z_t + B(L)\epsilon_t$ assumes that the coefficients are invariant to the intervention. A useful check of this assumption is to pretest the data by estimating the most appropriate ARIMA(p, d, q) models for both the pre- and postintervention periods. If the two ARIMA models are quite different, it is likely that the autoregressive and moving average coefficients have changed. Usually, there are not enough pre- and postintervention observations to estimate two separate models. In such instances, the researcher must be content to proceed using the best-fitting ARIMA model over the longest data span. The procedure described below is typical of most intervention studies.

STEP 1:   Use the longest data span (i.e., either the pre- or postintervention observations) to find a plausible set of ARIMA models.

You should be careful to ensure that the $\{y_t\}$ sequence is stationary. If you suspect nonstationarity, you can perform unit root tests on the longest span of data. Alternatively, you can use the Perron (1989) test for structural change discussed in Chapter 4. In the presence of d unit roots, estimate the intervention model using the dth difference of y_t (i.e., $\Delta^d y_t$).

In our study, we were interested in the effects of metal detectors on U.S. domestic skyjackings, transnational skyjackings (including those involving the United States), and all other skyjackings. Call each of these time series $\{DS_t\}$, $\{TS_t\}$, and $\{OS_t\}$ respectively. Since there are only 5 years of data (i.e., 20 observations) for the preintervention period, we estimated the best-fitting ARIMA model over the 1973:1 to 1988:4 period. Using the various criteria discussed in Chapter 2 (including diagnostic checks of the residuals), we selected an AR(1) model for the $\{TS_t\}$ and $\{OS_t\}$ sequences and a pure noise model (i.e., all autoregressive and moving average coefficients equal to zero) for the $\{DS_t\}$ sequence.

STEP 2:   Estimate the various models over the entire sample period including the effect of the intervention.

The installation of metal detectors was tentatively viewed as an immediate and permanent intervention. As such, we set $z_t = 0$ for $t < 1973{:}1$ and $z_t = 1$ beginning in 1973:1. The results of the estimations over the entire sample period are reported in Table 5.1. As you can see, the installation of metal detectors reduced each of the three types of skyjacking incidents. The most pronounced effect was on U.S. domestic skyjackings that immediately fell by over 5.6 incidents per quarter. All effects are immediate since the estimate of a_1 is zero. The situation is somewhat different for the $\{TS_t\}$ and $\{OS_t\}$ sequences since the estimated autoregressive coefficients are different from zero. On impact, transnational skyjackings and other types of skyjacking incidents fell by 1.29 and 3.9 incidents per quarter. The long-run effects are estimated to be -1.78 and -5.11 incidents per quarter.

STEP 3:   Perform diagnostic checks of the estimated equations.

Diagnostic checking is particularly important since we have merged the observations from the pre- and postintervention periods. To reiterate the discussion of ARIMA models, a well-estimated intervention model will have the following characteristics:

1. The estimated coefficients should be of "high quality." All coefficients should be statistically significant at conventional levels. As in all ARIMA modeling, we wish to use a parsimonious model. If any coeffi-

cient is not significant, an alternative model should be considered. Moreover, the autoregressive coefficients should imply that the $\{y_t\}$ sequence is convergent.

2. The residuals should approximate white noise. If the residuals are serially correlated, the estimated model does not mimic the actual data-generating process. Forecasts from the estimated model cannot possibly be making use of all available information. If the residuals do not approximate a normal distribution, the usual tests of statistical inference are not valid. If the errors appear to be ARCH, the entire intervention model can be reestimated as an ARCH process.

3. The tentative model should outperform plausible alternatives. Of course, no one model can be expected to dominate all others in all possible criteria. However, it is good practice to compare the results of the maintained model to those of reasonable rivals. In the skyjacking example, a plausible alternative was to model the intervention as a gradually increasing process. This is particularly true since the impact effect was immediate for U.S. domestic flights and convergent for transnational and other domestic flights. Our conjecture was that metal detectors were gradually installed in non–U.S. airports and, even when installed, the enforcement was sporadic. As a check, we modeled the intervention as gradually increasing over the year 1973. Although the coefficients were nearly identical to those reported in Table 5.1, the AIC and SBC were slightly lower (indicating a better fit) using the gradually increasing process. Hence, it is reasonable to conclude that metal detector adoption was more gradual outside of the United States.

Table 5.1 **Metal Detectors and Skyjackings**

	Preintervention Mean	a_1	Impact Effect (c_0)	Long-Run Effect
Transnational $\{TS_t\}$	3.032 (5.96)	0.276 (2.51)	−1.29 (−2.21)	−1.78
U.S. domestic $\{DS_t\}$	6.70 (12.02)		−5.62 (−8.73)	−5.62
Other skyjackings $\{OS_t\}$	6.80 (7.93)	0.237 (2.14)	−3.90 (−3.95)	−5.11

Notes:

1. t-statistics are in parentheses

2. The long–run effect is calculated as $\dfrac{c_0}{1-a_1}$

Estimating the Effect of the Libyan Bombing

We also considered the effects of the U.S. bombing of Libya on the morning of April 15, 1986. The stated reason for the attack was Libya's alleged involvement in the terrorist bombing of the La Belle Discotheque in West Berlin. Since 18 of the F-111 fighter-bombers were deployed from British bases at Lakenheath and Upper Heyford, England, the U.K. implicitly assisted in the raid. The remaining U.S. planes were deployed from aircraft carriers in the Mediterranean Sea. Now let y_t denote all transnational terrorist incidents directed against the United States and U.K. during month t. A plot of the $\{y_t\}$ sequence exhibited a large positive spike immediately after the bombing; the immediate effect seemed to be a wave of anti–U.S. and anti–U.K. attacks to protest the retaliatory strike.

Preliminary estimates of the monthly data from January 1968 to March 1986 indicated that the $\{y_t\}$ sequence could be estimated as a purely autoregressive model with significant coefficients at lags 1 and 5. We were surprised by a significant coefficient at lag 5, but both the AIC and SBC indicate that the fifth lag is important. Nevertheless, we estimated versions of the model with and without the fifth lag. In addition, we considered two possible patterns for the intervention series. For the first, $\{z_t\}$ was modeled as zero until April 1986 and 1 in all subsequent periods. Using this specification, we obtained the following estimates (with t-statistics in parentheses):

$$y_t = 5.58 + 0.336y_{t-1} + 0.123y_{t-5} + 2.65z_t$$
$$(5.56) \quad (3.26) \quad (0.84)$$
$$\text{AIC} = 1656.03, \quad \text{SBC} = 1669.95$$

Note that the coefficient of z_t has a t-statistic of 0.84 (which is not significant at the 0.05 level). Alternatively, when z_t was allowed to be 1 only in the month of the attack, we obtained

$$y_t = 3.79 + 0.327y_{t-1} + 0.157y_{t-5} + 38.9z_t$$
$$(5.53) \quad (2.59) \quad (6.09)$$
$$\text{AIC} = 1608.68, \quad \text{SBC} = 1626.06$$

In comparing the two estimates, it is clear that magnitudes of the autoregressive coefficients are similar. Although Q-tests indicated that the residuals from both models approximate white noise, the pulse specification is preferable. The coefficient on the pulse term is highly significant and both the AIC and SBC select the second specification. Our conclusion was that the Libyan bombing did not have the desired effect of reducing terrorist attacks against the United States and the U.K. Instead, the bombing caused an immediate increase of over 38 attacks. Subsequently, the number of attacks declined; 32.7% of these attacks are estimated to persist for one period ($0.327 \times 38.9 = 12.7$). Since the autoregressive coefficients imply convergence, the long-run consequences of the raid were estimated to be zero.

2. TRANSFER FUNCTION MODELS

A natural extension of the intervention model is to allow the $\{z_t\}$ sequence to be something other than a deterministic dummy variable. Consider the following generalization of the intervention model:

$$y_t = a_0 + A(L)y_{t-1} + C(L)z_t + B(L)\epsilon_t \qquad (5.3)$$

where $A(L)$, $B(L)$ and $C(L)$ = polynomials in the lag operator L

In a typical transfer function analysis, the researcher will collect data on the endogenous variable $\{y_t\}$ and exogenous variable $\{z_t\}$. The goal is to estimate the parameter a_0 and parameters of the polynomials $A(L)$, $B(L)$, and $C(L)$. The major difference between (5.3) and the intervention model is that $\{z_t\}$ is not constrained to have a particular deterministic time path. The intervention variable is allowed to be any exogenous stochastic process. The polynomial $C(L)$ is called the **transfer function** in that it shows how a movement in the exogenous variable z_t affects the time path of (i.e., is transferred to) the endogenous variable $\{y_t\}$. The coefficients of $C(L)$, denoted by c_i, are called transfer function weights. The impulse response function showing the effects of a z_t shock on the $\{y_t\}$ sequence is given by $C(L)/[1 - A(L)]$.

It is critical to note that transfer function analysis assumes that $\{z_t\}$ is an exogenous process that evolves independently of the $\{y_t\}$ sequence. Innovations in $\{y_t\}$ are assumed to have no effect on the $\{z_t\}$ sequence, so that $Ez_t\epsilon_{t-s} = 0$ for all values of s and t. Since z_t can be observed and is uncorrelated with the current innovation in y_t (i.e., the disturbance term ϵ_t), the current and lagged values of z_t are explanatory variables for y_t. Let $C(L)$ be $c_0 + c_1 L + c_2 L^2 + \cdots$. If $c_0 = 0$, the contemporaneous value of z_t does not directly affect y_t. As such, $\{z_t\}$ is called a **leading indicator** in that the observations z_t, z_{t-1}, z_{t-2}, ... can be used in predicting future values of the $\{y_t\}$ sequence.[2]

It is easy to conceptualize numerous applications for (5.3). After all, a large part of dynamic economic analysis concerns the effects of an "exogenous" or "independent" sequence $\{z_t\}$ on the time path of an endogenous sequence $\{y_t\}$. For example, much of the current research in agricultural economics concerns the effects of the macroeconomy on the agricultural sector. If we use (5.3), farm output $\{y_t\}$ is affected by its own past, as well as the current and past state of the macroeconomy $\{z_t\}$. The effects of macroeconomic fluctuations on farm output can be represented by the coefficients of $C(L)$. Here, $B(L)\epsilon_t$ represents the unexplained portion of farm output. Alternatively, the level of ozone in the atmosphere $\{y_t\}$ is a naturally evolving process; hence, in the absence of other outside influences, we should expect the ozone level to be well represented by an ARIMA model. However, many have argued that the use of fluorocarbons has damaged the ozone layer. Because of a cumulative effect, it is argued that current and past values of fluorocarbon usage affect the value of y_t. By letting z_t denote fluorocarbon usage in t, it is possible to model the effects of the fluorcarbon usage on the ozone layer using a model in the form of (5.3). The natural dissipation of ozone is captured through the coefficients of $A(L)$. Stochastic shocks to the ozone layer, possibly due to electrical storms and the presence of measurement errors, are captured by $B(L)\epsilon_t$. The contemporaneous effect of fluorocarbons on the ozone layer is captured by the coefficient c_0 and the lagged effects by the other transfer function weights (i.e., the values of the various c_i).

In contrast to the pure intervention model, there is no preintervention versus postintervention period, so that we cannot estimate a transfer function in the same fashion that we estimated an intervention model. However, the methods are very similar in that the goal is to estimate a parsimonious model. The procedure involved in fitting a transfer function model is easiest to explain by considering a simple case of (5.3). To begin, suppose $\{z_t\}$ is generated by a white-noise process that is uncorrelated with ϵ_t at all leads and lags. Also suppose that the realization of z_t affects the $\{y_t\}$ sequence with a lag of unknown duration. Specifically, let

$$y_t = a_1 y_{t-1} + c_d z_{t-d} + \epsilon_t \tag{5.4}$$

where $\{z_t\}$ and $\{\epsilon_t\}$ are white-noise processes such that $E(z_t \epsilon_{t-i}) = 0$; a_1 and c_d are unknown coefficients, and d is the "delay" or lag duration to be determined by the econometrician.

Since $\{z_t\}$ and $\{\epsilon_t\}$ are assumed to be independent white-noise processes, it is possible to separately model the effects of each type shock. Since we can observe the various z_t values, the first step is to calculate the **cross-correlations** between y_t and the various z_{t-i}. The cross-correlation between y_t and z_{t-i} is defined to be

$$\rho_{yz}(i) \equiv \text{cov}(y_t, z_{t-i})/\sigma_y \sigma_z \tag{5.5}$$

where σ_y and σ_z = the standard deviations of y_t and z_t, respectively

Notice that the standard deviation of each sequence is assumed to be time-independent.

Plotting each value of $\rho_{yz}(i)$ yields the cross-autocorrelation function (CACF) or **cross-correlogram.** In practice, we must use the cross-correlations calculated using sample data since we do not know the true covariances and standard deviations. The key point is that the sample cross-correlations provide the same type of information as the ACF in an ARMA model. To explain, solve (5.4) to obtain:

$$y_t = c_d z_{t-d}/(1 - a_1 L) + \epsilon_t/(1 - a_1 L)$$

Use the properties of lag operators to expand the expression $c_d z_{t-d}/(1 - a_1 L)$:

$$y_t = c_d(z_{t-d} + a_1 z_{t-d-1} + a_1^2 z_{t-d-2} + a_1^3 z_{t-d-3} + \cdots) + \epsilon_t/(1 - a_1 L)$$

Analogously to our derivation of the Yule–Walker equations, we can obtain the **cross-covariances** by the successive multiplication of y_t by $z_t, z_{t-1}, \ldots$ to form

$$y_t z_t = c_d(z_t z_{t-d} + a_1 z_t z_{t-d-1} + a_1^2 z_t z_{t-d-2} + a_1^3 z_t z_{t-d-3} + \cdots) + z_t \epsilon_t/(1 - a_1 L)$$
$$y_t z_{t-1} = c_d(z_{t-1} z_{t-d} + a_1 z_{t-1} z_{t-d-1} + a_1^2 z_{t-1} z_{t-d-2} + a_1^3 z_{t-1} z_{t-d-3} + \cdots) + z_{t-1} \epsilon_t/(1 - a_1 L)$$
$$\cdots$$
$$y_t z_{t-d} = c_d(z_{t-d} z_{t-d} + a_1 z_{t-d} z_{t-d-1} + a_1^2 z_{t-d} z_{t-d-2} + a_1^3 z_{t-d} z_{t-d-3} + \cdots) + z_{t-d} \epsilon_t/(1 - a_1 L)$$
$$y_t z_{t-d-1} = c_d(z_{t-d-1} z_{t-d} + a_1 z_{t-d-1} z_{t-d-1} + a_1^2 z_{t-d-1} z_{t-d-2} + a_1^3 z_{t-d-1} z_{t-d-3} + \cdots)$$
$$+ z_{t-d-1} \epsilon_t/(1 - a_1 L)$$
$$y_t z_{t-d-2} = c_d(z_{t-d-2} z_{t-d} + a_1 z_{t-d-2} z_{t-d-1} + a_1^2 z_{t-d-2} z_{t-d-2} + a_1^3 z_{t-d-2} z_{t-d-3} + \cdots)$$
$$+ z_{t-d-2} \epsilon_t/(1 - a_1 L)$$
$$\cdots$$

Now take the expected value of each of the above equations. If we continue to assume that $\{z_t\}$ and $\{\epsilon_t\}$ are independent white-noise disturbances, it follows that

$$Ey_t z_t = 0$$
$$Ey_t z_{t-1} = 0$$
$$\cdots$$
$$Ey_t z_{t-d} = c_d \sigma_z^2$$
$$Ey_t z_{t-d-1} = c_d a_1 \sigma_z^2$$
$$Ey_t z_{t-d-2} = c_d a_1^2 \sigma_z^2$$
$$\cdots$$

so that in compact form,

$$Ey_t z_{t-i} = 0 \text{ for all } i < d$$
$$= c_d a_1^{i-d} \sigma_z^2 \text{ for } i \geq d \qquad (5.6)$$

Dividing each value of $Ey_t z_{t-i} = \text{cov}(y_t, z_{t-i})$ by $\sigma_y \sigma_z$ yields the cross-correlogram. Note that the cross-correlogram consists of zeroes until lag d. The absolute value of height of the first nonzero cross-correlation is positively related to the magnitudes of c_d and a_1. Thereafter, the cross-correlations decay at the rate a_1. The decay of the correlogram matches the autoregressive patterns of the $\{y_t\}$ sequence.

The pattern exhibited by (5.6) is easily generalized. Suppose we allow both z_{t-d} and z_{t-d-1} to directly affect y_t:

$$y_t = a_1 y_{t-1} + c_d z_{t-d} + c_{d+1} z_{t-d-1} + \epsilon_t$$

Solving for y_t, we obtain

$$y_t = (c_d z_{t-d} + c_{d+1} z_{t-d-1})/(1 - a_1 L) + \epsilon_t/(1 - a_1 L)$$
$$= c_d(z_{t-d} + a_1 z_{t-d-1} + a_1^2 z_{t-d-2} + a_1^3 z_{t-d-3} + \cdots)$$
$$+ c_{d+1}(z_{t-d-1} + a_1 z_{t-d-2} + a_1^2 z_{t-d-3} + a_1^3 z_{t-d-4} + \cdots) + \epsilon_t/(1 - a_1 L)$$

so that

$$y_t = c_d z_{t-d} + (c_d a_1 + c_{d+1}) z_{t-d-1} + a_1 (c_d a_1 + c_{d+1}) z_{t-d-2} + a_1^2 (c_d a_1 + c_{d+1}) z_{t-d-3}$$
$$+ \cdots + \epsilon_t / (1 - a_1 L) \quad (5.7)$$

Forming the standardized cross-covariances reveals the following pattern:[3]

$$
\begin{aligned}
\mathrm{Cov}(y_t, z_{t-i})/\sigma_z^2 &= 0 && \text{for } i < d \\
&= c_d && \text{for } i = d \\
&= c_d a_1 + c_{d+1} && \text{for } i = d + 1 \\
&= a_1^{j-1}(c_d a_1 + c_{d+1}) && \text{for } i = d + j \quad (j > 0)
\end{aligned}
$$

The upper-left-hand graph (a) of Figure 5.3 shows the shape of the standardized cross-correlogram for $d = 3$, $c_d = 1$, $c_{d+1} = 1.5$, and $a_1 = 0.8$. Note that there are distinct spikes at lags 3 and 4 corresponding to the nonzero values of c_3 and c_4. Thereafter, the cross-correlations decay at the rate a_1. The upper-right-hand graph (b) of the figure replaces c_4 with the value -1.5. Again, all cross-correlations are zero until lag 3; since $c_3 = 1$, the standardized value of $\rho_{yz}(3) = 1$. To find the standardized value of $\rho_{yz}(4)$ form: $\rho_{yz}(4) = 0.8 - 1.5 = -0.7$. The subsequent values of $\rho_{yz}(i)$ decay at the rate 0.8. The pattern illustrated by these two examples generalizes to any intervention model of the form:

$$y_t = a_0 + a_1 y_{t-1} + C(L)z_t + B(L)\epsilon_t \quad (5.8)$$

The theoretical cross-correlogram has a shape with the following characteristics:

1. All $\rho_{yz}(i)$ will be zero until the first nonzero element of the polynomial $C(L)$.
2. The form of $B(L)$ is immaterial to the *theoretical* cross-correlogram. Since z_t is uncorrelated with ϵ_t at all leads and lags, the form of the polynomial $B(L)$ will not affect any of the theoretical cross-correlations $\rho_{yz}(i)$. Obviously, the intercept term a_0 does not affect any of the cross-covariances or cross-correlations.
3. A spike in the CACF indicates a nonzero element of $C(L)$. Thus, a spike at lag d indicates that z_{t-d} directly affects y_t.
4. All spikes decay at the rate a_1; convergence implies that the absolute value of a_1 is less than unity. If $0 < a_1 < 1$, decay in the cross-correlations will be direct, whereas if $-1 < a_1 < 0$, the decay pattern will be oscillatory.

Only the nature of the decay process changes if we generalize Equation (5.8) to include additional lags of y_{t-i}. In the general case of (5.3), the *decay pattern in the cross-correlations is* determined by the characteristic roots of the polynomial $A(L)$; the shape is precisely that suggested by the autocorrelations of a pure ARMA model. This should not come as a surprise; in the examples of (5.4) and (5.8), the

Figure 5.3 Standardized cross-correlograms.

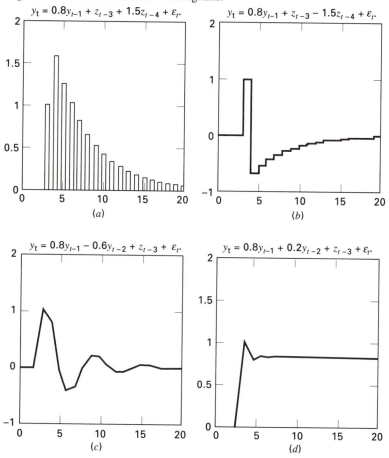

decay factor was simply the first-order autocorrelation coefficient a_1. We know that there will be decay since all characteristic roots of $1 - A(L)$ must be outside of the unit circle for the process to be stationary. Convergence will be direct if the roots are positive and will tend to oscillate if a root is negative. Imaginary roots impart a sine-wave pattern to the decay process.

The Cross-Covariances of a Second-Order Process

To use another example, consider the transfer function:

$$y_t = a_1 y_{t-1} + a_2 y_{t-2} + c_d z_{t-d} + \epsilon_t$$

Using lag operators to solve for y_t is inconvenient since we do not know the numerical values of a_1 and a_2. Instead, use the method of undetermined coefficients and form the **challenge solution:**

$$y_t = \sum_{i=0}^{\infty} W_i z_{t-i} + \sum_{i=0}^{\infty} V_i \epsilon_{t-i}$$

You should be able to verify that the values of W_i are given by

$$W_0 = 0$$
$$\cdots$$
$$W_d = c_d$$
$$W_{d+1} = c_d a_1$$
$$W_{d+2} = c_d(a_1^2 + a_2)$$
$$W_{d+3} = a_1 W_{d+2} + a_2 W_{d+1}$$
$$W_{d+4} = a_1 W_{d+3} + a_2 W_{d+2}$$
$$\cdots$$

Thus, for all $i > d + 1$, the successive coefficients satisfy the difference equation $W_i = a_1 W_{i-1} + a_2 W_{i-2}$. At this stage, we are not interested in the values of the various V_i, so that it is sufficient to write the solution for y_t as

$$y_t = c_d z_{t-d} + c_d a_1 z_{t-d-1} + c_d(a_1^2 + a_2)z_{t-d-2} + c_d(a_1^3 + 2a_1 a_2)z_{t-d-3} + \cdots + \Sigma V_i \epsilon_{t-i}$$

Next, use this solution for y_t to form all autocovariances using the Yule–Walker equations. Forming the expressions for $Ey_t z_{t-i}$, we get

$$Ey_t z_{t-i} = 0 \quad \text{for } i < d \quad (\text{since } Ez_t z_{t-i} = 0 \text{ for } i < d)$$
$$Ey_t z_{t-d} = c_d \sigma_z^2$$
$$Ey_t z_{t-d-1} = a_1 c_d \sigma_z^2$$
$$Ey_t z_{t-d-2} = c_d(a_1^2 + a_2)\sigma_z^2$$
$$\cdots$$

Thus, there is an initial spike at lag d reflecting the nonzero value of c_d. After one period, a_1 percent of the value c_d remains. After two periods—the number of autocorrelations in the transfer function—the decay pattern in the cross-covariances begins to satisfy the difference equation:

$$\rho_{yz}(i) = a_1 \rho_{yz}(i - 1) + a_2 \rho_{yz}(i - 2)$$

The lower-left-hand graph (c) of Figure 5.3 shows the shape of the CACF for the case of $d = 3$, $c_d = 1$, $a_1 = 0.8$, and $a_2 = -0.6$. The oscillatory pattern reflects the fact that the characteristic roots of the process are imaginary. For purposes of comparison, the lower-right-hand graph (d) shows the standardized CACF of a unit root process. The fact that one of the characteristic roots is equal to unity means that a z_{t-3} shock has a permanent effect on the $\{y_t\}$ sequence.[4]

The econometrician will rarely be so fortunate to work with a $\{z_t\}$ series that is white-noise. We need to further generalize our discussion of transfer functions to consider the case in which the $\{z_t\}$ sequence is a stationary ARMA process. Let the model for the $\{z_t\}$ sequence be an ARMA process such that

$$D(L)z_t = E(L)\epsilon_{zt}$$

where $D(L)$ and $E(L)_z$ = polynomials in the lag operator L
$\quad\quad\epsilon_{zt}$ = white-noise

At this point, we can use the methodology developed in Chapter 2 to estimate the ARMA process generating the $\{z_t\}$ sequence. The residuals from such a model, denoted by $\{\hat{\epsilon}_{zt}\}$, should be white-noise. The idea is to estimate the *innovations* in the $\{z_t\}$ sequence even though the sequence itself is not a white-noise process. At this point, it is tempting to think that we should form the cross-correlations between the $\{y_t\}$ sequence and $\{\hat{\epsilon}_{zt-i}\}$. However, this procedure would be inconsistent with the maintained hypothesis that the structure of the transfer function is given by (5.3). Reproducing (5.3) for your convenience, we get

$$y_t = a_0 + A(L)y_{t-1} + C(L)z_t + B(L)\epsilon_t$$

Here, $z_t, z_{t-1}, z_{t-2}, \ldots$ (and not simply the innovations) directly affect the value of y_t. Cross-correlations between y_t and the various $\hat{\epsilon}_{zt-i}$ would not reveal the pattern of the coefficients in $C(L)$. The appropriate methodology is to *filter* the $\{y_t\}$ sequence by multiplying (5.3) by the previously estimated polynomial $D(L)/E(L)$. As such, the filtered value of y_t is $D(L)y_t/E(L)$ and denoted by y_{ft}. Consider

$$D(L)y_t/E(L) = D(L)a_0/E(L) + D(L)A(L)y_{t-1}/E(L) + C(L)D(L)z_t/E(L)$$
$$+ B(L)D(L)\epsilon_t/E(L) \quad (5.9)$$

Given that $D(L)y_t/E(L) = y_{ft}$, $D(L)y_{t-1}/E(L) = y_{ft-1}$ and $D(L)z_t/E(L) = \epsilon_{zt}$, (5.9) is equivalent to

$$y_{ft} = D(L)a_0/E(L) + A(L)y_{ft-1} + C(L)\epsilon_{zt} + B(L)D(L)\epsilon_t/E(L) \quad (5.10)$$

Although you can construct the sequence $D(L)y_t/E(L)$, most software packages can make the appropriate transformations automatically. Now compare (5.3) and (5.10). You can see that y_t and $C(L)z_t$ will have the same correlogram as y_{ft} and $C(L)\epsilon_{zt}$. Thus, when we form the cross-correlations between y_{ft} and ϵ_{zt-i}, the cross-correlations will be the same as those from (5.3). As in the case in which $\{z_t\}$ was originally white-noise, we can inspect these cross-correlations for spikes and the decay pattern. In summary, the full procedure for fitting a transfer function entails:

STEP 1: Fit a ARMA model to the $\{z_t\}$ sequence. The technique used at this stage is precisely that for estimating any ARMA model. A properly estimated ARMA model should approximate the data-generating process for the $\{z_t\}$ sequence. The calculated residuals $\{\hat{\varepsilon}_{zt}\}$ are called the *filtered* values of the $\{z_t\}$ series. These filtered values can be interpreted as the pure innovations in the $\{z_t\}$ sequence. Calculate and store the $\{\hat{\varepsilon}_{zt}\}$ sequence.

STEP 2: Obtain the filtered $\{y_t\}$ sequence by applying the filter $D(L)/E(L)$ to each value of $\{y_t\}$; that is, use the results of Step 1 to obtain $D(L)/E(L)y_t \equiv y_{ft}$. Form the cross-correlogram between y_{ft} and $\hat{\varepsilon}_{zt-i}$. Of course, these sample correlations will not precisely conform to their theoretical values. Under the null hypothesis that the cross-correlations are all zero, the *sample variance* of cross-correlation coefficient i asymptotically converges to $(T - i)^{-1}$, where $T =$ number of usable observations. Let $r_{yz}(i)$ denote the sample cross-correlation coefficient between y_t and z_{t-i}. Under the null hypothesis that all the true values of $\rho_{yz}(i)$ are equal to zero, the variance of $r_{yz}(i)$ converges to

$$\mathrm{Var}[r_{yz}(i)] = (T - i)^{-1}$$

For example, with 100 usable observations, the standard deviation of the cross-correlation coefficient between y_t and z_{t-1} is the square root of 99 (approximately equal to 0.10). If the calculated value of $r_{yz}(1)$ exceeds 0.2 (or is less than −0.2), the null hypothesis can be rejected. Significant cross-correlations at lag i indicate that an innovation in z_t affects the value of y_{t+i}. To test the significance of the first k cross-correlations, use the statistic:

$$Q = T(T+2)\sum_{i=0}^{k} r_{yz}^2 (i)/(T-k)$$

Asymptotically, Q has a χ^2 distribution with $(k - p_1 - p_2)$ degrees of freedom, where p_1 and p_2 denote the number of nonzero coefficients in $A(L)$ and $C(L)$, respectively.

STEP 3: Examine the pattern of the cross-correlogram. Just as the ACF can be used as a guide in identifying an ARMA model, the CACF can help identify the form of $A(L)$ and $C(L)$. Spikes in the cross-correlogram indicate nonzero values of c_i. The decay pattern of the cross-correlations suggests plausible candidates for coefficients of $A(L)$. This decay pattern is perfectly analogous to the ACF in a traditional ARMA model. In practice, examination of the cross-correlogram will suggest several plausible transfer functions. Estimate each of these plausible models and select the "best-fitting" model. At this point, you will have selected a model of the form:

$$[1 - A(L)]y_t = C(L)z_t + e_t$$

where e_t denotes the error term that is not necessarily white-noise.

STEP 4: The $\{e_t\}$ sequence obtained in Step 3 is an approximation of $B(L)\epsilon_t$. As such, the ACF of these residuals can suggest the appropriate form for the $B(L)$ function. If the $\{e_t\}$ sequence appears to be white-noise, your task is complete. However, the correlogram of the $\{e_t\}$ sequence will usually suggest a number of plausible forms for $B(L)$. Use the $\{e_t\}$ sequence to estimate the various forms of $B(L)$ and select the "best" model for the $B(L)e_t$.

STEP 5: Combine the results of Steps 3 and 4 to estimate the full equation. At this stage, you will estimate $A(L)$, $B(L)$, and $C(L)$ simultaneously. The properties of a well-estimated model are such that the coefficients are of high quality, the model is parsimonious, the residuals conform to a white-noise process, and the forecast errors are small. You should compare your estimated model to the other plausible candidates from Steps 3 and 4.

There is no doubt that estimating a transfer function involves judgment on the part of the researcher. Experienced econometricians would agree that the procedure is a blend of skill, art, and perseverance that is developed through practice. Nevertheless, there are some hints that can be quite helpful.

1. After we estimate the full model in Step 5, any remaining autocorrelation in the residuals probably means that $B(L)$ is misspecified. Return to Step 4 and reformulate the form of $B(L)$ so as to capture the remaining explanatory power of the residuals.

2. After we estimate the full model in Step 5, if the residuals are correlated with $\{z_t\}$, the $C(L)$ function is probably misspecified. Return to Step 3 and reformulate the specifications of $A(L)$ and $C(L)$.

3. Instead of estimating $\{\epsilon_t\}$ as a pure autoregressive process, you can estimate $B(L)$ as an ARMA process. Thus, $e_t = B(L)\epsilon_t$ is allowed to have the form $e_t = G(L)\epsilon_t/H(L)$. Here, $G(L)$ and $H(L)$ are low-order polynomials in the lag operator L. The benefit is that a high-order autoregressive process can often be approximated by a low-order ARMA model.

4. The sample cross-correlations are not meaningful if $\{y_t\}$ and/or $\{z_t\}$ are not stationary. You can test each for a unit root using the procedures discussed in Chapter 4. In the presence of unit roots, Box and Jenkins (1976) recommend dif-

ferencing each variable until it is stationary. The next chapter considers unit roots in a multivariate context. For now, it is sufficient to note that this recommendation can lead to overdifferencing.

The interpretation of the transfer function depends on the type of differencing performed. Consider the following three specifications and assume that $|a_1| < 1$:

$$y_t = a_1 y_{t-1} + c_0 z_t + \epsilon_t \qquad (5.11)$$
$$\Delta y_t = a_1 \Delta y_{t-1} + c_0 z_t + \epsilon_t \qquad (5.12)$$
$$\Delta y_t = a_1 \Delta y_{t-1} + c_0 \Delta z_t + \epsilon_t \qquad (5.13)$$

In (5.11), a one unit shock in z_t has the initial effect of increasing y_t by c_0 units. This initial effect decays at the rate a_1. In (5.12), a one-unit shock in z_t has the initial effect of increasing *the change in* y_t by c_0 units. The effect on the *change* decays at the rate a_1, but the effect on the *level* of the $\{y_t\}$ sequence never decays. In (5.13), the change in z_t affects the change in y_t. Here, a pulse in the $\{z_t\}$ sequence will have a temporary effect on the level of $\{y_t\}$. Questions 1 and 2 at the end of this chapter are intended to help you gain familiarity with the different specifications.

3. ESTIMATING A TRANSFER FUNCTION

High-profile terrorist events (e.g., the hijacking of TWA flight 847 on June 14, 1985; the hijacking of the *Achille Lauro* cruise ship on October 7, 1985; and the Abu Nidal attacks on the Vienna and Rome airports on December 27, 1985) caused much speculation in the press about tourists changing their travel plans. Although opinion polls of prospective tourists suggest that terrorism affects tourism, the true impact, if any, can best be discovered through the application of statistical techniques. Polls conducted in the aftermath of significant incidents cannot indicate whether respondents rebooked trips. Moreover, polls cannot account for tourists not surveyed who may be induced by lower prices to take advantage of offers designed to entice tourists back to a troubled spot.

To measure the impact of terrorism on tourism, in Enders, Sandler, and Parise (1992), we constructed the quarterly values of total receipts from tourism for 12 countries.[5] The logarithmic share of each nation's revenues was treated as the dependent variable $\{y_t\}$ and the number of transnational terrorist incidents occurring within each nation as the independent variable $\{z_t\}$. The crucial assumption for the use of intervention analysis is that there be no feedback from tourism to terrorism. This assumption would be violated if changes in tourism induced terrorists to change their activities.

Consider a transfer function in the form of (5.3):

$$y_t = a_0 + A(L)y_{t-1} + C(L)z_t + B(L)\epsilon_t$$

where y_t = the logarithmic share of a nation's tourism revenues in quarter t

z_t = is the number of transnational terrorist incidents within that country during quarter t.[6]

If we use the methodology developed in the previous section, the first step in fitting a transfer function is to fit an ARMA model to the $\{z_t\}$ sequence. For illustrative purposes, it is helpful to consider the Italian case since terrorism in Italy appeared to be white-noise (with a constant mean of 4.20 incidents per quarter). Let $\rho_z(i)$ denote the autocorrelations between z_t and z_{t-i}. The correlogram for terrorist attacks in Italy is:

Correlogram for Terrorist Attacks in Italy

$\rho_z(0)$	$\rho_z(1)$	$\rho_z(2)$	$\rho_z(3)$	$\rho_z(4)$	$\rho_z(5)$	$\rho_z(6)$	$\rho_z(7)$	$\rho_z(8)$
1	0.13	0.02	−0.06	−0.04	0.11	−0.01	0.00	−0.13

Each value of $\rho_z(i)$ is less than two standard deviations from unity. The Ljung–Box Q-statistics for the significance of the first 4, 8, 12, and 16 lags are

$$Q(4) = 2.06, \quad \text{significance level} = 0.725$$
$$Q(8) = 4.52, \quad \text{significance level} = 0.807$$
$$Q(12) = 7.02, \quad \text{significance level} = 0.855$$
$$Q(16) = 8.06, \quad \text{significance level} = 0.947$$

Since terrorist incidents appear to be a white-noise process, we can skip Step 1; there is no need to fit an ARMA model to the series or filter the $\{y_t\}$ sequence for Italy. At this point, we conclude that terrorists randomize their acts, so that the number of incidents in quarter t is uncorrelated with the number of incidents in previous periods.

Step 2 calls for obtaining the cross-correlogram between tourism and terrorism. The cross-correlogram is

Cross-Correlogram Between Terrorism and Tourism in Italy

$\rho_{yz}(0)$	$\rho_{yz}(1)$	$\rho_{yz}(2)$	$\rho_{yz}(3)$	$\rho_{yz}(4)$	$\rho_{yz}(5)$	$\rho_{yz}(6)$	$\rho_{yz}(7)$	$\rho_{yz}(8)$
−0.18	−0.23	−0.24	−0.05	0.04	0.13	0.04	0.00	0.10

There are several interesting features of the cross-correlogram:

1. With T observations and i lags, the theoretical value of the standard deviation of each value of $\rho_{yz}(i)$ is $(T - i)^{-1/2}$. With 73 observations, $T^{-1/2}$ is approximately equal to 0.117. At the 5% significance level (i.e., two standard deviations), the sample value of $\rho_{yz}(0)$ is not significantly different from zero and $\rho_{yz}(1)$ and $\rho_{yz}(2)$ are just on the margin. However, the Q-statistic for $\rho_{yz}(0) = \rho_{yz}(1) = \rho_{yz}(2)$ = 0 is significant at the 0.01 level. Thus, there appears to be a strong negative re-

lationship between terrorism and tourism beginning at lag 1 or 2. The key issue is to find the most appropriate model of the cross-correlations.

2. It is good practice to examine the cross-correlations between y_t and leading values of z_{t+i}. If the current value of y_t tends to be correlated with *future* values of z_{t+i}, it might be that the assumption of no feedback is violated. The presence of a significant cross-correlation between y_t and leads of z_t might be due to the effect of the current realization of y_t on future values of the $\{z_t\}$ sequence.

3. Since $\rho_{yz}(0)$ is not significantly different from zero at the 5% level, it is likely that the delay factor is one quarter; it takes at least one quarter for tourists to significantly revise their travel plans. However, there is no obvious pattern to the cross-correlation function. It is wise to entertain the possibility of several plausible models at this point in the process.

Step 3 entails examining the cross-correlogram and estimating each of the plausible models. Based on the ambiguous evidence of the cross-correlogram, several different models for the transfer function were estimated. We experimented using delay factors of zero, one, and two quarters. Since the decay pattern of the cross-correlogram is also ambiguous, we allowed $A(L)$ to have the form: $a_1 y_{t-1}$ and $a_1 y_{t-1} + a_2 y_{t-2}$. Some of our estimates are reported in Table 5.2.

Model 1 has the form $y_t = a_0 + a_1 y_{t-1} + a_2 y_{t-2} + c_1 z_{t-1} + e_t$. The problem with this specification is that the intercept term a_0 is not significantly different from zero. Eliminating this coefficient yields model 2. Notice that all coefficients in model 2 are significant at conventional levels and that the magnitude of each is quite reasonable. The estimated value of c_1 is such that a terrorist incident reduces the logarithmic share of Italy's tourism by 0.003 in the following period. The point estimates of the autoregressive coefficients imply imaginary characteristic roots (the roots are

Table 5.2   **Terrorism and Tourism in Italy: Estimates from Step 2**

	a_0	a_1	a_2	c_0	c_1	c_2	AIC/SBC
Model 1	0.0249	0.795	−0.469		−0.0046		−5.09/4.01
	(1.25)	(2.74)	(−1.63)		(−2.34)		
Model 2		0.868	−0.696		−0.0030		−5.54/1.28
		(4.52)	(−3.44)		(−2.23)		
Model 3		1.09	−0.683	−0.0025			−4.94/1.89
		(4.51)	(−2.96)	(−2.10)			
Model 4					−0.0025	−0.0019	−4.84/3.27
					(−1.15)	(−0.945)	
Model 5		−0.217			−0.0025	−0.0027	−2.93/3.89
		(−0.221)			(−1.16)	(−0.080)	

Note: The numbers in parentheses are the t-statistics for the null hypothesis of a zero coefficient.

0.434 ± 0.69i). Since these roots lie inside the unit circle, the effect of any incident decays in a sine-wave pattern.

Model 3 changes the delay so as to allow z_t to have a contemporaneous effect on y_t. The point estimates of the coefficients are reasonable and all are more than two standard deviations from zero. However, both the AIC and SBC select model 2 over model 3. The appropriate delay seems to be one quarter.

Since the cross-correlogram seems to have two spikes and exhibits little decay, we allowed both z_{t-1} and z_{t-2} to directly affect y_t. You can see that models 4 and 5 are inadequate in nearly all respects. Thus, we tentatively select model 2 as the "best" model.

For Step 4, we obtained the $\{e_t\}$ sequence from the residuals of model 2. Hence,

$$e_t = y_t - [-0.003z_{t-1}/(1 - 0.868L + 0.676L^2)] \tag{5.14}$$

The correlogram of these residuals is:

$\rho(0)$	$\rho(1)$	$\rho(2)$	$\rho(3)$	$\rho(4)$	$\rho(5)$	$\rho(6)$	$\rho(7)$	$\rho(8)$
1.0	0.621	0.554	0.431	0.419	0.150	0.066	0.021	−0.00

The residuals were then estimated as an ARMA process using standard Box–Jenkins methods. Without going into details, we found that the best-fitting ARMA model of the residuals is

$$e_t = 0.485e_{t-1} + 0.295e_{t-2} + (1 + 0.238L^4)\epsilon_t \tag{5.15}$$

where the t-statistics for the coefficients = 4.08, 2.33, and 1.83 (significant at the 0.000, 0.023, and 0.071 levels), respectively

At this point, our tentative transfer function is

$$y_t = [-0.003z_{t-1}/(1 - 0.868L + 0.676L^2)]$$
$$+ [(1 + 0.293L^4)\epsilon_t/(1 - 0.485L - 0.246L^2)] \tag{5.16}$$

The problem with (5.16) is that the coefficients in the first expression were estimated separately from the coefficients in the second expression. In Step 5, we estimated all coefficients simultaneously and obtained

$$y_t = [-0.0022z_{t-1}/(1 - 0.876L + 0.749L^2)]$$
$$+ [(1 + 0.293L^4)\epsilon_t/(1 - 0.504L - 0.245L^2)] \tag{5.17}$$

Note that the coefficients of (5.17) are similar to those of (5.16). The t-statistics for the two numerator coefficients are −2.17 and 2.27, and the t-statistics for the four denominator coefficients are −7.78, 5.20, −4.31, and −1.94, respectively. The roots of the inverse characteristic equation for z_{t-1} are imaginary and outside the unit circle (the inverse characteristic roots are $0.585 \pm 0.996i$, so that the characteristic roots are $0.438 \pm 0.246i$). As in model 2, the effects of a terrorist incident decay in a sine-wave pattern. The roots of the inverse characteristic equation for ϵ_t are -3.29 and 1.238, so that the characteristic roots are -0.303 and 0.807. As an aside, note that you can obtain the original form of the model given in (5.3) by multiplying (5.17) by the two denominator coefficients.

The Ljung–Box Q-statistics indicate that the residuals of (5.17) appear to be white-noise. For example, $Q(8) = 6.54$ and $Q(16) = 12.67$ with significance levels of 0.587 and 0.696, respectively. Additional diagnostic checking included excluding the MA(4) term in the numerator (since the significance level was 5.5%) and estimating other plausible forms of the transfer functions. All other models had insignificant coefficients and/or larger values of the AIC and SBC and/or Q-statistics indicating significant correlation in the estimated residuals. Hence, we concluded that (5.17) best captures the effects of terrorism on tourism in Italy.

Our ultimate aim was to use the estimated transfer function to simulate the effects of a typical terrorist incident. Initializing the system such that all values of $y_0 = y_1 = y_2 = y_3 = 0$ and setting all $\{\epsilon_t\} = 0$, we let the value of $z_t = 1$. Figure 5.4 shows the **impulse response function** for this one-unit change in the $\{z_t\}$ sequence. As you can see from the figure, after a one-period delay, tourism in Italy declines sharply. After a sustained decline, tourism returns to its initial value in approximately 1 year. The system has a memory, and tourism again falls; notice the oscillating decay pattern.

Integrating over the actual values of the $\{z_t\}$ sequence allowed us to estimate Italy's total tourism losses. The undiscounted losses exceeded 600 million SDR; with a 5% real interest rate, the total value of the losses exceeded 861 million 1988 SDR (equal to 6% of Italy's annual revenues).

Figure 5.4   Italy's share of tourism (impulse response analysis).

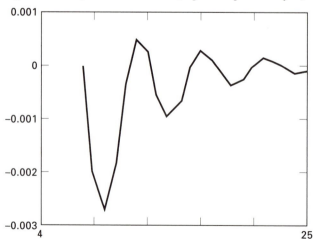

4. LIMITS TO STRUCTURAL MULTIVARIATE ESTIMATION

There are two important difficulties involved in fitting a multivariate equation such as a transfer function. The first concerns the goal of fitting a parsimonious model. Obviously, a parsimonious model is preferable to an overparameterized model. In the relatively small samples usually encountered in economic data, estimating an unrestricted model may so severely limit degrees of freedom as to render forecasts useless. Moreover, the possible inclusion of large but insignificant coefficients will add variability to the model's forecasts. However, in paring down the form of the model, two equally skilled researchers will likely arrive at two different transfer functions. Although one model may have a better "fit" (in terms of the AIC or SBC), the residuals of the other may have better diagnostic properties. There is substantial truth to the consensus opinion that fitting a transfer function model has many characteristics of an "art form." There is a potential cost to using a parsimonious model. Suppose you simply estimate the equation $y_t = A(L)y_{t-1} + C(L)z_t + B(L)\epsilon_t$ using long lags for $A(L)$, $B(L)$ and $C(L)$. As long as $\{z_t\}$ is exogenous, the estimated coefficients and forecasts are unbiased even though the model is overparameterized. Such is *not* the case if the researcher improperly imposes zero restrictions on any of the polynomials in the model.

The second problem concerns the assumption of no feedback from the $\{y_t\}$ sequence to the $\{z_t\}$ sequence. For the coefficients of $C(L)$ to be unbiased estimates of the impact effects of $\{z_t\}$ on the $\{y_t\}$ sequence, z_t must be uncorrelated with $\{\epsilon_t\}$ at all leads and lags. Although certain economic models may assert that policy variables (such as the money supply or government spending) are exogenous, there may be feedback such that the policy variables are set with specific reference to the state of other variables in the system. To understand the problem of feedback, suppose that you were trying to keep a constant 70° temperature inside your apartment by turning up or down the thermostat. Of course, the "true" model is that turning up the heat (the intervention variable z_t) warms up your apartment (the $\{y_t\}$ sequence). However, intervention analysis cannot adequately capture the true relationship in the presence of feedback. Clearly, if you perfectly controlled the inside temperature, there would be no correlation between the *constant* value of the inside temperature and the movement of the thermostat. Alternatively, you might listen to the weather forecast and turn up the thermostat whenever you expected it to be cold. If you underreact by not turning up the heat high enough, the cross-correlogram between the two variables would tend to show a negative spike reflecting the drop in room temperature with the upward movement in the thermostat setting. Instead, if you overreact by greatly increasing the thermostat setting, both the room temperature and the thermostat setting will rise together. However, the movement in room temperature will not be as great as the movement in the thermostat. Only if you moved the thermostat setting without reference to room temperature, would we expect to uncover the actual model.

The need to restrict the form of the transfer function and the problem of feedback or "reverse causality" led Sims (1980) to propose a nonstructural estimation strategy. To best understand the vector autoregression approach, it is useful to consider the state of macroeconometric modeling that led Sims to his then radical ideas.

Multivariate Macroeconometric Models: Some Historical Background

Traditionally, macroeconometric hypothesis tests and forecasts were conducted using large-scale macroeconometric models. Usually, a complete set of structural equations was estimated one equation at a time. Then, all equations were aggregated in order to form overall macroeconomic forecasts. Consider two of the equations from the Brookings quarterly econometric model of the United States as reported by Suits and Sparks (1965, p. 208):

$$C_{NF} = 0.0656Y_D - 10.93(P_{CNF}/P_C)_{t-1} + 0.1889(N + N_{ML})_{t-1}$$
$$\quad (0.0165) \qquad (2.49) \qquad\qquad (0.0522)$$
$$C_{NEF} = 4.2712 + 0.1691Y_D - 0.0743(ALQD_{HH}/P_C)_{t-1}$$
$$\quad (0.0127) \quad (0.0213)$$

where C_{NF} = personal consumption expenditures on food

$\quad\quad Y_D$ = disposable personal income

$\quad\quad P_{CNF}$ = implicit price deflator for personal consumption expenditures on food

$\quad\quad P_C$ = implicit price deflator for personal consumption expenditures

$\quad\quad N$ = civilian population

$\quad\quad N_{ML}$ = military population including armed forces overseas

$\quad\quad C_{NEF}$ = personal consumption expenditures for nondurables other than food

$\quad ALQD_{HH}$ = end-of-quarter stock of liquid assets held by households

and standard errors are in parentheses.

The remaining portions of the model contain estimates for the other components of aggregate consumption, investment spending, government spending, exports, imports, for the financial sector, various price determination equations, etc. Note that food expenditures, but not expenditures on other nondurables, are assumed to depend on relative price and population. However, expenditures for other nondurables are assumed to depend on real liquid assets held by households in the previous quarter.

Are such ad hoc behavioral assumptions consistent with economic theory? Sims (1980, p. 3), considers such multiequation models and argues that

> ... What "economic theory" tells us about them is mainly that any variable that appears on the right-hand side of one of these equations belongs in principle on the right-hand side of all of them. To the extent that models end up with very different sets of variables on the right-hand side of these equations, they do so not by invoking economic the-

ory, but (in the case of demand equations) by invoking an intuitive econometrician's version of psychological and sociological theory, since constraining utility functions are what is involved here. Furthermore, unless these sets of equations are considered as a system in the process of specification, the behavioral implications of the restrictions on all equations taken together may be less reasonable than the restrictions on any one equation taken by itself.

On the other hand, many of the monetarists used **reduced-form** equations to ascertain the effects of government policy on the macroeconomy. As an example, consider the following form of the so-called "St. Louis model" estimated by Anderson and Jordan (1968). Using U.S. quarterly data from 1952 to 1968, they estimated the following reduced-form GNP determination equation:

$$\Delta Y_t = 2.28 + 1.54\Delta M_t + 1.56\Delta M_{t-1} + 1.44\Delta M_{t-2} + 1.29\Delta M_{t-3}$$
$$+ 0.40\Delta E_t + 0.54\Delta E_{t-1} - 0.03\Delta E_{t-2} - 0.74\Delta E_{t-3} \qquad (5.18)$$

where ΔY = change in nominal GNP
ΔM = change in the monetary base
ΔE = change in "high employment" budget deficit

In their analysis, Anderson and Jordan used base money and the high employment budget deficit since these are the variables under the control of the monetary and fiscal authorities, respectively. The St. Louis model was an attempt to demonstrate the monetarist policy recommendations that changes in the money supply, but not changes in government spending or taxation, affected GNP. *t*-tests for the individual coefficients are misleading because of the substantial multicolinearity between each variable and its lags. However, testing whether the sum of the monetary base coefficients (i.e., $1.54 + 1.56 + 1.44 + 1.29 = 5.83$) differs from zero yields a *t*-value of 7.25. Hence, Anderson and Jordan concluded that changes in the money base translate into changes in nominal GNP. Since all the coefficients are positive, the effects of monetary policy are cumulative. On the other hand, the test that the sum of the fiscal coefficients ($0.40 + 0.54 - 0.03 - 0.74 = 0.17$) equals zero yields a *t*-value of 0.54. According to Anderson and Jordan, the results support "lagged crowding out" in the sense that an increase in the budget deficit initially stimulates the economy. Over time, however, changes in interest rates and other macroeconomic variables lead to reductions in private sector expenditures. The cumulated effects of the fiscal stimulus are not statistically different from zero.

Sims (1980) also points out several problems with this type of analysis. Sims' criticisms are easily understood by recognizing that (5.18) is a transfer function with two independent variables $\{M_t\}$ and $\{E_t\}$ and no lags of the dependent variable. As with any type of transfer function analysis, we must be concerned with:

1. Ensuring that lag lengths are appropriate. Serially correlated residuals in the presence of lagged dependent variables lead to biased coefficient estimates.

2. Ensuring that there is no feedback between GNP and the money base or the budget deficit. However, the assumption of no feedback is unreasonable since if the monetary authorities (or the fiscal authorities) deliberately attempt to alter nominal GNP, there is feedback. As in the thermostat example, if the monetary authority attempts to control the economy by changing the money base, we could not identify the "true" model. In the jargon of time-series econometrics, changes in GNP would "cause" changes in the money supply. One appropriate strategy would be to simultaneously estimate the GNP determination equation *and* money supply feedback rule.

Comparing the two types of models, Sims (1980, pp. 14–15) states:

> Because existing large models contain too many incredible restrictions, empirical research aimed at testing competing macroeconomic theories too often proceeds in a single- or few-equation framework. For this reason alone, it appears worthwhile to investigate the possibility of building large models in a style which does not tend to accumulate restrictions so haphazardly. . . . It should be feasible to estimate large-scale macromodels as unrestricted reduced forms, treating all variables as endogenous.

5. INTRODUCTION TO VAR ANALYSIS

When we are not confident that a variable is actually exogenous, a natural extension of transfer function analysis is to treat each variable symmetrically. In the two-variable case, we can let the time path of $\{y_t\}$ be affected by current and past realizations of the $\{z_t\}$ sequence and let the time path of the $\{z_t\}$ sequence be affected by current and past realizations of the $\{y_t\}$ sequence. Consider, the simple bivariate system:

$$y_t = b_{10} - b_{12}z_t + \gamma_{11}y_{t-1} + \gamma_{12}z_{t-1} + \epsilon_{yt} \qquad (5.19)$$
$$z_t = b_{20} - b_{21}y_t + \gamma_{21}y_{t-1} + \gamma_{22}z_{t-1} + \epsilon_{zt} \qquad (5.20)$$

where it is assumed (1) that both y_t and z_t are stationary; (2) ϵ_{yt} and ϵ_{zt} are white-noise disturbances with standard deviations of σ_y and σ_z, respectively; and (3) $\{\epsilon_{yt}\}$ and $\{\epsilon_{zt}\}$ are uncorrelated white-noise disturbances.

Equations (5.19) and (5.20) constitute a *first-order* vector autoregression (VAR) since the longest lag length is unity. This simple two-variable first-order VAR is useful for illustrating the multivariate higher-order systems that are introduced in Section 8. The structure of the system incorporates feedback since y_t and z_t are allowed to affect each other. For example, $-b_{12}$ is the contemporaneous effect of a unit change of z_t on y_t and γ_{21} the effect of a unit change in y_{t-1} on z_t. Note that the terms ϵ_{yt} and ϵ_{zt} are pure innovations (or shocks) in y_t and z_t, respectively. Of course, if b_{21} is not equal to zero, ϵ_{yt} has an indirect contemporaneous effect on z_t, and if b_{12} is not equal to zero, ϵ_{zt} has an indirect contemporaneous effect on y_t. Such a system could be used to capture the feedback effects in our temperature-thermostat example. The first equation allows current and past values of the thermostat setting to affect the time path of the temperature; the second allows for feedback between current and past values of the temperature and the thermostat setting.[7]

Equations (5.19) and (5.20) are not reduced-form equations since y_t has a contemporaneous effect on z_t and z_t has a contemporaneous effect on y_t. Fortunately, it is possible to transform the system of equations into a more usable form. Using matrix algebra, we can write the system in the compact form:

$$\begin{bmatrix} 1 & b_{12} \\ b_{21} & 1 \end{bmatrix} \begin{bmatrix} y_t \\ z_t \end{bmatrix} = \begin{bmatrix} b_{10} \\ b_{20} \end{bmatrix} + \begin{bmatrix} \gamma_{11} & \gamma_{12} \\ \gamma_{21} & \gamma_{22} \end{bmatrix} \begin{bmatrix} y_{t-1} \\ z_{t-1} \end{bmatrix} + \begin{bmatrix} \epsilon_{yt} \\ \epsilon_{zt} \end{bmatrix}$$

or

$$Bx_t = \Gamma_0 + \Gamma_1 x_{t-1} + \epsilon_t$$

where

$$B = \begin{bmatrix} 1 & b_{12} \\ b_{21} & 1 \end{bmatrix}, \quad x_t = \begin{bmatrix} y_t \\ z_t \end{bmatrix}, \quad \Gamma_0 = \begin{bmatrix} b_{10} \\ b_{20} \end{bmatrix}$$

$$\Gamma_1 = \begin{bmatrix} \gamma_{11} & \gamma_{12} \\ \gamma_{21} & \gamma_{22} \end{bmatrix}, \quad \epsilon_t = \begin{bmatrix} \epsilon_{yt} \\ \epsilon_{zt} \end{bmatrix}$$

Premultiplication by B^{-1} allows us to obtain the vector autoregressive (VAR) model in *standard* form:

$$x_t = A_0 + A_1 x_{t-1} + e_t \tag{5.21}$$

where $A_0 = B^{-1}\Gamma_0$
$A_1 = B^{-1}\Gamma_1$
$e_t = B^{-1}\epsilon_t$

For notational purposes, we can define a_{i0} as element i of the vector A_0, a_{ij} as the element in row i and column j of the matrix A_1, and e_{it} as the element i of the vector e_t. Using this new notation, we can rewrite (5.21) in the equivalent form:

$$y_t = a_{10} + a_{11}y_{t-1} + a_{12}z_{t-1} + e_{1t} \tag{5.22a}$$
$$z_t = a_{20} + a_{21}y_{t-1} + a_{22}z_{t-1} + e_{2t} \tag{5.22b}$$

To distinguish between the systems represented by (5.19) and (5.20) versus (5.22a) and (5.22b), the first is called a structural VAR or the primitive system and the second is called a VAR in standard form. It is important to note that the error terms (i.e., e_{1t} and e_{2t}) are composites of the two shocks ϵ_{yt} and ϵ_{zt}. Since $e_t = B^{-1}\epsilon_t$, we can compute e_{1t} and e_{2t} as

$$e_{1t} = (\epsilon_{yt} - b_{12}\epsilon_{zt})/(1 - b_{12}b_{21}) \tag{5.23}$$

$$e_{2t} = (\epsilon_{zt} - b_{21}\epsilon_{yt})/(1 - b_{12}b_{21}) \tag{5.24}$$

Since ϵ_{yt} and ϵ_{zt} are white-noise processes, it follows that both e_{1t} and e_{2t} have zero means, constant variances, and are individually serially uncorrelated. To derive the properties of $\{e_{1t}\}$, first take the expected value of (5.23):

$$Ee_{1t} = E(\epsilon_{yt} - b_{12}\epsilon_{zt})/(1 - b_{12}b_{21}) = 0.$$

The variance of e_{1t} is given by

$$
\begin{aligned}
Ee_{1t}^2 &= E[(\epsilon_{yt} - b_{12}\epsilon_{zt})/(1 - b_{12}b_{21})]^2 \\
&= (\sigma_y^2 + b_{12}^2\sigma_z^2)/(1 - b_{12}b_{21})^2
\end{aligned}
$$

Thus, the variance of e_{1t} is time-independent. The autocovariances of e_{1t} and e_{1t-i} are

$$Ee_{1t}e_{1t-i} = E[(\epsilon_{yt} - b_{12}\epsilon_{zt})(\epsilon_{yt-i} - b_{12}\epsilon_{zt-i})]/(1 - b_{12}b_{21})^2 = 0 \qquad \text{for } i \neq 0$$

Similarly, (5.24) can be used to demonstrate that e_{2t} is a stationary process with a zero mean, constant variance, and having all autocovariances equal to zero. A critical point to note is that e_{1t} and e_{2t} are correlated. The covariance of the two terms is

$$
\begin{aligned}
Ee_{1t}e_{2t} &= E[(\epsilon_{yt} - b_{12}\epsilon_{zt})(\epsilon_{zt} - b_{21}\epsilon_{yt})]/(1 - b_{12}b_{21})^2 \\
&= -(b_{21}\sigma_y^2 + b_{12}\sigma_z^2)/(1 - b_{12}b_{21})^2
\end{aligned}
\tag{5.25}
$$

In general, (5.25) will not be zero, so that the two shocks will be correlated. In the special case where $b_{12} = b_{21} = 0$ (i.e., if there are no contemporaneous effects of y_t on z_t and z_t on y_t), the shocks will be uncorrelated. It is useful to define the variance/covariance matrix of the e_{1t} and e_{2t} shocks as

$$\Sigma = \begin{bmatrix} \text{var}(e_{1t}) & \text{cov}(e_{1t}, e_{2t}) \\ \text{cov}(e_{1t}, e_{2t}) & \text{var}(e_{2t}) \end{bmatrix}$$

Since all elements of Σ are time-independent, we can use the more compact form:

$$\Sigma = \begin{bmatrix} \sigma_1^2 & \sigma_{12} \\ \sigma_{21} & \sigma_2^2 \end{bmatrix} \tag{5.26}$$

where $\text{var}(e_{it}) = \sigma_i^2$

$$\sigma_{12} = \sigma_{21} = \text{cov}(e_{1t}, e_{2t})$$

Stability and Stationarity

In the first-order autoregressive model $y_t = a_0 + a_1 y_{t-1} + \epsilon_t$, the stability condition is that a_1 be less than unity in absolute value. There is a direct analogue between this stability condition and the matrix A_1 in the first-order VAR model of (5.21). Using the brute force method to solve the system, iterate (5.21) backward to obtain

$$x_t = A_0 + A_1(A_0 + A_1 x_{t-2} + e_{t-1}) + e_t$$
$$= (I + A_1)A_0 + A_1^2 x_{t-2} + A_1 e_{t-1} + e_t$$

where $I = 2 \times 2$ identity matrix.

After n iterations,

$$x_t = (I + A_1 + \cdots + A_1^n)A_0 + \sum_{i=0}^{n} A_1^i e_{t-i} + A_1^{n+1} x_{t-n-1}$$

As we continue to iterate backward, it is clear that convergence requires the expression A_1^n vanish as n approaches infinity. As is shown below, stability requires that the roots of $(1 - a_{11}L)(1 - a_{22}L) - (a_{12}a_{21}L^2)$ lie outside the unit circle (the stability condition for higher-order systems is derived in the appendix to the next chapter). For the time being, assume the stability condition is met, so that we can write the particular solution for x_t as

$$x_t = \mu + \sum_{i=0}^{\infty} A_1^i e_{t-i} \tag{5.27}$$

where $\mu = [\bar{y} \quad \bar{z}]'$

and

$$\bar{y} = [a_{10}(1 - a_{22}) + a_{12}a_{20}]/\Delta, \qquad \bar{z} = [a_{20}(1 - a_{11}) + a_{21}a_{10}]/\Delta$$
$$\Delta = (1 - a_{11})(1 - a_{22}) - a_{12}a_{21}$$

If we take take the expected value of (5.27), the unconditional mean of x_t is μ; hence, the unconditional means of y_t and z_t are $\bar{y}$ and $\bar{z}$, respectively. The variances and covariances of y_t and z_t can be obtained as follows. First, form the variance/covariance matrix as

$$E(x_t - \mu)^2 = E\left[\sum_{i=0}^{\infty} A_1^i e_{t-i}\right]^2$$

Next, using (5.26), note that

$$Ee_t^2 = E\begin{bmatrix} e_{1t} \\ e_{2t} \end{bmatrix}\begin{bmatrix} e_{1t} & e_{2t} \end{bmatrix}$$
$$= \Sigma$$

Since $Ee_t e_{t-i} = 0$ for $i \neq 0$, it follows that

$$E(x_t - \mu)^2 = (I + A_1^2 + A_1^4 + A_1^6 + \cdots)\Sigma$$
$$= (I - A_1^2)^{-1}\Sigma$$

where   it is assumed that the stability condition holds, so that A_1^n approaches zero as n approaches infinity.

If we can abstract from an initial condition, the $\{y_t\}$ and $\{z_t\}$ sequences will be jointly covariance stationary if the stability condition holds. Each sequence has a finite and time-invariant mean, and a finite and time-invariant variance.

In order to get another perspective on the stability condition, use lag operators to rewrite the VAR model of (5.22a) and (5.22b) as

$$y_t = a_{10} + a_{11}Ly_t + a_{12}Lz_t + e_{1t}$$
$$z_t = a_{20} + a_{21}Ly_t + a_{22}Lz_t + e_{2t}$$

or

$$(1 - a_{11}L)y_t = a_{10} + a_{12}Lz_t + e_{1t}$$
$$(1 - a_{22}L)z_t = a_{20} + a_{21}Ly_t + e_{2t}$$

If we use this last equation to solve for z_t, it follows that Lz_t is

$$Lz_t = L(a_{20} + a_{21}Ly_t + e_{2t})/(1 - a_{22}L)$$

so that

$$(1 - a_{11}L)y_t = a_{10} + a_{12}L[(a_{20} + a_{21}Ly_t + e_{2t})/(1 - a_{22}L)] + e_{1t}$$

Notice that we have transformed the first-order VAR in the $\{y_t\}$ and $\{z_t\}$ sequences into a second-order stochastic difference equation in the $\{y_t\}$ sequence. Explicitly solving for y_t, we get

$$y_t = \frac{a_{10}(1 - a_{22}) + a_{12}a_{20} + (1 - a_{22}L)e_{1t} + a_{12}e_{2t-1}}{(1 - a_{11}L)(1 - a_{22}L) - a_{12}a_{21}L^2} \tag{5.28}$$

In the same fashion, you should be able to demonstrate that the solution for z_t is

$$y_t = \frac{a_{20}(1-a_{11})+a_{21}a_{10}+(1-a_{11}L)e_{2t}+a_{21}e_{1t-1}}{(1-a_{11}L)(1-a_{22}L)-a_{12}a_{21}L^2} \tag{5.29}$$

Both (5.28) and (5.29) have the same characteristic equation; convergence requires that the roots of the polynomial $(1 - a_{11}L)(1 - a_{22}L) - a_{12}a_{21}L^2$ lie outside the unit circle. (If you have forgotten the stability conditions for second-order difference equations, you might want to refresh your memory by reexamining Chapter 1.) As in any second-order difference equation, the roots may be real or complex and convergent or divergent. Notice that both y_t and z_t have the same characteristic equation; as long as both a_{12} and a_{21} do not equal zero, the solutions for the two sequences have the same characteristic roots. Hence, both will exhibit similar time paths.

Dynamics of a VAR Model

Figure 5.5 shows the time paths of four simple systems. For each system, 100 sets of normally distributed random numbers representing the $\{e_{1t}\}$ and $\{e_{2t}\}$ sequences were drawn. The initial values of y_0 and z_0 were set equal to zero, and the $\{y_t\}$ and $\{z_t\}$ sequences were constructed as in (5.22a) and (5.22b). The graph (a) uses the values:

$$a_{10} = a_{20} = 0, \qquad a_{11} = a_{22} = 0.7, \quad \text{and } a_{12} = a_{21} = 0.2$$

When we substitute these values into (5.27), it is clear that the mean of each series is zero. From the quadratic formula, the two roots of the inverse characteristic equation $(1 - a_{11}L)(1 - a_{22}L) - a_{12}a_{21}L^2$ are 1.111 and 2.0. Since both are outside the unit circle, the system is stationary; the two characteristic roots of the solution for $\{y_t\}$ and $\{z_t\}$ are 0.9 and 0.5. Since these roots are positive, real, and less than unity, convergence will be direct. As you can see in the figure, there is a tendency for the sequences to move together. Since a_{21} is positive, a large realization in y_t induces a large realization of z_{t+1}; since a_{12} is positive, a large realization of z_t induces a large realization of y_{t+1}. The cross-correlations between the two series are positive.

The second graph (b) illustrates a stationary process with $a_{10} = a_{20} = 0$, $a_{11} = a_{22}$ = 0.5, and $a_{12} = a_{21} = -0.2$. Again, the mean of each series is zero and the characteristic roots are 0.7 and 0.3. However, in contrast to the previous case, both a_{21} and a_{12} are negative, so that positive realizations of y_t can be associated with negative realizations of z_{t+1} and vice versa. As can be seen from comparing the second graph, the two series appear to be negatively correlated.

In contrast, graph (c) shows a process possessing a unit root; here, $a_{11} = a_{22} = a_{12}$ = $a_{21} = 0.5$. You should take a moment to find the characteristic roots. Undoubtedly, there is little tendency for either of the series to revert to a constant long-run value. Here, the intercept terms a_{10} and a_{20} are equal to zero, so that graph (c) rep-

Figure 5.5   Four VAR processes.

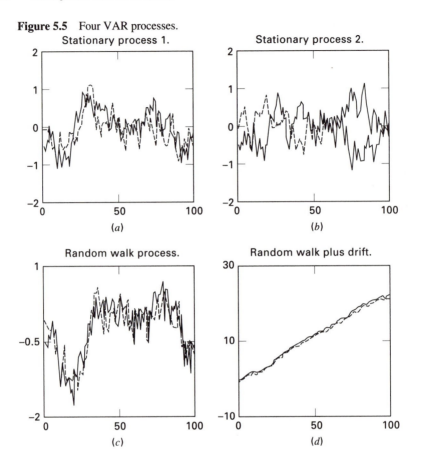

resents a multivariate generalization of the random walk model. You can see how
the series seem to meander together. In the fourth graph (d), the VAR process of
graph (c) also contains a nonzero intercept term ($a_{10} = 0.5$ and $a_{20} = 0$) that takes
the role of a "drift." As you can see from graph (d), the two series appear to move
closely together. The drift term adds a deterministic time trend to the nonstationary
behavior of the two series. Combined with the unit characteristic root, the $\{y_t\}$ and
$\{z_t\}$ sequences are joint random walk plus drift processes. Notice that the drift dominates the long-run behavior of the series.

6. ESTIMATION AND IDENTIFICATION

One explicit aim of the Box–Jenkins approach is to provide a methodology that
leads to parsimonious models. The ultimate objective of making accurate short-
term forecasts is best served by purging insignificant parameter estimates from the

model. Sims' (1980) criticisms of the "incredible identification restrictions" inherent in structural models argue for an alternative estimation strategy. Consider the following multivariate generalization of (5.21):

$$x_t = A_0 + A_1 x_{t-1} + A_2 x_{t-2} + \cdots + A_p x_{t-p} + e_t \qquad (5.30)$$

where x_t = an $(n \times 1)$ vector containing each of the n variables included in the VAR

         A_0 = an $(n \times 1)$ vector of intercept terms

         A_i = $(n \times n)$ matrices of coefficients

and e_t = an $(n \times 1)$ vector of error terms

Sims' methodology entails little more than a determination of the appropriate variables to include in the VAR and a determination of the appropriate lag length. The variables to be included in the VAR are selected according to the relevant economic model. Lag-length tests (to be discussed below) select the appropriate lag length. Otherwise, no explicit attempt is made to "pare down" the number of parameter estimates. The matrix A_0 contains n intercept terms and each matrix A_i contains n^2 coefficients; hence, $n + pn^2$ terms need to be estimated. Unquestionably, a VAR will be *overparameterized* in that many of these coefficient estimates can be properly excluded from the model. However, the goal is to find the important interrelationships among the variables and not make short-term forecasts. Improperly imposing zero restrictions may waste important information. Moreover, the regressors are likely to be highly colinear, so that the *t*-tests on individual coefficients may not be reliable guides for paring down the model.

Note that the right-hand side of (5.30) contains only predetermined variables and the error terms are assumed to be serially uncorrelated with constant variance.[3] Hence, *each equation in the system can be estimated using OLS.* Moreover, OLS estimates are consistent and asymptotically efficient. Even though the errors are correlated across equations, seemingly unrelated regressions (SUR) do not add to the efficiency of the estimation procedure since both regressions have identical right-hand-side variables.

The issue of whether the variables in a VAR need to be stationary exists. Sims (1980) and others, such as Doan (1992), recommend against differencing *even if the variables contain a unit root.* They argue that the goal of VAR analysis is to determine the interrelationships among the variables, *not* the parameter estimates. The main argument against differencing is that it "throws away" information concerning the comovements in the data (such as the possibility of cointegrating relationships). Similarly, it is argued that the data need not be detrended. In a VAR, a trending variable will be well approximated by a unit root plus drift. However, the majority view is that the form of the variables in the VAR should mimic the true data-generating process. This is particularly true if the aim is to estimate a structural model. We return to these issues in the next chapter; for now, it is assumed that all variables are stationary. Two sets of questions at the end of this chapter ask you to compare a VAR in levels to a VAR in first differences.

Identification

To illustrate the identification procedure, return to the structural two-variable/first-order VAR represented by (5.19) and (5.20). Due to the feedback inherent in the system, these equations cannot be estimated directly. The reason is that z_t is correlated with the error term ϵ_{yt} *and* y_t with the error term ϵ_{zt}. Standard estimation techniques require that the regressors be uncorrelated with the error term. Note there is no such problem in estimating the VAR system in standard form [i.e., in the form of (5.22a) and (5.22b)]. OLS can provide estimates of the two elements of A_0 and four elements of A_1. Moreover, by obtaining the residuals from the two regressions, it is possible to calculate estimates of the variance of e_{1t}, e_{2t}, and of the covariance between e_{1t} and e_{2t}. The issue is whether it is possible to recover all the information present in the primitive system from the estimated system (5.19) and (5.20). In other words, is the primative form identifiable given the OLS estimates of the VAR model in the form of (5.22a) and (5.22b)?

The answer to this question is "No, unless we are willing to appropriately restrict the primitive system." The reason is clear if we compare the number of parameters in the structural VAR with the number of parameters recovered from the standard form VAR model. Estimating (5.22a) and (5.22b) yields six coefficient estimates $(a_{10}, a_{20}, a_{11}, a_{12}, a_{21},$ and $a_{22})$ and the calculated values of var(e_{1t}), var(e_{2t}), and cov(e_{1t}, e_{2t}). However, the primitive system (5.19) and (5.20) contains 10 parameters. In addition to the two intercept coefficients b_{10} and b_{20}, the four autoregressive coefficients $\gamma_{11}, \gamma_{12}, \gamma_{21},$ and γ_{22}, and the two feedback coefficients b_{12} and b_{21}, there are the two standard deviations σ_y and σ_z. In all, the primitive system contains 10 parameters, whereas the VAR estimation yields only nine parameters. Unless one is willing to restrict one of the parameters, it is not possible to identify the primitive system; Equations (5.19) and (5.20) are underidentified. If exactly one parameter of the primitive system is restricted, the system is exactly identified, and if more than one parameter is restricted, the system is overidentified.

One way to identify the model is to use the type of **recursive** system proposed by Sims (1980). Suppose that you are willing to impose a restriction on the primitive system such that the coefficient b_{21} equals zero. Writing (5.19) and (5.20) with the constraint imposed yields

$$y_t = b_{10} - b_{12}z_t + \gamma_{11}y_{t-1} + \gamma_{12}z_{t-1} + \epsilon_{yt} \tag{5.31}$$
$$z_t = b_{20} + \gamma_{21}y_{t-1} + \gamma_{22}z_{t-1} + \epsilon_{zt} \tag{5.32}$$

Given the restriction (which might be suggested by a particular economic model), it is clear that z_t has a contemporaneous effect on y_t, but y_t affects the $\{z_t\}$ sequence with a one-period lag. Imposing the restriction $b_{21} = 0$ means that B^{-1} is given by:

$$B^{-1} = \begin{bmatrix} 1 & -b_{12} \\ 0 & 1 \end{bmatrix}$$

Now, premultiplication of the primitive system by B^{-1} yields:

$$\begin{bmatrix} y_t \\ z_t \end{bmatrix} = \begin{bmatrix} 1 & -b_{12} \\ 0 & 1 \end{bmatrix}\begin{bmatrix} b_{10} \\ b_{20} \end{bmatrix} + \begin{bmatrix} 1 & -b_{12} \\ 0 & 1 \end{bmatrix}\begin{bmatrix} \gamma_{11} & \gamma_{12} \\ \gamma_{21} & \gamma_{22} \end{bmatrix}\begin{bmatrix} y_{t-1} \\ z_{t-1} \end{bmatrix} + \begin{bmatrix} 1 & -b_{12} \\ 0 & 1 \end{bmatrix}\begin{bmatrix} \epsilon_{yt} \\ \epsilon_{zt} \end{bmatrix}$$

or

$$\begin{bmatrix} y_t \\ z_t \end{bmatrix} = \begin{bmatrix} b_{10} - b_{12}b_{20} \\ b_{20} \end{bmatrix} + \begin{bmatrix} \gamma_{11} - b_{12}\gamma_{21} & \gamma_{12} - b_{12}\gamma_{22} \\ \gamma_{21} & \gamma_{22} \end{bmatrix}\begin{bmatrix} y_{t-1} \\ z_{t-1} \end{bmatrix} + \begin{bmatrix} \epsilon_{yt} - b_{12}\epsilon_{zt} \\ \epsilon_{zt} \end{bmatrix} \qquad (5.33)$$

Estimating the system using OLS yields the theoretical parameter estimates:

$$y_t = a_{10} + a_{11}y_{t-1} + a_{12}z_{t-1} + e_{1t}$$
$$z_t = a_{20} + a_{21}y_{t-1} + a_{22}z_{t-1} + e_{2t}$$

where $a_{10} = b_{10} - b_{12}b_{20}$
$\quad\quad a_{11} = \gamma_{11} - b_{12}\gamma_{21}$
$\quad\quad a_{12} = \gamma_{12} - b_{12}\gamma_{22}$
$\quad\quad a_{20} = b_{20}$
$\quad\quad a_{21} = \gamma_{21}$
$\quad\quad a_{22} = \gamma_{22}$

Since $e_{1t} = \epsilon_{yt} - b_{12}\epsilon_{zt}$ and $e_{2t} = \epsilon_{zt}$, we can calculate the parameters of the variance/covariance matrix as

$$\text{Var}(e_1) = \sigma_y^2 + b_{12}^2\sigma_z^2 \qquad (5.34a)$$
$$\text{Var}(e_2) = \sigma_z^2 \qquad (5.34b)$$
$$\text{Cov}(e_1, e_2) = -b_{12}\sigma_z^2 \qquad (5.34c)$$

Thus, we have nine parameter estimates a_{10}, a_{11}, a_{12}, a_{20}, a_{21}, a_{22}, var(e_1), var(e_2), and cov(e_1, e_2) that can be substituted into the nine equations above in order to simultaneously solve for b_{10}, b_{12}, γ_{11}, γ_{12}, b_{20}, γ_{21}, γ_{22}, σ_y^2, and σ_z^2.

Note also that the estimates of the $\{\epsilon_{yt}\}$ and $\{\epsilon_{zt}\}$ sequences can be recovered. The residuals from the second equation (i.e., the $\{e_{2t}\}$ sequence) are estimates of the $\{\epsilon_{zt}\}$ sequence. Combining these estimates along with the solution for b_{12} allows us to calculate the estimates of the $\{\epsilon_{yt}\}$ sequence using the relationship $e_{1t} = \epsilon_{yt} - b_{12}\epsilon_{zt}$.

Take a minute to examine the restriction. In (5.32), the assumption $b_{21} = 0$ means that y_t does not have a contemporaneous effect on z_t. In (5.33), the restriction manifests itself such that both ϵ_{yt} and ϵ_{zt} shocks affect the contemporaneous value of y_t, but only ϵ_{zt} shocks affect the contemporaneous value of z_t. The observed values of e_{2t} are completely attributed to pure shocks to the $\{z_t\}$ sequence. Decomposing the residuals in this triangular fashion is called a **Choleski decomposition.**

Examples of Overidentified Systems

The interesting feature of overidentifying restrictions is that they can be tested. Suppose you wanted to further restrict (5.33) such that $\gamma_{12} = 0$. Such a restriction can have important economic implications; if $b_{21} = 0$ *and* $\gamma_{21} = 0$, contemporaneous ϵ_{yt} shocks *and* lagged values of y_{t-1} have no effect on z_t. Hence, the null hypothesis $b_{21} = \gamma_{12} = 0$ is equivalent to the hypothesis that $\{y_t\}$ is exogenous in that the $\{z_t\}$ sequence evolves independently of $\{y_t\}$. Given the form of (5.33), the test that $\gamma_{21} = 0$ is the test that a_{21} in the VAR model is zero. To perform this test, simply estimate (5.33) and use a t-test to test whether $a_{21} = 0$.

Not all testable restrictions are this straightforward. Consider another version of (5.19) and (5.20) such that $\gamma_{12} = \gamma_{21} = 0$:

$$y_t = b_{10} + \gamma_{11}y_{t-1} + b_{12}z_t + \epsilon_{yt}$$
$$z_t = b_{20} + b_{21}y_t + \gamma_{22}z_{t-1} + \epsilon_{zt}$$

To write the system in standard VAR form, we can use direct substitution:

$$y_t = b_{10} + \gamma_{11}y_{t-1} + b_{12}(b_{20} + b_{21}y_t + \gamma_{22}z_{t-1} + \epsilon_{zt}) + \epsilon_{yt}$$
$$z_t = b_{20} + b_{21}(b_{10} + \gamma_{11}y_{t-1} + b_{12}z_t + \epsilon_{yt}) + \gamma_{22}z_{t-1} + \epsilon_{zt}$$

It follows that

$$y_t = a_{10} + a_{11}y_{t-1} + a_{12}z_{t-1} + e_{1t}$$
$$z_t = a_{20} + a_{21}y_{t-1} + a_{22}z_{t-1} + e_{2t}$$

where
$$a_{10} = (b_{10} + b_{12}b_{20})/(1 - b_{12}b_{21})$$
$$a_{11} = \gamma_{11}/(1 - b_{12}b_{21})$$
$$a_{12} = b_{12}\gamma_{22}/(1 - b_{12}b_{21})$$
$$a_{20} = (b_{20} + b_{21}b_{10})/(1 - b_{12}b_{21})$$
$$a_{21} = b_{21}\gamma_{11}/(1 - b_{12}b_{21})$$
$$a_{22} = \gamma_{22}/(1 - b_{12}b_{21})$$

Since $e_{1t} = (\epsilon_{yt} + b_{12}\epsilon_{zt})/(1 - b_{12}b_{21})$ and $e_{2t} = (b_{21}\epsilon_{yt} + \epsilon_{zt})/(1 - b_{12}b_{21})$, it follows that

$$\text{Var}(e_{1t}) = (\sigma_y^2 + b_{12}^2\sigma_z^2)/(1 - b_{12}b_{21})^2$$
$$\text{Var}(e_{2t}) = (\sigma_z^2 + b_{21}^2\sigma_y^2)/(1 - b_{12}b_{21})^2$$
$$\text{Cov}(e_{1t}, e_{2t}) = (b_{21}\sigma_y^2 + b_{12}\sigma_z^2)/(1 - b_{12}b_{21})^2$$

OLS provides estimates of the six values of the a_{ij} and var(e_{1t}), var(e_{2t}), and cov(e_{1t}, e_{2t}). These nine estimated values can be used with any eight of the nine equations above to solve for b_{10}, b_{20}, b_{12}, b_{21}, γ_{11}, γ_{22}, σ_y, and σ_z. Since there is an *extra* equation, the system is overidentified. Unfortunately, the overidentifying restriction here leads to nonlinear restrictions on the various a_{ij}. Nevertheless, many software packages can test such nonlinear restrictions using the methodology discussed in Section 8.

7. THE IMPULSE RESPONSE FUNCTION

Just as an autoregression has a moving average representation, a vector autoregression can be written as a vector moving average (VMA). In fact, Equation (5.27) is the VMA representation of (5.21) in that the variables (i.e., y_t and z_t) are expressed in terms of the current and past values of the two types of shocks (i.e., e_{1t} and e_{2t}). The VMA representation is an essential feature of Sims' (1980) methodology in that it allows you to trace out the time path of the various shocks on the variables contained in the VAR system. For illustrative purposes, continue to use the two-variable/first-order model analyzed in the previous two sections. Writing (5.22a) and (5.22b) in matrix form, we get

$$\begin{bmatrix} y_t \\ z_t \end{bmatrix} = \begin{bmatrix} a_{10} \\ a_{20} \end{bmatrix} + \begin{bmatrix} a_{11} & a_{12} \\ a_{21} & a_{22} \end{bmatrix} \begin{bmatrix} y_{t-1} \\ z_{t-1} \end{bmatrix} + \begin{bmatrix} e_{1t} \\ e_{2t} \end{bmatrix} \tag{5.35}$$

or, using (5.27), we obtain

$$\begin{bmatrix} y_t \\ z_t \end{bmatrix} = \begin{bmatrix} \bar{y} \\ \bar{z} \end{bmatrix} + \sum_{i=0}^{\infty} \begin{bmatrix} a_{11} & a_{12} \\ a_{21} & a_{22} \end{bmatrix}^i \begin{bmatrix} e_{1t-i} \\ e_{2t-i} \end{bmatrix} \tag{5.36}$$

Equation (5.36) expresses y_t and z_t in terms of the $\{e_{1t}\}$ and $\{e_{2t}\}$ sequences. However, it is insightful to rewrite (5.36) in terms of the $\{\epsilon_{yt}\}$ and $\{\epsilon_{zt}\}$ sequences. From (5.23) and (5.24), the vector of errors can be written as

$$\begin{bmatrix} e_{1t} \\ e_{2t} \end{bmatrix} = [1/(1 - b_{12}b_{21})] \begin{bmatrix} 1 & -b_{12} \\ -b_{21} & 1 \end{bmatrix} \begin{bmatrix} \epsilon_{yt} \\ \epsilon_{zt} \end{bmatrix} \tag{5.37}$$

so that (5.36) and (5.37) can be combined to form

$$\begin{bmatrix} y_t \\ z_t \end{bmatrix} = \begin{bmatrix} \bar{y}_t \\ \bar{z}_t \end{bmatrix} + [1/(1 - b_{12}b_{21})] \sum_{i=0}^{\infty} \begin{bmatrix} a_{11} & a_{12} \\ a_{21} & a_{22} \end{bmatrix}^i \begin{bmatrix} 1 & -b_{12} \\ -b_{21} & 1 \end{bmatrix} \begin{bmatrix} \epsilon_{yt} \\ \epsilon_{zt} \end{bmatrix}$$

Since the notation is getting unwieldy, we can simplify by defining the 2×2 matrix ϕ_i with elements $\phi_{jk}(i)$:

$$\phi_i = \left[A_1^i / (1 - b_{12}b_{21}) \right] \begin{bmatrix} 1 & -b_{12} \\ -b_{21} & 1 \end{bmatrix}$$

Hence, the moving average representation of (5.36) and (5.37) can be written in terms of the $\{\epsilon_{yt}\}$ and $\{\epsilon_{zt}\}$ sequences:

$$\begin{bmatrix} y_t \\ z_t \end{bmatrix} = \begin{bmatrix} \bar{y} \\ \bar{z} \end{bmatrix} + \sum_{i=0}^{\infty} \begin{bmatrix} \phi_{11}(i) & \phi_{12}(i) \\ \phi_{21}(i) & \phi_{22}(i) \end{bmatrix} \begin{bmatrix} \epsilon_{yt-i} \\ \epsilon_{zt-i} \end{bmatrix}$$

or more compactly,

$$x_t = \mu + \sum_{i=0}^{\infty} \phi_i \epsilon_{t-i} \tag{5.38}$$

The moving average representation is an especially useful tool to examine the interaction between the $\{y_t\}$ and $\{z_t\}$ sequences. The coefficients of ϕ_i can be used to generate the effects of ϵ_{yt} and ϵ_{zt} shocks on the entire time paths of the $\{y_t\}$ and $\{z_t\}$ sequences. If you understand the notation, it should be clear that the four elements $\phi_{jk}(0)$ are **impact multipliers**. For example, the coefficient $\phi_{12}(0)$ is the instantaneous impact of a one-unit change in ϵ_{zt} on y_t. In the same way, the elements $\phi_{11}(1)$ and $\phi_{12}(1)$ are the one period responses of unit changes in ϵ_{yt-1} and ϵ_{zt-1} on y_t, respectively. Updating by one period indicates that $\phi_{11}(1)$ and $\phi_{12}(1)$ also represent the effects of unit changes in ϵ_{yt} and ϵ_{zt} on y_{t+1}.

The accumulated effects of unit impulses in ϵ_{yt} and/or ϵ_{zt} can be obtained by the appropriate summation of the coefficients of the impulse response functions. For example, note that after n periods, the effect of ϵ_{zt} on the value of y_{t+n} is $\phi_{12}(n)$. Thus, after n periods, the cumulated sum of the effects of ϵ_{zt} on the $\{y_t\}$ sequence is

$$\sum_{i=0}^{n} \phi_{12}(i)$$

Letting n approach infinity yields the **long-run multiplier**. Since the $\{y_t\}$ and $\{z_t\}$ sequences are assumed to be stationary, it must be the case that for all j and k,

$$\sum_{i=0}^{\infty} \phi_{jk}^2(i) \text{ is finite.}$$

The four sets of coefficients $\phi_{11}(i)$, $\phi_{12}(i)$, $\phi_{21}(i)$ and $\phi_{22}(i)$ are called the **impulse response functions**. Plotting the impulse response functions [i.e., plotting the coefficients of $\phi_{jk}(i)$ against i] is a practical way to visually represent the behavior of the $\{y_t\}$ and $\{z_t\}$ series in response to the various shocks. In principle, it might be possible to know all the parameters of the primitive system (5.19) and (5.20). With such knowledge, it would be possible to trace out the time paths of the effects of pure ϵ_{yt} or ϵ_{zt} shocks. However, this methodology is not available to the researcher since an estimated VAR is underidentified. As explained in the previous section, knowledge of the various a_{ij} and variance/covariance matrix Σ is not sufficient to identify the primitive system. Hence, the econometrician must impose an additional restriction on the two-variable VAR system in order to identify the impulse responses.

One possible identification restriction is to use Choleski decomposition. For example, it is possible to constrain the system such that the contemporaneous value of y_t does not have a contemporaneous effect on z_t. Formally, this restriction is represented by setting $b_{21} = 0$ in the primitive system. In terms of (5.37), the error terms can be decomposed as follows:

$$e_{1t} = \epsilon_{yt} - b_{12}\epsilon_{zt} \tag{5.39}$$
$$e_{2t} = \epsilon_{zt} \tag{5.40}$$

Thus, if we use (5.40), all the observed errors from the $\{e_{2t}\}$ sequence are attributed to ϵ_{zt} shocks. Given the calculated $\{\epsilon_{zt}\}$ sequence, knowledge of the values of the $\{e_{1t}\}$ sequence and the correlation coefficient between e_{1t} and e_{2t}, allows for the calculation of the $\{\epsilon_{yt}\}$ sequence using (5.39). Although this Choleski decomposition constrains the system such that an ϵ_{yt} shock has no direct effect z_t, there is an indirect effect in that lagged values of y_t affect the contemporaneous value of z_t. The key point is that the decomposition forces a potentially important asymmetry on the system since an ϵ_{zt} shock has contemporaneous effects on both y_t and z_t. For this reason (5.39) and (5.40) are said to imply an **ordering** of the variables. An ϵ_{zt} shock directly affects e_{1t} and e_{2t} but on ϵ_{yt} shock does not affect e_{2t}. Hence, z_t is "prior" to y_t.

Suppose that estimates of equations (5.22a) and (5.22b) yield the values $a_{10} = a_{20} = 0$, $a_{11} = a_{22} = 0.7$, and $a_{12} = a_{21} = 0.2$. You will recall that this is precisely the model used in the simulation reported in graph (a) of Figure 5.5. Also suppose that the elements of the Σ matrix are such that $\sigma_1^2 = \sigma_2^2$ and $\text{cov}(e_{1t}, e_{2t})$ is such that the correlation coefficient between e_{1t} and e_{2t} (denoted by ρ_{12}) is 0.8. Hence, the decomposed errors can be represented by[8]

$$e_{1t} = \epsilon_{yt} + 0.8\epsilon_{zt} \tag{5.41}$$
$$e_{2t} = \epsilon_{zt} \tag{5.42}$$

The top half of Figure 5.6, parts (a) and (b), traces out the effects of one-unit shocks to ϵ_{zt} and ϵ_{yt} on the time paths of the $\{y_t\}$ and $\{z_t\}$ sequences. As shown in the upper left-hand graph (a), a one unit-shock in ϵ_{zt} causes z_t to jump by one unit and y_t to jump by 0.8 units. [From (5.41), 80% of the ϵ_{zt} shock has a contemporaneous effect on e_{1t}.] In the next period, ϵ_{zt+1} returns to zero, but the autoregressive nature of the system is such that y_{t+1} and z_{t+1} do not immediately return to their long-run values. Since $z_{t+1} = 0.2y_t + 0.7z_t + \epsilon_{zt+1}$, it follows that $z_{t+1} = 0.86$ [$0.2(0.8) + 0.7(1) = 0.86$]. Similarly, $y_{t+1} = 0.7y_t + 0.2z_t = 0.76$. As you can see from the figure,

Figure 5.6   Two impulse reponse functions.

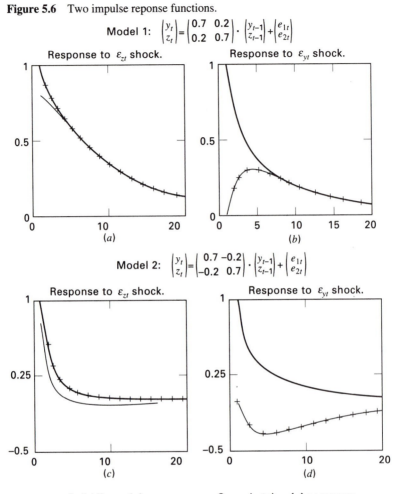

Model 1: $\begin{vmatrix} y_t \\ z_t \end{vmatrix} = \begin{vmatrix} 0.7 & 0.2 \\ 0.2 & 0.7 \end{vmatrix} \cdot \begin{vmatrix} y_{t-1} \\ z_{t-1} \end{vmatrix} + \begin{vmatrix} e_{1t} \\ e_{2t} \end{vmatrix}$

Response to ε_{zt} shock.   Response to ε_{yt} shock.

(a)   (b)

Model 2: $\begin{vmatrix} y_t \\ z_t \end{vmatrix} = \begin{vmatrix} 0.7 & -0.2 \\ -0.2 & 0.7 \end{vmatrix} \cdot \begin{vmatrix} y_{t-1} \\ z_{t-1} \end{vmatrix} + \begin{vmatrix} e_{1t} \\ e_{2t} \end{vmatrix}$

Response to ε_{zt} shock.   Response to ε_{yt} shock.

(c)   (d)

Solid line = $\{y_t\}$ sequence.   Cross-hatch = $\{z_t\}$ sequence.
note: In all cases $e_{1t} = 0.8v_t + \varepsilon_{yt}$ and $e_{2t} = \varepsilon_{zt}$.

the subsequent values of the $\{y_t\}$ and $\{z_t\}$ sequences converge to their long-run levels. This convergence is assured by the stability of the system; as found earlier, the two characteristic roots are 0.5 and 0.9.

The effects of a one-unit shock in ϵ_{yt} are shown in the upper-right-hand graph (b) of the figure. The asymmetry of the decomposition is immediately seen by comparing the two upper graphs. A one-unit shock in ϵ_{yt} causes the value of y_t to increase by one unit; however, *there is no contemporaneous effect on the value of* z_t, so that $y_t = 1$ and $z_t = 0$. In the subsequent period, ϵ_{yt+1} returns to zero. The autoregressive nature of the system is such that $y_{t+1} = 0.7y_t + 0.2z_t = 0.7$ and $z_{t+1} = 0.2y_t + 0.7z_t = 0.2$. The remaining points in the figure are the impulse responses for periods y_{t+2}

through y_{t+20}. Since the system is stationary, the impulse responses ultimately decay.

Can you figure out the consequences of reversing the Choleski decomposition in such a way that b_{12}, rather than b_{21}, is constrained to equal zero? Since matrix A_1 is symmetrical (i.e., $a_{11} = a_{22}$ and $a_{12} = a_{21}$), the impulse responses of an ϵ_{yt} shock would be similar to those in graph (a) and the impulse responses of an ϵ_{zt} would be similar to those in graph (b). The only difference would be that the solid line represents the time path of the $\{z_t\}$ sequence and the hatched line the time path of the $\{y_t\}$ sequence.

As a practical matter, how does the researcher decide which of the alternative decompositions is most appropriate? In some instances, there might be a theoretical reason to suppose that one variable has no contemporaneous effect on the other. In the terrorism/tourism example, knowledge that terrorist incidents affect tourism with a lag suggests that terrorism does not have a contemporaneous effect on tourism. Usually, there is no such a priori knowledge. Moreover, the very idea of imposing a structure on a VAR system seems contrary to the spirit of Sims' argument against "incredible identifying restrictions." Unfortunately, there is no simple way to circumvent the problem; identification necessitates imposing *some* structure on the system. The Choleski decomposition provides a minimal set of assumptions that can be used to identify the primitive model.[9]

It is crucial to note that *the importance of the ordering depends on the magnitude of the correlation coefficient between* e_{1t} *and* e_{2t}. Let this correlation coefficient be denoted by ρ_{12} so that $\rho_{12} = \sigma_{12}/\sigma_1\sigma_2$. Now suppose that the estimated model yields a value of Σ such that ρ_{12} is found to be equal to zero. In this circumstance, the ordering is immaterial. Formally, (5.41) and (5.42) become $e_{1t} = \epsilon_{yt}$ and $e_{2t} = \epsilon_{zt}$ when $\rho_{12} = 0$. Thus, if there is no correlation across equations, the residuals from the y_t and z_t equations are necessarily equivalent to the ϵ_{yt} and ϵ_{zt} shocks, respectively. At the other extreme, if ρ_{12} is found to be unity, there is a single shock in the system that contemporarily affects both variables. Under the assumption $b_{21} = 0$, (5.41) and (5.42) become $e_{1t} = \epsilon_{zt}$ and $e_{2t} = \epsilon_{zt}$; instead, under the assumption $b_{12} = 0$, (5.41) and (5.42) become $e_{1t} = \epsilon_{yt}$ and $e_{2t} = \epsilon_{yt}$. Usually, the researcher will want to test the significance of ρ_{12}; as a rule of thumb, if $|\rho_{12}| > 0.2$, the correlation is deemed to be significant. If $|\rho_{12}| > 0.2$, the usual procedure is to obtain the impulse response function using a particular ordering. Compare the results to the impulse response function obtained by reversing the ordering. If the implications are quite different, additional investigation into the relationships between the variables is necessary.

The lower half of Figure 5.6, parts (c) and (d), presents the impulse response functions for a second model; the sole difference between models 1 and 2 is the change in the values of a_{12} and a_{21} to -0.2. Model 2 was used in the simulation reported in graph (b) of Figure 5.5. The negative off-diagonal elements of A_1 weaken the tendency for the two series to move together. Using the impulse responses represented by (5.41) and (5.42) (d) shows that, $y_{t+1} = 0.7y_t - 0.2z_t = 0.7$ and $z_{t+1} = -0.2y_t + 0.7z_{t+1} = -0.2$. Tracing out the entire time path yields the lower-right-hand graph (d) of the figure. Since the system is stable, both sequences eventually converge to zero.

The lower-left-hand graph (c) traces out the effect of a one-unit ϵ_{zt} shock. In period t, z_t rises by one unit and y_t by 0.8 units. In period $(t + 1)$, ϵ_{zt+1} returns to zero, but the value of y_{t+1} is $0.7y_t - 0.2z_t = 0.36$ and the value of z_{t+1} is $-0.2y_t + 0.7z_t = 0.54$. The points represented by $t = 2$ through 20 show that the impulse responses converge to zero.

Variance Decomposition

Since unrestricted VARs are overparameterized, they are not particularly useful for short-term forecasts. However, understanding the properties of the forecast errors is exceedingly helpful in uncovering interrelationships among the variables in the system. Suppose that we knew the coefficients of A_0 and A_1 and wanted to forecast the various values of x_{t+i} conditional on the observed value of x_t. Updating (5.21) one period (i.e., $x_{t+1} = A_0 + A_1x_t + \epsilon_{t+1}$) and taking the conditional expectation of x_{t+1}, we obtain

$$E_t x_{t+1} = A_0 + A_1 x_t$$

Note that the one-step ahead forecast error is $x_{t+1} - E_t x_{t+1} = e_{t+1}$. Similarly, updating two periods, we get

$$\begin{aligned} x_{t+2} &= A_0 + A_1 x_{t+1} + e_{t+2} \\ &= A_0 + A_1(A_0 + A_1 x_t + e_{t+1}) + e_{t+2} \end{aligned}$$

If we take conditional expectations, the two-step ahead forecast of x_{t+2} is

$$E_t x_{t+2} = (I + A_1)A_0 + A_1^2 x_t$$

The two-step ahead forecast error (i.e., the difference between the realization of x_{t+2} and the forecast) is $e_{t+2} + A_1 e_{t+1}$. More generally, it is easily verified that the n-step ahead forecast is

$$E_t x_{t+n} = (I + A_1 + A_1^2 + \cdots + A_1^{n-1})A_0 + A_1^n x_t$$

and the associated forecast error is

$$e_{t+n} + A_1 e_{t+n-1} + A_1^2 e_{t+n-2} + \cdots + A_1^{n-1} e_{t+1} \tag{5.43}$$

We can also consider these forecast errors in terms of (5.38) (i.e., the VMA form of the model). Of course, the VMA and VAR models contain exactly the same information, but it is convenient (and a good exercise) to describe the properties of the forecast errors in terms of the $\{\epsilon_t\}$ sequence. If we use (5.38) to conditionally forecast x_{t+1}, the one-step ahead forecast error is $\phi_0\epsilon_{t+1}$. In general,

$$x_{t+n} = \mu + \sum_{i=0}^{\infty} \phi_i \epsilon_{t+n-i}$$

so that the n-period forecast error $x_{t+n} - E_t x_{t+n}$ is

$$x_{t+n} - E_t x_{t+n} = \sum_{i=0}^{n-1} \phi_i \epsilon_{t+n-i}$$

Focusing solely on the $\{y_t\}$ sequence, we see that the n-step ahead forecast error is

$$\begin{aligned}
y_{t+n} - E_t y_{t+n} &= \phi_{11}(0)\epsilon_{yt+n} + \phi_{11}(1)\epsilon_{yt+n-1} + \cdots + \phi_{11}(n-1)\epsilon_{yt+1} \\
&\quad + \phi_{12}(0)\epsilon_{zt+n} + \phi_{12}(1)\epsilon_{zt+n-1} + \cdots + \phi_{12}(n-1)\epsilon_{zt+1}
\end{aligned}$$

Denote the variance of the n-step ahead forecast error variance of y_{t+n} as $\sigma_y(n)^2$

$$\begin{aligned}
\sigma_y(n)^2 &= \sigma_y^2[\phi_{11}(0)^2 + \phi_{11}(1)^2 + \cdots + \phi_{11}(n-1)^2] \\
&\quad + \sigma_z^2[\phi_{12}(0)^2 + \phi_{12}(1)^2 + \cdots + \phi_{12}(n-1)^2]
\end{aligned}$$

Since all values of $\phi_{jk}(i)^2$ are necessarily nonnegative, the variance of the forecast error increases as the forecast horizon n increases. Note that it is possible to decompose the n-step ahead forecast error variance due to each one of the shocks. Respectively, the proportions of $\sigma_y(n)^2$ due to shocks in the $\{\epsilon_{yt}\}$ and $\{\epsilon_{zt}\}$ sequences are

$$\frac{\sigma_y^2[\sigma_{11}(0)^2 + \phi_{11}(1)^2 + \cdots + \phi_{11}(n-1)^2]}{\sigma_y(n)^2}$$

and

$$\frac{\sigma_z^2[\phi_{12}(0)^2 + \phi_{12}(1)^2 + \cdots + \phi_{12}(n-1)^2]}{\sigma_y(n)^2}$$

The **forecast error variance decomposition** tells us the proportion of the movements in a sequence due to its "own" shocks versus shocks to the other variable. *If ϵ_{zt} shocks explain none of the forecast error variance of $\{y_t\}$ at all forecast horizons, we can say that the $\{y_t\}$ sequence is exogenous.* In such a circumstance, the $\{y_t\}$ sequence would evolve independently of the ϵ_{zt} shocks and $\{z_t\}$ sequence. At the other extreme, ϵ_{zt} shocks could explain all the forecast error variance in the $\{y_t\}$ sequence at all forecast horizons, so that $\{y_t\}$ would be entirely endogenous. In applied research, it is typical for a variable to explain almost all its forecast error variance at short horizons and smaller proportions at longer horizons. We would expect this pattern if ϵ_{zt} shocks had little contemporaneous effect on y_t, but acted to affect the $\{y_t\}$ sequence with a lag.

Note that the variance decomposition contains the same problem inherent in impulse response function analysis. In order to identify the $\{\epsilon_{yt}\}$ and $\{\epsilon_{zt}\}$ sequences, it is necessary to restrict the B matrix. The Choleski decompostion used in (5.39) and (5.40) necessitates that all the one-period forecast error variance of z_t is due to ϵ_{zt}. If we use the alternative ordering, all the one-period forecast error variance of y_t would be due to ϵ_{yt}. The dramatic effects of these alternative assumptions are reduced at longer forecasting horizons. In practice, it is useful to examine the variance decomposition at various forecast horizons. As n increases, the variance decompositions should converge. Moreover, if the correlation coefficient ρ_{12} is significantly different from zero, it is customary to obtain the variance decompositions under various orderings.

Nevertheless, impulse response analysis and variance decompositions (together called **innovation accounting**) can be useful tools to examine the relationships among economic variables. If the correlations among the various innovations are small, the identification problem is not likely to be especially important. The alternative orderings should yield similar impulse responses and variance decompositions. Of course, the contemporaneous movements of many economic variables are highly correlated. Sections 10 through 13 consider two attractive methods that can be used to identify the structural innovations. Before examining these techniques, we consider hypothesis testing in a VAR framework and reexamine the interrelationships between terrorism and tourism.

8. HYPOTHESIS TESTING

In principle, there is nothing to prevent you from incorporating a large number of variables in the VAR. It is possible to construct an n-equation VAR with each equation containing p lags of all n variables in the system. You will want to include those variables that have important economic effects on each other. As a practical matter, degrees of freedom are quickly eroded as more variables are included. For example, with monthly data with 12 lags, the inclusion of one additional variable uses an additional 12 degrees of freedom. A careful examination of the relevant theoretical model will help you to select the set of variables to include in your VAR model.

An n-equation VAR can be represented by

$$
\begin{bmatrix} x_{1t} \\ x_{2t} \\ . \\ x_{nt} \end{bmatrix} = \begin{bmatrix} A_{10} \\ A_{20} \\ . \\ A_{n0} \end{bmatrix} + \begin{bmatrix} A_{11}(L) & A_{12}(L) & . & A_{1n}(L) \\ A_{21}(L) & A_{22}(L) & . & A_{2n}(L) \\ . & . & . & . \\ A_{n1}(L) & A_{n2}(L) & . & A_{nn}(L) \end{bmatrix} \begin{bmatrix} x_{1t-1} \\ x_{2t-1} \\ . \\ x_{nt-1} \end{bmatrix} + \begin{bmatrix} e_{1t} \\ e_{2t} \\ . \\ e_{nt} \end{bmatrix} \qquad (5.44)
$$

where A_{i0} = the parameters representing intercept terms
$A_{ij}(L)$ = the polynomials in the lag operator L.

The individual coefficients of $A_{ij}(L)$ are denoted by $a_{ij}(1)$, $a_{ij}(2)$, ... Since all equations have the same lag length, all the polynomials $A_{ij}(L)$ are of the same degree. The terms e_{it} are white-noise disturbances that may be correlated. Again, designate the variance/covariance matrix by Σ, where the dimension of Σ is $(n \times n)$.

In addition to the determination of the set of variables to include in the VAR, it is important to determine the appropriate lag length. One possible procedure is to allow for different lag lengths for each variable in each equation. However, in order to preserve the symmetry of the system (and to be able to use OLS efficiently), it is common to use the same lag length for all equations. As indicated in Section 6, as long as there are identical regressors in each equation, OLS estimates are consistent and asymptotically efficient. If some of the VAR equations have regressors not included in the others, seemingly unrelated regressions (SUR) provide efficient estimates of the VAR coefficients. Hence, when there is a good reason to let lag lengths differ across equations, estimate the so-called **near VAR** using SUR.

In a VAR, long lag lengths quickly consume degrees of freedom. If lag length is p, each of the n equations contains np coefficients plus the intercept term. Appropriate lag-length selection can be critical. If p is too small, the model is misspecified; if p is too large, degrees of freedom are wasted. To check lag length, begin with the longest plausible length or longest feasible length given degrees-of-freedom considerations. Estimate the VAR and form the variance/covariance matrix of the residuals. Using quarterly data, you might start with a lag length of 12 quarters based on the a priori notion that 3 years is sufficiently long to capture the system's dynamics. Call the variance/covariance matrix of the residuals from the 12-lag model Σ_{12}. Now suppose you want to determine whether eight lags are appropriate. After all, restricting the model from 12 to eight lags would reduce the number of estimated parameters by $4n$ in each equation.

Since the goal is to determine whether lag 8 is appropriate for all equations, an equation by equation F-test on lags 9 through 12 is not appropriate. Instead, the proper test for this **cross-equation** restriction is a likelihood ratio test. Reestimate the VAR *over the same sample period* using eight lags and obtain the variance/covariance matrix of the residuals Σ_8. Note that Σ_8 pertains to a system of n equations with $4n$ restrictions in each equation for a total of $4n^2$ restrictions. The likelihood ratio statistic is

$$(T)(\log|\Sigma_8| - \log|\Sigma_{12}|)$$

However, given the sample sizes usually found in economic analysis, Sims (1980) recommends using

$$(T - c)(\log|\Sigma_8| - \log|\Sigma_{12}|)$$

where T = number of usable observations

c = number of parameters estimated in each equation of the unrestricted system

$\log|\Sigma_n|$ = is the natural logarithm of the determinant of Σ_n.

In the example at hand, $c = 12n + 1$ since each equation of the unrestricted model has 12 lags for each variable term plus an intercept.

This statistic has the asymptotic χ^2 distribution with degrees of freedom equal to the number of restrictions *in the system*. In the example under consideration, there are $4n$ restrictions in each equation, for a total of $4n^2$ restrictions in the system. Clearly, if the restriction of a reduced number of lags is not binding, we would expect $\log|\Sigma_8|$ to be equal to $\log|\Sigma_{12}|$. Large values of this sample statistic indicate that only eight lags is a binding restriction; hence, a rejection of the null hypothesis that lag length = 8. If the calculated value of the statistic is less than χ^2 at a prespecified significance level, we would not be able to reject the null of only eight lags. At that point, we could seek to determine whether four lags were appropriate by constructing

$$(T - c)(\log|\Sigma_4| - \log|\Sigma_8|)$$

Considerable care should be taken in paring down lag length in this fashion. Often, this procedure will not reject the null hypotheses of eight versus 12 lags and four versus 8 lags, although it will reject a null of four versus 12 lags. The problem with paring down the model is that you may lose a small amount of explanatory power at each stage. Overall, the total loss in explanatory power can be significant. In such circumstances, it is best to use the longer lag lengths.

This type of likelihood ratio test is applicable to any type of cross-equation restriction. Let Σ_u and Σ_r be the variance/covariance matrices of the unrestriced and restricted systems, respectively. If the equations of the unrestricted model contain different regressors, let c denote the maximum number of regressors contained in the longest equation. Asymptotically, the test statistic:

$$(T - c)(\log|\Sigma_r| - \log|\Sigma_u|) \tag{5.45}$$

has a χ^2 distribution with degrees of freedom equal to the number of restrictions in the system.

To take another example, suppose you wanted to capture seasonal effects by including three seasonal dummies in each of the n equations of a VAR. Estimate the unrestricted model by including the dummy variables and estimate the restricted model by excluding the dummies. The total number of restrictions in the system is $3n$. If lag length is p, the equations of the unrestricted model have $np + 4$ parameters (np lagged variables, the intercept, and the three seasonals). For T usable observations, set $c = np + 4$ and calculate the value of (5.45). If for some prespecified significance level, this calculated value χ^2 (with $3n$ degrees of freedom) exceeds the critical value, the restriction of no seasonal effects can be rejected. Equation (5.45) can also be used to test the type of nonlinear restriction mentioned in Section 6. Estimate the restricted and unrestricted systems. Then compare the calculated value of (5.45) to the critical value found in a χ^2 table.

The likelihood ratio test is based on asymptotic theory that may not be very useful in the small samples available to time-series econometricians. Moreover, the likelihood ratio test is only applicable when one model is a restricted version of the other. Alternative test criteria to determine appropriate lag lengths and/or seasonality are the multivariate generalizations of the AIC and SBC:

$$\text{AIC} = T \log |\Sigma| + 2N$$
$$\text{SBC} = T \log |\Sigma| + N \log(T)$$

where $|\Sigma|$ = determinant of the variance/covariance matrix of the residuals
N = total number of parameters estimated *in all equations*.

Thus, if each equation in an n-variable VAR has p lags and an intercept, $N = n^2p + n$; each of the n equations has np lagged regressors and an intercept.

Adding additional regressors will reduce $\log |\Sigma|$ at the expense of increasing N. As in the univariate case, select the model having the lowest AIC or SBC value. Make sure that you adequately compare the models by using the same sample period. Note that these statistics are not based on any distributional theory; as such they are not used in *testing* the type of cross–equation restrictions discussed in Section 6.

Granger Causality

A test of causality is whether the lags of one variable enter into the equation for another variable. Recall that in (5.33), it was possible to test the hypotheses that $a_{21} = 0$ using a t-test. In a two-equation model with p lags, $\{y_t\}$ does not Granger cause $\{z_t\}$ if and only if all the coefficients of $A_{21}(L)$ are equal to zero. Thus, if $\{y_t\}$ does not improve the forecasting performance of $\{z_t\}$, then $\{y_t\}$ does not Granger cause $\{z_t\}$. The direct way to determine Granger causality is to use a standard F-test to test the restriction:

$$a_{21}(1) = a_{21}(2) = a_{21}(3) = \cdots = 0$$

In the n variable case in which $A_{ij}(L)$ represents the coefficients of lagged values of variable j on variable i, variable j does not Granger cause variable i if all coefficients of the polynomial $A_{ij}(L)$ can be set equal to zero.

Note that Granger causality is a weaker condition than the condition for exogeneity. A necessary condition for the exogeneity of $\{z_t\}$ is for current and past values of $\{y_t\}$ to not affect $\{z_t\}$. To explain, reconsider the VMA model. In our previous example of the two-variable VMA model, $\{y_t\}$ does *not* Granger cause $\{z_t)$ if and only if all coefficients of $\phi_{21}(i) = 0$ for $i > 0$. To sketch the proof, suppose that all coefficients of $\phi_{21}(i)$ are zero for $i > 0$. Hence, z_{t+1} is given by

$$z_{t+1} = \bar{z} + \phi_{21}(0)\epsilon_{yt+1} + \sum_{i=0}^{\infty} \phi_{22}(i)\epsilon_{zt+1-i}$$

If we forecast z_{t+1} conditional on the value of z_t, we obtain the forecast error $\phi_{21}(0)\epsilon_{yt+1} + \phi_{22}(0)\epsilon_{zt+1}$. Given the past value of z_t, information concerning past values of y_t does not aid in forecasting z_t. In other words, for the VAR(1) model under consideration, $E_t(z_{t+1} \mid z_t) = E_t(z_{t+1} \mid z_t, y_t)$.

The only additional information contained in y_t are the past values of $\{\epsilon_{yt}\}$. However, such values do not affect z_t and so cannot improve on the forecasting performance of the z_t sequence. Thus, $\{y_t\}$ does not Granger cause $\{z_t\}$. However, if $\phi_{21}(0)$ is not equal to zero, $\{z_t\}$ is not be exogenous to $\{y_t\}$. If $\phi_{21}(0)$ is not zero, pure shocks to y_{t+1} (i.e., ϵ_{yt+1}) affect the value of z_{t+1} even though the $\{y_t\}$ sequence does not Granger cause the $\{z_t\}$ sequence.

A **block exogeneity** test is useful for detecting whether to incorporate a variable into a VAR. Given the aforementioned distinction between causality and exogeneity, this multivariate generalization of the Granger causality test should actually be called a "block causality" test. In any event, the issue is to determine whether lags of one variable—say, w_t—Granger cause any other of the variables in the system. In the three-variable case with w_t, y_t, and z_t, the test is whether lags of w_t Granger cause either y_t or z_t. In essence, the block exogeneity restricts all lags of w_t in the y_t and z_t equations to be equal to zero. This cross-equation restriction is properly tested using the likelihood ratio test given by (5.45). Estimate the y_t and z_t equations using p lagged values of $\{y_t\}$, $\{z_t\}$, and $\{w_t\}$ and calculate Σ_u. Reestimate the two equations excluding the lagged values of $\{w_t\}$ and calculate Σ_r. Next, find the likelihood ratio statistic:

$$(T - c)(\log|\Sigma_r| - \log|\Sigma_u|)$$

As in (5.45), this statistic has a χ^2 distribution with degrees of freedom equal to $2p$ (since p lagged values of $\{w_t\}$ are excluded from each equation). Here, $c = 3p + 1$ since the two unrestricted y_t and z_t equations contain p lags of $\{y_t\}$, $\{z_t\}$, and $\{w_t\}$ plus a constant.

9. EXAMPLE OF A SIMPLE VAR: TERRORISM AND TOURISM IN SPAIN

In Enders and Sandler (1991), we used the VAR methodology to estimate the impact of terrorism on tourism in Spain during the period from 1970 to 1988. Most transnational terrorist incidents in Spain during this period were perpetrated by left-wing groups, which included the Anti-Fascist Resistance Group of October 1 (GRAPO), the ETA, the now defunct International Revolutionary Armed Front (FRAP), and Iraultza. Most incidents are attributed to the ETA (Basque Fatherland and Liberty) and its splinter groups, such as the Autonomous Anti-Capitalist Commandos (CAA). Right-wing terrorist groups included the Anti-Terrorist Liberation Group (GAL), Anti-Terrorism ETA, and Warriors of Christ the King. Catalan independence groups, such as Free Land (Terra Lliure) and Catalan Socialist Party for National Liberation, have been active in the late 1980s and often target U.S. businesses.

The transfer function model of Section 3 may not be appropriate because of feedback between terrorism and tourism. If high levels of tourism induce terrorist activities, the basic assumption of the transfer function methodology is violated. In fact, there is some evidence that the terrorist organizations in Spain target tourist hotels in the summer season. Since increases in tourism may generate terrorist acts, the VAR methodology allows us to examine the reactions of tourists to terrorism *and* those of terrorists to tourism. We can gain some additional insights into the interrelation between the two series by performing causality tests of terrorism on tourism and of tourism on terrorism. Impulse response analysis can quantify and graphically depict the time path of the effects of a typical terrorist incident on tourism.

We assembled a time series of all publicly available transnational terrorists incidents that took place in Spain from 1970 through 1988. In total, there are 228 months of observation in the time series; each observation is the number of terrorist incidents occurring that month. The tourism data are taken from various issues of the National Statistics Institute's (Estadistic Institute Nacional) quarterly reports. In particular, we assembled a time series of the number of foreign tourists per month in Spain for the 1970 to 1988 period.

Empirical Methodology

Our basic methodology involves estimating tourism and terrorism in a vector autoregression (VAR) framework. Consider the following system of equations:

$$n_t = \alpha_{10} + A_{11}(L)n_{t-1} + A_{12}(L)i_{t-1} + e_{1t} \tag{5.46}$$
$$i_t = \alpha_{20} + A_{21}(L)n_{t-1} + A_{22}(L)i_{t-1} + e_{2t} \tag{5.47}$$

where n_t = the number of tourists visiting Spain during time period t

i_t = the number of transnational terrorist incidents in Spain during t

α_{io} = are the 1×13 vectors containing a constant, 11 seasonal (monthly) dummy variables, and a time trend

A_{ij} = the polynomials in the lag operator L

e_{it} = independent and identically distributed disturbance terms such that $E(e_{1t}e_{2t})$ is not necessarily zero

Although Sims (1980) and Doan (1992) recommend against the use of a deterministic time trend, we decided not to heed their advice. We experimented with several alternative ways to model the series; the model including the time trend had yielded the best diagnostic statistics. Other variants included differencing (5.46) and (5.47) and simply eliminating the trend and letting the random walk plus drift terms capture any nonstationary behavior. Questions 5 and 6 at the end of this chapter ask you to compare these alternative ways of estimating a VAR.

The polynomials $A_{12}(L)$ and $A_{21}(L)$ in (5.46) and (5.47) are of particular interest. If all the coefficients of A_{21} are zero, then knowledge of the tourism series does not reduce the forecast error variance of terrorist incidents. Formally, tourism would not Granger cause terrorism. Unless there is a contemporaneous response of terrorism to tourism, the terrorism series evolves independently of tourism. In the same way, if all the coefficients of $A_{12}(L)$ are zero, then terrorism does not Granger cause tourism. The absence of a statistically significant contemporaneous correlation of the error terms would then imply that terrorism cannot affect tourism. If, instead, any of the coefficients in these polynomials differ from zero, there are interactions between the two series. In case of negative coefficients of $A_{12}(L)$, terrorism would have a negative effect on the number of foreign tourist visits to Spain.

Each equation was estimated using lag lengths of 24, 12, 6, and 3 months (i.e., for four estimations, we set $L = 24$, 12, 6, and 3). Because each equation has identical right-hand-side variables, ordinary least squares (OLS) is an efficient estimation technique. Using χ^2 tests, we determined that a lag length of 12 months was most appropriate (reducing the length from 24 to 12 months had a χ^2 value that was significant at the 0.56 level, whereas reducing the lag length to 6 months had a χ^2 value that was significant at the 0.049 level). The AIC indicated that 12 lags were appropriate, whereas the SBC suggested we could use only six lags. Since we were using monthly data, we decided to use the 12 lags.

To ascertain the importance of the interactions between the two series, we obtained the variance decompositions. The moving average representations of Equations (5.46) and (5.47) express n_t and i_t as dependent on the current and past values of both $\{e_{1t}\}$ and $\{e_{2t}\}$ sequences:

$$n_t = c_0 + \sum_{j=1}^{\infty}(c_{1j}e_{1t-j} + c_{2j}e_{2t-j}) + e_{1t} \tag{5.48}$$

$$i_t = d_0 + \sum_{j=1}^{\infty}(d_{1j}e_{1t-j} + d_{2j}e_{2t-j}) + e_{2t} \tag{5.49}$$

where c_0 and d_0 are vectors containing constants, the 11 seasonal dummies, and a trend; and c_{1j}, c_{2j}, d_{1j}, and d_{2j} are parameters.

Because we cannot estimate (5.48) and (5.49) directly, we used the residuals of (5.46) and (5.47) and then decomposed the variances of n_t and i_t into the percentages attributable to each type of innovation. We used the orthogonalized innovations obtained from a Choleski decomposition; the order of the variables in the factorization had no qualitative effects on our results (the contemporaneous correlation between e_{1t} and e_{2t} was -0.0176).

Empirical Results

With a 24-month forecasting horizon used, the variance decompositions are reported in Table 5.3, in which the significance levels are in parentheses. As expected, each time series explains the preponderance of its own past values; n_t explains over 91% of its forecast error variance, whereas i_t explains nearly 98% of its forecast error variance. It is interesting that terrorist incidents explain 8.7% of the forecast error variance of Spain's tourism, whereas tourism explains only 2.2% of the forecast error variance of terrorist incidents. More important, Granger causality tests indicate that the effects of terrorism on tourism are significant at the 0.006 level, whereas the effects of tourism on terrorism are not significant at conventional levels. Thus, causality is unidirectional: Terrorism affects tourism but not the reverse. We also note that the terrorism series appears to be autonomous in the sense that neither series Granger causes i_t at conventional levels. This result is consistent with the notion that terrorists randomize their incidents, so that any one incident is not predictable on a month-to-month basis.

Forecasts from an unrestricted VAR are known to suffer from overparameterization. Given the results of the variance decompositions and Granger causality tests, we reestimated (5.46) and (5.47) restricting all the coefficients of $A_{21}(L)$ to zero. Because the right-hand variables were no longer identical, we reestimated the equations with seemingly unrelated regressions (SUR). With the resulting coefficients from the SUR estimates, the effects of a typical terrorist incident on Spain's tourism can be depicted. In terms of the restricted version of (5.49), we set all e_{1t-j} and e_{2t-j} equal to zero for $j > 0$. We then simulated the time paths resulting from the effects of a one-unit shock to e_{2t}. The time path is shown in Figure 5.7, where the vertical axis measures the monthly impact on the number of foreign tourists and the horizontal axis the months following the shock. To smooth out the series,

Table 5.3 **Variance Decomposition Percentage of 24-Month Error Variance**

Percent of forecast error variance in	Typical shock in	
	n_t	i_t
n_t	91.3	8.7
	$(3 \times \text{E-15})$	(0.006)
i_t	2.2	97.8
	(17.2)	(93.9)

Note: The numbers in parentheses indicate the significance level for the joint hypothesis that all lagged coefficients of the variable in question can be set equal to zero.

Figure 5.7   Tourism response to a terrorist incident.

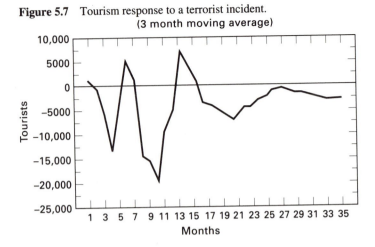
(3 month moving average)

we present the time path of a 3-month moving average of the simulated tourism response function.

After a "typical" terrorist incident, tourism to Spain begins to decline in the third month. After the sixth month, tourism begins to revert to its original level. There does appear to be a rebound in months 8 and 9. There follows another drop in tourism in month 9, reaching the maximum decline about 1 year after the original incident. Obviously, some of this pattern is due to the seasonality in the series. However, tourism slowly recovers and generally remains below its preincident level for a substantial period of time. Aggregating all 36 monthly impacts, we estimate that the combined effects of a typical transnational terrorist incident in Spain is to decrease the total number of foreign visits by 140,847 people. By comparison, a total of 5,392,000 tourists visited Spain in 1988 alone.

10. STRUCTURAL VARs

Sims' (1980) VAR approach has the desirable property that all variables are treated symmetrically, so that the econometrician does not rely on any "incredible identification restrictions." A VAR can be quite helpful in examining the relationships among a set of economic variables. Moreover, the resulting estimates can be used for forecasting purposes. Consider a first-order VAR system of the type represented by (5.21):

$$x_t = A_0 + A_1 x_{t-1} + e_t$$

Although the VAR approach yields only estimated values of A_0 and A_1, for exposition purposes, it is useful to treat each as being known. As we saw in (5.43), the

n-step ahead forecast error is

$$x_{t+n} - E_t x_{t+n} = e_{t+n} + A_1 e_{t+n-1} + A_1^2 e_{t+n-2} + \cdots + A_1^{n-1} e_{t+1} \qquad (5.50)$$

Even though the model is underidentified, an appropriately specified model will have forecasts that are unbiased and have minimum variance. Of course, if we had a priori information concerning any of the coefficients, it would be possible to improve the precision of the estimates and reduce the forecast-error variance. A researcher interested only in forecasting might want to trim down the overparameterized VAR model. Nonetheless, it should be clear that forecasting with a VAR is a multivariate extension of forecasting using a simple autoregression.

The VAR approach has been criticized as being devoid of any economic content. The sole role of the economist is to suggest the appropriate variables to include in the VAR. From that point on, the procedure is almost mechanical. Since there is so little economic input in a VAR, it should not be surprising that there is little economic content in the results. Of course, innovation accounting does require an ordering of the variables, but the selection of the ordering is generally ad hoc.

Unless the underlying structural model can be identified from the reduced-form VAR model, the innovations in a Choleski decomposition do not have a direct economic interpretation. Reconsider the two-variable VAR of (5.19) and (5.20):

$$y_t + b_{12} z_t = b_{10} + \gamma_{11} y_{t-1} + \gamma_{12} z_{t-1} + \epsilon_{yt}$$
$$b_{21} y_t + z_t = b_{20} + \gamma_{21} y_{t-1} + \gamma_{22} z_{t-1} + \epsilon_{zt}$$

so that it is possible to write the model in the form of (5.22a) and (5.22b):

$$y_t = a_{10} + a_{11} y_{t-1} + a_{12} z_{t-1} + e_{1t}$$
$$z_t = a_{20} + a_{21} y_{t-1} + a_{22} z_{t-1} + e_{2t}$$

where the various a_{ij} are defined as in (5.21). For our purposes, the important point to note is that the two error terms e_{1t} and e_{2t} are actually composites of the underlying shocks e_{yt} and e_{zt}. From (5.23) and (5.24),

$$\begin{bmatrix} e_{1t} \\ e_{2t} \end{bmatrix} = 1/(1 - b_{12} b_{21}) \begin{bmatrix} 1 & -b_{12} \\ -b_{21} & 1 \end{bmatrix} \begin{bmatrix} \epsilon_{yt} \\ \epsilon_{zt} \end{bmatrix}$$

Although these composite shocks are the one-step ahead forecast errors in y_t and z_t, they do not have a structural interpretation. Hence, there is an important difference between using VARs for forecasting and using them for economic analysis. In (5.50), e_{1t} and e_{2t} are forecast errors. If we are interested only in forecasting, the components of the forecast errors are unimportant. Given the economic model of (5.19) and (5.20), ϵ_{yt} and ϵ_{zt} are the autonomous changes in y_t and z_t in period t, respectively. If we want to obtain an impulse response function or a variance decomposition to trace out the effects of an innovation in y_t or z_t, it is necessary to use the structural shocks (i.e., ϵ_{yt} and ϵ_{zt}), not the forecast errors. The aim of a structural VAR is to use economic theory (rather than the Choleski decomposition) to recover the structural innovations from the residuals $\{e_{1t}\}$ and $\{e_{2t}\}$.

The Choleski decomposition actually makes a strong assumption about the underlying structural errors. Suppose, as in (5.32), we select an ordering such that $b_{21} = 0$. With this assumption, the two pure innovations can be recovered as

$$e_{zt} = e_{2t}$$

and

$$e_{yt} = e_{1t} + b_{12}e_{2t}$$

Forcing $b_{21} = 0$ is equivalent to assuming that an innovation in y_t does not have a contemporaneous effect on z_t. Unless there is a theoretical foundation for this assumption, the underlying shocks are improperly identified. As such, the impulse responses and variance decompositions resulting from this improper identification can be quite misleading.

If the correlation coefficient between e_{1t} and e_{2t} is low, the ordering is not likely to be important. However, in a VAR with several variables, it is improbable that all correlations will be small. After all, in selecting the variables to include in a model, you are likely to choose variables that exhibit strong comovements. When the residuals of a VAR are correlated, it is not practical to try all alternative orderings. With a four-variable model, there are 24 (i.e., 4!) possible orderings.

Sims (1986) and Bernanke (1986) propose modeling the innovations using economic analysis. To understand the procedure, it is useful to examine the relationship between the forecast errors and structural innovations in an n-variable VAR. Since this relationship is invariant to lag length, consider the first-order model with n variables:

$$
\begin{bmatrix}
1 & b_{12} & b_{13} & \cdots & b_{1n} \\
b_{21} & 1 & b_{23} & \cdots & b_{2n} \\
\cdot & \cdot & & \cdot & \\
b_{n1} & b_{n2} & b_{n3} & \cdots & 1
\end{bmatrix}
\begin{bmatrix}
x_{1t} \\
x_{2t} \\
\cdots \\
x_{nt}
\end{bmatrix}
=
\begin{bmatrix}
b_{10} \\
b_{20} \\
\cdots \\
b_{n0}
\end{bmatrix}
$$

$$
+
\begin{bmatrix}
\gamma_{11} & \gamma_{12} & \gamma_{13} & \cdots & \gamma_{1n} \\
\gamma_{21} & \gamma_{22} & \gamma_{23} & \cdots & \gamma_{2n} \\
\cdot & \cdot & \cdot & \cdot & \\
\gamma_{n1} & \gamma_{n2} & \gamma_{n3} & \cdots & \gamma_{nn}
\end{bmatrix}
\begin{bmatrix}
x_{1t-1} \\
x_{2t-1} \\
\cdots \\
x_{nt-1}
\end{bmatrix}
+
\begin{bmatrix}
\epsilon_{1t} \\
\epsilon_{2t} \\
\cdots \\
\epsilon_{nt}
\end{bmatrix}
$$

or in compact form,

$$Bx_t = \Gamma_0 + \Gamma_1 x_{t-1} + \epsilon_t$$

Equation (5.21) is obtained by premultiplying by B^{-1} to obtain

$$x_t = B^{-1}\Gamma_0 + B^{-1}\Gamma_1 x_{t-1} + B^{-1}\epsilon_t$$

Defining $A_0 = B^{-1}\Gamma_0$, $A_1 = B^{-1}\Gamma_1$, and $e_t = B^{-1}\epsilon_t$ yields the multivariate generalization of (5.21). The problem, then, is to take the observed values of e_t and restrict the system so as to recover ϵ_t as $\epsilon_t = Be_t$. However, the selection of the various b_{ij} cannot be completely arbitrary. The issue is to restrict the system so as to (1) recover the various $\{\epsilon_{it}\}$ and (2) preserve the assumed error structure concerning the independence of the various $\{\epsilon_{it}\}$ shocks. To solve this identification problem, simply count equations and unknowns. Using OLS, we can obtain the variance/covariance matrix Σ:

$$\Sigma = \begin{bmatrix} \sigma_1^2 & \sigma_{12} & \cdots & \sigma_{1n} \\ \sigma_{21} & \sigma_2^2 & \cdots & \sigma_{2n} \\ \cdot & \cdot & \cdot & \cdot \\ \sigma_{n1} & \sigma_{n2} & \cdots & \sigma_n^2 \end{bmatrix}$$

where each element of Σ is constructed as the sum:

$$\sigma_{ij} = (1/T)\sum_{t=1}^{T} e_{it}e_{jt}$$

Since Σ is symmetric, it contains only $(n^2 + n)/2$ distinct elements. There are n elements along the principal diagonal, $(n - 1)$ along the first off-diagonal, $n - 2$ along the next off-diagonal, . . . , and one corner element for a total of $(n^2 + n)/2$ free elements.

Given that the diagonal elements of B are all unity, B contains $n^2 - n$ unknown values. In addition, there are the n unknown values var(ϵ_{it}) for a total of n^2 unknown values in the structural model [i.e., the $n^2 - n$ values of B plus the n values var(ϵ_{it})]. Now, the answer to the identification problem is simple; in order to identify the n^2 unknowns from the known $(n^2 + n)/2$ independent elements of Σ, it is necessary to impose an additional $n^2 - [(n^2 + n)/2] = (n^2 - n)/2$ restrictions on the system. This result generalizes to a model with p lags: *To identify the structural model from an estimated VAR, it is necessary to impose $(n^2 - n)/2$ restrictions on the structural model.*

Take a moment to count the number of restrictions in a Choleski decomposition. In the system above, the Choleski decomposition requires all elements above the principal diagonal to be zero:

$$b_{12} = b_{13} = b_{14} = \cdots = b_{1n} = 0$$
$$b_{23} = b_{24} = \cdots = b_{2n} = 0$$
$$b_{34} = \cdots = b_{3n} = 0$$
$$\cdots$$
$$b_{n-1 n} = 0$$

Hence, there are a total of $(n^2 - n)/2$ restrictions; the system is exactly identified. To take a specific example, consider the following Choleski decomposition in a 3 variable VAR:

$$e_{1t} = \epsilon_{1t}$$
$$e_{2t} = c_{21}\epsilon_{1t} + \epsilon_{2t}$$
$$e_{3t} = c_{31}\epsilon_{1t} + c_{32}\epsilon_{2t} + \epsilon_{3t}$$

From the previous discussion, you should be able to demonstrate that ϵ_{1t}, ϵ_{2t}, and ϵ_{3t} can be identified from the estimates of e_{1t}, e_{2t}, e_{3t}, and variance/covariance matrix Σ. In terms of our previous notation, define matrix $C = B^{-1}$ with elements c_{ij}. Hence, $e_t = C\epsilon_t$. An alternative way to model the relationship between the forecast errors and the structural innovations is

$$e_{1t} = \epsilon_{1t} + c_{13}\epsilon_{3t}$$
$$e_{2t} = c_{21}\epsilon_{1t} + \epsilon_{2t}$$
$$e_{3t} = c_{31}\epsilon_{2t} + \epsilon_{3t}$$

Notice the absence of a triangular structure. Here, the forecast error of each variable is affected by its own structural innovation and the structural innovation in one other variable. Given the $(9 - 3)/2 = 3$ restrictions on C, the *necessary* condition for the exact identification of B and ϵ_t is satisfied. However, as illustrated in the next section, imposing $(n^2 - n)/2$ restrictions is not a sufficient condition for exact identification. Unfortunately, the presence of non-linearities means there are no simple rules that guarantee exact identification.

11. EXAMPLES OF STRUCTURAL DECOMPOSITIONS

To illustrate a Sims–Bernanke decomposition, suppose there are five residuals for e_{1t} and e_{2t}. Although a usable sample size of 5 is unacceptable for estimation purposes, it does allow us to do the necessary calculations in a simple fashion. Thus, suppose that the five error terms are

t	e_{1t}	e_{2t}
1	1.0	0.5
2	−0.5	−1.0
3	0.0	0.0
4	−1.0	−0.5
5	0.5	1.0

Since the $\{e_{1t}\}$ and $\{e_{2t}\}$ are regression residuals, their sums are zero. It is simple to verify that $\sigma_1^2 = 0.5$, $\sigma_{12} = \sigma_{21} = 0.4$, and $\sigma_2 = 0.5$; hence, the variance/covariance matrix Σ is

$$\Sigma = \begin{bmatrix} 0.5 & 0.4 \\ 0.4 & 0.5 \end{bmatrix}$$

Although the covariance between ϵ_{1t} and ϵ_{2t} is zero, the variances of ϵ_{1t} and ϵ_{2t} are presumably unknown. Let the variance/covariance matrix of these structural shocks be denoted by Σ_ϵ, so that

$$\Sigma_\epsilon = \begin{bmatrix} \mathrm{var}(\epsilon_1) & 0 \\ 0 & \mathrm{var}(\epsilon_2) \end{bmatrix}$$

The reason that the covariance terms are equal to zero is that ϵ_{1t} and ϵ_{2t} are deemed to be pure structural shocks. Moreover, the variance of each shock is time-invariant. For notational convenience, the time subscript can be dropped; for example, $\mathrm{var}(\epsilon_{1t}) = \mathrm{var}(\epsilon_{1t-1}) = \cdots = \mathrm{var}(\epsilon_1)$.

The relationship between the variance/covariance matrix of the forecast errors (i.e., Σ) and variance/covariance matrix of the pure shocks (i.e., Σ_ϵ) is such that $\Sigma_\epsilon = B\Sigma B'$. Recall that e_t and ϵ_t are the column vectors $(e_{1t}, e_{2t})'$ and $(\epsilon_{1t}, \epsilon_{2t})'$, respectively. Hence,

$$e_t e_t' = \begin{bmatrix} e_{1t}^2 & e_{1t}e_{2t} \\ e_{1t}e_{2t} & e_{2t}^2 \end{bmatrix}$$

so that

$$\Sigma = (1/T)\sum_{i=1}^{T} e_t e_t' \tag{5.51}$$

Similarly, Σ_ϵ is

$$\Sigma_\epsilon = (1/T)\sum_{t=1}^{T} \epsilon_t \epsilon_t' \tag{5.52}$$

To link the two variance/covariance matrices, note that the relationship between ϵ_t and e_t is such that $\epsilon_t = Be_t$. Substitute this relationship into (5.52) and recall that the transpose of a product is the product of the transposes [i.e., $(Be_t)' = e_t'B'$], so that

$$\Sigma_\epsilon = (1/T)\sum_{t=1}^{T} (Be_t)(e_t'B')$$

Hence, using (5.51), we obtain

$$\Sigma_\epsilon = B\Sigma B'$$

By using the specific numbers in the example, it follows that

$$\begin{bmatrix} \text{Var}(\epsilon_1) & 0 \\ 0 & \text{var}(\epsilon_2) \end{bmatrix} = \begin{bmatrix} 1 & b_{12} \\ b_{21} & 1 \end{bmatrix} \begin{bmatrix} 0.5 & 0.4 \\ 0.4 & 0.5 \end{bmatrix} \begin{bmatrix} 1 & b_{21} \\ b_{12} & 1 \end{bmatrix}$$

Since both sides of this equation are equivalent, they must be the same element by element. Carry out the indicated multiplication of $B\Sigma B'$ to obtain

$$\text{var}(\epsilon_1) = 0.5 + 0.8b_{12} + 0.5b_{12}^2 \tag{5.53}$$
$$0 = 0.5b_{21} + 0.4b_{21}b_{12} + 0.4 + 0.5b_{12} \tag{5.54}$$
$$0 = 0.5b_{21} + 0.4b_{12}b_{21} + 0.4 + 0.5b_{12} \tag{5.55}$$
$$\text{var}(\epsilon_2) = 0.5b_{21}^2 + 0.8b_{21} + 0.5 \tag{5.56}$$

As you can see, Equations (5.54) and (5.55) are identical. There are three independent equations to solve for the four unknowns b_{12}, b_{21}, $\text{var}(\epsilon_1)$, and $\text{var}(\epsilon_2)$. As we saw in the last section, in a two-variable system, one restriction needs to be imposed if the structural model is to be identified. Now consider the Choleski decomposition one more time. If $b_{12} = 0$, we find

$\text{Var}(\epsilon_1) = 0.5$

$\quad 0 = 0.5b_{21} + 0.4 \qquad$ so that $b_{21} = -0.8$

$\quad 0 = 0.5b_{21} + 0.4 \qquad$ so that again we find, $b_{21} = -0.8$

$\text{var}(\epsilon_2) = 0.5(b_{21})^2 + 0.8b_{21} + 0.5 \qquad$ so that $\text{var}(\epsilon_2) = 0.5(0.64) - 0.64 + 0.5 = 0.18$

Using this decomposition, we can recover each $\{\epsilon_{1t}\}$ and $\{\epsilon_{2t}\}$ as $\epsilon_t = Be_t$:

$$\epsilon_{1t} = e_{1t}$$

and

$$\epsilon_{2t} = -0.8e_{1t} + e_{2t}$$

Thus, the identified structural shocks are

t	ϵ_{1t}	ϵ_{2t}
1	1.0	−0.3
2	−0.5	−0.6
3	0.0	0.0
4	−1.0	0.3
5	0.5	0.6

If you want to take the time, you can verify that $\text{var}(\epsilon_1) = \Sigma(\epsilon_{1t})^2/5 = 0.5$, $\text{var}(\epsilon_{2t})$ $= \Sigma(\epsilon_{2t})^2/5 = 0.18$, and $\text{cov}(e_{1t}, e_{2t}) = \Sigma\epsilon_{1t}\epsilon_{2t}/5 = 0$. Instead, if we impose the alternative restriction of a Choleski decomposition and set $b_{21} = 0$, from (5.53) through (5.56), we obtain

$$\text{Var}(\epsilon_1) = 0.5 + 0.8b_{12} + 0.5b_{12}^2$$
$$0 = 0.4 + 0.5b_{12} \quad \text{so that } b_{12} = -0.8$$
$$0 = 0.4 + 0.5b_{12} \quad \text{so again } b_{12} = -0.8$$
$$\text{Var}(\epsilon_2) = 0.5$$

Since $b_{12} = -0.8$, $\text{var}(\epsilon_1) = 0.5 + 0.8(-0.8) + 0.5(0.64) = 0.18$. Now, B is identified as

$$B = \begin{bmatrix} 1 & -0.8 \\ 0 & 1 \end{bmatrix}$$

If we use the identified values of B, the structural innovations are such that $\epsilon_{1t} = e_{1t} - 0.8e_{2t}$ and $\epsilon_{2t} = e_{2t}$. Hence, we have the structural innovations:

t	ϵ_{1t}	ϵ_{2t}
1	0.6	0.5
2	0.3	−1.0
3	0.0	0.0
4	−0.6	−0.5
5	−0.3	1.0

In this example, the ordering used in the Choleski decomposition is very important. This should not be too surprising since the correlation coefficient between e_{1t} and e_{2t} is 0.8. The point is that the ordering will have important implications for the resulting variance decompositions and impulse response functions. Selecting the first ordering (i.e., setting $b_{12} = 0$) gives more importance to innovations in e_{1t} shocks. The assumed timing is such that ϵ_{1t} can have a contemporaneous effect on x_{1t} and x_{2t}, whereas ϵ_{2t} shocks can affect x_{1t} only with a one-period lag. Moreover, the amplitude of the impulse responses attributable to ϵ_{1t} shocks will be increased since the ordering affects the magnitude of a "typical" (i.e., one standard deviation) shock in ϵ_{1t} and decreases the magnitude of a "typical" ϵ_{2t} shock.

The important point to note is that *the Choleski decomposition is only one type of identification restriction.* With three independent equations among the four unknowns b_{12}, b_{21}, $\text{var}(\epsilon_{1t})$, and $\text{var}(\epsilon_{2t})$, any other linearly independent restriction will allow for the identification of the structural model. Consider some of the other alternatives:

1. *A Coefficient Restriction.* Suppose that we know that a one-unit innovation ϵ_{2t} has a one-unit effect on x_{1t}; hence, suppose we know that $b_{12} = 1$. By using

the other three independent equations, it follows that var(ϵ_{1t}) = 1.8, b_{21} = −1, var(ϵ_{2t}) = 0.2.

Given that $\epsilon_t = Be_t$, we obtain

$$\begin{bmatrix} \epsilon_{1t} \\ \epsilon_{2t} \end{bmatrix} = \begin{bmatrix} 1 & 1 \\ -1 & 1 \end{bmatrix} \begin{bmatrix} e_{1t} \\ e_{2t} \end{bmatrix}$$

so that $\epsilon_{1t} = e_{1t} + e_{2t}$ and $\epsilon_{2t} = -e_{1t} + e_{2t}$. If we use the five hypothetical regression residuals, the decomposed innovations become:

t	ϵ_{1t}	ϵ_{2t}
1	1.5	−0.5
2	−1.5	−0.5
3	0	0
4	−1.5	0.5
5	1.5	0.5

2. *A Variance Restriction.* Given the relationship between Σ_ϵ and Σ (i.e., $\Sigma_\epsilon = B\Sigma B'$), a restriction on the variances contained within Σ_ϵ will always imply multiple solutions for coefficients of B. To keep the arithmetic simple, suppose that we know var(ϵ_{1t}) = 1.8. The first equation yields two possible solutions for b_{12} = 1 and b_{12} = −2.6; unless we have a theoretical reason to discard one of these magnitudes, there are two solutions to the model. Thus, even in a simple 2-variable case, unique identification is not always possible. If b_{12} = 1, the remaining solutions are b_{21} = −1 and var(ϵ_{2t}) = 0.2. If b_{12} = −2.6, the solutions are $b_{21} = -1^2 \tfrac{1}{3}$ and var(ϵ_{2t}) = 0.556.

The two solutions can be used to identify two different {ϵ_{1t}} and {ϵ_{2t}} sequences and innovation accounting can be performed using both solutions. Even though there are two solutions, both satisfy the theoretical restriction concerning var(ϵ_{1t}).

3. *Symmetry Restrictions.* A linear combination of the coefficients and variances can be used for identification purposes. For example, the symmetry restriction $b_{12} = b_{21}$ can be used for identification. If we use Equation (5.54), there are two solutions: $b_{12} = b_{21}$ = −0.5 or $b_{12} = b_{21}$ = −2.0. For the first solution, var(ϵ_{1t}) = 0.225, and using the second solution, we get var(ϵ_{1t}) = 0.9.[10]

Nevertheless, for the first solution,

$$\begin{bmatrix} \epsilon_{1t} \\ \epsilon_{2t} \end{bmatrix} = \begin{bmatrix} 1 & -0.5 \\ -0.5 & 1 \end{bmatrix} \begin{bmatrix} e_{1t} \\ e_{2t} \end{bmatrix}$$

so that

t	ϵ_{1t}	ϵ_{2t}
1	0.75	0
2	0	−0.75
3	0	0
4	−0.75	0
5	0	0.75

Overidentified Systems

It may be that economic theory suggests more than $(n^2 - n)/2$ restrictions. If so, it is necessary to modify the method above. The procedure for identifying an overidentified system entails the following steps:

STEP 1: The restrictions on B or var(ϵ_{it}) do not affect the estimation of VAR coefficients. Hence, estimate the unrestricted VAR: $x_t = A_0 + A_1 x_{t-1} + \cdots + A_p x_{t-p} + e_t$. Use the standard lag length and block causality tests to help determine the form of the VAR.

STEP 2: Obtain the unrestricted variance/covariance matrix Σ. The determinant of this matrix is an indicator of the overall fit of the model.

STEP 3: Restricting B and/or Σ_ϵ will affect the estimate of Σ. Select the appropriate restrictions and maximize the likelihood function with respect to the free parameters of B and Σ_ϵ. This will lead to an estimate of the restricted variance/covariance matrix. Denote this second estimate by Σ_R.

For those wanting a more technical explanation, note that the log likelihood function is

$$-(T/2)\ln|\Sigma| - (1/2)\sum_{t=1}^{T}(e_t'\Sigma^{-1}e_t)$$

Fix each element of e_t (and e_t') at the level obtained using OLS; call these estimated OLS residuals $\hat{e}_t$. Now use the relationship $\Sigma_\epsilon = B\Sigma B'$ so that the log likelihood function can be written as

$$-(T/2)\ln\left|B^{-1}\Sigma_\epsilon(B')^{-1}\right| - (1/2)\sum_{t=1}^{T}(\hat{e}_t'B'\Sigma_\epsilon^{-1}B\hat{e}_t)$$

Now select the restrictions on B and Σ_ϵ and maximize with respect to the remaining free elements of these two matrices. The resulting estimates of B and Σ_ϵ imply a value of Σ that we have dubbed Σ_R.

STEP 4: If the restrictions are not binding, Σ and Σ_R will be equivalent. Let R = the number of overidentifying restrictions; that is, R = number of restrictions exceeding $(n^2 - n)/2$. Then, the χ^2 test statistic:

$$\chi^2 = |\Sigma_R| - |\Sigma|$$

with R degrees of freedom can be used to test the restricted system.[11] If the calculated value of χ^2 exceeds that in a χ^2 table, the restrictions can be rejected. Now allow for two sets of overidentifying restrictions such that the number of restrictions in R_2 exceeds that in R_1. In fact, if $R_2 > R_1 \geq (n^2 - n)/2$, the significance of the extra $R_2 - R_1$ restrictions can be tested as

$$\chi^2 = |\sigma_{R2}| - |\Sigma_{R1}| \qquad \text{with } R_2 - R_1 \text{ degrees of freedom}$$

Similarly, in an overidentified system, the t-statistics for the individual coefficients can be obtained. Sims warns that the calculated standard errors may not be very accurate.

Sims' Structural VAR

Sims (1986) uses a six-variable VAR of quarterly data over the period 1948:1 to 1979:3. The variables included in the study are real GNP (y), real business fixed investment (i), the GNP deflator (p), the money supply as measured by M1 (m), unemployment (u), and the treasury bill rate (r). An unrestricted VAR was estimated with four lags of each variable and a constant term. Sims obtained the 36 impulse response functions using a Choleski decomposition with the ordering $y \to i \to p \to m \to u \to r$. Some of the impulse response functions had reasonable interpretations. However, the response of real variables to a money supply shock seemed unreasonable. The impulse responses suggested that a money supply shock had little effect on prices, output, or the interest rate. Given a standard money demand function, it is hard to explain why the public would be willing to hold the expanded money supply. Sims' proposes an alternative to the Choleski decomposition that is consistent with money market equilibrium. Sims restricts the B matrix such that

$$
\begin{bmatrix}
1 & b_{11} & 0 & 0 & 0 & 0 \\
b_{21} & 1 & b_{23} & b_{24} & 0 & 0 \\
b_{31} & 0 & 1 & 0 & 0 & b_{36} \\
b_{41} & 0 & b_{43} & 1 & 0 & b_{46} \\
b_{51} & 0 & b_{53} & b_{54} & 1 & b_{56} \\
0 & 0 & 0 & 0 & 0 & 1
\end{bmatrix}
\begin{bmatrix}
r_t \\ m_t \\ y_t \\ p_t \\ u_t \\ i_t
\end{bmatrix}
=
\begin{bmatrix}
\epsilon_{rt} \\ \epsilon_{mt} \\ \epsilon_{yt} \\ \epsilon_{pt} \\ \epsilon_{ut} \\ \epsilon_{it}
\end{bmatrix}
$$

Notice that there are 17 zero restrictions on the b_{ij}; the system is overidentified; with six variables, exact identification requires only $(6^2 - 6)/2 = 15$ restrictions. Imposing these 16 restrictions, Sims' identifies the following six relationships among the contemporaneous innovations:

$$r_t = 71.20m_t + \epsilon_{rt} \tag{5.57}$$
$$m_t = 0.283y_t + 0.224p_t - 0.0081r_t + \epsilon_{mt} \tag{5.58}$$
$$y_t = -0.00135r_t + 0.132i_t + \epsilon_{yt} \tag{5.59}$$
$$p_t = -0.0010r_t + 0.045y_t - 0.00364i_t + \epsilon_{pt} \tag{5.60}$$
$$u_t = -0.116r_t - 20.1y_t - 1.48i_t - 8.98p_t + \epsilon_{ut} \tag{5.61}$$
$$i_t = \epsilon_{it} \tag{5.62}$$

Sims views (5.57) and (5.58) as money supply and demand functions, respectively. In (5.57), the money supply rises as the interest rate increases. The demand for money in (5.58) is positively related to income and the price level and negatively related to the interest rate. Investment innovations in (5.62) are completely autonomous. Otherwise, Sims sees no reason to restrict the other equations at any particular fashion. For simplicity, he chooses a Choleski-type block structure for GNP, the price level, and the unemployment rate. The impulse response functions appear to be consistent with the notion that money supply shocks affect prices, income, and the interest rate.

12. THE BLANCHARD AND QUAH DECOMPOSITION

Blanchard and Quah (1989) provide an alternative way to obtain a structural identification. Their aim is to reconsider the Beveridge and Nelson (1981) decomposition of real GNP into its temporary and permanent components. Toward this end, they develop a macroeconomic model such that real GNP is affected by demand-side and supply-side disturbances. In accord with the natural rate hypothesis, demand-side disturbances have no long-run affect on real GNP. On the supply side, productivity shocks are assumed to have permanent affects on output. In a univariate model, there is no unique way to decompose a variable into its temporary and permanent components. However, using a bivariate VAR, Blanchard and Quah show how to decompose real GNP and recover the two pure shocks.

To take a general example, suppose we are interested in decomposing an $I(1)$ sequence—say, $\{y_t\}$—into its temporary and permanent components. In a univariate framework [recall the discussion concerning Beveridge and Nelson (1981)], there is no unique way to perform the decomposition. However, let there be a second variable $\{z_t\}$ that is affected by the same two shocks. For the time being, suppose that $\{z_t\}$ is stationary. If we ignore the intercept terms, the bivariate moving average (BMA) representation of the $\{y_t\}$ and $\{z_t\}$ sequences will have the form:

$$\Delta y_t = \sum_{k=0}^{\infty} c_{11}(k)\epsilon_{1t-k} + \sum_{k=0}^{\infty} c_{12}(k)\epsilon_{2t-k} \tag{5.63}$$

$$z_t = \sum_{k=0}^{\infty} c_{21}(k)\epsilon_{1t-k} + \sum_{k=0}^{\infty} c_{22}(k)\epsilon_{2t-k} \tag{5.64}$$

or in a more compact form,

$$\begin{bmatrix} \Delta y_t \\ z_t \end{bmatrix} = \begin{bmatrix} C_{11}(L) & C_{12}(L) \\ C_{21}(L) & C_{22}(L) \end{bmatrix} \begin{bmatrix} \epsilon_{1t} \\ \epsilon_{2t} \end{bmatrix}$$

where ϵ_{1t} and ϵ_{2t} = independent white-noise disturbances, each having a constant variance

and the $C_{ij}(L)$ are polynomials in the lag operator L such that the individual coefficients of $C_{ij}(L)$ are denoted by $c_{ij}(k)$. For example, the third coefficient of $C_{21}(L)$ is $c_{21}(3)$. For convenience, the time subscripts on the variances and covariance terms are dropped and shocks normalized so that $\text{var}(\epsilon_1) = 1$ and $\text{var}(\epsilon_2) = 1$. If we call Σ_ϵ the variance/covariance matrix of the innovations, it follows that

$$\Sigma_\epsilon = \begin{bmatrix} \text{var}(\epsilon_1) & \text{cov}(\epsilon_1, \epsilon_2) \\ \text{cov}(\epsilon_1, \epsilon_2) & \text{var}(\epsilon_2) \end{bmatrix}$$

$$= \begin{bmatrix} 1 & 0 \\ 0 & 1 \end{bmatrix}$$

In order to use the Blanchard and Quah technique, both variables must be in a stationary form. Since $\{y_t\}$ is $I(1)$, (5.63) uses the first difference of the series. Note that (5.64) implies that the $\{z_t\}$ sequence is $I(0)$; if in your own work you find that $\{z_t\}$ is also $I(1)$, use its first difference.

In contrast to the Sims–Bernanke procedure, Blanchard and Quah do not directly associate the $\{\epsilon_{1t}\}$ and $\{\epsilon_{2t}\}$ shocks with the $\{y_t\}$ and $\{z_t\}$ sequences. Instead, the $\{y_t\}$ and $\{z_t\}$ sequences are the endogenous variables, and the $\{\epsilon_{1t}\}$ and $\{\epsilon_{2t}\}$ sequences represent what an economic theorist would call the exogenous variables. In their example, y_t is the logarithm of real GNP, z_t unemployment, ϵ_{1t} an aggregate demand shock, and ϵ_{2t} an aggregate supply shock. The coefficients of $C_{11}(L)$, for example, represent the impulse responses of an aggregate demand shock on the time path of change in the log of real GNP.[12]

The key to decomposing the $\{y_t\}$ sequence into its trend and irregular components is to assume that one of the shocks has a temporary effect on the $\{y_t\}$ sequence. It is this dichotomy between temporary and permanent effects that allows for the complete identification of the structural innovations from an estimated

VAR. For example, Blanchard and Quah assume that an aggregate demand shock has no long-run effect on real GNP. In the long run, if real GNP is to be unaffected by the demand shock, it must be the case that the cumulated effect of an ϵ_{1t} shock on the Δy_t sequence must be equal to zero. Hence, the coefficients $c_{11}(k)$ in (5.63) must be such that

$$\sum_{k=0}^{\infty} c_{11}(k)\epsilon_{1t-k} = 0 \tag{5.65}$$

Since the demand-side and supply-side shocks are not observed, the problem is to recover them from a VAR estimation. Given that the variables are stationary, we know there exists a VAR representation of the form:

$$\begin{bmatrix} \Delta y_t \\ z_t \end{bmatrix} = \begin{bmatrix} A_{11}(L) & A_{12}(L) \\ A_{21}(L) & A_{22}(L) \end{bmatrix} \begin{bmatrix} \Delta y_{t-1} \\ z_{t-1} \end{bmatrix} + \begin{bmatrix} e_{1t} \\ e_{2t} \end{bmatrix} \tag{5.66}$$

or to use a more compact notation,

$$x_t = A(L)x_{t-1} + e_t$$

where x_t = the column vector $(\Delta y_t, z_t)'$
           e_t = the column vector $(e_{1t}, e_{2t})'$
           $A(L)$ = the 2×2 matrix with elements equal to the polynomials $A_{ij}(L)$

and the coefficients of $A_{ij}(L)$ are denoted by $a_{ij}(k)$.[13]

The critical insight is that the VAR residuals are composites of the pure innovations ϵ_{1t} and ϵ_{2t}. For example, e_{1t} is the one-step ahead forecast error of y_t; that is, $e_{1t} = \Delta y_t - E_{t-1}\Delta y_t$. From the BMA, the one-step ahead forecast error is $c_{11}(0)\epsilon_{1t} + c_{12}(0)\epsilon_{2t}$. Since the two representations are equivalent, it must be the case that

$$e_{1t} = c_{11}(0)\epsilon_{1t} + c_{12}(0)\epsilon_{2t} \tag{5.67}$$

Similarly, since e_{2t} is the one-step ahead forecast error of z_t

$$e_{2t} = c_{21}(0)\epsilon_{1t} + c_{22}(0)\epsilon_{2t} \tag{5.68}$$

or, combining (5.67) and (5.68), we get

$$\begin{bmatrix} e_{1t} \\ e_{2t} \end{bmatrix} = \begin{bmatrix} c_{11}(0) & c_{12}(0) \\ c_{21}(0) & c_{22}(0) \end{bmatrix} \begin{bmatrix} \epsilon_{1t} \\ \epsilon_{2t} \end{bmatrix}$$

If $c_{11}(0)$, $c_{12}(0)$, $c_{21}(0)$, and $c_{22}(0)$ were known, it would be possible to recover ϵ_{1t} and ϵ_{2t} from the regression residuals e_{1t} and e_{2t}. Blanchard and Quah show that the relationship between (5.66) and the BMA model plus the long-run restriction of (5.65) provide exactly four restrictions that can be used to identify these four coefficients. The VAR residuals can be used to construct estimates of var(e_1), var(e_2) and cov(e_1, e_2).[14] Hence, there are the following three restrictions:

RESTRICTION 1

Given (5.67) and noting that $E\epsilon_{1t}\epsilon_{2t} = 0$, we see that the normalization var(ϵ_1) = var(ϵ_2) = 1 means that the variance of e_{1t} is

$$\text{Var}(e_1) = c_{11}(0)^2 + c_{12}(0)^2 \tag{5.69}$$

RESTRICTION 2

Similarly, if we use (5.68), the variance of e_{2t} is related to $c_{21}(0)$ and $c_{22}(0)$ as

$$\text{Var}(e_2) = c_{21}(0)^2 + c_{22}(0)^2 \tag{5.70}$$

RESTRICTION 3

The product of e_{1t} and e_{2t} is

$$e_{1t}e_{2t} = [c_{11}(0)\epsilon_{1t} + c_{12}(0)\epsilon_{2t}][c_{21}(0)\epsilon_{1t} + c_{22}(0)\epsilon_{2t}]$$

If we take the expectation, the covariance of the VAR residuals is

$$Ee_{1t}e_{2t} = c_{11}(0)c_{21}(0) + c_{12}(0)c_{22}(0) \tag{5.71}$$

Thus, equations (5.69), (5.70), and (5.71) can be viewed as three equations in the four unknowns $c_{11}(0)$, $c_{12}(0)$, $c_{21}(0)$, and $c_{22}(0)$. The fourth restriction is embedded in assumption that the $\{\epsilon_{1t}\}$ has no long-run effect on the $\{y_t\}$ sequence. The problem is to transform the restriction (5.65) into its VAR representation. Since the algebra is a bit messy, it is helpful rewrite (5.64) as

$$x_t = A(L)Lx_t + e_t$$

so that

$$[I - A(L)L]x_t = e_t$$

and by premultiplying by $[I - A(L)L]^{-1}$, we obtain

$$x_t = [I - A(L)L]^{-1}e_t \tag{5.72}$$

Denote the determinant of $[I - A(L)L]$ by the expression D. It should not take too long to convince yourself that (5.72) can be written as:

$$\begin{bmatrix} \Delta y_t \\ z_t \end{bmatrix} = (1/D) \begin{bmatrix} 1 - A_{22}(L)L & A_{12}(L)L \\ A_{21}(L)L & 1 - A_{11}(L)L \end{bmatrix} \begin{bmatrix} e_{1t} \\ e_{2t} \end{bmatrix}$$

or using the definitions of the $A_{ij}(L)$, we get

$$\begin{bmatrix} \Delta y_t \\ z_t \end{bmatrix} = (1/D) \begin{bmatrix} 1 - \Sigma a_{22}(k)L^{k+1} & \Sigma a_{12}(k)L^{k+1} \\ \Sigma a_{21}(k)L^{k+1} & 1 - \Sigma a_{11}(k)L^{k+1} \end{bmatrix} \begin{bmatrix} e_{1t} \\ e_{2t} \end{bmatrix}$$

where the summations run from $k = 0$ to infinity.

Thus, the solution for Δy_t in terms of the current and lagged values of $\{e_{1t}\}$ and $\{e_{2t}\}$ is

$$\Delta y_t = (1/D) \left\{ \left[1 - \sum_{k=0}^{\infty} a_{22}(k)L^{k+1} \right] e_{1t} + \sum_{k=0}^{\infty} a_{12}(k)L^{k+1} e_{2t} \right\} \tag{5.73}$$

Now, e_{1t} and e_{2t} can be replaced by (5.67) and (5.68). If we make these substitutions, the restriction that the $\{\epsilon_{1t}\}$ sequence has no long-run effect on y_t is

$$\left[1 - \sum_{k=0}^{\infty} a_{22}(k)L^{k+1} \right] c_{11}(0)\epsilon_{1t} + \sum_{k=0}^{\infty} a_{12}(k)L^{k+1} c_{21}(0)\epsilon_{1t} = 0$$

RESTRICTION 4

For all possible realizations of the $\{\epsilon_{1t}\}$ sequence, ϵ_{1t} shocks will have only temporary effects on the Δy_t sequence (and y_t itself) if

$$\left[1 - \sum_{k=0}^{\infty} a_{22}(k) \right] c_{11}(0) + \sum_{k=0}^{\infty} a_{12}(k) c_{21}(0) = 0$$

With this fourth restriction, there are four equations that can be used to identify the unknown values $c_{11}(0)$, $c_{12}(0)$, $c_{21}(0)$, and $c_{22}(0)$. To summarize, the steps in the procedure are as follows.

STEP 1: Begin by pretesting the two variables for time trends and unit roots. If $\{y_t\}$ does not have a unit root, there is no reason to proceed with the decomposition. Appropriately transform the two variables, so that the resulting sequences are both $I(0)$. Perform lag-length tests to find a reasonable approximation to the infinite-order VAR. The residuals of the estimated

VAR should pass the standard diagnostic checks for white-noise processes (of course, e_{1t} and e_{2t} can be correlated with each other).

STEP 2: Using the residuals of the estimated VAR, calculate the variance/covariance matrix; that is, calculate $\text{var}(e_1)$, $\text{var}(e_2)$, and $\text{cov}(e_1, e_2)$. Also calculate the sums:

$$1 - \sum_{k=0}^{p} a_{22}(k) \quad \text{and} \quad \sum_{k=0}^{p} a_{12}(k)$$

where p = lag length used to estimate the VAR

Use these values to solve the following four equations for $c_{11}(0)$, $c_{12}(0)$, $c_{21}(0)$, and $c_{22}(0)$:

$$\text{Var}(e_1) = c_{11}(0)^2 + c_{12}(0)^2$$
$$\text{Var}(e_2) = c_{21}(0)^2 + c_{22}(0)^2$$
$$\text{Cov}(e_1, e_2) = c_{11}(0)c_{21}(0) + c_{12}(0)c_{22}(0)$$
$$0 = c_{11}(0)[1 - \Sigma a_{22}(k)] + c_{21}(0)\Sigma a_{12}(k)$$

Given these four values $c_{ij}(0)$ and the residuals of the VAR $\{e_{1t}\}$ and $\{e_{2t}\}$, the entire $\{\epsilon_{1t}\}$ and $\{\epsilon_{2t}\}$ sequences can be identified using the formulas:[15]

$$e_{1t-i} = c_{11}(0)\epsilon_{1t-i} + c_{12}(0)\epsilon_{2t-i}$$

and

$$e_{2t-i} = c_{21}(0)\epsilon_{1t-i} + c_{22}(0)\epsilon_{2t-i}$$

STEP 3: As in a traditional VAR, the identified $\{\epsilon_{1t}\}$ and $\{\epsilon_{2t}\}$ sequences can be used to obtain impulse response functions and variance decompositions. The difference is that the interpretation of the impulses is straightforward. For example, Blanchard and Quah are able to obtain the impulse responses of the change in the log of real GNP to a typical supply-side shock. Moreover, it is possible to obtain the historical decomposition of each series. For example, set all $\{\epsilon_{1t}\}$ shocks equal to zero and use the actual $\{\epsilon_{2t}\}$ series (i.e., use the identified values of ϵ_{2t}) to obtain the permanent changes in $\{y_t\}$ as[16]

$$\Delta y_t = \sum_{k=0}^{\infty} c_{12}(k)\epsilon_{2t-k}$$

The Blanchard and Quah Results

In their study, Blanchard and Quah (1989) use the first difference of the logarithm of real GNP and the level of unemployment. They note that unemployment exhibits an apparent time trend and that there is a slowdown in real growth beginning in the mid–1970s. Since there is no obvious way to address these difficult issues, they estimate four different VARs. Two include a dummy allowing for the change in the rate of growth in output and two include a deterministic time trend in unemployment. Using quarterly GNP and unemployment data over the period 1950:2 through 1987:4, they estimated a VAR with eight lags.

Imposing the restriction that demand-side shocks have no long-run effect on real GNP, Blanchard and Quah identify the two types of shocks. The impulse response functions for the four VARs are quite similar:

1. The time paths of demand-side disturbances on output and unemployment are hump-shaped. The impulse responses are mirror images of each other; initially output increases while unemployment decreases. The effects peak after four quarters; afterward they converge to their original levels.

2. Supply-side disturbances have a cumulative effect on output. A supply disturbance having a positive effect on output also has a small positive initial effect on unemployment. After this initial increase, unemployment steadily decreases and the cumulated change becomes negative after four quarters. Unemployment remains below its long-run level for nearly 5 years.

Blanchard and Quah find that the alternative methods of treating the slowdown in output growth and the trend in unemployment affect the variance decompositions. Since the goal here is to illustrate the technique, consider only the variance decomposition using a dummy variable for the decline in output growth and detrended unemployment.

Percent of Forecast Error Variance due to Demand-Side Shocks

Forecasting Horizon (Quarters)	Output	Unemployment
1	99.0	51.9
4	97.9	80.2
12	67.6	86.2
40	39.3	85.6

At short-run horizons, the huge preponderance of the variation in output is due to demand-side innovations. Demand shocks account for almost all the movement in GNP at short horizons. Since demand shock effects are necessarily temporary, the findings contradict those of Beveridge and Nelson. The proportion of the forecast error variance falls steadily as the forecast horizon increases; the proportion converges to zero since these effects are temporary. Consequently, the contribution of supply-side innovations to real GNP movements increases at longer forecasting horizons. On the other hand, demand-side shocks generally account for increasing proportions of the variation in unemployment at longer forecasting horizons.

13. DECOMPOSING REAL AND NOMINAL EXCHANGE RATE MOVEMENTS: AN EXAMPLE

In Lee and Enders (1993), we decompose real and nominal exchange rate movements into the components induced by real and nominal factors. This section presents a small portion of the paper in order to further illustrate the methodology of the Blanchard and Quah technique. One aim of the study is to explain the deviations from purchasing power parity. As in Chapter 4, the real exchange rate (r_t) can be defined as[17]

$$r_t = e_t + p_t^* - p_t$$

where p_t^* and p_t refer to the logarithms of U.S. and Canadian wholesale price indices and e_t is the logarithm of the Canadian dollar/U.S. dollar nominal exchange rate.

To explain the deviations from PPP, we suppose there are two types of shocks: a real shock and nominal shock. The theory suggests that real shocks can cause permanent changes in the real exchange rate, but nominal shocks can cause only temporary movements in the real rate. For example, in the long run, if Canada doubles its nominal money supply, the Canadian price level will double and the Canadian dollar price of U.S. dollars will halve. Hence, in the long run, the real exchange rate remains invariant to a money supply shock.

For Step 1, we perform various unit root tests on the monthly Canadian/U.S. dollar real and nominal exchange rates over the 1973:1 to 1989:12 period. Consistent with other studies focusing on the post–Bretton Woods period, it is clear that real and nominal rates can be characterized by non-stationary processes. We use the first difference of the logarithm of each in the decomposition. Our BMA model has the form:

$$\begin{bmatrix} \Delta r_t \\ \Delta e_t \end{bmatrix} = \begin{bmatrix} C_{11}(L) & C_{12}(L) \\ C_{21}(L) & C_{22}(L) \end{bmatrix} \begin{bmatrix} \epsilon_{rt} \\ \epsilon_{nt} \end{bmatrix}$$

where ϵ_{rt} and ϵ_{nt} represent the zero-mean mutually uncorrelated real and nominal shocks, respectively.

The restriction that the nominal shocks have no long-run effect on the real exchange rate is represented by the restriction that the coefficients in $C_{12}(L)$ sum to zero; thus, if $c_{ij}(k)$ is the kth coefficient in $C_{ij}(L)$, as in (5.65), the restriction is

$$\sum_{k=0}^{\infty} c_{12}(k) = 0 \qquad (5.74)$$

The restriction in (5.74) implies that the cumulative effect of ϵ_{nt} on Δr_t is zero, and consequently, the long-run effect of ϵ_{nt} on the level of r_t itself is zero. Put another way, the nominal shock ϵ_{nt} has only short-run effects on the real exchange rate. Note that there is no restriction on the effects of a real shock on the real rate or on the effects of either real or nominal shocks on the nominal exchange rate.

For Step 2, we estimate a bivariate VAR model for several lag lengths. At conventional significance levels, formal tests indicate that one lag is sufficient. However, to avoid the possibility of omitting important effects at longer lags, we performed the entire analysis using lag lengths of 1 month, 6 months, and 12 months.

The variance decomposition using the actual $\{\epsilon_{nt}\}$ and $\{\epsilon_{rt}\}$ sequences allows us to assess the relative contributions of the real and nominal shocks to forecast error variance of the real and nominal exchange rate series.

Percent of Forecast Error Variance Accounted for by Real Shocks

Horizon	Δr_t	Δe_t
1 month	100%	81.5%
3 months	99.9	79.2
12 months	98.5	78.1
36 months	98.5	78.1

As is immediately evident, real shocks explain almost all the forecast error variance of the real exchange rate at any forecast horizon. Nominal shocks accounted for approximately 20% of the forecast error variance of the nominal exchange rate. Our interpretation is that real shocks are responsible for movements in real *and* nominal exchange rates. Hence, we should expect them to display sizable comovements.

Figure 5.8 shows the impulse response functions of the real and nominal exchange rates to both types of shocks. For clarity, the results are shown for the levels of exchange rates (as opposed to first differences) measured in terms of standard deviations. For real shocks:

1. The effect of a "real" shock is to cause an immediate increase in the real and nominal exchange rate. It is interesting to note that the jump in the real value of the dollar is nearly the same as that of the nominal dollar. Moreover, these changes are all of a permanent nature. Real and nominal rates converge to their new long-run levels in about 9 months.

Figure 5.8

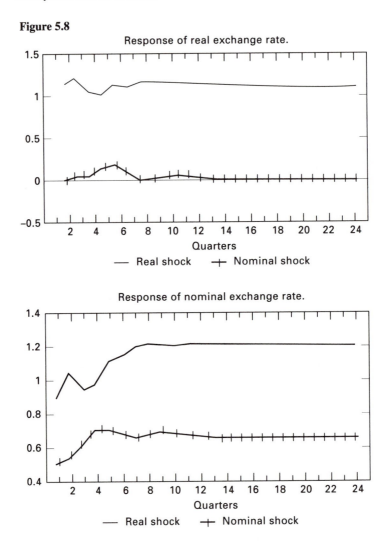

Response of real exchange rate.

— Real shock   —+— Nominal shock

Response of nominal exchange rate.

— Real shock   —+— Nominal shock

2. The movement in the real rate to its long-run level is almost immediate, whereas the nominal value of the U.S. dollar generally rises over time (i.e., the U.S. dollar price of the Canadian dollar falls). There is little evidence of exchange rate overshooting.

3. Long-run changes in the two rates are almost identical, but surprisingly, the long-run real rate jumps more rapidly than the nominal rate.

As required by our identification restriction, the effect of a nominal shock on the real exchange rate is necessarily temporary. Notice that the effects of typical "nominal" shocks of one standard deviation are all significantly smaller than the effects of typical "real" shocks. A typical nominal shock causes a rise in the nominal value of the U.S. dollar with no evidence of overshooting. Finally, the real U.S. dollar initially moves in the same direction as the U.S. nominal dollar.

It is instructive to examine the hypothetical time paths of the nominal rate that result from the decomposition. Normalize both rates such that January 1973 = 1.0. Figure 5.9 shows that if all shocks had been nominal shocks, the Canadian dollar would have declined (i.e., the U.S. dollar would have appreciated) rather steadily throughout the entire period; it appears that the rate of depreciation would have accelerated beginning in the early 1980s and continuing throughout 1989. The role of the "real" shock was generally reinforcing that of the nominal shock. It is particularly interesting to note that the real shock captures the major turning points of actual rates. The sharp depreciation beginning in 1978 and the sharp appreciation beginning around 1986 are the result of real, as opposed to nominal, factors.

Limitations of the Technique

A problem with this type of decomposition is that there are many types of shocks. As recognized by Blanchard and Quah (1989), the approach is limited by its ability to identify *at most* only as many types of distinct shocks as there are variables.

Figure 5.9   Decomposed real canadian dollars.

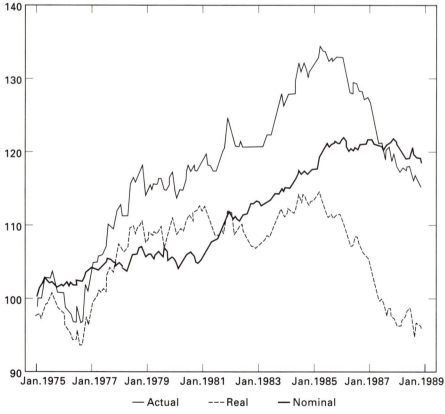

Blanchard and Quah prove several propositions that are somewhat helpful when the presence of three or more structural shocks is suspected. Suppose that there are several disturbances having permanent effects, but only one having a temporary effect on $\{y_t\}$. If the variance of one type of permanent disturbance grows "arbitrarily" small relative to the other, then the decomposition scheme approaches the correct decomposition. The second proposition they prove is that if there are multiple permanent disturbances (temporary disturbances), the correct decomposition is possible if and only if the individual distributed lag responses in the real and nominal exchange rate are sufficiently similar across equations. By "sufficiently similar," Blanchard and Quah mean that the coefficients may differ up to a scalar lag distribution. However, both propositions essentially imply that there are only two types of disturbances. For the first proposition, the third disturbance must be arbitrarily small. For the second proposition, the third disturbance must have a sufficiently similar path as one of the others. It is wise to avoid such a decomposition when the presence of three or more important disturbances is suspected.

SUMMARY AND CONCLUSIONS

Intervention analysis was used to determine the effects of installing metal detectors in airports. More generally, intervention analysis can be used to ascertain how any *deterministic* function affects an economic time series. Usually, the shape of the intervention function is clear as in the metal detector example. However, there is a wide variety of possible intervention functions. If there is an ambiguity, the shape of the intervention function can be determined using the standard Box–Jenkins criteria for model selection. The crucial assumption in intervention analysis is that the intervention function has only deterministic components.

Transfer function analysis is appropriate if the "intervention" sequence is stochastic. If $\{y_t\}$ is endogenous and $\{z_t\}$ exogenous, a transfer function can be fit using a five-step procedure discussed in Section 2. The procedure is a straightforward modification of the standard Box–Jenkins methodology. The resulting impulse response function traces out the time path of $\{z_t\}$ realizations on the $\{y_t\}$ sequence. The technique was illustrated by a study showing that terrorist attacks caused Italy's tourism revenues to decline by a total 600 million SDR.

With economic data, it is not always clear that one variable is dependent and the others are independent. In the presence of feedback, intervention and transfer function analysis are inappropriate. Instead, use a vector autoregression that treats all variables as jointly endogenous. Each variable is allowed to depend on its past realizations and the past realizations of all other variables in the system. There is no special attention paid to parsimony since the imposition of the "incredible identification restrictions" may be inconsistent with economic theory. Granger causality tests, block exogeneity, and lag-lengths tests can help select a more parsimonious model.

Ordinary least squares yield efficient estimates of the VAR coefficients. One difficulty with VAR analysis is that the underlying structural model cannot be recovered from estimated VAR. An arbitrary Choleski decomposition provides an extra equation necessary for identification of the structural model. For each variable in the system, innovation accounting techniques can be used to ascertain (1) the percentage of the forecast error variance attributable to each of the other variables and (2) the impulse responses to the various innovations. The technique was illustrated by examining the relationship between terrorism and tourism in Spain.

Another difficulty of VAR analysis is that the system of equations is overparameterized. The Bayesian approach combines a set of prior beliefs with the traditional VAR methods presented in the text. West and Harrison (1989) provides an approachable introduction to the Bayesian approach. Litterman (1981) proposed a sensible set of Bayesian priors that have become the standard in Bayesian VAR models. Todd (1984) and Leamer (1986) provide very accessible applications of the Bayesian approach.

An important development is the convergence of traditional economic theory and the VAR framework. Structural VARs impose an economic model on the contemporaneous movements of the variables. As such, they allow for the identification of the parameters of the economic model and the structural stocks. The Bernanke–Sims procedure can be used to identify (or overidentify) the structural innovations. The Blanchard and Quah methodology imposes long-run restrictions on the impulse response functions to exactly identify the structural innovations. An especially useful feature of the technique is that it provides a unique decomposition of an economic time series into its temporary and permanent components.

QUESTIONS AND EXERCISES

1. Consider three forms of the intervention variable:

   Pulse: $z_1 = 1$ and all other $z_i = 0$
   Pure jump: $z_1 = z_2 = \cdots = 1$ and all other $z_i = 0$
   Prolonged impulse: $z_1 = 1$, $z_2 = 0.75$, $z_3 = 0.5$, $z_4 = 0.25$, and all other values of $z_i = 0$

   A. Show how each of the following $\{y_t\}$ sequences responds to the three types of interventions:

      i. $y_t = 0.5y_{t-1} + z_t + \epsilon_t$
      ii. $y_t = -0.5y_{t-1} + z_t + \epsilon_t$
      iii. $y_t = 1.25y_{t-1} - 0.5y_{t-2} + z_t + \epsilon_t$
      iv. $y_t = y_{t-1} + z_t + \epsilon_t$
      v. $y_t = 0.75y_{t-1} + 0.25y_{t-2} + z_t + \epsilon_t$

   B. Notice that the intervention models in iv and v have unit roots. Show that the intervention variable $z_1 = 1$; $z_2 = -1$, and all other values of $z_i = 0$ have only a temporary effect on these two sequences.

C. Show that an intervention variable will not have a permanent effect on a unit root process if all values of z_i sum to zero.

D. Discuss the plausible models you might choose if the $\{y_t\}$ sequence is

   i. Stationary and you suspect that the intervention has a permanent effect on Ey_t.

   ii. Stationary and you suspect that the intervention has a growing and then a diminishing effect.

   iii. Nonstationary and you suspect that the intervention has a permanent effect on the level of $\{y_t\}$.

   iv. Nonstationary and you suspect that the intervention has a temporary effect on the level of the $\{y_t\}$.

   v. Nonstationary and you suspect that the intervention increases the trend growth of $\{y_t\}$.

2. Let the realized value of the $\{z_t\}$ sequence be such that $z_1 = 1$ and all other values of $z_i = 0$.

   A. Use Equation (5.11) to trace out the effects of the $\{z_t\}$ sequence on the time path of y_t.

   B. Use Equation (5.12) to trace out the effects of the $\{z_t\}$ sequence on the time paths of y_t and Δy_t.

   C. Use Equation (5.13) to trace out the effects of the $\{z_t\}$ sequence on the time paths of y_t and Δy_t.

   D. Would your answers to parts A through C change if $\{z_t\}$ was assumed to be a white-noise process and you were asked to trace out the effects of a z_t shock of the various $\{y_t\}$ sequences?

   E. Assume that $\{z_t\}$ is a white-noise process with a variance equal to unity.

      i. Use (5.11) to derive the cross-correlogram between $\{z_t\}$ and $\{y_t\}$.

      ii. Use (5.12) to derive the cross-correlogram between $\{z_t\}$ and $\{\Delta y_t\}$.

      iii. Use (5.13) to derive the cross-correlogram between $\{z_t\}$ and $\{\Delta y_t\}$.

      iv. Now suppose that z_t is the random walk process $z_t = z_{t-1} + \epsilon_{zt}$. Trace out the effects of an ϵ_{zt} shock on the Δy_t sequence.

3. Consider the transfer function model $y_t = 0.5y_{t-1} + z_t + \epsilon_t$, where z_t is the autoregressive process $z_t = 0.5z_{t-1} + \epsilon_{zt}$.

   A. Derive the CACF between the filtered $\{y_t\}$ sequence and $\{\epsilon_{zt}\}$ sequence.

   B. Now suppose $y_t = 0.5y_{t-1} + z_t + 0.5z_{t-1} + \epsilon_t$ and $z_t = 0.5z_{t-1} + \epsilon_{zt}$. Derive the cross-autocovariances between the filtered $\{y_t\}$ sequence and ϵ_{zt}. Show that the first two cross-autocovariances are proportional to the transfer function coefficients. Show that the cross-covariances decay at the rate 0.5.

4. Use (5.28) to find the appropriate second-order stochastic difference equation for y_t:

$$\begin{bmatrix} y_t \\ z_t \end{bmatrix} = \begin{bmatrix} 0.8 & 0.2 \\ 0.2 & 0.8 \end{bmatrix} \begin{bmatrix} y_{t-1} \\ z_{t-1} \end{bmatrix} + \begin{bmatrix} e_{1t} \\ e_{2t} \end{bmatrix}$$

A. Determine whether the $\{y_t\}$ sequence is stationary.

B. Discuss the shape of the impulse response function of y_t to a one-unit shock in e_{1t} and a one-unit shock in e_{2t}.

C. Suppose $e_{1t} = \epsilon_{yt} + 0.5\epsilon_{zt}$ and that $e_{2t} = \epsilon_{zy}$. Discuss the shape of the impulse response function of y_t to a one-unit shock in ϵ_{yt}. Repeat for a one-unit shock in ϵ_{zt}.

D. Suppose $e_{1t} = \epsilon_{yt}$ and that $e_{2t} = 0.5\epsilon_{yt} + \epsilon_{zt}$. Discuss the shape of the impulse response function of y_t to a one unit shock in ϵ_{yt}. Repeat for a one-unit shock in ϵ_{zt}.

E. Use your answers to C and D to explain why the ordering in a Choleski decomposition is important.

F. Using the notation in (5.21), find A_1^2 and A_1^3. Does A_1^n appear to approach zero (i.e., the null matrix)?

5. Using the notation of (5.21) suppose $a_{10} = 0$, $a_{20} = 0$, $a_{11} = 0.8$, $a_{12} = 0.2$, $a_{21} = 0.4$, and $a_{22} = 0.1$.

A. Find the appropriate second-order stochastic difference equation for y_t. Determine whether the $\{y_t\}$ sequence is stationary.

B. Answer parts B through F of Question 4 using these new values of a_{ij}.

C. How would the solution for y_t change if $a_{10} = 0.2$?

6. Suppose the residuals of a VAR are such that $\text{var}(e_1) = 0.75$, $\text{var}(e_2) = 0.5$, and $\text{cov}(e_{1t}, e_{2t}) = 0.25$.

A. Using (5.53) through (5.56) as guides, show that it is not possible to identify the structural VAR.

B. Using Choleski decomposition such that $b_{12} = 0$, find the identified values of b_{21}, $\text{var}(\epsilon_1)$, and $\text{var}(\epsilon_2)$.

C. Using Choleski decomposition such that $b_{21} = 0$, find the identified values of b_{12}, $\text{var}(\epsilon_1)$, and $\text{var}(\epsilon_2)$.

D. Using a Sims–Bernanke decomposition such that $b_{12} = 0.5$, find the identified values of b_{21}, $\text{var}(\epsilon_1)$, and $\text{Var}(\epsilon_2)$.

E. Using a Sims–Bernanke decomposition such that $b_{21} = 0.5$, find the identified values of b_{12}, $var(\epsilon_1)$, and $var(\epsilon_2)$.

F. Suppose that the first three values of e_{1t} are estimated to be 1, 0, and -1 and the first three values of e_{2t} are estimated to be -1, 0, and 1. Find the first three values of ϵ_{1t} and ϵ_{2t} using each of the decompositions in parts B through E.

7. This set of exercises uses data from the file entitled US.WK1. The first column contains the U.S. money supply (as measured by M1) and fifth column the U.S. GDP Deflator (1985 = 100) for the period 1960:Q1 through 1991:Q4. These two variables are labeled M1 and GDPDEF on the data disk. In Questions 7 through 10, your task is to uncover the relationship between the inflation rate and rate of growth of the money supply.

Economic theory suggests that many variables influence inflation and money growth. Some of these variables are included in the file US.WK1. Respectively, columns 2, 3, and 4 hold the Treasury bill rate (denoted by TBILL), 3-year government bond yield (denoted by R3), and 10-year government bond yield (denoted by R10). Column 6 contains real GDP in 1985 prices (denoted by GDP85) and column 7 nominal government purchases (denoted by GOVT). To keep the issues as simple as possible, consider only a bivariate VAR between money and inflation.

A. Construct the rate of growth of the money supply (GM1) and inflation rate (INF) as the following logarithmic changes:

$$GM1_t = \log(M1_t) - \log(M1_{t-1})$$
$$INF_t = \log(GDPDEF_t) - \log(GDPDEF_{t-1})$$

You should find that the constructed variables have the following properties:

Series	Observations	Mean	Standard Error	Minimum	Maximum
INF	127	0.0119070404	0.0066458391	−0.0039847906	0.0296770174
GM1	127	0.0149101522	0.0295263232	−0.0471790362	0.0781839833

B. The bivariate VAR might have the form given by (5.44). One problem with this specification is that $GM1_t$ has a strong seasonal component. In Exercise 5 of Chapter 2, you were asked to model the {M1} series using univariate methods. Recall that seasonal differencing was necessary. In VAR analysis, it is common practice to include seasonal dummy variables to capture the seasonality. Construct the dummy variables D_1, D_2, and D_3

where $D_i = 1$ in the ith quarter of each year and zero otherwise.

Interpret the effects of the seasonal dummies in the following bivariate VAR:

$$GM1_t = A_{10} + A_{10}(1)D_1 + A_{10}(2)D_2 + A_{10}(3)D_3 + A_{11}(L)GM1_{t-1}$$
$$+ A_{12}(L)INF_{t-1} + e_{1t}$$
$$INF_t = A_{20} + A_{20}(1)D_1 + A_{20}(2)D_2 + A_{20}(3)D_3 + A_{21}(L)GM1_{t-1}$$
$$+ A_{22}(L)INF_{t-1} + e_{2t}$$

C. Consider the bivariate VAR above using 12 lags of each variable and save the residuals.

   i. Explain why the estimation cannot begin earlier than 1963:Q2.

  ii. Estimate the model (with the seasonal dummies) using 12 lags of each variable and save the residuals. You should find that $\log(|\Sigma_{12}|) = -20.56126$

 iii. Estimate the same model *over the same sample period* now using only using eight lags of each variable. You should find $\log(|\Sigma_8|) = -20.42120$

 iv. Use (5.45) to construct the likelihood ratio test for the null hypothesis of eight lags. How many restrictions are there in the system? How many regressors are there in each of the unrestricted equations? If you answer correctly, you should find that the calculated value χ^2 with 16 degrees of freedom is 12.184668 with a significance level 0.73117262. Hence, it is not possible to reject the null of eight lags.

D. Repeat the procedure in part C in order to show that it is possible to further restrict the system to four lags of each variable. Now estimate models with eight and four lags over the sample period 1962:Q2 to 1991:Q4. (Note that the number of regressors in the unrestricted model is now 12.) You should find

$$\log(|\Sigma_8|) = -20.42791e$$
$$\log(|\Sigma_4|) = -20.30502$$
$$\chi^2_{16} = 12.165234 \text{ with significance level } 0.73252907$$

E. Show that it is inappropriate to restrict the system such that there is only one lag of each variable. Estimating the two models over the 1961:Q2 to 1991:Q4 period, you should find

$$\log(|\Sigma_4|) = -20.32279$$
$$\log(|\Sigma_1|) = -19.89689$$
$$\chi^2_{12} = 47.274603 \text{ with significance level } 0.00000418$$

8. Question 7 suggested using a bivariate VAR with four lags. Explain how it is possible to modify the procedure to in order to test for the presence of the seasonal dummy variables. Show that you can reject the restriction:

$$A_{10}(1)D_1 = A_{10}(2)D_2 = A_{10}(3)D_3 = A_{20}(1)D_1 = A_{20}(2)D_2 = A30(3)D_3 = 0$$

   i. How does this procedure differ from the following test?

$$A_{20}(1)D_1 = A_{20}(2)D_2 = A_{20}(3)D_3 = 0$$

9. Keep the seasonal dummies in both equations and estimate the bivariate VAR with four lags over the 1961:Q2 to 1991:Q4 period.

   A. How would you test to determine whether INF Granger causes GM1?

   B. Perform each of the indicated causality tests.

   i.   Verify that money growth Granger causes itself. The F-test for the restriction that all the coefficients of $A_{11}(L) = 0$ yields a value of 3.3602 with a significance level of 0.0122948.

   ii. Verify that inflation Granger causes money growth. The F-test for the restriction all $A_{12}(L) = 0$ yields a value of 2.1472 with a significance level of 0.0796779.

   iii. Verify that the F-test for the restriction all coefficients of $A_{21}(L) = 0$ yields a value of 0.7670 with a significance level of 0.5489179.

   iv. Verify that the F-test for the restriction all coefficients of $A_{22}(L) = 0$ yields a value of 56.1908 with a significance level of 0.0000000.

   C. The Granger causality test indicates that inflation Granger causes money growth and Granger causes itself. Money growth, however, only Granger causes itself. Explain why it is *not* appropriate to conclude that money growth has no affect on inflation! What if you knew that the correlation coefficient between innovations in money growth (i.e., e_{1t}) and inflation (i.e., e_{2t}) was identically equal to zero? Why might these results change in the presence of a third variable (such as GDP85)?

10. Consider a Choleski decomposition such that innovations in inflation (denoted by ϵ_{it}) do not have a contemporaneous effect on money growth, but money growth innovations (denoted by ϵ_{mt}) have a contemporaneous effect on inflation. Represent the relationship between the regression equation errors and pure money growth and inflation innovations in terms of (5.39) and (5.40).

   A. If you are using a software package capable of calculating variance decompositions, verify:

**Percent of forecast error variance
due to money shock**

Steps ahead	GM1	INF
1	100.00	0.1794
4	94.58	0.4632
12	93.24	2.0339
24	92.85	2.3442

Interpret the figures in the table.

B. Reverse the ordering of the Choleski decomposition, so that money growth innovations do not have a contemporaneous effect on inflation. Represent the relationship between the regression equation errors and pure money growth and inflation innovations in terms of (5.39) and (5.40).

C. Verify:

**Percent of forecast error variance
due to money shock**

Steps ahead	GM1	INF
1	99.82	0.0000
4	94.22	1.7180
12	93.15	2.3341
24	92.78	3.1891

Explain why this alternative ordering is nearly the same as that found in part A. What is the correlation coefficient between the regression error terms?

D. What are the major weaknesses of this bivariate VAR study? Comment on the following issues:

i.   The treatment of seasonality.

ii. Other variables that may affect the relationship between money growth and inflation. You may want to expand the VAR by including other variables in the file US.WK1.

iii. Changes in the conduct of monetary policy.

11. In the next set of questions, you are asked to analyze the relationship between short- and long-term interest rates. The data file US.WK1 contains some of the relevant variables for the period 1960:Q1 through 1991:Q4. Respectively, columns 2, 3, and 4 hold the Treasury bill rate (denoted by TBILL), 3-year government bond yield (denoted by R3), and 10-year government bond yield

(denoted by R10). Column 6 contains the U.S. GDP Deflator (denoted by GDPDEF, where 1985=100) and column 7 nominal government purchases (denoted by GOVT).

A. Certain economic theories suggest a relationship between real interest rates and real government spending. It seems sensible to analyze a trivariate VAR using TBILL, R10, and a measure of real government purchases of goods and services. Toward this end, construct the variable RGOVT as the ratio GOVT/GDPDEF. You should find

Series	Observa-tions	Mean	Standard Error	Minimum	Maximum
RGOVT	128	6255.9	1438.69	3511.256	8868.6
TBILL	128	6.3959	2.79151059	2.32000000	15.0900
R10	128	7.6299	2.76273472	3.79000000	14.8500

B. Pretest the variables for the presence of unit roots using Dickey–Fuller tests. Using four lags and a constant, you should find the t-statistics on the *lagged level* of each variable to be

$$RGOVT = -0.97872$$
$$TBILL = -2.21122$$
$$R10 = -1.90275$$

C. Estimate the trivariate VAR in levels including three seasonal dummy variables (see part B of Question 7 concerning the creation of the dummy variables). Construct a likelihood ratio test to determine whether it is possible to restrict the number of lags from 12 to eight. You should find:

$$\log(|\Sigma_{12}|) = 3.867667, \qquad \log(|\Sigma_8|) = 4.700780$$
$$\chi^2 \text{ (36 degrees of freedom)} = 63.316597 \text{ with significance level } 0.00327933$$

Hence, reject the hypothesis that eight lags are sufficient to capture the dynamic relationships in the data. (*Note:* For this test to be meaningful, the residuals of the regression equations used to construct Σ_{12} should be stationary.)

D. Using the model with 12 lags:

   i. Find the correlations between the innovations. Since the correlation between the innovations in TBILL and R10 is 0.808, explain why the ordering in a Choleski decomposition is likely to be important.

   ii. Show that each variable Granger causes the other variables at conventional significance levels.

E. Consider the variance decompositions using a Choleski decomposition such that RGOVT innovations contemporaneously affect themselves variables,

TBILL innovations contemporaneously affect themselves and R10, and R10 innovations contemporaneously affect only R10. Write down this structure in terms of a general form of (5.39) and (5.40). Using this ordering, verify that the proportions of 24-step ahead forecast error variance of RGOVT, TBILL, and R10 due to RGOVT, TBILL, and R10 innovations are

RGOVT = 89.07528, 9.21137, and 1.71335%, respectively
TBILL = 13.77804, 84.67659, and 1.54537%, respectively
R10 = 17.37698, 78.13322, and 4.48980%, respectively

Thus, TBILL innovations "explain" 78.13322% of the forecast error variance in R10, and R10 innovations explain only 1.54537% of the forecast error variance in TBILL.

F. Use the reverse ordering such that R10 innovations affect all variables contemporaneously, TBILL innovations contemporaneously affect TBILL and RGOVT, and RGOVT innovations contemporaneously affect only RGOVT. Compare your results to those in part E.

12. The results from Question 11B suggest that all variables are nonstationary. Now estimate the same trivariate VAR (including seasonals), but use first differences instead of levels.

A. Verify the following:

i. The lag-length tests for eight versus 12 lags yields

$\log(|\Sigma_{12}|) = 4.108633,$ $\log(|\Sigma_8|) = 4.700780$
χ^2 (36 degrees of freedom) = 58.544793 with significance level 0.01017107

ii. If we use 12 lags, the correlation between TBILL and R10 innovations is 0.7776.

iii. The change in RGOVT$_t$ (i.e., ΔRGOVT$_t$) does not Granger cause itself or ΔR10$_t$, but does Grange cause ΔTBILL$_t$ at the 0.016 significance level.

B. Use the same ordering as in Question 11E. Verify that the proportions of 24-step ahead forecast error variance of ΔRGOVT$_t$, ΔTBILL$_t$, and ΔR10$_t$ due to ΔRGOVT$_t$, ΔTBILL$_t$, and ΔR10$_t$ innovations are

ΔRGOVT = 71.54324, 18.22792, and 10.22885%, respectively
ΔTBILL = 19.02489, 70.99188, and 9.98323%, respectively
ΔR10 = 15.79140, 50.05796, and 34.15065%, respectively

C. Perform a block exogenity test to determine whether RGOVT helps to "explain" the movements in interest rates.

   D. Overall, compare the results of using the variables in levels to those using the variables in first differences.

ENDNOTES

1. In terms of the notation of the previous chapter, z_t is equivalent to the level dummy variable D_L.
2. In other words, if $c_0 \neq 0$, predicting y_{t+1} necessitates predicting the value of z_{t+1}.
3. In the identification process, we are primarily interested in the shape, not the height, of the cross-correlation function. It is useful to standardize the covariance by dividing through by σ_z^2; the shape of the correlogram is proportional to this standardized covariance. Hence, if $\sigma_y^2 = 1$, the two are equivalent. The benefit of this procedure is that we can obtain the CACF from the transfer function.
4. In such circumstances, Box and Jenkins (1976) recommend differencing y_t and/or z_t, so that the resulting series are both stationary. The modern view cautions against this approach; as shown in the next chapter, a linear combination of nonstationary variables may be stationary. In such circumstances, the Box–Jenkins recommendation leads to overdifferencing. For the time being, it is assumed that both $\{y_t\}$ and $\{z_t\}$ are stationary processes.
5. We were able to obtain quarterly data from 1970:I to 1988:IV for Austria, Canada, Denmark, Finland, France, West Germany, Greece, Italy, the Netherlands, Norway, the U. K. and the United States. The International Monetary Fund's *Balance of Payments Statistics* reports all data in special drawing rights (SDR). Our dependent variable is the logarithm of nation's revenues divided by the sum of the revenues for all 12 countries.
6. Tourism is highly seasonal; we tried several alternative deseasonalization techniques. The results reported here were obtained using seasonal dummy variables. Hence, y_t represents the deseasonalized logarithmic share of tourism receipts. The published paper reports results using quarterly differencing. When either type of deseasonalization was used, the final results were similar.
7. Expectations of the future can also be included in this framework. If the temperature $\{y_t\}$ is an autoregressive process, the expected value of next period's temperature (i.e., y_{t+1}) will depend on the current and past values. In (5.20), the presence of the terms y_t and y_{t-1} can represent how predictions regarding next period's temperature affect the current thermostat setting.
8. It is easily verified that this representation implies that $\rho_{12} = 0.8$. By definition, the correlation coefficient ρ_{12} is defined to be $\sigma_{12}/(\sigma_1\sigma_2)$ and the covariance is $Ee_{1t}e_{2t} = \sigma_{12}$. If we use the numbers in the example, $Ee_{1t}e_{2t} = E[\epsilon_{zt}(\epsilon_{yt} + 0.8\epsilon_{zt})] = 0.8\sigma_z^2$. Since the decomposition equates var(e_{2t}) with σ_z^2, it follows that $\rho_{12} = 0.8$ if $\sigma_1^2 = \sigma_2$.
9. Other types of identification restrictions are included in Sections 10 through 13.
10. In the example under consideration, the symmetry restriction on the coefficients means that var(ϵ_{1t}) is equal to var(ϵ_{2t}). This result does not generalize; it holds in the example because of the assumed equality var$(e_{1t}) = $ var(e_{2t}).
11. The value $|\Sigma_R| - |\Sigma|$ is asymptotically distributed as a χ^2 distribution with R degrees of freedom.
12. Since a key assumption of the technique is that $E(\epsilon_{1t}\epsilon_{2t}) = 0$, you might wonder how it is possible to assume that aggregate demand and supply shocks are independent. After all, if the stabilization authorities follow a feedback rule, aggregate demand will change in

response to aggregate supply shocks. The key to understanding this apparent contradiction is that ϵ_{1t} is intended to be the orthogonalized portion of the demand shock, that is, the portion of the demand shock that does not change in response to aggregate supply.

13. For example, $A_{11}(L) = a_{11}(0) + a_{11}(1)L + a_{11}(2)L^2 + \cdots$.

14. The VAR residuals also have a constant variance/covariance matrix. Hence, the time subscripts can be dropped.

15. Since two of the restrictions contain squared terms, there will be a positive value and an equal but opposite negative value for some of the coefficients. The set of coefficients to use is simply a matter of interpretation. In Blanchard and Quah's example, if $c_{11}(0)$ is positive, positive demand shocks have a positive effect of output, and if $c_{11}(0)$ is negative, the positive shock has a negative effect on output.

16. In doing so, it will be necessary to treat all $\epsilon_{2t-i} = 0$ for $t - i < 1$.

17. Here, Canada is treated as the home country, so that e_t is the Canadian dollar price of U.S. dollars and p_t^* refers to the U.S. price level.

Chapter 6

COINTEGRATION AND ERROR-CORRECTION MODELS

This chapter explores an exciting new development in econometrics: the estimation of a structural equation or VAR containing nonstationary variables. In univariate models, we have seen that a stochastic trend can be removed by differencing. The resulting stationary series can be estimated using univariate Box–Jenkins techniques. At one time, the conventional wisdom was to generalize this idea and difference all nonstationary variables used in a regression analysis. However, it is now recognized that the appropriate way to treat nonstationary variables is not so straightforward in a multivariate context. It is quite possible for there to be a linear combination of integrated variables that is stationary; such variables are said to be **cointegrated.** Many economic models entail such cointegrating relationships. The aims of this chapter are to:

1. Introduce the basic concept of cointegration and show that it applies in a variety of economic models. Any equilibrium relationship among a set of nonstationary variables implies that their stochastic trends must be linked. After all, the equilibrium relationship means that the variables cannot move independently of each other. This linkage among the stochastic trends necessitates that the variables be cointegrated.

2. Consider the dynamic paths of cointegrated variables. Since the trends of cointegrated variables are linked, the dynamic paths of such variables must bear some relation to the current deviation from the equilibrium relationship. This connection between the change in a variable and the deviation from equilibrium is examined in detail. It is shown that the dynamics of a cointegrated system are such that the conventional wisdom was incorrect. After all, if the linear relationship is already stationary, differencing the relationship entails a misspecification error.

3. Study the alternative ways to test for cointegration. The econometric methods underlying the test procedures stem from the theory of simultaneous difference equations. The theory is explained and used to develop the two most popular

cointegration tests. The proper way to estimate a system of cointegrated variables is examined. Several illustrations of each methodology are provided. Moreover, the two methods are compared by applying each to the same data set.

1. LINEAR COMBINATIONS OF INTEGRATED VARIABLES

Since money demand studies stimulated much of the cointegration literature, we begin by considering a simple model of money demand. Theory suggests that individuals want to hold a real quantity of money balances, so that the demand for nominal money holdings should be proportional to the price level. Moreover, as real income and the associated number of transactions increase, individuals will want to hold increased money balances. Finally, since the interest rate is the opportunity cost of holding money, money demand should be negatively related to the interest rate. In logarithms, an econometric specification for such an equation can be written as

$$m_t = \beta_0 + \beta_1 p_t + \beta_2 y_t + \beta_3 r_t + e_t \tag{6.1}$$

where m_t = long-run money demand
   p_t = price level
   y_t = real income
   r_t = interest rate
   e_t = *stationary* disturbance term
   β_i = parameters to be estimated

and all variables but the interest rate are expressed in logarithms.

The hypothesis that the money market clears allows the researcher to collect time-series data of the money supply (= money demand if the money market always clears), the price level, real income (possibly measured using real GNP), and an appropriate short-term interest rate. The behavioral assumptions require that $\beta_1 = 1$, $\beta_2 > 0$, and $\beta_3 < 0$; a researcher conducting such a study would certainly want to test these parameter restrictions. Be aware that the properties of the unexplained portion of the demand for money (i.e., the $\{e_t\}$ sequence) are an integral part of the theory. If the theory is to make any sense at all, any deviation in the demand for money must necessarily be temporary in nature. Clearly, if e_t has a stochastic trend, the errors in the model will be cumulative so that deviations from money market equilibrium will not be eliminated. Hence, a key assumption of the theory is that the $\{e_t\}$ sequence is stationary.

The problem confronting the researcher is that real GNP, the money supply, price level, and interest rate can all be characterized as nonstationary $I(1)$ variables. As such, each variable can meander without any tendency to return to a long-run level. However, the theory expressed in (6.1) asserts that there exists a linear combination of these nonstationary variables that is stationary! Solving for the error term, we can rewrite (6.1) as

$$e_t = m_t - \beta_0 - \beta_1 p_t - \beta_2 y_t - \beta_3 r_t \qquad (6.2)$$

Since $\{e_t\}$ must be stationary, it follows that the linear combination of integrated variables given by the right-hand side of (6.2) must also be stationary. Thus, the theory necessitates that the time paths of the four nonstationary variables $\{m_t\}$, $\{p_t\}$, $\{y_t\}$, and $\{r_t\}$ be linked. This example illustrates the crucial insight that has dominated much of the macroeconometric literature in recent years: *Equilibrium theories involving nonstationary variables require the existence of a combination of the variables that is stationary.*

The money demand function is just one example of a stationary combination of nonstationary variables. Within any equilibrium framework, the deviations from equilibrium must be temporary. Other important economic examples involving stationary combinations of nonstationary variables include:

1. *Consumption Function Theory.* A simple version of the permanent income hypothesis maintains that total consumption (c_t) is the sum of permanent consumption (c_t^p) and transitory consumption (c_t^t). Since permanent consumption is proportional to permanent income (y_t^p), we can let β be the constant of proportionality and write $c_t = \beta y_t^p + c_t^t$. Transitory consumption is necessarily a stationary variable, and consumption and permanent income are reasonably characterized as $I(1)$ variables. As such, the permanent income hypothesis requires that the linear combination of two $I(1)$ variables given by $c_t - \beta y_t^p$ be stationary.

2. *Unbiased Forward Market Hypothesis.* One form of the efficient market hypothesis asserts that the forward (or futures) price of an asset should equal the expected value of that asset's spot price in the future. If you recall the discussion of Corbae and Ouliaris (1986) in Chapter 4, you will remember that foreign exchange market efficiency requires the one-period forward exchange rate to equal the expectation of the spot rate in the next period. If we let f_t denote the log of the one-period price of forward exchange in t, and s_t the log of the spot price of foreign exchange in t, the theory asserts that $E_t s_{t+1} = f_t$. If this relationship fails, speculators can expect to make a pure profit on their trades in the foreign exchange market. If the agent's expectations are rational, the forecast error for the spot rate in $t + 1$ will have a conditional mean equal to zero, so that $s_{t+1} - E_t s_{t+1} = \epsilon_{t+1}$, where $E_t \epsilon_{t+1} = 0$. Combining the two equations yields $s_{t+1} = f_t + \epsilon_{t+1}$. Since $\{s_t\}$ and $\{f_t\}$ are $I(1)$ variables, the **unbiased forward market hypothesis** necessitates that there be a linear combination of nonstationary spot and forward exchange rates that is stationary.

3. *Commodity Market Arbitrage and Purchasing-Power Parity.* Theories of spatial competition suggest that in the short run, prices of similar products in varied markets might differ. However, arbiters will prevent the various prices from moving too far apart even if the prices are nonstationary. Similarly, the prices of Apple computers and PCs have exhibited sustained declines. Economic theory

suggests that these simultaneous declines are related to each other since prices of these differentiated products cannot continually widen.

Also, as we saw in Chapter 4, purchasing-power parity places restrictions on the movements on nonstationary price levels and exchange rates. If e_t denotes the log of the price of foreign exchange and p_t and p_t^*, denote respectively, the logs of the domestic and foreign price levels, long-run PPP requires that the linear combination $e_t + p_t^* - p_t$ be stationary.

All these examples illustrate the concept of **cointegration** as introduced by Engle and Granger (1987). Their formal analysis begins by considering a set of economic variables in long-run equilibrium when

$$\beta_1 x_{1t} + \beta_2 x_{2t} + \cdots + \beta_n x_{nt} = 0$$

If we let β and x_t denote the vectors $(\beta_1, \beta_2, \ldots, \beta_n)$ and $(x_{1t}, x_{2t}, \ldots, x_{nt})'$, the system is in long-run equilibrium when $\beta x_t = 0$. The deviation from long-run equilibrium—called the **equilibrium error**—is e_t, so that

$$e_t = \beta x_t$$

If the equilibrium is meaningful, it must be the case that the equilibrium error process is stationary. Engle and Granger (1987) provide the following definition of cointegration.

The components of the vector $x_t = (x_{1t}, x_{2t}, \ldots, x_{nt})'$ are said to be *cointegrated of order d, b,* denoted by $x_t \sim CI(d, b)$ if

1. All components of x_t are integrated of order d.
2. There exists a vector $\beta = (\beta_1, \beta_2, \ldots, \beta_n)$ such that linear combination $\beta x_t = \beta_1 x_{1t} + \beta_2 x_{2t} + \cdots + \beta_n x_{nt}$ is integrated of order $(d - b)$, where $b > 0$.

The vector β is called the **cointegrating vector.**[1]

In terms of equation (6.1), if the money supply, price level, real income, and interest rate are all $I(1)$ and the linear combination $m_t - \beta_0 - \beta_1 p_t - \beta_2 y_t - \beta_3 r_t = e_t$ is stationary, then the variables are cointegrated of order $(1, 1)$. The vector x_t is $(m_t, 1, p_t, y_t, r_t)'$ and the cointegrating vector β is $(1, -\beta_0, -\beta_1, -\beta_2, -\beta_3)$. The deviation from long-run money market equilibrium is e_t; since $\{e_t\}$ is stationary, this deviation is temporary in nature.

There are four very important points to note about the definition:

1. Cointegration refers to a *linear* combination of nonstationary variables. Theoretically, it is quite possible that nonlinear long-run relationships exist among a set of integrated variables. However, the current state of econometric practice is not able to test for nonlinear cointegrating relationships. Also note that the cointegrating vector is not unique. If $(\beta_1, \beta_2, \ldots, \beta_n)$ is a cointegrating vector, then for any nonzero value of λ, $(\lambda\beta_1, \lambda\beta_2, \ldots, \lambda\beta_n)$ is also a cointegrating vector. Typically, one of the variables is used to *normalize* the cointegrating vector by fixing its coefficient at unity. To normalize the cointegrating vector with respect to x_{1t}, simply select $\lambda = 1/\beta_1$.

2. All variables must be integrated of the same order.[2] Of course, this does not imply that all similarly integrated variables are cointegrated; usually, a set of $I(d)$ variables is *not* cointegrated. Such a lack of cointegration implies no long-run equilibrium among the variables, so that they can wander arbitrarily far from each other. If the variables are integrated of different orders, they cannot be cointegrated. Suppose x_{1t} is $I(d_1)$ and x_{2t} is $I(d_2)$ where $d_2 > d_1$. Question 6 at the end of this chapter asks you to prove that any linear combination of x_{1t} and x_{2t} is $I(d_2)$.

In a sense, the use of the term "equilibrium" is unfortunate since economic theorists and econometricians use the term in different ways. Economic theorists usually employ the term to refer to an equality between desired and actual transactions. The econometric use of the term makes reference to any long-run relationship among nonstationary variables. Cointegration does not require that the long-run (i.e., equilibrium) relationship be generated by market forces or the behavioral rules of individuals. In Engle and Granger's use of the term, the equilibrium relationship may be causal, behavioral, or simply a reduced-form relationship among similarly trending variables.

3. If x_t has n components, there may be as many as $n - 1$ linearly independent cointegrating vectors. Clearly, if x_t contains only two variables, there can be *at most* one independent cointegrating vector. The number of cointegrating vectors is called the **cointegrating rank** of x_t. For example, suppose that the monetary authorities followed a feedback rule such that they decreased the money supply when nominal GNP was high and increased the nominal money supply when nominal GNP was low. This feedback rule might be represented by

$$m_t = \gamma_0 - \gamma_1(y_t + p_t) + e_{1t}$$
$$= \gamma_0 - \gamma_1 y_t - \gamma_1 p_t + e_{1t} \tag{6.3}$$

where $\{e_{1t}\}$ = a stationary error in the money supply feedback rule

Given the money demand function in (6.1), there are two cointegrating vectors for the money supply, price level, real income, and interest rate. Let β be the (5×2) matrix:

$$\beta = \begin{bmatrix} 1 & -\beta_0 & -\beta_1 & -\beta_2 & -\beta_3 \\ 1 & -\gamma_0 & \gamma_1 & \gamma_1 & 0 \end{bmatrix}$$

The two linear combinations given by βx_t are stationary. As such, the cointegrating rank of x_t is 2. As a practical matter, if multiple cointegrating vectors are found, it may not be possible to identify the behavioral relationships from what may be reduced-form relationships.

4. Most of the cointegration literature focuses on the case in which each variable contains a single unit root. The reason is that traditional regression or time-series analysis applies when variables are $I(0)$ and few economic variables are integrated of an order higher than unity.[3] When it is unambiguous, many authors use the term "cointegration" to refer to the case in which variables are $CI(1, 1)$. The

remainder of the text follows this convention. Of course, many other possibilities arise. For example, a set of $I(2)$ variables may be cointegrated of order $CI(2, 1)$, so that there exists a linear combination that is $I(1)$.

Worksheet 6.1 illustrates some of the important properties of cointegration relationships. In Case 1, both the $\{y_t\}$ and $\{z_t\}$ sequences were constructed so as to be random walk plus noise processes. Although the 20 realizations shown generally decline, extending the sample would eliminate this tendency. In any event, neither series shows any tendency to return to a long-run level, and formal Dickey–Fuller tests are not able to reject the null hypothesis of a unit root in either series. Although each series is nonstationary, you can see that they do move together. In fact, the difference between the series $(y_t - z_t)$—shown in the second graph—is stationary; the "equilibrium error" term $e_t = (y_t - z_t)$ has a zero mean and constant variance.

WORKSHEET 6.1   Illustrating Cointegrated Systems

CASE 1   The $\{y_t\}$ and $\{z_t\}$ sequences are both random walk plus noise processes. Although each is nonstationary, the two sequences have the same stochastic trend; hence, they are cointegrated such that the linear combination $(y_t - z_t)$ is stationary. The equilibrium error term is an $I(0)$ process.

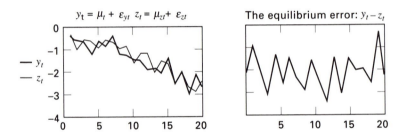

CASE 2   All three sequences are random walk plus noise processes. As constructed, no two are cointegrated. However, the linear combination $(y_t + z_t - w_t)$ is stationary; hence, the three are cointegrated. The equilibrium error is an $I(0)$ process.

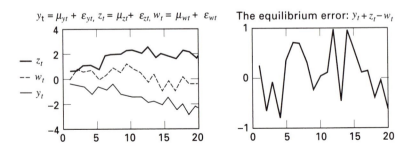

Case 2 illustrates cointegration among three random walk plus noise processes. As in Case 1, no series exhibits a tendency to return to a long-run level, and formal Dickey–Fuller tests are not able to reject the null hypothesis of a unit root in any of the three. In contrast to the previous case, no two of the series appear to be cointegrated; each series seems to "meander" away from the other two. However, as shown in the second graph, there exists a stationary linear combination of the three: $e_t = y_t + z_t - w_t$. Thus, it follows that the dynamic behavior of *at least* one variable must be restricted by the values of the other variables in the system.

Figure 6.1 displays the information of Case 1 in a scatter plot of $\{y_t\}$ against the associated value of $\{z_t\}$; each of the 20 points represents the ordered pairs (y_1, z_1), $(y_2, z_2), \ldots, (y_{20}, z_{20})$. Comparing Worksheet 6.1 and Figure 6.1, you can see that low values in the $\{y_t\}$ sequence are associated with low values in the $\{z_t\}$ sequence and values near zero in one series are associated with values near zero in the other. Since both series move together over time, there is a positive relationship between the two. The least-squares line in the scatter plot reveals this strong positive association. In fact, this line is the "long-run" equilibrium relationship between the series, and the deviations from the line are the stationary deviations from long-run equilibrium.

For comparison purposes, graph (a) in Worksheet 6.2 shows 100 realizations of two random walk plus noise processes that are not cointegrated. Each seems to me-

Figure 6.1 Scatter plot of cointegrated variables.

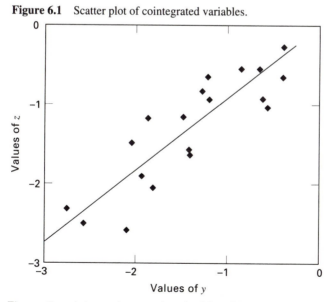

The scatter plot was drawn using the $\{y\}$ and $\{z\}$ sequences from Case 1 of Worksheet 6.1. Since both series decline over time, there appears to be a positive relationship between the two. The equilibrium regression line is shown.

ander without any tendency to approach the other. The scatter plot shown in graph (b) confirms the impression of no long-run relationship between the variables. The deviations from the straight line showing the regression of z_t on y_t are substantial. Plotting the regression residuals against time [see graph (c)] suggests that the regression residuals are not stationary.

WORKSHEET 6.2   Nonintegrated Variables

The $\{y_t\}$ and $\{z_t\}$ sequences are constructed to independent random walk plus noise processes. There is *no* cointegrating relationship between the two variables. As shown in (a), both seem to meander without any tendency to come together. Graph (b) shows the scatter plot of the two sequences and the regression line $z_t = \beta_0 + \beta_1 y_t$. However, this regression line is spurious. As shown in graph (c), the regression residuals are nonstationary.

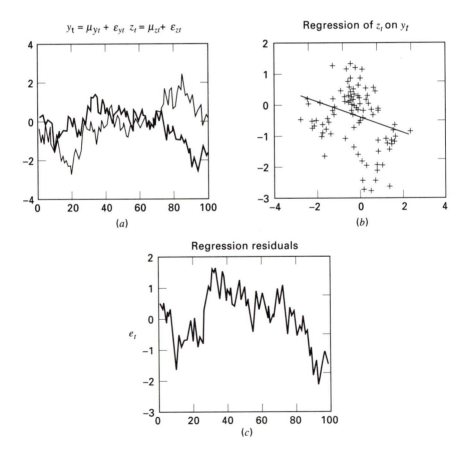

2. COINTEGRATION AND COMMON TRENDS

Stock and Watson's (1988) observation that cointegrated variables share common stochastic trends provides a very useful way to understand cointegration relationships.[4] For ease of exposition, return to the case in which the vector x_t contains only two variables, so that $x_t = (y_t, z_t)'$. Ignoring cyclical and seasonal terms, we can decompose each variable into a random walk plus an irregular (but not necessarily white-noise) component.[5] Hence, we can write

$$y_t = \mu_{yt} + \epsilon_{yt} \tag{6.4}$$
$$z_t = \mu_{zt} + \epsilon_{zt} \tag{6.5}$$

where μ_{it} = is a random walk process representing the trend in variable i in period t.
ϵ_{it} = the stationary (irregular) component of variable i in period t.

If $\{y_t\}$ and $\{z_t\}$ are cointegrated of order $(1, 1)$, there must be nonzero values of β_1 and β_2 for which the linear combination $\beta_1 y_t + \beta_2 z_t$ is stationary; that is,

$$\begin{aligned} \beta_1 y_t + \beta_2 z_t &= \beta_1(\mu_{yt} + \epsilon_{yt}) + \beta_2(\mu_{zt} + \epsilon_{zt}) \\ &= (\beta_1\mu_{yt} + \beta_2\mu_{zt}) + (\beta_1\epsilon_{yt} + \beta_2\epsilon_{zt}) \end{aligned} \tag{6.6}$$

For $\beta_1 y_t + \beta_2 z_t$ to be stationary, the term $(\beta_1\mu_{yt} + \beta_2\mu_{zt})$ must vanish. After all, if either of the two trends appears in (6.6), the linear combination $\beta_1 y_t + \beta_2 z_t$ will also have a trend. Since the second term in parenthesis is stationary, the necessary and sufficient condition for $\{y_t\}$ and $\{z_t\}$ to be $CI(1, 1)$ is

$$\beta_1\mu_{yt} + \beta_2\mu_{zt} = 0 \tag{6.7}$$

Clearly, μ_{yt} and μ_{zt} are variables whose realized values will be continually changing over time. Since we preclude both β_1 and β_2 from being equal to zero, it follows that (6.7) holds for all t if and only if

$$\mu_{yt} = -\beta_2\mu_{zt}/\beta_1$$

For nonzero values of β_1 and β_2, the only way to ensure equality is for the stochastic trends to be *identical* up to a scalar. Thus, up to the scalar $-\beta_2/\beta_1$, *two I(1) stochastic processes $\{y_t\}$ and $\{z_t\}$ must have the same stochastic trend if they are cointegrated of order (1, 1).*

Return your attention to Worksheet 6.1. In Case 1, the $\{y_t\}$ and $\{z_t\}$ sequences were constructed so as to satisfy

$$y_t = \mu_t + \epsilon_{yt}$$
$$z_t = \mu_t + \epsilon_{zt}$$

and

$$\mu_t = \mu_{t-1} + \epsilon_t$$

where ϵ_{yt}, ϵ_{zt}, and ϵ_t = independently distributed white-noise disturbances.

By construction, μ_t is a pure random walk process representing the same stochastic trend for both the $\{y_t\}$ and $\{z_t\}$ sequences. The value of μ_0 was initialized to zero and three sets of 20 random numbers were drawn to represent the $\{\epsilon_{yt}\}$, $\{\epsilon_{zt}\}$, and $\{\epsilon_t\}$ sequences. Using these realizations and the initial value of μ_0, we constructed the $\{y_t\}$, $\{z_t\}$, and $\{\mu_t\}$ sequences. As you can clearly determine, subtracting the realized value of z_t from y_t results in a stationary sequence:

$$y_t - z_t = (\mu_t + \epsilon_{yt}) - (\mu_t + \epsilon_{zt}) = \epsilon_{yt} - \epsilon_{zt}$$

To state the point using Engle and Granger's terminology, premultiplying the vector $x_t = (y_t, z_t)'$ by the cointegrating vector $\beta = (1, -1)$ yields the stationary sequence $\epsilon_t = \epsilon_{yt} - \epsilon_{zt}$. Indeed, the equilibrium error term shown in the second graph of Worksheet 6.1 has all the hallmarks of a stationary process. The essential insight of Stock and Watson (1988) is that the parameters of the cointegrating vector must be such that they purge the trend from the linear combination. Any other linear combination of the two variables contains a trend, so that the cointegrating vector is unique up to a normalizing scalar. For example, $\beta_3 y_t + \beta_4 z_t$ is not stationary unless $\beta_3/\beta_4 = \beta_1/\beta_2$.

Recall that Case 2 illustrates cointegration between three random walk plus noise processes. As in Case 1, each process is $I(1)$, and Dickey–Fuller unit root tests would not be able to reject the null hypothesis that each contains a unit root. As you can see in the lower portion of Worksheet 6.1, no pairwise combination of the series appears to be cointegrated. Each series seems to meander but, as opposed to Case 1, no one single series appears to remain close to any other series. However, by construction, the trend in w_t is the simple summation of the trends in y_t and z_t:

$$\mu_{wt} = \mu_{yt} + \mu_{zt}$$

Here, the vector $x_t = (y_t, z_t, w_t)'$ has the cointegrating vector $(1, 1, -1)$, so that the linear combination $y_t + z_t - w_t$ is stationary. Consider:

$$y_t + z_t - w_t = (\mu_{yt} + \epsilon_{yt}) + (\mu_{zt} + \epsilon_{zt}) - (\mu_{wt} + \epsilon_{wt})$$
$$= \epsilon_{yt} + \epsilon_{zt} - \epsilon_{wt}$$

The example illustrates the general point that cointegration will occur whenever the trend in one variable can be expressed as a linear combination of the trends in the other variable(s). In such circumstances, it is always possible to find a vector β such that the linear combination $\beta_1 y_t + \beta_2 z_t + \beta_3 w_t$ does not contain a trend. The result easily generalizes to the case of n variables. Consider the vector representation:

$$x_t = \mu_t + \epsilon_t \tag{6.8}$$

where x_t = the vector $(x_{1t}, x_{2t}, \ldots, x_{nt})'$
μ_t = the vector of stochastic trends $(\mu_{1t}, \mu_{2t}, \ldots, \mu_{nt})'$
ϵ_t = an $n \times 1$ vector of irregular components

If one trend can be expressed as a linear combination of the other trends in the system, it means that there exists a vector β such that

$$\beta_1 \mu_{1t} + \beta_2 \mu_{2t} + \cdots + \beta_n \mu_{nt} = 0$$

Premultiply (6.8) by this set of β_i's to obtain

$$\beta x_t = \beta \mu_t + \beta \epsilon_t$$

Since $\beta \mu_t = 0$, it follows that $\beta x_t = \beta \epsilon_t$. Hence, the linear combination βx_t is stationary. The argument easily generalizes to the case in which there are multiple linear relationships among the trends. If the cointegrating rank is r, there are $r < n$ linear relationships among the trends, so that we can write

$$\beta \mu_t = 0$$

where β = a $r \times n$ matrix consisting of elements β_{ij}

For example, if there are two cointegrating vectors among n variables, there are two independent cointegrating vectors of the form:

$$\begin{bmatrix} \beta_{11} & \beta_{12} & \cdots & \beta_{1n} \\ \beta_{21} & \beta_{22} & \cdots & \beta_{2n} \end{bmatrix}$$

Notice that it is possible to subtract β_{1i}/β_{2i} times row 2 from row 1 to yield another linear combination of the x_i that is stationary. However, there will be only $n - 1$ nonzero coefficients of the x_i in this combination. More generally, if there are r cointegrating vectors among n variables, there exists a cointegrating vector for each subset of $(n - r)$ variables.

3. COINTEGRATION AND ERROR CORRECTION

A principal feature of cointegrated variables is that their time paths are influenced by the extent of any deviation from long-run equilibrium. After all, if the system is to return to the long-run equilibrium, the movements of at least some of the variables must respond to the magnitude of the disequilibrium. For example, theories of the term structure of interest rates imply a long-run relationship between long- and short-term rates. If the gap between the long- and short-term rates is "large" relative to the long-run relationship, the short-term rate must ultimately rise relative to the long-term rate. Of course, the gap can be closed by (1) an increase in the short-term rate and/or a decrease in the long-term rate, (2) an increase in the long-term rate but a commensurately larger rise in the short-term rate, or (3) a fall in the long-term rate but a smaller fall in the short-term rate. Without a full dynamic specification of the model, it is not possible to determine which of the possibilities will occur. Nevertheless, the short-run dynamics must be influenced by the deviation from the long-run relationship.

The dynamic model implied by this discussion is one of **error correction**. In an error-correction model, the short-term dynamics of the variables in the system are influenced by the deviation from equilibrium. If we assume that both interest rates are $I(1)$, a simple error-correction model that could apply to the term structure of interest rates is[6]

$$\Delta r_{St} = \alpha_S(r_{Lt-1} - \beta r_{St-1}) + \epsilon_{St}, \qquad \alpha_S > 0 \qquad (6.9)$$
$$\Delta r_{Lt} = -\alpha_L(r_{Lt-1} - \beta r_{St-1}) + \epsilon_{Lt}, \qquad \alpha_L > 0 \qquad (6.10)$$

where r_{Lt} and r_{St} are the long- and short-term interest rates, respectively.

The two terms represented by ϵ_{St} and ϵ_{Lt} are white-noise disturbance terms that may be correlated and α_S, α_L, and β are positive parameters.

As specified, the short- and long-term interest rates change in response to stochastic shocks (represented by ϵ_{St} and ϵ_{Lt}) *and* to the previous period's deviation from long-run equilibrium. Everything else equal, if this deviation happened to be positive (so that $r_{Lt-1} - \beta r_{St-1} > 0$), the short-term interest rate would rise and the long-term rate would fall. Long-run equilibrium is attained when $r_{Lt} = \beta r_{St}$.

Here you can see the relationship between error-correcting models and cointegrated variables. By assumption, Δr_{St} is stationary, so that the left-hand side of (6.9) is $I(0)$. For (6.9) to be sensible, the right-hand side must be $I(0)$ as well. Given that ϵ_{St} is stationary, it follows that the linear combination $r_{Lt-1} - \beta r_{St-1}$ must also be stationary; hence, the two interest rates must be cointegrated with the cointegrating vector $(1, -\beta)$. Of course, the identical argument applies to (6.10). The essential point to note is that the error-correction representation necessitates the two variables be cointegrated of order $CI(1, 1)$. This result is unaltered if we formulate a more general model by introducing the lagged changes of each rate into both equations:[7]

$$\Delta r_{St} = a_{10} + \alpha_S(r_{Lt-1} - \beta r_{St-1}) + \Sigma a_{11}(i)\Delta r_{St-i} + \Sigma a_{12}(i)\Delta r_{Lt-i} + \epsilon_{St} \qquad (6.11)$$
$$\Delta r_{Lt} = a_{20} - \alpha_L(r_{Lt-1} - \beta r_{St-1}) + \Sigma a_{21}(i)\Delta r_{St-i} + \Sigma a_{22}(i)\Delta r_{Lt-i} + \epsilon_{Lt} \qquad (6.12)$$

Again, ϵ_{St}, ϵ_{Lt}, and all terms involving Δr_{St-i} and Δr_{Lt-1} are stationary. Thus, the linear combination of interest rates $(r_{Lt-1} - \beta r_{St-1})$ must also be stationary.

Inspection of (6.11) and (6.12) reveals a striking similarity to the VAR models of the previous chapter. This two-variable error-correction model is a bivariate VAR in first differences augmented by the error-correction terms $\alpha_S(r_{Lt-1} - \beta r_{St-1})$ and $-\alpha_L(r_{Lt-1} - \beta r_{St-1})$. Notice that α_S and α_L have the interpretation of *speed of adjustment* parameters. The larger α_S is, the greater the response of r_{St} to the previous period's deviation from long-run equilibrium. At the opposite extreme, very small values of α_S imply that the short-term interest rate is unresponsive to last period's equilibrium error. For the $\{\Delta r_{St}\}$ sequence to be unaffected by the long-term interest rate sequence, α_S *and* all the $a_{12}(i)$ coefficients must be equal to zero. Thus, *the absence of Granger causality for cointegrated variables requires the additional condition that the speed of adjustment coefficient be equal to zero.* Of course, at least one of the speed of adjustment terms in (6.11) and (6.12) must be nonzero. If both α_S and α_L are equal to zero, the long-run equilibrium relationship does not appear and the model is not one of error correction or cointegration.

The result is easily generalized to the n-variable model. Formally, the $(n \times 1)$ vector $x_t = (x_{1t}, x_{2t}, \ldots, x_{nt})'$ has an error-correction representation if it can be expressed in the form:

$$\Delta x_t = \pi_0 + \pi x_{t-1} + \pi_1 \Delta x_{t-1} + \pi_2 \Delta x_{t-2} + \cdots + \pi_p \Delta x_{t-p} + \epsilon_t \qquad (6.13)$$

where π_0 = an $(n \times 1)$ vector of intercept terms with elements π_{i0}
   π_i = $(n \times n)$ coefficient matrices with elements $\pi_{jk}(i)$
   π = is a matrix with elements π_{jk} such that one or more of the $\pi_{jk} \neq 0$
   ϵ_t = an $(n \times 1)$ vector with elements ϵ_{it}

Note that the disturbance terms are such that ϵ_{it} may be correlated with ϵ_{jt}.

Let all variables in x_t be $I(1)$. Now, if there is an error-correction representation of these variables as in (6.13), there is necessarily a linear combination of the $I(1)$ variables that is stationary. Solving (6.13) for πx_{t-1} yields

$$\pi x_{t-1} = \Delta x_t - \pi_0 - \Sigma \pi_i \Delta x_{t-i} - \epsilon_t$$

Since each expression on the right-hand side is stationary, πx_{t-1} must also be stationary. Since π contains only constants, each row of π is a cointegrating vector of x_t. For example, the first row can be written as $(\pi_{11}x_{1t-1} + \pi_{12}x_{2t-1} + \cdots + \pi_{1n}x_{nt-1})$. Since each series x_{it-1} is $I(1)$, $(\pi_{11}, \pi_{12}, \ldots, \pi_{1n})$ must be a cointegrating vector for x_t.

The key feature in (6.13) is the presence of the matrix π. There are two important points to note:

1. If all elements of π equal zero, (6.13) is a traditional VAR in first differences. In such circumstances, there is no error-correction representation since Δx_t does not respond to the previous preiod's deviation from long-run equilibrium.

2. If one or more of the π_{jk} differs from zero, Δx_t responds to the previous period's deviation from long-run equilibrium. Hence, *estimating x_t as a VAR in first dif-*

ferences is inappropriate if x_t has an error-correction representation. The omission of the expression πx_{t-1} entails a misspecification error if x_t has an error-correction representation as in (6.13).

A good way to examine the relationship between cointegration and error correction is to study the properties of the simple VAR model:

$$y_t = a_{11}y_{t-1} + a_{12}z_{t-1} + \epsilon_{yt} \tag{6.14}$$
$$z_t = a_{21}y_{t-1} + a_{22}z_{t-1} + \epsilon_{zt} \tag{6.15}$$

where ϵ_{yt} and ϵ_{zt} are white-noise disturbances that may be correlated with each other and, for simplicity, intercept terms have been ignored. Using lag operators, we can write (6.14) and (6.15) as

$$(1 - a_{11}L)y_t - a_{12}Lz_t = \epsilon_{yt}$$
$$-a_{21}Ly_t + (1 - a_{22}L)z_t = \epsilon_{zt}$$

The next step is to solve for y_t and z_t. Writing the system in matrix form, we obtain

$$\begin{bmatrix} (1-a_{11}L) & -a_{12}L \\ -a_{21}L & (1-a_{22}L) \end{bmatrix} \begin{bmatrix} y_t \\ z_t \end{bmatrix} = \begin{bmatrix} \epsilon_{yt} \\ \epsilon_{zt} \end{bmatrix}$$

Using Cramer's rule or matrix inversion, we can obtain the solutions for y_t and z_t as

$$y_t = \frac{(1 - a_{22}L)\epsilon_{yt} + a_{12}L\epsilon_{zt}}{(1 - a_{11}L)(1 - a_{22}L) - a_{12}a_{21}L^2} \tag{6.16}$$

$$z_t = \frac{a_{21}L\epsilon_{yt} + (1 - a_{11}L)\epsilon_{zt}}{(1 - a_{11}L)(1 - a_{22}L) - a_{12}a_{21}L^2} \tag{6.17}$$

We have converted the two-variable first-order system represented by (6.14) and (6.15) into two univariate second-order difference equations of the type examined in chapter 1. Note that both variables have the same inverse characteristic equation $(1 - a_{11}L)(1 - a_{22}L) - a_{12}a_{21}L^2$. Setting $(1 - a_{11}L)(1 - a_{22}L) - a_{12}a_{21}L^2 = 0$ and solving for L yield the two roots of the inverse characteristic equation. In order to work with the characteristic roots (as opposed to the inverse characteristic roots), define $\lambda = 1/L$ and write the characteristic equation as

$$\lambda^2 - (a_{11} + a_{22})\lambda + (a_{11}a_{22} - a_{12}a_{21}) = 0 \tag{6.18}$$

Since the two variables have the same characteristic equation, the characteristic roots of (6.18) determine the time paths of both variables. The following remarks summarize the time paths of $\{y_t\}$ and $\{z_t\}$:

1. If both characteristic roots (λ_1, λ_2) lie inside the unit circle, (6.16) and (6.17) yield stable solutions for $\{y_t\}$ and $\{z_t\}$. If t is sufficiently large or the initial conditions are such that the homogenous solution is zero, the stability condition guarantees that the variables are stationary. The variables cannot be cointegrated of order $(1, 1)$ since each will be stationary.

2. If either root lies outside the unit circle, the solutions are explosive. Neither variable is difference stationary, so that they cannot be $CI(1, 1)$. In the same way, if both characteristic roots are unity, the second difference of each variable will be stationary. Since each is $I(2)$, the variables cannot be $CI(1, 1)$.

3. As you can see from (6.14) and (6.15), if $a_{12} = a_{21} = 0$, the solution is trivial. For $\{y_t\}$ and $\{z_t\}$ to be unit root processes, it is necessary for $a_{11} = a_{22} = 1$. It follows that $\lambda_1 = \lambda_2 = 1$ and the two variables evolve without any long-run equilibrium relationship; hence, the variables cannot be cointegrated.

4. For $\{y_t\}$ and $\{z_t\}$ to be $CI(1, 1)$, it is necessary for one characteristic root to be unity and the other less than unity in absolute value. In this instance, each variable will have the same stochastic trend and the first difference of each variable will be stationary. For example, if $\lambda_1 = 1$, (6.16) will have the form:

$$y_t = [(1 - a_{22}L)\epsilon_{yt} + a_{12}L\epsilon_{zt}]/[(1 - L)(1 - \lambda_2 L)]$$

or multiplying by $(1 - L)$, we get

$$(1 - L)y_t = \Delta y_t = [(1 - a_{22}L)\epsilon_{yt} + a_{12}L\epsilon_{zt}]/(1 - \lambda_2 L)$$

which is stationary if $|\lambda_2| < 1$.

Thus, to ensure that the variables are $CI(1, 1)$, we must set one of the characteristic roots equal to unity and the other to a value that is less than unity in absolute value. For the larger of the two roots to equal unity, it must be the case that

$$0.5 * (a_{11} + a_{22}) + 0.5 * \sqrt{(a_{11}^2 + a_{22}^2) - 2a_{11}a_{22} + 4a_{12}a_{21}} = 1$$

so that after some simplification, the coefficients are seen to satisfy[8]

$$a_{11} = [(1 - a_{22}) - a_{12}\,a_{21}]/(1 - a_{22}) \tag{6.19}$$

Now consider the second characteristic root. Since a_{12} and/or a_{21} must differ from zero if the variables are cointegrated, the condition $|\lambda_2| < 1$ requires

$$a_{22} > -1 \tag{6.20}$$

and

$$a_{12}a_{21} + (a_{22})^2 < 1 \tag{6.21}$$

Equations (6.19), (6.20), and (6.21) are restrictions we must place on the coefficients of (6.14) and (6.15) if we want to ensure that the variables are cointegrated of order (1, 1). To see how these coefficient restrictions bear on the nature of the solution, write (6.14) and (6.15) as

$$\begin{bmatrix} \Delta y_t \\ \Delta z_t \end{bmatrix} = \begin{bmatrix} a_{11} - 1 & a_{12} \\ a_{21} & a_{22} - 1 \end{bmatrix} \begin{bmatrix} y_{t-1} \\ z_{t-1} \end{bmatrix} + \begin{bmatrix} \epsilon_{yt} \\ \epsilon_{zt} \end{bmatrix} \tag{6.22}$$

Now, (6.19) implies that $a_{11} - 1 = -a_{12}a_{21}/(1 - a_{22})$, so that after a bit of manipulation, (6.22) can be written in the form:

$$\Delta y_t = -[a_{12}a_{21}/(1 - a_{22})]y_{t-1} + a_{12}z_{t-1} + \epsilon_{yt} \tag{6.23}$$
$$\Delta z_t = a_{21}y_{t-1} - (1 - a_{22})z_{t-1} + \epsilon_{zt} \tag{6.24}$$

Equations (6.23) and (6.24) comprise an error-correction model. If both a_{12} and a_{21} differ from zero, we can normalize the cointegrating vector with respect to either variable. Normalizing with respect to y_t, we get

$$\Delta y_t = \alpha_y(y_{t-1} - \beta z_{t-1}) + \epsilon_{yt}$$
$$\Delta z_t = \alpha_z(y_{t-1} - \beta z_{t-1}) + \epsilon_{zt}$$

where $\alpha_y = -a_{12}a_{21}/(1 - a_{22})$
$\beta = (1 - a_{22})/a_{21}$
$\alpha_z = a_{21}$

You can see that y_t and z_t change in response to the previous period's deviation from long-run equilibrium: $y_{t-1} - \beta z_{t-1}$. If $y_{t-1} = \beta z_{t-1}$, y_t and z_t change only in response to ϵ_{yt} and ϵ_{zt} shocks. Moreover, if $\alpha_y < 0$ and $\alpha_z > 0$, y_t decreases and z_t increases in response to a positive deviation from long-run equilibrium.

You can easily convince yourself that conditions (6.20) and (6.21) ensure that $\beta \neq 0$ and at least one of the speed of adjustment parameters (i.e., α_y and α_z) is not equal to zero. Now, refer to (6.9) and (6.10); you can see this model is in exactly the same form as the interest rate example presented in the beginning of this section.

Although both a_{12} and a_{21} cannot equal zero, an interesting special case arises if one of these coefficients is zero. For example, if we set $a_{12} = 0$, the speed of adjustment coefficient $\alpha_y = 0$. In this case, y_t changes only in response to ϵ_{yt} as $\Delta y_t = \epsilon_{yt}$.[9] The $\{z_t\}$ sequence does all the correction to eliminate any deviation from long-run equilibrium.

To highlight some of the important implications of this simple model, we have shown:

1. *The restrictions necessary to ensure that the variables are CI(1, 1) guarantee that an error-correction model exists.* In our example, both $\{y_t\}$ and $\{z_t\}$ are unit root processes but the linear combination $y_t - \beta z_t$ is stationary; the normalized cointegrating vector is $[1, -(1 - a_{22})/a_{21}]$. The variables have an error-correction representation with speed of adjustment coefficients $\alpha_y = -a_{12}a_{21}/(1 - a_{22})$ and $\alpha_z = a_{21}$. It was also shown that an error-correction model for $I(1)$ variables necessarily implies cointegration. This finding illustrates the **Granger representation theorem** stating that for any set of $I(1)$ variables, error correction and cointegration are equivalent representations.

2. *Cointegration necessitates coefficient restrictions in a VAR model.* Let $x_t = (y_t, z_t)'$ and $\epsilon_t = (\epsilon_{yt}, \epsilon_{zt})'$, so that we can write (6.22) in the form:

$$\Delta x_t = \pi x_{t-1} + \epsilon_t \tag{6.25}$$

Clearly, it is inappropriate to estimate a VAR of cointegrated variables using only first differences. Estimating (6.25) without the expression πx_{t-1} would eliminate the error–correction portion of the model. It is also important to note that the rows of π are *not* linearly independent if the variables are cointegrated. Multiplying each element in row 1 by $-(1 - a_{22})/a_{12}$ yields the corresponding element in row 2. Thus, the determinant of π is equal to zero and y_t and z_t have the error-correction representation given by (6.23) and (6.24).

This two-variable example illustrates the very important insights of Johansen (1988) and Stock and Watson (1988) that *we can use the rank of π to determine whether or not two variables $\{y_t\}$ and $\{z_t\}$ are cointegrated.* Compare the determinant of π to the characteristic equation given by (6.18). If the largest characteristic root equals unity ($\lambda_1 = 1$), it follows that the determinant of π is zero and π has a rank equal to unity. If π were to have a rank of zero, it would be necessary for $a_{11} = 1$, $a_{22} = 1$, and $a_{12} = a_{21} = 0$. The VAR represented by (6.14) and (6.15) would be nothing more than $\Delta y_t = \epsilon_{yt}$ and $\Delta z_t = \epsilon_{zt}$. In this case, both the $\{y_t\}$ and $\{z_t\}$ sequences are unit root processes without any cointegrating vector. Finally, if the rank of π is full, then neither characteristic root can be unity, so that the $\{y_t\}$ and $\{z_t\}$ sequences are jointly stationary.

3. In general, both variables in a cointegrated system will respond to a deviation from long-run equilibrium. However, it is possible that one (but not both) of the speed of adjustment parameters is zero. In this circumstance, that variable does not respond to the discrepancy from long-run equilibrium and the other variable does all the adjustment. Hence, *it is necessary to reinterprete Granger causality in a cointegrated system.* In a cointegrated system, $\{z_t\}$ does not Granger cause $\{y_t\}$ if lagged values Δz_{t-i} do not enter the Δy_t equation and if y_t does not respond to the deviation from long-run equilibrium. For example, in the cointe-

grated system of (6.11) and (6.12), $\{r_{Lt}\}$ does not Granger cause $\{r_{St}\}$ if all $a_{12}(i) = 0$ and $\alpha_S = 0$.

The *n*-Variable Case

Little is altered in the *n*-variable case. The relationship between cointegration, error correction, and the rank of the matrix π is invariant to adding variables to the system. The interesting feature introduced in the *n*-variable case is the possibility of multiple cointegrating vectors. Now consider a more general version of (6.25):

$$x_t = A_1 x_{t-1} + \epsilon_t \tag{6.26}$$

where x_t = the $(n \times 1)$ vector $(x_{1t}, x_{2t}, \ldots, x_{nt})'$
   ϵ_t = the $(n \times 1)$ vector $(\epsilon_{1t}, \epsilon_{2t}, \ldots, \epsilon_{nt})'$
   A_1 = an $(n \times n)$ matrix of parameters

Subtracting x_{t-1} from each side of (6.26) and letting I be an $(n \times n)$ identity matrix, we get

$$\begin{aligned} \Delta x_t &= -(I - A_1)x_{t-1} + \epsilon_t \\ &= \pi x_{t-1} + \epsilon_t \end{aligned} \tag{6.27}$$

where π is the $(n \times n)$ matrix $-(I - A_1)$ and π_{ij} denotes the element in row i and column j of π. As you can see, (6.27) is a special case of (6.13) such that all $\pi_i = 0$.

Again, the crucial issue for cointegration concerns the rank of the $(n \times n)$ matrix π. If the rank of this matrix is zero, each element of π must equal zero. In this instance, (6.27) is equivalent to an *n*-variable VAR in first differences:

$$\Delta x_t = \epsilon_t$$

Here, each $\Delta x_{it} = \epsilon_{it}$, so that the first difference of each variable in the vector x_t is $I(0)$. Since each $x_{it} = x_{it-1} + \epsilon_{it}$, all the $\{x_{it}\}$ sequences are unit root processes and there is no linear combination of the variables that is stationary.

At the other extreme, suppose that π is of full rank. The long-run solution to (6.27) is given by the *n* independent equations:

$$\begin{aligned} \pi_{11}x_{1t} + \pi_{12}x_{2t} + \pi_{13}x_{3t} + \cdots + \pi_{1n}x_{nt} &= 0 \\ \pi_{21}x_{1t} + \pi_{22}x_{2t} + \pi_{23}x_{3t} + \cdots + \pi_{2n}x_{nt} &= 0 \\ &\vdots \\ \pi_{n1}x_{1t} + \pi_{n2}x_{2t} + \pi_{n3}x_{3t} + \cdots + \pi_{nn}x_{nt} &= 0 \end{aligned} \tag{6.28}$$

Each of these n equations is an independent restriction on the long-run solution of the variables; the n variables in the system face n long-run constraints. In this case, each of the n variables contained in the vector x_t must be stationary with the long-run values given by (6.28).

In intermediate cases, in which the rank of π is equal to r, there are r cointegrating vectors. If $r = 1$, there is a single cointegrating vector given by any row of the matrix π. Each $\{x_{it}\}$ sequence can be written in error-correction form. For example, we can write Δx_{1t} as

$$\Delta x_{1t} = \pi_{11} x_{1t-1} + \pi_{12} x_{2t-1} + \cdots + \pi_{1n} x_{nt-1} + \epsilon_{1t}$$

or, normalizing with respect to x_{1t-1}, we can set $\alpha_1 = \pi_{11}$ and $\beta_{ij} = \pi_{ij}/\pi_{11}$ to obtain

$$\Delta x_{1t} = \alpha_1(x_{1t-1} - \beta_{12} x_{2t-1} + \cdots + \beta_{1n} x_{nt-1}) + \epsilon_{1t} \tag{6.29}$$

In the long-run, the $\{x_{it}\}$ will satisfy the relationship:

$$x_{1t} + \beta_{12} x_{2t} + \cdots + \beta_{1n} x_{nt} = 0$$

Hence, the normalized cointegrating vector is $(1, \beta_{12}, \beta_{13}, \ldots, \beta_{1n})$ and the speed of adjustment parameter α_1. In the same way, with two cointegration vectors the long-run values of the variables will satisfy the two relationships:

$$\pi_{11} x_{1t} + \pi_{12} x_{2t} + \cdots + \pi_{1n} x_{nt} = 0$$
$$\pi_{21} x_{1t} + \pi_{22} x_{2t} + \cdots + \pi_{2n} x_{nt} = 0$$

which can be appropriately normalized.

The main point here is that there are two important ways to test for cointegration. The Engle–Granger methodology seeks to determine whether the residuals of the equilibrium relationship are stationary. The Johansen (1988) and Stock–Watson (1988) methodologies determine the rank of π. The Engle–Granger approach is the subject of the next three sections. Sections 7 through 10 examine the Johansen (1988) and Stock–Watson (1988) methodologies.

4. TESTING FOR COINTEGRATION: THE ENGLE–GRANGER METHODOLOGY

To explain the Engle–Granger testing procedure, let us begin with the type of problem likely to be encountered in applied studies. Suppose that two variables—say, y_t and z_t—are believed to be integrated of order 1 and we want to determine whether there exists an equilibrium relationship between the two. Engle and Granger (1987) propose a straightforward test whether two $I(1)$ variables are cointegrated of order $CI(1, 1)$.

STEP 1: Pretest the variables for their order of integration. By definition, cointegration necessitates that the variables be integrated of the same order. Thus, the first step in the analysis is to pretest each variable to determine its order of integration. The Dickey–Fuller, augmented Dickey–Fuller, and/or Phillips–Perron tests discussed in Chapter 4 can be used to infer the number of unit roots (if any) in each of the variables. If both variables are stationary, it is not necessary to proceed since standard time-series methods apply to stationary variables. If the variables are integrated of different orders, it is possible to conclude that they *are* not cointegrated.[10]

STEP 2: Estimate the long-run equilibrium relationship. If the results of Step 1 indicate that both $\{y_t\}$ and $\{z_t\}$ are $I(1)$, the next step is to estimate the long-run equilibrium relationship in the form:

$$y_t = \beta_0 + \beta_1 z_t + e_t \tag{6.30}$$

If the variables are cointegrated, an OLS regression yields a "super-consistent" estimator of the cointegrating parameters β_0 and β_1. Stock (1987) proves that the OLS estimates of β_0 and β_1 converge faster than in OLS models using stationary variables. To explain, reexamine the scatter plot shown in Figure 6.1. You can see that the effect of the common trend dominates the effect of the stationary component; both variables seem to rise and fall in tandem. Hence, there is a strong linear relationship as shown by the regression line drawn in the figure.

In order to determine if the variables are actually cointegrated, denote the residual sequence from this equation by $\{\hat{e}_t\}$. Thus, $\{\hat{e}_t\}$ is the series of the estimated residuals of the long-run relationship. If these deviations from long-run equilibrium are found to be stationary, the $\{y_t\}$ and $\{z_t\}$ sequences are cointegrated of order $(1, 1)$. It would be convenient if we could perform a Dickey–Fuller test on these residuals to determine their order of integration. Consider the autoregression of the residuals:

$$\Delta\hat{e}_t = a_1 \hat{e}_{t-1} + \epsilon_t \tag{6.31}$$

Since the $\{\hat{e}_t\}$ sequence is a residual from a regression equation, there is no need to include an intercept term; the parameter of interest in (6.31) is a_1. If we cannot reject the null hypothesis $a_1 = 0$, we can conclude that the residual series contains a unit root. Hence, we conclude that the $\{y_t\}$ and $\{z_t\}$ sequences are *not* cointegrated. The more precise wording is awkward because of a triple negative, but to be technically correct, *if it is not possible to reject the null hypothesis* $|a_1| = 0$, *we cannot reject the hypothesis that the variables are not cointegrated.* Instead, the rejection of the null hypothesis implies that the residual sequence is stationary.[11] Given that both $\{y_t\}$ and $\{z_t\}$ were found to be $I(1)$ and the residuals are stationary, we can conclude that the series are cointegrated of order $(1, 1)$.

In most applied studies, it is not possible to use the Dickey–Fuller tables themselves. The problem is that the $\{\hat{e}_t\}$ sequence is generated from a regression equation; the researcher does not know the actual error $\hat{e}_t$, only the estimate of the error $\hat{e}_t$. The methodology of fitting the regression in (6.30) selects values of β_0 and β_1 that minimize the sum of squared residuals. Since the residual variance is made as small as possible, the procedure is prejudiced toward finding a stationary error process in (6.31). Hence, the test statistic used to test the magnitude of a_1 must reflect this fact. Only if β_0 and β_1 were known in advance and used to construct the true $\{e_t\}$ sequence would an ordinary Dickey–Fuller table be appropriate. Fortunately, Engle and Granger provide test statistics that can be used to test the hypothesis $a_1 = 0$. When more than two variables appear in the equilibrium relationship, the appropriate tables are provided by Engle and Yoo (1987).

If the residuals of (6.31) do not appear to be white-noise, an augmented Dickey–Fuller test can be used instead of (6.31). Suppose that diagnostic checks indicate that the $\{\epsilon_t\}$ sequence of (6.31) exhibits serial correlation. Instead of using the results from (6.31), estimate the autoregression:

$$\Delta\hat{e}_t = a_1\hat{e}_{t-1} + \sum_{i=1}^{n} a_{i+1}\Delta\hat{e}_{t-i} + \epsilon_t \tag{6.32}$$

Again, if $-2 < a_1 < 0$, we can conclude that the residual sequence is stationary and $\{y_t\}$ and $\{z_t\}$ are $CI(1, 1)$.

STEP 3: Estimate the error-correction model. If the variables are cointegrated (i.e., if the null hypothesis of no cointegration is rejected), the residuals from the equilibrium regression can be used to estimate the error-correction model. If $\{y_t\}$ and $\{z_t\}$ are $CI(1, 1)$, the variables have the error-correction form:

$$\Delta y_t = \alpha_1 + \alpha_y\left(y_{t-1} - \beta_1 z_{t-1}\right) + \sum_{i=1}^{\infty} \alpha_{11}(i)\Delta y_{t-i} + \sum_{i=1}^{\infty} \alpha_{12}(i)\Delta z_{t-i} + \epsilon_{yt} \tag{6.33}$$

$$\Delta z_t = \alpha_2 + \alpha_z\left(y_{t-1} - \beta_1 z_{t-1}\right) + \sum_{i=1}^{\infty} \alpha_{21}(i)\Delta y_{t-i} + \sum_{i=1}^{\infty} \alpha_{22}(i)\Delta z_{t-i} + \epsilon_{zt} \tag{6.34}$$

where β_1 = the parameter of the cointegrating vector given by (6.30)

ϵ_{yt} and ϵ_{zt} = white-noise disturbances (which may be correlated with each other)

and α_1, α_2, α_y, α_z, $\alpha_{11}(i)$, $\alpha_{12}(i)$, $\alpha_{21}(i)$, and $\alpha_{22}(i)$ are all parameters.

Engle and Granger (1987) propose a clever way to circumvent the cross-equation restrictions involved in the direct estimation of (6.33) and (6.34). The value of the residual $\hat{e}_{t-1}$ estimates the deviation from long-run equilibrium in period $(t - 1)$. Hence, it is possible to use the saved residuals $\{\hat{e}_{t-1}\}$ obtained in Step 2 as an instrument for the expression $y_{t-1} - \beta_1 z_{t-1}$ in (6.33) and (6.34). Thus, using the saved residuals from the estimation of the long-run equilibrium relationship, we can estimate the error-correcting model as

$$\Delta y_t = \alpha_1 + \alpha_y \hat{e}_{t-1} + \sum_{i=1} \alpha_{11}(i)\Delta y_{t-i} + \sum_{i=1} \alpha_{12}(i)\Delta z_{t-i} + \epsilon_{yt} \qquad (6.35)$$

$$\Delta z_t = \alpha_2 + \alpha_z \hat{e}_{t-1} + \sum_{i=1} \alpha_{21}(i)\Delta y_{t-i} + \sum_{i=1} \alpha_{22}(i)\Delta z_{t-i} + \epsilon_{zt} \qquad (6.36)$$

Other than the error-correction term $\hat{e}_{t-1}$, $\hat{e}$ Equations (6.35) and (6.36) constitute VAR in first differences. This *near VAR* can be estimated using the same methodology developed in Chapter 5. All the procedures developed for a VAR apply to the near VAR. Notably:

1. OLS is an efficient estimation strategy since each equation contains the same set of regressors.

2. Since all terms in (6.35) and (6.36) are stationary [i.e., Δy_t and its lags, Δz_t and its lags, and $\hat{e}_{t-1}$ are $I(0)$], the test statistics used in traditional VAR analysis are appropriate for (6.35) and (6.36). For example, lag lengths can be determined using a χ^2 test and the restriction that all $\alpha_{jk}(i) = 0$ can be checked using an F-test. If there is a single cointegrating vector, restrictions concerning α_y or α_z can be conducted using a t-test. Asymptotic theory indicates α_y and α_z converge to a t-distribution as sample size increases.

STEP 4:   Assess model adequacy. There are several procedures that can help determine whether the estimated error-correction model is appropriate.

1. You should be careful to assess the adequacy of the model by performing diagnostic checks to determine whether the residuals of the near

VAR approximate white noise. If the residuals are serially correlated, lag lengths may be too short. Reestimate the model using lag lengths that yield serially uncorrelated errors. It may be that you need to allow longer lags of some variables than on others.

2. The *speed of adjustment* coefficients α_y and α_z are of particular interest in that they have important implications for the dynamics of the system.[12] If we focus on (6.36), it is clear that for any given value of $\hat{e}_{t-1}$, a large value of α_z is associated with a large value of Δz_t. If α_z is zero, the change in z_t does not at all respond to the deviation from long-run equilibrium in $(t-1)$. If α_z is zero and all $\alpha_{21}(i) = 0$, then it can be said that $\{\Delta y_t\}$ does not Granger cause $\{\Delta z_t\}$. We know that one or both of these coefficients should be significantly different from zero if the variables are cointegrated. After all, if both α_y and α_z are zero, there is no error correction and (6.35) and (6.36) comprise nothing more than a VAR in first differences. Moreover, the absolute values of these speed of adjustment coefficients must not be too large. The point estimates should imply that Δy_t and Δz_t converge to the long-run equilibrium relationship.[13]

3. As in a traditional VAR analysis, Lutkepohl and Reimers (1992) show that innovation accounting (i.e., impulse responses and variance decomposition analysis) can be used to obtain information concerning the interactions among the variables. As a practical matter, the two innovations ϵ_{yt} and ϵ_{zt} may be contemporaneously correlated if y_t has a contemporaneous effect on z_t and/or z_t has a contemporaneous effect on y_t. In obtaining impulse response functions and variance decompositions, some method—such as Choleski decomposition—can be used to orthogonalize the innovations.

The shape of the impulse response functions and results of the variance decompositions can indicate whether the dynamic responses of the variables conform to theory. Since all variables in (6.35) and (6.36) are $I(0)$, the impulse responses should converge to zero. You should reexamine your results from each step if you obtain a nondecaying or explosive impulse response function.

5. ILLUSTRATING THE ENGLE–GRANGER METHODOLOGY

Figure 6.2 shows three simulated variables that can be used to illustrate the Engle–Granger procedure. Inspection of the figure suggests that each is nonstationary and there is no visual evidence that any pair is cointegrated. As detailed in Table 6.1, each series is constructed as the sum of a stochastic trend component plus an autoregressive irregular component.

Figure 6.2   Three cointegrated series.

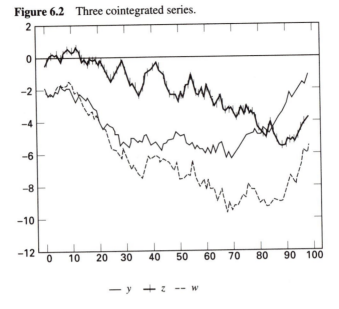

The first column of the table contains the formulas used to construct the $\{y_t\}$ sequence. First, 150 realizations of a white-noise process were drawn to represent the $\{\epsilon_{yt}\}$ sequence. Initializing $\mu_{y0} = 0$, we constructed 150 values of the random walk process $\{\mu_{yt}\}$ using the formula $\mu_{yt} = \mu_{yt-1} + \epsilon_{yt}$ (see the first cell of the table). Another 150 realizations of a white-noise process were drawn to represent the $\{\eta_{yt}\}$ sequence; given the initial condition $\delta_{y0} = 0$, these realizations were used to construct $\{\delta_{yt}\}$ as $\delta_{yt} = 0.5\delta_{yt-1} + \eta_{yt}$ (see the next lower cell). Adding the two constructed series yields 150 realizations for $\{y_t\}$. To help ensure randomness, only the last 100 observations are used in the simulated study.

The $\{z_t\}$ sequence was constructed in a similar fashion; the $\{\epsilon_{zt}\}$ and $\{\eta_{zt}\}$ sequences are each represented by two different sets of 150 random numbers. The trend $\{\mu_{zt}\}$ and autoregressive irregular term $\{\delta_{zt}\}$ were constructed as shown in the second column of the table. The $\{\delta_{zt}\}$ sequence can be thought of as a pure irregular component in the $\{z_t\}$ sequence. In order to introduce correlation between the

Table 6.1   The Simulated Series

	$\{y_t\}$	$\{z_t\}$	$\{w_t\}$
Trend	$\mu_{yt} = \mu_{yt-1} + \epsilon_{yt}$	$\mu_{zt} = \mu_{zt-1} + \epsilon_{zt}$	$\mu_{wt} = \mu_{yt} + \mu_{zt}$
Pure Irregular	$\delta_{yt} = 0.5\delta_{yt-1} + \eta_{yt}$	$\delta_{zt} = 0.5\delta_{zt-1} + \eta_{zt}$	$\delta_{wt} = 0.5\delta_{wt-1} + \eta_{wt}$
Series	$y_t = \mu_{yt} + \delta_{yt}$	$z_t = \mu_{zt} + \delta_{zt} + 0.5\delta_{yt}$	$w_t = \mu w_t + \delta_{wt} + 0.5\delta_{yt} + 0.5\delta_{zt}$

$\{y_t\}$ and $\{z_t\}$ sequences, the irregular component in $\{z_t\}$ was constructed as the sum $\delta_{zt} + 0.5\delta_{yt}$. In the third column, you can see that the trend in $\{w_t\}$ is the simple summation of the trends in the other two series. As such, the three series have the cointegrating vector $(1, 1, -1)$. The irregular component in $\{w_t\}$ is the sum of pure innovation δ_{wt} and 50% of the innovations δ_{yt} and δ_{zt}.

Now pretend that we do not know the data-generating process. The issue is whether the Engle–Granger methodology can uncover the essential details of the data-generating process. The first step is to pretest the variables in order to determine their order of integration. Consider the augmented Dickey–Fuller regression equation for $\{y_t\}$:

$$\Delta y_t = \alpha_0 + \alpha_1 y_{t-1} + \sum_{i=1}^{n} \alpha_{i+1}\Delta y_{t-i} + e_t$$

If the data happened to be quarterly, it would be natural to perform the augmented Dickey–Fuller tests using lag lengths that are multiples of 4 (i.e., $n = 4, 8, \ldots$). For each series, the results of the Dickey–Fuller test and augmented test using four lags are reported in Table 6.2.

With 100 observations and a constant, the 95% critical value of the Dickey–Fuller test is -2.89. Since, in absolute value, all t-statistics are well below this critical value, we cannot reject the null hypothesis of a unit root in any of the series. Of course, if there was any serious doubt about the presence of a unit root, we could use the procedures in Chapter 4 to (1) test for the presence of the constant term, (2) test for the presence of a deterministic trend, and/or (3) perform Phillips–Perron tests if the errors do not appear to be white-noise. If various lag lengths yield different results, we would want to test for the most appropriate lag length.

The luxury of using simulated data is that we can avoid these potentially sticky problems and move on to Step 2.[14] Since all three variables are presumed to be jointly determined, the long-run equilibrium regression can be estimated using either y_t, z_t, or w_t as the "left-hand-side" variable. The three estimates of the long-run

Table 6.2   Estimated α_1 and the Associated t-statistic

	No lags	4 Lags
Δy_t	−0.01995	−0.02691
	(−0.74157)	(−1.0465)
Δz_t	−0.02069	−0.25841
	(−0.99213)	(−1.1437)
Δw_t	−0.03501	−0.03747
	(−1.9078)	(−1.9335)

relationship (with *t*-values in parentheses) are

$$y_t = -0.4843 - 0.9273z_t + 0.97687w_t + e_{yt} \qquad (6.37)$$
$$(-0.5751) \ (-38.095) \ (53.462)$$
$$z_t = -0.0589 - 1.0108y_t + 1.02549w_t + e_{zt} \qquad (6.38)$$
$$(-0.6709) \ (-38.095) \ (65.323)$$
$$w_t = -0.0852 + 0.9901y_t + 0.95347z_t + e_{wt} \qquad (6.39)$$
$$(-1.0089) \ (52.462) \ (65.462)$$

where e_{yt}, e_{zt}, and e_{wt} = the residuals from the three equilibrium regressions

The essence of the test is to determine whether the residuals from the equilibrium regression are stationary. Again, in performing the test, there is no presumption that any one of the three residual series is preferable to any of the others. If we use each of the three series to estimate an equation in the form of (6.31) and (6.32), the estimated values of a_1 are as given in Table 6.3.

Engle and Yoo (1987) report the critical values of the *t*-statistic as −3.93. Hence, using any one of the three equilibruim regressions, we can conclude that the series are cointegrated of order (1, 1). Fortunately, all three equilibrium regressions yield this same conclusion. We should be very wary of a result indicating that the variables are cointegrated using one variable for the normalization, but are not cointegrated using another variable for the normalization. This possible ambiguity is a weakness of the test; other methods can be tried if mixed results are found.

Avoid the temptation to conduct significance tests in (6.37) through (6.39). The coefficients *do not* have asymptotic *t*-distributions unless the right hand side variables are actually independent and there exists a single cointegrating vector.

Step 3 entails estimating the error-correction model. Consider the first-order system shown with *t*-statistics in parentheses:

$$\Delta y_t = 0.009 + 0.441e_{wt-1} + 0.190\Delta y_{t-1} + 0.332\Delta z_{t-1} - 0.380\Delta w_{t-1} + \epsilon_{yt} \quad (6.40)$$
$$(0.291) \quad (2.94) \qquad (1.15) \qquad (2.05) \qquad (-2.35)$$
$$\Delta z_t = -0.042 + 0.054e_{wt-1} + 0.139\Delta y_{t-1} + 0.253\Delta z_{t-1} - 0.304\Delta w_{t-1} + \epsilon_{zt} \quad (6.41)$$
$$(-1.11) \quad (0.304) \qquad (0.711) \qquad (1.32) \qquad (-1.59)$$
$$\Delta w_t = -0.041 - 0.065e_{wt-1} + 0.157\Delta y_{t-1} + 0.302\Delta z_{t-1} - 0.421\Delta w_{t-1} + \epsilon_{wt} \quad (6.42)$$
$$(-0.31) \quad (-0.907) \qquad (0.688) \qquad (1.35) \qquad (-1.88)$$

where $e_{wt-1} = w_{t-1} + 0.0852 - 0.9901y_{t-1} - 0.95347z_{t-1}$

That is, e_{wt-1} is the lagged value of the residual from (6.39).

Equations (6.40) through (6.42) comprise a first-order VAR augmented with the single error-correction term e_{wt-1}. Again, there is an area of ambiguity since the residuals from any of the "equilibrium" relationships could have been used in the estimation. The signs of the speed of adjustment coefficients are in accord with convergence toward the long-run equilibrium. In response to a positive discrepancy

Table 6.3 **Estimated a_1 and the Associated t-statistic**

	No lags	4 Lags
Δe_{yt}	−0.44301	−0.59525
	(−5.17489)	(−4.0741)
Δe_{zt}	−0.45195	−0.59344
	(−5.37882)	(−4.2263)
Δe_{wt}	−0.45525	−0.60711
	(−5.3896)	(−4.2247)

in e_{wt-1}, both y_t and z_t tend to increase while w_t tends to decrease. The error-correction term, however, is significant only in (6.40).

Finally, the diagnostic methods discussed in the last section should be applied to (6.40) through (6.42) in order to assess the model's adequacy. If you use actual data, lag-length tests and the properties of the residuals need to be considered. Moreover, innovation accounting could help determine whether the model is adequate. These tests are not performed here since there is no economic theory associated with the simulated data.

6. COINTEGRATION AND PURCHASING-POWER PARITY

Unfortunately, the simplicity of simulated data is rarely encountered in applied econometrics. To illustrate the Engle–Granger methodology using "real world" data, reconsider the theory of purchasing-power parity (PPP). Respectively, if e_t, p_t^*, and p_t denote the logarithms of the price of foreign exchange, foreign price level, and domestic price level, long-run PPP requires that $e_t + p_t^* - p_t$ be stationary. The unit root tests reported in Chapter 4 indicate that real exchange rates—defined as $r_t = e_t + p_t^* - p_t$—appear to be nonstationary. Cointegration offers an alternative method to check the theory; if PPP holds, the sequence formed by the sum $\{e_t + p_t^*\}$ should be cointegrated with the $\{p_t\}$ sequence. Call the constructed dollar value of the foreign price level f_t; that is, $f_t = e_t + p_t^*$. Long-run PPP asserts that there exists a linear combination of the form $f_t = \beta_0 + \beta_1 p_t + \mu_t$ such that $\{\mu_t\}$ is stationary *and* the cointegrating vector is such that $\beta_1 = 1$.

As reported in Chapter 4, in Enders (1988), I used price and exchange rate data for Germany, Japan, Canada, and the United States for both the Bretton Woods (1960–1971) and post–Bretton Woods (1973–1988) periods.[15] Pretesting the data indicated that for each period, both the U.S. price level $\{p_t\}$ and dollar values of the foreign price levels $\{e_t + p_t^*\}$ both contained a single unit root. With differing orders of integration, it would have been possible to immediately conclude that long-run PPP failed.

The next step was to estimate the long-run equilibrium relation by regressing each $f_t = e_t + p_t^*$ on p_t:

$$f_t = \beta_0 + \beta_1 p_t + \mu_t \tag{6.43}$$

Absolute PPP asserts that $f_t = p_t$, so that this version of the theory requires $\beta_0 = 0$ and $\beta_1 = 1$. The intercept β_0 is consistent with the relative version of PPP requiring only that domestic and foreign price levels move proportionately to each other. Unless there are compelling reasons to omit the constant, the recommended practice is to include an intercept term in the equilibrium regression. In fact, Engle and Granger's (1987) Monte Carlo simulations all include intercept terms.

The estimated values of β_1 and their associated standard errors are reported in Table 6.4. Note that five of the six values are estimated to be quite a bit below unity. Be especially careful not to make too much of these findings. It is *not* appropriate to conclude that each value of β_1 is significantly different from unity simply because the values of $(1 - \beta_1)$ exceed two or three standard deviations. The assumptions underlying this type of t-test are not applicable here unless the variables are actually cointegrated and p_t is the independant variable.[16]

The residuals from each regression equation, called $\{\hat{\mu}_t\}$, were checked for unit roots. The unit root tests are straightforward since the residuals from a regression equation have a zero mean and do not have a time trend. The following two equations were estimated using the residuals from each long-run equilibrium relationship:

$$\Delta\hat{\mu}_t = a_1\hat{\mu}_{t-1} + \epsilon_t \tag{6.44}$$

and

$$\Delta\hat{\mu}_t = a_1\hat{\mu}_{t-1} + \Sigma a_{i+1}\Delta\hat{\mu}_{t-i} + \epsilon_t \tag{6.45}$$

Table 6.4   **The Equilibrium Regressions**

	Germany	Japan	Canada
1973–1986			
Estimated β	0.5374	0.8938	0.7749
Standard error	(0.0415)	(0.0316)	(0.0077)
1960–1971			
Estimated β	0.6660	0.7361	1.0809
Standard Error	(0.0262)	(0.0154)	(0.0200)

Table 6.5 reports the estimated values of a_1 from (6.44) and (6.45) using a lag length of four. It bears repeating that failure to reject the null hypothesis $a_1 = 0$ means we cannot reject the null of no cointegration. Alternatively, if $-2 < a_1 < 0$, it is possible to conclude that the $\{\hat{\mu}_t\}$ sequence does not have a unit root and the $\{f_t\}$ and $\{p_t\}$ sequences are cointegrated. Also note that it is not appropriate to use either of the confidence intervals reported in Dickey and Fuller. The Dickey–Fuller statistics are inappropriate because the residuals used in (6.44) and (6.45) are not the actual error terms. Rather, these residuals are estimated error terms that are obtained from the estimate of the equilibrium regression. If we knew the magnitudes of the actual errors in each period, we could use the Dickey–Fuller tables.

Engle and Granger (1987) perform their own set of Monte Carlo experiments to construct confidence intervals for a_1 in (6.44) and (6.45). Under the null hypothesis hypothesis $a_1 = 0$, the critical values for the t-statistic depend on whether or not lags are appropriately included.[17] The critical values at the 1, 5, and 10% significance levels are given by

Critical Values for the Null of No Cointegration

	1%	5%	10%
No lags	−4.07	−3.37	−3.03
Lags	−3.73	−3.17	−2.91

Comparing the results of Table 6.5 with the critical values provided by Engle and Granger indicates that for only Japan during the fixed exchange rate period is it possible to reject the null hypothesis of no cointegration. By using four lags, the t-statistic for the null $a_1 = 0$ is calculated to be −3.437. At the 5% significance level, the critical value of t is −3.17. Hence, at the 5% significance level, we can reject the null of no cointegration (i.e., accept the alternative that the variables are cointegrated) and find in favor of PPP. For the other countries in each time period, we cannot reject the null hypothesis of no cointegration and must conclude that PPP generally failed.

The third step in the methodology entails estimation of the error-correction model. Only the Japan/U.S. model needs estimation since it is the sole case for which cointegration holds. The final error-correction models for Japanese and U.S. price levels during the 1960 to 1971 period were estimated to be

$$\Delta f_t = 0.00119 - 0.10548\hat{\mu}_{t-1} \tag{6.46}$$
$$(0.00044) \quad (0.04184)$$
$$\Delta p_t = 0.00156 + 0.01114\hat{\mu}_{t-1} \tag{6.47}$$
$$(0.00033) \quad (0.03175)$$

where $\hat{\mu}_{t-1}$ is the lagged residual from the long-run equilibrium regression

That is, $\hat{\mu}_{t-1}$ is the estimated value of $f_{t-1} - \beta_0 - \beta_1 p_{t-1}$ and standard errors are in parentheses.

Table 6.5   **Dickey–Fuller Tests of the Residuals**

	Germany	Japan	Canada
1973–1986			
no lags			
Estimated a_1	−0.0225	−.0151	−0.1001
Standard error	(0.0169)	(0.0236)	(0.0360)
t-Statistic for $a_1 = 0$	−1.331	−0.640	−2.781
4 lags			
Estimated a_1	−0.0316	−0.0522	−0.0983
Standard error	(0.0170)	(0.0236)	(0.0388)
t-Statistic for $a_1 = 0$	−1.859	−2.212	−2.533
1960–1971			
no lags			
Estimated a_1	−0.0189	−0.1137	−0.0528
Standard error	(0.0196)	(0.0449)	(0.0286)
t-Statistic for $a_1 = 0$	−0.966	−2.535	−1.846
4 lags			
Estimated a_1	−0.0294	−0.1821	−0.0509
Standard error	(0.0198)	(0.0530)	(0.0306)
t-Statistic for $a_1 = 0$	−1.468	−3.437	−1.663

Lag-length tests (see the discussion of χ^2 and F-tests for lag lengths in the previous chapter) indicated that lagged values of Δf_{t-i} or Δp_{t-i} did not need to be included in the error-correction equations. Note that the point estimates in (6.46) and (6.47) indicate a direct convergence to long-run equilibrium. For example, in the presence of a one-unit deviation from long-run PPP in period $t - 1$, the Japanese price level falls by 0.10548 units and the U.S. price level rises by 0.01114 units. Both these price changes in period t act to eliminate the positive discrepancy from long-run PPP present in period $t - 1$.

Notice the discrepancy between the magnitudes of the two speed of adjustment coefficients; in absolute value, the Japanese coefficient is approximately 10 times that of the U.S. coefficient. As compared to the Japanese price level, the U.S. price level responded only slightly to a deviation from PPP. Moreover, the error-correction term is about $\frac{1}{3}$ of a standard deviation from zero for the United States (0.01114/0.03175 = 0.3509) and approximately 2.5 standard deviations from zero for Japan (0.10548/0.04184 = 2.5210). Hence, at the 5% significance level, we can conclude that the speed of adjustment term is insignificantly different from zero for the United States but not for Japan. This result is consistent with the idea that the United States was a large country relative to Japan—movements in U.S. prices evolved independently of events in Japan, but movements in exchange rate adjusted Japanese prices responded to events in the United States.

7. CHARACTERISTIC ROOTS, RANK, AND COINTEGRATION

Although the Engle and Granger (1987) procedure is easily implemented, it does have several important defects. The estimation of the long-run equilibrium regression requires that the researcher place one variable on the left-hand side and use the others as regressors. For example, in the case of two variables, it is possible to run the Engle–Granger test for cointegration by using the residuals from either of the following two "equilibrium" regressions:

$$y_t = \beta_{10} + \beta_{11}z_t + e_{1t} \tag{6.48}$$

or

$$z_t = \beta_{20} + \beta_{21}y_t + e_{2t} \tag{6.49}$$

As the sample size grows infinitely large, asymptotic theory indicates that the test for a unit root in the $\{e_{1t}\}$ sequence becomes equivalent to the test for a unit root in the $\{e_{2t}\}$ sequence. Unfortunately, the large sample properties on which this result is derived may not be applicable to the sample sizes usually available to economists. In practice, it is possible to find that one regression indicates the variables are cointegrated, whereas reversing the order indicates no cointegration. This is a very undesirable feature of the procedure since the test for cointegration should be invariant to the choice of the variable selected for normalization. The problem is obviously compounded using three or more variables since any of the variables can be selected as the left-hand-side variable. Moreover, in tests using three or more variables, we know that there may be more than one cointegrating vector. The method has no systematic procedure for the separate estimation of the multiple cointegrating vectors.

Another serious defect of the Engle–Granger procedure is that it relies on a *two-step* estimator. The first step is to generate the error series $\{\hat{e}_t\}$ and the second step uses these generated errors to estimate a regression of the form $\Delta \hat{e}_t = a_1 \hat{e}_{t-1} + \cdots$. Thus, the coefficient a_1 is obtained by estimating a regression using the residuals from another regression. Hence, any error introduced by the researcher in Step 1 is carried into Step 2. Fortunately, several methods have been developed that avoid these problems. The Johansen (1988) and Stock and Watson (1988) maximum likelihood estimators circumvent the use of two-step estimators *and* can estimate and test for the presence of multiple cointegrating vectors. Moreover, these tests allow the researcher to test restricted versions of the cointegrating vector(s) and speed of adjustment parameters. Often, we want to test a theory by drawing statistical inferences concerning the magnitudes of the estimated coefficients.

Both the Johansen (1988) and Stock and Watson (1988) procedures rely heavily on relationship between the rank of a matrix and its characteristic roots. The

Appendix to this chapter reviews the essentials of these concepts; those of you wanting more details should review this appendix. For those wanting an intuitive explanation, notice that the Johansen procedure is nothing more than a multivariate generalization of the Dickey–Fuller test. In the univariate case, it is possible to view the stationarity of $\{y_t\}$ as being dependent on the magnitude $(a_1 - 1)$, that is,

$$y_t = a_1 y_{t-1} + \epsilon_t$$

or

$$\Delta y_t = (a_1 - 1)y_{t-1} + \epsilon_t$$

If $(a_1 - 1) = 0$, the $\{y_t\}$ process has a unit root. Ruling out the case in which $\{y_t\}$ is explosive, if $(a_1 - 1) \neq 0$ we can conclude that the $\{y_t\}$ sequence is stationary. The Dickey–Fuller tables provide the appropriate statistics to formally test the null hypothesis $(a_1 - 1) = 0$. Now consider the simple generalization to n variables; as in (6.26), let

$$x_t = A_1 x_{t-1} + \epsilon_t$$

so that

$$\begin{aligned}
\Delta x_t &= A_1 x_{t-1} - x_{t-1} + \epsilon_t \\
&= (A_1 - I)x_{t-1} + \epsilon_t \\
&= \pi x_{t-1} + \epsilon_t
\end{aligned} \tag{6.50}$$

where $\quad x_t$ and ϵ_t are $(n \times 1)$ vectors
$\qquad A_1 = $ an $(n \times n)$ matrix of parameters
$\qquad I \;\; = $ an $(n \times n)$ identity matrix
$\qquad$ and π is defined to be $(A_1 - I)$.

As indicated in the discussion surrounding (6.27), the rank of $(A_1 - I)$ equals the number of cointegrating vectors. By analogy to the univariate case, if $(A_1 - I)$ consists of all zeros, so that rank$(\pi) = 0$, all the $\{\Delta x_{it}\}$ sequences are unit root processes. Since there is no linear combination of the $\{x_{it}\}$ processes that is stationary, the variables are not cointegrated. If we rule out characteristic roots that are greater than unity, if rank$(\pi) = n$, (6.50) represents a convergent system of difference equations, so that all variables are stationary.

There are several ways to generalize (6.50). The equation is easily modified to allow for the presence of a drift term; simply let

$$\Delta x_t = A_0 + \pi x_{t-1} + \epsilon_t \tag{6.51}$$

where $\quad A_0 = $ a $(n \times 1)$ vector of constants $(a_{01}, a_{02}, \ldots a_{0n})'$

The effect of including the various a_{0i} is to allow for the possibility of a linear time trend in the data-generating process. You would want to include the drift term if the variables exhibited a decided tendency to increase or decrease. Here, the rank of π can be viewed as the number of cointegrating relationships existing in the "detrended" data. In the long run, $\pi x_{t-1} = 0$ so that each $\{\Delta x_{it}\}$ sequence has an expected value of a_{i0}. Aggregating all such changes over t yields the deterministic expression $a_{i0}t$.

Figure 6.3 illustrates the effects of including a drift in the data-generating process. Two random sequences with 100 observations each were generated; denote these sequences as $\{\epsilon_{yt}\}$ and $\{\epsilon_{zt}\}$. Initializing $y_0 = z_0 = 0$, we constructed the next 100 values of the $\{y_t\}$ and $\{z_t\}$ sequences as

$$\begin{bmatrix} \Delta y_t \\ \Delta z_t \end{bmatrix} = \begin{bmatrix} -0.2 & 0.2 \\ 0.2 & -0.2 \end{bmatrix} \begin{bmatrix} y_{t-1} \\ z_{t-1} \end{bmatrix} + \begin{bmatrix} \epsilon_{yt} \\ \epsilon_{zt} \end{bmatrix}$$

so that the cointegrating relationship is

$$-0.2y_{t-1} + 0.2z_{t-1} = 0$$

In the top graph (a) of Figure 6.3, you can see that each sequence resembles a random walk process and neither wanders too far from the other. The next graph (b) adds drift coefficients such that $a_{10} = a_{20} = 0.1$; now, each series tends to increase by 0.1 in each period. In addition to the fact that each sequence shares the same stochastic trend, note that each has the same deterministic time trend also. The fact that each has the same deterministic trend is *not* a result of the equivalence between a_{10} and a_{20}; the general solution to (6.51) necessitates that each have the same linear trend. For verification, the next graph (c) of Figure 6.3 sets $a_{10} = 0.1$ and $a_{20} = 0.4$. Again, the sequences have the same stochastic and deterministic trends. As an aside, note that increasing a_{20} and decreasing a_{10} would have an ambiguous effect on the slope of the deterministic trend. This point will be important in a moment; by appropriately manipulating the elements of A_0, it is possible to include a constant in the cointegrating vector(s) without imparting a deterministic time trend to the system.

One way to include a constant in the cointegrating relationships is to restrict the values of the various a_{i0}. For example, if π has a rank$(\pi) = 1$, the rows of π can differ only a scalar, so that it is possible to write each $\{\Delta x_{it}\}$ sequence in (6.51) as

$$\Delta x_{1t} = \pi_{11}x_{1t-1} + \pi_{12}x_{2t-1} + \cdots + \pi_{1r}x_{nt-1} + a_{10} + \epsilon_{1t}$$
$$\Delta x_{2t} = s_2(\pi_{11}x_{1t-1} + \pi_{12}x_{2t-1} + \cdots + \pi_{1r}x_{nt-1}) + a_{20} + \epsilon_{2t}$$
$$\cdots$$
$$\Delta x_{nt} = s_n(\pi_{11}x_{1t-1} + \pi_{12}x_{2t-1} + \cdots + \pi_{1r}x_{nt-1}) + a_{n0} + \epsilon_{nt}$$

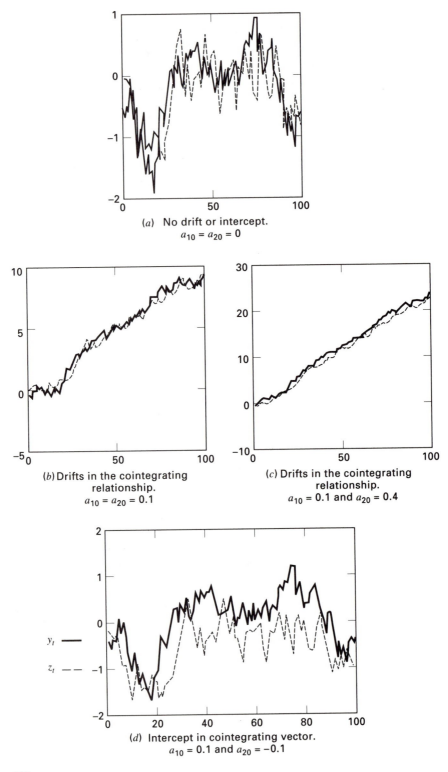

(a) No drift or intercept.
$a_{10} = a_{20} = 0$

(b) Drifts in the cointegrating
relationship.
$a_{10} = a_{20} = 0.1$

(c) Drifts in the cointegrating
relationship.
$a_{10} = 0.1$ and $a_{20} = 0.4$

y_t ——
z_t — —

(d) Intercept in cointegrating vector.
$a_{10} = 0.1$ and $a_{20} = -0.1$

where s_i = scalars such that $s_i \pi_{1j} = \pi_{ij}$

If the a_{i0} can be restricted such that $a_{i0} = s_i a_{10}$, it follows that all the Δx_{it} can be written with the constant included in the cointegrating vector:

$$\Delta x_{1t} = (\pi_{11} x_{1t-1} + \pi_{12} x_{2t-1} + \cdots + \pi_{1n} x_{nt-1} + a_{10}) + \epsilon_{1t}$$
$$\Delta x_{2t} = s_2(\pi_{11} x_{1t-1} + \pi_{12} x_{2t-1} + \cdots + \pi_{1n} x_{nt-1} + a_{10}) + \epsilon_{2t}$$
$$\cdots$$
$$\Delta x_{1n} = s_n(\pi_{11} x_{1t-1} + \pi_{12} x_{2t-1} + \cdots + \pi_{1n} x_n + a_{10}) + \epsilon_{nt}$$

or in compact form,

$$\Delta x_t = \pi^* x_{t-1} + \epsilon_t \tag{6.52}$$

where $x_t = (x_{1t}, x_{2t}, \ldots, x_{nt})'$
$x^*_{t-1} = (x_{1t-1}, x_{2t-1}, \ldots, x_{nt-1}, 1)'$

$$\pi^* = \begin{bmatrix} \pi_{11} & \pi_{12} & \cdots & \pi_{1n} & a_{10} \\ \pi_{21} & \pi_{22} & \cdots & \pi_{2n} & a_{20} \\ \cdot & \cdot & \cdots & \cdot & \cdot \\ \pi_{n1} & \pi_{n2} & \cdots & \pi_{nn} & a_{n0} \end{bmatrix}$$

The interesting feature of (6.52) is that the linear trend is purged from the system. In essence, the various a_{i0} have been altered in such a way that the general solution for each $\{x_{it}\}$ does not contain a time trend. The solution to the set of difference equations represented by (6.52) is such that all Δx_{it} are expected to equal zero when $\pi_{11} x_{1t-1} + \pi_{12} x_{2t-1} + \cdots + \pi_{1n} x_{nt-1} + a_{10} = 0$.

To highlight the difference between (6.51) and (6.52), the last graph (d) of Figure 6.3 illustrates the consequences of setting $a_{10} = 0.1$ and $a_2 = -0.1$. You can see that neither sequence contains a deterministic trend. In fact, for the data shown in the figure, the trend will vanish so long as we select values of the drift terms maintaining the relationship $a_{10} = -a_{20}$. (You are asked to demonstrate this result in the Questions and Exercises section at the end of this chapter.)

As with the augmented Dickey–Fuller test, the multivariate model can also be generalized to allow for a higher-order autoregressive process. Consider

$$x_t = A_1 x_{t-1} + A_2 x_{t-2} + \cdots + A_p x_{t-p} + \epsilon_t \tag{6.53}$$

Figure 6.3   Drifts and intercepts in cointegrating relationships. (a) No drift or intercept. (b) and (c) Drifts in the cointegrating relationship. (d) Intercept in the cointegrating vector.

where x_t = the $(n \times 1)$ vector $(x_{1t}, x_{2t}, \ldots, x_{nt})'$
  ϵ_t = is an independently and identically distributed n-dimensional vector with zero mean and variance matrix Σ_ϵ[18]

Equation (6.53) can be put in a more usable form by subtracting x_{t-1} from each side to obtain

$$\Delta x_t = (A_1 - I)x_{t-1} + A_2 x_{t-2} + A_3 x_{t-3} + \cdots + A_p x_{t-p} + \epsilon_t$$

Now add and subtract $(A_1 - I)x_{t-2}$ to obtain

$$\Delta x_t = (A_1 - I)\Delta x_{t-1} + (A_2 + A_1 - I)x_{t-2} + A_3 x_{t-3} + \cdots + A_p x_{t-p} + \epsilon_t$$

Next add and subtract $(A_2 + A_1 - I)x_{t-3}$ to obtain

$$\Delta x_t = (A_1 - I)\Delta x_{t-1} + (A_2 + A_1 - I)\Delta x_{t-2} + (A_3 + A_2 + A_1 - I)x_{t-3} + \cdots + A_p x_{t-p} + \epsilon_t$$

Continuing in this fashion, we obtain

$$\Delta x_t = \sum_{i=1}^{p-1} \pi_i \Delta x_{t-i} + \pi x_{t-p} + \epsilon_t$$

$$(6.54)$$

where

$$\pi = -\left(I - \sum_{i=1}^{p} A_i \right)$$

$$\pi_i = -\left(I - \sum_{j=1}^{i} A_j \right)$$

Again, the key feature to note in (6.54) is the rank of the matrix π; the rank of π is equal to the number of independent cointegrating vectors. Clearly, if rank$(\pi) = 0$, the matrix is null and (6.54) the usual VAR model in first differences. Instead, if π is of rank n, the vector process is stationary. In intermediate cases, if rank$(\pi) = 1$, there is a single cointegrating vector and the expression πx_{t-p} is the error-correction factor. For other cases in which $1 < $ rank$(\pi) < n$, there are multiple cointegrating vectors.

As detailed in the appendix, the number of distinct cointegrating vectors can be obtained by checking the significance of the characteristic roots of π. We know that the rank of a matrix is equal to the number of its characteristic roots that differ from zero. Suppose we obtained the matrix π and ordered the n characteristic roots such that $\lambda_1 > \lambda_2 > \cdots > \lambda_n$. If the variables in x_t are *not* cointegrated, the rank of π is zero and all these characteristic roots will equal zero. Since $\ln(1) = 0$, each of the expressions $\ln(1 - \lambda_i)$ will equal zero if the variables are not cointegrated. Similarly, if the rank of π is unity, $0 < \lambda_1 < 1$ so that the first expression $\ln(1 - \lambda_1)$ will be negative and all the other $\lambda_i = 0$ so that $\ln(1 - \lambda_2) = \ln(1 - \lambda_3) = \cdots = \ln(1 - \lambda_n) = 0$.

In practice, we can obtain only estimates of π and the characteristic roots. The test for the number of characteristic roots that are insignificantly different from unity can be conducted using the following two test statistics:

$$\lambda_{\text{trace}}(r) = -T \sum_{i=r+1}^{n} \ln(1 - \hat{\lambda}_i) \tag{6.55}$$

$$\lambda_{\text{max}}(r, r+1) = -T \ln(1 - \hat{\lambda}_{r+1}) \tag{6.56}$$

where $\hat{\lambda}_i$ = the estimated values of the characteristic roots (also called eigenvalues) obtained from the estimated π matrix

T = the number of usable observations

When the appropriate values of r are clear, these statistics are simply referred to as λ_{trace} and λ_{max}.

The first statistic tests the null hypothesis that the number of distinct cointegrating vectors is less than or equal to r against a general alternative. From the previous discussion, it should be clear that λ_{trace} equals zero when all $\lambda_i = 0$. The further the estimated characteristic roots are from zero, the more negative is $\ln(1 - \lambda_i)$ and the larger the λ_{trace} statistic. The second statistic tests the null that the number of cointegrating vectors is r against the alternative of $r + 1$ cointegrating vectors. Again, if the estimated value of the characteristic root is close to zero, λ_{max} will be small.

Johansen and Juselius (1990) provide the critical values of the λ_{trace} and λ_{max} statistics obtained using simulation studies. The critical values are reproduced in Table B at the end of this text. The distribution of these statistics depends on:

1. The number of nonstationary components under the null hypothesis (i.e., $n - r$).
2. The form of the vector A_0. Use the middle portion of Table B if you do not include a constant in the cointegrating vector or a drift term. Use the top portion of the table if you include the drift term A_0. Use the bottom portion of the table if you include a constant in the cointegrating vector.

Using quarterly data for Denmark over the sample period 1974:1 to 1987:3, Johansen and Juselius (1990) let the x_t vector be represented by

$$x_t = (m2_t, y_t, i_t^d, i_t^b)'$$

where $m2$ = log of the real money supply as measured by M2 deflated by a price index

y = log of real income

i^d = deposit rate on money representing a direct return on money holding

i^b = bond rate representing the opportunity cost of holding money

Including a constant in the cointegrating relationship (i.e., augmenting x_{t-p} with a constant), they report that the residuals from (6.54) appear to be serially uncorrelated. The four characteristic roots of the estimated π matrix are given in the first column below.[19]

	$\lambda_{max} = -T\ln(1 - \hat{\lambda}_{r+1})$	$\lambda_{trace} = -T\Sigma \ln(1 - \hat{\lambda}_i)$
$\hat{\lambda}_1 = 0.4332$	30.09	49.14
$\hat{\lambda}_2 = 0.1776$	10.36	19.05
$\hat{\lambda}_3 = 0.1128$	6.34	8.69
$\hat{\lambda}_4 = 0.0434$	2.35	2.35

The second column reports the various λ_{max} statistics as the number of usable observations ($T = 53$) multiplied by $\ln(1 - \hat{\lambda}_i)$. For example, $-53 \ln(1 - 0.0434) = 2.35$ and $-53 \ln(1 - 0.1128) = 6.34$. The last column reports the λ_{trace} statistics as the summation of the λ_{max} statistics. Simple arithmetic reveals that $8.69 = 2.35 + 6.34$ and $19.05 = 2.35 + 6.34 + 10.36$.

To test the null hypothesis $r = 0$ against the general alternative $r = 1, 2, 3,$ or 4, use the λ_{trace} statistic. Since the null hypothesis is $r = 0$ and there are four variables (i.e., $n = 4$), the summation in (6.55) runs from 1 to 4. If we sum over the four values, the calculated value of λ_{trace} is 49.14. Since Johansen and Juselius (1990) include the constant in the cointegrating vector, this calculated value of 49.14 is compared to the critical values reported in the bottom portion of Table B. For $n - r = 4$, the critical values of λ_{trace} are 49.925, 53.347, and 60.054 at the 90, 95, and 99% levels, respectively. Thus, at the 90% level, the restriction is *not* binding, so that the variables are *not* cointegrated using this test.

To make a point and give you practice in using the table, suppose you want to test the null hypothesis $r \leq 1$ against the alternative $r = 2, 3,$ or 4. Under this null hypothesis, the summation in (6.55) runs from 2 to 4, so that the calculated value of λ_{trace} is 19.05. For $n - r = 3$, the critical values of λ_{trace} are 32.093, 35.068, and 40.198 at the 90, 95, and 99% levels, respectively. The restriction $r = 0$ or $r = 1$ is not binding.

In contrast to the λ_{trace} statistic, the λ_{max} statistic has a specific alternative hypothesis. To test the null hypothesis $r = 0$ against the specific alternative $r = 1$, use Equation (6.56). The calculated value of the $\lambda_{max}(0, 1)$ statistic is $-53 \ln(1 - 0.4332) = 30.09$. For $n - r = 4$, the critical values of λ_{max} are 25.611, 28.167, 30.262, and 33.121 at the 90, 95, 97.5, and 99% levels, respectively. Hence, it is possible to reject the null hypothesis $r = 0$ at the 95% level (but not the 97.5% level) and conclude that there is only one cointegrating vector (i.e., $r = 1$). Before reading on, you should take a moment to examine the data and convince yourself that the null hypothesis $r = 1$ against the alternative $r = 2$ cannot be rejected at conventional levels. You should find that the calculated value of the λ_{max} statistic for $r = 1$ is 10.36 and the critical value at the 90% level 19.796. Hence, there is no significant evidence of more than one cointegrating vector.

The example illustrates the important point that the results of the λ_{max} and λ_{trace} tests can conflict. The λ_{max} test has the sharper alternative hypothesis. It is usually preferred for trying to pin down the number of cointegrating vectors.

8. HYPOTHESIS TESTING IN A COINTEGRATION FRAMEWORK

In the Dickey-Fuller tests discussed in Chapter 4, it was important to correctly ascertain the form of the deterministic regressors. A similar situation applies in the Johansen procedure. As you can see in Table B, the critical values of the λ_{trace} and λ_{max} statistics are smallest with a drift term and largest with an intercept term included in the cointegrating vector. Instead of cavalierly positing the form of A_0, it is possible to test restricted forms of the vector.

One of the most interesting aspects of the Johansen procedure is that it allows for testing restricted forms of the cointegrating vector(s). In a money demand study, you might want to test restrictions concerning the long-run proportionality between money and prices, the size of the income and interest rate elasticities of demand for money. In terms of Equation (6.1) (i.e., $m_t = \beta_0 + \beta_1 p_t + \beta_2 y_t + \beta_3 r_t + \epsilon_t$), the restrictions of interest are: $\beta_1 = 1$, $\beta_2 > 0$, and $\beta_3 < 0$.

The key insight to all such hypothesis tests is that *if there are r cointegrating vectors, only these r linear combinations of the variables are stationary.* All other linear combinations are nonstationary. Thus, suppose you reestimate the model restricting the parameters of π. If the restrictions are not binding, you should find that the number of cointegrating vectors has *not* diminished.

To test for the presence of an intercept in the cointegrating vector as opposed to the unrestricted drift A_0, estimate the two forms of the model. Denote the ordered characteristic roots of unrestricted π matrix by $\hat{\lambda}_1, \hat{\lambda}_2, \ldots, \hat{\lambda}_n$ and the characteristic roots of the model with the intercept(s) in the cointegrating vector(s) by $\hat{\lambda}_1^*, \hat{\lambda}_2^*, \ldots, \hat{\lambda}_n^*$. Suppose that the unrestricted form of the model has r non-zero characteristic roots. Asymptotically, the statistic:

$$-T \sum_{i=r+1}^{n} \left[\ln(1 - \hat{\lambda}_i^*) - \ln(1 - \hat{\lambda}_i) \right] \tag{6.57}$$

has a χ^2 distribution with $(n - r)$ degrees of freedom.

The intuition behind the test is that all values of $\ln(1 - \hat{\lambda}_i^*)$ and $\ln(1 - \hat{\lambda}_i)$ should be equivalent if the restriction is not binding. Hence, small values for the test statistic imply that it is permissible to include the intercept in the cointegrating vector. However, the likelihood of finding a stationary linear combination of the n variables is greater with the intercept in the cointegrating vector than if the intercept is absent from the cointegrating vector. Thus, a large value of $\hat{\lambda}_{r+1}^*$ [and a corresponding large value of $-T \ln(1 - \hat{\lambda}_{r+1}^*)$], implies that the restriction artificially inflates the number of cointegrating vectors. Thus, as proven by Johansen (1991), if the test statistic is sufficiently large, it is possible to reject the null hypothesis of an intercept in the cointegrating vector(s) and conclude that there is a linear trend in the variables. This is precisely the case represented by the middle portion of Figure 6.3.

Johansen and Juselius (1990) test the restriction that their estimated Danish money demand function does not have a drift. Since they found only one cointegrating vector among $m2$, y, i^d, and i^b, set $n = 4$ and $r = 1$. The calculated value of the χ^2 statistic in (6.57) is 1.99. With three degrees of freedom, this is insignificant at conventional levels; they conclude that the data do not have a linear time trend, and find it appropriate to include the constant in the cointegrating vector.

In order to test restrictions on the cointegrating vector, Johansen defines the two matrices α and β, both of dimension $(n \times r)$, where r is the rank of π. The properties of α and β are such that

$$\pi = \alpha\beta'$$

The matrix β is the matrix of cointegrating parameters, and the matrix α the matrix of weights with which each cointegrating vector enters the n equations of the VAR. In a sense, α can be viewed as the matrix of the speed of adjustment parameters. Due to the cross-equation restrictions, it is not possible to estimate α and β using OLS.[20] However, with maximum likelihood estimation, it is possible to (1) estimate (6.53) as an error-correction model; (2) determine the rank of π; (3) use the r most significant cointegrating vectors to form β'; and (4) select α such that $\pi = \alpha\beta'$. Question 5 at the end of this chapter asks you to find several such α and β' matrices.

It is easy to understand the process in the case of a single cointegrating vector. Given that rank(π) = 1, the rows of π are all linear multiples of each other. Hence, the equations in (6.54) have the form:

$$\Delta x_{1t} = \cdots + \pi_{11}x_{1t-p} + \pi_{12}x_{2t-p} + \cdots + \pi_{1n}x_{nt-p} + \epsilon_{1t}$$
$$\Delta x_{2t} = \cdots + s_2(\pi_{11}x_{1t-p} + \pi_{12}x_{2t-p} + \cdots + \pi_{1n}x_{nt-p}) + \epsilon_{st}$$
$$\cdots$$
$$\Delta x_{nt} = \cdots + sn(\pi_{11}x_{1t-p} + \pi_{12}x_{2t-p} + \cdots + \pi_{1n}x_{nt-p}) + \epsilon_{nt}$$

where the s_i are scalars

and for notational simplicity, the matrices $\pi_i\Delta x_{t-i}$ have not been written out.

Now define $\alpha_i = (s_i\pi_{ij})$, so that each equation can be written as

$$\Delta x_{it} = \cdots + \alpha_i(x_{1t-p} + \beta_2 x_{2t-p} + \cdots + \beta_n x_{nt-p}) + \epsilon_{it} \qquad (i = 1, \ldots, n)$$

or in matrix form,

$$\Delta x_t = \sum_{i=1}^{p-1} \pi_i \Delta x_{t-i} + \alpha\beta' x_{t-p} + \epsilon_t \qquad (6.58)$$

where the single cointegrating vector is $\beta = (1, \beta_2, \beta_3, \ldots, \beta_n)'$ and the speed of adjustment parameters are given by $\alpha = (\alpha_1, \alpha_2, \ldots, \alpha_n)'$.

Once α and β' are determined, testing various restrictions on α and β' is straightforward if you remember the fundamental point that if there are r cointegrating vectors, only these r linear combinations of the variables are stationary. Thus, the test statistics involve comparing the number of cointegrating vectors under the null and alternative hypotheses. Again, let $\hat{\lambda}_1, \hat{\lambda}_2, \ldots, \hat{\lambda}_n$ and $\hat{\lambda}_1^*, \hat{\lambda}_2^*, \ldots, \hat{\lambda}_n^*$ denote the ordered characteristic roots of the unrestricted and restricted models, respectively. To test restrictions on β, form the test statistic:

$$ T \sum_{i=1}^{r} [\ln(1 - \hat{\lambda}_i^*) - \ln(1 - \hat{\lambda}_i)] \tag{6.59} $$

Asymptotically, this statistic has a χ^2 distribution with degrees of freedom equal to the number of restrictions placed on β. Small values of $\hat{\lambda}_i^*$ relative to $\hat{\lambda}_i$ (for $i \leq r$) imply a reduced number of cointegrating vectors. Hence, the restriction embedded in the null hypothesis is binding if the calculated value of the test statistic exceeds that in a χ^2 table.

For example, Johansen and Juselius test the restriction that money and income move proportionally. Their estimated long-run equilibrium relationship is:

$$ m2_{t-p} = 1.03 y_{t-p} - 5.21\, i^b_{t-p} + 4.22 i^d_{t-p} + 6.06 $$

They restrict the coefficient of income to be unity and find the restricted values of the $\hat{\lambda}_i^*$ to be such that

	$\hat{\lambda}_i^*$	$T \ln(1 - \hat{\lambda}_i^*)$
$i = 1$	0.433	-30.04
$i = 2$	0.172	-10.01
$i = 3$	0.044	-2.36
$i = 4$	0.006	-0.32

Given that the unrestricted model has $r = 1$ and $-T \ln(1 - \hat{\lambda}_1) = 30.09$, (6.59) becomes: $-30.04 + 30.09 = 0.05$. Since there is only 1 restriction imposed on β, the test statistic has a χ^2 distribution with 1 degree of freedom. A χ^2 table indicates that 0.05 is not significant; hence, they conclude that the restriction is not binding.

Restrictions on α can be tested in the same way. The procedure is to restrict α and compare the r most significant characteristic roots for the restricted and unrestricted models using (6.59). If the calculated value of (6.59) exceeds that from a χ^2 table, with degrees of freedom equal to the number of restrictions placed on α, the restrictions can be rejected. For example, Johansen and Juselius (1990) test the restriction that only money demand (i.e., m2$_t$) responds to the deviation from long run equilibrium. Formally, they test the restriction that $\alpha_2 = \alpha_3 = \alpha_4 = 0$. Restricting the three values of α_i to equal zero, they find the largest characteristic root in the restricted model is such that $T \ln(1 - \hat{\lambda}_1^*) = -23.42$. Since the unrestricted model is such that $T \ln(1 - \hat{\lambda}_1) = -30.09$, equation (6.59) becomes $-23.42 - (-30.09) = 7.67$. The χ^2 statistic with 3 degrees of freedom is 7.81 at the 5% significance level. Hence, they find mild support for the hypothesis that the restriction is not binding.

If there is a single cointegrating vector, the Engle–Granger and Johansen methods have the same asymptotic distribution. If it can be determined that only one cointegrating vector exists, it is common to rely on the estimated error-correction model to test restrictions on α. If $r = 1$, and a single value of α is being tested, the usual t-statistic is asymptotically equivalent to the Johansen test.

9. ILLUSTRATING THE JOHANSEN METHODOLOGY

An interesting way to illustrate the Johansen methodology is to use exactly the same data shown in Figure 6.2. Although the Engle–Granger technique did find that the simulated data were cointegrated, a comparison of the two procedures is useful. Use the following four steps when implementing the Johansen procedure.

STEP 1:   Pretests and lag length. It is good practice to pretest all variables to assess their order of integration. Plot the data to see if a linear time trend is likely to be present in the data-generating process. Although forms of the Johansen tests can detect differing orders of integration, it is wise not to mix variables with different orders of integration.

The results of the test can be quite sensitive to the lag length so it is important to be careful. The most common procedure is to estimate a vector autoregression using the *undifferenced* data. Then use the same lag-length tests as in a traditional VAR. Begin with the longest lag length deemed reasonable and test whether the lag length can be shortened. For example, if we want to test whether lags 2 through 4 are important, we can estimate the following two VARs:

$$x_t = A_0 + A_1 x_{t-1} + A_2 x_{t-2} + A_3 x_{t-3} + A_4 x_{t-4} + \epsilon_{1t} \tag{6.60}$$
$$x_t = A_0 + A_1 x_{t-1} + e_{2t} \tag{6.61}$$

where x_t = the $(n \times 1)$ vector of variables
        A_0 = $(n \times 1)$ matrix of intercept terms
        A_i = $(n \times n)$ matrices of coefficients
        e_{1t} and e_{2t} = $(n \times 1)$ vector of error terms

Estimate (6.60) with four lags of each variable in each equation and call the variance/covariance matrix of residuals Σ_4. Now estimate (6.61) using only one lag of each variable in each equation and call the variance/covariance matrix of residuals Σ_1. Even though we are working with nonstationary variables, the likelihood ratio test statistic recommended by Sims (1980) is the same as that reported in Chapter 5:

$$(T - c)(\log |\Sigma_1| - \log |\Sigma_4|)$$

where T = number of observations
  c = number of parameters in the unrestricted system
  $\log |\Sigma_i|$ = natural logarithm of the determinant of Σ_i.

Following Sims, use the χ^2 distrubution with degrees of freedom equal to the number of coefficient restrictions. Since each A_i has n^2 coefficients, constraining $A_2 = A_3 = A_4 = 0$ entails $3n^2$ restrictions. Alternately, you can select lag length p using the multivariate generalizations of the AIC or SBC.

STEP 2: Estimate the model and determine the rank of π. Many time-series statistical software packages contain a routine to estimate the model. Here, it suffices to say that OLS is not appropriate since it is necessary to impose cross-equation restrictions on the π matrix. You may choose to estimate the model in three forms: (1) with all elements of A_0 set equal to zero, (2) with a drift, or (3) with a constant term in the cointegrating vector.

With the simulated data in Figure 6.2 such that $x_t = (y_t, z_t, w_t)'$, an intercept term in the cointegrating vector(s) was included even though the data-generating process did not contain an intercept. As we saw in the last section, it is possible to test for the presence of the intercept. Lag-length tests indicate setting $p = 2$, so that the estimated form of the model is

$$\Delta x_t = A_0 + \pi_1 \Delta x_{t-1} + \pi x_{t-2} + e_t \qquad (6.62)$$

where the drift term A_0 was constrained so as to force the intercept to appear in the cointegrating vector.

As always, carefully analyze the properties of the residuals of the estimated model. Any evidence that the errors are not white-noise usually means that lag lengths are too short. Figure 6.4 shows the deviations of y_t from the long run equilibrium relationship ($\mu_t = -0.01331 - 1.0000y_t - 1.0350z_t + 1.0162w_t$) and one of the short-run error sequences [i.e., the $\{e_{yt}\}$ sequence that equals the residuals from the y_t equation in (6.62)]. Both sequences conform to their theoretical properties in that the residuals from the long-run equilibrium relationship appear to be stationary and the estimated values of the $\{\epsilon_{yt}\}$ sequence approximate a white-noise process.

The estimated values of the characteristic roots of the π matrix in (6.62) are

$$\lambda_1 = 0.32600, \quad \lambda_2 = 0.14032, \quad \text{and } \lambda_3 = 0.033168$$

Figure 6.4 Long- and short-run errors.

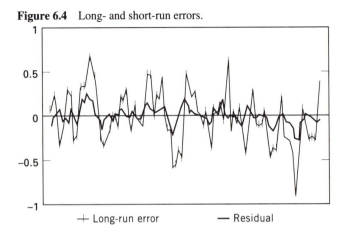

Since $T = 98$ (100 observations less the two lost as a result of using two lags), the calculated values of λ_{max} and λ_{trace} for the various possible values of r are reported in the center column of Table 6.6.

Consider the hypothesis that the variables are not cointegrated (so that the rank $\pi = 0$). Depending on the alternative hypothesis, there are two possible test statistics to use. If we are simply interested in the hypothesis that the variables are not cointegrated ($r = 0$) against the alternative of one or more cointegrating vectors ($r > 0$), we can calculate the $\lambda_{trace}(0)$ statistic:

$$\lambda_{trace}(0) = -T[\ln(1 - \lambda_1) + \ln(1 - \lambda_2) + \ln(1 - \lambda_3)]$$
$$= -98\,[\ln(1 - 0.326) + \ln(1 - 0.14032) + \ln(1 - 0.033168)]$$
$$= 56.786$$

Table 6.6 **The λ_{max} and λ_{trace} Tests**

Null Hypothesis	Alternative Hypothesis		95% Critical Value	90% Critical Value
λ_{trace} *tests*		λ_{trace} *value*		
$r = 0$	$r > 0$	56.786	35.068	32.093
$r \le 1$	$r > 1$	18.123	20.168	17.957
$r \le 2$	$r > 2$	3.306	9.094	7.563
λ_{max} *tests*		λ_{max} *value*		
$r = 0$	$r = 1$	38.663	21.894	19.796
$r = 1$	$r = 2$	14.817	15.252	13.781
$r = 2$	$r = 3$	3.306	9.094	7.563

Since 56.786 exceeds the 95% critical value of the λ_{trace} statistic (in the bottom portion of Table B, the critical value is 35.068), it is possible to reject the null hypothesis of no cointegrating vectors and accept the alternative of one or more cointegrating vectors. Next, we can use the $\lambda_{\text{trace}}(1)$ statistic to test the null of $r \le 1$ against the alternative of two or three cointegrating vectors. In this case, the $\lambda_{\text{trace}}(1)$ statistic is

$$\begin{aligned}
\lambda_{\text{trace}}(1) &= -T[\ln(1 - \lambda_2) + \ln(1 - \lambda_3)] \\
&= -98 \, [\ln \, (1 - 0.14032) + \ln(1 - 0.033168)] \\
&= 18.123
\end{aligned}$$

Since 18.123 is less than the 95% critical value of 20.168, we cannot reject the null hypothesis at this significance level. However, 18.123 does exceed the 90% critical value of 17.957; some researchers might reject the null and accept the alternative of two or three cointegrating vectors. The $\lambda_{\text{trace}}(2)$ statistic indicates no more than two cointegrating vectors at the 90% level significance level.

The λ_{max} statistic does not help to clarify the issue. The null hypothesis of no cointegrating vectors ($r = 0$) against the specific alternative $r = 1$ is clearly rejected. The calculated value $\lambda_{\text{max}}(0, 1) = -98 \ln(1 - 0.326) = 38.663$ exceeds the 95% critical value of 21.894. Note that the test of the null hypothesis $r = 1$ against the specific alternative $r = 2$ cannot be rejected at the 95% level, but can be rejected at the 90% level. The calculated value of $\lambda_{\text{max}}(1, 2)$ is $-98 \ln(1 - 0.14032) = 14.817$, whereas the critical values at the 95 and 90% significance levels are 15.752 and 13.781, respectively. Even though the actual data-generating process contains only one cointegrating vector, the realizations are such that researchers willing to use the 90% significance level would incorrectly conclude that there are two cointegrating vectors. Failing to reject an incorrect null hypothesis is always a danger of using wide confidence intervals.

STEP 3: Analyze the normalized cointegrating vector(s) and speed of adjustment coefficients. If we select $r = 1$, the estimated cointegrating vector ($\beta_0 \; \beta_1 \; \beta_2 \; \beta_3$) is

$$\beta = (0.00553 \; 0.41532 \; 0.42988 \; -0.42207)$$

If we normalize with respect to β_1, the normalized cointegrating vector and speed of adjustment parameters are

$$\begin{aligned}
\beta &= (-0.01331 \; -1.0000 \; -1.0350 \; 1.0162) \\
\alpha_y &= 0.54627 \\
\alpha_z &= 0.16578 \\
\alpha_w &= 0.21895
\end{aligned}$$

Recall that the data were constructed imposing the long-run relationship $w_t = y_t + z_t$, so that the estimated coefficients of the normalized β vector are close to their theoretical values of $(0, -1, -1, 1)$. Consider the following tests:

1. The test that $\beta_0 = 0$ entails one restriction on one cointegrating vector; hence, the likelihood ratio test has a χ^2 distribution with one degree of freedom. The calculated value of $\chi^2 = 0.011234$ is not significant at conventional levels. Hence, we cannot reject the null hypothesis that $\beta_0 = 0$. Thus, it is possible to use the form of the model in which there is neither a drift nor an intercept in the cointegrating vector. Thus, to clarify the issue concerning the number of cointegrating vectors, it would be wise to reestimate the model excluding the constant from the cointegrating vector.

2. To restrict the normalized cointegrating vector such that $\beta_2 = -1$ and $\beta_3 = 1$ entails two restrictions on one cointegrating vector; hence, the likelihood ratio test has a χ^2 distribution with two degrees of freedom. The calculated value of $\chi^2 = 0.55350$ is not significant at conventional levels. Hence, we cannot reject the null hypothesis that $\beta_2 = -1$ and $\beta_3 = 1$.

3. To test the joint restriction $\beta = (0, -1, -1, 1)$ entails the three restrictions $\beta_0 = 0$, $\beta_2 = -1$, and $\beta_3 = 1$. The calculated value of χ^2 with three degrees of freedom is 1.8128, so that the significance level is 0.612. Hence, we cannot reject the null hypothesis that the cointegrating vector is $= (0, -1, -1, 1)$.

STEP 4: Innovation accounting. Finally, innovation accounting and causality tests on the error-correction model of (6.62) could help to identify a structural model and determine whether the estimated model appears to be reasonable. Since the simulated data have no economic meaning, innovation accounting is not performed here.

10. GENERALIZED PURCHASING-POWER PARITY

Most studies of purchasing-power parity (PPP) find the theory inadequate to explain price and exchange rate movements for low inflation countries during the post–World War II period. The theory of generalized purchasing-power parity (G-PPP) was developed in Enders and Hurn (1994) to explain the observed nonstationarity of real exchange rate behavior. The idea is that traditional PPP can fail because the fundamental macroeconomic variables that determine real exchange rates—such as real output levels and expenditure patterns—are nonstationary; thus, the real rates themselves will tend to be nonstationary.[21] Although bilateral real exchange rates are generally nonstationary, G-PPP hypothesizes that they will exhibit common stochastic trends if the fundamental variables (i.e, the forcing variables) are sufficiently interrelated.

G-PPP can be interpreted in terms of optimum currency areas. In the two-country case, the real exchange rate between the two countries comprising the domain of a currency area should be stationary. In a multicountry setting, within an appropriately defined currency area, the forcing variables will be sufficiently interrelated, so that the real exchange rates themselves will share common trends. Hence, within a currency area we would expect there to be at least one linear combination of the various bilateral real exchange rates that is stationary.

To test the theory, we obtained wholesale prices and exchange rates from the IMF data tapes over the period January 1973 to December 1989 for Australia, Germany, India, Indonesia, Japan, Korea, Philippines, Singapore, Thailand, the U.K., and the United States.[22] The real exchange rate series were constructed using Japan as the base country; for each country, we defined the real bilateral exchange rate with Japan to be the log of the domestic WPI plus the log of the domestic currency price of the yen minus the log of the Japanese WPI. All were then normalized, so that the real rates in January 1973 are all equal to zero (for Indonesia, January 1974 = 0). If we use augmented Dickey–Fuller (1979, 1981) and Phillips–Perron (1988) tests with 12 lags (since monthly data are used), it is not possible to reject a null of a unit root at conventional significance levels for any of the series. These findings are hardly surprising; they simply confirm what other studies have concluded about the nonstationarity of real exchange rates in the post–Bretton Woods period. You can use the data contained in the file REALRATE.PRN along with the discussion below.

In accord with G-PPP, suppose that m of the countries in an n-country world comprise the domain of a currency area; for these m countries, there exists a long-run equilibrium relationship between the $m - 1$ bilateral real rates such that:

$$r_{12t} = \beta_0 + \beta_{13}r_{13t} + \beta_{14}r_{14t} + \cdots + \beta_{1m}r_{1mt} + e_t \qquad (6.63)$$

where the r_{1it} = the bilateral real exchange rates in period t between country 1
   (Japan in our empirical estimations) and country i
   β_0 = an intercept term
   β_{1i} = the parameters of the cointegrating vector
   e_t = a stationary stochastic disturbance term

For the special case in which all the β_{1i} are zero, Equation (6.63) becomes the familiar PPP relationship between domestic prices, foreign prices, and the exchange rate.

Empirical Tests

Our first step is to consider whether there exists a cointegrating vector between the three real rates for Germany, the U.K., and the United States. Using Japan as the base country, we calculate the following values for the λ_{trace} and λ_{max} tests:

H_0	λ_{trace}	λ_{max}
$r = 2$	3.32	3.32
$r = 1$	12.74	9.42
$r = 0$	28.95	16.21

Using the λ_{trace} test, we cannot reject the null hypothesis that $r = 0$. The calculated value of 28.95 is less than the 90% critical value of 32.093. If we use the more specific λ_{max} test, a null of $r = 0$ against the alternative of $r = 1$ cannot be rejected at the 80% level of significance (the critical value being 17.474 at the 80% significance level). Thus, the three real exchange rates are not cointegrated; G-PPP does *not* hold among these countries, so it is possible to conclude that these four countries do not comprise a currency area.

Still using Japan as the base country, we next examine whether there exist cointegrating relationships among the German, U.K., and U.S. rates with the rates of other Pacific Rim nations. Consider the following four-variable equation:

$$r_{1it} = \beta_0 + \beta_{13}r_{13t} + \beta_{14}r_{14t} + \beta_{15}r_{15t} + e_t \tag{6.64}$$

where r_{1i}, r_{13}, r_{14}, and r_{15}, refer respectively, to the logarithms of the bilateral real exchange rates of country i, the United States, Germany, and the U.K.[23]

For each of the seven countries listed in Table 6.7, the $\lambda_{\text{trace}}(0)$ statistic is reported in column 2. With 4 variables, at the 95% level, the critical value of λ_{trace} is 53.347. For all countries except India, we can reject a null of no cointegration. If we examine India in more detail, the λ_{max} statistic for the null of $r = 0$ against the alternative $r = 1$ cannot be rejected at the 90% level. Therefore, we conclude that G-PPP does not hold for India. However, G-PPP *does* hold for each of the other Pacific Rim countries with Germany, Japan, the U.K., and the United States. Since G-PPP does not hold between Japan, the United States, Germany, and the U.K. alone, the natural interpretation is that the real exchange rate of each of the smaller Pacific Rim nations (except India) follows a time path dictated by events in the larger countries.

Table 6.7   **Values of λ_{trace} for $r = 0$**

	λ_{trace}	β_{13}	β_{14}	β_{15}	α
Australia	60.35	0.202	0.586	−0.549	−0.07
India	46.49	1.436	0.985	1.302	0.02
Indonesia	56.93	1.513	1.390	1.750	−0.04
Korea	63.11	−0.497	1.443	−0.995	−0.05
Philippines	56.91	0.720	−0.352	0.253	−0.47
Thailand	64.25	0.986	0.893	0.383	0.04
Singapore	55.44	1.173	0.681	0.638	0.066

The interrelationships among the various real exchange rates are reflected by the coefficients of the equilibrium relationship reported in columns 3 to 5 of Table 6.7. The straightforward interpretation of the various β_{1j} are as long-run elasticities. For example, the Australian bilateral real rate with Japan changes by 0.202% in response to a 1% change in the U.S./Japanese bilateral real exchange rate. Notice that the absolute values of the β_{1j} are generally quite large; only five of the 21 estimated coefficients are less than 0.5 in absolute value.

The sixth column of Table 6.7 reports the weights or "speed of adjustment" coefficients with which a discrepancy from G-PPP affects the real rate between country i and Japan. The speed of adjustment coefficients for the large countries are not significant and not shown in the table. Note that for all countries except the Philippines, the speed of adjustment coefficients are rather small; thus, any deviation from G-PPP can be expected to persist for a relatively long period of time.[24]

The Australia, Korea, Philippines Group

Since we had reason to believe that the rates for Australia, Korea, and the Philippines are interrelated, it is interesting to examine this group in greater detail. Letting rau, rko, and rph denote the logs of the Australian, Korean, and Philippine real bilateral exchange rates with Japan, we estimated the following long-run equilibrium relation:

$$11.62 \text{ rau} - 6.65 \text{ rko} - 9.58 \text{ rph} + 3.152 = 0 \qquad (6.65)$$

or normalizing with respect to the Austrialian real rate, we get

$$\text{rau}_t = 0.572 \text{ rko}_t + 0.825 \text{ rph}_t - 0.271 \qquad (6.66)$$

In the formal tests for cointegration, the calculated λ_{trace} test statistic for the null $r = 0$ equals 39.95; this null can be strongly rejected at the 99% significance level. Moreover, both the λ_{trace} and λ_{max} tests indicate that this cointegrating vector is unique (so that $r = 1$).

The Johansen procedure allows us to test restrictions on the cointegrating vector. We tested the following restrictions on equation (6.66):

H_1: The coefficients on rko and rph sum to unity

If the sum of these two coefficients is equal to unity, (6.66) can be rewritten solely in terms of the Australian bilateral rate with Korea and Korean bilateral rate with the Philippines. The calculated χ^2 statistic is 11.36; with one degree of freedom (since $r = 1$ and $n - s = 1$), $\chi^2_{0.01} = 6.63$ and we reject the restriction; thus, we can reject the hypothesis that the Japanese price level does not enter into Equation (6.65).

H_2: Zero restrictions

Restricting the coefficient on rko to equal zero yields a χ^2 value of 7.90; restricting for the coefficient on rph yields a χ^2 value of 12.94. Again, with one degree of freedom, we reject the restriction at the 1% significance level.

H_3: Equality restrictions

Restricting the coefficients on rko and rph to be equal yields a χ^2 statistic of 4.83. We can reject the restriction at the 5% (but not the 1%) significance level since $\chi^2_{0.05} = 3.84$. The restricted cointegration vector becomes:

$$rau = 0.653(rko + rph) - 0.271 \qquad (6.67)$$

Certainly, there is strong evidence that G-PPP holds among this subset of countries. The question is whether Australia, Korea, and the Philippines *as a group* form their own currency area with Japan. Next, we compare the residual variances of rau, rko, and rph when estimated in the system given by (6.64) versus the residual variances when the rates are estimated by Equation (6.65).

Variances of Residuals

	Equation 6.64	Equation 6.65
rau	0.00105	0.00114
rko	0.00066	0.00073
rph	0.00087	0.00105

Notice that for each of the three real rates, the residuals have the smallest variance when estimated as in Equation (6.64). Thus, for Australia, Korea, and the Philippines, real exchange rate movements are more heavily influenced by Germany, Japan, the U.K., and the United States than each other. Since these three countries are the most likely of the Pacific Rim nations to constitute a currency area, there is little evidence that any subgroup of Pacific Rim nations constitutes a currency area. Rather, each Pacific nation has its own real rate influenced by the set of the larger nations.

SUMMARY AND CONCLUSIONS

Many economic theories imply that a linear combination of certain nonstationary variables must be stationary. For example, if the variables $\{x_{1t}\}$, $\{x_{2t}\}$, and $\{x_{3t}\}$ are $I(1)$ and the linear combination $e_t = \beta_0 + \beta_1 x_{1t} + \beta_2 x_{2t} + \beta_3 x_{3t}$ is stationary, the variables are said to be cointegrated of order (1, 1). The vector $(\beta_0, \beta_1, \beta_2, \beta_3)$ is called the cointegrating vector. Cointegrated variables have the same stochastic trends and so cannot drift too far apart. Cointegrated variables have an error-correction representation such that each responds to the deviation from "long-run equilibrium."

One way to check for cointegration is to examine the residuals from the long-run equilibrium relationship. If these residuals have a unit root, the variables cannot be cointegrated of order (1, 1). Another way to check for cointegration among $I(1)$

variables is to estimate a VAR in first differences and include the lagged level of the variables in some period $t - p$. If we use a multivariate generalization of the Dickey–Fuller test, the vector can be checked for the presence of unit roots. In an n equation system, n minus the number of unit roots equals the number of cointegrating vectors.

The λ_{trace} and $\lambda_{\max}$ test statistics can be used to help determine the number of cointegrating vectors. These tests are sensitive to the presence of the deterministic regressors included in the cointegrating vector(s). Restrictions on the cointegrating vector(s) and/or speed of adjustment parameters can be tested using χ^2 statistics.

The Johansen and Juselius tables are extended to allow for more than five variables in Osterwald–Lenum (1992). Also, there is a growing body of work considering hypothesis testing in a cointegration framework. Park (1992) develops a non–parametric method for the estimation and testing of cointegrating vectors. Johansen and Juselius (1992) and Horvath and Watson (1993) discuss the testing of structural hypotheses within a cointegration framework. A useful review of the hypothesis testing is provided by Johansen (1991).

The literature is proceeding in several interesting directions. Friedman and Kuttner (1992) use cointegration tests to show that significant relationships between money, income, and interest rates break down in the 1980s. The paper makes an excellent companion piece with this chapter since it also uses innovation accounting techniques. Another interesting money demand study using the techniques in this chapter is Baba, Hendry, and Starr (1992). Gregory and Hansen (1992) consider the possibility of a structural break in a cointegrated system. The intercept and/or slope coefficients of the cointegrating vector are allowed to experience a regime shift at an unknown date. King et al. (1991) combine cointegration tests with the type of structural decompositions considered in Chapter 5.

QUESTIONS AND EXERCISES

1. Let Equations (6.14) and (6.15) contain intercept terms such that

$$y_t = a_{10} + a_{11}y_{t-1} + a_{12}z_{t-1} + \epsilon_{yt} \quad \text{and} \quad z_t = a_{20} + a_{21}y_{t-1} + a_{22}z_{t-1} + \epsilon_{zt}$$

A. Show that the solution for y_t can be written as

$$y_t = [(1 - a_{22}L)\epsilon_{yt} + (1 - a_{22})a_{10} + a_{12}L\epsilon_{zt} + a_{12}a_{20}] / [(1 - a_{11}L)(1 - a_{22}L) - a_{12}a_{21}L^2]$$

B. Find the solution for z_t.

C. Suppose that y_t and z_t are $CI(1, 1)$. Use the conditions in (6.19), (6.20), and (6.21) to write the error-correcting model. Compare your answer to (6.22) and (6.23). Show that the error-correction model contains an intercept term.

D. Show that $\{y_t\}$ and $\{z_t\}$ have the same deterministic time trend (i.e., show that the slope coefficient of the time trends is identical).

E. What is the condition such that the slope of the trend is zero? Show that this condition is such that the constant can be included in the cointegrating vector.

2. The data file COINT6.PRN contains the three simulated series used in Sections 5 and 9. You should find that the properties of the data are such that

Series	Observations	Mean	Standard Error	Minimum	Maximum
Y	100	−4.2810736793	1.4148612773	−6.3307043375	−1.2512548288
Z	100	−2.1437335637	1.7951179043	−5.7040632238	0.6257029853
W	100	−6.3677952867	2.3914380011	−9.6848404427	−1.4460513399

A. Use the data to reproduce the results in Section 5

B. Use the data to reproduce the results in Section 9.

3. The data file REALRATE.PRN contains the real exchange rate series used in Section 10. Use the series to reproduce the results in Section 10.

4. The second, third, and fourth columns of the file labeled US.PRN contain the interest rates paid on U.S. 3-month, 3-year, and 10-year U.S. government securities. The data run from 1960:Q1 to 1991:Q4. These columns are labeled TBILL, $r3$, and $r10$, respectively. You should find that the properties of the data are such that

Series	Observations	Mean	Standard Error	Minimum	Maximum
TBILL	128	6.3959	2.7915	2.3200	15.0900
r3	128	7.3666	2.8113	3.3700	15.7900
r10	128	7.6299	2.7627	3.7900	14.8500

A. Pretest the variables to show that all the rates act as unit root processes. Specifically, perform augmented Dickey–Fuller tests with 1, 4, and 8 lags. You should obtain

Series	Statistic	Sample	Observations	Without Trend	With Trend
TBILL	ADF(1)	60Q3 91Q4	126	−2.3007(−2.8844)	−2.2850(−3.4458)
	ADF(4)	61Q2 91Q4	123	−2.2112(−2.8849)	−2.0101(−3.4466)
	ADF(8)	62Q2 91Q4	119	−2.0913(−2.8857)	−1.8901(−3.4478)

Series	Statistic	Sample	Observations	Without Trend	With Trend
r3	ADF(1)	60Q3 91Q4	126	−1.8902(−2.8844)	−1.7706(−3.4458)
	ADF(4)	61Q2 91Q4	123	−1.9902(−2.8849)	−1.6882(−3.4466)
	ADF(8)	62Q2 91Q4	119	−1.6772(−2.8857)	−1.1362(−3.4478)
r10	ADF(1)	60Q3 91Q4	126	−1.6974(−2.8844)	−1.5642(−3.4458)
	ADF(4)	61Q2 91Q4	123	−1.9028(−2.8849)	−1.8007(−3.4466)
	ADF(8)	62Q2 91Q4	119	−1.5170(−2.8857)	−.89269(−3.4478)

95% critical values appear in brackets.

B. Estimate the cointegrating relationships using the Engle–Granger procedure. Perform augmented Dickey–Fuller tests on the residuals. Using TBILL as the "dependent" variable, you should find

$$TBILL_t = 0.050882 + 2.2535r3_t - 1.3441r10_t$$
$$(0.35017) \quad (21.3184) \quad (-12.4961)$$

where *t*-statistics are in parentheses.

Unit root tests for residuals

Statistic	Sample	Value
ADF(1)	60Q3 91Q4	−5.3486
ADF(4)	61Q2 91Q4	−4.5669
ADF(8)	62Q2 91Q4	−3.4573
ADF(12)	63Q2 91Q4	−3.0687

The 95% critical value is about 3.81. Based on this data, do you conclude that the variables are cointegrated?

C. Repeat part B using *r*10 as the "dependent" variable. You should find that

Unit root tests for residuals

Statistic	Sample	Value
ADF(1)	60Q3 91Q4	−4.9209
ADF(4)	61Q2 91Q4	−3.33
ADF(8)	62Q2 91Q4	−2.1910
ADF(12)	63Q2 91Q4	−1.4109

D. Estimate an error-correcting model using only one lag of each variable. For the TBILL equation, you should find

$$\Delta \text{TBILL}_t = 0.011346 + 0.24772\hat{e}_{t-1} - 0.15598\Delta \text{TBILL}_{t-1} + 0.73044\Delta r3_{t-1} - 0.48743\Delta r10_{t-1} + \epsilon_{\text{TBILL}t}$$

where $\hat{e}_{t-1}$ is the lagged residual from your estimate in part B.

Diagnose the problems with this regression equation. You should find

   i. All coefficients are insignificant.

   ii. The $\{\epsilon_{\text{TBILL}t}$ sequence exhibits serial correlation.

   iii. Large volatility of the residuals in the early 1980s.

How would you attempt to correct these problems?

E. Estimate the model using the Johansen procedure. Use four lags and include an intercept in the cointegrating vector. You should find that

List of characteristic roots (i.e., eigenvalues) in descending order:

0.15307   0.10840   0.031092

Trace Tests			**Maximum Eigenvalue Tests**		
Null	**Alternative**	λ_{trace}	**Null**	**Alternative**	λ_{max}
$r = 0$	$r \geq 1$	38.7453	$r = 0$	$r = 1$	20.6006
$r \leq 1$	$r \geq 2$	18.1447	$r = 1$	$r = 2$	14.2280
$r \leq 2$	$r = 3$	3.9167	$r = 2$	$r = 3$	3.9167

   i. Explain why the λ_{trace} test strongly suggests that there is exactly one cointegrating vector.

   ii. To what extent is this result reinforced by the λ_{max} test?

   iii. Explain why there may be a discrepancy in the results.

F. Given that there is one cointegrating vector, verify that the normalized cointegrating vector is

$$\text{TBILL}_t = 1.8892r3_t - 0.95116r10_t - 0.27438$$

   i. Compare this result to your answer in part C.

   ii. Show that the speed of adjustment parameters for the normalized TBILL, $r3$, and $r10$ equations are

       TBILL: -0.096246 $r3$: -0.38181 $r10$: -0.3538

iii. What do the negative signs imply about the adjustment process?

G. Test the restriction $\beta_0 = 0$. You should find that the estimated cointegrating vector is

$$\text{TBILL}_t = 1.9459r3_t - 1.0376r10_t$$

and the χ^2 statistic with one degree of freedom is 0.80839.

H. Estimate the model assuming that there is a drift. You should find that the characteristic roots are

$$0.15298 \qquad 0.10619 \qquad 0.025545$$

Given that $r = 1$, verify that the summation indicated by (6.57) yields

$$-124[\ln(1 - 0.10840) + \ln(1 - 0.031092) - \ln(1 - 0.10619)$$
$$- \ln(1 - 0.025545)] = 1.01$$

Do you conclude there is a drift term?

5. Suppose you estimate π to be:

$$\pi = \begin{bmatrix} 0.6 & -0.5 & 0.2 \\ 0.3 & -0.25 & 0.1 \\ 1.2 & -1.0 & 0.4 \end{bmatrix}$$

A. Show that the determinant of π is zero.

B. Show that two of the characteristic roots are zero and that the third is 0.75.

C. Let $\beta' = (3 \; -2.5 \; 1)$ be the single cointegrating vector normalized with respect to x_3. Find the (3×1) vector α such that $\pi = \alpha\beta'$. How would α change if you normalized β with respect to x_1?

D. Describe how you could test the restriction $\beta_1 + \beta_2 = 0$.
Now suppose you estimate π to be:

$$\pi = \begin{bmatrix} 0.8 & 0.4 & 0.0 \\ 0.1 & 0.1 & 0.0 \\ 0.75 & 0.25 & 0.5 \end{bmatrix}$$

E. Show that the three characteristic roots are 0.0, 0.5, 0.9.

F. Select β such that:

$$\beta = \begin{bmatrix} 0.8 & 0.75 \\ 0.4 & 0.25 \\ 0.0 & 0.5 \end{bmatrix}$$

Find the (3×2) matrix α such that $\pi = \alpha\beta'$.

6. Suppose that x_{1t} and x_{2t} are integrated of orders 1 and 2, respectively. You are to sketch the proof that any linear combination of x_{1t} and x_{2t} is integrated of order 2. Towards this end:

A. Allow x_{1t} and x_{2t} to be the random walk processes

$$x_{1t} = x_{1t-1} + \epsilon_{1t}$$

and

$$x_{2t} = x_{2t-1} + \epsilon_{2t}$$

i. Given the initial conditions x_{10} and x_{20}, show that the solution for x_{1t} and x_{2t} have the form $x_{1t} = x_{10} + \Sigma\epsilon_{1t-i}$ and $x_{2t} = x_{20} + \Sigma\epsilon_{2t-i}$.

ii. Show that the linear combination $\beta_1 x_{1t} + \beta_2 x_{2t}$ will generally contain a stochastic trend.

iii. What assumption is necessary to ensure that x_{1t} and x_{2t} are $CI(1, 1)$?

B. Now let x_{2t} be integrated of order 2. Specifically, let $\Delta x_{2t} = \Delta x_{2t-1} + \epsilon_{2t}$. Given initial conditions for x_{20} and x_{21}, find the solution for x_{2t}. [You may allow ϵ_{1t} and ϵ_{2t} to be perfectly correlated].

Is there any linear combination of x_{1t} and x_{2t} that contains only a stochastic trend?

Is there any linear combination of x_{1t} and x_{2t} that does not contain a stochastic trend?

C. Provide an intuitive explanation for the statement: If x_{1t} and x_{2t} are integrated of orders d_1 and d_2 where $d_2 > d_1$, any linear combination of x_{1t} and x_{2t} is integrated of order d_2.

ENDNOTES

1. To include an intercept term, simply set all realizations of one $\{x_{it}\}$ sequence equal to unity. In the text, the long-run relationship with an intercept will be denoted by $\beta_0 + \beta_1 x_{1t} + \cdots + \beta_n x_{nt} = 0$. Also note that the definition rules out the trivial case in which all elements of β equal zero. Obviously if all the $\beta_i = 0$, $\beta x_t' = 0$.

2. Suppose that x_{1t} and x_{2t} are $I(2)$ and x_{3t} is $I(1)$. If x_{1t} and x_{2t} are $C(2, 1)$, there exists a linear combination of the form $\beta_1 x_{1t} + \beta_2 x_{2t}$ is $I(1)$. It is possible that *this* combination of x_{1t} and x_{2t} is cointegrated with x_{3t} such that the linear combination $\beta_1 x_{1t} + \beta_2 x_{2t} + \beta_3 x_{3t}$ is stationary.

3. As a technical point, note that if all elements of x_t are $I(0)$, it is possible for e_t to be integrated of order -1. However, this case is of little interest for economic analysis. Also note that if $\{x_t\}$ is stationary, $\Delta^d x_t$ is stationary for all $d > 0$.

4. The issue is trivial if both trends are deterministic. Simply detrend each of the variables using a deterministic polynomial time trend of the form $\alpha_0 + \alpha_1 t + \alpha_2 t^2 + \cdots$.

5. From Chapter 3 you will recall that the decomposition of an $I(1)$ variable into a random walk plus a noise term is not unique. Stock and Watson confine their analysis to trends that are random walks.

6. The error-correction term could have been written in the form $\alpha_S'(\beta_1 r_{Lt-1} - \beta_2 r_{St-1})$. Normalization with respect to the long-term rate yields (6.9), where $\alpha_S = \alpha_S' \beta_1$ and $\beta = \beta_2/\beta_1$. Here, the cointegrating vector is $(1, -\beta)$.

7. Note that (6.11) and (6.12) represent a system of first-order difference equations. The stability conditions place restrictions on the magnitudes of α_S, α_L, and the various values of $a_{ij}(k)$.

8. Equation (6.18) can be written as $\lambda^2 = a_1 \lambda + a_2$, where $a_1 = (a_{11} + a_{22})$ and $a_2 = (a_{12}a_{21} - a_{11}a_{22})$. Now refer all the way back to Figure 1.5 in Chapter 1. For $\lambda_1 = 1$, the coefficients of (6.18) must lie along line segment BC. Hence, $a_1 + a_2 = 1$, or $a_{11} + a_{22} + a_{12}a_{21} - a_{11}a_{22} = 1$. Solving for a_{11} yields (6.21). For $|\lambda_2| < 1$, the coefficients must lie inside region $A0BC$. Given (6.19), the condition $a_2 - a_1 = 1$ is equivalent to that in (6.21).

9. Another interesting way to obtain this result is to refer back to (6.14). If $a_{12} = 0$, $y_t = a_{11}y_{t-1} + \epsilon_{yt}$. Imposing the condition $\{y_t\}$ is a unit root process is equivalent to setting $a_{11} = 1$, so that $\Delta y_t = \epsilon_{yt}$.

10. As mentioned above, with three or more variables, various subsets may be cointegrated. For example, a group of $I(2)$ variables may be $CI(2, 1)$ or $CI(2, 2)$ or a subset of $I(1)$ variables may be $CI(1, 1)$. Moreover, a set of $CI(2, 1)$ variables may be cointegrated with a set of $I(1)$ variables. Form the $CI(2, 1)$ relation and determine whether the resultant is cointegrated with the $I(1)$ variables.

11. The stability/stationarity condition is such that $-2 < a_1 < 0$. Hence, if a_1 is found to be sufficiently negative, we need to be able to reject the null hypothesis $a_1 = -2$.

12. As shown in Section 3, the values of α_y and α_z are directly related to the characteristic roots of the difference equation system. Direct convergence necessitates that α_y be negative and α_z positive.

13. Engle and Granger (1987) does provide a statistic to test the joint hypothesis $\alpha_y = \alpha_z = 0$. However, their simulations suggest this statistic is not very powerful and recommend against its use.

14. If a variable is found to be integrated of a different order than the others, the remaining variables can be tested for cointegration.

15. Wholesale prices and period average exchange rates were used in the study. Each series was converted into an index number such that each series was equal to unity at the beginning of its respective period (either 1960 or 1973). In the fixed exchange rate period, all values of $\{e_t\}$ were set equal to unity.

16. A second set of regressions of the form $p_t = \beta_0 + \beta_1 f_t + \mu_t$ was also estimated. The results using this alternative normalization are very similar to those reported here.

17. Use (6.44) only if the residuals from the equilibrium regression are serially uncorrelated. Any evidence that ϵ_t is not white-noise necessitates using the augmented form of the test

[i.e., Equation (6.45)]. Engle and Granger recommend using the augmented tests when there is any doubt about the nature of the data-generating process. The unaugmented tests have very low power if (6.44) is estimated when lags are actually present in the data-generating process.

18. In Section 3, we allowed the disturbance to be serially correlated. Since we want to perform significance tests, we need the error terms to be white-noise disturbances.

19. The numbers are slightly different from those reported by Johansen and Juselius (1990) due to rounding.

20. The Johansen procedure consists of the matrix of vectors of the squared canonical correlations between the residuals of x_t and Δx_{t-1} regressed on lagged values of Δx_t. The cointegrating vectors are the rows of the normalized eigenvectors.

21. Long-run money neutrality guarantees that nominal variables have only temporary effects on real exchange rates. Proportional movements in prices and exchange rates may be observed in high inflation countries since the temporary effects of the vast money supply movements dwarf the consequences of the nonstationary changes in real variables.

22. The price series for Singapore runs from January 1974 through December 1989 and the series for Indonesia from January 1973 through April 1986. Unfortunately, it was not possible to obtain wholesale price indices for Hong Kong, Malaysia, or Taiwan. Although consumer price indices are readily available, the large weights given to nontradables such as housing and services make them less appropriate for PPP comparisons.

23. Respectively, Japan, the United States, Germany, and the U.K. are denoted as country 1, 3, 4, and 5. Notice that the values of β_{13}, β_{14}, and β_{15} will differ for each country i; when there is a possible ambiguity, we use the notation $\beta_{1j,i}$ to denote the coefficient of r_{1j} in the cointegrating relationship for country i.

24. As in any difference equation system, the speed of adjustment term can be positive or negative. The critical factor is whether the characteristic roots of the system are all less than unity in absolute value. Notice that these roots are the estimated values of λ_i from the matrix of canonical correlations. In a sense, the Johansen (1988) procedure is a method to determine whether the characteristic roots of the difference equation system represented by an error-correction system imply convergence.

APPENDIX: Characteristic Roots, Stability, and Rank

Characteristic Roots Defined

Let A be an $(n \times n)$ square matrix with elements a_{ij} and x an $(n \times 1)$ vector. The scalar λ is called a characteristic root of A if

$$Ax = \lambda x \tag{A6.1}$$

Let I be an $(n \times n)$ identity matrix, so that we can rewrite (A6.1) as

$$Ax - \lambda x = 0$$

or

$$(A - \lambda I)x = 0 \tag{A6.2}$$

Since x is a vector containing values not identically equal to zero, (A.62) requires that the rows of $(A - \lambda I)$ be linearly dependent. Equivalently, (A6.2) requires that the determinant $|A - \lambda I| = 0$. Thus, we can find the characteristic root(s) of (A6.1) by finding the values of λ that satisfy

$$|A - \lambda I| = 0 \tag{A6.3}$$

Example 1

Let A be the matrix:

$$A = \begin{bmatrix} 0.5 & -0.2 \\ -0.2 & 0.5 \end{bmatrix}$$

so that

$$|A - \lambda I| = \begin{vmatrix} 0.5 - \lambda & -0.2 \\ -0.2 & 0.5 - \lambda \end{vmatrix}$$

Solving for the value of λ such that $|A - \lambda I| = 0$ yields the quadratic equation:

$$\lambda^2 - \lambda + 0.21 = 0$$

The two values of λ that solve the equation are $\lambda = 0.7$ and $\lambda = 0.3$. Hence, 0.7 and 0.3 are the two characteristic roots.

Example 2

Now change A such that each element in column 2 is twice the corresponding value in column 1. Specifically,

$$A = \begin{bmatrix} 0.5 & 1 \\ -0.2 & -0.4 \end{bmatrix}$$

Now,

$$|A - \lambda I| = \begin{vmatrix} 0.5 - \lambda & 1 \\ -0.2 & -0.4 - \lambda \end{vmatrix}$$

Again, there are two values of λ that solve $|A - \lambda I| = 0$. Solving the quadratic equation $\lambda^2 - 0.1\lambda = 0$ yields the two characteristic roots $\lambda_1 = 0$ and $\lambda_2 = 0.1$.

Characteristic Equations

Equation (A6.3) is called the characteristic equation of the square matrix A. Notice that the characteristic equation will be an nth-order polynomial in λ. The reason is that the determinant $|A - \lambda I| = 0$ contains the nth degree term λ^n resulting from the expression:

$$(a_{11} - \lambda)(a_{22} - \lambda)(a_{33} - \lambda) \ldots (a_{nn} - \lambda)$$

As such, the characteristic equation will be an nth-order polynomial of the form:

$$\lambda^n + b_1\lambda^{n-1} + b_2\lambda^{n-2} + b_3\lambda^{n-3} + \cdots + b_{n-1}\lambda + b_n = 0 \qquad \text{(A6.4)}$$

From (A6.4), it immediately follows that an $(n \times n)$ square matrix will necessarily have n characteristic roots. As we saw in Chapter 1, some of the roots may be repeating and some may be complex. In practice, it is not necessary to actually calculate the values of the roots solving (A6.4). The necessary and sufficient condition for all characteristic roots to lie within the unit circle are given in the appendix to Chapter 1.

Notice that the term b_n is of particular relevance since $b_n = (-1)^n |A|$. After all, b_n is the only expression resulting from $|A - \lambda I|$ that is not multiplied by λ. In terms of (A6.4), the expressions λ^n and b_n will have the same sign if n is even and opposite signs if n is odd. In Example 1, the characteristic equation is $\lambda^2 - \lambda + 0.21 = 0$, so that $b_2 = 0.21$. Since $|A| = 0.21$, it follows that $b_2 = (-1)^2(0.21)$. Similarly, in Example 2, the characteristic equation is $\lambda^2 - 0.1\lambda = 0$, so that $b_2 = 0$. Since it is also the case that $|A| = 0$, it also follows that $b_2 = (-1)^2 |A|$. In Example 3 below, we consider the case in which $n = 3$.

Example 3

Let A be such that

$$|A - \lambda I| = \begin{bmatrix} 0.5 - \lambda & 0.2 & 0.2 \\ 0.2 & 0.5 - \lambda & 0.2 \\ 0.2 & 0.2 & 0.5 - \lambda \end{bmatrix}$$

The characteristic equation is

$$\lambda^3 - 1.5\lambda^2 + 0.63\lambda - 0.081 = 0$$

and the characteristic roots are

$$\lambda_1 = 0.9, \qquad \lambda_2 = 0.3, \qquad \lambda_3 = 0.3$$

The determinant of A is 0.081, so that $b_3 = -0.081 = (-1)^3 |A|$.

Determinants and Characteristic Roots

The determinant of an $(n \times n)$ matrix is equal to the product of its characteristic roots, that is

$$|A| = \prod_{i=1}^{n} \lambda_i \qquad \text{(A6.5)}$$

where $\lambda_1, \lambda_2, \ldots, \lambda_n =$ the n characteristic roots of the $(n \times n)$ matrix A

The proof of this important proposition is straightforward since the values $\lambda_1, \lambda_2,$ $\ldots, \lambda_n$ solve (A6.4). However, from the algebra of polynomials, the product of the factors of (A6.4) is equal to $(-1)^n b_n$:

$$\prod_{i=1}^{n} \lambda_i = (-1)^n b_n$$

From the second section above, we also know that $(-1)^n b_n = |A|$. Hence, (A6.5) must hold in that the product $(\lambda_1)(\lambda_2) \ldots (\lambda_n) = (-1)^n b_n = |A|$.

Examples 1 to 3 continued:

In Examples 1 and 2, the characteristic equation is quadratic of the form $\lambda^2 + b_1 \lambda + b_2 = 0$. To find the roots of this quadratic equation, we seek the factors λ_1 and λ_2 such that

$$(\lambda - \lambda_1)(\lambda - \lambda_2) = 0$$

or

$$\lambda^2 - (\lambda\lambda_1 + \lambda\lambda_2) + \lambda_1\lambda_2 = 0$$

or

$$\lambda^2 - (\lambda_1 + \lambda_2)\lambda + \lambda_1\lambda_2 = 0$$

Clearly, the values $\lambda_1\lambda_2$ must equal b_2. To check the formulas in Example 1, recall that the characteristic equation is $\lambda^2 - \lambda + 0.21 = 0$. In this problem, the value of b_2 is 0.21, the product of the characteristic roots $\lambda_1\lambda_2 = (0.7)(0.3) = 0.21$, and the determinant of A $(0.5)^2 - (0.2)^2 = 0.21$. In Example 2, the characteristic equation is $\lambda^2 - 0.1\lambda = 0$, so that $b_2 = 0$. The product of the characteristic roots is $\lambda_1\lambda_2 = (0.0)(0.1) = 0.0$, and the determinant of A $(0.5)(0.4) - (0.2) = 0$.

In Example 3, the characteristic equation is cubic: $\lambda^3 - 1.5\lambda^2 + 0.63\lambda - 0.081 = 0$. The value of b_2 is -0.081, the product of the characteristic roots $(0.9)(0.3)(0.3) = 0.081$, and the determinant of A 0.081.

Characteristic Roots and Rank

The rank of a square $(n \times n)$ matrix A is the number of linearly independent rows (columns) in the matrix. The notation rank(A) = r means that the rank of A is equal to r. The matrix A is said to be of full rank if rank(A) = n.

From the discussion above, it follows that *the rank of A is equal to the number of its nonzero characteristic roots.* Certainly, if all rows of A are linearly independent, the determinant of A is not equal to zero. From (A6.5), it follows that none of the characteristic roots can equal zero if $|A| \neq 0$. At the other extreme, if rank$(A) = 0$, each element of A must equal zero. When rank$(A) = 0$, the characteristic equation degenerates into $\lambda^n = 0$ with the solutions $\lambda_1 = \lambda_2 = \cdots = \lambda_n = 0$. Consider the intermediate cases in which $0 < \text{rank}(A) = r < n$. Since interchanging the various rows of a matrix does not alter the absolute value of its determinant, we can always rewrite $|A - \lambda I| = 0$ such that the first r rows comprise the r linearly independent rows of A. The determinant of these first r rows will contain r characteristic roots. The other $(n - r)$ roots will be zeros.

In Example 2, rank$(A) = 1$ since each element in row 1 equals -2.5 times the corresponding element in row 2. For this case, $|A| = 0$ and exactly one characteristic root is equal to zero. In the other two examples, A is of full rank and all characteristic roots differ from zero.

Example 4

Now consider a (3×3) matrix A such that rank$(A) = 1$. Let

$$|A - \lambda I| = \begin{bmatrix} 0.5 - \lambda & 0.2 & 0.2 \\ 1 & 0.4 - \lambda & 0.4 \\ -0.25 & -0.1 & -0.1 - \lambda \end{bmatrix}$$

The rank of A is unity since row 2 is twice row 1 and row 3 is -0.5 times row 1. The determinant of A equals zero and the characteristic equation is given by

$$\lambda^3 - 0.8\lambda^2 = 0$$

The three characteristic roots are $\lambda_1 = 0.8$, $\lambda_2 = 0$, and $\lambda_3 = 0$.

Stability of a First-Order VAR

Let x_t be the $(n \times 1)$ vector $(x_{1t}, x_{2t}, \ldots, x_{nt})'$ and consider the first-order VAR

$$x_t = A_0 + A_1 x_{t-1} + \epsilon_t \tag{A6.6}$$

where A_0 = an $(n \times 1)$ vector with elements a_{i0}
  A = an $(n \times n)$ square matrix with elements a_{ij}
  ϵ_t = the $(n \times 1)$ vector of white-noise disturbances $(\epsilon_{1t}, \epsilon_{2t}, \ldots, \epsilon_{nt})'$.

To check the stability of the system, we need only examine the homogeneous equation:

$$x_t = A_1 x_{t-1} \tag{A6.7}$$

We can use the method of undetermined coefficients and for each x_{it} posit a solution of the form:

$$x_{it} = c_i \lambda^t \tag{A6.8}$$

where c_i = an arbitrary constant

If (A6.8) is to be a solution, it must satisfy each of the n equations represented by (A6.7). Substituting $x_{it} = c_i \lambda^t$ and $x_{it-1} = c_i \lambda^{t-1}$ for each of the x_{it} in (A6.7), we get

$$c_1\lambda^t = a_{11}c_1\lambda^{t-1} + a_{12}c_2\lambda^{t-1} + \cdots + a_{1n}c_n\lambda^{t-1}$$
$$c_2\lambda^t = a_{21}c_1\lambda^{t-1} + a_{22}c_2\lambda^{t-1} + \cdots + a_{2n}c_n\lambda^{t-1}$$
$$c_3\lambda^t = a_{31}c_1\lambda^{t-1} + a_{32}c_2\lambda^{t-1} + \cdots + a_{3n}c_n\lambda^{t-1}$$
$$\cdots$$
$$c_n\lambda^t = a_{n1}c_1\lambda^{t-1} + a_{n2}c_2\lambda^{t-1} + \cdots + a_{nn}c_n\lambda^{t-1}$$

Now, divide each equation by λ^{t-1} and collect terms to form

$$
\begin{array}{llll}
c_1(a_{11} - \lambda) + c_2 a_{12} & + c_3 a_{13} & \cdots + c_n a_{1n} & = 0 \\
c_1 a_{21} & + c_2(a_{22} - \lambda) + c_3 a_{23} & \cdots + c_n a_{2n} & = 0 \\
\cdots & \cdots & \cdots & \cdots \\
c_1 a_{n1} & + c_2 a_{n2} & + c_3 a_{n3} \cdots + c_n(a_{nn} - \lambda) & = 0
\end{array}
$$

so that the following system of equations must be satisfied:

$$
\begin{bmatrix}
a_{11} - \lambda & a_{12} & a_{13} & \cdots & a_{1n} \\
a_{21} & a_{22} - \lambda & a_{23} & \cdots & a_{2n} \\
\cdots & \cdots & \cdots & \cdots & \cdots \\
a_{n1} & a_{n2} & a_{n3} & \cdots & a_{nn} - \lambda
\end{bmatrix}
\begin{bmatrix}
c_1 \\ c_2 \\ \cdots \\ c_n
\end{bmatrix}
=
\begin{bmatrix}
0 \\ 0 \\ 0 \\ 0
\end{bmatrix}
$$

For a nontrivial solution to the system of equations, the following determinant must equal zero:

$$
\begin{vmatrix}
(a_{11} - \lambda) & a_{12} & a_{13} & \cdots & a_{1n} \\
a_{21} & (a_{22} - \lambda) & a_{23} & \cdots & a_{2n} \\
\cdots & \cdots & \cdots & \cdots & \cdots \\
a_{n1} & a_{n2} & a_{n3} & \cdots & (a_{nn} - \lambda)
\end{vmatrix}
= 0
$$

The determinant will be an nth-order polynomial that is satisfied by n values of λ. Denote these n characteristic roots by $\lambda_1, \lambda_2, \ldots, \lambda_n$. Since each is a solution to the homogeneous equation, we know that the following linear combination of the homogeneous solutions is also a homogeneous solution:

$$x_{it} = d_1\lambda_1^t + d_2\lambda_2^t + \cdots + d_n\lambda_n^t$$

Note that each $\{x_{it}\}$ sequence will have the same roots. The necessary and sufficient condition for stability is that all characteristic roots lie within the unit circle.

Cointegration and Rank

The relationship between the rank of a martix and its characteristic roots is critical in the Johansen procedure. Using the notation from Section 7, let:

$$x_t = A_1 x_{t-1} + \epsilon_t$$

so that

$$\Delta x_t = (A_1 - I)x_{t-1} + \epsilon_t$$
$$= \pi x_{t-1} + \epsilon_t$$

If the rank of π is unity, all rows of π can be written as a scalar multiple of the first. Thus, each of the $\{\Delta x_{it}\}$ sequences can be written as

$$\Delta x_{it} = s_i(\pi_{11}x_{1t-1} + \pi_{12}x_{2t-1} + \cdots + \pi_{1n}x_{nt-1}) + \epsilon_{1t}$$

where $s_1 = 1$
      $s_i = \pi_{ij}/\pi_{1j}$

Hence, the linear combination $\pi_{11}x_{1t-1} + \pi_{12}x_{2t-1} + \cdots + \pi_{1n}x_{nt-1} = (\Delta x_{it} - \epsilon_{it})/s_i$ is stationary since both Δx_{it} and ϵ_{it} are stationary.

The rank of π equals the number of cointegrating vectors. If rank$(\pi) = r$, there are r linearly independent combinations of the $\{x_{it}\}$ sequences that are stationary. If rank$(\pi) = n$, all variables are stationary.

The rank of π is equal to the number of its characteristic roots that differ from zero. Order the roots such that $\lambda_1 > \lambda_2 > \cdots > \lambda_n$. The Johansen methodology allows you to determine the number of roots that are statistically different from zero. The relationship between A_1 and π is such that if all characteristic roots of A_1, are in the unit circle, π is of full rank.

STATISTICAL TABLES

Table A   **Empirical Cumulative Distribution of τ**

Probability of a Smaller Value								
Sample Size	**0.01**	**0.025**	**0.05**	**0.10**	**0.90**	**0.95**	**0.975**	**0.99**
No Constant or Time ($a_0 = a_2 = 0$)				τ				
25	−2.66	−2.26	−1.95	−1.60	0.92	1.33	1.70	2.16
50	−2.62	−2.25	−1.95	−1.61	0.91	1.31	1.66	2.08
100	−2.60	−2.24	−1.95	−1.61	0.90	1.29	1.64	2.03
250	−2.58	−2.23	−1.95	−1.62	0.89	1.29	1.63	2.01
300	−2.58	−2.23	−1.95	−1.62	0.89	1.28	1.62	2.00
∞	−2.58	−2.23	−1.95	−1.62	0.89	1.28	1.62	2.00
Constant ($a_2 = 0$)				τ_τ				
25	−3.75	−3.33	−3.00	−2.62	−0.37	0.00	0.34	0.72
50	−3.58	−3.22	−2.93	−2.60	−0.40	−0.03	0.29	0.66
100	−3.51	−3.17	−2.89	−2.58	−0.42	−0.05	0.26	0.63
250	−3.46	−3.14	−2.88	−2.57	−0.42	−0.06	0.24	0.62
500	−3.44	−3.13	−2.87	−2.57	−0.43	−0.07	−0.24	0.61
∞	−3.43	−3.12	−2.86	−2.57	−0.44	−0.07	0.23	0.60
Constant + time				τ_τ				
25	−4.38	−3.95	−3.60	−3.24	−1.14	−0.80	−0.50	−0.15
50	−4.15	−3.80	−3.50	−3.18	−1.19	−0.87	−0.58	−0.24
100	−4.04	−3.73	−3.45	−3.15	−1.22	−0.90	−0.62	−0.28
250	−3.99	−3.69	−3.43	−3.13	−1.23	−0.92	−0.64	−0.31
500	−3.98	−3.68	−3.42	−3.13	−1.24	−0.93	−0.65	−0.32
∞	−3.96	−3.66	−3.41	−3.12	−1.25	−0.94	−0.66	−0.33

Source: This table was constructed by David A. Dickey using Monte Carlo methods. Standard errors of the estimates vary, but most are less than 0.20. The table is reproduced from Wayne Fuller. *Introduction to Statistical Time Series*. (New York: John Wiley). 1976.

Table B **Distribution of the λ_{max} and λ_{trace} Statistics**

	80%	90%	95%	97.5%	99%
		λ_{max} and λ_{trace} statistics with trend drift			
n-r		λ_{max}			
1	1.699	2.816	3.962	5.332	6.936
2	10.125	12.099	14.036	15.810	17.936
3	16.324	18.697	20.778	23.002	25.521
4	22.113	24.712	27.169	29.335	31.943
5	27.889	30.774	33.178	35.546	38.341
		λ_{trace}			
1	1.699	2.816	3.962	5.332	6.936
2	11.164	13.338	15.197	17.299	19.310
3	23.868	26.791	29.509	32.313	35.397
4	40.250	43.964	47.181	50.424	53.792
5	60.215	65.063	68.905	72.140	76.955
		λ_{max} and λ_{trace} statistics without trend or constant			
		λ_{max}			
1	4.905	6.691	8.083	9.658	11.576
2	10.666	12.783	14.595	16.403	18.782
3	16.521	18.959	21.279	23.362	26.154
4	22.341	24.917	27.341	29.599	32.616
5	27.953	30.818	33.262	35.700	38.858
		λ_{trace}			
1	4.905	6.691	8.083	9.658	11.576
2	13.038	15.583	17.844	19.611	21.962
3	25.445	28.436	31.256	34.062	37.291
4	41.623	45.248	48.419	51.801	55.551
5	61.566	65.956	69.977	73.031	77.911
		λ_{max} and λ_{trace} statistics a constant in the cointegrating vector			
		λ_{max}			
1	5.877	7.563	9.094	10.709	12.740
2	11.628	13.781	15.752	17.622	19.834
3	17.474	19.796	21.894	23.836	26.409
4	22.938	25.611	28.167	30.262	33.121
5	28.643	31.592	34.397	36.625	39.672
		λ_{trace}			
1	5.877	7.563	9.094	10.709	12.741
2	15.359	17.957	20.168	22.202	24.988
3	28.768	32.093	35.068	37.603	40.198
4	45.635	49.925	53.347	56.449	60.054
5	66.624	71.472	75.328	78.857	82.969

Table C   **Empirical Distribution of Φ**

Probability of a Smaller Value

Sample size n	0.01	0.025	0.05	0.10	0.90	0.95	0.975	0.99
				Φ_1				
25	0.29	0.38	0.49	0.65	4.12	5.18	6.30	7.88
50	0.29	0.39	0.50	0.66	3.94	4.86	5.80	7.06
100	0.29	0.39	0.50	0.67	3.86	4.71	5.57	6.70
250	0.30	0.39	0.51	0.67	3.81	4.63	5.45	6.52
500	0.30	0.39	0.51	0.67	3.79	4.61	5.41	6.47
∞	0.30	0.40	0.51	0.67	3.78	4.59	5.38	6.43
				Φ_2				
25	0.61	0.75	0.89	1.10	4.67	5.68	6.75	8.21
50	0.62	0.77	0.91	1.12	4.31	5.13	5.94	7.02
100	0.63	0.77	0.92	1.12	4.16	4.88	5.59	6.50
250	0.63	0.77	0.92	1.13	4.07	4.75	5.40	6.22
500	0.63	0.77	0.92	1.13	4.05	4.71	5.35	6.15
∞	0.63	0.77	0.92	1.13	4.03	4.68	5.31	6.09
				Φ_3				
25	0.74	0.90	1.08	1.33	5.91	7.24	8.65	10.61
50	0.76	0.93	1.11	1.37	5.61	6.73	7.81	9.31
100	0.76	0.94	1.12	1.38	5.47	6.49	7.44	8.73
250	0.76	0.94	1.13	1.39	5.39	6.34	7.25	8.43
500	0.76	0.94	1.13	1.39	5.36	6.30	7.20	8.34
∞	0.77	0.94	1.13	1.39	5.34	6.25	7.16	8.27

REFERENCES

Anderson, L. and J. Jordan. "Monetary and Fiscal Actions: A Test of their Relative Importance in Economic Stabilization." *Federal Reserve Bank of St. Louis Review* (Nov. 1968), 11–24.

Baba, Yoshihisa, David F. Hendry, and Ross M. Starr. "The Demand for M1 in the U.S.A., 1960–1988." *Review of Economic Studies* 59 (Jan. 1992), 25–61.

Bell, W. and S. Hilmer. "Issues Involved with the Seasonal Adjustment of Economic Time Series." *Journal of Business and Economic Statistics* 2 (1984), 291–320.

Bernanke, Ben. "Alternative Explanations of Money-Income Correlation." *Carnegie-Rochester Conference Series on Public Policy* 25 (1986), 49–100.

Beveridge, Stephen and Charles Nelson. "A New Approach to Decomposition of Economic Time Series into Permanent and Transitory Components with Particular Attention to Measurement of the Business Cycle." *Journal of Monetary Economics* 7 (March 1981), 151–74.

Blanchard, Oliver and Danny Quah. "The Dynamic Effects of Aggregate Demand and Supply Disturbances." *American Economic Review* 79 (Sept. 1989), 655–673.

Bollerslev, Tim. "Generalized Autoregressive Conditional Heteroscedasticity." *Journal of Econometrics* 31 (1986), 307–27.

Box, George and D. Pierce. "Distribution of Autocorrelations in Autoregressive Moving Average Time Series Models." *Journal of the American Statistical Association* 65 (1970), 1509–26.

Box, George and Gwilym Jenkins. *Time Series Analysis, Forecasting, and Control.* San Francisco, Calif.: Holden Day, 1976.

Box, George and D. Cox. "An Analysis of Transformations." *Journal of the Royal Statistical Society,* Series B.26 (1964), 211–52.

Bureau of the Census. *X-11 Information for the User,* U.S. Department of Commerce. Washington D.C.: U.S. Government Printing Office, 1969.

Cagan, Phillip. "The Monetary Dynamics of Hyperinflation." Milton Friedman, ed., *Studies in the Quantity Theory of Money.* Chicago, Ill.: University of Chicago Press, 1956, pp. 25–120.

Campbell, John Y. and Pierre Perron. "Pitfalls and Opportunities: What Macroeconomists Should Know About Unit Roots." *Technical Working Paper 100,* NBER Working Paper Series. April 1991.

Corbae, Dean and Sam Ouliaris. "Robust Tests for Unit Roots in the Foreign Exchange Market." *Economic Letters* 22 (1986), 375–80.

Dickey, David and Wayne A. Fuller. "Distribution of the Estimates for Autoregressive Time Series with a Unit Root." *Journal of the American Statistical Association* 74 (June 1979), 427–31.

___. "Likelihood Ratio Statistics for Autoregressive Time Series with a Unit Root." *Econometrica* 49 (July 1981), 1057–72.

Dickey, David, W. Bell, and R. Miller. "Unit Roots in Time Series Models: Tests and Implications." *American Statistician* 40 (1986), 12–26.

Dickey, David and S. Pantula. "Determining the Order of Differencing in Autoregressive Processes." *Journal of Business and Economic Statistics* 15 (1987), 455–61.

Doan, Thomas. *RATS User's Manual.* Evanston, Ill.: Estima, 1992.

Doldado, Juan, Tim Jenkinson, and Simon Sosvilla-Rivero. "Cointegration and Unit Roots." *Journal of Economic Surveys* 4 (1990), 249–73.

Dornbusch, Rudiger. "Expectations and Exchange Rate Dynamics." *Journal of Political Economy* 84 (1976), 1161–76.

Enders, Walter. "ARIMA and Cointegration Tests of Purchasing Power Parity." *Review of Economics and Statistics* 70 (Aug. 1988), 504–08.

Enders, Walter and Stan Hurn. "The Theory of Generalized Purchasing Power Parity: Tests in the Pacific Rim." *Review of International Economics* 2 (1994), 179–90.

Enders, Walter and Todd Sandler. "Causality Between Transnational Terrorism and Tourism: The Case of Spain." *Terrorism* 14 (Jan. 1991), 49–58.

Enders, Walter, Todd Sandler, and Jon Cauley. "Assessing the Impact of Terrorist-Thwarting Policies: An Intervention Time Series Approach." *Defense Economics* 2 (Dec. 1990), 1–18.

Enders, Walter, Todd Sandler, and Gerald F. Parise. "An Econometric Analysis of the Impact of Terrorism on Tourism." *Kyklos* 45 (1992), 531–554.

Engle, Robert F. "Autoregressive Conditional Heteroscedasticity with Estimates of the Variance of United Kingdom Inflation." *Econometrica* 50 (July 1982), 987–1007.

Engle, Robert E. and Tim Bollerslev. "Modelling the Persistence of Conditional Variances." *Econometric Reviews* 5 (1986), 1–50.

Engle, Robert E. and Clive W. J. Granger. "Cointegration and Error-Correction: Representation, Estimation, and Testing. *Econometrica* 55 (March 1987), 251–76.

Engle, Robert F. and David Kraft. "Multiperiod Forecast Error Variances of Inflation Based on the ARCH Model." A. Zellner, ed., *Applied Time Series Analysis of Economic Data.* Washington, D.C.: Bureau of the Census, 1983, pp. 293–302.

Engle, Robert F., David Lilien, and Russell Robins. "Estimating Time Varying Risk Premia in the Term Structure: The ARCH-M Model." *Econometrica* 55 (March 1987), 391–407.

Engle, Robert F. and B. Yoo. "Forecasting and Testing in Cointegrated Systems." *Journal of Econometrics* 35 (1987) 143–59.

Evans, G. and N. Savin. "Testing for Unit Roots: 1." *Econometrica* 49 (1981), 753–79.

Farmer, Roger E. *The Macroeconomics of Self-Fulfilling Prophecies.* Cambridge, Mass.: MIT Press, 1993.

Friedman, Benjamin and Kenneth Kuttner. "Money, Income, Prices, and Interest Rates." *American Economic Review* 82 (June 1992), 472–92.

Granger, Clive and P. Newbold. "Spurious Regressions in Econometrics." *Journal of Econometrics* 2 (1974), 111–20.

Gregory, Allen and Bruce Hansen. "Residual Based Tests for Cointegration in Models with Regime Shifts." Kingston: Queens University, 1992.

Harvey, Andrew. *Forecasting, Structural Time Series Models, and the Kalman Filter.* Cambridge: Cambridge Univ. Press, 1989.

Hendry, David, A. Neale, and N. Ericsson. *PC-NAIVE: An Interactive Program for Monte Carlo Experimentation in Econometrics.* Institute for Economics and Statistics: Oxford University, 1990.

Holt, Matthew and Satheesh Aradhyula. "Price Risk in Supply Equations: An Application of GARCH Time-Series Models to the U.S. Broiler Market." *Southern Economic Journal* 57 (July 1990), 230–42.

Horvath, Michael and Mark Watson. "Testing for Cointegration When Some of the Cointegrating Vectors are Known." Chicago, Ill.: Federal Reserve Bank of Chicago, 1993.

Hylleberg, S., R. Engle, C. Granger, and B. Yoo. "Seasonal Integration and Cointegration." *Journal of Econometrics* 44 (1990), 215–38.

Johansen, Soren. "Statistical Analysis of Cointegration Vectors." *Journal of Eocnomic Dynamics and Control* 12 (June–Sept. 1988), 231–54.

___. "Estimation and Hypothesis Testing of Cointegrating Vectors in Gaussian Vector Autoregressive Models." *Econometrica* 59 (Nov. 1991), 1551–80.

Johansen, Soren and Katerina Juselius. "Maximum Likelihood Estimation and Inference on Cointegration with Application to the Demand for Money." *Oxford Bulletin of Economics and Statistics* 52 (1990), 169–209.

___. "Testing Structural Hypotheses in a Multivariate Cointegration Analysis of PPP and the UIP for UK." *Journal of Econometrics* 53 (1992), 211–44.

King, Robert, Charles Plosser, James Stock, and Mark Watson. "Stochastic Trends and Economic Fluctuations." *American Economic Review* 81 (Sept. 1991), 819–40.

Leamer, Edward. "A Bayesian Analysis of the Determinants of Inflation." P. A. Belsey and E. Kuh, eds., *Model Reliability.* Cambridge, Mass.: MIT Press, 1986, pp. 62–89.

Lee, Bong-Soo and Walter Enders. "Accounting for Real and Nominal Exchange Rate Movements in the post-Bretton Woods Period." Ames, Iowa: *Iowa State University Working Paper* (June, 1993).

Lee, Bong-Soo and Walter Enders. "Decomposing Real and Nominal Exchange Rate Movements." Iowa State University, 1993.

Litterman, Robert. "A Bayesian Procedure for Forecasting with Vector Autoregressions." Federal Reserve Bank of Minneapolis, Minneapolis, 1981.

Ljung, G. and George Box. "On a Measure of Lack of Fit in Time Series Models." *Biometrica* 65 (1978), 297–303.

Lutkepohl, Helmut and Hans-Eggert Reimers. "Impulse Response Analysis of Cointegrated Systems." *Journal of Economic Dynamics and Control* 16 (Jan. 1992), 53–78.

Meese, R. and Ken Singleton. "On Unit Roots and Empirical Modeling of Exchange Rates." *Journal of Finance* 37 (1982), 1029–35.

Muth, John. "Optimal Properties of Exponentially Weighted Forecasts." *Journal of the American Statistical Association* 55 (1960), 299–306.

Nelson, Charles and Charles Plosser. "Trends and Random Walks in Macroeconomic Time Series: Some Evidence and Implications." *Journal of Monetary Economics* 10 (1982), 130–62.

Osterwald-Lenum, Michael. "A Note with Quantiles of the Asymptotic Distribution of the Maximum Likelihood Cointegration Rank Test Statistics." *Oxford Bulletin of Economics and Statistics* 54 (1992), 461–71.

Park, Joon. "Canonical Cointegrating Regressions." *Econometrica* 60 (Jan. 1992), 119–43.

Perron, Pierre. "The Great Crash, the Oil Price Shock, and the Unit Root Hypothesis." *Econometrica* 57 (Nov. 1989), 1361–1401.

Perron, Pierre and Timothy Vogelsang. "Nonstationary and Level Shifts with an Application to Purchasing Power Parity." *Journal of Business and Economic Statistics* 10 (1992), pp. 301–20.

Phillips, Peter. "Understanding Spurious Regressions in Econometrics." *Journal of Econometrics* 33 (1986), 311–40.

Phillips, Peter and Pierre Perron. "Testing for a Unit Root in Time Series Regression." *Biometrica* 75 (June 1988), 335–46.

Quah, Danny. "The Relative Importance of Permanent and Transitory Components: Identification and Some Theoretical Bounds." *Econometrica* 60 (Jan. 1992), 107–18.

Said, S. and David Dickey. "Testing for Unit Roots in Autoregressive-Moving Average Models with Unknown Order." *Biometrica* 71 (1984), 599–607.

Samuelson, Paul. "Interactions Between the Multiplier Analysis and Principle of Acceleration." *Review of Economics and Statistics* 21 (May 1939), 75–78.

___. "Conditions That the Roots of a Polynomial Be Less than Unity in Absolute Value." *Annals of Mathematics Statistics* 12 (1941), 360–64.

Schmidt, Peter. "Dickey–Fuller Tests with Drift." *Advances in Econometrics* 8 (1990), 161–200.

Sims, Christopher. "Macroeconomics and Reality." *Econometrica* 48 (Jan. 1980), 1–49.

___. "Are Forecasting Models Usable for Policy Analysis?" *Federal Reserve Bank of Minneapolis Quarterly Review* (Winter 1986), 3–16.

___. "Bayesian Skepticism on Unit Root Econometrics." *Journal of Economic Dynamics and Control* 12 (1988), 463–74.

Stock, James. "Asymptotic Properties of Least-Squares Estimators of Cointegrating Vectors." *Econometrica* 55 (1987), 1035–56.

Stock, James and Mark Watson. "Testing for Common Trends." *Journal of the American Statistical Association* 83 (Dec. 1988), 1097–1107.

Suits, Daniel and Gorden Sparks. "Consumption Regressions with Quarterly Data." T. S. Duesenberry, G. Fromm, L. R. Klein, and E. Kuh, eds., *The Brookings Quarterly Econometric Model of the United States.* Chicago, Ill.: Rand McNally, 1965, pp. 203–23.

Todd, Richard M. "Improving Economic Forecasting with Bayesian Autoregression." *Federal Reserve Bank of Minnesota Quarterly Review* (Fall 1984), 18–29.

Watson, Mark. "Univariate Detrending Methods with Stochastic Trends." *Journal of Monetary Economics* 18 (1986), 49–75.

West, Mike and Jeff Harrison. *Bayesian Forecasting and Dynamic Models.* New York: Springer-Verlag, 1989.

Zellner, Arnold. "Bayesian Analysis in Econometrics." *Journal of Econometrics* 37 (1988), 27–50.

AUTHOR INDEX

SUBJECT INDEX

HOGG and KLUGMAN · Loss Distributions
HOLLANDER and WOLFE · Nonparametric Statistical Methods
HOSMER and LEMESHOW · Applied Logistic Regression
HUBERTY · Applied Discriminary Analysis
IMAN and CONOVER · Modern Business Statistics
JACKSON · A User's Guide to Principle Components
JOHN · Statistical Methods in Engineering and Quality Assurance
JOHNSON · Multivariate Statistical Simulation
JOHNSON and KOTZ · Distributions in Statistics
        Continuous Univariate Distributions—2
        Continuous Multivariate Distributions
JOHNSON, KOTZ, and BALAKRISHNAN · Continuous Univariate Distributions,
 Volume I, *Second Edition*
JOHNSON, KOTZ, and KEMP · Univariate Discrete Distributions, *Second Edition*
JUDGE, GRIFFITHS, HILL, LÜTKEPOHL, and LEE · The Theory and Practice of
 Econometrics, *Second Edition*
JUDGE, HILL, GRIFFITHS, LÜTKEPOHL, and LEE · Introduction to the Theory and
 Practice of Econometrics, *Second Edition*
KALBFLEISCH and PRENTICE · The Statistical Analysis of Failure Time Data
KASPRZYK, DUNCAN, KALTON, and SINGH · Panel Surveys
KISH · Statistical Design for Research
KISH · Survey Sampling
LANGE, RYAN, BILLARD, BRILLINGER, CONQUEST, and GREENHOUSE · Case
 Studies in Biometry
LAWLESS · Statistical Models and Methods for Lifetime Data
LEBART, MORINEAU, and WARWICK · Multivariate Descriptive Statistical Analysis:
 Correspondence Analysis and Related Techniques for Large Matrices
LEE · Statistical Methods for Survival Data Analysis, *Second Edition*
LePAGE and BILLARD · Exploring the Limits of Bootstrap
LEVY and LEMESHOW · Sampling of Populations: Methods and Applications
LINHART and ZUCCHINI · Model Selection
LITTLE and RUBIN · Statistical Analysis with Missing Data
MAGNUS and NEUDECKER · Matrix Differential Calculus with Applications in
 Statistics and Econometrics
MAINDONALD · Statistical Computation
MALLOWS · Design, Data, and Analysis by Some Friends of Cuthbert Daniel
MANN, SCHAFER, and SINGPURWALLA · Methods for Statistical Analysis of
 Reliability and Life Data
MASON, GUNST, and HESS · Statistical Design and Analysis of Experiments with
 Applications to Engineering and Science
McLACHLAN · Discriminant Analysis and Statistical Pattern Recognition
MILLER · Survival Analysis
MONTGOMERY and PECK · Introduction to Linear Regression Analysis, *Second Edition*
NELSON · Accelerated Testing, Statistical Models, Test Plans, and Data Analyses
NELSON · Applied Life Data Analysis
OCHI · Applied Probability and Stochastic Processes in Engineering and Physical
 Sciences
OKABE, BOOTS, and SUGIHARA · Spatial Tesselations: Concepts and Applications of
 Voronoi Diagrams
OSBORNE · Finite Algorithms in Optimization and Data Analysis
PANKRATZ · Forecasting with Dynamic Regression Models
PANKRATZ · Forecasting with Univariate Box-Jenkins Models: Concepts and Cases
PORT · Theoretical Probability for Applications
PUTERMAN · Markov Decision Processes: Discrete Stochastic Dynamic Programming
RACHEV · Probability Metrics and the Stability of Stochastic Models
RÉNYI · A Diary on Information Theory
RIPLEY · Spatial Statistics
RIPLEY · Stochastic Simulation
ROSS · Introduction to Probability and Statistics for Engineers and Scientists